Twentieth Century Europe

Twentieth Century Europe

Alexander Rudhart

J. B. Lippincott Company
Philadelphia   New York   Toronto

ISBN 0-397-47311-7

Library of Congress Catalog Card Number 74-14620

Printed in the United States of America

1 3 5 7 9 8 6 4 2

Library of Congress Cataloging in Publication Data

Rudhart, Alexander.
  Twentieth century Europe.

  Bibliography: p.
  1. Europe — Politics — 1871-1918. 2. Europe — Politics — 1918-1945.
I. Title.
D443.R79   320.9'4'05   74-14620
ISBN 0-397-47311-7

To the memory of Hugo Hantsch

Foreword

André Malraux has told us recently that "there is no such thing as Europe, there never was."

Whether one is able to agree with this assessment or not, it is clear and self-evident that the European image in the world, as well as the European self-image have undergone a profound change since the beginning of this century.

It is part of the purpose of this book to examine the reasons that have prompted this change during the first half of the twentieth century: the European failure to answer the challenge of industrialism in a satisfactory manner; the relapse of the European state system into the prewar pattern of diplomacy and international relations, following the brief American initiative under the League; and the return to strident nationalism after the short Indian summer of the mid 1920's.

Speaking as a European, Conrad Ahlers, the former *Spiegel* editor and subsequent government spokesman for Willy Brandt, has referred to the era of European history since World War II as "A time without history." What he obviously had in mind was the passing of the age, in which the European state system was, or at any rate still seemed to be, master over its own destiny and planner of its own future. This book is chiefly concerned with that period, the first half of the twentieth century.

This is the place for thanks to be given and appreciation to be expressed to all those who have helped me in completing this volume. To Professor Christa Graf, I extend my profound gratitude for having read the entire manuscript; to Mrs. Bess Polkowski, I give my thanks for typing the whole manuscript under often difficult and trying circumstances; my special thanks, however, go out to my many students, both graduate and under-graduate, whose genuine interest in the subject has so greatly stimulated me and affirmed my impression that European history, far from suffering a decline in appeal, is alive and well among American students. It is to them that I dedicate this work with affection.

Alexander Rudhart
Brigantine, N.J. August 1974

Contents

Contents

Contents

Contents

Illustrations

Illustrations

1 | Europe on the Eve of the First World War

To the generation of Europeans entering upon maturity in the early 1900's, the new century held out the promise of unprecedented material gain, emancipation from disease, and heightened individual dignity through law, social progress, and education. After the birth pangs of the French Revolutionary Age of the latter 18th century and those of the early Industrial Revolution of the first decades of the 19th century, Europe and the Western world at large appeared to have entered upon the age of rational progress which the Enlightenment had postulated two centuries before. If European civilization still showed many imperfections, there was reason to hope that it was moving in the direction of a more perfect state than had been attained at any previous time. Through the genius and effort of its ancestors, the Europe of the early 20th century had reached a summit which opened up new visions of a world transformed through the conscious choice of man.

Material progress in the lives of nations and of Western man was as measurable and seemingly predictable as was the exploration of the physical universe through the laws and methods of classical, Newtonian physics. In a process of cross fertilization, science had perfected the tools of technology and these more perfect engineering tools had accelerated the rate of scientific investigation and discovery throughout the 19th century. The twin thrusts of science and technology had turned the civilization of Western man into the most action-oriented of any age or region.

By 1900 Europe had freed itself from the ancient mass epidemics of cholera, typhoid, and the plague and was well on its way towards curbing tuberculosis and diphtheria. The breakthrough in bacteriology, improved hygiene, as well as increased farm yields resulted in a tremendous growth of Europe's population, which, having doubled between 1750 and 1850, more than doubled again in the hundred years after 1850, to reach 576 million by the mid-20th century, the population of Russia included. As the population of Europe increased, so did the productivity of the individual through the mechanization of production and automation, which made its debut in industrial society in the early 1900's. At the same time, technology and science made available new sources of energy to satisfy the needs of the industrial economies, adding oil and electrical power to the older staple power source of coal.

1

The rate of scientific-technological change of European society was not, to be sure, uniform, vast discrepancies existing between the more developed parts of Western Europe and the relatively backward parts of Eastern Europe. By 1913 Great Britain, Germany, France, Italy, Belgium, and Sweden accounted for 74 per cent of all goods manufactured in Europe. The question of a more thorough and rapid industrialization of Eastern Europe was not one of "if" but rather of "when," however, as the foundations of future industrial growth were being laid. Even the backward regions of Europe appeared as one with the more advanced, however, from the standpoint of the non-European world, as all Great European Powers, regardless of the state of their development, employed the weapons of the industrial age in the assertion of worldwide imperialist claims.

The primacy of Europe in the world, based on its industrial-scientific civilization, was indeed taken as much for granted as were the beneficial effects of material progress itself. From Europe had issued the spark of scientific discovery; Europe had given birth to the Industrial Revolution; and Europe continued to lead in world trade and the world manufacture of goods. From Europe had flowed the greatest mass migration in history: twenty-five million individuals had settled in the American hemisphere and the "white colonies" of the British Empire in the three decades after 1870. Europe also remained the chief supplier of the world's capital until the First World War. The United States, to be sure, had already grown into the largest industrial power of the world, outproducing each of the three leading industrial nations of Europe — Germany, Great Britain, and France — in steel, coal, and numerous other commodities by 1913. The combined economic power of Britain, France, and Germany retained its world pre-eminence, however, these three nations possessing over half the world's industries and controlling half the world's trade. Most important, perhaps, in the European estimation of the global balance, it was European power — economic, political, and military — which had transformed virtually all of the world's land and oceans, save for the American hemisphere, into a sphere of European influence, both open and disguised.

Nineteen fourteen was to mark the great unhinging of the age of European primacy and confidence, wreaking upon Europe as great and sudden a change as modern physics, launched in the early 1900's by Albert Einstein and Max Planck, wrought on the established categories of space, time, matter, and causality in Newtonian physics. From the summit of its knowledge and power, Europe, after 1914, would no longer perceive the vision of orderly and rational progress but of a horizon darkened by the resurgence of irrational forces. In the crucible of war, the social, political, and national ferment of pre-war Europe would ripen into an explosive charge of worldwide repercussions, rendering the 20th century the most revolutionary of ages since the beginning of modern European history in the 16th century.

In its quest for progress, the scientific-industrial civilization of pre-war Europe had left an ever-diminishing scope of human affairs to chance; yet it was from chance and accident, more than design, that the immediate causes of the war of 1914 sprang. The deeper reason for the Great Power collision lay, no doubt, in the divisions of Europe, divisions which the industrial age had aggravated rather than overcome.

THE DIVISIONS OF EUROPE: FROM THE AGE OF BISMARCK TO THE REALIGNMENT OF THE POWERS AFTER 1900

By 1914 Europe had enjoyed nearly a half century of peace, no war between the Great Powers having been fought since the Franco-Prussian war of 1870/1871, and none engulfing the entire continent of Europe since the collapse of the First Napoleonic Empire in 1815. The unification of the German states into the Hohenzollern Empire in 1871 – the most disturbing revision of the European state system as constituted by the Congress of Vienna in 1815 – did not initiate a new series of wars, as had been widely feared in Europe.

In the age of Bismarck, from 1871 to 1890, the new German Empire, rather, developed into a factor of European stability, and the system of Bismarck's alliances came to serve the cause of peace. Basic to the European alliance system of the 1870's and 1880's was Bismarck's desire to preserve the European *status quo* of 1871. Having annexed Alsace-Lorraine from France in the Treaty of Frankfurt of May, 1871, Bismarck desired no further territorial gain in Europe. Outside Europe, Bismarck entered the colonial race with reservation and delay, the first German colony being established in Africa in 1884. Although welcoming the imperialism of other European powers as a means of deflecting their energies from Europe, Bismarck deemed imperialism a luxury and hazard for the German Empire, which it could ill afford in its early stages. Unlike many of his countrymen, intoxicated by their victory over France in 1871, Bismarck never lost sight of the limitations imposed on German power by virtue of Germany's geography in the heart of Europe and the suspicion which the mere fact of German national unification was likely to arouse among the established powers of Europe.

France, the nation most aggrieved by the outcome of the war of 1871 and the one most inclined to challenge it, was unable to find a single ally during Bismarck's chancellorship. Old ties of dynasty and friendship connected the Prussian-German Empire under the Hohenzollerns with an autocratic Russia, and no quarrel of territory or prestige divided the Russian from the German nation. The moderation shown by Bismarck towards Austria in her defeat by Prussia in 1866 made possible the restoration of cordial ties between Vienna and Berlin, once Habsburg Austria had reconciled herself to the reality of Germany united under Prussia.

A lasting union between the three conservative empires of Central and Eastern Europe – Germany, Russia, and Austria-Hungary – such as Bismarck attempted to fashion with the first and second Three Emperors' League of 1873 and 1881, eluded his diplomatic skill. In Bismarck's time the Balkans provided the chief obstacle to fruitful Austro-Russian relations, as they would still a generation later on the eve of the First World War.

The Balkan Peninsula was a region distinguished neither by the advanced level of its civilization nor the wealth of its resources, as they were known to exist in the 19th century. Yet Austria-Hungary and Russia attached the greatest importance to it. To Austria-Hungary the Balkans formed a strategic hinterland, which it was no more willing to see controlled by another Great Power than Britain would tolerate the domination of the Low Lands by a great continental power. To Russia the Balkans formed the gateway to the Aegean Sea, to Constantinople and the Dardanelles, which Russia had claimed as the "keys to her Empire" since the latter 18th century.

In the latter 19th century, the Austro-Russian rivalry in the Balkans was compounded by the spread of nationalism to the Christian subject peoples of the Moslem Turkish Empire, with Serbia, Montenegro, Bulgaria, and Rumania all clamoring for nationhood and independence. Prior to Russia's appearance in the Balkans, Austria had been the sole European power engaged in the reduction of the Moslem Turkish Empire in the Balkans, and the 18th-century victories of Austria's Prince Eugene over the Turks established a long memory of Balkan hegemony in the Austrian mind. In the 19th century, bonds of ethnic affinity between the Balkan Slavs and Russia made Russia, not Austria, appear in the role of liberator and patron of the Christian Balkan peoples. Moreover, by the latter 19th century, Austria no longer desired the complete expulsion of Turkey from Christian Europe but on the contrary, aspired to its preservation both as a bulwark against Russian expansion and as a curb to South Slav nationalism.

The Austro-Russian Balkan rivalry, first brought into sharp focus during the Crimean War in the middle of the 19th century, narrowly avoided open warfare in the wake of the Russo-Turkish war of 1877/1878. Russia had defeated Turkey and the most objectionable feature of the Peace of San Stefano, which Russia imposed on Turkey in March, 1878, was the creation of a large Bulgarian state, stretching from the Black Sea to the Aegean. Both Austria-Hungary and Great Britain objected to the establishment of a large and independent Bulgaria; both viewed it as a Russian satellite and springboard for future Russian expansion. Both

Austria-Hungary and Britain threatened war unless the San Stefano Treaty was revised.

The peace of Europe was saved in 1878 as a result of the revision of the San Stefano Peace by the Congress of Berlin. In effect, the Congress of Berlin provided for a partial dismemberment of European Turkey by the Great Powers acting in concert. Britain gained the island of Cyprus and Austria-Hungary was authorized to occupy and administer, though not to annex, the provinces of Bosnia and Hertsegovina. The small Balkan nations of Serbia, Montenegro, and Rumania obtained independence from Turkey. The chief loser of the Berlin settlement was Russia. Although Russia retained her gains in Asia Minor, such as Batum, which she had seized from Turkey in the San Stefano Peace, she failed in her plans of establishing a large Bulgarian satellite. Bulgaria north of the Balkan mountains was turned into an autonomous principality; the remainder, East Rumelia and Macedonia, stayed under Turkish control.

The Congress of Berlin saved the peace between the Great Powers, but it accomplished little towards a lasting solution of the Balkan problems themselves. The Balkan states, though independent, were not satisfied with the frontiers that were drawn. Implicit in the Congress of Berlin settlement were the territorial disputes which resulted in the Balkan wars of 1912 and 1913 as well as the Austro-Serbian confrontation of 1914.

The Congress of Berlin also cast the first shadow on Russo-German relations, since Russia blamed Bismarck, the chairman of the Congress, for her diplomatic defeat. Russian hostility towards Germany after the Congress of Berlin prompted Bismarck to conclude the Dual Alliance with Austria-Hungary in October, 1879. The Dual Alliance was a defensive alliance pledging Germany and Austria-Hungary to come to each other's aid if either were attacked by Russia or Russia allied with another power. If attacked by a power other than Russia, either member of the Dual Alliance pledged to observe benevolent neutrality.

The Dual Alliance was intended to serve as Germany's warning to Russia, rather than as a final rebuff. Bismarck served notice that Germany regarded the preservation and integrity of Austria-Hungary as indispensable to the general peace of Europe. Once Russia recognized that fact, the obstacle towards restoration of the first Three Emperors' League shattered by the Balkan crisis of 1877/1878, would be removed.

Towards Austria-Hungary, Bismarck emphasized the defensive nature of the alliance. It was designed to protect Austria-Hungary in her present state, not to encourage her in the pursuit of an aggressive and expansionist Balkan policy. In Bismarck's time, the defensive character of the Dual Alliance was preserved. Afterwards, Austria-Hungary increasingly viewed the alliance of 1879 as insurance against the risks of her own Balkan imperialism.

In the years immediately following its conclusion, the Dual Alliance produced the sobering effect on Russia which Bismarck had intended. In 1881 Russia, Germany, and Austria-Hungary formed the second Three Emperors' League, pledging neutrality of all three if one were attacked by a fourth power. Yet the Second Three Emperors' League established no more than a truce in the Austro-Russian Balkan quarrels. The truce was ended in 1885/1886 in the wake of a new Balkan crisis following the union of autonomous Bulgaria with East Rumelia.

Russia refused to renew the Second Three Emperors' League when it expired in 1887. The connection between Vienna and St. Petersburg was severed once again, but not between St. Petersburg and Berlin. In 1887 Russia and Germany concluded the Reinsurance Treaty, which was occasioned both by the disintegration of the Second Three Emperors' League and by the resurgence of revanchist feeling against Germany in France.

The Reinsurance Treaty was a German-Russian neutrality agreement, in which Germany, at first sight, appeared to have paid the heavier price. Germany and Russia pledged benevolent neutrality in the event of war with a third power. The obligation of neutrality did not apply to an aggressive war by Russia against Austria-Hungary or Germany against France. Germany recognized Russia's historic rights in the Balkans and specifically, Russia's preponderant influence in Bulgaria. Moreover, Germany promised moral and diplomatic support should Russia seek control over the Dardanelles.

Bismarck's heavy commitment to Russian Balkan interests, which potentially conflicted with the spirit, if not the letter, of the Dual Alliance of 1879, was counterbalanced, however, by the Mediterranean League. The latter, concluded in 1887 between Britain, Italy, and Austria-Hungary, guaranteed the integrity of the Turkish Empire as well as Turkish control over the Dardanelles. Although Germany was not a partner to the League, it was chiefly as a result of Bismarck's initiative that it was formed. The mere fact of the Mediterranean League, of whose existence Russia knew despite its secret terms, lessened the probability of Germany's having to pay the price for Russian neutrality which the Reinsurance Treaty had stipulated.

The Reinsurance Treaty and the Mediterranean League marked the pinnacle of Bismarck's system of alliances, in which Italy, by her own request, had also been included in 1882. Historically and sentimentally, the sympathies of Italy were largely on the side of France, Austria having been the major obstacle to Italian national unification before 1859 and France having given the support without which Austria could not have been evicted from Italy in 1859. Yet France became Italy's main colonial rival in North Africa when it seized Tunisia in 1881 while Italy herself was poised to turn Tunisia into her own colony. The

Italian motive in seeking an alliance with Germany and Austria-Hungary at the turn of 1881/1882 thus sprang chiefly from the desire to overcome Italy's isolation and to obtain the necessary backing for Italy's colonial pursuits in Africa. At the behest of Italy, Germany, Austria-Hungary, and Italy concluded the Triple Alliance in May, 1882, which pledged Italian support to Germany and German-Austrian support to Italy in the event of French attack. The Triple Alliance, it should be noted, did not replace or supersede the Dual Alliance of 1879. Both alliances retained their separate identity, the Triple Alliance soon losing its force and meaning, the Dual Alliance lasting until the end of the First World War.

By 1890 Bismarck had drawn every major power on the European continent, save France, into his alliance system. Bismarck's last diplomatic project, prior to his downfall in 1890, to conclude a defensive alliance with Great Britain, failed over the polite rejection of the British Prime Minister, Lord Salisbury. In 1890, when Britain deemed her isolation still "splendid," she had no need for permanent allies. Otherwise, Anglo-German relations were friendly, having suffered only one brief set-back in 1884/1885 at the time of Germany's first colonial venture in Africa.

A greater asset to the peace of Europe than the alliances themselves was the prestige of Bismarck and the trust which the restraint of German power in his hands had engendered among the governments of Europe generally. The dismissal of Bismarck from the German chancellorship in March, 1890, by the young Emperor William II was thus an event of European significance.

THE REALIGNMENT OF THE EUROPEAN POWERS AFTER BISMARCK: FROM THE TRIPLE ALLIANCE TO THE TRIPLE ENTENTE

In 1890, after Bismarck's fall, Germany failed to renew the Reinsurance Treaty with Russia, despite the latter's plea for a continuation of the neutrality agreement. Bismarck's successors, less skillful than the master by their own admission, simply regarded Bismarck's alliance system as too complex and as a source of possible conflict of interest between the Austro-German and the German-Russian alliances. The dropping of the Reinsurance Treaty by Germany set the stage for the first major revision of the European alignment of powers since Bismarck. Russia mistakenly interpreted the German rebuff of 1890 as a clear sign of a major German policy shift, away from Russia and towards Great Britain. In 1894, after extended negotiations, Russia and France concluded a secret military alliance, designed to counterbalance the Triple Alliance of 1882; Russia and France would answer the mobilization of any one member of the Triple Alliance with mobilizations of their own;

Russia promised to support France, if France were attacked by Germany, or Italy supported by Germany; France would support Russia, if Russia were attacked by Germany, or Austria supported by Germany. The duration of the Franco-Russian alliance was conditioned on that of the Triple Alliance.

The division of continental Europe into two military blocs, of Triple Alliance and Franco-Russian alliance, did not immediately assume the threatening aspects it was to attain on the eve of the First World War. During the first decade of the new Franco-Russian alliance, European Great Power interest and concern shifted instead to the far corners of the world with the approaching climax of the age of European imperialism.

In carving up the colonial world, the European powers acted in fierce competition, rather than in concert; joint actions, such as the suppression of the Chinese "Boxer" Rebellion in 1900 by the European powers and the United States, were the exception rather than the rule. At the turn of the century, the most serious friction among the competing imperialist rivals was that between Britain and France over Egypt and the Egyptian Sudan and that between Britain and Russia over the control of Persia, Afghanistan, and Tibet. In 1898 Britain and France narrowly avoided war over the Sudan, following the near clash of a French force under Captain Marchand and an Anglo-Egyptian army under General Kitchener at Fashoda.

THE END OF BRITISH ISOLATION

By the turn of the century, Britain regarded her isolation as no longer "splendid" but dangerous amidst the onrush of not one but several imperialist competitors throughout the world. The extent of British isolation as well as of anti-British feeling among the continental powers was demonstrated during Britain's war of conquest against the Boer Republics of Transvaal and Orange Free State in South Africa between 1899 and 1902. Public opinion in continental Europe was overwhelmingly hostile to the British cause and official government reaction only a little less so. Nicholas II of Russia, for one, castigated Britain for her alleged "implacable egoism" and "avidity."

Britain needed and wanted allies and it was Germany that she turned to first. Between 1898 and 1902 Britain approached Germany on several occasions with proposals for a bilateral alliance. The proposal for alliance with Germany was initiated by the British Colonial Secretary Joseph Chamberlain and put into concrete form by the Foreign Secretary Lord Lansdowne. In his speech at Leicester of November, 1899, Joseph Chamberlain even proposed the creation of a new global Triple Alliance of Britain, the United States, and Germany as the best guarantee of world peace.

The Germany of 1900 was not the same as Bismarck's Germany. Though honoring the memory of Bismarck, the German Empire no longer displayed the moderation which had been the chief source of European trust in Bismarck's statesmanship. A new generation had come of age since Bismarck, dazzled by the many signs of Germany's growing industrial strength and rapidly expanding population. By 1900 Germany had become the leading industrial power of continental Europe and had begun to surpass Great Britain in key areas of industrial production, such as steel. The voice of moderation of the 1880's had given way to a boisterous assertion of power, as Germany acquired a new island empire in the Pacific with the purchase of the Carolines and Marianas from Spain in 1898 and established a foothold in China with the lease of Kiaochow on the Shantung Peninsula in 1897.

The German quest for world power was not unique, but rather part of the imperialist pattern of the age. In the expansion of its power, Germany was more confident than others, however, and it was over-confidence as well as a misreading of Great-Power relations which determined Germany's reply to the British offer of alliance.

Germany rejected Britain's alliance offer in the form in which it was made. In so doing, Germany assumed that time was on her side, that the power of the British Empire was in decline while that of Germany was increasing. Britain's failure to win speedy victory in the Boer War seemed only to confirm the German estimate of Britain's waning strength. Likewise, Germany assumed the Anglo-French friction over Egypt and that between Britain and Russia over Persia to be permanent and irremovable features of the imperialist age. A Britain hemmed in by France and Russia and conscious of its relative decline would have no choice, in the German estimate, but to return to Germany with a proposal of alliance on better terms than those of 1899 or 1900. A further German motive was suspicion. Germany was willing to join Britain in alliance, provided that alliance was the Triple Alliance of 1882. Britain's refusal to join the Triple Alliance confirmed the German view that Britain desired the advantages of an alliance with Germany without assuming corresponding risks. In the words of the German chancellor Bernhard Bülow, Britain wished Germany merely to "pull her chestnuts out of the fire."

Time was not on the German side, as Bülow and William II had so confidently assumed in 1900, nor were the imperialist rivalries of Britain, France, and Russia beyond compromise. Rebuffed by Germany, Britain settled her colonial differences with France in the colonial settlement of 1904 known as the *Entente Cordiale*. In essence, the *Entente Cordiale,* or cordial understanding, allotted Egypt to the British sphere of influence and Morocco to that of France. The threat of Russian imperialism to British interests in Asia was first countered by the Anglo-Japanese alliance of 1902 and, more importantly for the realignment of the European powers, resolved through compromise in the Anglo-Russian *entente* of 1907. The Anglo-Russian *entente* was an agreement similar to that between Britain and France of 1904, removing old sources of imperialist friction. Persia was divided threefold into a northern Russian, a southern British, and a central neutral zone. In Afghanistan, where British-Indian and Russian forces had clashed repeatedly in the 1880's, British influence was to prevail. Tibet was turned into a buffer.

In the realignment of the European powers after 1900, personalities were as important as the issues, which led to the Anglo-French and Anglo-Russian compromise. In France, the principal architect of the *Entente Cordiale* was Foreign Minister Théophile Delcassé, who always regarded Anglo-French imperialist rivalries secondary to the threat posed by Germany to France in Europe. In Britain, the Liberal Foreign Secretary Sir Edward Grey and Undersecretary Arthur Nicolson actively strove towards a colonial settlement with Russia in order to create a new power balance in Europe between Triple Alliance and Triple Entente. The cause of Anglo-Russian reconciliation in 1907 was greatly aided also by the fact of German naval armaments, of which more will be said presently, as well as the appearance of German interests in Turkey with the project of a German-built railroad from Constantinople to Basra on the Persian Gulf. The project of the so-called Bagdad railroad was equally disturbing to Russia and Great Britain: to Russia, because it constituted a German invasion of an area considered by Russia to be her own sphere of influence; to Britain, because the Bagdad railroad threatened to establish an alternate land route in the Middle East to the Suez Canal.

THE GERMAN CHALLENGE TO THE REALIGNMENT OF THE POWERS: THE MOROCCO CRISIS AND NAVAL ARMAMENTS

To the German Empire, the realignment of the powers after 1904 did not appear as a new balance between Triple Alliance and Triple Entente but rather as a policy of encirclement of Germany. The awareness of having suffered a major diplomatic defeat in 1904 and the anxiety over "being encircled" resulted in a German policy of threats, designed to reverse the changed diplomatic situation of 1904 and after. In 1905 Germany deliberately provoked a European crisis over Morocco, charging the incompatibility of the Anglo-French agreement on Morocco of 1904 with the provisions of the Madrid Convention, concluded between the powers and Morocco in 1880. The latter had upheld the integrity of Morocco and established the most favored nation principle for Morocco's economic relations with the Madrid powers.

Although Germany's economic interests in Morocco were real, she was less concerned with the protection of her economic interest than with the political disruption of the Anglo-French Entente. By demanding an international conference for the review of the Morocco question, Germany hoped to isolate France and to demonstrate the worthlessness of British friendship for France in time of crisis. The German aim, in Chancellor Bülow's words, was to "confront France with the possibility of war" and to knock France, "the continental dagger," out of Britain's hands. The German hopes for French submission in 1905 seemed all the more justified, as Russian military power was fully absorbed in the Russo-Japanese war, the Russian army having been beaten by Japan in the Battle of Mukden and the Russian navy having met with a similar fate in the Battle of Tsushima.

The conference, which Germany demanded and which France resisted in vain, was held at Algeciras in early 1906. Although the Algeciras Conference paid lip service to the integrity of Morocco and the principle of the Open Door, it marked a major diplomatic defeat for Germany, since Britain and all other powers save Austria-Hungary, voted with France on the important issues. To all intents and purposes, Morocco was opened to further French penetration and the *Entente Cordiale,* far from being shattered, had been strengthened in response to German pressure. Beginning with 1906, the British Foreign Secretary Sir Edward Grey authorized the holding of conferences between the British and French military staffs.

The Morocco crisis of 1905 had far-reaching consequences whose effects were being felt as late as 1914. In Germany and Austria-Hungary, the precedent of the Algeciras vote produced a lasting aversion to international conferences for the settlement of Great-Power conflicts. In Britain, the Morocco crisis awakened the suspicion that behind every major European crisis, which was to follow after 1906, there lurked the German motive of wrecking Britain's entente with France and, after 1907, with Russia.

The year 1905, which at first had promised to be one of diplomatic opportunities for Germany, brought the German Empire yet another defeat. In July, 1905, Emperor William II and Tsar Nicholas II had concluded a personal alliance at the Finnish island of Björkö on the occasion of the Emperor's summer cruise in the Baltic Sea. The Björkö Treaty pledged Germany and Russia to mutual support in the event of an attack by a third power in Europe. Concluded at the time of the Russo-Japanese war, the Björkö Treaty reflected the Tsar's momentary anger at Great Britain, with which Russia had almost come to blows in October, 1904, over the Dogger Bank Incident. The latter involved the Russian fleet and English fishing boats in the North Sea. The Russian fleet, on its way to the Far East, had opened fire on the fishing boats in the mistaken belief that they were a flotilla of Japanese torpedo boats in European waters.

The Björkö Treaty, if allowed to stand, would have repudiated the Franco-Russian alliance of 1894. For that very reason the Russian foreign office rejected it, as soon as it learned of its conclusion. The Björkö Treaty, signed in a fit of dynastic amity between the monarchs of Russia and Germany, remained an episode without consequence.

THE ALIENATION OF ITALY FROM THE TRIPLE ALLIANCE

While the Anglo-French entente withstood successfully the challenge of German power, the old Triple Alliance of 1882 was losing its force and meaning in the early 1900's. In 1902 Italy concluded a secret agreement with France, pledging neutrality if France became the object of direct or indirect aggression or if France waged war in defense of her national honor. In 1909 Italy concluded a secret agreement with Russia at Racconigi, on the occasion of the Tsar's visit to Italy. In the Racconigi Agreement, Italy and Russia pledged to maintain the status quo in the Balkans and to consult one another if a threat of "foreign," meaning Austrian, "domination" developed in the Balkans. Both agreements violated the spirit of the Triple Alliance, and one of them—the agreement with France—violated its letter.

The reasons for Italy's alienation from the Triple Alliance were essentially two: (1) Italian membership in the Triple Alliance had always been conditioned on friendly relations between the members of the Triple Alliance on the one hand, and Great Britain on the other. In the early 1900's this condition no longer obtained, especially with the sharpening of the Anglo-German naval race. (2) As noted earlier, among Italy's motives in seeking an alliance with Germany and Austria-Hungary in 1882, support for Italy's colonial expansion in Africa was paramount. In fact, Germany and Austria-Hungary had given no such support. Yet Italy was as anxious as any European power to rank among the great colonial nations, especially after the Italian bid to conquer Ethiopia had ended with the defeat of Italian troops by a native army in the Battle of Adowa of 1896. Italian imperialists, speaking in the pages of the imperialist mouthpiece *Il Regno,* coined the phrase "proletarian nation" to describe Italy, whose only major export was people. The emigration of Italians to the United States and Latin America amounted, in the Italian imperialists' view, to a "hemorrhage." "Emigration," wrote the leading imperialist Enrico Corradini, "is a phenomenon, if not of an inferior people, at least of a people at an inferior stage of existence." Italy wanted her colonial empire in Africa, and both France and Russia, in the agreements of 1902 and 1909 respectively, had recognized Tripoli as an Italian sphere of influence.

In September, 1911, Italy invaded Tripoli, which was still under Turkish rule. The Italian-Turkish war lasted longer than Italy had calculated. Unable to defeat the Turkish defenses at Tobruk and Benghazi in the first rush, Italy carried the war to the Turkish islands in the Aegean and the Dardanelles. Not until October, 1912, did Turkey concede defeat and surrender Tripoli to Italian rule, after the payment of an Italian indemnity to Turkey. In carrying the war into the area of the Balkans, Italy aroused the ill will of Austria-Hungary. Austria's Chief of Staff, Conrad von Hötzendorff, would have preferred an Austrian preventive war against Italy in 1911 as the best means of settling accounts with the estranged Italian ally. By 1911 the atmosphere of Austro-Italian relations was as fully charged with mutual suspicion and dislike as it had been at the time of Italian national unification a half century before.

THE ANGLO-GERMAN NAVAL RACE

The most disconcerting manifestation of German power in the early 20th century from the British standpoint was the growth of German naval strength. Until the turn of the century, German naval power had been comparatively insignificant, German naval expenditures ranking behind those of France and Russia. The appointment of Alfred von Tirpitz as Secretary of the Navy in 1897 marked the turning point in German naval history. Tirpitz launched a program of naval expansion with the naval bill of 1898, which was followed by a series of naval bills between 1900 and 1912. The first naval bill of 1898, providing for the addition of seven battleships, two heavy cruisers, seven light cruisers as well as a number of smaller vessels, did not yet arouse undue concern in Great Britain. German naval armaments became a menace only when Germany doubled the projected number of naval vessels in 1900 and duplicated the new British "Dreadnought" design of super-battleships after 1904.

The motives behind the naval policy of Tirpitz were several. They included the expansion of Germany's colonial empire into the Pacific and the Far East in the 1890's and the increase of German overseas trade and interests, both of which appeared to justify increased naval armaments. When acquiring the first German colonies in Africa in 1884, Bismarck had pointed to the German colonial empire as proof of Germany's good will towards Britain, because the communications between Germany and her colonies, unprotected by German sea power, depended on friendly Anglo-German relations. The Germany of William II no longer wished to rely exclusively on British goodwill, nor could it always do so after 1900.

Tirpitz' navy was designed to serve purposes other than those of protection, however. The Tirpitz navy was intended as a challenge to Great Britain, as a means of asserting the equality of Germany as a world power. Britain's supremacy at sea rested on the so-called two-power standard, adopted by the British admiralty in 1888. To retain its pre-eminence, the British fleet, according to the two-power standard, must exceed the combined naval strength of Britain's two nearest naval rivals. Against the British concept of the two-power standard, Tirpitz posed the German concept of the "risk navy." Although Germany could not hope to match British naval power, she could build a fleet large enough to act as a deterrent. Should Britain engage the German "risk navy" in battle, British casualties would be severe enough to destroy the two-power standard.

German navalism of the early 1900's was strongly influenced by the thesis of Alfred Mahan, the American author of *The Influence of Sea Power upon History,* of 1890. In due time, naval armaments became a highly popular cause in Germany, inextricably tied to considerations of national prestige. In the early 1900's naval power came to be viewed as the ultimate strategic weapon, to influence the balance of the world, not unlike air power in the middle of the 20th century or missile power since the 1960's.

The British response to German naval power was an increase in Britain's own naval strength, a policy which the Liberal government of Britain between 1906 and 1914 resented all the more since it was committed to large expenditures for domestic social reform. The need for higher taxes, to cover both, increased naval spending and social reform, caused a severe political and constitutional crisis in Great Britain in 1909. In 1881, when explaining to Russia the limits of German support to that country in the event of a Russo-British war over the Dardanelles, Bismarck had observed that the German army "will not be able to swim to London." The implications of German naval power in the early 20th century were, however, that a German army might indeed attempt such an undertaking in the future. To Britain, German naval power was as much a provocation as the establishment of a British conscript army in peace time would have been to Germany. Short of a negotiated agreement on the limitations of German naval power, Britain had no choice but to keep abreast of German naval armaments.

THE HALDANE MISSION: THE FAILURE OF ANGLO-GERMAN NAVAL TALKS

The new crisis over Morocco in 1911 dramatically highlighted the extent of Anglo-German animosity, fuelled by the naval issue. The French military occupation of the Moroccan capital of Fez had prompted Germany to dispatch the gunboat *Panther* to the Moroccan port of Agadir. Ostensibly, the purpose of the *Panther's* mission was the protection of German mining interests in Morocco. In truth, it served the purpose of pressuring France into colonial "compensation" as a price for German recognition of a French protectorate over Morocco. The British government, fearing the establishment of a German naval base in West Morocco, responded to the "*Panther's* leap" much more sharply than it had to the first Morocco crisis of 1905. In July, 1911, Lloyd George, the British Chancellor of the Exchequer, delivered a stern warning to Germany, declaring that peace at the price of surrender of Britain's "great and beneficent" position would be an intolerable humiliation. Under British pressure Germany settled for a much smaller colonial compensation from France than she had expected to obtain. Instead of receiving the entire French Congo, Germany got only a few worthless strips.

Although the crisis of 1911 had inflamed public opinion in Germany and Britain, it also resulted, at least in Britain, in growing public and parliamentary concern over the state of Anglo-German relations. The House of Commons wished at least to explore the possibility of an Anglo-German naval accord, and it was for that purpose that the British Minister of War Lord Haldane arrived in Berlin in February, 1912.

Though conducted in a friendly atmosphere, the Anglo-German naval talks of February, 1912, produced no agreement. Britain insisted that Germany recognize British supremacy at sea and also alter the new naval bill of 1912, extending the building program from the projected six to twelve years. Germany refused concessions in the building program unless a binding neutrality agreement were obtained from Britain in return. Such an agreement Britain was no longer in a position to grant in view of her moral commitments under the Triple Entente, to which specific military arrangements had been added in the wake of the Morocco crisis of 1911. In July, 1911, the French and British staffs had worked out detailed plans for the deployment of a British expeditionary force of 170,000 men to France in case of war. After the failure of the Haldane mission, Germany enacted the naval bill of 1912, which called for the addition of a third battle squadron to the German North Sea fleet. In response, Britain and France agreed to shift the British battleship squadron in the Mediterranean to the North Sea while France transferred the bulk of her naval forces from the North Sea to the Mediterranean. Henceforth, France took the protection of her Atlantic seaboard by British naval power for granted. To all intents and purposes, the Anglo-French entente had become a military alliance.

The principal obstacle to a naval agreement in 1912 between Britain and Germany was Admiral Tirpitz. The German Chancellor Bethmann-Hollweg favored an accord and offered his resignation when none was achieved. In a prophetic warning to his imperial master, Bethmann-Hollweg stated, after the failure of the Haldane mission, that for Germany to provoke a war without her honor or vital interests being at stake would be a sin against her fate. "Your majesty's navy will fight heroically," Bethmann declared in 1912, "but we cannot count on victory over the British and French fleets." In naval, as in army matters, it was the judgment of admirals and generals, however, not of political leaders, which determined policy in the imperial Germany of 1912.

After the failure of the Haldane mission, Britain and Germany persisted in their effort to find areas of agreement. But such agreements as they succeeded in concluding on the eve of the First World War, such as the compromise on the Bagdad railroad, leaving its final stretch to Britain, or the tentative accord on the division of the Portuguese colonial empire in Africa between Germany and Britain, were merely peripheral to the differences between them.

THE RETURN OF CRISIS TO THE BALKANS:
1908 TO 1914

At the turn of the century, the Balkans had been free from major crisis, largely because of Russian preoccupation with problems in the Far East and because of the Russian-Austrian agreement of 1897. That agreement had pledged both powers to preserve the Balkan *status quo* and to cooperate against any other power seeking Balkan territorial gains.

The Balkan truce of 1897 was shortlived, as others had been before. After the turn of the century, the Balkan truce was broken by a combination of factors which rekindled the dormant national and imperialist fires. These factors may be summarized under the broad categories of resumption of an active Russian Balkan role, following Russia's defeat by Japan in 1905, the revival of Austrian Balkan imperialism, the progressive weakening of the Turkish Empire, and the growing appetite for territorial expansion on the part of the Balkan states at the expense of both the Turkish and the Habsburg empires. Any one of these developments would have sufficed to turn the Balkans into an area of major crisis in the early 1900's. The coincidence, combination, and interaction of the several Balkan crises in the last decade before 1914 rendered the Balkan Peninsula more explosive than ever.

THE ANNEXATION OF
BOSNIA-HERTSEGOVINA

The Young Turk revolution of the summer of 1908 in many ways acted as the trigger for the several ensuing Balkan crises. Young Turkish officers, among whom Mustafa Kemal of World War One and postwar fame was prominent, staged a coup against the Sultan in an attempt to rejuvenate the Ottoman Empire. In July, 1908, the Young Turk revolution compelled Sultan Abdul Hamid to restore the Turkish liberal constitution of 1876, and in the following year it replaced Abdul Hamid with the more pliable Mohammed V. The Sultan lost his power to dissolve parliament, and the government was made responsible to parliament. Apart from modernizing the machinery of government, the Young Turk revolution strove to imbue all subjects of the Ottoman Empire, regardless of their nationality, with a new Turkish national consciousness.

The eff- was the exact opposite. The non-Turkish nationalities asserted their separate identity, and the Great Powers, Russia and Austria-Hungary, were prompted into new action lest the Turkish national revolution should actually succeed. In September, 1908, the foreign ministers of Russia and Austria-Hungary, Izvolsky and Aehrenthal, concluded an agreement at Buchlau whereby Russia acquiesced in Austria-Hungary's annexation of the Turkish provinces of Bosnia and Hertsegovina, which Austria-Hungary had administered since the Congress of Berlin. In return, Austria-Hungary promised not to oppose the opening of the Dardanellas to Russian warships. Although the subject of the Buchlau agreement was precise, the timing of its implementation was not, no date for the Austrian annexation having been agreed upon.

In early October, 1908, Austria-Hungary surprised Russia and the world by announcing the annexation of Bosnia and Hertsegovina. The nation most angered by the Austrian move, next to Russia, was Serbia, which coveted the area in question as part of her plan of creating a Yugoslav state under her leadership. In March, 1909, Russia accepted the Austrian *fait accompli* after receiving a stiff warning from Germany that to do otherwise would entail the risk of conflict. In 1909 Russia was too near the ill effects of her defeat in Asia in 1905 to accept the Austro-German challenge. She bowed to Austro-German pressure and advised Serbia to do likewise. The annexation crisis of 1908/1909 not only ended Austro-Russian cooperation in the Balkans but intensified Austro-Serb antagonism, which had been growing since 1902.

Between its emancipation from Turkish rule at the Congress of Berlin in 1878 and the beginning of the 20th century, Serbia had been, if not a satellite of Austria, her client state. In 1881 Serbia was tied to Austria-Hungary, both by commercial and political agreements, the latter stipulating that Serbia would not conclude any political treaty with another government without a previous understanding with Austria-Hungary. In 1903 the rule of the pro-Austrian Serb dynasty of Obrenovich ended with the assassination of King Alexander in an army plot. The new king of Serbia, Peter of the Karageorgevich dynasty, as well as Serbia's long-term prime minister, Nicholas Pašić, looked towards Russia for political support while receiving loans and armaments from France.

THE BALKAN WARS OF 1912/1913

The political program of Serbia after 1903 became the union of the South Slavs under Serbian leadership. The Serbian plan of creating a greater Yugoslavia was frustrated, however, as long as Austria-Hungary remained in possession of Bosnia-Hertsegovina and Turkey in control of

Macedonia. Of the two obstacles in the path of Serbia's ambitions, the Turkish Empire was the weaker. The Italian-Turkish war from September, 1911, to October, 1912, previously discussed, confirmed the vulnerability of Turkey. In March of 1912 Serbia formed the Balkan League with Bulgaria, with the encouragement of Russia. The Balkan League was the overture to the impending Bulgarian-Serb attack on Turkey, which was delivered in October, 1912. At the time of its attack on Turkey, the Balkan League had been expanded to include Greece and Montenegro as well.

The Balkan League had little difficulty in defeating Turkey, but it encountered major trouble in dividing the spoils of its victory. Macedonia, which Russia had proposed to unite with Bulgaria in the San Stefano Treaty of 1878 after the Russo-Turkish war of 1877/1878, was the prize coveted by all three — Serbia, Bulgaria, and Greece. The rival claims on Macedonia were based on the ethnic divisions of the Macedonian population, which contained elements of all three Balkan nations. Serbia, in addition to its Macedonian claims, demanded Albania as well, which had been conquered from the Turks.

By December, 1912, the Great Powers intervened in the Balkan crisis with the formation of the Ambassadors' Conference in London, consisting of the ambassadors of France, Italy, Russia, Austria-Hungary, and Germany and presided over by the British Foreign Secretary Sir Edward Grey. For the first time since the Congress of Berlin in 1878, the Great Powers thus acted in concert in dealing with the problem of the Balkans. With the aid of the Ambassadors' Conference, peace was concluded between Turkey and the Balkan League in the Treaty of London of May, 1913. Turkey surrendered its European territory except for Constantinople, a strip along the Dardanelles, and the island of Crete. Albania, at the insistence of Austria-Hungary and Italy, neither of which desired a Serbia entrenched in Albania, was to be constituted as an autonomous principality.

No sooner had the Treaty of London been signed than the members of the Balkan League went to war with one another over the division of the Turkish spoils. In late June, 1913, Bulgaria responded to the formation of a new Greek-Serbian alliance with an attack on both powers. Greece and Serbia were quickly joined by Montenegro, Rumania, and even Turkey, all of whom overwhelmed Bulgaria by August, 1913. Peace was restored in the Treaty of Bucharest of August, 1913. Turkey regained Adrianople, Serbia obtained the northern and central parts of Macedonia, and Greece secured the southern part of Macedonia together with the port of Saloniki. Bulgaria, in addition to losing virtually all gains of the first Balkan war, also had to cede the better part of the Dobroja to Rumania.

The petty haggling over Balkan territory might have remained

TERRITORIAL CHANGES IN
THE BALKANS, 1856-1914

150 MILES

RUSSIAN

EMPIRE
1914

VIENNA

AUSTRIA-

Budapest

HUNGARY
1914

DRAVE

DANUBE

TISZA

MAROS

SAVE

DNIESTER

1812

PRUT

SERETH

BESSARABIA

1812

1856-
1878

BLACK

BOSNIA-
HERZEGOVINA
OCCUP., 1878
ANNEXED, 1908

Sarajevo

Belgrade

SERBIA
INDEP., 1878

RUMANIA
INDEP.,
1878

Bucharest

1878

DOBRUDJA

DANUBE

1878

SEA

1878

1878

1878

1913

MONTE-
NEGRO

1912-13

1878

BULGARIA
INDEP., 1908

Sofia

1885

EASTERN RUMELIA

ADRIATIC SEA

ITALY

Tirana

ALBANIA
INDEP.
1912-13

1912-13

1886-1913

Constantinople

OTTOMAN

1913

1881

AEGEAN

SEA

EMPIRE

1914

IONIAN

SEA

Smyrna

BOUNDARY OF THE
OTTOMAN EMPIRE
1815

GREECE
INDEP.
1830

Athens

AEGEAN IS.
TO GR.
1913

DODECANESE IS.
TO ITALY
1912

MEDITERRANEAN

CRETE
AUTONOMOUS, 1908
UNITED TO GREECE, 1908-13

SEA

TRM

19

a minor, though tedious, issue for the Great Powers, but for its effect on the larger confrontation of Austrian and Russian interests. Austria-Hungary feared and resented the territorial expansion of Serbia, if only because it increased Serbian self-confidence as well as the appeal of Great-Serbian propaganda within the South Slav areas of Austria-Hungary. The Balkan League had in itself constituted a major gain for Russian Balkan influence. Although the jealousy between Serbia and Bulgaria had smashed the Balkan League after the first Balkan War, Austria-Hungary's position in the Balkans had improved little. Bulgaria, to be sure, now looked towards Austria-Hungary, pleading for an alliance with the latter, in order to counter the combined pressure of the remaining Balkan nations. Among the latter, the influence of Austria-Hungary was waning. Rumania, though formally associated with the Triple Alliance since 1883, had ceased to be a reliable Austrian ally, largely because Rumania, like Serbia, had territorial claims against Austria-Hungary. The territory in question was Transylvania, an area containing a large Rumanian population. Greece, although considered friendly by Germany because of dynastic ties between the Greek and German ruling families, had aligned behind Serbia since 1912.

The Balkan Wars of 1912/1913 thus brought Austro-Serbian tensions to their highest pitch since 1909. After the Peace of Bucharest of August, 1913, Serbia defied the decision of the London Ambassadors' Conference by refusing to evacuate its troops from Albania. On October 18, 1913, Austria-Hungary, acting independently of the other Great Powers, delivered a one-week ultimatum to Serbia, demanding Serbian evacuation of Albania and threatening war as the alternative. In October, 1913, Serbia complied with Austria's ultimatum on the advice of Russia. Within less than a year, another Austrian ultimatum to Serbia would lead to general war. Serbia's enforced evacuation of Albania did not affect her basic aim, which Russian Foreign Minister Sazonov had described in May, 1913: "Serbia has only gone through the first stage of her historic road . . . Serbia's promised land lies in the territory of present-day Hungary. . . . In these circumstances it is a vital interest of Serbia to obtain the necessary degree of preparedness for the future inevitable struggle."

THE DIPLOMATIC CRISIS OF 1914

The peace of Europe had been broken twice in the course of the 19th century as a result of Austrian opposition to the establishment of nation states; between 1859 and 1860, Austria had opposed Italian national unification, and in 1866 she had resisted the national unification of the German states. Neither conflict had resulted in general wars, encompassing the whole of Europe, because both wars were brief and relatively localized. In 1914, however, the whole system of the European states was drawn into the crisis which grew from Austria's opposition to yet another movement of national unification, that of the South Slavs under Serbian leadership. The cause itself was peripheral or unrelated to the more serious issues which had unsettled Europe since the early 1900's, such as the Anglo-German naval race, the bullying of France by Germany in the Morocco crises, or Germany's peremptory demand of 1909 that Russia acquiesce in Austria-Hungary's annexation of Bosnia. None of these issues had led to war, though most had been more serious than the Austro-Serbian confrontation would be in 1914.

The cumulative effect of the recurring crises during the last decade before the war was not to make for greater caution among the powers but rather to increase the determination to avoid past failures. There was, in 1914, as yet no balance of terror, such as has apparently rendered the alternatives to war more acceptable than war itself in the nuclear age. There was only a balance of power, and both the members of the Triple Entente on the one hand and Germany and Austria-Hungary on the other pursued the Austro-Serbian crisis to its bitter end, lest the triumph of one or the other upset the balance as either alliance understood it to exist.

Well might a general European war between the power blocs have started at a later date over another issue. Whether it actually would have broken out must necessarily remain a matter of conjecture. Explosive issues, carelessly attended to, abounded in the Europe of the early 20th century. The fact that general war was triggered by the assassination of Austria-Hungary's Archduke Francis Ferdinand was rooted both in logic and in accident.

THE ASSASSINATION
OF FRANCIS FERDINAND

On June 28, 1914, six Serbian-trained assassins, together with an uncounted number of welcomers, awaited the arrival of Archduke Francis Ferdinand, heir to the Austrian throne, in Sarajevo, capital of Bosnia. The assassins belonged to the Serbian terrorist organization "Black Hand" *(Crna Ruka)*, founded in 1911, dedicated to the liberation of Serbs under Turkish and Austrian rule and previously active in Macedonia and Bosnia. The Serbian government was aware of the existence of the "Black Hand," disapproved of its methods but dared not suppress it for fear of suffering a fate similar to that which had overtaken the Serbian King Alexander, murdered by individuals subsequently active in the "Black Hand." Of the six assassins only one, Gabrilo Princip, found both the opportunity and the courage to carry out his mission. The motive of the assassination, in Princip's own words after his arrest, was that "the archduke was a German, an enemy of the Slavs." More basic to the murder than Francis Ferdinand's nationality was his intention to reorganize the Austro-Hungarian Empire into a Triple Monarchy with greater freedom and autonomy for Austria's South Slav subjects. If he had been given an opportunity to carry out his plans, Austria's own Serbian subjects might have lost some of their enthusiasm for union with Serbia.

Austria-Hungary was anxious to implicate the Serbian government in Princip's deed, chiefly to justify before the world the reprisal she was about to take against Serbia. The proof was not established. In Austria-Hungary, however, official Serbian involvement in the assassination was simply taken for granted. The Belgrade press was jubilant over Francis Ferdinand's assassination. The Austrian request, submitted to the Serbian government, to dampen the enthusiasm of the Belgrade press evoked the answer that Serbia's press was free.

From the beginning of the crisis which followed the assassination, Austria-Hungary was resolved not to settle for another diplomatic victory over Serbia, such as she had obtained in 1909 and 1913 after Serbia's withdrawal from Albania, but rather to seek the elimination of Serbia as an independent state. Before taking action against Serbia, the Foreign Minister of Austria-Hungary, Count Berchtold, sought to obtain assurances of German support. Meeting with Berchtold's emissary, Alexander Hoyos, at Potsdam, William II issued a "blank check" to Austria-Hungary on July 5, 1914. In so doing, the German Emperor urged his Austrian ally to act with speed, however. It was the hope both of Germany and Austria-Hungary to keep the Austro-Serbian crisis localized and to prevent the alliance systems from becoming drawn into it. Both powers were conscious of the risks of general war, however, and both accepted them. In the event, William II doubted the preparedness for war of either France or Russia in 1914.

THE EXPANSION OF THE CRISIS

The Austro-Serbian crisis could not be localized, as Germany and Austria-Hungary hoped, largely because a full month passed between the assassination of Francis Ferdinand and Austria-Hungary's declaration of war on Serbia on July 28, 1914. The delay was due to a variety of factors. Time was needed to complete Austria-Hungary's legal inquiry into the origins of the assassination, to justify the Habsburg cause. Time was needed also to settle the debate within the government of Austria-Hungary over the future disposition of Serbian territory. The Hungarian Prime Minister Tisza, a powerful voice in the affairs of the Dual Monarchy, opposed the annexation of Serbia. Reflecting the Hungarian aversion towards Slavs in general and South Slavs in particular, Tisza feared the increase in Austria-Hungary's own South Slav population if Serbia were incorporated. It was thus agreed in Vienna that assurances be given to the powers that Austria-Hungary would not seek the annexation of Serbian territory.

It was also agreed, however, that an ultimatum be delivered to Serbia, containing unacceptable demands. The Austrian ultimatum was to serve the sole purpose of a formal prelude to war, not as the basis for a negotiated settlement with Serbia. The crucial points of the ultimatum were Austria-Hungary's demands for the suppression of all anti-Austrian propaganda, conducted by Serbia on its own territory as well as that of the Dual Monarchy and, more important, the participation of Austrian officials in Serbian proceedings against persons connected with the Sarajevo crime.

Finally, the delay in Austria-Hungary's action against Serbia was due to military factors, the Austro-Hungarian army being unprepared for an immediate invasion. The gathering of the summer harvest on Austria-Hungary's farms was also deemed desirable before the induction of reserves. Not until July 23, 1914, was Austria-Hungary's 48-hour ultimatum delivered to Serbia.

The skillfully drafted Serbian reply was conciliatory in form while rejecting those parts of the ultimatum incompatible with Serbian sovereignty. In 1914, unlike 1909 and 1913, Russia did not pressure Serbia into compliance with Austrian demands.

The Austro-Hungarian declaration of war set into motion the chain reaction of mobilizations among the Great Powers which quickly destroyed all hopes of a diplomatic solution of the crisis. On July 28, 1914, Russia, having received French assurances of support, began a partial mobilization of her army against Austria-Hungary. Russian partial mobilization was intended to put pressure on Austria-Hungary without unduly provoking Germany. The order for partial mobilization was changed by the Tsar into one for full Russian mobilization on July 29 when it was learned that no Russian general staff plans for partial mobilization existed. On the same day, Nicholas II, overwhelmed by the responsibility of sending thousands of men to their death, countermanded the order for general mobilization. On July 30, 1914, submitting to the pressure of the Russian military, the Tsar reissued the order for general mobilization.

News of the Russian general mobilization caused a near panic in Germany, which had not yet mobilized. To await the full deployment of the Russian army along her borders without immediate countermeasures would have jeopardized Germany's strategic plans for a two-front war, which General Schlieffen had devised in 1905. As will be discussed more fully in the chapter on the First World War, the Schlieffen plan was premised on the quick defeat of France by the bulk of the German army before the full weight of Russian military power could be brought to bear on Germany's eastern borders.

As of July 30, military considerations dictated German policy. On July 31, Germany sent an ultimatum to Russia as well as France. Russia was asked to stop general mobilization within twelve hours; when she failed to reply, Germany also mobilized on August 1 and, on the same day, declared war on Russia. France was given eighteen hours to declare her intentions. If they were peaceful, Germany demanded proof through the surrender of the French key fortresses of Toul and Verdun. France, having rejected the ultimatum, mobilized on August 1. On August 2, Germany delivered an ultimatum to Belgium, demanding the right of military passage, promising evacuation and restitution of damages after the war in the event of Belgian compliance and threatening war in the event of Belgian refusal. Belgium refused on August 3. On the same day, Germany declared war on France and invaded Belgium, providing thereby the immediate cause for Britain's declaration of war on Germany on August 4, 1914.

THE FAILURE OF BRITISH MEDIATION

Even before the Austrian ultimatum of July 23 and Austria's declaration of war on Serbia of July 28 had set the fateful mechanisms of mobilization into motion, British Foreign Secretary Sir Edward Grey had launched a policy of mediation. In so doing, Grey acted on the assumption that the lack of formal alliances between Great Britain and any European power gave her unique advantages as a mediator in the thickening crisis between the continental power blocs. Beginning with July 20, 1914, Grey initiated a series of proposals in rapid succession, beginning with the idea of direct Austro-Russian talks and continuing with the proposal for a four-power conference of Britain, France, Germany, and Italy. On July 26, 1914, Grey proposed an ambassadors' conference in London under his own chairmanship. The ambassadors' conference was to be identical with that which had worked successfully in the Balkan crisis of 1912/1913.

Grey's mediation proposals were flatly rejected by Austria-Hungary and Germany while receiving only qualified support from the entente powers. For Germany and Austria-Hungary, there was the memory of the Algeciras Conference and hence the fear of being outvoted once again in an international conference such as Grey proposed. Austria-Hungary had special reasons to oppose Grey's proposal for an ambassadors' conference. The ambassadors' conference of 1912/1913 may well have been a suitable instrument for the settlement of disputes between Serbia, Montenegro, Bulgaria, and Greece. But to invoke an ambassadors' conference in the crisis of July, 1914, in which Austria

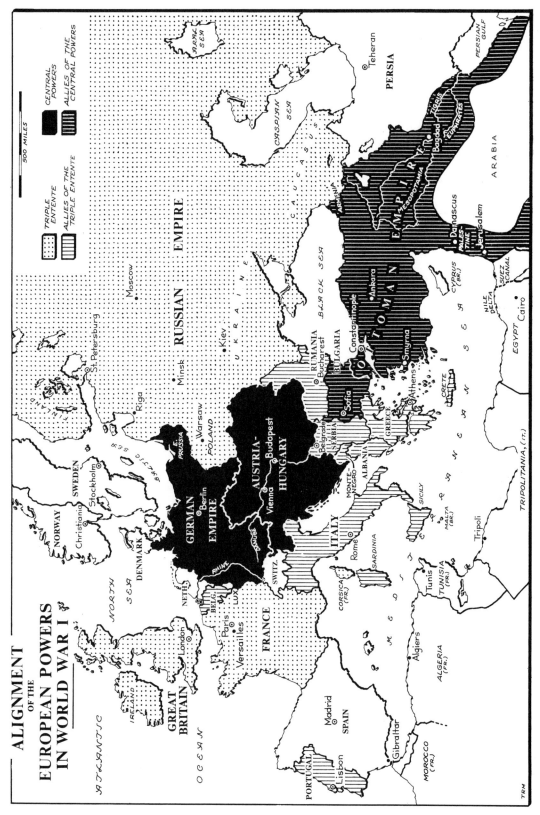

ALIGNMENT
OF THE
EUROPEAN POWERS
IN WORLD WAR I

TRIPLE ENTENTE
ALLIES OF THE TRIPLE ENTENTE

CENTRAL POWERS
ALLIES OF THE CENTRAL POWERS

500 MILES

ATLANTIC OCEAN

GREAT BRITAIN
IRELAND
London

NORTH SEA

NORWAY
Christiania
SWEDEN
Stockholm
DENMARK

BALTIC SEA

FINLAND
St. Petersburg
Riga

RUSSIAN EMPIRE
Moscow
Minsk
Kiev
UKRAINE

GERMAN EMPIRE
Berlin
E. PRUSSIA
Warsaw
POLAND

NETH.
BELG.
LUX.
Paris
Versailles
FRANCE

SWITZ.
Vienna
AUSTRIA-HUNGARY
Budapest

RHINE
DANUBE

ITALY
Rome
Corsica (FR.)
Sardinia

Madrid
SPAIN
PORTUGAL
Lisbon
Gibraltar

MOROCCO (FR.)
Algiers
ALGERIA (FR.)
Tunis
TUNISIA (FR.)
Tripoli
TRIPOLITANIA (IT.)

MEDITERRANEAN SEA

SICILY
MALTA (BR.)

RUMANIA
Bucharest
BULGARIA
Sofia
SERBIA
Belgrade
MONTE-NEGRO
ALBANIA
GREECE
Athens
CRETE

BLACK SEA

CAUCASUS
CASPIAN SEA

Constantinople
Ankara
Smyrna
OTTOMAN EMPIRE
ARMENIA
MESOPOTAMIA
TIGRIS
EUPHRATES
Bagdad

PERSIA
Teheran
PERSIAN GULF

ARABIA
Damascus
Jerusalem
PALESTINE

CYPRUS (BR.)
SUEZ CANAL
NILE DELTA
EGYPT
Cairo

AEGEAN SEA

TRM

25

was centrally involved, would, in the Austrian estimate, have lowered the Dual Monarchy to the level of Serbia. It was the desperate clinging to the rank and status of a great power, however, whether such rank befitted Austria-Hungary any longer or not, which was the driving force behind all Austrian actions in the diplomatic crisis of 1914.

In 1876, when Russia, Austria-Hungary, and Germany attempted to settle the Balkan troubles of the Turkish Empire through joint action, without consulting Britain, British Prime Minister Disraeli angrily retorted that Britain would not be treated like Montenegro or Bosnia. In 1914, that, essentially, was also the Austrian sentiment. The feeling was perhaps a trifle stronger in Austria-Hungary, since the Serbian question of 1914 did not, for her, involve a distant issue but a problem of internal security and survival as a major power.

The most promising of Grey's mediation proposals was the last. On July 29, Britain suggested the "Halt-in-Belgrade" proposal, permitting Austria-Hungary to occupy the Serbian capital on condition of halting her forces and accepting Great Power mediation afterwards. Germany, alarmed by the prospect of Britain's entering the European conflict, advanced an identical proposal to Vienna, urging its acceptance in strong terms. While the German Chancellor, Bethmann-Hallweg, urged moderation on Vienna on July 30, 1914, the German Chief of Staff, Moltke, alarmed by the Russian general mobilization, advised Austria-Hungary to mobilize against Russia forthwith. It was on the advice of Moltke, not Bethmann-Hollweg, that Austria-Hungary acted.

Russia, for her part, was less interested in British mediation than in a clear and unequivocal statement of British support. The July crisis, Russian Foreign Minister Sazonov warned, was not a matter between Austria and Serbia but one between the Triple Entente and the Austro-German alliance. If Britain openly supported her friends, peace would be saved. If she did not, war would result and Britain would have to join her friends after the outbreak.

The fear that British aid would reach her friends too late also haunted Sir Edward Grey's advisers in the Foreign Office, Under Secretary Nicolson and Assistant Secretary Crowe. Both men had strongly urged, long before 1914, that the Triple Entente be converted into a written alliance. Grey had rejected such a course and with good reason, for it was doubtful whether the British public and the House of Commons would have endorsed it. The German invasion of Belgium, however, was a provocation and a threat to British security understood by all, and none in the House of Commons doubted that it must be answered with a British declaration of war on Germany.

2 | The First World War

THE NATURE OF THE CONFLICT

The relative decline, which all major European powers, save Russia, have suffered in relation to the world at large since August, 1914, has given the First World War increasingly the meaning of a European Civil War, equally damaging in its long-range results to the interests of all European participants. Having directed their energies, inventiveness and resources towards their own internal development as well as towards global conquest during the imperialist age, the Great Powers of Europe turned their strength against one another in 1914. The ultimate consequences of such a struggle for Europe, though dreaded by a few men, such as Britain's Foreign Secretary Sir Edward Grey, were neither anticipated nor even imagined by the political-military leadership of pre-war Europe.

Since the 1870's the Great Powers had been surging forward, their primary interest being the fulfillment of their respective national potentials, rather than the upholding of European primacy in general. This, to be sure, was no departure from earlier patterns of European behavior ever since the emergence of European nation states. During the half century preceding the First World War, the policy and diplomacy of European powers had changed little from the pre-industrial age. The pre-war alliances, conceived in the spirit of secret diplomacy, differed but little in form or purpose from those customary in the Age of Louis XIV. By contrast, the industrial-scientific revolution of the 19th and early 20th centuries had conferred upon Western man unprecedented powers of creation as well as of destruction. Whereas international relations continued to be governed by the principles and practices adopted since the Treaty of Westphalia in 1648, suited to limited wars with limited objectives, the Industrial Age had changed the nature of war into *total* war, capable of the total destruction of warring nations. By 1914 European civilization had achieved revolutionary progress in man's mastery over nature; it had failed to match its revolution in science and technology, however, with an awareness of the urgent need for new approaches to the relations between members of the European family of nations. Having plunged into a universal war through the failures of the old diplomacy, the European state system proceeded to the task of mutual self-destruction through the power of the new technology. Significantly, the paralysis of Europe was not broken until the United States provided the Allied cause with fresh resources and new ideas, which assured Allied victory and promised an alternative to Europe's pre-war system of alliances and hostile blocs.

THE ECONOMIC DIMENSIONS OF
TOTAL WAR

That the war of 1914 would be more destructive than previous wars was foreseen; the new weapons of the Industrial Age had proven their fearful power in the Russo-Japanese War of 1904/1905 as well as in the Boer War. The sheer size of Europe's standing armies — all major powers except England had introduced conscription since 1870 — together with their modern armaments, gave rise to the illusion, however, that the war would be brief. Only few military men of vision, such as Prussia's Chief of Staff Helmut Moltke, had prophesied as far back as 1890 that a future war between the fully armed powers of Europe would in all likelihood not be decided in a few campaigns but might become a "seven years' war" or even a "thirty years' war."

The wedding of technology to war made the offensive by mass armies as costly as the defense, however, a fact which turned the First World War into a four-year stalemate, in which the millions killed in the attack were matched by other millions consumed in the defense. At the outset of the First World War, the general staffs of Europe had considered their available stocks of matériel as well as the troops at their disposal as adequate for the entire war. No sooner had the war of rapid movement of the early weeks given way to the stalemate in the trenches than all armies experienced an acute shortage of ammunition and the huge gaps torn into the armies of August, 1914, had to be filled, often with hastily trained reserves.

To meet the insatiable appetite for shells and other implements of war, the belligerents were forced into a spectacular expansion of armaments production through the wholesale mobilization of their human and industrial resources. Each power responded to the needs of total war with different measures, though the overall effect of greatly increased government controls over the economy, as well as over the individual, was universal. The mobilization of industry and labor for war purpose was most successful in the advanced nations of Britain, France, and Germany. It was least productive in Imperial Russia, where dynastic suspicions of popular initiative stifled the war effort of Russia's patriotic middle and upper classes. The policy of "war socialism" reached its most extreme form in Imperial Germany, where the Surpreme Command imposed stringent controls upon management and labor, to be more fully described later.

The American Civil War had demonstrated the decisive weight of industrial power in modern war. Yet the European belligerents had omitted long-range economic planning from the strategic equation of 1914. The statement, attributed to the French Prime Minister Clemenceau, that war was too important to be left to the generals, was proven correct, as the initiative for industrial mobilization came chiefly from energetic civilians rather than the military.

THE WAR ECONOMY IN BRITAIN AND FRANCE

In Britain, Lloyd George, as Minister of Munitions, was instrumental in putting the economy on a war-time footing and expanding armaments production. Having entered the war with only 1,330 machine guns, the British army was supplied with over 240,000 machine guns in the course of war, in addition to receiving over 28,000 pieces of artillery and 55,000 aircraft. To fill the man-power gaps caused in vital industries through enlistments, the government recruited unskilled labor and women, partly through the special war-time powers under the Defense of the Realm Act (D.O.R.A.) of August, 1914, mostly with the voluntary collaboration of the unions. Although labor's freedom of movement was temporarily restricted through the requirement of "leaving certificates" as a deterrent to rapid job shifting, Britain never resorted to the wholesale drafting of civilian labor which Germany was to adopt in 1916. Nor did the British government embark on large-scale plant construction, as did the Germans after 1916, Britain's armaments being supplied chiefly through private industry. The latter produced 90 per cent of British guns and 97 per cent of all aircraft manufactured during the war.

In France the problem of increased armaments production was complicated by the fact that half of the French coal mines and two thirds of the French steel industries remained in German hands for the better part of the war. These handicaps notwithstanding, French munitions industries achieved remarkable production feats: daily shell output increased from an average of 9,000 in September, 1914, to 300,000 in 1915: over the same period, the total number of machine guns rose to 300,000, and the amount of artillery increased to 36,000 guns. Aircraft, at first regarded more as a curiosity than a serious weapon, grew in number from little over one hundred in 1914 to 35,000 by war's end; Renault and Schneider-Creuzot produced a total of 5,000 tanks.

THE WAR ECONOMY IN GERMANY

In Germany, the industrialist Walther Rathenau awakened the military leadership to the need of stockpiling and allocating strategic raw materials for a prolonged war as early as August, 1914, when a Raw

Materials Board *(Kriegsrohstoffabteilung)* was established in Berlin at Rathenau's initiative. The requirement of rationing strategic raw materials as well as of finding substitutes for those in short supply became all the more urgent in the German case, as German industry was cut off from its overseas supplies virtually from the first day of the war by the British blockade. Germany and Austria-Hungary possessed an adequate supply of the basic raw materials coal and iron, but they were lacking in such other essentials as nitrates (for the production of explosives and chemical fertilizer), foodstuffs, oil, fats, and non-ferrous metals, especially copper and cotton. Germany's territorial conquests during the First World War did little to ease the shortage of these supplies; the loot of the port of Antwerp brought no more than temporary relief, as did the stripping of Belgium and Russian Poland of many industries. It was raw materials, rather than factories, that Germany required most to keep her war economy going. The German conquest of Rumania in 1916 and the occupation of the Ukraine in 1918 yielded some grain and oil, though not the expected amount.

The German raw materials bottleneck was partly overcome through substitutes and synthetics. Whereas half of Germany's nitrogen needs had been covered through the import of Chilean nitrates before the war, the processes developed by Haber-Bosch and Franck-Caro provided Germany with sufficient nitrogen for the explosives industry. Rayon became a substitute for cotton, while synthetic rubber and gasoline covered only a fraction of the needs.

The effect of the British blockade was most pronounced on the German food supply. Although pre-war Germany had attained 80 per cent self-sufficiency in food, the shortage of farm labor and chemical fertilizer, as well as poor weather, resulted in a sharp decline of German farm output. Daily rations decreased from 1,350 calories in 1916 to a starvation diet of 1,000 calories in 1917. Following the poor potato harvest of 1916, a large part of Germany's civilian population subsisted on turnips in the winter of 1916/1917, appropriately called *Rübenwinter* (turnip winter) in Germany. Starvation casualties reached an estimated 750,000 by the end of the war. Although opinions vary as to the overall significance of the British blockade — the German interpretation emphasizing its decisive role, the British maintaining that it served as a convenient excuse for the German military defeat — the evidence of Germany's progressive economic emasculation was clear enough by 1918.

Although food for the urban masses became increasingly short in supply, the year 1916 marked the beginning of Germany's most ambitious program of industrial mobilization during the First World War. Prompted by the experience of the Somme battles, in which the western powers had amassed unprecedented amounts of war matériel, Germany launched the "Somme program" for the expansion of armaments production. The "Somme program" was surpassed by the "Hindenburg program," following the appointment of Hindenburg and Ludendorff to the German Supreme Command. The Supreme Command organized industry and labor along military lines, the former through the war-companies, the latter through the Auxiliary Service Law of December 5, 1916. The Auxiliary Service Law subjected all males between the ages of 17 and 60 to compulsory work in assigned tasks. Moreover, the government launched an extensive building program for the construction of blast furnaces, steel and aluminum industries, and armament plants. By 1917 Germany produced 14,000 machine guns per month, by 1918 2,500 field guns per month. The paradox of the Hindenburg program was that it supplied more armaments than could be used by trained military personnel. In this respect, the Hindenburg program bore a striking resemblance to Germany's armaments program under the direction of Albert Speer during the Second World War, when German output of aircraft exceeded the supply of trained pilots. Moreover, the Hindenburg program overtaxed Germany's overall resources, with crippling effects not only upon nonessential industries but upon such vital areas as transportation as well. The effects of Germany's total war effort between 1916 and 1918 outlasted Germany's defeat. The Hindenburg program accelerated the concentration of big business, a feature characteristic of the German pre-war economy and fatal to the Germany democracy which was to emerge from the ruins of defeat in 1918.

U. S. ARMAMENTS

The United States, "arsenal of democracy" and the world's leading armaments manufacturer during the Second World War, contributed a relatively minor share to the stock of arms and ammunitions of its European allies during the First World War. Although the United States became the chief supplier of Allied credit, and although the United States raised an army of four million men and a navy of 800,000 sailors after entering the European war in April, 1917, American forces on the battlefields of Europe were chiefly supplied with European artillery, aircraft, and tanks. Although the American contribution in manpower, finance, and strategic resources was thus decisive to Allied victory in 1918, the American economy did not become geared up for mass production of armaments in time to meet the massive orders. Of the more than 20,000 tanks ordered in the United States, less than 30 were delivered before the armistice of November, 1918; of some 2,200 guns used by the U. S. Army in Europe, only 130 were of American origin, and of the 9 million shells expended by American forces, little more than 200,000 came from the United States.

ARMAMENTS AND STRATEGY

The industrial-scientific revolution of the 19th century, which had altered the texture of Western civilization in peace, likewise changed the face of war beyond recognition. On land, rapid-fire artillery and the machine gun made their debut in mass, to which were added, in the course of war, poison gas, first employed by Germany in 1915; the tank, introduced by Britain in 1916; the flame-thrower, developed by the French; and long-range artillery with a range of up to 70 miles, perfected by Germany with the "Paris gun" of 1918. Communications on land, sea, and in the air were revolutionized by radio and telephone, although artillery fire continued to be directed by rocket signals throughout the war.

The phenomenal development of 20th-century technology was foreshadowed by the growth of air power, less than two decades after man's first flight in a heavier-than-air device by the Wright brothers. The future range of air power was suggested by the unbroken flight of a German Zeppelin (dirigible) from Germany to East Africa, as well as the sporadic Zeppelin attacks on London and Allied air attacks on German cities and military bases. The application of air power in the First World War was chiefly tactical, however, rather than strategic, the airplane being used as a supporting weapon of field troops. The airplane's potential as a strategic weapon for the destruction of communications, industries, and indeed entire cities was only dimly realized towards the end of the First World War and advocated soon after the war by such prophets of strategic air power as Giulio Douhet in Italy and William Mitchell in the United States.

On the high seas the battleship ruled supreme, though the aircraft carrier, which was to overshadow it in the Second World War, made its appearance towards the end of the First World War. In July, 1918, aircraft launched from the British carrier *Furious* attacked German Zeppelin bases on the North Sea Coast. The submarine had become an operational weapon since its fitting with Diesel engines for surface cruising in 1910. It proved a potent weapon beyond expectation with momentous political consequences, providing the immediate cause for the American entry into the First World War in April, 1917.

The new weapons of the 20th century had vastly increased the fire power of all armies, but the mobility of the armies had not grown apace. The internal combustion engine was widely used, to be sure, for the propulsion of aircraft, submarines, and, less so, surface ships, which employed steampower. Troops, artillery, and supplies continued to rely on the horse and the mule, however, in spite of the growing number of trucks. The railroads made possible the swift mobilization of armies at the beginning of the war and the rapid transfer of troops behind the battle lines; railroads contributed nothing to the mobility of troops in the field, however, where advance and retreat had to be undertaken on foot or horseback. The armies of the First World War thus employed many of the weapons which would still form the backbone of armies in the Second World War, but they moved about the battlefield by means essentially unchanged since Napoleon's time.

The disproportion between firepower and mobility gave the First World War its peculiar form of a war of siege, fought between frozen lines of trenches. The concentration of superior artillery and massed infantry upon a single point thus enabled the attacker to break into the enemy's defenses, but rarely through them. For the exploitation of the break-in for a break-through, mobility was lacking. Invariably, the defender was given sufficient time to haul up reserves, while the attacker spent an equal amount of time replenishing his battered assault troops and bringing up his slow-moving, horse-drawn artillery. The superiority of defense in depth over the attack was thus demonstrated time and again — in the German assault on Verdun and the Allied offensives on the Somme in 1916, in the French attacks on the Aisne in 1917, and in the Ludendorff offensive of 1918. The armored division and motorized infantry, whose breakthrough tactics were devised after the First World War by Liddell Hart in England, Charles DeGaulle in France, and Heinz Guderian in Germany, restored mobility to the battlefields of the Second World War. Although the tank made its battlefield debut in the First World War, it was used neither in sufficient numbers nor effectively enough to alter the strategic stalemate.

The strategic stalemate was more pronounced on the western front than in the east, chiefly because the armies facing one another in the west were more evenly matched in the technology of their armaments and the fighting morale of the combatants. Where major breakthroughs occurred in the east, such as in the German-Austrian conquest of Russian Poland in 1915 or Brusilov's victory over the Austrians in 1916, an acute shortage of arms or the demoralization of the defeated accounted for the changed pattern of warfare.

If Allied and German strategy on the western front seemed to be lacking in imagination, it must be recognized that the nature of the First World War imposed severe limitations on the most fertile of military minds. The most astonishing aspect of the war of siege was perhaps not the lack of good generalship but the discipline and obedience with which the doomed legions marched towards certain death. That discipline broke, but rarely. The most painful outcry of men who had witnessed senseless slaughter occurred in the French army, following the collapse of General George R. Nivelle's offensive on the Aisne in April, 1917. The French army mutinied; the troops refused to leave the trenches, and reserves, marching through villages on their way to the front, issued shouts of "bah-bah-bah" to suggest their fate as helpless sheep being driven to slaughter. The French mutiny of April, 1917, remained an episode in the continuing drama of the First World War, in which the opposing armies, bound together by the common knowledge and experience of trench warfare, often felt greater kinship for each other than for the remote and unreal civilian world of their respective countries.

THE MILITARY PLANS AND THE CAMPAIGNS
OF 1914

ALLIED PLANS

The military plans of all great continental European powers, prepared long in advance of the outbreak of hostilities and implemented in August, 1914, were offensive. On the Allied side, France and Russia had coordinated their strategy against Germany and Austria-Hungary ever since the conclusion of the French-Russian alliance of 1894. Under its terms, both powers agreed to mobilize their forces immediately in response to the mobilization of any one member of the Triple Alliance and to advance on Germany from west and east with "emphasis and speed." Russia, considering Austria-Hungary her principal enemy and rival, would have preferred to concentrate all her forces against the latter. Not without good reason, France insisted on the priority of Germany's defeat, Germany being the stronger of the two opponents. Once Germany was beaten, Russia could deal with Austria-Hungary as she pleased. By 1912 Russia had given a definite promise of launching an offensive against Germany with 800,000 men on the fifteenth day of mobilization. The Russian promise was to have fateful consequences for the eastern campaigns of 1914, as the division of the Russian forces between the German and Austrian fronts became a major cause of Russia's defeat at Tannenberg in August, 1914.

The French army under Chief of Staff Joseph Jacques Joffre had abandoned its earlier defensive strategy in favor of the doctrine of "*offensive à outrance*" (offensive to the limit), advocated by Colonel de Grandmaison. As implemented in Plan XVII of the French General Staff, the French army was to launch frontal attacks on either side of the German stronghold of Metz into Germany proper. Joffre's earlier plan of invading Germany via neutral Belgium had been vetoed by the French government, in view of the adverse reaction which a French violation of Belgian neutrality would inevitably produce in Great Britain.

As early as 1911, Britain had pledged to send her small but highly trained expeditionary force of six divisions to France in the event of war with Germany. As the British army took Germany's violation of Belgian neutrality for granted, General Sir John French, the commander of the BEF, would have preferred the movement of the BEF towards the vital port of Antwerp. In fact, the BEF was subordinated to the role of an auxiliary force on the left wing of the French army and, though retaining formal independence of command, was subjected to overall French strategy.

CENTRAL POWER PLANS
        Among the Central Powers, few preparations towards a co-ordinated strategy of the armed forces of Germany and Austria-Hungary had been made, despite the fact that the Dual Alliance of October, 1879, was the oldest among the pre-war alliances of Europe. During Bismarck's term of office as chancellor (1871-90), there were good political reasons for this omission, since Bismarck regarded the Dual Alliance as strictly defensive. A definite German military commitment to Austria, Bismarck feared, might induce the latter to pursue an adventurist and aggressive Balkan policy against Russia and subvert the original purpose of the Dual Alliance. Bismarck's Chief of Staff Helmut Moltke (the elder) neverthe-less drafted plans for a two-front war as early as 1871, which envisaged a French-Russia coalition against Germany and Austria-Hungary. Moltke's intention was to fight defensively against France while launching a joint German-Austrian offensive against Russia. Austria, for the reason stated, was not informed of these plans.
        Although German dependence on Austria-Hungary had grown by the early 20th century and German restraint of Austrian Balkan ventures had correspondingly decreased, the military collaboration of the two powers had for these reasons not become more intimate. As France and Russia had disagreed on the priorities of their respective military efforts, so did Germany and Austria-Hungary. Whereas Austria-Hungary favored a knock-out blow against Russia first, Germany's Chief of Staff Alfred von Schlieffen had decided at the turn of the century in favor of a "France first" strategy. France and Britain being the stronger of the Central Powers' foes, the fate of Austria-Hungary, in the German view, would be decided on the Seine, not the river San in Poland.
        Conceived in 1905, the Schlieffen plan proceeded from the assumption that Germany's chances of survival in an extended conflict were minimal in view of the superior resources of Germany's probable enemies and British command at sea. Where the elder Moltke had still thought in terms of a negotiated compromise peace after limited German military successes in west and east, Schlieffen wished to inflict total defeat on France by concentrating virtually the entire German army against the latter. The protection of Germany's eastern border against Russian invasion was to be left to a single German army in East Prussia and such support as Austria-Hungary might be able to afford. As a speedy German penetration of the strongly fortified French border of 150 miles length was beyond question, the Schlieffen plan called for the encirclement of the entire French army by means of a bold march through Belgium, Holland,

and northern France. After crossing the Seine at Rouen, the German armies were to pass Paris to the south and complete their scythe-like movement by marching eastward towards the Moselle and the German border. The French army, facing eastward, was to be crushed between the hammer of the moving German armies and the anvil of the German fortresses in Lorraine. To assure German superiority on the advancing front, Schlieffen demanded the massing of strength on the German right wing, to consist of 53 divisions, leaving only 9 divisions to guard the French-German border and a further 10 divisions to mask the French fortress of Verdun in the center. Anticipating the defeat of France within six weeks, Schlieffen proposed the shifting of German troops to the east thereafter, in the hope that the slowness of the Russian mobilization would delay the full employment of Russian manpower during the crucial campaign in France.

Schlieffen's successor, Helmut Moltke the younger, name-sake and nephew of the Prussian Chief of Staff of 1870, modified the Schlieffen plan in essential points. Moltke ruled out the invasion of Holland, as a neutral Holland might be useful to German overseas trade in time of war. Moreover, Moltke, fearful lest France might overwhelm the weak German defenses along the French border, strengthened the German left wing, though not, as is often erroneously assumed, at the expense of the advancing right wing.

However brilliant in its conception, the Schlieffen plan contained serious risks and flaws which might have caused its failure even if applied without change in 1914. Apart from the problem of mobility, previously mentioned, Schlieffen overlooked the need for further troops to invest the Belgian fortresses not overrun in the first onrush of the German invasion. Likewise Schlieffen underestimated the significance which the small British Expeditionary Force was to assume in the early phases of the campaign. Above all, the Schlieffen plan committed Germany to the violation of an innocent neutral country, with all the political consequences and Allied propaganda advantages which the violation of Belgian neutrality entailed. Joffre, as has been seen, was also tempted to violate Belgian neutrality, but had been overruled by his government. It was indicative of the role of the military in pre-war Germany that Schlieffen merely informed the German Foreign Office of the "military necessity" of invading Belgium and that the German government neither protested nor vetoed that decision. The younger Moltke expressed his regrets about the violation of Belgian neutrality with the observation that "it is not pleasant to begin a campaign with the violation of a neutral neighbour's territory."

Austria-Hungary was kept in the dark about the Schlieffen plan. Other than general assurances that the bulk of German troops would be transferred to the east within six weeks after the beginning of military operations in the west, Austria's Chief of Staff Conrad elicited no information from his German counterpart, Moltke. Germany and Austria-Hungary, though tied together in the Dual Alliance, had thus paradoxically achieved far less military coordination by 1914 than had Britain and France. These two, though not officially allied, had prepared the joint deployment of their armies against Germany during many years of confidential staff talks.

Although it was clear that Austria-Hungary would stand virtually alone against Russia during the initial phase of the war, Conrad had not settled for a defensive strategy consistent with the limited military power at his command. Austria's pugnacious chief of staff would have liked to destory his enemies all at once, having advocated preventive war against Russia and Serbia ever since 1909. In 1910 Conrad had included Italy among the nations to be defeated in a preventive war as he suspected Italy of disloyalty to her partners in the Triple Alliance. In 1914 Austrian military plans called for offensives against both Serbia and Russian Poland, a goal which far exceeded Austrian military power.

THE CLASH IN THE WEST

At the outset of the western campaigns, the opposing forces were nearly evenly matched in numbers, seventy-eight German divisions, organized in seven armies, facing sixty-two French divisions, comprising five armies, as well as four, later six, British and seven Belgian divisions. In application of Plan XVII, the French armies launched frontal attacks against the fortified German borders north and south of Metz, beginning with August 14. The ensuing battles, known collectively as the Battle of the Frontier, cost France 300,000 casualties without yielding lasting results. By the end of August the French were driven from Lorraine by the armies of Crown Prince Rupprecht of Bavaria and had suffered defeat in the Ardennes. Charles DeGaulle has aptly described the shock which German fire power inflicted upon the high-spirited French advance: "With effected calm, the officers let themselves be killed standing upright . . . bugles sounded the charge, isolated heroes made fantastic leaps, but all to no purpose. In an instant it had become clear that not all the courage in the world could withstand this fire."

While Plan XVII was being shattered to pieces, the four northern armies of the German front had begun to execute the Schlieffen plan with the invasion of Belgium and Luxembourg on August 4, 1914. Although the small Belgian army under King Albert was no match for the colossus from the east, the strong Belgian fortresses in and around Liége delayed the German advance until August 16, 1914. The German advance did not gain momentum until August 18, after which the German armies broke into northern France with alarming speed, covering 180 miles in fifteen days and reaching Amiens on September 1. Though most of Belgium had been overrun, the Belgian army continued to exist, rendering in fact crucial service to the Allies well into October, 1914. Albert and his battered army withdrew into Antwerp, which was held until October 10. Germany was thus compelled to leave far larger forces behind than she could afford, as the battle was approaching its climax in northern France. Moreover, the demolition of Belgian rolling stock and rail tracks rendered the supply of the advancing German armies increasingly difficult. The thrusting wing of the German front was weakened further towards the end of August through the withdrawal of two army corps to East Prussia, where Russian armies had meanwhile broken through.

Nevertheless, until the end of August the western battlefield gave every appearance of unbroken German mastery and initiative, the French having been beaten on the German border and no effective roadblock thrown as yet astride the German breakthrough into northern France. British attacks at Mons and Le Cateau were beaten off, as were those of the French Fifth Army under General Lanrezac. The spearhead of the German advance, Kluck's First and Bulow's Second Armies had reached the Marne by September 2, and German advance units could see the needle of the Eiffel tower on the horizon. On the same day, the French government left Paris for Bordeaux, entrusting the defense of the capital to the military governor, Galliéni.

Yet there were disquieting notes on the German side, which caused a groundswell of pessimism in the German headquarters, far to the rear in Luxembourg. The German troops were exhausted and few prisoners had been taken. The French army had been pushed back but had remained a force in being. There had been no battle comparable to that of Sedan, which had decided the outcome of the Franco-Prussian war in September, 1870.

THE SCHLIEFFEN PLAN ABORTED:
THE BATTLE OF THE MARNE

At first General Joffre had been taken by surprise by the ambitious reach of the German invasion, having credited the Germans with fewer reserves than they possessed and having counted on a more limited German advance. By the end of August, Joffre took effective countermeasures, which included the purging of French generals, including Fifth Army Commander Lanrezac, who had displayed a lack of aggressiveness, as well as the transfer of troops from Lorraine to Paris. A newly constituted French army (the Sixth) under General Maunoury prepared to strike at the flank of the German First Army on the Marne. Among the replacements of the purged French generals, officers with long-time service in the colonies were conspicuous, such as Franchet d'Esperey, Mangin, Degoutte, and Guillaumat, who, like Joffre himself, had proven their initiative abroad. Of the French colonial officers, it was said that they developed more initiative in six months of service overseas than those stationed in France would show in a lifetime. As a result of the French troop transfers, Joffre achieved a numerical superiority over his enemy on the Marne, at the decisive moment.

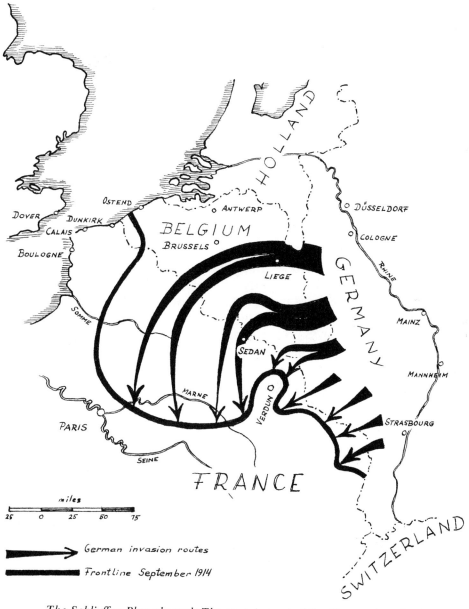

The Schlieffen Plan aborted: The containment of the German invasion of France in September 1914.

Disturbed by the growing strength of the French armies in his path, Moltke changed the initial goal of the Schlieffen plan by early September. Rather than swing around the far side of Paris, the German armies were to pass its near side and, in conjunction with a German attack launched in the south between Toul and Épinal, accomplish the encirclement of the French army. Moltke's alternative bore all the features of à desperate improvisation, as a German frontal assault through the French belt of fortresses between Toul and Épinal had little chance of succeeding. Had Schlieffen considered such a venture promising, he would not have burdened Germany with the odium of violating Belgian neutrality.

Before Moltke's plan could be implemented, the French Sixth Army, reinforced from Paris by taxi-cab–borne reserves, had struck Kluck's First Army on September 5. The French attack forced Kluck to turn his army westward, resulting in a thirty-mile gap between himself and the neighboring German Second Army, through which the British Expeditionary Force advanced. News of the battle of the Marne induced the shaken Moltke to urge the withdrawal of both the German First and Second Armies from the Marne by September 8. Not the least important cause of Moltke's panic was the news that British troops had landed in the German rear at Ostend, coupled with the rumor that Russia had sent an expeditionary corps to fight alongside the British. The Ostend landings involved, in fact, a mere three battalions of British marines who were withdrawn within forty-eight hours. The rumors concerning Russian troops on the western front proved groundless.

By September 11, the German front in France was in general retreat which halted behind the river Aisne along a line from Noyon to Verdun. The Battle of the Marne represented an immense strategic victory for the Allies, since it thwarted the German bid for a swift victory over France. The dejected Moltke informed the German Emperor that Germany had lost the war. Although it took the Allies four more years to prove the point, the judgment was essentially correct when made in September, 1914, as prospects of a German victory in an extended war of attrition were slim. On September 14, 1914, Moltke was relieved as Chief of Staff, to be succeeded by the Prussian Minister of War, Erich von Falkenhayn.

Since the German military leadership, though not the general public, recognized the magnitude of the strategic setback on the Marne, a bitter controversy ensued over its causes. The most easily identifiable scapegoat was Colonel Hentsch, the officer who transmitted Moltke's order for retreat on September 8, verbally and without written instructions. The cause of the German defeat ran, without doubt, much deeper and may be summarized as a disproportion between the high aims of the Schlieffen plan and existing German military strength. Even Schlieffen had not remained free of doubt whether the German army could fulfill the task he had assigned it. Falkenhayn came perhaps closest to the truth with his charge that the naval funds, if applied to the German army before 1914, would have given Germany enough troops to defend East Prussia and conquer France at the same time. The German navy was indeed useless to the German war effort of 1914. Never once did it attempt to interfere with British troop transports across the English Channel.

After the hardening of the battle line behind the Aisne in mid-September, both sides attempted to outflank each other in what became popularly known as a "race to the sea." The military operations shifted from the Aisne to Flanders, a no-man's land in which no major campaign had been fought thus far. Britain, as previously noted, had landed weak forces at Antwerp and Ostend in a futile attempt to raise the German siege of Antwerp. The British forces at Ostend succeeded, however, in covering the retreat of the Belgian army along the Flanders coast after the fall of Antwerp on October 10.

By October, the Germans had missed their chance of seizing the channel ports of Calais and Boulogne, which British forces had evacuated during the general Allied retreat of August, 1914. By shifting the BEF from the Aisne to Flanders, the Allies had extended their front to the North Sea in conjunction with the Belgian army. The Flanders front withstood the furious German assaults in the first Battle of Ypres, which lasted until November 11, 1914. Ypres became the grave for thousands of German students, whose scanty military training did not match their enthusiasm for combat. For Britain, the Battle of Ypres provided the lesson that an army, far larger than the original BEF would be required. By the end of 1914, British voluntary enlistments, responding to the call of War Secretary Lord Kitchener, had grown to one million.

After the clash of Ypres, the western front became stationary along a line of twisted trenches which stretched from Switzerland to Nieuport on the North Sea. Having dashed across the plains of northern France and the fields of Flanders during the summer and fall of 1914 in anticipation of an early victory, the armies of the western front went underground in preparation of four years of siege.

THE EASTERN FRONT IN 1914: RUSSIA'S AND AUSTRIA'S ABORTIVE BIDS FOR EARLY VICTORY; THE STALEMATE OF DECEMBER, 1914

Geography determined eastern strategy in 1914, with Russian Poland, extending westward into the flank of the Central Powers, forming a convenient springboard for Russian attack, as well as presenting a tempting target for German-Austrian invasion from north and south. Russia enjoyed numerical superiority, although only one third of her army had been fully mobilized by late August, 1914. Russia's larger numbers were offset by the superior mobility of the armies of Germany and Austria behind the front line, the Central Powers possessing superior rail communications in East Prussia, Silesia, and Austrian Galicia. As a result, the German armies, in particular, achieved a higher rate of concentration in the decisive eastern battles of 1914 than did their Russian opponents, German troops being shifted over distances of up to 500 miles and in as many as 700 trains at a given time.

Responding to the pleas of his French ally, the Russian Commander-in-Chief, Grand Duke Nicholas, dispatched two armies into East Prussia between August 17 and August 21, 1914. The Russian First (Njemen) and Second (Narev) Armies, under the command of Pavel Rennenkampf and Alexander Samsonov respectively, faced a single German army under Max von Prittwitz. Communications between the two Russian armies, separated by over 100 miles, were poor, as were the personal relations between their commanders, both veterans of the Russo-Japanese war of 1904/1905. The battle plans of the invading Russians were no secret to the outnumbered Germans, since Russian radio messages were exchanged without the benefit of code.

THE BATTLE OF TANNENBERG

In its first encounter with the Njemen army at Gumbinnen on August 20, 1914, the German Eighth Army was thrown back and Prittwitz contemplated a withdrawal behind the Vistula, leaving East Prussia to the Russians. Moltke thereupon replaced Prittwitz with Paul von Hindenburg, an elderly general recalled from retirement, and appointed Erich Ludendorff as Hindenburg's chief of staff. Ludendorff had acquired fame in the West through his storming of the fortress of Liége. Upon taking command in East Prussia, Hindenburg and Ludendorff implemented a battle plan prepared by one of Prittwitz' staff officers, Max Hoffman. Leaving only a cavalry screen to observe the slow-moving Njemen army, the German Eighth Army was moved by railroad 130 miles to the south to meet the Narev army. The latter was encircled and virtually destroyed in the Battle of Tannenberg between August 23 and August 30, with 125,000 Russian prisoners taken at a cost of 13,000 German casualties. Among the Russian casualties was General Samsonov, who died, presumably, by his own hand.

Reinforced by the two army corps which had been withdrawn from the Marne and which had arrived only after the Battle of Tannenberg, the German Eighth Army was shifted north in four days to deal with Rennenkampf's Njemen army. The Germans were denied a second Tannenberg, however, by the timely withdrawal of Rennenkampf, following the Battle of Masurian lakes on September 10, 1914.

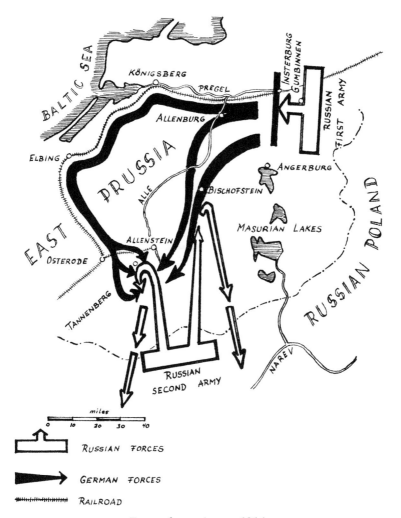

Tannenberg, August 1914.

Tannenberg marked a great tactical and psychological victory for the German army which propelled Hindenburg and Ludendorff to national fame. The fame was less deserved in the case of Hindenburg, whose calm exterior in the midst of crisis was widely misinterpreted as an expression of superior strategic gifts.

On the Tannenberg site Germany was to build a huge war memorial in the style of the fortified castles of the Order of Teutonic Knights. The Tannenberg memorial was appropriately demolished by the retreating German armies during the final stages of the Second World War, when no miracle halted the westward march of the Soviet armies.

Upon the Russians, Tannenberg left a lasting psychological scar, which robbed the Russian leadership of self-confidence in future encounters with the German army during the First World War.

THE AUSTRIAN DEFEAT IN GALICIA

While suffering defeat in East Prussia, the Russian armies had achieved spectacular success against the Austrian armies in Galicia. Where the German mobilization had been a model of efficient planning, that of Austria-Hungary was characterized by confusion. Initially, Austria-Hungary had planned to concentrate superior forces against Serbia to assure quick victory over the latter. The outbreak of war between Austria-Hungary and Russia on August 6, 1914, necessitated the withdrawal of Austrian forces to the Russian front which had already been committed to battle against Serbia. Accordingly, the Austrian forces remaining on the Serbian front were too weak to overwhelm the Serbs, while those transferred to Galicia arrived piecemeal and not in time for the opening of the Austrian offensive of August 23, 1914.

The Austrian campaign against Serbia thus ended with a humiliating setback. Between August and December, Austria-Hungary launched three invasions against Serbia, the first and second being repulsed in August and September, while the third resulted in the Austrian capture of Belgrade on December 2, 1914. No sooner had Austria begun to celebrate the fall of the Serbian capital than General Putnik, the able commander of the Serbian troops, evicted Austria from Belgrade and forced a general Austrian retreat in mid-December.

In Galicia, Austria-Hungary's chief of staff Conrad had opened an offensive against four Russian armies under General Ivanov between the rivers Vistula and Bug on August 23. The Austrian attack did not come as a surprise, Russia being fully acquainted with the Austrian plans as a result of their betrayal prior to the war by the Austrian staff officer Alfred Redl. After initial Austrian gains at Krasnik and Komarov in late August, Conrad was forced to retire along a line between the Vistula and the Carpathian Mountains. Austria-Hungary had sustained 350,000 casualties and lost the provinces of Eastern Galicia and Bukovina to Russia.

The surprising aspect of Austria-Hungary's military performance was not that the Austrian army fought poorly, but that it fought as well as it did, considering the ethnic turmoil which had embittered relations among the nationalities before the war. Apart from the Czechs, who showed little enthusiasm for the war from its beginning, most of the other nationalities fought loyally under the Habsburg scepter. The South-Slav Bosnians, in particular, soon gained a reputation as fearless fighters in the Habsburg cause.

The Austrian debacle in Galicia prompted Russia to seek a

second invasion of Germany, with seven Russian armies marching towards the province of Silesia in Nobember, 1914. As at Tannenberg, Germany again made up for numerical inferiority with superior mobility by railroad. Having slowed down the westward movement of the Russian armies through the demolition of Polish rail communications, one German army was moved via German railroads to strike at the Russian northern flank. The German flank attack at Lodz on November 11 paralyzed the Russian advance and resulted in a general retreat behind the rivers Bzura and Ravka in December, 1914. As in the west, stalemate followed the war of movement in the east by the end of the year. Along the Turkish front in the Caucasus, Russia had scored a brilliant defensive victory over the Turkish army which had attempted the seizure of Kars and Ardahan as a first step towards the invasion of Georgia. The Turkish troops under the command of the Turkish Minister of War Enver Pasha suffered more casualties from the rigors of the Caucasian winter than from the actual engagement with the Russian army. Having started out with 95,000 troops in November, 1914, Enver Pasha retired to Turkey with 18,000 survivors, following his defeat at Sarikamis in January, 1915.

Although the Allied powers, Britain, France and Russia, were lacking in a unified command, the campaigns in France, East Prussia, and Poland had resulted in a close interdependence of the western and the eastern fronts. The Russian invasion of East Prussia had prompted Germany to withdraw forces from France with victory seemingly within the German grasp in the west; the squandering of German forces on the western front in early November, 1914, in the Battle of Ypres, conversely deprived Hindenburg and Ludendorff of that additional strength which otherwise might well have turned the Battle of Lodz into another Tannenberg. By the end of 1914 Falkenhayn, the German Chief of Staff, concluded that Germany would not be in a position to inflict a strategic defeat on any Allied power unless she managed to obtain a separate peace in either the east or the west.

1915:
THE HARDENING OF THE STALEMATE;
ALLIED CAMPAIGNS IN FRANCE;
THE LANDINGS AT GALLIPOLI AND
MESOPOTAMIA

Joffre attributed the western stalemate of the latter part of 1914 to the lack of Allied strength in artillery. With adequate artillery and superiority in manpower, the Allies, in Joffre's view, would be able to inflict a decisive defeat upon Germany in the west in 1915.

The objective of French strategy was the crushing of the German salient which extended from Flanders to the Vosges in the south, its western apex a mere sixty miles from Paris. The so-called Noyon bulge was to be shattered by converging blows from Artois in the north and the Champagne in the south. A third blow, delivered from Verdun, would cut the German lateral rail communications behind the front and force Germany to evacuate France. Joffre expected to reach the Rhine by autumn, 1915.

Britain, less sanguine than the French about a breakthrough in the west, searched for alternative solutions. Hoping to escape the horrors of attrition, Britain wished to strike at the enemy's flanks in the tradition of British peripheral strategy with minimum use of land power and maximum employment of Britain's superior sea power. Accordingly, a variety of schemes were discussed at the beginning of 1915: Sir John French, commander of the BEF, hoped to turn the German flank in Flanders through an amphibious operation against Ostend and Zeebrugge, behind the German front; Lord Fisher, the First Sea Lord, proposed British landings in Schleswig-Holstein, an idea which had occurred to the British army ten years before the war; Lloyd George wished to transfer the bulk of the BEF to the Balkans, where it would drive Austria-Hungary out of the war with the aid of Greece and Rumania; Winston Churchill, First Lord of the Admiralty, proposed the seizure of the Dardanelles. The Allied capture of the Turkish straits would, in all likelihood, force Turkey out of the war and open a short and secure supply route to hard-pressed Russia.

Of all the schemes proposed, that of Churchill was adopted, after Grand Duke Nicholas had sent an urgent plea for a British naval demonstration against Turkey, to ease the Turkish pressure on the Caucasus front. Churchill's Dardanelles campaign was as brilliant in conception as it was faulty in execution. Initially, Britain and France hoped to force the passage through the Straits with sea power only. A combined fleet bombarded the Turkish forts on the Gallipoli Peninsula in two raids of February 19 and 25. Although the Allied naval bombardment was effective, the Turkish mine barrier remained intact, claiming four British and French battleships when the Allied fleet returned for a third assault on March 18, 1915. To force the passage, the Allies decided on a major landing operation on the Gallipoli Peninsula. The element of surprise having been lost, the Turks increased their defenses, which had numbered only two divisions in February. Beginning with April 25, 1915, 78,000 British troops, composed chiefly of Australian and New Zealand forces of the Anzac Corps, were landed under the command of Sir Ian Hamilton. In due course, Allied strength was to increase to 410,000.

The Gallipoli campaign soon became a small-scale replica of the trench war in France. Malaria took a growing toll of the Allied troops, while German submarines and Turkish surface vessels continued to disturb the Allied presence at sea. A British surprise landing

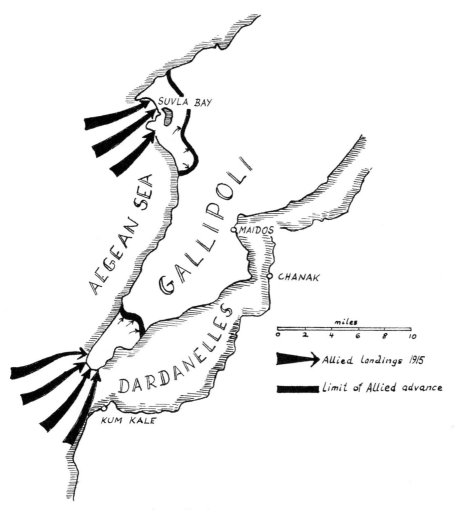

The Gallipoli Campaign, 1915.

at Suvla Bay on the far side of Gallipoli in August, 1915, failed to break the deadlock for want of rapid exploitation. The Turkish defenses, organized by Liman von Sanders, the head of the German military mission in Turkey, stood firm in the face of all Allied attacks. Among the Turkish local commanders, Mustafa Kemal, soon to emerge as the leader of the Turkish national revolution of 1919, excelled.

After Lord Kitchener's fact-finding mission to Gallipoli, the Allies decided on evacuation in November, 1915. The evacuation was completed by January 9, 1916, without the loss of a single Allied soldier. Withdrawal became the most efficiently conducted phase of the Allied operation. Overall Allied casualties exceeded 250,000, the Turks losing an almost equal number of men.

Gallipoli claimed the heads of famous men in England: Fisher and Churchill resigned, and a reputation for strategic eccentricity and amateurishness continued to haunt Churchill well into the Second World War. In military history, men are less often remembered for their brilliant ideas than for their results. Kitchener's prestige suffered, as did that of Prime Minister Herbert Asquith.

Whether an Allied capture of Gallipoli and the Dardanelles would have had a decisive impact on the war and whether the opening of an Allied supply route to Russia would have prevented Russia's revolution and collapse in 1917 must forever remain subjects of conjecture. That Germany interpreted the Gallipoli campaign as one of the most decisive of the war was attested by the opinions of her military leaders. The fall of the Dardenelles, in Falkenhayn's view, meant the defeat of the Central Powers.

THE BRITISH ADVANCE IN THE MIDDLE EAST

While the attention of the world was focused on the Dardanelles, Britain had launched a major campaign against the Turkish Middle East. British troops, composed chiefly of Indian divisions, had landed in Mesopotamia as early as late 1914, in order to protect the oil installations on Abadan Island in the Persian Gulf. After the capture of Basra the British force, under the command of General John Nixon, advanced inland as far as the confluence of the Tigris and Euphrates, reaching Kut al Amara by September, 1915. From a protective operation, the Mesopotamian landings thus developed into an ambitious offensive with the city of Bagdad as its goal. Although Bagdad possessed little strategic value in itself, its capture would produce favorable headlines in Britain and obscure the Allied defeat in the Gallipoli campaign. The advance on Bagdad was undertaken with insufficient strength, however, the two Indian divisions, withdrawn from France and earmarked for the Middle East not arriving at their destination until January, 1916. Accordingly, a British force under General Townshend was surrounded at Kut and forced to surrender after a Turkish siege which lasted from December, 1915, to April, 1916. As at Gallipoli, German military assistance had been instrumental in the Turkish victory at Kut, overall command of the Turkish forces in Mesopotamia being under Field Marshal von der Goltz, who was well acquainted with the area from his extensive pre-war travels.

While suffering defeat on the Tigris, Britain had beaten off a Turkish attack on the Suez Canal in early February, 1915. After dragging their own pontoons across the forbidding Sinai Peninsula, 20,000 Turks had arrived on the eastern bank of the Canal on February 2. Only a few managed to cross the Canal before the Turkish force was repulsed by naval gunfire. With the arrival of troops from Gallipoli, Britain reinforced her Suez defenses through the establishment of the Egyptian Expeditionary Force.

THE FRENCH FRONT IN 1915

On the main Allied front in France, the increase in the strength of Allied artillery had failed to achieve the decisive results which Joffre had confidently predicted at the beginning of 1915. In vain, British and French attacks in Artois and the Champagne were hurled against the Noyon salient between February and October, 1915. The single Battle of Loos of September, 1915, cost Britain 60,000 casualties, while the assault in the Champagne during October resulted in 150,000 French casualties. Sir John French lost his command to Sir Douglas Haig, but the change in command did not alter the deadlock on the western front. "Strategy," in the words of the British military historian Liddell Hart, "became the hand maiden of tactics, while tactics became a cripple." The Allied penetrations measured 3,000 yards at their furthest points. Well might Lord Kitchener exclaim: "I don't know what is to be done — this isn't war!"

In Flanders, Germany had sprung an unpleasant surprise on the Allies with a gas attack on the Ypres salient on April 22, 1915. By May the Ypres salient was crushed and Allied casualties reached 70,000. As the German attack was not the beginning of a larger offensive but rather served the aim of concealing troop withdrawals to the Russian front, Germany failed to exploit the success achieved by surprise.

Nineteen fifteen witnessed the expansion of aerial combat over France, with mass formations of Allied and German aircraft engaged in dog fights high above the trenches. The air aces, Fonck, Guynemer, Nungesser on the Allied side, Richthofen, Boelcke and Immelmann on the German, achieved quick fame, as aerial combat seemed to have restored a human dimension to an otherwise inhuman war. In the air, individual skill and bravery stood out against the anonymity of mass suffering among the slogging armies on the ground.

ITALY'S ENTRY INTO THE FIRST WORLD WAR

Having declared her neutrality at the outset of the First World War, Italy made the continuation of her neutrality dependent upon territorial concessions by Austria-Hungary. Although the latter had disclaimed any intention of annexing Serbian territory, Italy invoked Article VII of the Triple Alliance, which entitled her to territorial compensation in the event of Austria's annexations in the Balkans. In her demands, Italy was emboldened by the poor military showing of the Habsburg

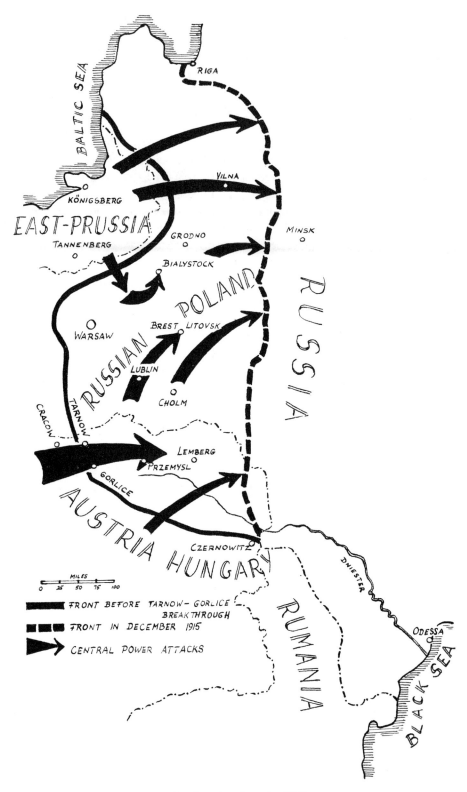

BALTIC SEA

RIGA

KÖNIGSBERG

EAST-PRUSSIA

TANNENBERG

VILNA

GRODNO

MINSK

BIALYSTOCK

POLAND

RUSSIA

WARSAW

BREST LITOVSK

RUSSIAN

LUBLIN

CHOLM

CRACOW

TARNOW

LEMBERG

PRZEMYSL

GORLICE

AUSTRIA HUNGARY

CZERNOWITZ

DNIESTER

RUMANIA

ODESSA

BLACK SEA

MILES
0   25   50   75   100

FRONT BEFORE TARNOW-GORLICE BREAKTHROUGH

FRONT IN DECEMBER 1915

CENTRAL POWER ATTACKS

The Russian front in 1915.

50

monarchy in Serbia and Poland. Austria could ill-afford to face another enemy and possibly two, as an Italian declaration of war might induce Rumania to follow suit.

Italy's territorial demands against Austria-Hungary included the South Tirol, Trentino, Goricia, as well as some of the Dalmatian Islands. Triest was to be internationalized. The Italian demands might well have revived in Vienna the memory of Bismarck's observation that Italy's appetite was large but her teeth were poor. Under existing military conditions, even a weak bite in the Austrian flank could be fatal, however, in view of Austria-Hungary's overextended forces.

Prince Bülow, Germany's ambassador to Rome, attempted vainly to mediate between Vienna and Rome, urging Austria to make at least limited territorial concessions. Reluctantly, Austria offered the Trentino by March, 1915, but no more. As Italy was being promised all she had demanded of Austria and more, in the secret Treaty of London on April 26, 1915, with the Allies, she declared war on Austria on May 23, 1915. War on Germany was not declared until August, 1916.

The war with Italy united Slavs and Austro-Germans of the Habsburg monarchy as few other events of the First World War could, both nationalities possessing a long history of common aversion to their neighbor in the south. The Italian declaration of war even induced the aging former Austrian Foreign Minister Berchtold to volunteer for military service against Italy.

Italy's military contribution to the Allied war effort of 1915 was minor. Between June and November, 1915, Count Luigi Cadorna, Italy's Chief of Staff, tried in vain to storm the Austrian front on the Isonzo River in the four Isonzo battles. The Italian attacks did not create a strong enough diversion to prevent the conquest of Serbia by the Central Powers in the fall of 1915.

THE CENTRAL POWERS' INITIATIVE
IN THE EAST

The fall and winter battles on the eastern front had very nearly exhausted Russia's stocks of ammunitions by the turn of 1914/1915. Quite often, Russian reserves would be sent into battle without rifles of their own, depending for their arms on the equipment of their fallen comrades in the first waves of the attack. Russia's shortage of ammunitions, plus the proven superiority of the German troops in the defensive battles of Tannenberg and Lodz, encouraged Hindenburg and Ludendorff to attempt to drive Russia out of the war in 1915.

Ludendorff hoped to destroy the bulk of the Russian army in Poland through a battle of wide encirclement, proceeding from East Prussia into Lithuania and thence to the south. The Ludendorff plan would have required the shifting of substantial German troop strength from west to east, however, which Falkenhayn, the German Chief of Staff, opposed out of fear of an Allied breakthrough in the west. Accordingly, the Central Powers settled for a more limited attack in western Galicia, whose mentor was the Austrian Chief of Staff Conrad.

THE BREAKOUT AT TARNOV AND GORLICE

Between May 2 and 5, 1915, a combined German-Austrian force, under the command of Field Marshall August von Mackensen, broke through the Russian front between Tarnov and Gorlice. In timing, strength, and place, the Central Powers' attack achieved full surprise. Within two weeks Mackensen's armies had advanced one hundred miles. Warsaw was captured on August 4, the fortress of Brest-Litovsk taken by the end of August. Towards the end of 1915, the Central Powers had conquered all of Poland, Lithuania, as well as one half of Latvia, while recapturing Austrian Galicia. The eastern front now ran from the Rumanian frontier in the south to the Gulf of Riga in the north along a nearly straight line of 600 miles. Russia had lost 3,000 guns and 300,000 prisoners.

The pace of the German-Austrian offensive had begun to slacken by September, 1915, largely because of the impending invasions of Serbia. As Allied pressure mounted in the Gallipoli campaign, Falkenhayn had decided on the conquest of Serbia, in order to open a direct route to Turkey and provide the latter with much-needed military assistance.

To assure quick victory over Serbia, the Central Powers induced Bulgaria to enter the war on their side through a secret agreement of September 6, 1915. King Ferdinand of Bulgaria, who had been seeking an alliance with Austria-Hungary before the war, secured parliamentary approval of his decision to join the Central Powers by the narrow margin of 250 against 200 deputies. Though anxious to obtain revenge against her rival Serbia, Bulgaria had held back until the Russian defeats of 1915 suggested the ascendancy of the Central Powers in the east.

In early October, 1915, German, Austrian, and Bulgarian troops invaded Serbia from the north and east. Bulgaria severed the Serbian rail communications with Greece and thereby isolated the Anglo-French expeditionary force under General Maurice Serrail, which had landed at Salonika on October 3, 1915, with the intention of relieving Serbia from the south. Accordingly, Serbia was quickly overrun, Belgrade having been captured on October 9. By January, 1916, Austria had conquered the larger part of Albania as well, with Italy retaining a foothold in the south of Albania. The remnants of the Serbian army were evacuated to the Greek island of Corfu.

The Allied expeditionary force at Salonika, though it eventually grew to 600,000 men, remained isolated, on guard both against the Bulgarians to its north as well as the uncertain Greeks around it. Officially, Greece remained a neutral in the war despite the uninvited Allied military presence at Salonika. Allied pressure eventually forced the pro-German King Constantine to abdicate on June 12, 1917. On June 29, 1917, Greece, under the pro-Allied Prime Minister Venizelos, declared war on Germany, Bulgaria, and Turkey.

The Central Powers' military operations in the east, from Russia to Serbia and Gallipoli, achieved no more than the securing of a stronger defensive position. However impressive the Central Powers' victories, they had failed to push Russia out of the war. The stalemate between the warring blocs had merely hardened by the end of 1915.

1916:
TOWARDS MUTUAL EXHAUSTION;
VERDUN, THE SOMME, GALICIA;
RUMANIA'S ENTRY INTO THE WAR

The strategic initiative had rested with the Central Powers through most of 1915, largely because the Allies had failed to develop a coordinated strategy of their own. The Allied military conference at Joffre's headquarters in Chantilly between December 5 and 8, 1915, which was attended by representatives of Britain, Belgium, Italy, Russia, and even Japan, was designed to remedy this deficiency. The Allies decided to launch simultaneous offensives in west and east in the spring of 1916, thereby denying Germany the advantage of interior lines and preventing her from shifting troops between her fronts. At Chantilly it was further decided to strengthen Britain's Suez defenses.

Of all the promising plans agreed upon at Chantilly, the Allies were able to implement only those relating to the Turkish Middle East. After the British defeat in Mesopotamia at Kut in April, 1916, Britain assembled a new striking force of about 160,000 troops under Sir Stanley Maude, which resumed the offensive on December 12, 1916. After a slow advance up the Tigris, supported by air power and river gun boats, Maude captured Bagdad on March 11, 1917. In Egypt Sir Archibald Murray improved the Suez defenses by establishing a forward line of defense along the eastern borders of the Sinai Peninsula. Murray's advance, which took the better part of 1916, involved a considerable logistical effort, as a brand-new railroad as well as a truck route had to be thrown across the trackless Sinai. A Turkish attack, carried out with German support at Romani on August 4, 1916, was beaten off.

In the main theaters of France and Russia, Allied plans for a coordinated strategy were quickly overtaken by the German offensive against Verdun.

While Allied military leaders were conferring at Chantilly, Falkenhayn had hatched his strategic plans for 1916. Falkenhayn was a "westerner" among German generals, who considered Britain Germany's main enemy and France England's "best sword" on the continent of Europe. Regarding Russia as paralyzed by the German blows of 1915, Falkenhayn wished to cripple France in 1916 in a battle of attrition, which would bleed the French army white and leave France, in Falkenhayn's words, "nothing to hope for." The German attack was directed at the French fortress of Verdun, which France could ill-afford to abandon both for reasons of prestige as well as for the sake of its strategic significance as the anchor of the French northeastern front. Falkenhayn's western strategy also included a stepped-up submarine campaign against England. With France beaten on the continent and Britain severed from her vital overseas imports, Germany's chances of victory would greatly increase.

The German assault on Verdun was postponed from February 12 to 21, 1916, because of bad weather. The delay was significant to the outcome of the battle, as Germany would have enjoyed a far greater superiority in numbers had the assault begun on the scheduled date. France accepted Falkenhayn's challenge, defending Verdun in what became the longest and most cruel of all the long and cruel battles of the First World War. Verdun became the finest hour of the French army, but it also sowed the seeds of future French despair and defeatism, whose effects were still being felt in 1940.

To save the defenders from obliteration, Philippe Pétain, who took command of Verdun on February 25, 1916, rotated his sixty-six divisions throughout the battle, which lasted from February to July. By June, 1916, the German troops, under the command of the Crown Prince, had stormed two of the key forts, Douaumont and Vaux, without, however, being able to cut the lifeline of Verdun, the "Sacred Way," a highway over which French reinforcements continued to pour into Verdun at a rate of up to six thousand trucks in twenty-four hours.

In response to the French agony at Verdun, the Allies, Russia, Italy, and Britain, mounted relief offensives, whose timing was dictated more by the German pressure on Verdun than by their own calculations. In Italy Cadorna resumed his futile hammering along the Isonzo front with the Fifth Battle of the Isonzo between March 11 and 29. Russia, which had not planned on striking until June, 1916, launched a hasty attack in March against the German Baltic flank at Lake Naroch, which was as costly to the Russian army as it was futile in its results. Britain, having taken over the western front all the way from Ypres to the Somme, mounted a relief attack on the Somme on July 1, 1916.

The Somme offensive was Britain's greatest effort on the western front to date, the size of the British army having been further ex-

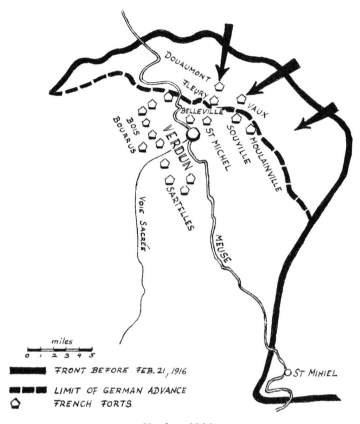

Verdun, 1916.

panded since the introduction of conscription under the Military Service Acts of April, 1916. The morale of the British army was high, but many of the recruits who marched to battle on the Somme were raw, lacking the experience of their French allies and German foes. The British infantry advanced from its trenches in close formation as the armies of Frederick the Great might have done in an earlier century. The march was uphill against thoroughly prepared German defenses, which claimed 58,000 British casualties between sunrise and dusk on July 1, 1916. On the Somme, the infantry of both sides soon became, in the words of an observer, "compressed cannon fodder for artillery consumption." By mid-September, 1916, Douglas Haig attempted another push, in which Britain revealed for the first time her "secret weapon" of the First World War, the tank.

The history of the tank, like that of most other revolutionary weapons, was a tortuous path of official indifference and petty obstruction by established military authority. Chief credit for the development of the tank belonged to Colonel Ernest Swinton and Winston Churchill. The former conceived the idea of the tank in late 1914, calling for the development of the tractor into a bullet-proof trench-crossing machine. The latter, as First Lord of the Admiralty, furthered the project through testing, the first prototype, "Big Willie," performing satisfactorily in February, 1916.

On September 15, 1916, the tank was thrown into battle on the Somme in insufficient numbers—only thirty-two were committed, of which nine broke down—and with faulty tactics. The tank made a mighty impression on the Germans, but it failed to influence the overall course of the Somme battle. The Battle of the Somme had yielded Britain only a slight penetration of six miles in depth. It was instrumental, however, in bringing the German attack on Verdun to a halt. After July 1, 1916, no German reinforcements went to Verdun. France went over to the offensive on the Verdun front, recapturing the forts of Douaumont and Vaux in October, 1916, as well as much of the territory lost in the spring. At Verdun and on the Somme, the Allies had suffered 1.2 million casualties, their German opponent 800,000.

Of Falkenhayn, it has been rightly said that he was "penny

FIGURE 1 *French troops during the Battle of Verdun, 1916.*

wise and pound foolish" in the employment of his troops. While consigning irreplaceable German reserves to a fiery death in the furnace of Verdun, the German chief of staff missed splendid strategic opportunities in Italy and exposed the Central Powers' front in Russia to the most serious risks. Austria's Chief of Staff, Conrad, whose imagination forever outran his military strength, had proposed a decisive strike against Italy, to be launched from the Trentino towards the back of the Italian front on the Isonzo. Were Germany and Austria to concentrate their forces against Italy in 1916, as they had done against Serbia in 1915, Conrad was certain that Italy would capitulate.

Falkenhayn doubted whether Italy would sue for peace even if she suffered a decisive military defeat in the far north, simply because Britain and France would veto a separate Italian surrender. Conrad thus launched his attack from the Trentino on May 15, 1916, without German aid. In order to achieve the desired strength, Conrad withdrew his best divisions from the Russian front, having pleaded vainly that their position be taken up by German troops. The Austrian offensive achieved a twelve-mile penetration and cost Italy 300 guns and 45,000 prisoners; Italy's overall casualties in the Trentino offensive of May and June, 1916, were estimated as high as 280,000. The Austrian attack had fallen far short of its strategic and political goals, however, the unhinging of the Italian Isonzo front and the surrender of Italy.

By early June, 1916, Austria hastily broke off the Trentino offensive, as disaster threatened to envelop her armies in Galicia and Bukovina.

THE BRUSILOV OFFENSIVE

The Russian giant, stunned and staggering after the blows of 1915, though far from paralyzed as Falkenhayn had hoped, had struck against the brittle wall of Austria's eastern front in one last mighty effort of the war. Beginning in June 4, 1916, four Russian armies under General Brusilov had broken through the Austrian lines at Luck and seized the province of Bukovina with its capital Czernowitz by June 16. The Russian breakthrough resulted less from a superiority of numbers than from surprise and from the mass surrender of disaffected Czech and Ruthenian troops in the Austrian army. Brusilov bagged the greatest number of prisoners of any Russian victory during the First World War, with 350,000. Brusilov's own casualties climbed to over one million, however, as German reinforcements restored the Austrian front by October, 1916.

The military and political repercussions of Brusilov's attack ranged far and wide: Falkenhayn was forced to divert German strength to the east, originally earmarked for a counterstroke against the British on the Somme; Conrad, as previously noted, had to abandon the Trentino drive; most important, Rumania was emboldened to enter the war against

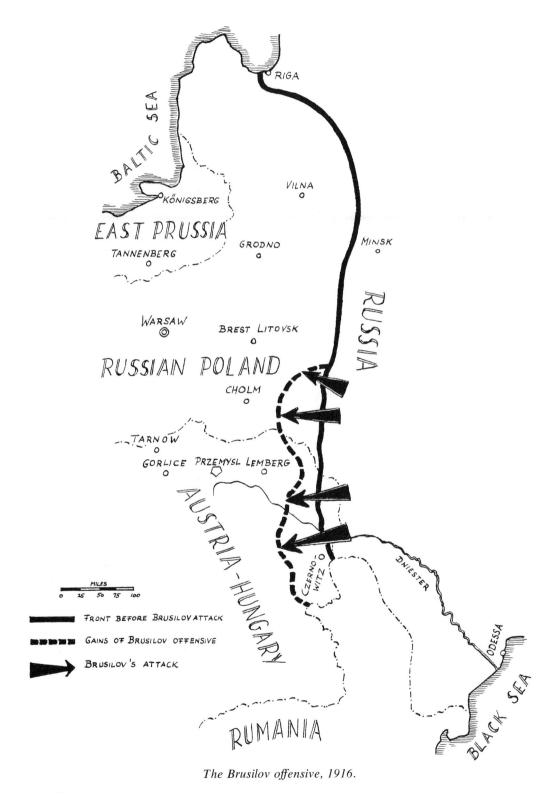

The Brusilov offensive, 1916.

the Central Powers on August 27, 1916, having been promised Transylvania and Bukovina as a prize by the Allies. Among the casualties of
Brusilov's offensive was also Falkenhayn, who was dismissed as Chief
of Staff in August, his strategy in shambles.

Rumania had postponed her entry into the war a trifle too long,
as Austria's debacle was being mastered by late August, and Germany
and Austria, in conjunction with Bulgaria and Turkey, were able to scrape
together enough troops for the defeat of Rumania. The Rumanians were
so anxious to secure Transylvania, the Hungarian border province to their
north, which they had coveted since before the war, that they mounted a
rash invasion of Transylvania, rather than hold the easily defensible
passes in the Transylvanian Alps. By September, 1916, Falkenhayn, now
in the role of an army commander in the field, chased the Rumanian army
out of Hungary and invaded Rumania proper in conjunction with a mixed
Bulgarian-Turkish-German force, which had advanced from Bulgaria.
Among the officers of Falkenhayn's invading army was a young unknown
by the name of Erwin Rommel, who was to achieve fame in another war
and another theater. On December 5, 1916, Bucharest was taken by the
Central Powers; the oil field of Ploesti fell the following day. What remained of the Rumanian army was confined to the province of Moldavia,
adjacent to the Russian front, until Russia's own collapse in 1917.

THE WAR AT SEA AND OVERSEAS

During the decade preceding the outbreak of the First World
War, Britain and Germany, as has been noted earlier, had engaged in an
expensive naval race, which had materially contributed to the worsening
of their mutual relations. As an anti-climax to the feverish preparations
for naval warfare, neither power committed the bulk of its fleet to battle
for nearly two years after the outbreak of war.

As Britain's Grand Fleet enjoyed a numerical superiority of
about 3:2 over the German High Seas Fleet, the latter risked annihilation
in an open confrontation on the seas. German naval strategy thus planned
to lure the Grand Fleet into battle close to the German North Sea coast,
where mine barriers and submarines would offset superior British strength
in surface vessels. It was hoped that Britain would accept battle on German terms. The German naval command counted on an aggressive British
naval strategy in the Nelsonian tradition as well as on the enforcement of
a "close blockade" against German shipping near the North Sea coast. A
further consideration in German naval strategy was the desire to preserve
the German fleet intact until after the hoped-for defeat of France and
Russia, as a means of persuading Britain into a favorable peace settlement.

Although the British public desired a "Trafalgar," a decisive
naval victory over Germany, at the outset of the war, the Grand Fleet

settled for the less exciting strategy of a "distant blockade," which yielded all the benefits of superior British sea power without the risks inherent in a major battle near the German coast. While the old battleships of the British Channel Fleet guarded the English Channel, the Grand Fleet controlled the sea lanes from the Atlantic into the North Sea from its bases in the Orkneys.

With both battle fleets confined to their bases, the few naval engagements in the early months of the war were in the nature of skirmishes, involving cruiser forces in the North Sea or German commerce raiders on the far oceans. A German cruiser force under the command of Graf Spee sank the British cruisers *Good Hope* and *Monmouth* under Admiral Christopher Cradock's command off Coronel, Chile, on November 1, 1914. Spee, in turn, was hunted down and his armored cruisers *Scharnhorst* and *Gneisenau* destroyed at the Falkland Islands on December 8, 1914. The German commerce raider *Emden,* which had inflicted considerable damage on Allied shipping in the Atlantic and Indian oceans, was sunk on November 9, 1914, by the Australian cruiser *Sydney.*

THE BATTLE OF JUTLAND

In the North Sea the British and German cruiser forces under the command of Vice Admiral Beatty and Admiral Hipper, respectively, had been baiting each other with raids close to the enemy coasts, Beatty as early as August 28, 1914, with a raid into the Heligoland Bight, Hipper with a raid to the Dogger Bank on January 24, 1915, which resulted in the loss of the German cruiser *Blücher.* On May 31, 1916, Admiral Reinhard Scheer sent out Hipper's cruisers towards the Jutland Straits (Skagerrak) to entice the British cruisers within range of the German High Seas Fleet. Britain accepted the challenge by sending the Grand Fleet under Admiral Jellicoe into the North Sea. In the ensuing Battle of Jutland, 28 battleships and 9 battle cruisers of the Grand Fleet clashed with 22 battleships and 5 battle cruisers of the German High Seas Fleet. Counting the escorting smaller vessels, 250 ships fought at Jutland under 25 admirals. In the first and only encounter of both fleets, the stakes were high, more so for Jellicoe than his opponent Scheer. If Scheer was defeated, Germany would lose a battle; if Jellicoe succumbed, Britain might well risk the existence of her Empire, based on control of the seas. It was in this context that Churchill called Jellicoe the "only man who could lose the war in an afternoon."

The Battle of Jutland was as brief as it was violent, the main forces making contact only after 6 P.M. on May 31, 1916. The outcome of the battle was determined as much by superior British numbers as by superior German gunnery and better armor plating. Against Britain's loss of three battle cruisers, three armored cruisers, and eight destroyers stood German losses of one battle cruiser, one old battleship, four light cruisers, and five destroyers. Over 6,000 British sailors gave their lives as against 2,500 German.

Though Britain's prestige was impaired by suffering the greater casualties, her command at sea was not, as Jutland had left the naval balance unaltered. To break the increasingly effective British distant blockade, Germany would soon return to unrestricted submarine warfare, which she had first employed in early 1915, but abandoned after the Lusitania Incident, to be discussed more fully in the context of the U. S. entry into the First World War.

On balance, the battle fleet served Germany no useful purpose in the First World War; it neither lifted the British blockade nor protected a single German overseas colony from rapid Allied seizure. Indeed, the German battle fleet, status symbol of empire, showpiece of German industrial achievement, and pride of Emperor William II, was to become the seedbed of mutiny and revolution, which in November, 1918, swept the Hohenzollern dynasty from its throne.

THE CONQUEST OF THE GERMAN COLONIES

In the Far East, Japan had occupied the undefended German islands of the Carolines, Marshalls, and Marianas and had taken the German fortress of Tsingtao on November 7, 1914, with British help. Also in 1914, New Zealand had seized Samoa, Australia had seized New Pomerania, renamed New Britain with the capital of Rabaul of World War II fame. In Africa, South Africa's General Louis Botha conquered diamond-rich German South-West Africa by July, 1915, while Togo and the Cameroons fell to a combined Anglo-French force. In East Africa alone, Germany's richest and largest colony, was German resistance sustained and successful, chiefly because of the resourcefulness of the German commander Lettow-Vorbeck. Though Britain had captured the principal port of Dar-es-Salaam as well as the East African railroad by 1916, the conquest of German East Africa was not completed until November, 1917. Lettow-Vorbeck and his few thousand troops, chiefly African, eluded their pursuers even after that date, having crossed into Portuguese East Africa and holding out until the German surrender in Europe on November 11, 1918.

1917:
WAR-WEARINESS, WAR AIMS, AND PEACE FEELERS; THE COLLAPSE OF RUSSIA

By early 1917 the strain of total war began to take its toll on the morale both of the fighting troops and of the populations at home. The deadlock of attrition on the battlefields of Europe had swept from power many of the political and military leaders who had led peoples and armies into war three years earlier with the promise of an early victory. In Britain, Lloyd George had replaced Herbert Asquith as Prime Minister on December 7, 1916, with the promise of a more determined prosecution of the war. In Germany, the resignation of Chancellor Bethmann-Hollweg on July 12, 1917, ended the contest between civilian and military authority and paved the way for the establishment of a virtual military dictatorship under Ludendorff. In Austria-Hungary, Emperor Francis Joseph had died on November 21, 1916, bequeathing his tottering empire to the irresolute and inexperienced hands of young Emperor Charles I. In Russia Tsar Nicholas II had assumed personal command over the Russian armies after the disastrous defeat in the spring of 1915, thereby identifying his person and dynasty with Russia's subsequent reverses and preparing his downfall in March, 1917. In Italy Prime Minister Salandra had fallen from power in 1915 in the wake of Italy's defeat on the Trentino front. In France Prime Minister Briand was to yield to Georges Clemenceau in November, 1917, when French spirits were at their lowest and the need for inspired and resolute leadership at its greatest. In the United States, President Wilson had been reelected in November, 1916, chiefly on his promise of keeping the United States out of war.

The changes in the military and naval commands were equally sweeping. In France Joffre gave way to Nivelle in December, 1916; in Germany, as previously noted, Falkenhayn was succeeded by Hindenburg with Ludendorff as his deputy; Haig remained in command of the British army in France, while Kitchener was killed on June 5, 1916, when his British cruiser *Hampshire,* en route to Russia, was sunk by a German mine. Tirpitz, the father of the German navy, resigned as Naval Minister in 1916 in protest against his government's opposition to unrestricted submarine warfare; Austria's Chief of Staff Conrad was replaced in early 1917, while Cadorna lost his command to Armando Díaz following the Italian disaster of Caporetto in the fall of 1917.

The strain of war had opened cracks in the morale of ordinary soldiers and sailors. The French army, as previously noted, suffered a moral collapse in April, 1917, following the Nivelle offense. Although no mutinies occurred in the British army, the confidence of common soldiers in their leadership was undermined after the slaughter on the Somme. An Australian soldier, who fought at the Somme, expressed the mood of many comrades when he complained about the "murder" of British troops "through the incompetence, callousness, and personal vanity of those high in authority." Sailors' mutinies broke out at the Austro-Hungarian naval base of Cattaro in February, 1917, and the German naval base at Kiel in August, 1917. In Austria-Hungary, the Slavic nationalities became increasingly restless over the failure of Emperor Charles I to implement immediate and sweeping reforms in the structure of the Dual Monarchy.

In the United Kingdom, the divisive issue of Irish Home Rule exploded in the Easter Rebellion during Easter week of 1916 in Dublin. Whereas the more moderate Irish Nationalist Party under John Redmond had acquiesced in the suspension of the Irish Home Rule Bill of 1914 for the duration of the First World War, the radical Sinn Fein ("We Ourselves" in Gaelic) had sought German help in the fulfillment of its goals. Sir Roger Casement had gone so far as to attempt, without success, the raising of a volunteer Irish Legion from British prisoners of war in Germany. Casement landed in Ireland from a German submarine on Good Friday, 1916. On Easter Monday, the rebels seized control of Dublin and proclaimed the Irish Republic. Britain crushed the ill-organized uprising quickly by dispatching a force under General John Maxwell. Casement, together with several other rebel leaders, was executed. Eamon de Valera was spared, thanks to American intervention. An attempt to calm the Irish issue by granting immediate home rule to twenty-six counties, excluding the six counties of Ulster, failed, owing to Parliamentary opposition. The Easter Rebellion and its aftermath contributed to the fall of Prime Minister Asquith in December, 1916.

Whereas Britain had snuffed out the Sinn Fein insurrection without lasting damage to her war effort, the Empire of Russia was consumed in the conflagration of social, national, and political revolution, beginning with the overthrow of Tsar Nicholas II on March 15, 1917. The causes of the Russian revolution of March, 1917, and its subsequent course until the Bolshevik seizure of power in November, 1917, will be described more fully in the discussion of Russia's internal developments. In the context of the First World War, the most important factors in the coming of the Russian Revolution were the demoralization of the front-line troops, owing to the blood toll and poor leadership, and the moral and political bankruptcy of the dynasty among the Russian middle and upper classes. War-weariness prevented the Provisional Governments under Prince Lvov and Alexander Kerensky, which followed the overthrow of the monarchy in March, 1917, from maintaining a sustained war effort against the Central Powers for the remainder of 1917. While the Petrograd Soviet, the rival organ of Lvov's Provisional Government, issued the call for a negotiated peace without annexations and indemnities, the command structure of the Russian Army collapsed through the formation of soliders' councils (soviets) among the troops in the field and the garrisons. Except for the Kerensky offensive, launched on July 1, 1917, in Galicia under pressure of the western Allies, Russia ceased to play an active part in the military affairs of 1917. After a few gains against the Austrians, the Kerensky offensive was crushed by a German counteroffensive on July 19. The pitiful state of Russia's defenses was further revealed by the German capture of Riga on the Baltic on September 3, 1917. Having overthrown the Provisional Government of Kerensky on November 7, 1917, the new Bolshevik government of Lenin, in fulfillment of its pledge to end the war, signed a separate armistice with the Central Powers in December, 1917. Russia, for all intents and purposes, had left the war.

Before the Russian Revolution of March, 1917, had dramatically reversed the strategic balance of the war in Germany's favor, Germany launched an initiative for peace negotiations in the fall of 1916. During the American election campaign, the German government appealed to Woodrow Wilson to use his good offices for the convocation of a general peace conference. Germany did not wish the United States to be part of the proposed peace conference, however, hoping to divide the Allies more easily at the peace table without the presence of the United States.

President Wilson had unsuccessfully explored the possibilities of a peace negotiated through his own efforts before, by sending his adviser Colonel House to the belligerent capitals of Europe in January, 1915, and January, 1916.

In Berlin, Colonel House was told that the restoration of Belgium and the return of Russian Poland were no longer negotiable. In London, House promised that the United States would call a peace conference whenever Britain and France considered the moment favorable. In the House-Grey Memorandum of February 22, 1916, the United States even intimated that it might join the Allies in the event of German refusal to accept an invitation to a peace conference. In early 1916, the Allies did not consider the time opportune for a peace conference, however.

When President Wilson did not immediately respond to the German initiative of October, 1916, Germany issued an invitation for peace negotiations directly to the Allies on December 12, 1916, which was timed to coincide with the successful conclusion of German operations in Rumania. The German note stated the war aims of the Central Powers in the vaguest of terms, citing as objectives the "existence, honor, and freedom of development" of the peoples of the Central Powers. The German conditions were thus flexible enough to cover any territorial annexations that Germany might desire. The Allies rejected the German offer as a political maneuver designed to impress favorably the neutrals and confuse the Allies.

On December 18, 1916, Wilson addressed a call to both the Allies and the Central Powers to state their war aims, in order to determine whether a common basis for a negotiated peace did, in fact, exist. Germany agreed to participate in peace discussions, without, however, answering the core of Wilson's question. The Allies submitted a list of war aims to Wilson on January 10, 1917, which included the restoration of Belgium, Serbia and Montenegro, the German evacuation of all occupied territory in France and Russia, the restitution of territories seized by force in the past (a reference to Alsace-Lorraine), and the liberation of Italians, Slavs, Rumanians, and Czechoslovaks from "foreign domination." The latter demand implied the dismemberment of Austria-Hungary. The Allies also demanded the exclusion of the Ottoman Empire from Europe. Disappointed by both the Allied and German response, President Wilson outlined his own ideas for peace in a speech before the Senate of January 22, 1917, which suggested some of the principles of the Fourteen Points of January, 1918. The President called for a "peace without victory," based on the equality of all nations and a world organization for peace, for freedom of the seas, and for a reduction of armaments.

The Allies were displeased by Wilson's phrase "peace without victory." The Germans had revealed none of their war aims, the Allies not all of theirs. By 1916 the Allies had concluded far-reaching secret agreements among themselves for territorial acquisition after the war. The secret agreements, to be discussed more fully in the context of the Paris Peace Conference of 1919, included the Treaty of London with Italy in 1915, the Sykes-Picot Agreement of 1916 for the dismemberment of the Turkish Empire, the promise of Constantinople to Russia in 1915, and a French-Russian agreement of February, 1917, for the detachment of the Rhineland from Germany.

GERMAN WAR AIMS

The German Empire, in turn, had secretly outlined a program of vast annexations in expectation of a *Siegfrieden* (peace based on victory) as early as September, 1914. On September 9, 1914, when Germany's war aims were still officially described as defensive, Bethmann-Hollweg had drafted a confidential memorandum on annexations, which remained the basis of German intentions for the rest of the war. Belgium was to be brought under permanent German political and economic control; France was to yield the iron ore mines of Briey as well as the channel coast from Dunkirk to Boulogne. France was to be forced into paying heavy reparations, which would not only cover Germany's own war costs but weaken France sufficiently to prevent her rearmament for years to come. Luxembourg was to be annexed outright. German economic domination of continental Europe was to be assured through a customs union with France, Austria-Hungary, the Scandinavian countries, Holland, and Belgium. In Africa a compact German colonial empire was to be created in central Africa, including the mineral-rich Belgian Congo as well as French and Portuguese colonies. In the East, Bethmann-Hollweg wished to retain a "frontier strip" in Russian Poland. On November 5, 1916, the Central Powers proclaimed the establishment of a separate kingdom of Poland, which was, however, to remain tied to Germany and Austria-Hungary. As an attempt to enlist Polish nationalism on the side of the

Central Powers, the proclamation of November 5, 1916, was a failure. Contrary to Ludendorff's expectation, only a handful of Poles repaid the gesture by military service on the Central Powers' side.

The collapse of the Russian Empire in 1917 whetted the German appetite for annexations in the east. Under the pretext of promoting the national self-determination of the non-Russian nationalities of the Russian Empire, Ludendorff brought the western and southern borderlands of European Russia ranging from Finland, the Baltic provinces, and Poland, to the Ukraine and the Caucasus, under various forms of German political, economic, or military control in 1918. The Peace of Brest-Litovsk between the Bolshevik government and the Central Powers on March, 1918, was to bring the German Empire within reach of its overall war aim in the First World War—the securing of world power, based on the space and resources of the Eurasian land mass from the Caucasus to the Rhine.

AUSTRIAN PEACE FEELERS

Austria-Hungary, pursuing far less grandiose schemes than her German ally, would have been glad to emerge from the First World War with her frontiers of 1914 intact. By 1917 the Dual Monarchy had ceased to be its free agent, however, being chained for better or for worse to the destiny of Germany. Emperor Charles, acting through his brother-in-law Prince Sixtus of Bourbon-Parma, made several unsuccessful attempts to secure a separate peace between himself and the western powers in 1916 and 1917. Austria-Hungary's temptation to desert her German ally increased with the collapse of Russia, since Russia had been Austria's principal enemy and since the Habsburgs had had no quarrel with the western powers before 1914. The Austrian maneuver failed because of the territorial demands of Italy. When the French Prime Minister Clemenceau disclosed the Austrian peace feelers of 1917, the embarrassed Emperor Charles was forced to submit to far-reaching German controls in the Agreement of Spa of May 12, 1918. The Spa Agreement turned the Dual Monarchy into a virtual satellite of Germany, with the result that Austrian economic, military, and foreign policies fell increasingly under German domination.

THE POPE'S PEACE INITIATIVE

"Peace without victory," as a peaceful and secure America wished it for war-torn Europe in 1917, proved impossible in the light of German and Allied war aims. Self-restraint in the common interest of Europe had been notably absent from Great Power relations in peace time before 1914. It was not likely to materialize under conditions of war. Accordingly, the peace initiative of Pope Benedict XV on August 1, 1917, proved no more successful than Wilson's had been in January. The pope proposed a "just and durable" peace, based on "the moral force of right," rather than "the material force of arms." All conquered territories were to be restored and plebiscites held in such disputed areas as Poland, the Trentino, and Alsace-Lorraine.

THE REICHSTAG PEACE RESOLUTION

On the initiative of Matthias Erzberger, a Catholic deputy, the German Reichstag had passed a "peace resolution" a few weeks before the Pope's initiative, on July 19, 1917. The resolution called for a "peace of understanding and permanent reconciliation of nations" and opposed "forced concessions of territory and political, economic and financial impositions." The Reichstag peace resolution failed to convince the Allies and the United States, however, as it contained no specific pledge concerning the restoration of Belgium. Moreover, the terms "forced concessions of territory" did not exclude the possibility of German annexations in Russia under the guise of negotiated agreements. Most important, the Reichstag peace resolution was lacking in credibility because Hindenburg and Ludendorff, virtual military dictators of Germany by 1917, decided German foreign policy, rather than the Reichstag. At best, the peace resolution was an expression of the growing doubts of German parliamentary deputies in the policy of *Siegfrieden* which Ludendorff espoused. Specific papal inquiries as to Germany's readiness to restore Belgium did not elicit an affirmative reply from the German government.

THE GERMAN SUBMARINE OFFENSIVE; THE AMERICAN ENTRY INTO THE WAR

The appointment of Hindenburg and Ludendorff to the German Supreme Command ended the debate in Germany over submarine warfare in favor of those who advocated its unrestricted use. In a crown council of January 9, 1917, William II sanctioned the launching of an unrestricted submarine campaign as of February 1, 1917. The American government, after being advised of the German decision on January 31, 1917, by the German Ambassador, Bernstorff, broke off diplomatic relations with Germany on February 4.

The rupture of diplomatic relations climaxed a long and bitter controversy between the United States and Germany over the violation of American neutral rights by German submarine action. In retaliation against Britain's declaration of the entire North Sea as a military area on November 2, 1914, Germany had established a war zone around the British Isles on February 4, 1915. Both the British blockade and the German counterblockade by submarine departed from the accepted rules of sea war, Britain extending the lists of contraband to virtually all German imports, including grain, and Germany destroying Allied merchant ships on sight, without previous search or care for surviving passengers. Neither side obeyed the rules on naval warfare, adopted in the London Declaration of 1909, which, having been rejected by the British House of Lords, was not ratified by the other powers. Upon American inquiry, Germany pledged to abide by the London Declaration if the Allies would do likewise. Britain, in effect, refused compliance.

THE SINKING OF THE LUSITANIA

The United States protested against both the British and the German practices, insisting not only on the preservation of its trading rights but the right of American citizens to travel unharmed on belligerent passenger ships. This meant, in practice, travel of American citizens on British ships, as no German oceanliners crossed the Atlantic after August, 1914. Incidents soon occurred. On March 28, 1915, one American life was lost in the torpedoing of the British liner *Falaba.* On May 7, 1915, the British liner *Lusitania,* carrying both passengers and ammunition, was sunk with 128 American lives lost. On the day of its departure from New York, American citizens had been warned through newspaper ads, placed by Germany, not to sail on British vessels. While diplomatic notes were being exchanged between Washington and Berlin, in which the United States demanded compensation as well as an end to German attacks on passenger liners, another British liner, the *Arabic,* was sunk with American passengers aboard. The *Arabic* Incident of August 19, 1915, very nearly resulted in the rupture of American-German relations. It was avoided by Germany's promise to desist from further attacks on unarmed passenger liners. As of September, 1915, Germany had abandoned unrestricted submarine warfare.

German submarine attacks on merchant vessels were resumed in February, 1916, however, as part of Falkenhayn's overall western strategy against France and Britain. The sinking of the French channel boat *Sussex* on March 24, 1916, causing injury to American passengers aboard, again threatened to lead to a break in American-German relations. Once more, Germany abandoned submarine attacks on merchant vessels, while appealing to the United States to urge Britain into stopping its blockade practices.

THE RESUMPTION OF
UNRESTRICTED SUBMARINE WARFARE

The German decision of January 9, 1917, to resume unrestricted submarine warfare was thus taken in full knowledge of the consequences. The German military authorities considered an American declaration of war an acceptable risk, however, as the German navy confidently predicted the collapse of Britain through starvation "before the harvest" of 1917. Admiral Holtzendorff, the naval chief of staff, went so far as to pledge his "word of honor" that no American troop ship would escape the German submarine patrols. In any event, American military aid, in Germany's estimation, could not reach the Allies before 1918, by which time hostilities might well be ended.

THE AMERICAN DECLARATION OF WAR

The break in American-German diplomatic relations on February 4, 1917, did not yet mean war, and President Wilson still hoped to avoid it. Germany did her best to make it inevitable by attacking American merchant ships and by launching a clumsy diplomatic maneuver with the Zimmermann Note. In February, 1917, the German Foreign Secretary Alfred Zimmermann offered Mexico an alliance with the promise of returning New Mexico, Arizona, and Texas to Mexico in the event of war between Germany and the United States. Britain intercepted and decoded the Zimmermann Note and made its text available to the United States. On April 6, 1917, Congress declared war on Germany.

Since the sinking of the *Lusitania,* the American public, though anxious to stay out of war, had steadily moved closer to the Allied cause. The drowning of men, women, and children strengthened the impression of German brutality which British war propaganda had done its best to advertise in the United States. The report of Lord Bryce, concerning German atrocities in Belgium, though unsubstantiated, had its effects and seemed confirmed by the mass deportations of Belgian forced labor to Germany, which even German sources criticized. Although many Irish- and German-Americans sympathized with the Central Powers, Americans born in Austria-Hungary or descended from its Slavic nationalities hoped for the emancipation of their brothers in Europe from Habsburg domination. Most important, by 1917 the war in Europe had decidedly assumed the nature of an ideological contest between democracy and autocracy. It was for the purpose of "making the world safe for democracy" that Wilson asked the Congress of the United States to declare war. The collapse of tsarist Russia and the beginnings of what appeared, from a distance, to be a Russian democratic revolution in March, 1917, made the American decision to fight alongside the Allies much easier.

Although the United States was unprepared to send troops into battle immediately, the American declaration of war lifted the morale of the exhausted Allies beyond measure. The first large contingent of American forces did not reach France until May, 1918. Meanwhile, the small regular army and National Guard units, numbering little over 200,000 in April, 1917, served as a cadre for the mass army, which was to grow into a force of over 4 million, with more than 2 million reaching

Europe before the end of the war. Major General John J. Pershing, Commander of the American Expeditionary Force, wisely insisted on creating a separate American army, rather than permit the distribution of individual divisions among French and British troops, as the Allies had initially requested.

The American navy was ready for immediate action and played a decisive role in the containment of the German submarine threat. At the beginning of 1917 Germany had 110 submarines in service, while the Allies possessed over 21 million tons of merchant shipping. A minimum of 15 million tons was considered essential for Britain's survival. If the rate of German sinkings, which had reached over 880,000 tons for the month of April, 1917, continued into the fall of 1917, Britain's position would become desperate. Once Allied shipping space fell below fifteen million tons, Britain could neither maintain her domestic economy nor supply her overseas armies in Europe. In planning her strategy of starvation, Germany counted as much on actual sinkings as on frightening neutrals from sailing into British ports.

THE CONTAINMENT OF THE SUBMARINE THREAT

By October, 1917, the submarine threat was being mastered, chiefly through the convoy system, whose adoption Lloyd George, Admiral Beatty, and Admiral William S. Sims, U. S. Navy, had urged. After the first successful trial of the convoy system on the Gibraltar to Britain route in May, 1917, regular convoys sailed across the Atlantic in both directions beginning with August, 1917. While Allied convoys soon reduced their losses to one per cent, German submarines continued to inflict serious losses on the unescorted Scandinavian convoys. The United States Navy, in addition to providing destroyer escorts, laid a mine barrage between Norway and the Orkneys of some 70,000 mines over a distance of 180 miles, which closed the North Sea exit into the Atlantic to German submarines. Air patrols and depth charges increased German submarine losses to a total of 199 by the end of the First World War.

The Allied campaign against the submarine was less successful in the Mediterranean, where over 800 Allied ships were sunk by German and Austrian submarines between February and December, 1917. Lacking sufficient numbers of armed escorts, Britain had to rely on French, Italian, and even Japanese destroyers in the Mediterranean. The Allied attempt to contain submarines in the Adriatic through a mine barrier across the Otranto Straits between Italy and Albania brought limited success only, since the depth of the Otranto Straits enabled submarines to pass under the mines.

By the end of 1917 the German threat of starving Britain "before the harvest" had been proven an empty boast. The United States had gained sufficient time to bring to bear the full weight of its manpower on the battlefields of France. Not a single American troop ship was lost to submarine attack.

THE ALLIED CRISIS IN FRANCE; THE ITALIAN DEBACLE AT CAPORETTO

At the turn of 1916/1917 Italy's Chief of Staff Cadorna had vainly pleaded with his French and British allies to send strong forces to Italy for a decisive battle that would drive Austria-Hungary out of the war. General Nivelle rejected the Italian plan, as Allied numerical superiority over Germany on the western front seemed to augur well for Allied victory in France. Where his predecessor Joffre had failed, Nivelle was determined to win the war in one great battle, which was scheduled for April, 1917. The attack on the German lines in Champagne was to be a French effort, with the British army further to the north playing a subsidiary role.

The plans for the Allied spring offensive were upset, however, by Ludendorff's voluntary withdrawal from the Noyon bulge on March 12, 1917, towards a straight front with thoroughly prepared defenses. The German retreat, code-named operation *Alberich,* turned the evacuated territory into a wasteland of poisoned wells, dynamited villages, and booby traps, rendering it useless as a staging area for an Allied offensive.

By doing the unexpected, Ludendorff shortened his front line and gained new reserves. Behind the new Hindenburg Line (called Siegfried Line by the Germans), he awaited the Allied spring offensive, which began on April 9, 1917, at Arras on the British sector. The battle of Arras repeated the pattern of the western battles of 1916, gaining Britain the strategic height of Vimy Ridge at a cost of 84,000 casualties. The German casualties were not much lower, with 75,000. On April 16, 1916, Nivelle opened his great offensive on the Aisne with 54 French divisions. The battle ended with 120,000 French lives lost and the morale of the French army broken. Pétain, who succeeded the discredited Nivelle, arrested the mutinies, which had spread to sixteen army corps, less by a show of force than his paternal care for the welfare of the common soldier. The shattered morale of the French army may be gauged from the sharp increase in desertions, from only 500 in 1914 to over 21,000 in 1917.

After April, 1917, the British army, contrary to Nivelle's expectations, carried the main burden of the fighting, while Pétain nursed the French army back to health. Haig delivered his main blow in the third Battle of Ypres, beginning on July 31, 1917. The aim of the British attack was the capture of the Belgian channel ports of Ostende and Zeebrugge, which Haig mistakenly believed to be major German submarine bases. The Ypres attack bogged down in the soggy terrain of Passchendaele, made impassable to men, mules, and horses by the steady rains and the destruction of the intricate drainage system after ten days of uninterrupted British artillery fire. After three months Haig broke off the battle, the Belgian channel ports still beyond his reach. The use of a new type of gas by the German defense, called "mustard gas," compounded the agony of the rain-soaked British troops.

A British tank attack, launched with nearly 400 tanks over dry ground at Cambrai on November 20, 1917, achieved the greatest success of all Allied attacks of 1917. The British were lacking in infantry reserves to exploit the penetration of the tanks, however, having suffered a quarter million casualties in the futile Battle of Ypres. Upon news of the successful tank assault, church bells were rung in London. By November 30, 1917, the Germans had regained the lost ground at Cambria. The Battle of Cambria, nevertheless, gave a convincing demonstration of the tank's potential.

CAPORETTO

Italy suffered her greatest defeat of the World War in October, 1917, following a combined German-Austrian attack between Tolmino and Caporetto on October 24. The Italian troops, exhausted from Cadorna's ceaseless attacks in the eleven battles on the Isonzo, collapsed more quickly than anyone had expected. From the Isonzo the Central Powers advanced to Udine and crossed the Tagliamento by late October, 1917. Venice itself seemed threatened before the Italian army made a stand on the Piave on November 7, 1917. For a while it appeared as though Italy would share the fate of Rumania in 1916 and Serbia in 1915. Ludendorff had committed only six German divisions to the Caporetto attack, however. The British pressure at Ypres prevented the shifting of German reserves to Italy. Italy had suffered 300,000 casualties, of which some 260,000 were prisoners. Britain and France rushed troops to Italy, helping to restore Italian morale and build a stable front.

In the Middle East alone Britain achieved notable success in the course of 1917 with the capture of Jerusalem on December 9, 1917, by a British force under General Sir Edmund Allenby, nicknamed "the bull." Allenby's invasion of Palestine from Sinai was aided by the romantic desert hero T. E. Lawrence, a master of guerilla warfare, who stirred the Arabs into revolt against the Turks. "The Arab army," Lawrence wrote, "never tried to maintain or improve an advantage, but would move off and strike again somewhere else. It used the smallest force in the quickest time at the farthest place. . . ." Strategically, the capture of Jerusalem was no more significant than the conquest of Bagdad had been. The British victories in the Middle East served as a tonic, however, to British morale, after the dreary and inconclusive battles in France. They also earned Britain squatter's rights in the future disposition of the Middle East.

1918:
THE LUDENDORFF OFFENSIVE; THE ALLIED COUNTERSTROKE; THE COLLAPSE OF THE CENTRAL POWERS

The fall of Russia enabled Ludendorff to transfer sufficient numbers of troops from east to west to achieve, for the first time in the war, superior strength over the combined armies of Britain and France along the western front. In addition, the German armies had been resupplied with vast amounts of ammunition and armaments as a result of the Hindenburg program. A less ambitious strategist than Ludendorff might have seized the favorable moment of early 1918 and made a compromise peace offer to the western powers while preparing a strategic defense in France.

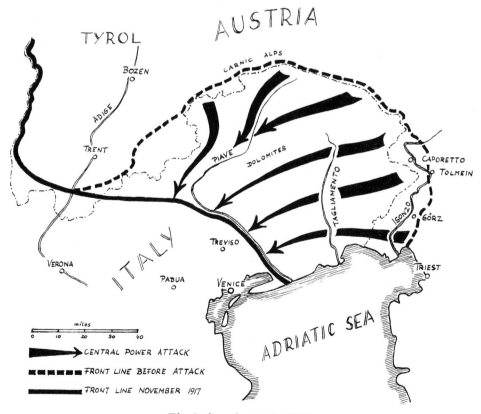

The Italian theater in 1917.

A peace program, such as President Wilson proposed in his Fourteen Points on January 8, 1918, was wholly unacceptable to Ludendorff. When Germany had at last been freed from fighting a two-front war, the German Supreme Command did not contemplate the surrender of Alsace-Lorraine, the evacuation of occupied Russian territory, the restoration of Belgium, and the establishment of an independent Poland, all of which were part of the Fourteen Points. On the contrary, Ludendorff wished to reap the full benefits of Russia's collapse by expanding eastward, while dealing the western Allies a mortal blow before the arrival of American forces in France could redress the balance in the Allies' favor. To achieve his territorial and political ambitions in the east, Ludendorff left one million German troops in Russia, which, if promptly shifted to the west, might have spelled the difference between German victory and defeat in France

Following the Treaty of Brest-Litovsk on March 3, 1918, with Russia, Germany turned the Ukraine into a virtual colony, while German troops occupied the Crimea. From the Crimea German troops advanced into the Caucasus and towards the Caspian Sea, Baku being occupied in September, 1918. In the Baltic, Germany strove towards the consolidation of Courland, Estonia, and Livonia into a single state, tied to the German Empire through personal union under William II. German influence was extended into Finland, following the conclusion of German-Finnish agreements on March 7, 1918, which granted Germany the right to establish naval bases. On October 9, 1918, only a few weeks before the German surrender in the West, Finland elected a German prince, Frederick Charles of Hesse, as king. To Rumania, Germany had dictated the Peace of Burcharest on May 7, 1918, which established German economic dominance over Rumania. Rumania's rail transport, Danube shipping, oil, and grain trade fell under German control, while Constanza on the Black Sea was turned into a free port.

In France, between March 21 and July 15, 1918, Ludendorff delivered altogether five major blows which brought the war to its fiery climax. The first blow of March 21 was delivered at the seam of the British and French fronts on the Somme and aimed at the annihilation of the British army in France. The German attack split open the seam, and for a while it appeared as though the French would fall back on Paris while the British prepared for evacuation from the channel ports. Britain sustained 160,000 casualties, France 70,000. The creation of a unified Allied command under Marshal Ferdinand Foch on April 3, 1918, was instrumental in containing the German Somme offensive. The second German blow again fell upon the British, at Lys south of Ypres on April 9. The objective of the German attack was the capture of the channel ports to cut off the British evacuation route. The situation became desperate for the British, and Haig issued the order to hold each position "to the last man." French reserves, rushed to the British by Foch, helped save the situation. To replace losses, Britain had to transfer divisions from Palestine and Salonika to France. The third German attack of May 27 fell upon the French and resulted in a German breakthrough to the Marne at Château-Thierry, less than sixty miles from Paris on June 2, 1918. At Château-Thierry the Germans had their first encounter with large American forces. The fourth German assault of June 9 attempted to link together the two German bulges at Amiens and the Marne; it failed. The fifth German attack, delivered on either side of Reims on July 15, resulted in the Second Battle of the Marne, the German aim being less the capture of Paris than the crippling of the French army to deny Britain any relief in future attacks along the British front.

THE ALLIED COUNTER STROKE

By mid-July, 1918, American strength in France was approaching the million mark, a figure equal to the casualties of France and Britain since March, 1918. Throughout the summer of 1918, American troops poured into Europe at a rate of 200,000 per month. By September, 29 American divisions held one fourth of the entire western front. The American blood transfusion restored offensive power to the anemic body of the Allied armies. Germany, by contrast, could not replace the losses of the spring. German reserves consisted more and more of the very young and the very old. After July, 1918, the combat value of German divisions in France declined.

The Second Battle of the Marne, like the first in September, 1914, became a turning point. After crossing the Marne, the German troops were thrown back by French and American forces, supported by 600 tanks. On August 8, which Ludendorff called "the black day" of the German army, the British Fourth Army, supported by 456 tanks, broke through the German lines east of Amiens. The British breakthrough shattered German morale more than the Second Battle of the Marne.

By September 25, 1918, the German front had been driven back to the Hindenburg Line through a combination of superior Allied manpower, air superiority, and masses of tanks. The Hindenburg Line was not broken until November 1, 1918. The U. S. First Army (Pershing) had meanwhile eliminated the German salient at St. Mihiel, which had been a thorn in the French front south of Verdun since 1914. The U. S. First Army, together with the French Fourth, launched the final drives of the war on the Meuse-Argonne front in September and October, 1918. Two American commanders who would play a leading role in the Second World War made their battlefield debut at St. Mihiel and Argonne — George C. Marshall, a staff officer of the First Army, and Douglas MacArthur, Commander of the Rainbow Division.

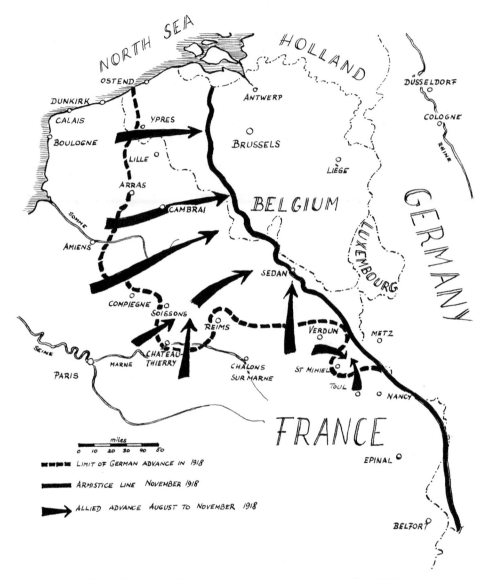

The Allied offensive in France, August to November 1918.

THE COLLAPSE OF BULGARIA, TURKEY, AND AUSTRIA-HUNGARY

Since its establishment in 1915, the Allied bridgehead at Salonika had contributed little to the overall Allied war effort, and Bulgaria had beaten off all Allied attacks in Macedonia in 1916 and 1917. The Germans referred to the Macedonian front derisively as an "internment camp"; Allied cartoonists called it "the bird cage." The Macedonian front assumed great significance in the final months of the war, however, as the Allied forces under General Franchet d'Esperey shattered the Bulgarian front on September 15 and thereby set in motion a chain reaction of collapse among Germany's allies. Bulgaria, weakest of the Central Powers, concluded an armistice with the Allies on September 30. The Bulgarian surrender opened the path to Serbia and Rumania, while threatening Turkey from the north.

The Ottoman Empire, too, had reached the end of its strength, following the British offensive of September, 1918, in which Allenby captured Damascus and routed the Turkish army. On October 30, Turkey concluded the Armistice of Mudros, signed aboard the British battleship *Agamemnon.* On November 12, an Allied fleet sailed past Gallipoli towards Constantinople.

Austria-Hungary had launched a last and abortive offensive across the Piave and from the Trentino on June 13, 1918. By 1918 Italian morale had recovered from the defeat of Caporetto, and British and French forces stood in the Italian line. Austrian morale had, by contrast, deteriorated since 1917 because of Austria's near starvation and the growing restlessness of the Slavic nationalities. On October 24, 1918, an Allied offensive crossed the Piave, and Austrian resistance quickly collapsed as the Hungarian divisions were ordered withdrawn from battle by Budapest. On November 3, 1918, Austria-Hungary concluded an armistice with the Allies at Villa Giusti, which was not to go into effect until the following day. Three-hundred thousand Austrian troops, believing that hostilities had ended on November 3, were taken prisoner by Italy at Vittorio Veneto after the signing of the armistice.

The collapse of Germany's allies and the turning of the tide on the western front caused Ludendorff to panic. On September 29, he announced that the condition of the army demanded "an immediate armistice" to avoid a catastrophe. Having rejected Wilson's Fourteen Points in January, 1918, the German government appealed to Wilson for an armistice, based on the Fourteen Points, on October 4, 1918. After protracted negotiations between the United States and Germany, on the one hand, and the United States and the Allies, on the other, the Armistice of Compiègne ended the struggle on November 11, 1918.

As many as ten million men may have given their lives in the First World War, with another twenty-two million wounded. The greatest casualties were suffered by Germany, Russia, France, and the peoples of Austria-Hungary and the British Empire. The late entry of the United States into the war kept American losses at the relatively low figure of slightly more than 116,000 killed. The material cost of war may have run as high as $330 billion.

More harmful to Europe than the loss of life and property was the spiritual damage and the realization that European civilization, like others before it, was vulnerable and perishable. Politically, the First

World War heralded the beginning of the end of European primacy in the world. Never again would Europe be the undisputed master of the non-European world or, indeed, master of its own destiny. Socially, the First World War aggravated, rather than solved, the problems engendered by the Industrial Age. From the trenches of 1918 emerged not only the happy survivors of the war but the shadows of Communism, Fascism, and Nazism.

The Collapse of the Old Order of Eastern Europe at the End of the First World War

3

THE RUSSIAN EMPIRE AND THE FIRST WORLD WAR

The outbreak of the First World War presented Tsar Nicholas II with a unique opportunity of instilling new loyalties for the Romanov dynasty in the masses of the Russian Empire by identifying the national struggle of Russia with the person of the Tsar. In sharp contrast to the outbreak of the Russo-Japanese war in 1904, which had been received by the masses with indifference, the outbreak of the First World War was greeted with patriotic fervor, uniting classes, nationalities, and parties as no other event had done during the reign of Nicholas II. With the exception of the five Bolshevik deputies, who voted against the war credits, the Duma (Parliament) stood united behind Nicholas II during its session of August 8, 1914. The call to arms in 1914 seemed to have restored the mystique of union between the autocrat and the masses, as Russian men and women knelt before Nicholas II during the Tsar's address from the Winter Palace.

Tsar Nicholas and the Duma interpreted the national unity of August, 1914, in opposite ways, however. To the Tsar the unity was proof of the unbroken loyalty of his subjects, which the Duma and the whole concept of constitutional government had endangered before the war. In war time, when the very survival of the Empire was at stake, the Duma's aspirations to power appeared an even greater threat than in times of peace. The Tsar wished to relegate the Duma to the role of patriotic sounding board rather than accept it as a partner in the decisions of war.

The members of the Duma, on the other hand, together with the representatives of the municipalities, speaking from a profound patriotic concern, feared that the old bureaucratic machine would be inadequate to the demands of total war. The Duma's apprehensions were borne out fully by the disastrous course of events within the first year of the World War. The military reverses at the hands of Germany, the acute shortage of munitions, and the chaos created by the evacuation of millions of civilian refugees from the war zone, all attested to the incompetence of the Tsar's leading ministers and the old bureaucracy.

At the outset of the war, the Tsar had limited the war activities of the Duma to Red Cross work, which was coordinated by the Zemgor organization. Under the impact of military defeat and the mismanagement of the war economy, the Tsar yielded to the demand for broader Duma participation in the war effort and authorized the formation of special councils for defense, transport, fuel, and food supplies, as well as a War Industries Committee. The new agencies mobilized managerial and administrative talent for the Russian war effort and, in the case of the War Industries Committee, united representatives of management and labor in one administrative body for the first time.

The dismissal of the incompetent Minister of War Sukhomlinov in response to Duma pressure in the summer of 1915 appeared to be another encouraging step towards a more efficient war effort and a greater role of the Duma in running the war. On August 1, 1915, the Cadet and Octobrist Duma representatives adopted a resolution demanding a government "enjoying the confidence of the country." The resolution was, in effect, a call for a government responsible to the Duma and thus a demand for a change of the semi-autocracy into a parliamentary monarchy.

In September, 1915, Tsar Nicholas took the fateful step of assuming personal command over the army against the advice of the Duma majority. The Tsar's step, undertaken largely under the influence of Empress Alexandra, marked a turning point in the political fortunes of the Russian Empire. It was a grave psychological mistake, for it identified the throne with the shifting fortunes of war, making it co-responsible for every defeat of Russian arms. More seriously, the Tsar's departure to military headquarters at Mogilev left politics in the capital increasingly in the hands of the unpopular Empress, nicknamed "nemka" (the German) by the people because of her German birth, and in the hands of Rasputin.

Cadets, Octobrists, and moderates in the Duma responded angrily to the Tsar's decision by forming a Progressive bloc, which comprised some 300 out of a total of 425 Duma deputies. On September 3, 1915, the Progressive bloc drew up a political program to safeguard the legality of the administration, to limit the powers of the military, and to achieve greater liberalization for the municipalities and labor unions. Some members of the Progressive bloc even contemplated the revolutionary step of turning the Duma into a Constituent Assembly, to write a constitution and limit the crown's prerogatives.

In the ensuing struggle between Duma and crown, the latter prevailed, mainly because the Duma, for all its voices of protest, lacked the courage to take revolutionary action.

As the Romanov Empire rushed towards the abyss of revolution, Rasputin became the dark symbol of a dying social and political order. An illiterate Siberian peasant and self-styled monk, Rasputin had won the confidence of Nicholas and Alexandra before the war through his alleged faith-healing powers over the hemophiliac Alexis, the Tsar's only son and successor to the throne. After 1915 Rasputin's growing political influence at the court made him the unofficial prime minister of Russia, on whose advice the Tsar appointed and removed ministers and plotted military strategy. Rasputin made and unmade ministers, claiming among his victims some of Russia's most distinguished statesmen, such as Foreign Minister Sazonov. Within a year after the Tsar's departure for Mogilev, no less than three ministers of war, four ministers of agriculture and five ministers of the interior succeeded one another in a whirl of intrigue and backstage politicking. The Old Regime, in the words of Alexander Guchkov, founder of the Octobrist party, had become a government of "favorites, conjurers, and clowns." With the Duma powerless and the Tsar absent from Petrograd, Rasputin and Alexandra ruled supreme. Russia had become an autocracy without an autocrat.

Towards the end of 1916, the accumulated frustrations and despair of Russia's upper classes burst forth in open protest. At the Duma meeting of November 14, 1916, Paul Miliukov, the Cadet leader, accused the Empress and Prime Minister Sturmer of stupidity and treason. Both the Moscow congress of municipalities and the congress of towns called upon the Duma to take the leadership in ending corruption in the highest places. "The government, which is being used as a tool by the forces of darkness," a resolution of the congress of towns charged, "is heading Russia along the path of ruin and shaking the foundations of the throne. The time limit given us by history has run out."

By December, 1916, plots abounded in the Russian capital among Duma and high army circles to save the monarchy from itself by a coup d'etat from above. Guchkov, Miliukov, and Chief of Staff Alexeyev discussed plans to force the abdication of Nicholas II and install a regency under the Tsar's brother Michael on behalf of the young Alexis. The Progressive bloc even prepared a list for a "shadow cabinet" to assume power after the Tsar's overthrow. Others talked openly of assassination, hoping that the example of Tsar Paul, who had been assassinated in 1801 in another moment of national crisis, would be repeated. On February 27, 1917, Alexander Kerensky, the Duma labor deputy who would soon emerge on the revolutionary scene, openly called for the Tsar's death in Duma session.

As in September, 1915, the Duma's angry words were not matched by action in December, 1916. Instead, the leaders of the Duma, of the army, and even the Allied ambassadors in Petrograd pleaded with the Tsar to close the gap between the throne and people. Nicholas II replaced the unpopular Sturmer as Prime Minister in November, 1916, with the equally unpopular A. F. Trepov, who in turn was ousted in January, 1917, by Prince N. D. Golitsyn. The mere reshuffling of cabinets and prime ministers no more solved the dynastic crisis than did the murder of Rasputin on December 30, 1916.

THE MOOD OF THE MASSES

While the leaders of the Duma protested loudly against corruption and inefficiency, the broad masses of the Russian people were stirred by the more elemental forces of hunger and fear of further bloodshed. The calling to arms of nearly fourteen million men, the shortage of farm machinery and chemical fertilizer, which had been imported chiefly from Germany before the war, and the inadequacies of Russian transport and distribution had caused a serious food shortage in the cities by early 1917. On the eve of the revolution of March, 1917, the bread supply of Petrograd and Moscow was adequate for a few weeks only.

To the food shortage in the towns was added the problem of inflation which had driven food prices up by as much as 800 per cent, while workers' wages had risen by little more than 100 per cent since the beginning of the war. The long lines of shoppers in front of food stores and the growing number of strikes in the cities were testimony to the plight of urban Russia in the third year of the war.

The deepest impression made by the war and the one most responsible for the revolutionary temper of the masses was the tremendous bloodletting of the Russian armies. Of an estimated seven million casualties, nearly two million men had been killed. The great sacrifices in blood seemed all the more intolerable to the masses because they were no longer claimed in the interest of national defense alone, but for the sake of conquest. In December, 1916, the publication by the government of Russia's aim to seize Constantinople and the Straits only reminded the people that its blood was being spent in the pursuit of annexationist aims. At the beginning of 1917, the great majority of Russians desperately longed for peace.

THE REVOLUTION OF MARCH, 1917:
THE OVERTHROW OF THE RUSSIAN
MONARCHY

In Petrograd the year 1917 had opened with workers' demonstrations in January in memory of "Bloody Sunday" of 1905. On February 11, 1917, the Minister of the Interior, A. D. Protopopov, had provoked the workers of Petrograd by ordering the arrest of the labor representatives on the War Industries Committee. At the beginning of

March, 1917, a lockout of thousands of workers from the Putilov plant led to sympathy strikes from other factories and quickly merged with food demonstrations into a general disturbance which spread from the industrial suburbs to the heart of the capital. Initially, the demonstrations of early March, 1917, did not suggest the momentous political events that were to flow from them in short time. They were spontaneous, without central direction or political purpose. They appeared to be no more than a continuation of the strike movement which had grown since 1915 in proportion to the rising urban plight. Empress Alexandra, for one, regarded the events of early March, 1917, as just another demonstration, a "hooligan movement" which would soon subside "if only the Duma behaved itself."

The persistence of the demonstrators and the refusal of the great majority of the 160,000 soldiers of the Petrograd garrison to fire on the crowds turned the spontaneous mass uprising into revolution. By March 12, 1917, the police had lost all control over Petrograd.

Nicholas II had responded to the disturbances in characteristic fashion, by ordering the Duma prorogued and commanding the Petrograd garrison to fire on the crowds. In a last-minute appeal, Rodzianko, the Duma president, urged the Tsar to adopt a more enlightened course. "The last hour has come," Rodzianko telegraphed to Nicholas, "when the fate of the fatherland and the dynasty is being decided."

By March 12, 1917, however, events had overtaken any measures that Nicholas II might still have chosen. On March 11, the Progressive bloc had elected a twelve-man "Provisional Committee," whose members included the "shadow cabinet" prepared by the Progressive bloc before the March disturbance, as well as two Socialists, Alexander Kerensky and Chkeidze. On March 12, the Petrograd Soviet was constituted out of left Duma deputies, factory representatives, and the released labor members of the Central War Industries Committee.

Tsar Nicholas, unable to reach the capital from Mogilev, was prevailed upon to abdicate on March 15, 1917, by leaders of the army and the conservative Duma leaders Guchkov and Shulgin. At first, Nicholas had hoped to save the throne for his son Alexis and install his brother Michael as regent. In view of Alexis' illness, the Tsar changed his mind and designated Michael as his successor. Grand Duke Michael accepted on condition that a constituent assembly would endorse his candidacy. Michael's reservation was no more than an empty gesture, for in 1917 the Romanov dynasty stood isolated and discredited before a bewildered and suffering nation. On March 15, 1917, no hand was raised in Petrograd or in the vastness of the Russian Empire to save the monarchy. No Allied statesman or ambassador offered support to Nicholas, as France had bolstered the autocracy during the stormy days of the 1905 revolution.

The people of Russia and the Allied governments, though for different reasons, greeted the swift overthrow of Nicholas II with relief. Russia had become a de facto republic.

THE PROVISIONAL GOVERNMENT AND THE PETROGRAD SOVIET: THE DUALISM OF POWER

The Western Allies welcomed the outbreak of the Russian revolution in the belief that a democratic Russia would revive the sagging spirits of the Russian army and strengthen Russia's war effort. The Allied press, in its initial response to the fall of the Russian monarchy, was apt to draw comparisons between the French revolution of 1789 and the Russian revolution of March, 1917. The Western illusion of a Russia strengthened by revolution persisted well after many contrary indications had been given.

The Duma, it soon became all too clear, was not the Russian equivalent of the French National Assembly of 1789; the Duma leaders were not the chosen spokesmen of the vast majority of Russians. Owing to the restrictive suffrage under which the Duma had been elected in 1912, neither the peasantry, the urban workers, nor the leaders of the non-Russian nationalities were adequately represented in its ranks.

When the temporal committee proclaimed itself the Provisional Government of Russia on March 16, 1917, it thus lacked a mandate from the people at large and represented no one but the Progressive Duma bloc from which it had emerged. The first Provisional Government under Prime Minister Prince Lvov thus consisted entirely of Cadet, Octobrist, and conservative Duma leaders with the single exception of Alexander F. Kerensky, a Socialist Duma deputy, who became Minister of Justice. From the start, the leading personalities in Lvov's cabinet were the Cadet leader Paul Miliukov as Foreign Minister and the Octobrist Guchkov as Minister of War.

The mass of urban workers and peasants looked instinctively for leadership to the Petrograd Soviet and the numerous soviets which had been formed throughout Russia, for it was in the soviets that the two leading socialist parties, the Mensheviks and Social Revolutionaries, predominated.

In March, 1917, both ideological and political reasons prevented the formation of a broad coalition between the Provisional Government and the soviets.

The Socialist parties shunned power and partnership with the Provisional Government because they interpreted the Russian revolution of March, 1917, on the basis of the Marxist dogma of successive revolutions. Accordingly, they viewed the downfall of the monarchy as the end of the feudal stage of Russian history, which must be followed by the bourgeois-capitalist stage. The socialist revolution would have to await the full maturing of the capitalist-bourgeois order. Meanwhile, the role of the Socialist parties would be one of support, but not of leadership, in the bourgeois revolution

On the political level, the Petrograd Soviet agreed to recognize the Provisional Government as the supreme executive authority until the convocation of a Russian Constituent Assembly. This formal arrangement belied the true balance of power between soviets and Provisional Government, however. Owing to the disappearance of the old bureaucracy in many parts of Russia with the fall of the monarchy, the Provisional Government had great difficulty in extending its authority beyond Petrograd, where the old ministerial bureaucracy continued to serve the new government loyally. The Petrograd Soviet and its Menshevik and Social Revolutionary majority, on the other hand, were in close contact with the masses throughout Russia through the numerous local soviets and peasants' committees that had emerged since early March, 1917.

The dualism of power involved a paradox. The Provisional Government, though claiming formal power, lacked the means of enforcing it, while the Petrograd soviet, though declining formal power, in fact exercised it by virute of its mass support.

Of this paradox, the famous Order Number One, issued by the Petrograd Soviet on March 14, 1917, was the most striking example. The order abolished the rule requiring off-duty servicemen to salute officers, encouraged the soldiers to elect soviets, and entrusted control over arms and armored cars to the soldiers' soviets. Most important of all, Order Number One made the military orders of the Provisional Government dependent on the consent of the Petrograd Soviet. With Order Number One the Petrograd Soviet assumed de facto command over the army and contributed to the latter's progressive demoralization by breaking down the old standards of discipline.

THE CLASH BETWEEN THE PROVISIONAL GOVERNMENT AND THE PETROGRAD SOVIET; THE FALL OF THE FIRST LVOV CABINET

The fall of tsarism on March 15, 1917, had unleashed not one but several revolutions in the Russian Empire, which grew from both pent-up pre-war grievances and those raised by the war itself. The upper middle class, represented by Cadets and Octobrists, viewed the revolution mainly as political in content and aimed at the establishment of a representative democracy. The peasantry interpreted the fall of the monarchy as a promise for sweeping land reform that would realize the age-old peasant dream of expropriating all lands of the state, the church, and the nobility; the urban workers hoped for social betterment, while the non-Russian nationalities, which comprised over 50 per cent of all inhabitants of the Empire, aspired to national autonomy within a federated Empire, or, in the case of Poland, to complete independence. Moreover, the fall of tsarism had raised the expectations of an early, compromise peace among the war-weary soldiers and hungry civilian masses.

The first Provisional Government, though aware of the multiple pressures of the revolution, refused to satisfy them fully in advance of the Constituent Assembly. Consistent with its provisional nature, the government would take only preparatory measures. These measures included the introduction of universal suffrage, the establishment of elective municipal and provinical governments, the restoring of Finnish autonomy, and the promise of Polish independence. Through its Land Decree, the government set up a Land Committee for the orderly transfer of land to those who worked on it. In response to the nationality movement, the government granted limited concessions to the Ukrainian demands for autonomy and invited the nationalities of the Caucasus, Turkestan, and the Baltic provinces to participate in the new administration. In response to soviet demands, the government abolished capital punishment, liberalized labor legislation, and rescinded all tsarist decrees discriminating against national and religious minorities.

Only a fraction of the government's sweeping measures would have been sufficient to prevent the outbreak of revolution if adopted before March, 1917. After March, 1917, however, the masses were no longer satisfied with the promise of change, but demanded the immediate fulfillment of their expectations. Above all, they expected the government to end the war quickly.

THE ISSUE OF WAR

Although the Provisional Government's views were diametrically opposed to tsarism on all domestic issues, its leading personalities, Foreign Minister Miliukov and War Minister Guchkov, were in agreement with its foreign policy aims. Miliukov was determined to maintain the alliance with the Western powers and secure for Russia the annexations promised in the secret war-time treaties. In Miliukov's words, "Constantinople was victory and victory Constantinople."

The Petrograd Soviet, although opposed to peace at any price, particularly a separate peace with the Central Powers, repudiated the imperialism of tsarist Russia and called for a general peace without annexations or indemnities. In the declaration of March 27, 1917, the Petrograd Soviet appealed to the peoples of the world to overthrow their governments, if necessary, and discontinue their service under "kings, landowners and bankers."

Miliukov's assurance to the Allies on May 2, 1917, which pledged the continuity of Russia's foreign policy, led to violent demonstrations and clashes in Petrograd between supporters of the Provisional Government and the Petrograd Soviet. The vast majority of the people and of the enlisted men in the army sided with the Petrograd Soviet. By May, 1917, the disintegration of the armed forces was far advanced, partly through mass desertions, partly as a result of the formation of national units within the army. Soon the number of deserters reached two million, consisting mostly of peasant soldiers, anxious to return to their villages to share in the distribution of the land. The peasant soldier, in Lenin's words, voted for peace "with his feet." Ukrainian, White Russian, and Polish soldiers in the Russian army, responding to the call of their respective national leaders, formed their own units to advance the cause of national autonomy or complete separation from Russia.

The state of the armed forces and the angry response of the people to Miliukov's announcement of war aims led to the fall of the first Provisional Government by May 15, 1917. After the resignation of Miliukov and Guchkov, Prince Lvov reorganized his government on a broader basis, including, for the first time, five socialist ministers. Upon its dissolution, the first Provisional Government issued a somber warning to the people of Russia: "Before Russia rises the terrible specter of civil war and anarchy, carrying destruction to freedom. There is a somber and grievous course of peoples, a course well known in history, leading from freedom through civil war and anarchy to reaction and the return to despotism. . . ."

LENIN'S RETURN TO RUSSIA

With the granting of political amnesty by the first Provisional Government, thousands of Russian revolutionaries began to stream back to Petrograd from the far corners of the world, from tsarist prisons, or from Siberian exile. The returning émigrés included the well known and the obscure, some with long records of past revolutionary activity, others soon to play a leading part in the momentous events of the future. Plekhanov, the father of Russian Marxism, returned from his French exile, Trotsky from New York. Among the exiles returning from tsarist prisons were Felix Dzerzhynski, the future organizer of the Bolshevik secret police, and Joseph Stalin. Because of their well-known radicalism and opposition to the war, not all the returning exiles were welcomed by the Provisional Government, but the Petrograd Soviet had forced the government's hand in the matter of exiles, as it had in other questions.

By far the most important group of returning exiles were the Bolsheviks under Lenin, who had returned to Russia via Germany and Sweden. The German government had aided in Lenin's return to Russia in full knowledge of his anti-war views and in the hope that his return would further the collapse of the Provisional Government. So important did Lenin appear to the German Supreme Command that it offered to slip him through the German front lines into Russia should Sweden bar his transit to Finland.

Prior to Lenin's arrival in Petrograd on April 16, 1917, the Bolshevik party was a divided and insignificant splinter group on the Russian Revolutionary scene, with fewer than 25,000 members. Imprisonment and Siberian exile had left only the "second team" of Bolshevik leaders in Petrograd when the Revolution of March broke out. Nor were the leaders who returned from Siberian exile agreed on their attitude towards the Provisional Government. The Party paper *Pravda* extended conditional support to the Provisional Government.

Within a few weeks after his return, Lenin imposed his own views on the party leadership, views which originally differed vastly from theirs, and forced his will upon the party's organization as a first step towards the Bolshevik conquest of power.

MARXISM-LENINISM

In 1914, Lenin alone among European socialists remained faithful to the anti-war resolutions adopted by the Second International in its pre-war conferences. The resolutions of the International, adopted at Stuttgart in 1907 and Basel in 1912, had warned the governments of Europe that a world war would spell the end of capitalist society and the beginning of proletarian revolution everywhere. "Let the governments be mindful of the fact," the Basel resolution warned, "that they cannot let loose a war without danger to themselves. Let them recall that the Franco-German War was followed by the revolutionary uprising of the Commune, that the Russo-Japanese War set in motion the revolutionary forces of the peoples of the Russian Empire. . . . It would be sheer madness for the governments to fail to realize that the very thought of the monstrosity of a world war would inevitably call forth the indignation and revolt of the working class."

In September, 1914, while European socialists followed their governments' call to arms, Lenin, in his *Seven Theses on the War,* repeated the message of the Second International, calling on all socialists to turn their weapons against their governments, rather than their "brothers, the hired slaves of other lands." Lenin's voice went unheard, and, as the war progressed, he alternated between hopes for the imminence of world revolution and despair that he would not live to witness its arrival. As late as January, 1917, Lenin expressed the view that "we, of the older generation, may not live to see the decisive battles of this coming revolution. . . ."

The Russian revolution of March, 1917, caught Lenin by surprise, but not unprepared. From the beginning, he regarded the Russian revolution, not as an isolated event, but as the signal for revolution throughout Europe, for which the world war had set the stage.

The First World War, Lenin asserted in his study *Imperialism, the Highest Stage of Capitalism,* resulted from the struggle of finance capitalism for colonies and markets throughout the world. With the advent of finance capitalism, capitalism had entered its final stage, which Karl Marx had not foreseen. Having outgrown its national limitations, capitalism had added the exploitation of colonial peoples to that of the industrial proletariat in the advanced nations. The task of the socialists was to transform the world imperialist war into a world revolution.

The proletarian revolution, Karl Marx had predicted in *Das Kapital,* could occur only in an industrially advanced country with a fully developed capitalist-bourgeois society. "A society cannot skip over the natural phases of development nor can it replace them by decree," Marx had written.

Lenin contradicted this Marxist thesis with his own thesis of imperialism. In the imperialist age, Lenin argued, capitalism chained the economies of the entire world. The chain would snap first in its weakest link, in a relatively underdeveloped country with sharp social contrasts, such as Russia. Revolution in a backward country was "justified," according to Lenin, if it sparked revolutions in the industrially advanced west.

Concerning the method of the proletarian revolution, Karl Marx had expressed three views. In the *Communist Manifesto* of 1848, Marx had viewed the revolution as the result of a conscious, organized political action of the proletariat; in *Das Kapital* of 1867, revolution was seen more as a spontaneous, inevitable event, marking the transition of capitalism towards socialism according to the "immanent laws" of history. In 1872, Marx hinted at the possibility of a peaceful change from one order into the other, in countries with a democratic franchise, such as England or the United States. Whatever the method of change from capitalism to socialism, Marx had assumed that it would not occur before the industrial proletariat had become the majority.

Based on his thesis of imperialism, Lenin argued that in a backward country the industrial proletariat need not constitute the majority in order to effect the change from capitalism into socialism, provided that certain other conditions were met: the proletariat must be led by a disciplined, revolutionary party; the proletarian party must enter into alliances with other revolutionary, though non-proletarian forces. Socialist revolution, to Lenin, was the conscious deed of a professional, dedicated, revolutionary elite, rather than a spontaneous occurrence or the result of parliamentary majorities.

Applying his revolutionary creed to Russia, Lenin had urged

the alliance of workers, peasants, and liberals to achieve the overthrow of tsarism. Once the monarchy had fallen, he demanded that the industrial proletariat advance immediately towards the proletarian, Communist revolution. In the second, proletarian stage of revolution, the proletariat would ally itself with the poor peasants and the national minorities of Russia to destroy the Russian liberals and their bourgeois following. The goal of the proletarian revolution would be the dictatorship of the proletariat or, more precisely, the dictatorship of the Communist party on behalf of the proletariat, which Lenin described as "a government unlimited by any laws, and absolutely unhampered by any rules, and relying directly on force."

Lenin intended to win the allegiance of the Russian peasants by satisfying the ancient peasant hunger for land, immediately and without conditions. He wooed the non-Russian nationalities to his cause by recognizing the right of national self-determination, including the right to full secession from Russia. In neither case did Lenin intend to honor his promises in the long run. Instead, the promises of land and national self-determination were tactical devices, designed to win for the Bolshevik party the mass support that was essential to the conquest of political power. "To whom and how should the confiscated lands be given?" Lenin asked in 1905. "At first we will support the peasant to the end," Lenin replied, "up to confiscation, and against the landowner — but later we will support the proletariat against the peasant in general."

Similarly, for Lenin, Russia's nationality problem was not a problem to be solved, but to be exploited in the cause of the proletarian revolution. In the Leninist interpretation, the right of national self-determination was limited to the proletariat of the various non-Russian nationalities. Since the Bolshevik party claimed to be the exclusive spokesman of the proletariat everywhere in Russia, the disposition of the nationalities would be in Bolshevik hands.

Lenin's gift for exploiting the revolutionary currents of his time for the benefit of socialist revolution also explains his deviation from the orthodox Marxist view on nationalism in general. Whereas Karl Marx had dismissed nationalism as a transitory force which would disappear with the fall of capitalism and the fulfillment of the classless socialist order, Lenin perceived in the awakening nationalism of the colonial peoples a force that could be profitably exploited by the worldwide Communist movement. The nationalism of the colonial peoples of Africa and Asia was seen by Lenin as an ally of socialism in its struggle against imperialist capitalism.

LENIN AND THE OTHER SOCIALISTS
OF HIS TIME

The Socialist leaders of Europe had spent the decades between the death of Marx and the outbreak of the First World War in unending debate over the correct interpretation of "Marxism." In so doing, they were continually baffled by the contradictions between the picture of the world which Marx had drawn and the reality which surrounded them at the beginning of the 20th century. Many of the developments which Marx foretold had not occurred. Capitalism was stronger in 1914 than it had been in 1867; the industrial proletariat, though more numerous in 1914 than in the time of Marx, was better off than at any time before. Nationalism, far from disappearing, had become one of the prime movers of European history. Not class solidarity, but allegiance to nation, had swayed the workers of all belligerents at the beginning of the war. The outbreak of the First World War had shattered the Second International and, with it, the faith of the socialist leaders in the scientific infallibility of Marxism. Marxism had become a stumbling block to socialist action, rather than its inspiration. Those who still believed in the inevitability of the socialist revolution, relegated it to the distant future.

Among European socialists, Lenin was the formidable exception. Lenin's pragmatism had cut the Gordian knot of Marxist theory, had borrowed from it what was useful and discarded what was not. Lenin had approached the theory of Marx not only as a scholar—as had the German socialists, Karl Kautsky foremost among them—but as a pragmatic revolutionary. Although doctrinaire in his interpretation of the master, Lenin remained the most flexible of politicians in his method. Marxism, to Lenin, was not a dogma but a guide to action. "Grey is all theory," Lenin was fond of quoting from the German poet Goethe, "and green the tree of life."

Among European socialists, socialist revolution had become the subject of academic debate by 1914. In Lenin, by contrast, burned the fires of revolution, set by a long line of Russian progenitors as far back as N. G. Chernyshevsky and Peter Tkachev. It was in the tradition of the latter that Lenin was not content with revolutionary theory but longed for personal involvement in revolutionary action. Among his mentors were not only Marx and Engels but Clausewitz, the Prussian military strategist, and Cluseret, the French general, who had written on the subject of street-fighting. Looking at the labor parties which had sprung up in Europe after the appearance of *Das Kapital,* Marx had said contemptuously: "I have sowed dragons and reaped a harvest of fleas." With the advent of Lenin, the dragon seed of Karl Marx took root in the soil of revolutionary Russia.

THE APRIL THESES:
THE RISE OF BOLSHEVIK POWER

When he arrived in Petrograd on April 16, 1917, Lenin was greeted by the Menshevik president of the Petrograd Soviet, N. S. Chkheidze, with the cautious advice that the main problem of revolutionary democracy in Russia was the defense of the revolution against all attacks "from within or without." Lenin responded to this thinly veiled threat against the Bolshevik party with his April theses, which outlined his revolutionary program for the near future: "the unique quality of the present moment for Russia," Lenin told the Bolshevik party, "consists in the transition from the first stage of revolution, which gave power to the bourgeoisie, . . . to its second stage, which should place power in the hands of the proletariat and the poorest strata of the peasantry."

The April Theses constituted Lenin's declaration of war on the Provisional Government. Lenin denounced the Provisional Government as "capitalist" and attacked it for continuing the war for the sake of territorial acquisition. He rejected the goal of a parliamentary republic as a step backward and called instead for a soviet republic, to be modelled after the Paris Commune of 1871. *The April Theses* further demanded the immediate transfer of all land to the peasants' soviets, the nationalization of all banks, and the establishment of a new Communist International to promote world revolution. The Russian Socialists were to change their party name to *Communist* party.

Lenin's revolutionary program not only shocked the moderate Socialists but astonished his own Bolshevik followers in its extremism. Plekhanov, Lenin's erstwhile teacher, called *The April Theses* the "ravings of a madman"; *Pravda,* the Bolshevik paper, dismissed them as Lenin's personal opinion.

Lenin's first task was thus to win the Bolshevik party over to his views, a task which he accomplished by May, 1917, at the Bolshevik Party Congress in Petrograd. The party adopted the slogan "all power to the soviets."

For the moment, however, Lenin cautioned his party to avoid open clashes with the Provisional Government. The Bolsheviks' first task was to win control over the soviets, to outmaneuver the Mensheviks and Social Revolutionaries, who were still the majority in the soviets, by explaining their "errors" in a "patient, systematic and persistent manner."

THE PROVISIONAL GOVERNMENT
AFTER MAY, 1917

Following the resignation of Miliukov and Guchkov, three Social Revolutionaries, among them Victor Chernov, the leader of the Social Revolutionary party, and two Mensheviks, joined the Provisional Government of Prince Lvov. The inclusion of Socialist ministers in the reorganized government on May 18, 1917, with the approval of the Petrograd Soviet, at first raised hopes of greater unity among the revolutionary forces, a better rapport between the government and the masses, and a more fruitful relationship between the soviets and the government.

Alexander Kerensky, who continued to serve in the government as Minister of War, soon emerged as the dominant figure in the second Provisional Government. Well known for his role of defense lawyer in revolutionary cases before the war, Kerensky brought to his office as minister a passionate belief in the ideal of democracy. As a political leader, however, he was sorely lacking in an appreciation for power, mistaking the spoken word for action. Although he possessed great oratorical gifts, the effect of his speeches was often greater on himself than on his audience.

Although the new Provisional Government included Socialists, it proved no more effective in finding rapid answers to the foreign and domestic problems of revolutionary Russia. In its approach to the issues of land reform, autonomy for national minorities, and the urban labor crisis, it retained the gradualist and legalistic attitude that had characterized its predecessor. The new foreign minister, Michael B. Tereshchenko, had repudiated Miliukov's imperialism, but his efforts to persuade Russia's western Allies into a similar declaration as a prelude to a negotiated peace, failed.

The Western Allies, far from willing to repudiate their own annexationist aims, expected greater Russian military efforts in the common cause. Although Kerensky was well aware of the state of the Russian army through his personal inspection, he agreed to whip his tired forces into one last military effort in the hope that a Russian victory would deflect public attention from the unsolved domestic issues. The so-called "Kerensky offensive," launched against the Galician front on July 1, 1917, revealed the hopeless state of Russia's defenses. After initial gains it turned into a rout of the Russian army, whose soldiers turned into a pillaging and raping mob during their confused retreat. "Authority and obedience exist no longer," the army reported to the Provisional Government, ". . . all Russia should be told the truth."

The collapse of the Kerensky offensive was the beginning of the end of the Provisional Government. Through its demonstrated inability to achieve either victory or a negotiated peace, the government stirred both the revolutionary and the counter-revolutionary forces into greater opposition.

The unpopularity of the Provisional Government increased as a result of the worsening domestic crisis which coincided with the military failure of July, 1917. By then, inflation had reached new heights with the issuing of worthless paper money, popularly known as the "Kerensky Rubels"; factory output had fallen by more than half, owing to the takeover of entire plants by workers; the non-Russian nationalities, no longer satisfied with the promise of national autonomy, demanded its immediate fulfillment. On June 23, 1917, a Ukrainian Rada (Council) proclaimed Ukrainian autonomy and formed its own national Ukrainian army. Kerensky, although opposed to any settlement of the nationality question before the meeting of the Constituent Assembly, was forced to compromise with the forces of Ukrainian nationalism. Kerensky's concession in turn so angered the Cadet ministers that they resigned from the government in protest.

As the government's powers grew more feeble, Bolshevik propaganda gained converts among the workers and the soldiers, for whose benefit the Bolshevik party printed special propaganda papers, such as *Okopnaya Pravda* (Trench Truth) and *Soldatskaya Pravda* (Soldiers' Truth).

FIRST ALL-RUSSIAN SOVIET CONGRESS

At the First All Russian Congress of Soviets on June 16, 1917, the Bolsheviks were still in the minority with only 105 representatives, as against 248 Mensheviks and 285 Social Revolutionaries. Lenin nevertheless used the Soviet congress as a propaganda forum by identifying the moderate Socialists with the failure of the Provisional Government. At the Soviet congress Lenin demanded publication of the secret treaties of the tsarist government and denounced the Provisional Government, as well as Mensheviks and Social Revolutionaries, for resisting genuine autonomy for the Ukraine. Lenin told the congress that the Bolshevik party was ready to seize power, overthrow the Provisional Government, and "hang one hundred of the most prominent capitalists." Lenin's threats evoked the laughter of the moderate Socialists, but the subsequent street demonstrations of July 17, 1917, revealed the great strength which the Bolsheviks had accumulated since *The April Theses*.

THE JULY DAYS

The impatience of the Petrograd masses with the Provisional Government exploded in the street demonstrations of July 17, 1917, which were originally organized by the Soviet congress but which threatened to develop into a coup against the Provisional Government in the hands of Bolshevik agitators. The demonstrators moved to the Tauride Palace, the seat of the Petrograd Soviet, and demanded that it seize power from the government. The Provisional Government weathered the storm of the July days largely because the Petrograd Soviet, dominated by the Mensheviks and the Social Revolutionaries, refused to be stampeded by the mob. On July 18, the Provisional Government struck back at the Bolshevik party by seizing the offices of *Pravda* and ordering the arrest of the Bolshevik leaders, including Lenin who was accused of being a German agent.

The July days marked a serious setback for the Bolsheviks, though not as serious as it appeared to the Bolshevik leaders at the time. Lenin had gone into hiding in Finland, and most of the other Bolshevik leaders were in government custody. The government's charge that Lenin was a German spy was widely believed, coming on the heels of the defeat of the Kerensky offensive. The government failed to exploit its triumph over the Bolsheviks, however, and soon reverted to its earlier routine of inaction.

THE KORNILOV AFFAIR

On July 21, 1917, Prince Lvov, Prime Minister of the Provisional Government since March, resigned over disagreements with the Social Revolutionaries on the land question. Alexander Kerensky succeeded Lvov, thus becoming Prime Minister in name as well as fact. In an effort to unite all political forces other than the Bolsheviks behind his person, Kerensky summoned the so-called All-Russian State Conference to Moscow, which met from August 24 to August 28, 1917. Kerensky's strategy of using ad-hoc assemblies, such as the Moscow State Conference, as props of the Provisional Government, failed of its purpose, for it mistook transitory gatherings of politicians for instruments of political power. Moreover, the Moscow State Conference revealed the deep political divisions which the past failures of the government had opened up between the left and right.

The most important figure to emerge from the Moscow State Conference was General Lavr G. Kornilov, the recently appointed Commander-in-Chief of the army. Kornilov shared the contempt and the impatience with which the Allied governments had come to regard the "Kerensky Democracy" of Russia. Both Kornilov and the Allies blamed the soviets for the political confusion and military paralysis. Both regarded Kerensky as too subservient to soviet demands.

Kornilov intended to restore "discipline, honor and order" to revolutionary Russia. With the connivance of the Allied ambassadors, he planned to crush the Petrograd Soviet, with Kerensky's aid if possible, against Kerensky if necessary. Aside from ardent patriotism, the general had few qualifications to carry out his delicate scheme. He was, above all, completely lacking in any political gifts and remained, throughout the "Kornilov affair," a simple cossack soldier "with the heart of a lion and the brain of a lamb." Although Kornilov and Kerensky shared a common fear of the Bolsheviks, they shared little else. Whereas Kerensky hoped to realize Russian democracy with the aid of the soviets, Kornilov saw in the soviets only the agents of political anarchy and military demoralization.

Matters were brought to a head between Kornilov and Kerensky by the clumsy intervention of Vladimir N. Lvov (unrelated to the former Prime Minister Prince Lvov), who wished to act as intermediary between the army and the government. Through Lvov, Kerensky learned of Kornilov's intention of establishing a military dictatorship in which Kerensky was to serve on in some capacity, if he desired. Kornilov's plan was presented in the form of an ultimatum, however, prompting Kerensky to dismiss Kornilov as Commander-in-Chief on September 9, 1917. Kornilov struck back the following day with a proclamation demanding the ouster of the Provisional Government. Kornilov's troops, under command of General Alexander M. Krimov, advanced on Petrograd.

Kerensky called on all socialists, including the Bolsheviks, to help defend Petrograd against the threatening military counter-revolution. Mensheviks, Social Revolutionaries, and Bolsheviks formed a Committee for Struggle Against Counter-Revolution. The government released the Bolshevik leaders, imprisoned since the July days, and opened its arsenals to the Petrograd workers and sailors from the Kronstadt naval base, who sympathized with the Bolsheviks. Lenin, directing his party from his hiding place in Finland, advised his followers to aid in the crushing of Kornilov, not out of sympathy for Kerensky, but rather to expose his weakness. The army that rose against Kornilov, Trotsky observed later, was the future army of the November revolution.

By September 14, 1917, Kornilov's coup had collapsed. His troops were unable to use the railroads for their advance on the capital because of a strike by the railroad workers. They melted away under the impact of the propaganda which Bolshevik agitators skillfully spread among their ranks. General Krimov had committed suicide, the other conspiring generals, Kornilov and Denikin, were in government custody.

THE AFTERMATH OF THE KORNILOV COUP

The swift collapse of the military coup of September, 1917, gave the false impression that the Provisional Government, having survived the attacks of both the extreme left in July and the extreme right in September, had successfully defended the democratic center. In truth, the Kornilov plot had seriously weakened both the foreign and domestic position of Kerensky. The Allies, disappointed over the failure of Kornilov, treated the Kerensky government with condescension and disrespect. An Allied note of October 9, 1917, admonished Kerensky to show by acts his "resolve to employ all proper means to revive discipline and true military spirit among the fighting troops." Failing this, the Allies threatened to cut off all further military aid to Russia. Moreover, the Allies refused to answer Kerensky's continued pleas for an official change in the Allied position on war aims. Although the Allies promised to hold a conference on war aims at Paris towards the end of November, 1917, they refused to admit any representatives of the Petrograd Soviet. Kerensky's efforts to enlist the support of the United States, untarnished by any secret war-time agreement, likewise failed. President Wilson's Fourteen Points, which came closest to the Soviet's formula of peace without annexations and idemnities, were not announced until January, 1918.

The Allied attitude towards Kerensky aided the Bolshevik effort to portray the Prime Minister of Russia as a "lackey" of the western capitalist bourgeoisie. Kerensky's failure to elicit from the Allies or the United States any statement on war aims that would have appeased the great yearning of the Russian masses for peace must be counted among the major causes of his government's fall in November, 1917.

The Allies' contemptuous treatment of Kerensky was matched by the desertion of Kerensky's domestic allies throughout September and October. Although Kerensky had at last fixed the date for the election of the Constituent Assembly for late November, 1917, it was doubtful whether his government could maintain itself during the last, crucial weeks of its existence. Most serious for Kerensky was the resignation of Victor Chernov, the leader of the Social Revolutionary party, as Minister of Agriculture over Kerensky's failure to deal effectively with the land problem. Lenin was jubilant over the Chernov-Kerensky split, for it robbed the Provisional Government of whatever support it may still have enjoyed among the peasants. Moreover, the Social Revolutionary Party had begun to break up into two wings, since June, 1917, with the Left Social Revolutionaries moving closer to the Bolshevik position. Finally, the government's support within the soviets dwindled rapidly with the resurgence of Bolshevik strength.

Once more, Kerensky resorted to the makeshift device of loosely organized, short-lived assemblies with ill-defined objectives, to prop up his government. The Democratic Conference, in session from September 27 to October 5 was one such gathering, composed of representatives of the army, the trade unions, and the soviets. Instead of giving the government support, the Conference succumbed to factional quarreling. The left-wing delegates qualified their support of Kerensky by demanding the ouster of the remaining Cadet ministers from the government.

Before disbanding, the Democratic Conference created yet another interim assembly, the "Pre-Parliament," which was to serve until the convocation of the Constituent Assembly. Trotsky, speaking at the opening session of the Pre-Parliament, accused the Provisional Government of "murderous intrigue" against the people and the intention of destroying the revolution by surrendering Petrograd to the Germans.

THE BOLSHEVIK SEIZURE OF POWER

While Kerensky was attempting to maintain his strength on the shifting sands of rapidly changing majorities in the Democratic Conference and the Pre-Parliament, the Bolsheviks had taken enormous strides towards winning control over the soviets. The turning point in Bolshevik fortunes had come with the Kornilov affair. Kornilov's clumsy attempt to seize power not only led to the release of Bolshevik leaders and the arming of Bolshevik workers, but enabled the Bolsheviks to claim credit for the defeat of the counter-revolution. By September, 1917, Bolshevik strength in the soviets had increased from 10 per cent to over 50 per cent; Bolshevik party strength to over 240,000. Most important, the Bolsheviks had captured control of both the Petrograd and Moscow soviets with the election of Trotsky and Nogin to the chairmanship of these bodies.

After becoming chairman, Trotsky withdrew the support of the Petrograd Soviet from the Provisional Government and called for the convocation of a second All-Russian Soviet Congress, to which all power was to be transferred.

From his vantage point in Finland, Lenin had closely followed the rise of his own party's strength and the growing problems of the Kerensky government throughout September, 1917. With the Bolshevik capture of the Petrograd and Moscow soviets, Lenin was convinced that the moment most favorable to a Bolshevik seizure of power had arrived. "Having obtained a majority in the Soviets of Workers' and Soldiers' Deputies of Moscow and Petrograd," Lenin wrote to the Bolshevik Central Committee in Petrograd in late September, "the Bolsheviks can and must seize state power." Lenin proposed the slogan "power to the Soviets, land to the peasants, peace to the peoples and bread to the hungry" for the Bolshevik uprising.

Not all of Lenin's associates in the Bolshevik Central Committee shared his conviction that "victory was assured, and there are nine chances out of ten that it will be bloodless." Kamenev, who had opposed Lenin's *April Theses,* as well as Zinoviev, the future head of the Communist International, opposed Lenin out of fear that the Provisional Government was still too strong and the Bolshevik party too weak. To change the Central Committee's mind, Lenin bombarded it with a barrage of letters, threatened to resign from the Central Committee, and, finally, on October 23, 1917, attended the Central Committee's crucial meeting in person. With a vote of 10 to 2, the Central Committee decided in favor of an armed Bolshevik uprising and elected from its midst a Political Bureau (Politbureau) to direct the revolution. The two dissenters, Kamenev and Zinoviev, unconvinced of Lenin's arguments, aired their opposition in a non-Bolshevik newspaper and thereby made the Bolshevik plan an open secret in Petrograd.

Lenin had committed his party to revolution, but it remained for Trotsky to supervise the detailed planning. To camouflage the Bolshevik preparations, Trotsky skillfully used the Military Revolutionary Committee for Bolshevik ends. The Military Revolutionary Committee had been formed by the Petrograd Soviet, ironically on Menshevik initiative, for the defense of Petrograd, which, it had been rumored, Kerensky intended to leave to the Germans without a fight. What appeared to be a

Soviet organ for the defense of the capital was in truth the Bolshevik General Staff for insurrection. Significantly, all members of the Military Revolutionary Committee were either Bolshevik or Left Social Revolutionaries. "The Revolution," in Stalin's words, "masked the offensive acts with a cover of defense so that it might more easily draw into its orbit the irresolute, vacillating elements."

On November 5, 1917, the Provisional Government took belated action against the threat of Bolshevik revolution, but the response remained ill-organized and feeble to the last. Kerensky ordered the seizure of the Bolshevik printing plants and the withdrawal of the cruiser *Aurora* from Petrograd, which was manned by Bolshevik sailors and moored within shelling distance of the Winter Palace, the seat of the government. On November 6, 1917, the Bolshevik newspapers appeared as usual and the order to move the *Aurora* was countermanded by the Military Revolutionary Committee.

On November 6, 1917, Kerensky made his last appearance before the Pre-Parliament, asking for its support and declaring a state of insurrection. The Pre-Parliament, although condemning the Bolshevik insurrection, also blamed Kerensky for having led Russia to the point of Bolshevik revolution. In vain, the Mensheviks urged Kerensky to counter the Bolshevik insurrection by the immediate convocation of the Constituent Assembly and the publication of decrees on land and peace. In a spirit of resignation, Kerensky instead called for support against the Bolshevik uprising. Not without cause did Trotsky characterize the Provisional Government as a "pitiful, helpless, half-government," which awaited "the historical broom to sweep it off."

The actual armed uprising came as an anti-climax to the thorough Bolshevik preparations. Without bloodshed, the Bolsheviks seized the strategic points of Petrograd during the night of November 6, 1917. Only at the Winter Palace did any fighting develop, when Cossacks, military cadets, and a Women's Batallion tried to defend Kerensky's ministers, huddled in a committee room of the Palace. The cruiser *Aurora* added the roar of its cannon to the fray, but since the cruiser's batteries fired blanks, the effect was more psychological than physical.

After the fall of the Winter Palace shortly after midnight of November 7, the Military Revolutionary Committee declared the capital under its control and the Provisional Government deposed. Power, according to the announcement, was "in the hands of the Revolutionary Committee of the Petrograd Soviet." In truth, it was in Bolshevik hands.

THE ESTABLISHMENT OF BOLSHEVIK POWER

The Bolsheviks had overthrown the Provisional Government of Russia with an apparent ease that surprised the world and even some of the Bolshevik leaders themselves. At first, however, the Bolshevik victory seemed to many but another phase in the continuing chaos of revolutionary Russia, which would eventually give way to more orderly and conventional forms of social and political life. Few credited the Bolsheviks with the ability to govern; fewer still appreciated the Bolsheviks' deadly determination to hold onto power and transform Russia according to their own vision of the future.

The first task that confronted the Bolshevik leaders after seizing power in Petrograd on November 7, 1917, was the establishment of a stable revolutionary government and the extension of its power over the vast Russian Empire. Secondly, the Bolsheviks had to come to grips with the problem of Russia's disintegration into separate nationality states and the still unsolved problem of the war with the Central Powers—two dilemmas that the Bolsheviks themselves had ruthlessly exploited on their road to power between April and November, 1917.

The problem of power was solved quickly, at least for the Great Russian parts of Russia, by the Bolshevik conquest of key cities, such as Moscow, which was under Bolshevik control by November 15, 1917; by the establishment of an all-Bolshevik government in Petrograd; and by the progressive elimination of all political freedoms, culminating in the dispersal of the Constituent Assembly in January, 1918.

THE SOVNARKOM

Trotsky had synchronized the Bolshevik coup with the meeting of the Second All Russian Congress of Soviets on November 7, 1917, in order to present it with the *fait accompli* of the overthrow of the Provisional Government. The Menshevik delegates to the Soviet Congress still hoped to persuade the Bolsheviks—after their triumph—into forming a coalition government of Mensheviks, Bolsheviks, and Social Revolutionaries. Such illusions were quickly dispelled by Trotsky, who advised the Mensheviks in his customary vitriolic style to betake themselves to the "garbage heap of history." The Mensheviks and Right Social Revolutionaries thereupon left the Soviet Congress in protest and organized a "Committee of Salvation," which proved no serious threat to the Bolsheviks. By leaving the Soviet Congress, the Mensheviks and Right Social Revolutionaries had left the field to the Bolsheviks and their Left Social Revolutionary allies.

On November 8, 1917, the Soviet Congress accordingly installed a new Soviet government, the Council of People's Commissars (called Sovnarkom after the Russian initials), with Lenin as chairman and an all-Bolshevik cabinet. Some Bolshevik leaders, notably Kamenev and Zinoviev, demurred at the exclusively Bolshevik composition of the Sovnarkom and warned that an all-Bolshevik government "will lead to the establishment of an irresponsible regime and the ruin of the revolution and the country." In response to this criticism, Lenin admitted three Left Social Revolutionaries to the Sovnarkom on December 22, 1917. The Bolshevik–Left Social Revolutionary coalition ended with March 15, 1918, however, as a result of the bitter controversy over the peace of Brest-Litovsk.

Before adjourning, the Second All-Russian Congress approved the Bolshevik decrees on land and peace. The decree on land abolished all private property on land and assigned its use to those who tilled it. The decree on peace called upon all belligerent nations to begin immediate negotiations towards an armistice and a "democratic peace without annexations and indemnities." Although the Bolsheviks called the peace decree a formal offer to all belligerent governments, the decree addressed itself significantly to the "class-conscious workers of France, England and Germany." The ideological overtones of the Bolshevik peace offer were revealed further by the announcement of the forthcoming publication of all secret treaties between the former tsarist government and the Allies.

CURTAILMENT OF POLITICAL FREEDOMS; THE CHEKA

Following the adjournment of the Second All-Russian Soviet Congress on November 10, 1917, the Bolshevik regime moved swiftly to destroy the democratic freedoms which the revolution of March, 1917, had bestowed on Russia. Aside from censuring the press, the Bolshevik dictatorship dissolved the Cadet Party on December 11, 1917, and arrested its leaders. The Mensheviks and Right Social Revolutionaries, though not disbanded formally, were little more than tolerated. On December 20, 1917, the Sovnarkom decreed the establishment of the "All-Russian Extraordinary Commission," or Cheka (after the Russian initials), the new secret police. In the hands of Felix Dzerzhinski, the Cheka soon developed into an instrument of indiscriminate terror that surpassed the tsarist Okhrana in violence. By 1918 the Cheka, in the words of one official, "no longer waged war against separate individuals but exterminated the bourgeoisie as a class."

As the Bolshevik regime revealed its true face of violence and terror against "class enemies" and political dissenters, western socialists, with their deeply ingrained tradition of democracy, took issue with the Bolshevik practice of Marxism. The prominent German theorist of Marxism, Karl Kautsky, whom Lenin had once accepted as an authority, bitterly assailed Lenin's dictatorship in *The Dictatorship of the Proletariat*. Kautsky's *Dictatorship of the Proletariat* and Lenin's equally bitter reply, *The Proletarian Revolution and the Renegade Kautsky,* set the tone for the acrimonious debate that was to mark all future exchanges between western Social Democrats and Russian Communists.

THE CONSTITUENT ASSEMBLY

When the Sovnarkom was installed by the Second All-Russian Congress of Soviets on November 8, 1917, it was created as a *temporary* or *provisional* government only, to act until the convocation of the Constituent Assembly. The Constituent Assembly presented the Bolshevik regime with an acute dilemma. As in the questions of peace, land reform, and national autonomy, the Bolsheviks had assailed the Provisional Government for its failure to act with speed in the convocation of the Constituent Assembly. On the other hand, the Bolshevik concept of dictatorship was wholly incompatible with the idea of a democratic assembly. The Bolsheviks thus permitted the election to the assembly to proceed on November 25, 1917, as scheduled, but the Bolshevik Central Committee decided on December 24, 1917, to break up the assembly as soon as it convened.

The election results of November 25, 1917, were a clear repudiation of the Bolshevik dictatorship by the majority of the Russian electorate. Out of a total 707 seats, the Social Revolutionaries gained 370, the Bolsheviks 175, the Left Social Revolutionaries 40, the Mensheviks 16, and the Cadets 17 seats. The remaining strength was divided among various national minorities.

The Bolshevik government, having surrounded the Marinsky Opera House, the assembly's meeting place, with troops, permitted the elected deputies exactly one day for the practice of parliamentary government. Victor Chernov, the elected assembly president, ignoring the political realities of Russia, still urged a reconciliation among the Socialist parties of Russia and called for a government of both the soviets and the Constituent Assembly. The Bolshevik answer was to close the assembly by threat of arms on January 19, 1918, and to scatter the pro-assembly demonstrations with bursts of gun-fire. As tsarist guns had spilled the blood of freedom-seeking Russians on Bloody Sunday in January, 1905, the Bolshevik dictatorship stamped out the glow of liberty in January, 1918. The debates and resolutions on land reform and peace, which had filled the assembly's only day of business on January 18, 1918, were the swan song of Russian democracy.

At the meeting of January 23, 1918, the third All-Russian Congress of Soviets endorsed the closing of the Constituent Assembly and proceeded to lay the groundwork for a formal soviet constitution of Russia, which was adopted on July 10, 1918, by the Fifth All-Russian Congress of Soviets. Within less than a year after the Bolshevik seizure of power in Petrograd, the soviets had been relegated to the role of masking the dictatorship of the Bolshevik party. But even within that party a free debate on political issues had become impossible for the majority of its members. Even before the Bolshevik seizure of power, the Bolshevik Party Congress of August, 1917, had resolved that "Party factions in state, municipal, soviet and other institutions . . . subordinate themselves to all decisions of the Party and the respective leading Party centers." By virtue of its organization and its principles, the Bolshevik Party was well on the road towards becoming the "irresponsible regime" of which Kamenev had warned in November, 1917.

THE BOLSHEVIK DICTATORSHIP AND THE NATIONALITY PROBLEM

At the time of the Bolshevik seizure of power, the non-Russian nationalities of the Empire, ignoring the dilatory tactics of the Provisional Government, had taken matters into their own hands. With the exception of the Poles and Finns, who demanded full independence, the Baltic, White Russian, Ukrainian, and Caucasian nationalities decided at the Congress of national representatives at Kiev in September, 1917, to settle for autonomy within a federated Russia.

The Bolshevik seizure of power and the subsequent Bolshevik suppression of other political parties after November, 1917, had the effect, however, of strengthening the centrifugal tendencies among the nationalities. The nationalities which had been satisfied with autonomy before November, 1917, aspired to full secession from a Bolshevik-dominated Russia after November, 1917. Following the example of the Ukraine, Estonia, White Russia and the Caucasian states of Armenia, Azerbaidjan and Georgia seceded from Russia after the establishment of national councils. Finland declared its independence on December 19, 1917, under the national government of Per Svinhufvud. The Bolsheviks responded to the national break-up of Russia by asserting the right of national self-determination in principle while denying its exercise in practice. Thus, the Second All-Russian Soviet Congress had passed a decree on national autonomy on November 8, 1917, which was confirmed by the Declaration to the Peoples of Russia of November 15, by Lenin and Stalin, who was Commissar of Nationalities in the Sovnarkom. On December 31 the Sovnarkom also recognized the independence of Finland, but the case of Finland proved to be an exception to the Bolshevik nationality policy. "Autonomy is a form," Stalin explained; what mattered was its "class content." "The Soviet Power is not against autonomy—it is for autonomy, but only for an autonomy where all power rests in the hands of workers and peasants."

Since the various national governments which had seceded from Russia were not "proletarian" by Bolshevik definition, the Bolshevik regime moved to crush them at the turn of 1917/1918. The Bolshevik masters of Russia were also motivated by the fear that the seceding borderlands might become springboards for foreign intervention. The recognition of Ukrainian independence by Britain and France gave ample warning of that possibility. Moreover, behind Bolshevik words was often hidden the Great Russian nationalism of Bolshevik leaders, who were, in principle, opposed to genuine nationality rights for the non-Russians. "Scratch many a Communist," Lenin would say, "and you will find a Great Russian chauvinist."

Having overthrown the anti-Bolshevik White Russian Rada (Council), the Bolsheviks moved against the Ukraine, capturing the Ukrainian capital of Kiev on February 8, 1918. The Bolshevik reconquest of the seceding areas was halted, however, by the peace of Brest-Litovsk, which proved an even greater challenge to the survival of the Bolshevik regime than did the problem of the nationalities.

THE BOLSHEVIK DICTATORSHIP AND THE PROBLEM OF PEACE

At the very beginning of Bolshevik rule, the Bolshevik leaders held a somewhat simplified view of the complex problem of peace, which had so greatly contributed to the fall of Kerensky. In this respect, they were to a large extent the prisoners of their ideological illusion that world revolution must spring from the World War and victims of their belief that the moral condition of the other belligerent armies equalled that of the Russian army of 1917. The Bolsheviks initially hoped to secure peace by appealing directly to the peoples of the warring nations and by inciting the peoples to revolution against their governments should the latter persist in the war. Formal diplomacy would be a thing of the past. "What sort of diplomatic work will we be doing anyway?" Trotsky was reported to have said upon becoming Foreign Commissar in the Sovnarkom. "I shall issue a few revolutionary proclamations to the people and then close up shop."

Within a few weeks after seizing power, the Bolsheviks were brought face to face with the political and military realities of the war, which dispelled their myth of world revolution and plunged the Bolshevik leadership into its deepest crisis since the assumption of power. That the Bolshevik dictatorship mastered the crisis was due mainly to the flexibility of Lenin, whose pragmatic grasp triumphed once more over all ideological illusions.

The propagandistic soviet peace offer of November 8, 1917, evoked no other official Allied response than a condemnation of the Bolshevik intention to sign a separate peace with Germany if a general peace conference failed to materialize. The Allied outrage at soviet behavior mounted when Trotsky made good the Bolshevik threat and published the secret Allied-Russian Treaties on November 22, 1917, in order to expose the "robber alliances" and hasten the overthrow of the "rule of capital" in the west.

The German response to the Bolshevik peace offer was swift and positive. Lenin had ordered the Russian Commander-in-Chief, General Nicolai Dukhonin, on November 20, 1917, to initiate armistice talks with the Germans. When Dukhonin refused to carry out the order, he was dismissed and shortly afterwards lynched. Dukhonin's successor, the Bolshevik Ensign Krylenko, secured a series of local armistice agreements in advance of the general armistice, signed at Brest-Litovsk on December 15, 1917. A formal peace conference between the Central Powers and the Soviet government opened at Brest-Litovsk, the headquarters of the German army in Russia, on December 22, 1917. Although all Central Powers were represented at the peace conference, the principal negotiations were conducted between Foreign Minister Richard Kühlmann and General Max Hoffmann, the chiefs of the German delegation, and Adolf Joffe, the Soviet representative.

THE GERMAN CONDITIONS AT BREST-LITOVSK

Germany was anxious to end the war with Russia as quickly as possible in order to transfer its Eastern divisions to the Western front, where Ludendorff prepared his great blow against the Western Allies. Although speed was of the essence, the Germans meant to reap the maximum territorial and economic benefits from their advantageous position in the east, which the weak Bolshevik government would be unable to resist.

In substance, the German peace conditions aimed at the break-up of the former tsarist empire, with Bolshevik Russia being confined to the territory inhabited by Great Russians. The western and southern borderlands of Great Russia, Finland, the Baltic area, Poland, and the Ukraine would pass under various forms of German domination, from outright annexation in the Baltic to economic and political control over the Ukraine.

THE SOVIET RESPONSE

The Soviet government had begun the peace negotiations at Brest-Litovsk in the hope that Germany would accept the soviet formula of peace "without annexations and indemnities" by evacuating the conquered eastern territories. The soviet formula for peace was elaborated further in Adolf Joffe's Six Points of December 22, 1917, which barred "forcible annexations" of territory seized and reaffirmed the right of national self-determination. In the German interpretation, the right of national self-determination implied, however, soviet recognition of the secession of the non-Russian nationalities and their submission under German power.

Having learned the true meaning of the German conditions of peace, Trotsky assumed personal direction of the soviet negotiations at Brest-Litovsk on January 8, 1918, in the hope of gaining better terms through delaying tactics. The Germans ended the debate on January 18 by threatening to end the armistice and presenting a map which outlined their demands in detail.

The German ultimatum plunged the Bolshevik Central Committee into a severe crisis and split the Bolshevik leadership three ways. Lenin favored acceptance of the German terms, fearing that their rejection would lead to harsher terms later or even the ouster of the Bolshevik government by German military power.

Trotsky, still hoping for the outbreak of proletarian revolution in the west, wished to gain time, in order to bring Bolshevik propaganda to bear on the armies and workers of the Central Powers. The outbreak of mass strikes in Vienna, Budapest, and Berlin at the beginning of 1918, which were, in part, related to the Brest-Litovsk deadlock, strengthened Trotsky's optimism. In his search for an escape from the Bolshevik peace dilemma, Trotsky even looked towards the United States for help. President Wilson's Fourteen Points, delivered in the midst of the Brest-Litovsk deadlock on January 8, 1918, specifically demanded in Point VI "the evacuation of all Russian territory" by Germany. In the end, however, Bolshevik hopes for American support against German imperialism succumbed to the Bolshevik suspicion that the United States government, as a "capitalist" government, could only desire the destruction of the Bolshevik regime. Trotsky went so far as to charge the United States with collusion in the preparation of the German peace conditions.

The third Bolshevik faction under Bukharin, certain that Bolshevik acceptance of the German conditions would mean the end of Bolshevik power, advocated a "revolutionary war" against Germany, a Bolshevik *"levée en masse"* which would free Russia from German occupation.

On January 22, 1918, the Bolshevik Central Committee voted in favor of Trotsky's policy of delay, which was to be implemented by the startling formula "No Peace, no War." The Bolshevik government would declare the war ended but refuse to sign peace on the German conditions.

Trotsky's formula of "No Peace, no War" remained what Lenin had claimed it to be all along—an empty political demonstration. After recovering from their surprise over the unorthodoxy of Bolshevik diplomacy, the Germans signed a separate peace with the non-Bolshevik government of the Ukraine on February 8, 1918. On February 18, 1918, the Germans terminated the armistice with Russia and resumed their military advance, which turned, in General Hoffmann's words, into a "military excursion by rail and car." With the Russian capital itself threatened by the German advance, the Bolshevik government was forced, as Lenin had predicted, to accept harsher terms on February 23, 1918. The Bolshevik government was forced to evacuate all forces from Finland, the Ukraine, Estonia, and Latvia. All Bolshevik propaganda in German-occupied territory was forbidden and Russia forced to make border concessions to Turkey. A new German-Russian trade agreement was to be signed on terms favorable to Germany.

It required Lenin's threat of resignation to secure the necessary majority in the Bolshevik Central Committee for acceptance of the German terms. On March 3, 1918, the peace of Brest-Litovsk was signed. There remained the final hurdle of ratification of the treaty by the Fourth All-Russian Soviet Congress, which met in Moscow on March 12, 1918. Owing to strong opposition to the treaty in Bolshevik ranks and especially among the Left Social Revolutionaries, ratification was more than a routine business of the Congress. Trotsky, fearful of the possibility of rejection, once more looked towards the United States for last-minute help, and even Lenin expressed his willingness to accept "potatoes and arms from the bandits of Anglo-American imperialism." By March, 1918, Lenin was more concerned, however, about the danger of western intervention against his government than the resumption of war with Germany. On March 14, 1918, the All-Russian Soviet Congress, following Lenin's advice, ratified the treaty of Brest-Litovsk. President Wilson had sent a message to the Soviet Congress on the same day in the hope of blocking ratification. The President's message, besides conveying the sympathy of the American people, conveyed little else and evoked a cynical reply from the Soviet Congress. In its reply the Soviet Congress expressed the hope for the overthrow of capitalism and the advent of social revolution in the United States in the near future.

The peace of Brest-Litovsk virtually pushed European Russia back to its pre-Petrine frontiers before Russia's expansion to the Baltic and the Black seas. The territories lost represented approximately 32 per cent of Russia's arable land, 75 per cent of her coal and iron ore resources, 33 per cent of her factories, and 26 per cent of her railroads. For all its enormous sacrifice, the treaty remained a conditional settlement, however, pending the outcome of the military struggle in the West. Whether German power would continue to hold sway from Finland to the Ukraine, whether the right of national self-determination would prevail in its western, or German, interpretation in the borderlands of Russia, all depended on the nature of the peace, which the Allies and Germany would ultimately conclude in the West. The characterization of the Brest-Litovsk treaty by William II as one of the "greatest successes of world history" was thus premature.

More correct was Lenin's comparison of the Brest-Litovsk treaty to the treaty of Tilsit in 1807, between Alexander I and Napoleon. As the Tilsit treaty had marked but a phase in the unfolding of Napoleonic imperialism, so Brest-Litovsk was not the final confirmation of a German triumph. As the kingdom of Prussia had risen from the ashes of defeat after 1807, Lenin predicted that Bolshevik Russia would prevail over her enemies and live to broadcast the message of social revolution to the world. By satisfying German territorial greed, Lenin had deflected German military might to the West, where it would prolong the war, delay foreign intervention, and increase the chances of Bolshevik survival. As in the days before the Bolshevik assumption of power in Russia, Lenin was guided by a mixture of Marxist doctrine and political pragmatism in his search for peace. "The road to Revolution" Lenin advised his lieutenants, "is not covered with roses. We shall walk in mud up to our knees, if necessary, to reach the Communist goal. . . ." When the Marxist prognosis of world revolution had proven false, when the proletarian masses of Europe had failed to emulate the Russian Revolution, Lenin urged his followers to discard their ideological illusions and accommodate themselves to the facts of German power. In so doing, the Bolshevik regime had not assured itself of ultimate survival, but it had made its survivial more probable. Once again Lenin had acted in accordance with his favorite maxim, borrowed from Napoleon: *"On s'engage et puis on voit,"* "one enters a struggle and sees what happens."

4 | The Collapse of the Old Order of Central Europe at the End of the First World War

The collapse of Russia and the Russian Revolution had a twofold effect on the German Empire. On the one hand, Russia's withdrawal from the war and the Treaty of Brest-Litovsk had strengthened the hand of the German Supreme Command and brought Ludendorff closer to the fulfillment of his fondest annexationist dreams. On the other hand, the yearning of the Russian masses for peace and the skillful pacifist propaganda of the Bolsheviks had left a deep impression on the German working class. Distrust of the government's motives and war aims spread over an ever larger segment of the German working class at the turn of 1917/1918, as it had among Russian workers and peasants a year earlier.

Nineteen seventeen, the year of the Russian revolution, thus became also the year of the sharpest confrontation between German annexationist forces and the war-weary and hungry masses. The two principal issues of the German confrontation were the debate over war aims and the renewed pressure for domestic reform. Embedded in these closely related issues were also the roots of the German revolution of 1918. To clarify the origins of this revolution, it would be helpful to survey the unsettled political and constitutional problems inherited by Germany from pre-war times.

POLITICAL AND CONSTITUTIONAL ISSUES OF PRE-WAR GERMANY

In its economic and industrial development, the Germany of 1914 was a nation far removed from the Germany which Bismarck had united in 1871. By contrast, the political facade and constitutional structure of Wilhelmian Germany had remained essentially unchanged from Bismarck's times. The Germany of 1914 was still the semi-autocratic empire under the predominant influence of Prussia that Bismarck had created in league with the German dynasties in 1871.

With the change of Germany from a predominantly agrarian

society into an industrial-urban one, the autocratic features of Prussia-Germany came under increasing attack. On the federal level the Reichstag, the lower house of the legislature, pressed for the introduction of parliamentary government and the adoption of the principle of ministerial responsibility. Under the Imperial Constitution of 1871, the chancellor was immune from the censure of the Reichstag. The chancellor required the consent of a Reichstag majority for the enactment of his legislative program, but failing to secure one, he could dissolve the Reichstag and order new elections. The political parties elected to the Reichstag could discuss or even oppose the chancellor's policies, but they could not alter them. The Reichstag was thus more than a mere advisory body but less than a genuine parliament in the Western, democratic sense, since the appointment and dismissal of the chancellor remained the sole prerogative of the crown.

The universal manhood suffrage for Reichstag elections which Bismarck had granted as concession to liberalism was thus largely deprived of its political meaning. Its significance in national politics was further reduced by the preponderance of the Bundesrat, the upper house of the federal legislature, whose members were appointed by the states. Furthermore, the electoral districts for the Reichstag elections remained unchanged throughout the history of the Empire, resulting in the over-representation of the rural at the expense of the urban districts.

The state constitution of Prussia, dating back to 1850, provided for an unequal three-class suffrage for the election of the Prussian Diet that heavily discriminated against the mass of voters in favor of the propertied and educated classes. The Prussian suffrage was not only a matter of internal Prussian politics, however, because of the size of the Prussian state and the favoring of the states over the federal government in the distribution of powers. In size Prussia was larger than all the other German federal states put together. Its political preponderance was anchored in the union of the Prussian royal and the German imperial crown and in the Prussian veto power in the Bundesrat, which could block any amendment of the German federal constitution. Since the legislative preponderance was with the states and not the federal government, the state laws of Prussia were often of greater importance than the national laws of Germany.

THE AGENTS OF REFORM

It was significant for the political history of the Hohenzollern Empire that the main pressure for reform did not originate in the middle class or the landed aristocracy. Of all political parties of the Empire, the Prussian Conservatives, stronghold of the landed Junker aristocracy, were least inclined to alter the political conditions of Prussia-Germany. On the contrary, they had viewed Bismarck's merger of Prussia with the rest of Germany with great suspicion, for fear that the national unification of Germany might lead to the Germanization of Prussia rather than the Prussianization of Germany.

The German middle class, on the other hand, had largely lost its revolutionary zeal and liberal convictions. Of its twin goals of national unification and liberalism, it had sacrificed the latter to the former after its efforts to achieve both had failed in the German revolution of 1848 and after Bismarck had offered the alternative of unification without liberalism. After Bismarck, the industrial middle class increasingly identified with the "New Course" of William II and its offspring of navalism, colonialism, and imperialism. A further incentive to preserve the political status quo was the middle-class fear of the rising strength of German Social Democracy. The middle-class parties, which included National Liberals and Progressives and the Catholic Center, might, on occasion, criticize the Emperor's abuse of power or express indignation at the excesses of Prussian militarism, such as in the Zabern Affair. In the latter incident Colonel von Reuter, a regular army officer, arrested and detained twenty-eight citizens of the small Alsatian town of Zabern in November, 1913, merely because they had taken part in a demonstration. Far from being punished for his illegal behavior, Colonel von Reuter was decorated by the army for his action. They might also, in a general way, deplore the inability of the Reichstag to influence the course of German foreign policy, as the last pre-war governments under Bülow and Bethmann-Hollweg staggered from crisis to crisis on the road to world war. They would not, however, challenge the dynasty into making meaningful concessions on the issues of parliamentary government or reform of the Prussian suffrage. Such a challenge, to be successful, would have required the collaboration of the Social Democrats. The middle class was separated from the Social Democrats, however, by a wide chasm of social discrimination and ideological suspicion.

THE SOCIAL DEMOCRATIC DILEMMA

The Social Democratic Party (SPD), by 1910 the largest political party of Germany with 110 Reichstag-seats, was the only mass party dedicated to the democratic reform of Prussia and the Empire. Its political effectiveness as an agent of reform was seriously undermined, however, by its ideological dilemma and the increased isolation which that dilemma entailed. At the time of its founding in 1875 and for some years after, the Social Democratic Party had assumed a defiant, revolutionary, and strongly Marxist stance, reflected in the party programs of Gotha (1875) and Erfurt (1891). For this, both the economic conditions of the German industrial revolution and the political persecution of the party by Bismarck were largely responsible. After Bismarck, and with greater participation by the working class in the fruits of capitalist expansion, the Social Democrats abandoned all serious thought of revolution and turned into a reformist party, in which the democratic outweighed the socialist element.

The change in tactics did not lead to a formal repudiation of revolutionary Marxism, however, in spite of strong urgings by the "revisionist" party theorists, notably Eduard Bernstein. In his *Preconditions of Socialism,* a brilliant analysis of the party's metamorphosis from a revolutionary into an evolutionary movement, Bernstein called upon his party to rid itself of the "deadweight" of revolutionary Marxism and assume the role of "lawful heir of German liberalism."

This the party refused to do, for fear that an abrupt ideological turnabout would lead to a split in the powerful party organization. It also feared to lose its prestige in the Second International, in which it was widely admired for its organizational strength and doctrinal pronouncements. To both their foreign admirers and their domestic foes, the German Social Democrats thus retained the false image of a revolutionary party. For that reason, the party shocked foreign socialists through its support of the Empire when the World War broke out, and alienated the German middle-class parties before the war which might otherwise have supported it. As the Social Democratic Party remained a force apart from all other political parties, so did the working class from the rest of German pre-war society. By custom, if not law, Social Democrats were excluded from serving in the government or civil service. They could not even qualify, in the words of SPD chairman Friedrich Ebert, for "imperial night watchmen."

The most profound impact which the four decades of Hohenzollern rule had on the politics of Prussia-Germany was in preventing the development of political skill and articulate leadership among the political parties of the Empire. The absence of a bill of rights and of the principle of popular sovereignty from the Imperial Constitution of 1871 was but a formal expression of the gap which still separated the "state" from the "people." In his hostility to the German political parties, Bismarck had called them "fragments" and tried to reduce them to the level of economic interest groups. By 1914 the political parties of Germany had not significantly advanced from that position.

THE IMPACT OF WAR ON THE POLITICS OF THE EMPIRE

The outbreak of the First World War ended temporarily in Germany, as it had elsewhere, the dissension between classes and parties. The parties concluded a political truce, the *Burgfrieden,* which they pledged not to violate for the duration of the conflict. The Social Democrats found it easier to reconcile their supporting vote for the war credits with their conscience because they believed Germany to have been attacked. In a defensive war, especially against tsarist Russia, they were anxious to give full support, since the Germany of William II seemed to them a veritable haven of political liberty by comparison with the Russia of Nicholas II.

COLLAPSE OF THE BURGFRIEDEN

By 1917 the Burgfrieden broke down under the weight of the war aims debate and the renewed pressure for political reform, spearheaded by the Social Democrats. Ebert had pledged not to make political reform the "object of barter" in the midst of war. By 1917, however, several factors combined to renew the pre-war demands for the liberalization of Prussia and the democratization of the Empire. The Social Democrats felt that the great sacrifices which the millions of ordinary men made on behalf of the dynasty entitled them to political equality at home. Hence, the renewed demand for the abolition of the unequal Prussian suffrage.

More important than the Prussian question, in the context of war, was the growing pressure of the Reichstag to make itself heard on the matter of war aims and foreign policy. It was against the monopoly of power which the Supreme Command had acquired in all questions related to war aims since 1916, that the SPD, the Center, and the Progressives banded together in the Reichstag Peace Resolution of July 19, 1917. The three parties, which together constituted a majority of the Reichstag, demanded a peace of understanding and "lasting reconciliation" without annexations and reparations.

The military-monarchical powers met the dual challenge of domestic reform and compromise with the foreign enemy by a policy that mixed token concessions with a show of force. In the reform question the monarchy was on the defensive, partly because of mass sentiment, partly because of the impact of the Russian March revolution and the condemnation of Prussian militarism by the United States after its entry into the war.

As a gesture to the spirit of reform, William II, in his "easter gift" of April 8, 1917, promised a change in the Prussian suffrage, to be carried out after the war. On the question of war aims, the regime remained adamant. Ludendorff showed his contempt for the Reichstag majority when he forced Bethmann-Hollweg, who had supported the reform drive, to resign and replaced him with Georg Michaelis, without consulting the Reichstag. To counter the spirit of the Reichstag Peace Resolution, he launched the Fatherland Party, an organization composed of annexationists and firm backers of the Supreme Command.

BREAK-UP OF THE SPD INTO TWO RIVAL FACTIONS

The military and political gains of the German Supreme Command at the beginning of 1918 seemed to vindicate its tough policy against the opposition of 1917. The same Reichstag which had passed the Peace Resolution of July, 1917, endorsed the annexationist Peace of Brest-Litovsk in March, 1918. The chief victim of the political crisis of 1917 was the Social Democratic Party, which broke into two factions under the stress of the war aims debate. In April, 1917, the orthodox Marxists combined with socialist pacifists to from the new Independent Social Democratic Party (USPD). Of all political parties the USPD alone opposed the Treaty of Brest-Litovsk in the Reichstag. The SPD merely abstained from voting.

The self-confidence of the German military authorities, boosted by the defeat of Russia, continued to soar for some time after the Treaty of Brest-Litovsk and the initial gains of the Ludendorff offensive in the west. William II, when informed of these gains, exclaimed on March 26, 1918, that if an English delegation came to sue for peace, "it must kneel before the German flag," for it was a question here of a victory of the monarchy over democracy.

THE MILITARY COLLAPSE AND THE ATTEMPT AT CONTROLLED REVOLUTION FROM ABOVE

The sudden prospect of a German military defeat in France after the failure of the Ludendorff offensive and the danger of imminent collapse of Germany's allies—Austria-Hungary, Bulgaria and Turkey— sent Ludendorff and William II on a frantic search for ways of preventing revolution at home and avoiding unconditional surrender to the Allies. Having gambled away Germany's last offensive reserves, the Supreme Command was anxious to relinquish all political responsibility for the consequences of defeat to a German civilian government. On September 29, 1918, a panic-stricken Ludendorff urged the Emperor to broaden the basis of the German government at once and have the new government appeal to President Wilson for an armistice. On September 30, 1918, William II announced that henceforth "men who enjoyed the confidence of the nation should partake extensively of the rights and duties of government."

After the resignation of the aged chancellor Hertling, too steeped in conservatism to preside over the democratization of the Empire, Prince Max of Baden formed the first parliamentary government of the Empire in early October, 1918. The cabinet was recruited from the parties of the Peace Resolution of 1917, including the Social Democrats. In less than four weeks the new government put into effect reforms which the Empire had resisted for forty years. The Prussian suffrage was replaced by a universal, equal, and secret suffrage. On the federal level the principle of ministerial responsibility was adopted and civilian control over the military assured. When Ludendorff balked at Wilson's armistice terms, he was promptly replaced by General Gröner. Gröner was one of the few military leaders of the Empire who had supported democratic reforms even before the military collapse had made their adoption appear politically expedient.

The controlled revolution from above might well have accomplished its purpose of saving the dynasty, but for the failure of Prince Max to secure an immediate armistice. With the exception of the Conservatives on the far right and the USPD on the far left, all parties accepted the constitutional changes of October, 1918, with satisfaction. What radicalized the masses and snapped the tight discipline of the German army and navy, however, was the impatient yearning for an immediate end to the war, once the news of the German armistice request of October 3, 1918, had become public knowledge. As the armistice negotiations between the American and German governments dragged on through the entire length of October, 1918, the German public blamed William II for the delay and demanded his abdication.

Although the United States did not expressly demand the abdication of William II, the Emperor's continued presence on the German throne was, in fact, the main reason for Wilson's caution in dealing with the new German government. In reply to the first German note of October 3, 1918, the President therefore asked whether Prince Max was speaking "merely for the constituted authorities of the empire." Only after receiving repeated assurances that the peace negotiations were being conducted by a democratic German government did Wilson agree to an armistice based on his Fourteen Points, subject to certain reservations made by Britain and France.

In order to save the monarchy from being overthrown by growing public resentment against William II, Prince Max and the Social Democrats, more concerned than ever about the prospect of violent revolution, had meanwhile tried to secure the Emperor's abdication in favor of his grandson, for whom a regency was to be set up. Even among the military the Emperor now enjoyed little support, as indicated by General Gröner's advice that William join his troops and seek death in battle. All plans and schemes to save the monarchy were condemned to failure by the Emperor's refusal to yield the throne and the military mutiny which the Emperor's attitude helped precipitate in the early days of November, 1918.

THE FAILURE OF THE CONTROLLED REVOLUTION

The military mutiny began with a sailors' revolt at the naval base at Kiel on November 3, 1918, in response to rumors that the German fleet was to be sent on a "death cruise" against the British to avoid the humiliation of surrender. The German navy had witnessed earlier cases of insubordination in 1917. Whereas the authorities had dealt swiftly with the incidents of 1917, they no longer possessed the self-confidence to do so in the tense atmosphere of November, 1918. The sailors' revolt thus mushroomed overnight into a movement of national scope, involving most of the fleet and the home army. Concurrently with the military mutiny, sailors', soldiers', and workers' councils sprang up throughout Germany in imitation of the Russian soviets. Their chief political demand was the abdication of the Emperor.

That the spark of revolution should have originated in the German navy was both ironic and logical. It was ironic because the German navy, built at tremendous expense to the Empire, had always been the source of the Emperor's special pride and joy. It was logical because morale in the German navy had been low throughout the war, as a result of its inaction and the hostility between officers and men which reflected sharp pre-war class antagonisms. The anti-war propaganda of the Independent Social Democrats had fallen on fertile soil among the disgruntled sailors, and rumors of impending world revolution were rife among the ranks. The sailors of Kiel even claimed to have seen British vessels in the North Sea flying the red flag.

The first major political repercussion of the mutiny was the proclamation of a republic in Bavaria by the USPD leader Kurt Einsner on November 8, 1918. In Berlin the leaders of the Social Democrats had decided on drastic steps under the pressure of revolutionary developments in north and south Germany and in response to the revolutionary groundswell among Berlin factory workers. On November 7, 1918, the SPD issued an ultimatum to Prince Max, demanding the abdication of the Emperor and threatening to withdraw from the cabinet in the event of the Emperor's refusal. Prince Max, in a last effort to save the monarchy, announced the abdication of William II on November 9, on his own authority. When faced with the mass demonstrations of Berlin workers, who fraternized with the troops, the Prince relinquished his powers to Ebert with the understanding that a constituent assembly would be called as soon as practicable. Philip Scheidemann, another SPD leader, without the express authority of his party, thereupon proclaimed the German republic from the balcony of the German Reichstag to a cheering crowd.

THE SPONTANEOUS REVOLUTION: THE GOALS AND TACTICS OF THE GERMAN LEFT

To many, the swift overthrow of the Hohenzollern dynasty and the old military regime, seemingly unshakable in their power as late as September, 1918, appeared as an incredible event. Otto Braun, the

SPD leader and future Prime Minister of Prussia, reflected the general amazement in these words: "Should the century-old, seemingly powerful Hohenzollern regime have collapsed so completely and miserably? Who was to assume the inheritance, an inheritance frightful to behold. Two million dead, millions of widows, orphans and cripples . . . the undernourished children lay in bed with papershirts and all metal had been used up for ammunition, down to the last church bell and the last doorknob."

With the wholesale abdication of the German dynasties and the retreat of a frightened bourgeoisie, the political field was relinquished for the moment to the German left, more deeply divided in its goals than it had been before November 9, 1918. Outwardly, the revolution of November 9 bore many resemblances to the Russian revolution of 1917. In Berlin soldiers and demonstrating workers had fraternized and trucks with revolutionary banners and machine guns had raced through the streets. Soldiers' councils, elected from the ranks, had stripped officers of the power of military command — and occasionally of their war decorations. Even at the Supreme Headquarters at Spa, a soldiers' council had installed itself under the very noses of Hindenburg and Gröner.

SPARTACISTS AND REVOLUTIONARY SHOP STEWARDS

Of the various factions within the German labor movement, however, only the extreme left wing, represented by the Spartacists and the Revolutionary Shop Stewards, desired a Bolshevik-style revolution in Germany in 1918. Both groups were loosely associated with Independent Social Democrats but appeared as independent political agents during the revolution. The Spartacists, founded during the war by Rosa Luxemburg and Karl Liebknecht, were a well-publicized group of flamboyant Marxist intellectuals, who had engaged in anti-war propaganda. Rosa Luxemburg, an indefatigable author of pamphlets, articles, and revolutionary manifestos, was among the foremost German connoisseurs of Marxist ideology and an oldtime critic of SPD revisionism. Although she had agreed with the aims of Lenin's revolution, she sharply disagreed with its tactics of force and terror.

The Revolutionary Shop Stewards, by contrast, were an underground conspiratorial group, drawn mostly from the radical Berlin metal workers. Unlike the Spartacists, they had little faith in spontaneous, revolutionary mass action. The Revolutionary Shop Stewards were the true counterpart of the Russian Bolsheviks. Among all German radical organizations, they alone had made preparations for an armed uprising and the forceful seizure of power for early November, 1918. Their preparations, well financed and supported by the Soviet embassy in Berlin before its closing, were overtaken by the sailors' mutiny, however.

Both the Spartacists and the Revolutionary Shop Stewards agreed with the Bolshevik thesis of world revolution. In keeping with the Russian Communist expectation of the day, they regarded the extension of the Bolshevik revolution into industrial Germany as their principal task. As the Bolsheviks had used the soviets as the stepping stone to Communist revolution, so the German radicals intended to turn the German soldiers' and workers' councils into vehicles of Communist revolution. What distinguished the German radicals from the Bolsheviks, however, was the absence of a strong unified command. The extreme German left produced no Lenin during the revolution of November, 1918. Neither Luxemburg nor Liebknecht of the Spartacists, nor Ledebour, Müller, and Däumig of the Revolutionary Shop Stewards could equal Lenin's persuasive powers of leadership and singleness of purpose.

GOALS OF THE SPD

The Social Democrats believed that their chief task during the revolution was to preserve the political gains made as a result of the constitutional changes of October, 1918, until the people at large could confirm these gains in a freely elected constituent assembly. What drove the Social Democrats to the political forefront on November 9, 1918, was not the desire to initiate revolution, but rather the anxiety that the radical left would wrest control over the masses from the SPD unless the Social Democrats took charge themselves. In proclaiming the republic, Philip Scheidemann had significantly added that "all that is politically attainable, has been attained."

The chief policy aims of Ebert during the revolution thus were: to sign an armistice as quickly as possible; to protect Germany's frontiers against Polish incursions in the East and against French-supported separation in the Rhineland; to preserve the political unity and the federal structure of Germany, although the disappearance of the German dynasties made the abandonment of the latter appear logical; to improve the food supply, especially of the cities, which were threatened with starvation; to encourage the entire administrative and judicial staff of the old regime, from state secretaries down to local officials, to remain at their posts; to enact the broadest possible suffrage for all men and women above the age of twenty for the election of a constituent assembly; and to fix the earliest possible election date compatible with the repatriation and demobilization of the millions of veterans.

In keeping with their scrupulous adherence to the rules of political democracy, the Social Democrats opposed any sweeping social or economic changes during the revolution which might prejudice the wishes of the constituent assembly. They thus opposed any nationalization of industries or seizure of private property. During the German revolution not a single factory, bank, or landed estate was taken over by the state. The most radical social reform which the SPD achieved between November, 1918, and January, 1919, was the introduction of the eight-hour day in industry and the recognition of the unions as agents of collective bargaining.

It was difficult to assess the relative strength of the various factions of the German labor movement under the conditions of November, 1918, or to determine the following which radicals and moderates enjoyed among the masses. It was safe to assume, however, that the mood and the expectation of the masses had become more radical as a result of war-weariness and hunger. Many workers, who had otherwise remained loyal to the Social Democrats, found the economic policy of their party too cautious and conservative. The expectation that the revolution would lead to the wholesale nationalization of basic industries was all the greater in view of the deep structural changes which the "Hindenburg program" had effected in the German war-time economy. In the interest of greater efficiency and a higher armaments output the military had fostered the trend towards cartels and trusts, had founded new factories with public funds, the *Kriegsgesellschaften,* and had closed down many private enterprises. The trend towards economic concentration and the founding of the *Kriegsgesellschaften* appeared, in the minds of many workers, to be the first step towards the nationalization of industry.

As a concession to such expectations, the Social Democrats installed a commission to study the problem of nationalization. Beyond issuing a cautious report, the commission took no action. One major reason for Social Democratic restraint on the nationalization issue was the fear that nationalized industries, as a property of the state, would be the first to be claimed and seized by the Allies for reparations.

Considerations of national policy merged with party interests also in the Social Democratic handling of the German soviets. As exponents of liberal democracy, the Social Democrats regarded the soviets as agents of "revolutionary disorder" and desired their earliest possible removal. To prevent their use by the radicals, the Social Democrats packed the soviets with their own supporters, however, and thus effectively neutralized them. In no way did the Social Democrats wish to integrate the soviets into the final political structure of postwar Germany. Any semblance of a sovietized Germany, Ebert feared, would give the Allies an excuse for open intervention in the internal affairs of Germany with possibly harmful consequences to the political unity of the German republic. Marshal Foch had already gone on record that France would not negotiate a peace treaty with a German soviet government.

THE CENTERS OF REVOLUTIONARY POWER

ALLIANCE OF SPD AND USPD

To minimize the threat from the extreme left, the Social Democrats entered into an open alliance with the Independent Social

Democrats while relying on the secret collaboration of the army. The USPD, as previously noted, was itself ideologically split between its Communist left wing and the socialist pacifists on the right. On November 10, 1918, Ebert invited the USPD to join in the formation of a Provisional Government, called the Council of People's Representatives, in which both parties were to be represented by three men each. By drawing the Independents into the government, Ebert hoped not only to isolate the extreme left but to pave the way for an eventual merger of SPD and USPD. The latter purpose was especially important to the Social Democrats in view of the elections, in which a reunited workers' party had greater chances of winning a majority of seats in the constituent assembly.

The USPD accepted the invitation in spite of bitter opposition from its left wing. The SPD-USPD coalition was tenuous from the start, however, since the Independent members of the Provisional Government, Haase, Barth and Dittmann, wished to postpone the constituent assembly as long as possible in order to effect radical social and economic changes in the meantime. Through the overriding influence of Ebert, the Provisional Government followed the Social Democratic Party line in all important questions until its collapse in late December, 1918.

ALLIANCE BETWEEN EBERT AND GRÖNER

While Ebert hoped to have achieved a "vaccination against Communism" through the inclusion of the USPD in the Provisional Government, he formed a personal and secret alliance with General Gröner, Ludendorff's successor at the Supreme Command. By securing the support of the army, Ebert hoped to gain added protection against the radicals should they resort to force in the pursuit of their goals. General Gröner, on his part, gladly offered his support, for he regarded the Social Democrats as the best available safeguard against Communist revolution. Beyond that, the dependence of the Provisional Government on the good will of the army offered Gröner the opportunity of gaining an important place for the old army in the new republic. Beginning on November 10, 1918, the Reichchancellory in Berlin and the Supreme Command at Kassel were connected by a secret telephone line which remained open even during the most turbulent events of the coming weeks in Berlin.

The secret Gröner-Ebert alliance has often been deplored in the light of the subsequent role played by the German army in undermining the Weimar Republic. Yet such were the conditions of the German revolution that the Social Democrats were unable to raise an effective republican guard, independent of the army. The few armed units recruited from among Social Democratic workers soon proved to be ineffective when faced with Communist violence, largely because of their feeling for class solidarity. Since the Communists did not always reciprocate such sentiments, Ebert relied increasingly on the army for his own political survival and the defense of his goals.

Field Marshal Hindenburg sanctioned the Gröner-Ebert alliance, for he too regarded Ebert as the man best qualified to combat Communism under the circumstances. However, the Field Marshal's basic hostility to the new republic, of which he was to become president in 1925, was indicated by his observation that the Germans would always look foolish "with a Jacobin hat on their heads."

THE BERLIN EXECUTIVE COUNCIL

The Revolutionary Shop Stewards and Spartacists sought to counter Social Democratic strategy by making the Berlin Executive Council their chief organ of power. The Executive Council had been chosen by the soldiers' and workers' councils of Berlin on November 10, 1918, and claimed to speak for all German soldiers' and workers' councils. Like the Provisional Government, the Berlin Executive Council consisted of an equal number of Social Democrats and Independents, but the influence of the radicals outweighed that of the SPD, largely because of Richard Müller. Müller fought for the victory of the soviet system over the constituent assembly. To his opponents he was known, not without humor, as "dead-body Müller" for his statement that the constituent assembly would be convened only over his dead body. Müller claimed supreme power for the Berlin Executive Council over all other political, administrative, military, and judicial agencies. The Executive Council thus issued decrees, undertook arrests, and generally interfered in the business of the Provisional Government to the best of its ability. The slogans "all power to the soviets" and "constituent assembly" came to symbolize the struggle between the two centers of revolutionary power.

In the struggle between Ebert and the Berlin Executive Council, the latter soon lost ground. The chief weakness of the radicals was the lack of interest in, and support for, their goals shown by the German soldiers' and workers' councils themselves. The German soviets, far from becoming a revolutionary organization of their own, merely reflected in their membership the relative strength of the competing factions within the German labor movement. Not only did the Social Democrats outnumber the radicals in the workers' councils, but the soldiers' councils, in particular, soon emerged as a strongly conservative force in support of Ebert. Once the basic issue of the German revolution, which was the choice between soviet dictatorship and constituent assembly, had been understood, the majority within the soldiers' and workers' councils favored the dissolution of the soviets.

ALL-GERMAN SOVIET CONGRESS

The weak following of the radicals among the soldiers' and workers' councils was strikingly revealed in the All-German Soviet Congress, which opened on December 16 in Berlin. The Chief purposes of the Congress were to decide which of the rival goals the German soviets should support and to elect a new Central Council, to take the place of the Berlin Executive Council.

The radicals would have liked the Soviet Congress to declare itself the revolutionary parliament of Germany and to proceed with the immediate drafting of a soviet constitution. To this end, the radicals put pressure on the Congress through frequent demonstrations and interruptions to sway its vote. The debate over the merits of the soviet system as opposed to liberal democracy revealed, however, that not all German radicals wished merely to copy the Russian example. Many German radicals believed that the soviet system offered Germany a third choice, between western democracy and Bolshevik dictatorship, in the form of a direct workers' democracy. The radicals feared that a mere copying of representative democracy by the German revolution would not eradicate the deep-seated German aversion to politics or the national proclivity for carrying out orders uncritically. A government resting on elected workers' councils, they argued, would awaken a sense of political responsibility among the masses through their direct involvement in public affairs. Fritz Heckert, a leading advocate of soviet democracy, issued a prophetic warning about the failure of representative democracy in Germany. The German people, he said, expected that the constituent assembly would solve the problems of peace and bread. Since the assembly would lack the means for their solution, the people, angry and disappointed, would curse their leaders and their parliament "and the misery will be all the greater."

The great majority of the Congress members did not share the radicals' faith in soviet democracy, since the soviet system, under whatever guise, implied to the moderates the dictatorship of a minority over the majority. With over four hundred against fifty votes, the Congress thus adopted the Social Democratic resolution to hold elections for the constituent assembly on January 19, 1919. The Congress ended with tumultuous scenes between the rival factions which foreshadowed the violent clashes between moderates and radicals in the streets. Having suffered defeat on the political level, the radicals were determined to challenge Ebert and the Social Democrats by force of arms.

THE BREAK-UP OF THE PROVISIONAL GOVERNMENT; THE COMMUNIST UPRISINGS OF 1919

On December 23, 1918, only a few days after the closing of the all-German Soviet Congress, the first serious armed clashes between government forces and the radicals occurred in Berlin. The street battles, involving regular troops and the so-called People's Sailors' Division, a force of revolutionary sailors, were inconclusive. The regular troops were reluctant to open fire on the armed demonstrators, who included many women and children. General Gröner, alarmed by the lack of resolve among his troops, began to recruit volunteer units, the Free Corps, which could be relied upon to fight the radicals under any circumstances. The Free Corps volunteers were mainly drawn from the most militarist and reactionary residue of the imperial army, whose hatred for Communism was matched by their contempt for democracy. Communism being the more immediate threat, the Free Corps placed its services at the disposal of Ebert as the lesser of two evils. From the ranks of the Free Corps were to emerge in later years some of the most bitter enemies of the Weimar Republic, assassins of republican politicians and recruits for Hitler's storm troopers.

The three Independent Social Democrats of the Provisional Government used the bloodshed of Berlin as an excuse to withdraw from the government. Caught in the power struggle between Ebert and the radicals, the Independents followed the pull of their left wing when violence began to overtake political debate. The Social Democrats, filling the vacancies with their own men, were thus in complete control of the government by the end of December, 1918. The polarization of forces continued when the radicals constituted themselves as the Communist Party of Germany (KPD) on December 31, 1918.

At the beginning of 1919 the only Independent Social Democrat to hold high office was the police commissioner of Berlin, Emil Eichhorn. When the government asked for his resignation, the Communists seized on the demand as a pretext for revolution against the Ebert government. A revolutionary committee of fifty-three, mostly Communist, declared the Ebert government deposed, and formed a revolutionary counter-government under Liebknecht. In Berlin the Communists seized strategic points and the building of the SPD party newspaper *Vorwärts*. With the cry "Down with the tyranny of Ebert and Scheidemann. . . . Long live revolutionary, international socialism!" the Communists appealed to the workers of Berlin to join in battle against the government.

Rosa Luxemburg, one of the founders of the German Communist Party, had wisely counseled against the armed insurrection of January 5, 1919, but had been unable to restrain the revolutionary impatience of the inflammable Liebknecht. Not only was the timing of the German Communist revolution ill chosen, but Communist strength throughout Germany had not yet been organized for a concerted revolutionary effort. The insurrection of January, 1919, was thus largely confined to the German capital, where the Free Corps found little difficulty in crushing the Communists in a week's bitter street fighting. Among the Communist casualties were Liebknecht and Luxemburg, who were shot by their captors without trial. To the end Rosa Luxemburg, as militantly Communist as she was anti-Leninist, held firm to her belief that the great mass of German workers truly desired a Communist revolution but that they needed to be radicalized first through a series of ever larger mass strikes.

The pattern of Communist violence and its repression by the Free Corps was repeated throughout the spring of 1919, as the Communists spent their force in piecemeal revolts in Saxony and Bavaria.

In Bavaria the assassination of Kurt Eisner in February, 1919, by a reactionary student precipitated civil war that climaxed in the establishment of a Communist Soviet Republic of Bavaria in April, 1919. The leading role which the Russian Communists Eugen Levine and Max Levien played in the Bavarian Communist revolution, together with the earlier victory of the Hungarian Communists under Bela Kun, raised fears once more in Germany that the Bolshevik revolution might yet succeed in spreading westward and gaining a permanent foothold in central Europe.

During its brief existence, the Bavarian Communist regime was marked by a reign of terror, which was reciprocated in full by the Free Corps when it marched against Munich and crushed the Soviet Republic by May 1, 1919. Not surprisingly, Munich soon developed into a hotbed of reactionary and bitterly anti-republican associations in the aftermath of Communist terror and Free Corps reprisals. The National Socialists that Hitler joined were but one of these associations.

In Berlin a second outburst of violence had meanwhile been put down in March, 1919, with greater loss of life than was sustained during the uprisings of January. Prominent in crushing both the January and March uprisings was Gustav Noske, the Social Democratic leader with the most military mind and the most cordial relations with the army and the Free Corps. So great was Noske's popularity with the military that some officers wished to make him head of a military dictatorship. Noske refused to capitalize on his anti-Communist exploits, however. Among Berlin workers of all political persuasions, his forceful policy and his association with the military made him unpopular and earned him the epithet of "bloodhound."

ELECTIONS TO THE CONSTITUENT ASSEMBLY

In spite of the flaring up of civil war in various parts of Germany between January and May, 1919, the elections to the Constituent Assembly took place without disturbance on the assigned date, January 19, 1919. The political parties which entered the contest—only the Communists boycotted the election—were essentially those of the Empire, although some regrouping and changing of names had occurred since the revolution. The old Conservatives reappeared as the Nationalists, and gained 44 seats. The right wing of the former National Liberals, reconstituted as the People's Party, polled only 19 seats. The left wing of the former National Liberals had fused with the Progressives to form the Democratic Party, which gained an impressive 75 seats. No merger between the SPD and USPD having been achieved during the revolution, the two parties ran separately under the old labels, the SPD gaining 165, the USPD 22 seats. The Catholic Center, with 91 seats, essentially retained its prewar strength.

Although the Social Democrats, much against their expectation and to their great regret, failed to win a simple majority of seats, they formed, together with the Center and the Progressives, a powerful democratic bloc. The three parties, SPD, Center, and Democrats (the former Progressives), had stood together in the Reichstag Peace Resolution of 1917 and had worked together in the shortlived coalition government under Prince Max in October, 1918. During the revolution the common ground and understanding among the three parties had become wider still, outweighing such differences as still existed, especially between the Catholic Center and the SPD on such matters as religion. Above all, the three parties shared a firm commitment to the cause of parliamentary democracy. When Ebert surrendered the powers of the Provisional Government to the newly elected Constituent Assembly in February, 1919, he invoked the memory of the German revolution of 1848/1849, whose goals the Social Democrats claimed to have fulfilled. The solid democratic majority of the Weimar assembly gave substance to the Social Democratic claim and held out the promise of a viable German democracy for the future.

DANGERS TO GERMAN DEMOCRACY

The election results of January, 1919, notwithstanding, there existed many forces hostile and dangerous to the German democratic experiment from the time of birth of the German republic. The attack from the far left, although greatly magnified in its impression by violence and bloodshed, was never very dangerous to the democratic cause during the revolution. Not only had radical strategy been confused and disorganized, but the conditions, which the Marxists liked to call "objective," for a successful Communist revolution were not present in the Germany of 1918. It was precisely because the German working class was more numerous than the Russian, better organized politically, and more conscious of its interests, that it rejected the Communist call for a complete destruction of the old society. Having acquired a significant stake in the old order, the working class stood more to lose from its destruction than it stood to gain from its reform. Moreover, pre-revolutionary Germany did not suffer from the same acute land and peasant problem that had plagued Russia and so greatly aided Lenin in the establishment of a Bolshevik dictatorship.

A greater threat to German democracy was its association

with national defeat and the exploitation of that fact by the nationalist right. Political liberty had entered Germany on the heels of defeat and partly under foreign pressure. It had also come, however, as a result of growing agitation, as witnessed by pre-war political strife and new demands raised in the midst of war. At the turn of 1918/1919, an indigenous German democratic wave merged with the high tide of victorious Allied democracy, when democracy promised to become the prevailing form of European governments west of Russia.

The Social Democratic leaders tried to bolster the forces of German democracy, not only by drawing a direct line from 1848 to 1918, but by invoking the memory of the humanist traditions of Weimar as well. Weimar, the city where the first German constituent assembly met in early 1919, was also the city of Goethe and the symbol of the "other Germany," the Germany of "poets and thinkers." By infusing the new republic with the spirit of Germany's greatest cultural epoch, the founders of the republic hoped to forge new ties to the liberal west, which the Prussianized Germany of Bismarck and the imperialist Germany of William II had severed.

The nationalist right, having emerged from hiding almost as soon as the revolution ended, made full use of the new political freedom to attack and discredit the new republic. The main thrust of the nationalist attack consisted in the planting of misconceptions about the origins of the revolution and the motives of its leaders. In the nationalist version, revolution had been the cause, rather than the effect, of military defeat. In its effort to free the old authorities from all association with the consequences of defeat, the nationalist right portrayed the revolution as the stab in the back of a heroically fighting army. None other than Field Marshall Hindenburg gave credence to the thesis of the "stab in the back," an endorsement all the more fateful since it came from a revered public figure.

Against the thesis of the "stab in the back," the founders of the Weimar Republic mustered only a feeble defense. The efforts of the Social Democrats to pinpoint the responsibility of the Supreme Command and of the Emperor for the precipitate armistice request of October and the outbreak of revolution in November, 1918, were soon drowned out in the national uproar over the Treaty of Versailles.

The failure of the democratic parties to set the record of the revolution straight and to free the liberal democracy of Weimar from an odious association with national defeat must be rated as the chief weakness of the new democracy and the principal failure of the German revolution. The weak response of the democratic parties to this challenge from the nationalist right betrayed a lack of self-confidence arising from the absence of any previous example of successful revolution in the German past. Unlike the Third French Republic, also born in national defeat and after the fall of empire in 1870, the Weimar Republic could not look back on a long history of successful liberal revolution for both the political and the national inspiration of its citizens.

THE COLLAPSE OF AUSTRIA-HUNGARY; THE FAILURE OF THE CONSTITUTIONAL COMPROMISE OF 1867

During the half century preceding the outbreak of the First World War, the Habsburg monarchy had failed to cope with its most serious internal problem, the strife among the nationalities. The revolutionary wave of 1848/1849 had first revealed the full force which western national ideas and Russian Pan-Slavism could exert on the multilingual and multinational Danubian Empire. Although the Habsburg dynasty had weathered the crisis of the 1848/1849 revolution, the fires of nationalism continued to smolder under the surface until they consumed the whole edifice of the Danubian Empire under the impact of the First World War.

If the nationality problem of the Habsburg monarchy appeared keener than that of Russia before the First World War, it was chiefly because of the deeper ethnic divisions among Slavs, Germans, Magyars, Italians, and Rumanians within the Habsburg monarchy and the fact that the old historic bonds which had united these ethnic blocs under the Habsburg scepter had largely lost their significance in the age of nationalism. The common threat of Moslem Turkish invasion, which had united Hungary, Bohemia, and Austria in the 16th century had disappeared when Turkey itself became the scene of national revolutions and the victim of Great Power imperialism in the 19th century. Also the old supra-national feudal aristocracy, upon which Emperor Francis Joseph continued to draw for the government of the monarchy, increasingly lost touch with the nationality-conscious middle classes of the various ethnic blocs.

Following its expulsion from Italy in 1859 and Germany in 1866, the Habsburg dynasty hoped to calm the nationality strife by granting the Magyars, the most numerous and vociferous of the non-German nationalities, an equal share in the control of the multi-national empire. The constitutional compromise (*Ausgleich*) of 1867 divided the Habsburg monarchy into a western or Austrian and eastern or Hungarian half and thereby replaced the former German hegemony with a German-Magyar dualism.

The constitutional arrangement of 1867, though satisfactory to the Magyars, did not pacify the non-German and non-Magyar nationalities, which, taken together, constituted a majority within the fifty-two million people who composed the Dual Monarchy of Austria-Hungary on the eve of World War I. In the Austrian half of the monarchy, ethnic Germans accounted for a mere 35 per cent of the population, the remainder being composed of roughly 23 per cent Czechs, 17 per cent Poles, 12 per cent Ukrainians, 4.5 per cent Slovenes, 2.8 per cent Serbo-Croats, 2.7 per cent Italians, and 1 per cent Rumanians. In the kingdom of Hungary, the privileged Magyars accounted for 48 per cent of the population; 10 per cent were German, 9.4 per cent Slovak, 14 per cent Rumanian, 2 per cent Ukrainian, 8.8 per cent Croat, and 5.3 per cent Serb.

Although Magyar and German treatment of the "subject races" differed, neither half of the Dual Monarchy offered a nationality policy during the half century following the Ausgleich which satisfied the underprivileged nationalities. The Magyars, though granting limited autonomy to the South-Slav Croats in a "sub-dual" arrangement of 1868, relied in the main on a policy of ruthless Magyarization of Slavs and Rumanians. Before World War I only 6 per cent of the population of Hungary were enfranchised and, of over 450 parliamentary deputies in Budapest, a mere 50 were listed as being non-Magyar. Magyar influence over the nationality policy of the Dual Monarchy reached beyond the borders of Hungary, however, since the emperor of Austria, as king of Hungary, was bound by oath to uphold the Ausgleich of 1867. The Magyars jealously guarded the privileged position of Germans and Magyars in the Dual Monarchy and thus vetoed any effort of the Habsburg dynasty to extend autonomy to other nationalities, such as Emperor Francis Joseph contemplated briefly in the 1870's for the Czechs.

Although Austria had granted universal manhood suffrage to all its nationalities in 1907 for election to the Austrian parliament, or *Reichsrat,* the Austro-Slavs, foremost among them the economically and culturally advanced Czechs, resented the centralist government in Vienna with its overtones of German cultural and political hegemony. The hope of the Habsburg dynasty that universal manhood suffrage and the resulting growth of mass political parties would help erase national distinctions, at least in the Austrian half, was not fulfilled. Mass political parties, such as Victor Adler's Austrian Social Democrats or the Christian Socialists, continued to reflect national divisions in spite of their common social or religious appeals. In pre-war Austria, national loyalties far outweighed the common bonds of social class or religious affiliation, and prevented supranational allegiance to the dynasty or monarchy from taking root. Not without justification could a Czech Reichsrat deputy exclaim during the First World War: "I only know of a Czech, a Polish, a Ruthenian (Ukrainian), an Italian, a Yugoslav patriotism. . . . An Austrian patriotism is an artificially encouraged plant."

Far from becoming an agent of national reconciliation, the Vienna Reichsrat developed into a sounding board of discontent, in which national passions led to bitter verbal and physical clashes. In March, 1914, several months before the outbreak of the First World War, the Reichsrat was suspended and the government forced to govern by emergency decree under Article 14 of the Austrian Constitution.

The irredentist pull of South Slavs, who looked towards Serbia, of Rumanians and Italians, who expected liberation from their fellow nationals across the border, and of Czechs, who demanded equality with Austro-Germans, might have been countered by a thoroughgoing reform of the Habsburg monarchy along federal-ethnic lines. Proposals of this kind were not wanting in pre-war Austria, coming from such well-intentioned men as the pro-Habsburg Rumanian Aurel Popovici and Karl Renner, the leader of the moderate wing of Austrian Social Democracy. Aurel Popovici proposed a "United States of Greater Austria," to consist of fifteen federal states. Renner's reform proposals added the novel concept of "personal cultural autonomy" for the citizen regardless of his place of residence within the monarchy. Austrian socialists, such as Karl Renner, were even optimistic that Austria, once she had solved her own nationality problem, could point the way towards a general solution of the European nationality problem, a key source of pre-war instability and tension.

The failure of Emperor Francis Joseph, who had been on the throne since 1848, to grant autonomy to all major ethnic blocs was rooted not merely in the immobility of old age but in formidable political obstacles as well. Chief among the latter was the Hungarian veto against any alteration of the 1867 *status quo* and the fact that the national divisions ran among the Slavs as well as between the German-Magyar bloc and other nationalities. The Austro-Poles, though anxious to secure autonomy for themselves, opposed its extension to the Austro-Ukrainians, who lived in varying degrees of exploitation under Polish rule. Francis Ferdinand, heir to the Habsburg Empire, had given promise of breaking the Hungarian veto against the changing of the dualist system of 1867, by force if necessary. Whatever plans for reform he may have entertained were cut short by his assassination by a Yugoslav nationalist on June 28, 1914.

THE IMPACT OF THE WAR; 1917, THE YEAR OF LOST OPPORTUNITIES

The Austrian government, forewarned by pre-war strife among the nationalities, responded to the outbreak of war by tightening its police and military controls over the non-German nationalities. The Reichsrat in Vienna remained closed, the parliament in Budapest, still under the safe control of the Magyar oligarchy and Prime Minister Stephen Tisza, remained open. In spite of many provocations, such as the German characterization of the First World War as a life-and-death struggle between Slavs and Germans, the Slavic peoples of Austria-Hungary showed a surprising degree of dynastic loyalty in the first two years of the war.

Beginning in November, 1916, several decisive changes at home and abroad disrupted the domestic tranquility of the Dual Monarchy. With the death of Emperor Francis Joseph in November, 1916, the most venerable symbol of unity among the nationalities disappeared. Although widely criticized for his pedantic personality and bureaucratic approach to the emotional issue of nationalism, Francis Joseph was held in high esteem by Slavs, Magyars, and Germans alike, partly because of his stoical attitude towards the many personal misfortunes of his long reign. The Emperor's son, Rudolf, had committed suicide in 1889, and the Empress Elizabeth had been assassinated in 1898, as was the Emperor's nephew and successor to the throne, Francis Ferdinand, in 1914.

The ascension of Charles I, youthful, optimistic, and yet unmarred by any personal encounter with the national dilemma of Austria-Hungary, aroused widespread hope for sweeping change at home and for peace with the Allies. The mood of expectation among the nationalities was strengthened in 1917 by the double impact of the Russian March revolution and the entry of the United States into World War I. Encouraged by the liberal nationality policy of the Kerensky government and the democratic promise of the American nation, many of whose citizens had emigrated from the Dual Monarchy, the Habsburg nationalities confidently awaited a great liberating gesture of the new ruler.

Charles I, though well-intentioned, lacked the fortitude which the solution of the nationality problem in the midst of war and the securing of a compromise peace with the Allies would have required. Both his domestic and foreign policy initiatives, launched in 1917, soon ended up as half measures, earning for the new monarch the reputation of duplicity among friend and foe alike. By 1917 the issues of peace and internal reform had become inextricably interrelated. Austria's failure to withdraw from the war raised the specter of the Allies' championing the cause of liberation of the Habsburg nationalities. In January, 1917, the Allies, responding to Wilson's inquiry about their war aims, had spoken of the "liberation of Italians, of Slavs, of Rumanians and Czecho-Slovaks from foreign domination." In view of Germany's uncompromising attitude on the question of a compromise peace with the Allies, a separate peace seemed Austria-Hungary's only hope of extricating the Habsburg monarchy from the war essentially intact. The temptation to seek a separate peace had become all the greater for Austria-Hungary at the turn of 1917/1918, because of Russia's collapse. Since tsarist Russia had been Austria-Hungary's chief enemy, its collapse seemed to open the path to a negotiated peace with the western Powers, with which the Habsburgs did not have a real quarrel before 1914.

The several peace feelers which Emperor Charles sent out before the spring of 1918, notably through his brother-in-law Prince Sixtus of Bourbon-Parma, came to nothing because of the conditions set by the Allies and because Germany strengthened its grip on the Habsburg monarchy when news of Charles's efforts for a separate peace leaked out. Having missed the opportunity to gain a separate peace by rejecting Italian territorial demands, Emperor Charles had to submit to far-reaching German control in the Spa Agreement of May 12, 1918, with Emperor William II. The Spa Agreement deprived the Habsburg monarchy of the last semblance of independence by subordinating Austria-Hungary's economic, military, and foreign policy decisions to German leadership and interest.

Charles' domestic policies were equally vacillating and indecisive. To placate the non-German nationalities of Austria, the Emperor reopened the Reichsrat in May, 1917, and issued a political amnesty for imprisoned leaders of the nationalities, such as the Czech patriot Karel Kramar. The Emperor's freedom to effect sweeping changes in the dualist system of 1867 was limited from the start, however, when Charles took the oath to uphold the Ausgleich during the coronation ceremonies in Budapest in December, 1916.

The Emperor's failure to follow up the reconvening of the Reichsrat with grants of national autonomy to the Slavs, quickly changed the latter's mood from hopeful expectation into bitter opposition. As late as January, 1917, the Czech Reichsrat deputies had disassociated themselves from the Allied aim of liberating "the Czecho-Slovaks from foreign domination" and had reaffirmed their loyalty to the Habsburg dynasty. After a year of disappointment, the same Czech deputies demanded, in the so-called Epiphany Resolution of January 6, 1918, the "union of the Czech nation with the Slovaks in a state enjoying complete independence and possessing all the attributes of sovereignty." The Reichsrat had returned to its customary pre-war turmoil, in which Slavic and German deputies traded insults and blows. "In a menagerie," an Austro-German Reichsrat deputy thundered, "one does not go to work with promises but with a whip."

The Austro-Poles were thoroughly disillusioned with the new monarch when Austria-Hungary submitted to German pressures during the negotiations at Brest-Litovsk. In the separate peace between the Central Powers and the Ukraine, Germany awarded the Cholm district, with a heavy Polish population, to the Ukraine in the expectation of large Ukrainian grain deliveries.

Torn by the strife of nationalities and critically short of food supplies for its large cities, the Dual Monarchy in early 1918 resembled tsarist Russia on the eve of the March revolution of 1917. By early 1918 Austria's food shortage led the government to seize grain shipments destined for Germany. Textiles were in such short supply that the authorities recommeded the burial of the dead without clothes. As in Germany, the cutting of the food rations in January, 1918, precipitated major strikes among industrial workers, which engulfed the two capitals, Vienna and Budapest, as well as numerous other industrial centers, and led to the formation of workers' soviets. Although the strikes of January, 1918, were suppressed, they were followed in early February by a naval mutiny at the Kotor naval base in the Adriatic. The Kotor naval mutiny was inspired by both left-wing socialist and nationalist revolutionaries, with Czech, South Slav, Polish, and Italian sailors of the Austro-Hungarian navy playing a prominent part in the formation of a sailors' central soviet. Soon after the government's suppression of the Kotor mutiny, Slavic nationalist demonstrations and anti-Habsburg rallies swept the monarchy. In May, 1918, the Czech National Theater festivities in Prague turned into a mass demonstration of Czech-Yugoslav solidarity in the struggle against the dynasty. In August, 1918, a Pan-Slav congress of Slovenes, Czechs, and Poles in Ljubljana gave further proof of the growing power of the Slavic independence movement within the Dual Monarchy

To stamp out the fires of mutiny and national revolution, often set by returning prisoners of war from Russia, the government was forced to draw increasingly on its military reserves. Of the Austro-Hungarian troops set free by the Peace of Brest Litovsk, a full seven divisions were diverted to the home front for policing purposes. By the summer of 1918 the Habsburg armies were waging a two-front war against the foreign enemy and the rising tide of national and social revolution at home.

THE PREPARATION OF NATIONAL INDEPENDENCE BY THE EXILE LEADERS

As long as there appeared a possibility of persuading Emperor Charles into signing a separate peace with the Allies, the Allied governments had generally spoken with caution on the subject of Austro-Hungarian dismemberment. As late as January, 1918, Lloyd George had declared that the break-up of the Austro-Hungarian Empire was "no part of our war aims," and Wilson's call for the "freest opportunity for autonomous development" for the peoples of Austria-Hungary under Point 10 of the Fourteen Points was still compatible with the federalization of the Habsburg monarchy.

Only after the failure of Austro-Allied peace talks and under the impact of the powerful Ludendorff offensive, which threatened to overwhelm the Allied front in France, did the hard-pressed Allied governments take up the cause of Austro-Hungarian dismemberment. Just as the

German Supreme Command had hastened the collapse of tsarist Russia by exploiting its nationality strife, the Allies hoped to shatter the multinational Habsburg army by advocating independence for the Slavs.

The shift in Allied policy focused attention on the exiled leaders of the Habsburg Slavs, who had agitated for the dismemberment of Austria-Hungary through national committees and councils in the Allied capitals almost from the outset of the war. Before Russia's collapse some Slavic leaders, such as Karel Kramar in Bohemia or Roman Dmowski, the Polish National Democrat, had looked towards Russia as the liberator of the Habsburg Slavs in the tradition of 19th-century Pan-Slavism. After the Bolshevik coup, however, the center of secessionist and independence propaganda shifted to the capitals of the western Allies, Paris becoming the site of the Czech National Council and the Polish National Committee, London the site of the South Slav Committee

The organizers of the exiles' committees and councils were invariably men of scholarly or artistic distinction who pursued the cause of national liberation with skill and stubbornness in the face of great obstacles. For the better part of the First World War, the exiles could be certain neither of majority support among their fellow nationals in Austria-Hungary nor of ultimate Allied endorsement of their aims. Leading among the Czech and Slovak exiles were Jan Masaryk, Eduard Benes, and the Slovak Colonel Milan Stefanik, who had fought on Russia's side until 1917. Ante Trumbic headed the South Slav Committee, while Ignace Paderewski, the world famous Polish pianist, won influential friends and supporters for the cause of Polish independence in the United States.

Even before the Allied shift in policy on the issue of Austro-Hungarian dismemberment, the cause of Czechoslovak and South Slav independence had received vigorous support from Wickham Steed, the foreign editor of the London *Times,* and Hugh Seton-Watson, historian and leading British expert on Austria-Hungary and editor of the periodical *New Europe.* To Wickham Steed the Dual Monarchy was a "carcass suffocating within the wrinkles of its parchment a number of young peoples striving to be born." Both Steed and Seton-Watson regarded the Dual Monarchy as little more than a tool of German imperialism in eastern Europe and hoped that the Slavic peoples of Austria-Hungary, once emancipated, would form a federation for the containment of German power. In their capacity as advisers to Lord Northcliffe, the Director of Propaganda in the British Ministry of Information, both men wielded considerable influence in the shaping of British public opinion and policy.

Between the summers of 1917 and 1918, the exiles made extensive preparations of their own in expectation of national independence. In July, 1917, the Serbian prime minister, Pasic, issued the Declaration of Corfu together with Ante Trumbic of the South Slav Committee, pledging the equality of Croats and Slovenes with the Serbs in a future Yugoslav kingdom. Jan Masaryk sponsored the Treaty of Pittsburgh, Pennsylvania, in May, 1918, in which the Slovaks were promised equal status with the Czechs in the projected Czechoslovak state. To overcome Italian opposition to the union of the South Slavs, which conflicted with Italian claims on Dalmatia, Wickham Steed organized the Rome Congress of Oppressed Nationalities in April, 1918. Attended by Poles, Czechs, South Slavs, Rumanians, and Italians, as well as French officials, the Rome Congress was also designed to impress the Allied governments with the exiles' unity and to win Allied recognition of their aims. The Rome Congress thus petitioned the Allied governments to admit as combatants "all those expressing their desire to be liberated from the German-Magyar yoke and made independent states." Although the Congress achieved the publicity it desired, it failed to reconcile the conflicting territorial claims of the nationalities represented. The question of Dalmatia remained unsettled between Italians and South Slavs, as did the rival claims between Czechs and Poles, Rumanians and Czechs, and South Slavs and Rumanians. Seton-Watson's hope for a Slavic federation seemed doomed before the Habsburg monarchy began to fall apart.

ALLIED RECOGNITION OF THE EXILES' AIMS

The Polish exiles were the first to secure Allied recognition of their goals, largely through Paderewski's effort in the United States. As early as January, 1917, President Wilson had announced that "statesmen everywhere are agreed that there should be a united independent and autonomous Poland." In January, 1918, the President called, under Point 13 of his Fourteen Points, for the establishment of "an independent Polish state," including "the territories inhabited by indisputably Polish populations, which should be assured a free and secure access to the sea. . . ."

Whereas the United States had taken the lead in recognizing Polish independence, France was first to accord the Czech National Council in Paris recognition, on June 28, 1918. After British and American recognition had also been secured, Eduard Benes announced the formation of a provisional Czechoslovak government in Paris.

With Italy's declaration of September 9, 1918, that the liberation of the Yugoslavs was in harmony with Allied war aims, the chief obstacle to the union of Serbs, Croats, and Slovenes appeared removed.

Of great significance in securing recognition for the nationalities was their military contribution to the Allied cause through the formation of volunteer units, recruited mostly from deserters and prisoners of the Habsburg armies. These units fought side by side with Allied armies in Italy and France, and, through their sacrifice in blood, established the exiles' claim to co-belligerent status. Most spectacular among the exiles' armies was the Czech Legion, recruited from Habsburg prisoners of war in Russia. Originally scheduled for repatriation to the west after the Bolshevik revolution, the Legion soon became involved in the Russian civil war and fought the Bolsheviks successfully in Siberia. By retaining command over the Czech Legion in Russia, the Czech exiles in Paris gained new significance in the eyes of Allied military leaders, who wished to use the well-armed and disciplined Czech Legion to crush the Bolshevik regime. In the summer of 1918 Jan Masaryk even referred to himself as "master of Siberia."

LAST EFFORTS OF AUSTRIA-HUNGARY TO PRESERVE THE HABSBURG EMPIRE

While the exiles were forming governments in the Allied capitals, Emperor Charles tried to stave off the disintegration of his monarchy through last-minute appeals for a separate peace and promises of major concessions to the nationalities. Both moves came far too late and offered far too little to influence the attitude of the Allies or that of the Slavic nationalities of Austria-Hungary. The appeal of the Austro-Hungarian foreign minister, Burian, on September 14, 1918, to all belligerents for a confidential exchange of peace conditions remained without effect. The Austrian request for an armistice based on the Fourteen Points, sent to President Wilson on October 4, 1918, was answered by the President on October 20 with the reply that, not the President, but the nationalities of Austria-Hungary must be the judges of what action on the part of the Austro-Hungarian government will satisfy their aspirations. Wilson's shift from mere autonomy to full independence for the nationalities of Austria-Hungary had been foreshadowed by the President's Mount Vernon speech of July 4, 1918, in which he had rejected "compromise" and "half-way decisions" as a solution of the Habsburg nationality problem.

The October Manifesto, issued by Emperor Charles on October 16, 1918, which promised a federal reorganization of the Dual Monarchy was, in fact, no more than a "half-way decision." The Manifesto proposed the establishment of a federal union of Austro-Germans, Czechs, South Slavs, and Ukrainians. Austro-Poland (Galicia) was to be united with a free Poland and the port of Triest, with its large Italian population, granted special status. Significantly, Hungary and its Rumanian and Slavic subjects were not to be included in the proposed federalization, since the Magyars, even at this late stage, were adamantly opposed to any relaxation of their discriminatory nationality policy.

Against the background of the nationality strife at home and the success of the exile politicians abroad, the October Manifesto came as an anti-climax. In view of its limited application to the Austrian half of the monarchy, it would not even have satisfied the Slavic nationalities in May, 1917, when their mood was still predominantly loyal to the Habsburg dynasty. Not without humor, a leading American newspaper referred to the October Manifesto of Emperor Charles as "a worthy production in the home of musical comedy." By October, 1918, the Slavs of the Dual Monarchy demanded not autonomy but, in the words of the Czech nationalist leader Frantisek Stanek, a "front of Slav states to extend from Danzig by way of Prague to the Adriatic."

THE COURSE OF NATIONAL REVOLUTIONS IN THE DUAL MONARCHY

The October Manifesto acted as a signal for the exile leaders to join forces with those who had agitated for independence from within the Dual Monarchy. Beginning in October, 1918, national committees sprang up in the Czech, Slovak, Polish, South Slav, and Rumanian parts of the Dual Monarchy, which either proclaimed their national independence in conjunction with the exile leaders or united with adjacent countries of their fellow nationals. The national committees thus not only aided in the union of exile and home leaders of the various independence movements but of political parties of varying social and ideological background as well. In so doing, the national committees helped to contain the threat of social revolution, which might otherwise have engulfed the Danube Basin under Bolshevik influence, and to assure the predominantly bourgeois and national character of the revolution in Austria-Hungary.

The transfer of power from the old Habsburg authorities was accomplished peacefully in most cases and without serious opposition, partly because the Habsburg authorities often believed that the national committees were merely implementing the October Manifesto of Emperor Charles rather than seeking full independence. Hungary alone resisted the transfer of power and had to be forced into yielding its Slovak, South Slav, and Rumanian provinces to the successor states.

CZECHOSLOVAK INDEPENDENCE

Following Masaryk's declaration of Czechoslovak independence in Paris on October 21, 1918, the Czech National Committee, constituted in Prague, adopted the "Law on the establishment of an independent Czechoslovak state" on October 28. A Slovak National Committee thereupon declared its linguistic, cultural, and historical solidarity with the Czechoslovak nation. On October 30, 1918, the Austrian Premier, Lammasch, acknowledged the *fait accompli* of Czechoslovak independence when he greeted the Czech envoy, Vlastimil Tusar, with the words: "I take pleasure in welcoming you as ambassador of the Czechoslovak state," to which Tusar replied: "The pleasure is all mine."

Following negotiations between Czech exiles and Prague political leaders in Switzerland, a new Czechoslovak government, consisting of representatives of both, was formed with Jan Masaryk as president, Karel Kramar as prime minister, and Benes as minister of foreign affairs.

POLAND

The formation of an independent Poland did not proceed as swiftly and smoothly as the Union of Czechs and Slovaks, mainly because the rapport between Polish exile leaders and Polish patriots at home was not as strong and partly because of the opposition of the Austro-Ukrainians (Ruthenians) to their inclusion in the new Poland. Leading in the union of the "three parts of Poland" were the Regents Council of Warsaw, installed by the Central Powers in 1916, Joseph Pilsudski, who had fought on the Central Power side against Russia until his imprisonment in Germany in 1917, the newly constituted National Committee in Cracow, and the Polish National Committee in Paris under Roman Dmowski. The Cracow National Committee took over power from the Austrian authorities in Galicia through a Commission of Liquidation, while the Warsaw Regency Council entrusted Pilsudski with the formation of a Polish government on November 14, 1918. The reconciliation between Pilsudski's forces and those of the Paris National Committee was not accomplished until the beginning of 1919 when Paderewski formed a new coalition government with Pilsudski as chief of state and Dmowski as foreign minister.

Efforts of Ukrainian nationalists to establish a "Ukrainian Peoples' Government" in the eastern part of Austrian Galicia were crushed by Pilsudski's forces with the seizure of Lvov on November 22, 1918. In east and west, Poland's frontiers remained fluid, however, and awaited the final verdict of the Paris Peace Conference. The border dispute with the new German republic was foreshadowed by armed clashes in West Prussia which led to the severing of diplomatic relations with Germany on December 19, 1918.

THE KINGDOM OF SERBS,
CROATS, AND SLOVENES

South Slav secession from the Dual Monarchy began with the formation of a national committee by Serbs, Croats, and Slovenes in Zagreb on October 6, 1918, which repudiated the October Manifesto of Emperor Charles. On October 30, 1918, the Croat Diet of Zagreb cut all ties with the Dual Monarchy and declared the former Habsburg South Slav provinces to be part of the "state of the Serbs, Croats, and Slovenes." On November 1, 1918, the Zagreb National Committee took over Bosnia and Hertsegovina and for a while also gained control over the Austro-Hungarian navy before its seizure by Italian forces. Having retaken the

Serbian capital of Belgrade, the Serbian army restored Prince Regent Alexander, who proclaimed the formation of a Yugoslav kingdom on December 1, 1918, following the union with Montenegro on November 19. The new Yugoslav government under premier Protic included Trumbic from the London South Slav Committee and the two representatives of the Zagreb National Committee, Korosec and Pribicevic As in the case of Poland, the final drawing of Yugoslavia's frontiers with her neighbors, Austria, Italy, Hungary, and Rumania, awaited the decision of the Paris peace conference.

RUMANIA

Rumania, like Poland, reaped substantial benefits from the collapse of both the Russian and the Austro-Hungarian empires. Having seized Bessarabia from Russia in the wake of the Bolshevik revolution, Rumania supported its irredenta in eastern Hungary and Transylvania as the end of the Dual Monarchy approached. After the establishment of a Rumanian National Committee in Arad in October, 1918, Maniu, the leader of the Rumanian independence party in Hungary, demanded the union of Transylvania with Rumania. A Rumanian national assembly, convened at Alba Julia on December 1, 1918, effected the union with the aid of Allied forces under the command of General Henri Berthelot. The union of the Bukovina, a Habsburg province with a mixed Rumanian-Ukrainian population, and Rumania was declared on November 28, 1918, by a Rumanian National Committee formed at Cernauti Rumanian-Yugoslav rival claims on the Banat, promised in its entirety to Rumania in the Bucharest Treaty of April, 1918, were not resolved until 1919, with the partitioning of the Banat into a Rumanian and Yugoslav part.

GERMAN-AUSTRIA

Concurrently with the establishment of national committees in various parts of the Dual Monarchy, a Provisional National Assembly was formed in Vienna of Austro-German Reichsrat deputies on October 21, 1918. Heinrich Lammasch, the last imperial prime minister, and Count Julius Andrassy, the foreign minister, were mainly concerned with the orderly liquidation of the Empire and the securing of an armistice for the multinational Habsburg army, still fighting in Italy as national revolutions were spreading in its rear. Julius Andrassy, in a last futile effort of winning the Allies' sympathy, severed the Dual Alliance with the German empire on October 27, 1918, almost exactly thirty-nine years after its conclusions by Andrassy's father and Bismarck. On November 3, 1918, the Allies signed a separate armistice with the Habsburg monarchy at Villa Giusti near Padua, when the Dual Monarchy had, in fact, ceased to exist. Hungary, which had recalled its troops from the Italian front on October 24, 1918, signed a separate agreement with the Allies on November 13 at Belgrade. So sweeping were the terms of Habsburg surrender that Clemenceau, when informed of them, remarked that the only condition omitted was the demand for Emperor Charles's breeches.

On October 30, 1918, the Provisional National Assembly in Vienna had proclaimed the establishment of a state of German-Austria, which also claimed sovereignty over the German-speaking portions of Bohemia and Moravia, the "Sudeten provinces." On November 11, 1918, Emperor Charles I, now dubbed "Charles the Last" by the Viennese, signed his abdication and soon went into Swiss exile. After several unsuccessful attempts at a political comeback in Hungary, he died in exile on Madeira in 1922. Following the abdication of Charles the Vienna National Assembly proclaimed Austria a republic and sought admission into the German republic by a unanimous vote. Although neither Britain nor the United States had serious objections to the *Anschluss* of Austria and Germany, France soon vetoed it emphatically. Karl Renner, the moderate Austrian Social Democrat formed the first provisional government of the Austrian republic, with the support of all Austro-German parties of the former Reichsrat.

HUNGARY

In Hungary both national and social revolution swept aside the Magyar oligarchy which had resisted national emancipation of the Slavs and the democratization of the Hungarian government to the bitter end. Symbolic of Magyar reaction was the statement of Count Stephen Tisza, Hungarian prime minister until May, 1917: "Radical tendencies must be resisted, even if the wheel of universal history passes over the body of him who resists." Equally symbolic of the change ushered in by the revolution was Tisza's assassination in October, 1918.

On October 31, 1918, a new Hungarian government emerged under Count Michael Karolyi from a Hungarian National Council, established on October 25 out of liberal and Social Democratic forces. On November 16, 1918, Karolyi disbanded the parliament in Budapest, proclaimed a Hungarian republic and severed all ties with Austria. Although a foe of aristocratic privilege and a sincere advocate of democratic and social reform, Karolyi's Magyar nationalism differed little from that of earlier Hungarian governments. While spearheading a Hungarian social revolution Karolyi hoped to stave off national revolutions of Slavs and Rumanians in Hungary and to preserve the territorial integrity of pre-war Hungary. The vision of an "eastern Switzerland" was short lived, however, with the secession of Slovaks, South Slavs and Rumanians accomplished between October and November, 1918. It was Karolyi's failure to prevent the break-up of the old Hungary that undermined his popularity and forced his resignation in March, 1919, followed by the launching of the soviet dictatorship of Bela Kun and Garbai.

THE PROMISE AND THE PROBLEMS OF
THE "SUCCESSOR STATES"

The collapse of the three empires of eastern and central Europe, Russia, Germany and the Dual Monarchy, at the end of the First World War seemed to signal the triumph of the western ideals of democracy and national independence over reaction and national oppression in the vast corridor formed by the "successor states" from Finland to the Balkans. The joy of national emancipation of peoples who had, for centuries, lived under foreign domination outweighed and overshadowed all other long-range consequences of the collapse of the three eastern empires.

The viability of the new states of north and central eastern Europe and the peace of the entire region from the Baltic to the Adriatic depended, however, on the measure of mutual cooperation between the "successor states" and the backing which the western democracies were willing to give. Even at the time of their birth the new states showed signs of bickering, however, over rival border claims which rendered hopes of regional associations illusory from the beginning. Moreover, the union even of affiliated nationalities, such as that of the Czechs and Slovaks, or of Croats, Slovenes and Serbs failed to put to rest the old strife among the nationalities as a result of the leadership claims of one Slavic nationality over another. Economically, the passing of the Dual Monarchy spelled the break up of a large common market with a sound industrial-agricultural balance, and its replacement by the separate national economies of the successor states, divided by tariff walls and barriers.

The Austro-Hungarian empire, an old Austrian proverb claimed, was but the reflection of the world at large in microcosm. Only time could tell, whether the failure of the Dual Monarchy to solve its nationality problem reflected also the world's inability to cope with the problem of 20th-century nationalism.

5 | The Attempt at Building a New Political Order for Europe and the World

THE ARMISTICE OF NOVEMBER 11, 1918

The armistice agreements with Bulgaria at Salonika on September 30, 1918, with Turkey at Mudros on October 30, and with Austria-Hungary at Padua on November 3, had presented few difficulties to the Allies, as none of the lesser Central Powers was in a condition to insist on surrender terms of their choosing. At the time of the armistice, large parts of the Ottoman Empire were under Allied occupation; the Dual Monarchy of Austria-Hungary had, in fact, ceased to exist by early November, 1918. In none of these armistice agreements were President Wilson's Fourteen Points mentioned as a basis for peace. The United States took no part in the armistice agreements with Bulgaria and Turkey since war had not been declared between these two countries and the U.S. The appeal of Austria-Hungary to the United States of October 4, 1918, to arrange for an armistice on the basis of the Fourteen Points had been declined on the grounds that the nationalities of Austria-Hungary must themselves be "the judges of what action on the part of the Austro-Hungarian government will satisfy their aspirations."

The German appeal to the United States of October 3, 1918, which asked the United States to arrange an armistice on the basis of Wilson's Fourteen Points, raised, by contrast, serious problems in American-Allied relations as well as within the United States. The reaction of the Allied and Associated Powers to the German armistice request was of two kinds: American military leaders, notably generals Bliss and Pershing, opposed a negotiated armistice with Germany on the grounds that it would obscure the fact of German military defeat. Since this defeat was taken for granted by the U.S. Army, Bliss and Pershing advocated an Allied occupation of Berlin, to be followed by a dictated armistice. The sentiment was shared, from all available evidence, by a significant part of the American public as well as many leaders of the Republican Party. Theodore Roosevelt, for one, preferred a peace dictated by "hammering guns" to the "chatting about peace" accompanied by clicking typewriters.

The military leaders of France and Britain, Foch and Haig, were less sanguine about the fact of German military defeat than were

141

their American counterparts. At the time of the German armistice request, no German territory of significant size had been conquered; although the number of German prisoners had sharply risen in September, 1918, the German lines remained unbroken. The German army seemed to have enough strength left to inflict new heavy casualties on the Allies. Foch favored an early armistice, on condition that it would render the resumption of German hostilities impossible.

Although President Wilson was aware of the popular currents against a negotiated armistice, he decided to accept the German initiative in order to prevent further bloodshed. As it was transparent that the government of the German Empire had discovered the virtues of the Fourteen Points only in the hour of approaching defeat, the President insisted on the destruction of the "arbitrary power" which had "hitherto controlled the German Nation." The outbreak of the German revolution, discussed previously, and the resulting abdication of William II on November 9, 1918, gave promise of a fundamental change in the political and constitutional make-up of Germany. To Germany, the Fourteen Points were a decided advantage in defeat because they offered the likelihood of peace conditions far more agreeable than those which Britain and France might draw up by themselves. Conversely, the European Allies of the United States, as well as Japan, had cause to fear the adoption of the Fourteen Points as a formal basis of peace, since the Wilsonian peace concept clashed in many respects with the Allied war aims under the secret treaties. Through the American initiative in armistice negotiations, the Fourteen Points changed from an instrument of Allied war propaganda into a basis for peace negotiations. As such, they aroused resentment among the Allies, giving rise to reservations and protest. Britain, whose blockade against Germany had been decisive in the German defeat, objected to Point II, concerning "absolute freedom of navigation upon the seas . . . alike in peace and war." Both Britain and France entertained serious reservations on Point V, concerning "a free, open-minded, and absolutely impartial adjustment of all colonial claims." Italy, having been promised territory that was not purely Italian in ethnic composition in the Treaty of London of 1915, took exception to Point IX, which pledged the readjustment of Italian frontiers "along clearly recognizable lines of nationality."

Not until after the United States had threatened to sign a separate armistice with Germany did the Allies agree to the Fourteen Points as a basis for peace, subject to two reservations: first, Britain reserved judgment on the principle of the freedom of the seas; and, second, reparations, covered only in a general manner in the Fourteen Points, were defined as "compensation made by Germany for all damage done to the civilian population of the Allies and their property by the aggression by Germany by land, by sea, and from the air." On November 5, 1918,

U.S. Secretary of State Robert Lansing informed Germany of the Allied acceptance of the Fourteen Points subject to these two reservations. The Lansing note of November 5 and the affirmative German reply came to be known as the Pre-Armistice Agreement between Germany and the Allied and Associated Powers. On the German side, the Pre-Armistice Agreement gave rise to false hopes of an easy peace. Such hopes were strengthened by the orderly return of the German army from occupied territories after the Armistice and the lack of visible signs of defeat in the field. To a large segment of the German public, Germany had not ceased fighting because of dire necessity but because of her free consent to a negotiated peace, proposed by the impartial President of the United States. The German Provisional Government, emerging from the revolutionary turmoil of November 9, 1918, was both too preoccupied with internal problems and too dependent on the German High Command in its struggle against Communist insurrection, to give sober warning to the German public. Having been ill-informed about the true state of the war by the German High Command before October, 1918, the German public remained unenlightened about the nature of the peace it might expect. An Allied invasion of Germany, as advocated by generals Bliss and Pershing in October, 1918, may well have eased the task of making and enforcing the peace with Germany.

THE TERMS OF THE ARMISTICE

The actual drafting of the Armistice terms was left chiefly to French military and British naval experts. Consistent with the American and Allied aim of denying Germany the means of resuming hostilities, the Armistice demanded the surrender of huge quantities of arms, and rail and motor transport, as well as of all German submarines, and the bulk of the German surface fleet. Germany was to surrender "in good condition" 5,000 pieces of artillery, 25,000 machine guns, 3,000 mortars, and 1,700 military aircraft. German troops were to be evacuated within two weeks, not only from Belgium, France, Luxembourg, and Alsace-Lorraine, but from the left (western) bank of the Rhine as well. Allied troops, in addition to occupying the left bank of the Rhine, would move into the three principal Rhine crossings at Mainz, Koblenz, and Cologne and occupy bridgeheads of twenty miles depth on the right bank. All Allied prisoners were to be returned without reciprocity. The Allied blockade against Germany was not lifted. After the Armistice it became, in fact, more severe, owing to the free access of Allied war ships into the Baltic, previously closed by German naval power. Allied food shipments into Germany did not begin until March, 1919, owing less to a deliberate Allied attempt to worsen the critical food situation in Germany than to the difficulty of agreeing on the means of payment and transportation.

In its Eastern provisions, the Armistice declared the German peace treaties of Brest-Litovsk with Russia and of Bucharest with Rumania null and void. Although the Armistice demanded German troop withdrawal from all occupied territory of the former tsarist Empire in principle, it left the date of withdrawal to Allied discretion, because of the unsettled conditions of the Russian Civil War.

On November 11, 1918, a German armistice delegation, headed by the civilian Mathias Erzberger, accepted the Allied terms in the railroad coach of Marshall Foch in the forest of Compiègne. The coach, soon to be turned into a French national shrine, was used by Germany on June 22, 1940, for the signing of another armistice, imposed on fallen France by Hitler after the Battle of France.

THE ORGANIZATION OF THE PEACE CONFERENCE

The choice of Paris as the site of the Peace Conference, though logical in recognition of French sacrifices in the Allied cause, was not welcome on all sides. Britain would have preferred a neutral city, preferably Swiss, to shield the Peace Conference from the pressures of an inflamed public and of an inquisitive press corps, which France could and did use as a sounding board for her official position in the peace negotiations. To British and American delegates, who had not shared the French experience of living under German guns for four years, the Paris of 1919 seemed a "shell-shocked" city, a place ill-suited to the drafting of a peace designed to look beyond the passions of the war. Moreover, the choice of Paris as host city of the Peace Conference virtually assured the election of the French Prime Minister Clemenceau as President of the Conference, with all the power of initiative and leadership implied by this role.

From the beginning of the Peace Conference on January 18, 1919, its proceedings and decisions were dominated by the five Great Powers, the United States, Britain, France, Italy, and Japan. The Big Five organized the Council of Ten (or Supreme Council), composed of President Wilson, the Prime Ministers of Britain, France, and Italy — Lloyd George, Clemenceau, and Orlando — and the Japanese representative, Marquis Kimmochi Saionji — as well as their senior assistants. In due course, the Council of Ten was changed into the Council of Four, consisting of Wilson, Lloyd George, Clemenceau, and Orlando only, owing to the preoccupation of the western powers with European issues. When Orlando staged his dramatic walkout from the Conference in April, 1919, over the issue of Fiume, the Council of Four became the Council of Three, which determined the major questions of the peace with Germany.

The lesser Allied powers not unnaturally resented their virtual exclusion from the decision-making process of the Conference. The business of "getting things done," in Clemenceau's words, could not be accomplished, however, by the unwieldy body of the plenary session, consisting of all thirty-two Allied and Associated powers. The plenary session, called only six times during the Conference, thus merely recorded the decisions reached in the more than 140 meetings of the Council of Four (and Three). Clemenceau dismissed the protests of the smaller Allies with the assertion that the Big Five represented twelve million armed men; were it not for the concept of the League of Nations, the French Prime Minister added, the Great Powers might not even have invited the small powers.

Initially it had been planned to limit the task of the Paris Peace Conference to the drafting of a preliminary peace only, containing essential territorial and reparation provisions. The preliminary peace was to be imposed on Germany; the remaining provisions of the settlement were to be worked out in a final peace, negotiated between the Allied and Associated Powers on the one hand and the defeated Central Powers on the other. The official title of the Paris Peace Conference remained, in fact, that of Preliminary Conference of the Allied and Associated Powers. The idea of expanding the Peace Conference into a peace congress by admitting enemy representatives was soon abandoned. There were several reasons for this decision. The admission of a German delegate, it was feared, would add to the divisions among the Allies; Germany was not to profit from the quarrels among the victors, as Talleyrand had benefitted from the divisions of the Congress of Vienna. Moreover, France feared that peace-making in two stages would ease the pressure on Germany as Allied troops were being demobilized, and Wilson feared that a delayed peace settlement would sidetrack the League of Nations covenant, which he considered to be the heart of the entire peace. The Treaty of Versailles, originally drafted as a basis for negotiations with Germany, was thus presented as a final treaty of peace to Germany on May 7, 1919. Although Germany was permitted to reply to the treaty in writing and although she managed to secure some changes in this manner, the Treaty of Versailles was essentially not a negotiated peace.

Negotiations among the Great Powers at the Peace Conference were conducted in secret, except when it suited Clemenceau to release confidential information to the French press in order to rally French public opinion on a controversial issue. President Wilson also broke the rule of secrecy, when he aired the American-Italian controversy over Fiume in an appeal to the press on April 23, 1919. The press of Britain and the United States, taking notice of the fact of secrecy, charged Wilson with having violated the first of his Fourteen Points, calling for "open covenants of peace, openly arrived at." The charge was not without importance in the United States, where Wilson's failure to inform the public and the Congress on the details of his proposed League had increased distrust of the President's mission to Europe.

The element of time had a great bearing, not only on procedure, but on the substance of the peace. The delay in opening the Peace Conference until January 18, 1919, was due in part to the British elections on December 14, 1918, in which Prime Minister Lloyd George won a resounding victory on the strength of his promise to make Germany pay the full cost of the war. President Wilson, journeying to Europe on the *George Washington,* a former German transatlantic liner, did not arrive in France until December 13, 1918. Upon his arrival, Wilson spent several weeks touring the Allied capitals of Europe. Wherever the President went, he was given an enthusiastic reception, being greeted as "Wilson the Just" in France and "God of Peace" in Italy. The almost religious fervor with which the masses of Europe received the American President was a highly gratifying experience for Wilson, since it confirmed his own conviction that he, rather than the hard-boiled politicians of France, England, and Italy, truly embodied the hopes of Europe for a better future. However, his reception was more an expression of European gratitude for American services during the war than an endorsement of whatever decisions he would make on the complex issues of peace. The time consumed in Wilson's European tour might thus have been more profitably spent on the actual preparation of the peace, for time was at a premium once formal peace negotiations among the Allies had begun. The Peace Conference worked under the dual pressure of an increasingly impatient Allied and American public and a rising revolutionary tide, which threatened to engulf defeated Germany and much of central eastern Europe at the beginning of 1919. Moreover, both President Wilson and Prime Minister Lloyd George were forced to leave the Peace Conference for weeks on end to attend to urgent matters of domestic politics. Wilson returned to the United States on February 15, 1919, to explain the recently completed draft of the League Covenant and did not rejoin the Peace Conference until mid-March. The Treaty of Versailles thus bore many marks of haste since some Allied statesmen had not had the opportunity to study the entire treaty before its official presentation to Germany on May 7, 1919.

THE CLASH OF AIMS AND PERSONALITIES AT PARIS

The Paris Peace Conference of 1919 has often been compared to the Congress of Vienna of 1815, because both gatherings were charged with the task of fashioning comprehensive peace settlements after prolonged periods of European conflict. However, the restoration of peace and the design of a new order were infinitely more complex tasks in 1919 than they had been a century earlier. After they had thwarted the Napoleonic drive for hegemony over Europe, the peacemakers of Vienna had a relatively easy task of restoring a European balance of power since they could redraw the borders of Europe without regard to nationality: Holland and Belgium could be united as a buffer against resurgent French power; Norway could be offered to Sweden as a compensation for the Swedish loss of Finland to Russia; Prince Metternich could preserve the pre-eminence of Austria in central Europe and on the Italian Peninsula by devising the German Confederation and by dismissing Italian national aspirations with the remark that Italy was a term of geography, not nationhood; the balance of power in eastern Europe could be restored by a fresh dismemberment of Poland between Austria, Prussia, and Russia. Above all, the collapse of Napoleonic Europe brought with it a certain finality to the struggle that had unsettled Europe ever since 1789. Although the fires of nationalism and liberalism, which the Vienna Congress had done its best to stamp out, continued to smolder in many corners of the new Europe, they failed to converge into a universal conflagration, such as had passed over Europe before 1815.

The conflict of 1914 had been global in nature, drawing into its vortex not only the United States but China and Japan as well. As the war ended in Europe, the seeds of new struggles and revolutions had taken root in Russia with the establishment of Bolshevik power. No sooner had the victorious alliance of the First World War mastered the challenge of German imperialism than it was brought face to face with a new challenge, potentially more sweeping in its destructive force since it advanced, not along traditional national lines, but along the fissures of the exhausted industrial societies of the West.

The war of 1914 had climaxed the development of European nationalism and in so doing had awakened and stimulated nationalism all over the world in areas which had been colonized and kept under European tutelage during the half century preceding the First World War. In Europe, the application of the principle of nationality in the broad area from the Baltic to the Black and Adriatic seas was fraught with new tensions and rivalries owing to the mixed and overlapping settlement of nationalities.

Coming at an advanced stage in the Industrial Revolution of the West, the war of 1914 had mobilized the total human and economic resources of the principal belligerents. As a result, individual citizens identified to an unprecedented degree with national war aims, shifting quarrels between nations to the level of personal passion and hatred. The atmosphere of the Paris Peace Conference thus differed markedly from that of the Vienna Congress of 1815, where emotion had played no comparable role in the deliberations of the peacemakers. No moral stigma of aggression was attached to defeated France in 1815 once Napoleon had been safely exiled and the Bourbon dynasty restored to France. The community of interest among the restored dynasties of Europe and those dynasties which had survived the onslaught of Napoleonic France rendered the task of European unity far easier in 1815 than after the First World War. The First World War, in addition to being a war between nations, had been a war of ideologies, in which the Western ideal of democracy clashed with principles of German autocracy. The gulf which separated the vanquished from the victors was thus infinitely wider in 1919 and far more difficult to bridge; nor was it narrowed by the German revolution of November, 1918, and the liberal democracy of the Weimar Republic which it produced, since the latter owed its birth largely to the Allied victory of 1918.

THE LEAGUE

It was part of the vision of Woodrow Wilson that he, better than the Allied statesmen of Europe, grasped the revolutionary meaning of the First World War and hence was searching for new forms and principles of international relations, which could provide a better answer to the challenges of the new century than the traditional concepts of Old World diplomacy. The instrumentality of Wilson's New Order was to be the League of Nations, defined in the Fourteenth Point as "a general association of nations—under specific covenants for the purpose of affording mutual guarantees of political independence and territorial integrity to great and small States alike." What distinguished the Wilsonian concept of an international association of nations from earlier similar ideas—some of which could be traced as far back as the "Grand Design" of Henry IV of France and the 18th-century writings of the Abbé de St. Pierre and Montesquieu—was its universality, i.e., openness to all states of the world and its permanent statute. To Wilson, agreement on the League of Nations was the first and most important task of the Peace Conference, as it would provide the entire peace settlement with a new moral foundation as well as the machinery for the eventual adjustment of its inequities. Towards this end, the League of Nations covenant was to be made an integral part of each peace treaty.

The European Allies, though not averse to the ideas of the League—the League concept had a strong following, especially in Great Britain—wished to reverse the procedure and agree on the peace treaties first. To the Allies, building the League in advance of the peace treaties was like completing the roof before the foundations of the house had been properly laid. Moreover, there existed wide disagreement on the nature of the proposed League, particularly between France and the United States. The 77-year-old Clemenceau, old enough to have experienced the German conquest of France in 1871, wished to turn the League into an expanded alliance of the victors of 1918, for the preservation of the status quo, backed by a permanent international army, preferably under French command. A League of this kind was neither desirable from Wilson's point of view nor constitutionally permissable under the American system of government, which reserved decisions over war and peace to the Congress.

Wilson's views on the League prevailed when the plenary session of the Peace Conference resolved on January 25, 1919, that the League should form "an integral part of the general treaty of peace." A League of Nations Commission under the chairmanship of Woodrow Wilson, consisting of representatives of fourteen Allied governments, was established to draft the League Covenant. Proceeding from an American draft, which Wilson had prepared with his adviser Colonel House before going to Europe, the League Commission completed the Covenant in ten meetings. Such amendments as were made to the original American draft stemmed largely from Lord Robert Cecil and General Jan C. Smuts of South Africa. On February 14, 1919, Wilson presented the Covenant to the plenary session with the proud and hopeful remark that "a living thing" had been born.

The League Covenant rested in its main outlines on American and British, rather than French, concepts. Conceived as a universal body, the League offered equal representation to all its members in the Assembly, as a quasi-world parliament. Permanent membership in the Upper House, or League Council, which acted as the executive organ of the League, was reserved to the "Big Five." The remaining four seats on the League Council were to be filled by smaller states, elected by the League Assembly for limited periods of time. The core of the League covenant was Article Ten, pledging all League members to "respect and preserve as against external aggression the territorial integrity and existing political independence of all Members of the League." The principles of collective security and the indivisibility of peace were anchored in the provision that "any war or threat of war" was the concern of the whole League. League members which were party to a dispute were obligated to submit their quarrel either to arbitration or to the inquiry of the League Council. To provide for a "cooling off" period, the Covenant imposed a three-month period before the opening of hostilities, in the event of failure of arbitration. An attack of one League member upon another in violation of these rules would *ipso facto* constitute an act of war against all League members. Among the penalties cited were the severance of trade and financial relations, expulsion from the League, and effective military, naval, and air action.

As a precaution against secret diplomacy, which Wilson held responsible in part for the First World War, the Covenant required that international agreements between League members be registered with the Secretariat of the League of Nations, which published all registered treaties.

The Covenant took a first step towards general disarmament by stipulating that the maintenance of peace required the reduction of national armaments "to the lowest point consistent with national security." To the defeated powers, the Covenant held out the prospect of treaty revision. According to Article 19 of the Covenant, the League Assembly was empowered to recommend the reconsideration of treaties which had become inapplicable and to consider international conditions "whose continuance might endanger the peace of the world." The Covenant did not include the statement on equality of races which the Japanese delegate, Baron Makino, had asked the League Commission to include in the preamble. The Japanese request reflected Japan's keen desire for formal, Western recognition of Japanese equality as a Great Power. The First World War, Makino stated, had carried the "wave of national and democratic spirit — to remote corners of the world and has given additional impulse to the aspirations of all peoples; this impulse once set in motion . . . cannot be stifled, and it would be imprudent to treat this symptom lightly." By adding a plank on racial equality to the platform of the League, Japan also hoped to reduce discrimination against Japanese immigration into the United States and the dominions of the British Empire. It was for this very reason that Australian Prime Minister Hughes, in particular, strongly objected to the adoption of the Japanese proposal. In the event of its acceptance, Australia threatened to take the issue before the plenary session of the Peace Conference with possibly explosive consequences. Wilson had cause to fear an airing of the Japanese-Australian controversy because of its effects on anti-Japanese sentiment in the western states of the United States. The League Commission rejected the Japanese proposal. Because Wilson was President of the Commission, Japan blamed the United States more than Australia for the defeat of its proposal. As a result, this incident contributed to the postwar deterioration of Japanese-American relations.

The League Covenant, though satisfactory to Wilson, was subjected to severe criticism by the American press and Republican leaders when first publicized in February, 1919. Bowing to the objections raised in the United States, the President secured amendments of the original Covenant on four major issues: (1) the competency of the League was removed from domestic issues, such as immigration and tariff legislation; (2) the Monroe Doctrine was formally recognized in the Covenant; (3) League members could refuse a mandate over former enemy colonies; (4) members could withdraw from the League on two years' notice. The need for further amendments was embarrassing to Wilson, as it publicized the weakness of his own position among the American electorate. This weakness had been first revealed by the election of a Republican majority to both Houses of Congress on November 5, 1918, as well as Theodore Roosevelt's statement after the election that "Mr. Wilson has no authority whatever to speak for the American people at this time. His leadership has just been emphatically repudiated by them. . . ." Although the Allies did not oppose the amendments to the Covenant, they expected in return American concessions on the peace treaties.

THE PEACE WITH GERMANY

The German problem overshadowed all others at the Paris Peace Conference, and it was on the German question that opinions and expectations among the Great Powers collided most sharply. The decisions on Germany were mainly reached by Britain, France, and the United States, since the German peace involved no Japanese interests, with the exception of German rights in China and the German islands in the Pacific. Similarly, the interests of Italy were centered elsewhere, in the Adriatic, the Alps, and the fringes of the Balkans.

GERMAN WAR GUILT

There was little disagreement among the Big Three on the question of Germany's responsibility for the outbreak of the First World War and on the German obligation to make restitution in some form for the damages inflicted on the Allied nations. A German request to have the question of war guilt examined and judged by a commission of neutrals, with full access to the documents on foreign policy of all belligerents, was rejected by the Allies in March, 1919, on the grounds that German war guilt was, in their opinion, an established fact.

THE GERMAN COLONIES

Beyond this issue of German war guilt, however, agreement among the Big Three ceased. The first divisive issue was that of the German colonies. To Britain and the Dominions, as well as France and Japan, it was a foregone conclusion that the German colonies, all of which had been conquered by their respective armed forces, should pass into their ownership. The representatives of the Dominions—Hughes of Australia, Massey of New Zealand, Smuts of South Africa, and Borden of Canada—all argued for annexation on the grounds of security and as a reward for the sacrifices of the Dominion forces in the war. Japan invoked the secret agreement of 1917 with Britain and France which had promised her the German rights in the Chinese province of Shantung as well as the German Pacific islands north of the equator, which comprised the Marianas and the Marshall and Caroline islands. In support of the claim for annexation, Lloyd George advanced the moral argument of German maladministration of her colonies before the war. This argument might well have been invoked against the Belgian administration of the Congo, but Allied colonies were not a subject of debate in Paris.

President Wilson concurred with the Allies that the conquered German colonies ought not to be restored to Germany; he opposed the outright annexation of the colonies, however, because it ran counter to his own desire to elevate the peace settlement to a higher moral plane. In the case of the Japanese claims on China and the Pacific islands, the President was also guided by considerations of American public opinion. Since the first display of Japanese power against China in the 1890's American public opinion had favored the cause of China. Wilson's dilemma was that his acceptance of the Japanese claims might have resulted in the repudiation of the peace by the U. S. Senate while his rejection of their claims might have prompted the Japanese to walk out of the Peace Conference and to boycott the League. Having been defeated on the issue of racial equality in the League, Japan would not have accepted the added humiliation of a denial of her war-time conquests. Wilson's own solution of the problem of the German colonies was a system of mandates, under which the former German colonies would be administered under League supervision, not by the Allied conquerors but preferably by neutral powers, such as Holland and the Scandinavian countries. The final settlement was a compromise: the Mandate system was adopted, but the administration remained in the hands of the conquerors. Three types of Mandates were devised, A, B, and C, depending on the development stage of the indigenous population. The stated purpose of the Mandate system was to guide the mandated territories towards eventual independence. The former German colonies of Togoland and Cameroon, divided between France and Britain, were designated as B Mandates. German East Africa became a British B Mandate, South-West Africa a C Mandate under the Union of South Africa. Ruanda-Urundi was added to the Belgian Congo. The Mandate system was also applied to the Arab portions of the Turkish Empire, at the Allied conference at San Remo, to be presently discussed. The title of all Mandates remained vested in the League; the Mandate Powers were prohibited fortifications or military bases in the Mandate territories or the military training of natives for purposes other than the defense of the territory and police duties. The economic value of the German colonies, which German experts estimated to be as high as $9 billion — an estimate considered far in excess of their actual value — was not credited to the German reparations debt.

Although the mandate system appeared to some as a cynical compromise between imperialism and Wilsonian idealism, chiefly at the expense of the latter, Wilson welcomed the Mandate system as an opportunity to boost League prestige. The troublesome issue of the Japanese colonial claims was not resolved until April, 1919. An Allied compromise proposal that Japan hand back the German concessions in Shantung to the Allies, who would subsequently work out a settlement fair to Japanese interests, was indignantly rejected by Japan. In the end, Japan was awarded the German Pacific islands north of the equator as C Mandates. Japan also received the German rights and holdings in Shantung. In a declaration, separate from the Treaty of Versailles, Japan promised an eventual withdrawal of her troops from Shantung while retaining the German economic assets. Although Japan kept her promise by returning the Shantung province to Chinese sovereignty in 1922, the agreement aroused a storm of indignation in the United States, where the settlement was denounced as a "Far-Eastern Alsace-Lorraine" and the "Crime of Shantung." The negative American reaction to the concessions awarded Japan contributed to the ultimate defeat of the peace settlement in the U. S. senate. The Chinese delegation at Paris responded to the Shantung agreement by leaving the Peace Conference, "leaving judgment of the decision to history." China was the sole power among the Allied and Associated Powers which refused to sign the Treaty of Versailles.

THE RHINELAND AND THE SAAR
While the Japanese issue dragged on into April, 1919, compromise had been reached on the more immediate problems of the German peace. The principal difference between France on the one hand and Britain and the United States on the other centered around the question of French security. Taking advantage of the Allied military occupation of the Rhineland plus the eastern bridgeheads of Cologne, Mainz, and Trier under the Armistice of November 11, 1918, France wished to detach the entire left bank of the Rhine from Germany. The Rhineland, an area of 10,000 square miles containing a German population of five million, was to be turned into a buffer state or a number of buffer states under permanent French military control. Ideally, from the French viewpoint, the objective of French security could be best achieved by undoing Bismarck's work of German national unification, which had coincided with the French defeat of 1871. The goal of the political dismemberment of Germany remained uppermost in the French military mind for several years after 1919. Clemenceau, much as he might have agreed to such a policy in his heart, realized, however, that the demand for a complete break-up of Germany into separate states was unrealistic, as neither the United States nor Britain would agree to it. In addition to demanding a Rhineland buffer state, France wished to annex the German Saar, whose population was predominantly German. For its demand for the Saar, France could muster convincing economic arguments and less substantial claims of history. The rich coal mines of the Saar, which had yielded 17 million tons of coal per year before the war, would serve as just compensation for the destruction of the French coal mines by the retreating German army in 1918. The historic French claim on the Saar rested on the fact that part of it had belonged to France between 1793 and 1815.

Britain and the United States, though sympathetic to French security requirements and the French need for German coal, opposed the French annexation of the Saar and the amputation of the Rhineland. Lloyd George feared the creation of a new Alsace-Lorraine in Europe with the likely prospect of renewed conflict and renewed involvement of Britain in a continental war. Wilson objected on the grounds of national self-determination, as the Germans of the Saar and of the Rhineland clearly preferred to stay with Germany. The Treaty of Versailles resolved the Saar controversy by awarding France the coal mines of the Saar while placing the area of the Saar under League administration. After a period of fifteen years, a plebiscite was to determine whether the Saar should pass under French sovereignty or return to Germany. Germany retained the option of repurchasing the Saar mines from France, should the plebiscite go in favor of Germany.

GERMAN DISARMAMENT

The Rhineland problem was solved in the larger context of the disarmamant provisions of the Treaty of Versailles. Whereas the Rhineland remained part of Germany, the left bank of the Rhine, together with a strip thirty miles in depth on the right bank, was to be permanently demilitarized. Demilitarization meant that Germany was barred from erecting fortifications or stationing troops in the demilitarized zone. Moreover, the Rhineland was divided into three zones of occupation from which the Allies would withdraw after periods of five, ten, and fifteen years respectively. The Rhineland occupation could be extended beyond these periods, however, in the event of German violations of the treaty. As an added measure of security for France, Wilson and Lloyd George signed a security treaty with France, pledging American and British assistance in the event of renewed German aggression. The offer of a military pact, in peace time and in advance of actual hostilities, marked an extraordinary departure from the traditions of both the United States and Britain. Only thirteen years before the First World War, Lord Salisbury had characterized the British attitude on permanent commitments to foreign powers in times of peace in these words: "The British government cannot undertake to declare war, for any purpose, unless it is a purpose of which the electors of this country would approve. If the government promised to declare war for an object which did not commend itself to public opinion, the promise would be repudiated and the government would be turned out." The significance of the Anglo-American guarantee was lessened, however, by the provision that the failure of one guaranteeing power to ratify the security treaty would automatically free the other from the obligation promised. Both the French chamber of deputies and the French senate ratified the security treaty with alacrity; the House of Commons and the House of Lords likewise ratified the agreement without a dissenting voice. In the United States, however, the security treaty failed to reach even the Senate floor, dying a quiet death in the Senate foreign relations committee.

Although the Anglo-American security treaty failed to materialize, the Treaty of Versailles contained stringent disarmament provisions which, if adhered to, would reduce Germany to a third-rate military power. Universal military training was abolished and the German army reduced to 100,000 men, including 4,000 commissioned officers. To prevent its use as a cadre army for the training of reserves—as defeated Prussia had used its army of 40,000 after the Treaty of Tilsit in 1807—long-term enlistments were prescribed for both enlisted men and officers. Germany was forbidden to possess any of the weapons which the technology of the First World War had either created or developed to an advanced stage: tanks, military aircraft, and dirigibles, poison gas and heavy artillery. The German general staff was abolished.

The German navy, limited to 15,000 men, was forbidden to possess any submarines; capital ships were limited to six pocket battleships of no more than 10,000 tons displacement. An Allied control commission was installed in Germany with free access to all military facilities.

REPARATIONS

Apart from the issues of the Saar and French security, German reparations constituted the major obstacle to agreement among the Big Three. As previously stated, the Lansing note of November 5, 1918, had defined German reparations as "compensation made by Germany for all damage done to the civilian population of the Allies and their property by the aggression by Germany by land, by sea, and from the air." Prior to the opening of the Peace Conference, however, both Britain and France openly demanded German compensation for the full cost of the war; Germany, in the words of the British Minister of Transport Eric Geddes, should be squeezed "like a lemon, until you can hear the pips squeak."

The demand for German reparations beyond civilian damage appeared justified by the fact that the Allies themselves were forced to borrow some $10 billion from the United States during the war and the armistice period and by the further fact that Wilson refused to consider a reduction or cancellation of the Allied debt to the United States at the Peace Conference. Moreover, the war had greatly increased the internal debt of the Allies, who, with the exception of Great Britain, had financed the war chiefly through borrowing. Although Great Britain had covered as much as 28 per cent of her war cost through increased taxation, her national debt was fourteen times higher at the end of the war than before its outbreak. The huge British war loans to Russia, which exceeded Britain's debt of 850 million pounds to the United States, were lost when the Bolsheviks repudiated the tsarist debt. The limitation of German reparations to civilian damages was unsatisfactory to Britain and the Dominions for the added reason that Britain had sustained little civilian damage beyond the loss of shipping. As the latter was to be compensated through the surrender of the bulk of the German merchant fleet, Britain would receive little cash. Lloyd George, supported by South Africa's Smuts, therefore proposed to include the pensions of veterans, widows, and orphans in the category of civilian damages, thereby tripling the expected reparations total.

France, in addition to demanding restitution of the entire war cost, also asked for the repayment of the French indemnity to Germany of 1871, amounting to $1 billion, plus five per cent interest.

Although the United States opposed the Allied demand for German compensation of the full war cost (except in the case of Belgium), Wilson agreed to include veterans', widows', and orphans' pensions in the reparations debt. Fixing a definitive reparations amount depended, however, on a consensus between the United States and the Allies on the German capacity to pay reparations; it was on the question of German capacity that no agreement could be reached at the Peace Conference. Whereas the French estimates of German capacity to pay ranged as high as $200 billion, those of Britain quoted the sum of $130 billion. American experts assessed the German capacity at no more than $30 billion. No compromise having been reached, the Peace Conference installed a Reparations Commission. Composed of representatives of the United States, Britain, France, Italy, Belgium, and Yugoslavia, the Reparations Commission was to produce a final reparations sum by May 1, 1921. In the meantime, Germany was to make preliminary reparations payments in cash and kind to the amount of $5 billion. Moreover, all German assets in the United States and Allied nations, valued at $2 billion, were seized. For a period of five years, the Allies were to enjoy the advantage of the most favored nation principle in their trade relations with Germany without reciprocity.

The deferment of the decision on Germany's total reparations sum did not, as the United States had hoped, result in an economically sound reparations settlement. The failure of the United States to ratify the Treaty of Versailles reduced the American position on the Reparations Commission to that of a non-voting observer. The final reparations sum, fixed at $33 billion in the London Ultimatum of May, 1921, was arrived at without American participation. The controversy over the German capacity to pay reparations was not settled with the London Ultimatum, but merely postponed until the American intervention in the reparations crisis of 1923/1924. Not until the drafting of the Dawes plan, to be more fully explained in the discussion of the enforcement of the peace, were reparations removed from the area of politics into the field of economic and financial expertise.

The reparations clauses of the Treaty of Versailles assumed a significance beyond their economic content because of the wording of Article 231, which opened the section of the Treaty on reparations: "The Allied and Associated Governments affirm and Germany accepts the responsibility of Germany and her allies for causing all the losses and damage to which the Allied and Associated Governments . . . have been subjected as a consequence of the war imposed upon them by the aggression of Germany and her allies." Although the Allies had omitted a specific "war guilt" clause from the treaty, on the advice of Allied experts entrusted with the study of the origins of the war, Germany was quick to interpret Article 231 as a moral indictment rather than a legal basis for Allied reparations claims. It was largely in response to the German publicity given to Article 231 and the German pose of moral indignation that the Allies stressed German moral responsibility for the First World War in the strongly worded Allied note of June 16, 1919, drafted by Philip Kerr, Lloyd George's private secretary. The note accused the German Empire of having willfully planned the subjugation of Europe and the imposition of Prussian militarism.

THE GERMAN FRONTIERS

Once the Rhineland issue had been disposed of by the compromise described previously, the drawing of Germany's new frontiers posed few difficulties except for those with Poland. The loss of Alsace-Lorraine to France had been anticipated in the armistice conditions of November 11, 1918. The Treaty of Versailles made minor border corrections in Belgium's favor at Eupen, Malmedy, and Moresnet and ordered a plebiscite in the mixed German-Danish area of North Schleswig, which Bismarck had promised in 1866 but which had not been held. The plebiscite held in March, 1920, restored part of the province to Denmark. In the east the small Hultschin district was awarded to Czechoslovakia without a plebiscite. The new republic of Austria of six and a half million ethnic Germans was barred from union with Germany, contrary to the wishes expressed by the Austrian parliament and the sentiments revealed on the subject of union with Germany in several plebiscites in the provinces of Austria. Although the ban on Austro-German union conflicted with the principle of national self-determination, which the Peace Conference applied to other areas of Europe, Britain and the United States accepted the French objection to union on the grounds that it would unduly strengthen defeated Germany.

The drawing of Germany's frontiers with Poland created difficulties, because of the absence of a clear ethnic division between Germans and Poles and the Allied promise of giving Poland access to the Baltic Sea. In his Thirteenth Point President Wilson had called for an independent Poland, including the territories "inhabited by indisputably Polish populations, which should be assured a free and secure access to the sea." The port of Danzig, Poland's natural outlet to the sea, was, however, an indubitably German city. The dilemma of Danzig was resolved by turning Danzig into a free city, governed by a High Commissioner of the League. Poland, in addition to enjoying the free use of its port facilities, also took charge of the foreign relations of Danzig. The larger parts of West Prussia and Poznania were surrendered to Poland, resulting in the Polish Corridor which severed East Prussia from the rest of Germany. Plebiscites were to decide the fate of the districts of Allenstein and Marienwerder. The plebiscites, held in 1920, resulted in German majorities of 93 and 97 per cent respectively. Upper Silesia, Germany's second largest industrial-mining complex after the Ruhr, was awarded outright to Poland in the original draft of the Versailles Treaty, although the population of the area was not predominantly Polish. Owing largely to the initiative of Lloyd George, who was sympathetic to the German protests, the status of Upper Silesia was to be decided by plebiscite. Although the plebiscite of March 20, 1921, resulted in a 60 per cent German majority, Upper Silesia was partitioned in accordance with the local plebiscite results, with 40 per cent of the territory and most of its industrial-mining assets going to Poland. The full significance of the territorial changes, as effected by the Treaty of Versailles, was reflected in the economic loss which they represented for Germany. The areas ceded permanently or, in the case of the Saar, temporarily, represented 26 per cent of German hard coal output, 75 per cent of German iron ore, 35 per cent of pig iron, and 25 per cent of German steel production. The surrender of Lorraine left the blast furnaces of the German steel industry, of which only 25 per cent had been located in Lorraine and the Saar, without their traditional ore supply. The eastern territories lost to Poland represented 16 per cent of Germany's grain-producing area, 18 per cent of its potato producing area, and 11 per cent of its livestock.

ACCEPTANCE OF THE TREATY

The Treaty of Versailles was presented to the German delegation under Foreign Minister Brockdorff-Rantzau on May 7, 1919. Clemenceau opened the ceremony at the Trianon Palace Hotel with the remark that "the time has now come for a heavy reckoning of accounts. You have asked for peace. We are prepared to offer you peace." Germany was given fifteen days in which to reply to the Treaty in writing. The choice of Brockdorff-Rantzau as head of the German peace delegation was an unfortunate one, for the German foreign minister did not advance the cause of Republican Germany either by the substance of his remarks or the manner of their delivery. Whereas Clemenceau had delivered his remarks standing, Brockdorff-Rantzau remained seated. After criticizing the Allies for having taken six weeks to grant an armistice and six months to draw up a peace treaty, the German foreign minister accused the Allies of having caused the death of "hundreds of thousands of noncombatants" through the blockade: "Remember that, when you speak of guilt and atonement."

Apart from a general repudiation of Germany's sole responsibility for the outbreak of the First World War, the written German counterproposals centered on six main points: (1) Germany requested an immediate admission to the League, instead of having to serve a probationary period of unspecified length; (2) Germany offered a specific reparations sum of 100 billion gold marks ($25 billion), to be paid over an indefinite period of time without interest; (3) certain items, such as seized German war matériel, were to be deducted from the reparations sum; (4) Germany requested plebiscites for the areas to be ceded, including Alsace-Lorraine, where Germany had not permitted a plebiscite in 1871; (5) Germany wished to share in the assignment of colonial Mandates; (6) Germany took exception to the so-called "honor clauses" of the treaty, which demanded the surrender of various individuals as war criminals to the Allies, including former Emperor William II, Hindenburg, and Ludendorff.

Except for the change concerning Upper Silesia, the Peace Conference did not alter the conditions of the Treaty of Versailles. In Germany, where the terms of the Peace Treaty caused the resignation of the first government of the Weimar Republic under Chancellor Scheidemann, various alternatives to the acceptance of the Treaty of Versailles were briefly considered. The German situation of June, 1919, was in many ways not unlike that of Bolshevik Russia in March, 1918. As Germany had presented the Treaty of Brest-Litovsk in the form of an ultimatum to Soviet Russia, the Allies threatened to terminate the armistice unless Germany accepted the Treaty of Versailles unconditionally. Among the various alternatives to acceptance of the peace, which were discussed but in the end abandoned, was the proposal for an alliance with Communist Russia against the West, advanced by the German advocates of "national Bolshevism." Walther Rathenau, the prominent industrialist and future foreign minister of the Weimar Republic, even suggested that nonacceptance of the Treaty and an Allied occupation of Germany were preferable to acceptance, since the Treaty could not be fulfilled by Germany. Some extremist officers proposed to sever East Prussia from Germany and to use East Prussia as a base from which to resume hostilities against the Allies. In the end, acceptance of the Treaty seemed preferable because the proposed alternatives entailed the risk of destroying the political unity of Germany, which the Treaty of Versailles had left intact. On June 28, 1919, the fifth anniversary of the assassination of Arch-Duke Francis Ferdinand, the Treaty of Versailles was signed in the Hall of Mirrors of Versailles, the scene of Bismarck's proclamation of the German Empire in 1871.

John Meynard Keynes, whose *Economic Consequences of the Peace* of 1920 was influential in shaping public reaction to the Treaty of Versailles both in Britain and the United States, denounced the peace as "Carthaginian." As an economist, Keynes criticized the peacemakers for having neglected the economic needs of Europe in their alleged preoccupation with frontiers and questions of sovereignty. The Europe which the

Peace Conference bequeathed to future generations was, in Keynes' opinion, "inefficient, unemployed, disorganized, . . . torn by internal strife and international hate, fighting, starving, pillaging, and lying." The French economist Etienne Mantoux, writing more than two decades after Keynes, in the midst of the Second World War, refuted Keynes' thesis in his *The Carthaginian Peace or the Economic Consequences of Mr. Keynes* on the grounds that the peace of 1919 had not prevented Germany from rearming for another world war. Denunciation of the Treaty of Versailles as too harsh or as not harsh enough omitted the all-important question of the enforcement of the peace. The Treaty of Versailles had left the greatest asset of German political and economic strength, the political unity of the German nation, unimpaired. That Germany was able to mobilize her economic and political assets once more for purposes of aggression was less the fault of the Treaty of Versailles than of its enforcement.

It was in the latter context that the American retreat into isolationism, following the Senate rejection of the Treaty of Versailles and of the League covenant on March 20, 1920, was of supreme significance. The American withdrawal from the political and military affairs of Europe robbed the peace settlement of 1919 of the very premise upon which it had been designed. It was for this reason that Clemenceau and Lloyd George followed the feud between Wilson and the Republican opposition under Senator Lodge with growing apprehension. The Allied statesmen of Europe would have preferred a limited or conditional American participation in the League to none at all. President Wilson contributed to the collapse of his own vision of a world community of power, which was to overcome the hazards of the traditional European concept of balance of power, by his refusal to compromise on Article Ten of the League covenant, the feature most objectionable to the Republican opposition. Wilson's extraordinary speaking tour through twenty-nine cities in September, 1919, to popularize the cause of the League proved its swan song, as an increasingly isolationist America turned its attention to domestic problems. For France, the American repudiation of Woodrow Wilson reopened the security question in all its frightening prospects, since France, unlike the United States and Britain, was not, in the words of a French diplomat "protected from Germany by the seas."

THE NEW FRONTIERS OF EASTERN EUROPE: THE PEACE TREATIES OF ST. GERMAIN WITH AUSTRIA, TRIANON WITH HUNGARY, NEUILLY WITH BULGARIA

Whereas the German problem had loomed largest at the Peace Conference, the establishment of a stable state system in Eastern Europe was a task of equal urgency. The end of the First World War had created stable conditions in Western Europe owing to the clear-cut military defeat of Germany. It had left the situation in Eastern Europe fluid and uncertain, however, because of the Russian Civil War between Bolsheviks and Whites and the often conflicting territorial ambitions of the lesser Allied nations of Eastern Europe—Poland, Czechoslovakia, the emerging state of Yugoslavia, Rumania, and Greece.

Although Russia was not represented at the Paris Peace Conference, the Russian Civil War, which entered its most violent stage only in 1919, was never far removed from the attention of the peacemakers. Whereas France and, to a lesser degree, Britain favored open Western intervention in the Russian Civil War, the United States did not, for reasons to be more fully explained in the discussion of the Russian Civil War. The Western decision not to launch a full-scale intervention in Russia, reached in March, 1919, thus left the ultimate determination of the frontiers of the Baltic states, of Finland, and of eastern Poland, to a future date. The territories of the Baltic states—Estonia, Latvia, and Lithuania—formed, in fact, part of the battleground on which the Russian Civil War was being waged. Soviet Russia recognized the independence of Finland and the Baltic states in 1920, when peace treaties were signed with Finland on October 14 at Dorpat, with Estonia on February 2 at Dorpat, with Lithuania on July 12 at Moscow, and with Latvia on August 11 at Riga. In the Peace of Dorpat, Finland succeeded in gaining Petsamo with its important nickel mines but failed to make good its claim on Eastern Karelia. In the Peace of Moscow, Russia recognized the city of Vilna as being in the possession of Lithuania, a decision soon overturned by Poland. Vilna, whose population was predominantly Polish and Jewish, rather than Lithuanian, had been claimed by both Poland and Lithuania since 1918. Poland seized Vilna by a military coup in October, 1920, and incorporated the city in March, 1922. Lithuania, on her part, seized the port of Memel in January, 1923, when the attention of the Great Powers was focused on the Ruhr crisis between France and Germany. The Allies, to whom Memel had been ceded by Germany in the Treaty of Versailles pending a future disposition of the predominantly German city, acquiesced in the Lithuanian coup in 1924.

THE TESCHEN DISPUTE

Whereas Poland's western frontiers had been defined in the Treaty of Versailles, the Polish borders with Czechoslovakia and Russia were not given final shape until 1920 and 1921 respectively. Poland and Czechoslovakia quarreled over Teschen, a district rich in coal with a population of over 400,000 predominantly Polish-speaking people. Historically, Teschen had formed part of the kingdom of Bohemia and was therefore claimed by Czechoslovakia. After fighting had broken out between Polish and Czech troops in Teschen, the Allied Supreme Council ordered a plebiscite in September, 1919, which both sides refused. In July, 1920, the Allies partitioned Teschen, Poland receiving the city of Teschen together with one third of the area, Czechoslovakia retaining the coal mines. Poland remained unreconciled to the division of Teschen for the next twenty years, a fact which explains the coolness in Polish-Czechoslovak relations and Poland's eventual participation in the dismemberment of Czechoslovakia in 1938.

THE CURZON LINE

In the east, Poland claimed her historic frontiers of 1772, a claim which not only clashed with the Allied concept of national self-determination but provoked conflict with Soviet Russia. On December 8, 1919, the Allies recommended the drawing of the Russo-Polish frontier along an ethnographic line, subsequently known as the Curzon Line. Though acceptable to Russia, Poland rejected the Curzon Line and attacked Russia in April, 1920, precipitating the Russo-Polish war, to be discussed more fully in the treatment of the Russian Civil War. The final Russo-Polish border, as drawn in the peace of Riga on March 18, 1921, though to the west of Poland's borders of 1772, ran considerably east of the Curzon Line, leaving some five million Ukrainians and White Russians under Polish rule.

THE CZECHOSLOVAK BORDERS

The frontiers of Czechoslovakia were fixed in the Treaty of Versailles, the Treaty of St. Germain with Austria of September 10, 1919, and the Treaty of Trianon with Hungary of June 4, 1920. In addition to receiving the Hultschin district from Germany, Czechoslovakia retained the Sudeten provinces with a German minority of over three million, although the latter had expressed their desire to join the new Republic of Austria or, failing that, Germany. Britain had voiced the strongest reservations against leaving the Sudeten provinces under Czech rule, but the Peace Conference ruled in favor of the Czechoslovak claim because of the industrial significance of the area and the fact that it was within the historic frontiers of the kingdom of Bohemia. Moreover, Czechoslovakia assured the Allied governments of its intention to become a "sort of Switzerland" with full equality for all its national minorities.

THE PEACE OF TRIANON

The Peace of Trianon, whose signing was delayed until June, 1920, owing to the interlude of the Communist regime of Bela Kun, recognized the cession of Slovakia, together with a broad strip of the northern plains of Hungary, containing 700,000 Magyars. The argument of historic frontiers, which Czechoslovakia had invoked successfully in support of her claim on the Sudeten provinces, was rejected when made by Hungary on behalf of Slovakia. The Hungarian plea that Slovakia had formed a part of the kingdom of Hungary "for a thousand years" was answered with the statement that "an injustice does not cease to be an injustice because it has lasted for a thousand years."

The Carpatho-Ukraine, though containing few Czechs or Slovaks, was awarded Czechoslovakia chiefly for strategic reasons, as its passes commanded the communications from the Danube Basin into Poland and Rumania. The Carpatho-Ukraine gave Czechoslovakia a common border with Rumania, deemed friendly by the Czechs, and prevented a link-up between Poland and Hungary, both of which were considered hostile by Czechoslovakia.

THE PEACE OF ST. GERMAIN

The Peace of St. Germain, in addition to repeating the ban on Austro-German union, first stated in the Treaty of Versailles, compelled the new republic to change its name from German-Austria into Austria. The Austrian borders with Italy were drawn in accordance with the Treaty of London, which had promised Italy the Brenner frontier and South Tyrol. Although the surrender of South Tyrol meant the transfer of 240,000 German-Austrians to Italian rule without a plebiscite, President Wilson, against the advice of his American experts, did not object. Austria's borders with Yugoslavia were not settled until a plebiscite was held on October 10, 1920, as a result of which Yugoslavia withdrew her claim to the previously occupied province of Carynthia (Kärnten). In the east, Austria obtained the predominantly German-speaking Burgenland from Hungary, an area of 1,500 square miles, with the exception of the city of Ödenburg (Sopron), which opted for Hungary in a plebiscite of December, 1921. A proposal of Czechoslovakia and Yugoslavia to turn the Burgenland into a corridor, linking the two nations together, was turned down by the Peace Conference.

RUMANIAN GAINS

Rumania emerged from the vicissitudes of war, in which she had first been defeated by Germany only to declare war on Germany again a few days before the Allied Armistice of November 11, 1918, with substantial gains. In the peace settlement Rumania enlarged her territory by more than twice its original size while increasing her population from seven and a quarter million to fifteen and three quarters of a million. From Russia, Rumania had taken Bessarabia in 1918, a gain which Soviet Russia never recognized between the wars; the Allies (but not the United States) formally recognized the seizure of Bessarabia in March, 1920. The Peace of Trianon awarded Rumania Transylvania from Hungary, and the Peace of St. Germain granted her the former Austrian crown land of the Bukovina. The Hungarian Bánát, jointly claimed by Rumania and Yugoslavia, was partitioned between these two in the Treaty of Sevres on August 10, 1920. The southern Dobruja, seized by Bulgaria during the war, was restored to Rumania in the Peace of Neuilly with Bulgaria.

In addition to this loss, Bulgaria surrendered all of western Thrace to Greece in the Treaty of Neuilly, thereby losing access to the Aegean Sea. Although promised access rights to the Aegean under the Peace Treaty, none were in fact granted to Bulgaria. Macedonia was divided between Bulgaria and Yugoslavia along the lines drawn after the second Balkan war of 1913.

THE FIUME CONTROVERSY

The problems of the Yugoslav-Italian frontiers as well as those pertaining to Albania assumed significance beyond the scope of other eastern questions, since they involved the claims of one of the Great Powers. Italy had followed the establishment of a Yugoslav state with undisguised displeasure, as the union of the South (Yugo) Slavs challenged the Italian design for hegemony over the western Balkans. At the Peace Conference, Italy thus demanded, not only the territories promised her in the Treaty of London, but the port of Fiume as well, which had not been mentioned in the agreement of 1915. Fiume was, however, Yugoslavia's natural sea port on the Adriatic, such as had been promised Serbia in Point XI of Wilson's Fourteen Points. To counter the Italian demands, Yugoslavia claimed for herself not only Fiume but Triest, as well as all of Dalmatia and Istria. The chief opposition to the Italian claim on Fiume came from President Wilson, who, having made no issue over South Tyrol, rejected the Italian claim on Fiume on moral and legal grounds. The American-Italian confrontation over Fiume reached its climax, as previously stated, with Wilson's taking the issue to the press in April, 1919, causing the heads of the Italian peace delegation to depart in anger. In Italy angry crowds, which had cheered the President five months earlier, changed their chant from "Wilson, Wilson" to *"vil sono"* (I am vile). The Italian withdrawal from Paris was politically unwise because major decisions, such as the division of the German colonies and the Greek landings in Turkey, were made during Italy's absence. The attempt of the Italian poet Gabriele d'Annunzio to create a *fait accompli* by seizing Fiume in September, 1919, with a band of nationalists did not achieve the results for Italy which the Polish seizure of Vilna would accomplish for Poland in the following year. The controversy over Fiume was temporarily solved by the treaty of Rapallo of November, 1920, between Italy and Yugoslavia. Fiume was established as a free state (without League involvement); Italy obtained in the main the Istrian frontier of the Treaty of London, while renouncing her claim to Dalmatia except for the city of Zara. In September, 1923, taking advantage of the Ruhr crisis in western Europe, Italy annexed Fiume, a fact recognized by Yugoslavia in the Pact of Rome of January, 1924.

Albania, which had emerged from the Balkan wars of 1912/13 as an independent principality without clearly defined frontiers, became the scene of rival claims from Italy, Greece, and Yugoslavia at the Peace Conference. By 1920 Italy withdrew from Albania in the face of rising Albanian nationalism. When Yugoslavia failed to follow suit, Britain, France, Italy, and Japan issued a joint declaration in November, 1921, pronouncing the independence of Albania "a matter of international concern." Upon Yugoslavia's withdrawal, an Allied border commission was to establish the frontiers of Albania. By the mid-1920's, Italy would return to an active policy of intervention in Albanian affairs.

THE DISMEMBERMENT OF THE OTTOMAN EMPIRE; THE TREATIES OF SÈVRES AND LAUSANNE

The complexity of the Turkish problem stemmed from the fact that the secret agreements and promises made between the Allies as well as to Arab nationalism and the young Zionist movement were often contradictory. Among themselves, Britain, France, Russia, and Italy had agreed on the dismemberment of the Ottoman Empire in the secret agreements between 1915 and 1917. Britain had taken the first step towards dismemberment with the establishment of a British protectorate over Egypt in December, 1914. In March, 1915, Russia had been promised Constantinople and the Straits; the Treaty of London of 1915 recognized the Italian claim to the Dodecanese Islands and Adalia (Antalya) in Asia Minor; the Sykes-Picot agreement of April, 1916, between France and Britain, to which Russia also adhered, had divided the Arab Middle East into prospective British and French spheres of influence, reserving Syria, together with the oil-rich territory of Mosul, to France, and Iraq to Britain; Palestine was to be placed under international administration. The Agreement of St. Jean de Maurienne of April, 1917, further defined Italian claims on Turkey, pending Russian consent. In addition to Adalia, Italy was to receive the city of Smyrna (Ismir), together with surrounding territory totalling 70,000 square miles.

To the Arabs, the British High Commissioner for Egypt Sir Henry McMahon had promised independence after the war, in his negotiations with the Sharif of Mecca, the Amir Hussein Similarly, a joint Anglo-French declaration of November 8, 1918, had pledged both nations to "encourage and assist in the establishment of indigenous governments and administrations in Syria and Mesopotamia." By contrast, the Balfour Declaration of November 2, 1917, had promised British support in the establishment of a national home for the Jewish people in Palestine.

The imperial war-time arrangements for Turkey, inasmuch as they included Russia, had been rendered meaningless by the Russian Revolution and the Bolshevik repudiation of the secret treaties as "robber alliances." Moreover, Britain and France considered the St. Jean de Maurienne agreement with Italy as no longer binding upon themselves, since Russia's consent had not been secured. Prior to the opening of the Peace Conference, France had surrendered her claim to Mosul to Britain and agreed to the inclusion of Palestine in the British sphere of influence in exchange for British support of French demands on the Rhineland question. France upheld her claim to Syria, however, even after the American King-Crane commission, dispatched by Wilson to ascertain the wishes of the Syrian people, had reported overwhelming Syrian opposition to a French mandate.

The final partitioning of the Arab Middle East was left to the Allied conference of San Remo in 1920. The division into French and British mandates followed essentially the outlines of the Sykes-Picot Agreement: Syria and Lebanon became French mandates, Iraq and Palestine (including Transjordan) British mandates. The mid-eastern mandates were classified as "A" type mandates, obliging the mandate powers in theory to render "administrative advice and assistance" until such time as the mandates were able to stand alone.

THE GREEK INVASION OF TURKEY

The disposition of Turkey proper at the Paris Peace Conference was complicated by the claims of Greece, whose Prime Minister Venizelos wished to include Greek communities of western Turkey in his projected Greek Empire of the Aegean Venizelos, who enjoyed the support of Lloyd George and won the sympathy of Wilson, was authorized by the Big Three during Italy's absence from the Peace Conference to effect Greek landings in Smyrna and to occupy eastern Thrace Italian troops had landed in Asia Minor a few weeks earlier at Adalia in late April, 1919.

The Greek landings at Smyrna, though initially successful, precipitated a violent national reaction in Turkey, which ultimately forced not only Greece but Italy, France, and Britain to withdraw from Asia Minor. Mustafa Kemal, the successful defender of Gallipoli in 1915, emerged as the leader of the Turkish national movement. Within days of the Greek landings at Smyrna on May 15, 1919, Mustafa Kemal laid the foundations of a nationalist *de facto* government which challenged the authority of the Sultan's government at Constantinople

The aim of the nationalist movement under Kemal was not the restoration of the Ottoman Empire to its former, multinational expanse, but rather Turkish national independence, territorially, politically, judicially, and economically. The territorial demands of the nationalists were defined in the National Pact, adopted by the nationalist deputies at Ankara, the seat of Kemal's government. In addition to demanding the withdrawal of all foreign troops from Turkish soil, the National Pact called for plebiscites in western Thrace, Kars, Ardahan, and Batum.

By contrast, the Peace Treaty of Sèvres, presented by the Allies to the Sultan's government on May 11, 1920, provided for the partial dismemberment of Turkey proper, in addition to severing the Arab Middle East. Smyrna, together with its hinterland, was to remain under Greek occupation for five years, its ultimate fate to be determined in a plebiscite. Armenia was to become independent, and Kurdistan autonomous. Italy received full title to the Dodecanese, and Greece obtained eastern Thrace to within twenty miles of Constantinople. Cilicia, a region adjacent to Syria, became a French sphere of influence. The Straits were demilitarized. The peace of Sèvres, accepted by the government of Sultan Mehmed VI on August 10, 1920, was rejected by Kemal on the grounds that the Sultan was the virtual prisoner of the Allied High Commissioners in Constantinople.

Through a mixture of skillful diplomacy and the judicious use of his growing armed might, Mustafa Kemal forced the Allies into revising the Peace of Sèvres within less than three years of its signing. The Greek military advance on Ankara, designed to oust Kemal's *de facto* government, was turned into a hasty retreat after the disastrous Greek defeat at Sakarya in August, 1921. By September, 1922, the Greek armies were driven off Asia Minor entirely and the British garrison at Constantinople was brought face to face with Kemal's victorious army.

The military successes of nationalist Turkey were due in no small measure to the diplomacy of Kemal, which divided the Allies and secured the assistance of Soviet Russia. Although Soviet Russia had no illusions about the non-Communist character of the Kemalist movement, it willingly rendered diplomatic and armed support to nationalist Turkey, hoping that the Turkish nationalist revolution would impair British imperialism in western Asia. On March 16, 1921, Russia thus concluded the Treaty of Moscow with nationalist Turkey, in which both powers pledged not to recognize any peace treaties imposed upon either by force; the Treaty of Moscow also settled the outstanding border disputes between Russia and Turkey in a manner acceptable to the latter. Although Batum remained with Russia, Kars and Ardahan were recognized as Turkish.

Among the western powers, Italy was the first to withdraw from the Turkish theater. In return for the promise of economic advantages, Italy withdrew from Adalia in March, 1921. The Treaty of Ankara of October 20, 1921, in which France evacuated Cilicia, signalled the French withdrawal from the Allied front against Turkey. By October, 1922, Great Britain, isolated except for the support of defeated Greece, faced nationalist Turkey alone. The restraint of Mustafa Kemal, who avoided an armed clash with the British garrison at Constantinople, as well as the growing opposition to Lloyd George's Turkish policy in Britain and especially the Dominions, set the stage for the armistice of Mudanya, concluded between the Allies and nationalist Turkey on October 11, 1922. A new Allied peace conference, in which Turkey participated as an equal, produced the Treaty of Lausanne of August 23, 1923. Turkey recognized the loss of her former Arab provinces, but retained all of Anatolia, eastern Thrace, and the islands of Imbros and Tenedos. The Straits remained demilitarized, and the Capitulations, granting foreigners special privileges in Turkey, were abolished. The Anglo-Turkish dispute over Mosul, which Britain claimed for Iraq, was not resolved until December, 1925, when the League awarded Mosul to Iraq. The hostility between Greeks and Turks, which had sparked the nationalist movement of Kemal in 1919, was alleviated, if not altogether removed, by an exchange of Turkish and Greek minorities. By agreement of January 30, 1923, the Greek minority of Turkey, except for that of Constantinople, was repatriated to Greece, and the Moslem minority of Greece, except for that in western Thrace, was transported to Turkey.

In fulfilling most of the demands of the National Pact, the Treaty of Lausanne aided in the establishment of a stable Turkish Republic, which was formally proclaimed on October 29, 1923. It also facilitated the rapprochement between Turkey and Britain and Turkey's eventual alignment with the western democracies in the League and against Fascist Italy in the 1930's.

THE MEANING OF THE EASTERN SETTLEMENT, 1919/1923

The unfulfilled national aspirations of the peoples of Eastern Europe, from the Baltic Sea to Turkey, had been among the principal causes of instability not only in Eastern Europe but in Europe as a whole for nearly a century before 1919. Russian Poland had been gripped by three revolutions, in 1830, 1848, and 1863, in which Polish nationalists had tried, without success, to shake off Russian domination The Dual Monarchy of Austria-Hungary had been the scene of prolonged nationality strife ever since the onslaught of the national and liberal revolutions of 1848, without devising a compromise that was satisfactory to the majority of its subject peoples. The stirrings of South Slav nationalism against the overlordship of the Ottoman Empire had brought the Great Powers of Europe to the brink of a general war in the wake of the Russo-Turkish war of 1877/1878. The Congress of Berlin of 1878, though removing the immediate threat of war among the Great Powers, had merely postponed, not solved, the problem of South Slav nationalism. By the beginning of the 20th century, the South Slav struggle for emancipation from Turkish rule merged with the South Slav attack upon the hegemony of Austria-Hungary over the western Balkans, thereby creating the conditions for the Great Power confrontation of July, 1914.

The fulfillment of national aspirations from Finland to the

Aegean Sea thus gave rise to hopes among the peacemakers of 1919 that the forces of Eastern European nationalism would change from a disruptive into a stabilizing element for Europe as a whole. The determination of the new frontiers of Eastern Europe was, as we have seen, far from perfect, leaving or creating new national minorities. In Poland and Czechoslovakia one out of every three citizens belonged to a national minority; in Rumania, one out of every four. Six and a half million Austrians were barred from union with Germany; and three million Magyars, one third of all the Magyars in Europe, were distributed among the new neighbors of Hungary. Where principles of nationality conflicted with the strategic and economic demands of the Allied nations in Eastern Europe, the conflict was resolved, in most cases, in favor of the latter The Western powers had hoped to minimize the inequities of the Eastern settlement, however, by compelling the Allied states of Eastern Europe to guarantee the new minorities religious freedom, equality before the law, and the right to cultivate their native language, either through minority treaties or a formal declaration. The minority treaties thus constituted an integral part of the Eastern settlement in the minds of its Western authors. That the minority treaties afforded little protection in practice was less the fault of the peace settlement of 1919 than of its enforcement.

More significant to the stability of the Eastern state system than the protection of the new minorities was the need for outside economic aid, the reaching of a general consensus on foreign policy and military questions among the "satisfied" states of Eastern Europe, and the development of the League into a viable instrument for the rule and enforcement of international law With few exceptions, such as Czechoslovakia, the states of Eastern Europe were predominantly rural, requiring outside aid if their economies were to advance from their pre-war underdeveloped state. In the decade following the First World War, only the great Western powers could have furnished such assistance American investments, which poured into Europe in large amounts beginning in 1924, were chiefly directed towards the established industrial nations, however, particularly Germany, where prospects of a good return were high. France, which had been among the chief suppliers of foreign capital to pre-war Russia, was neither willing nor fully able to invest huge sums in Eastern Europe after having lost 16 billion gold francs as a result of the Bolshevik repudiation of the tsarist debt. In the second decade after the Peace Settlement, the states of Eastern Europe, particularly those of the Balkans, looked increasingly to Germany for economic aid, a development fraught with grave political risk, since Germany's objective in Eastern Europe was not the preservation of the *status quo* of 1919 but its change.

The hoped-for foreign political and military consensus among the states of Eastern Europe failed to materialize because of their bickering over frontiers and the lack of a unifying territorial and strategic out-look. In effect, the new states of Eastern Europe subordinated what should have been their overriding common concern—the power of Russia and Germany—to the lesser issue of frontier disputes involving small areas with a few hundred thousand inhabitants. Relations between Poland and Czechoslovakia remained hostile because of the Teschen dispute, as did those between Poland and Lithuania over Vilna. No permanent regional alliances emerged in Eastern Europe, except for the Little Entente between Czechoslovakia, Rumania, and Yugoslavia, which did not survive the stresses of the late 1930's. Nor did the great Western powers, with whose assistance the new states of Eastern Europe had come into being, preserve the unity of outlook essential to the stability of the Eastern state system. The French view, that the preservation of the Eastern *status quo* was essential to the preservation of peace in Western Europe was not fully shared by Great Britain until Hitler's direct assault on the Eastern state system in 1939. Italy, herself a dissatisfied power after the First World War, was to contribute to the undermining of the Eastern settlement of 1919 by her alignment with the dissatisfied powers of Eastern Europe—Hungary, Austria, and Bulgaria—beginning with the early 1930's and by her intermittent pressures on Yugoslavia, Greece, and Turkey. The League, thought to be the ultimate shield of the new order of 1919, including that of Eastern Europe, suffered irreparable harm through the American withdrawal and the division among the great Western Powers, France, Italy, and Great Britain, beginning in 1935. By the time Germany and Russia, the two Great Powers least reconciled to the new Eastern European order, had regained their capacity for military and political initiatives in the 1930's, few preparations of an economic, military, or political nature had been undertaken for the defense of an independent Eastern Europe. It was only after the destruction of Eastern European independence, first by Germany between 1939 and 1944, later by Soviet Russia, that the virtues of the Eastern settlement of 1919 appeared more readily discernible. Against the background of the Second World War and its aftermath, the freedoms enjoyed by the nationalities of Eastern Europe as a result of the peace settlement of 1919 appear both unsurpassed and unprecedented in the history of 20th-century Europe.

6 | The Enforcement of the Peace I

THE PACIFIC SEQUEL TO THE PARIS PEACE SETTLEMENT: THE WASHINGTON CONFERENCE OF 1921/1922

In addition to the problem of Soviet Russia, one of the major issues left unsolved by the Paris Peace Conference was the new balance of power in Asia and the Pacific. In the Far East, Japan had benefitted from both the collapse of Imperial Germany in 1918 as well as the Russian Revolution of 1917. Not only had the Treaty of Versailles surrendered a portion of the former German Pacific Empire to Japan, but Japan had advanced into eastern Siberia and had occupied northern Sakhalin under the guise of intervention in the Russian Civil War. The destruction of German and Russian sea power had left Japan the third ranking naval power of the world behind Great Britain and the United States. Since her emergence as a major power after 1867, Japan had not been presented with a more favorable opportunity for expansion than was provided by the outcome of the First World War. Nor did Japan regard her territorial and maritime ambitions in Asia and the Pacific as any more provocative than the expansion of Western imperialism into Asia prior to the outbreak of the First World War. In Japanese eyes the Western powers controlled a disproportionately large share of the world's land area in general and of Asia in particular, counting British rule in India, French rule in Indo-China, and Russian control over Siberia. The will to imperial expansion was thus motivated not only by Japan's awareness of her increased power but by the conviction that Japan's survival as a Great Power depended on the acquisition of new sources of raw material and new outlets for her growing population surplus. The Paris squabble over Shantung and the German North Pacific islands had only confirmed Japanese suspicions of Western discrimination since Japanese claims involved territories and rights far more modest than those already possessed in Asia by the established colonial powers. Nor did Japan put great faith in the American principle of the Open Door for China; the "Caucasian nations," from the Japanese viewpoint, were too firmly entrenched in Asia by reason of their priority and their accumulated wealth to allow "non-Caucasians" a fair chance to compete with them by launching new enterprises.

The phenomenon of expanding Japanese power in Asia was

far less alarming to the European Allies than it was to the United States. Britain's policy towards Japan had been based on imperial partnership, rather than competition, ever since the conclusion of the Anglo-Japanese alliance of 1902, which was due for renewal in 1921. The Anglo-Japanese alliance of 1902 had been conceived in the spirit of Britain's Colonial Secretary Joseph Chamberlain, who had urged the abandonment of Britain's traditional attitude of "splendid isolation" in favor of a policy of alliances to protect the worldwide interests of empire. Prime Minister Lloyd George considered the Anglo-Japanese alliance of 1902 still useful to Britain after the First World War.

France had welcomed Japanese power during the First World War, if only as a means of redressing the European military balance in the Allies' favor. In 1917, Prime Minister Clemenceau had thus asked for the westward advance of Japanese troops as far as the Urals, in order to enlist Japanese help in the rebuilding of a fighting front against Germany in Russia. At the Paris Peace Conference the United States had, in the French view, applied its idealism in Germany's favor and to the detriment of France, while pursuing a policy of realism in the defense of its own interests vis à vis Japan.

To the United States, Japan appeared headed towards a policy of Asian hegemony, threatening not only the principle of the Open Door in China but American strategic interests in the Western Pacific. The exclusion of Japanese immigration from the United States, following the American veto against a clause on racial equality in the League Covenant, added an emotional element to the strained relations between the United States and Japan. By 1921 the United States had shifted the bulk of its naval power from the Atlantic to the Pacific.

The American-Japanese confrontation created a dilemma for Great Britain and her Dominions, as Britain was allied with Japan and tied to the United States by bonds of friendship and the common war effort against Germany. The United States asked for the abrogation of the Anglo-Japanese alliance or, in the event of its continuation, a modification to render it harmless to American interests; Lloyd George favored the renewal of the Anglo-Japanese alliance unchanged. The United States had greatly expanded its naval power as a result of the First World War and the increased American building program since 1918; Lloyd George, unwilling to accept naval parity with the United States, proposed to keep abreast of American naval armaments through an increase in British naval construction. A truce, informally agreed upon by Wilson and Lloyd George at the Paris Peace Conference, to forestall an Anglo-American naval race, was nullified by the American repudiation of Wilson's policy. Wilson had agreed to slow the tempo of American naval expansion in exchange for Britain's support of the American amendments to the League Covenant of March, 1919.

British views on the Anglo-Japanese alliance and on naval

competition with the United States, defiant of American wishes in 1919, became accommodating to American interests by 1921 as a result of economic necessity and political pressure from the Dominions. After the pre-war naval race with Imperial Germany and the expenditures of the First World War, Britain could ill afford the strain of a new naval race with the United States. By 1921 Britain was willing to accept naval parity with the United States. The Dominions, including Canada, Australia, and New Zealand, shared the American rather than the British interest in Pacific and Asian questions by reason of geography and strategic necessity. Having asserted their *de facto* independence from Great Britain at the Paris Peace Conference, the Dominions prevailed upon Lloyd George in the Imperial Conference of July, 1921, to discontinue the Anglo-Japanese alliance. After 1921 the weight of the Dominion's interest was to become an increasingly important factor in shaping British policy towards Europe as well, as evidenced by the Anglo-Turkish crisis of 1922, the British response to the Geneva Protocol in 1924, the Anglo-Italian confrontation over Ethiopia in 1935, and the Czechoslovak crisis of 1938.

To resolve the problem of naval armaments and the related problem of Anglo-American–Japanese interests in Asia and the Pacific, the Nine Power Washington Conference opened in November, 1921. In addition to the major naval powers of the world, Great Britain, the United States, Japan, France, and Italy, the Washington Conference included the lesser powers, China, Portugal, the Netherlands, and Belgium. The choice of Washington as the Conference site signified the redistribution of power, caused by the First World War, as did the choice of the U. S. Secretary of State, Charles Evans Hughes, as chairman of the Conference.

The Washington Conference produced three agreements: (1) In the Four Power Treaty, concluded between the U. S., Britain, Japan, and France for a ten-year period, the signatories pledged to respect each others' rights in their Pacific island possessions. Disputes arising among the Four Powers with regard to their Pacific island possessions were to be submitted to a conference of all four signatories; the Anglo-Japanese alliance of 1902 was formally abrogated. (2) The Five Power Treaty between the U. S., Britain, Japan, France, and Italy, concluded for a fifteen-year period, set the ratio of capital ships and aircraft carriers at 5 (U. S.); 5 (Britain); 3 (Japan); 1.67 (France); 1.67 (Italy). The United States and Britain agreed not to fortify their Pacific island possessions, with the exception of Hawaii and the islands adjacent to Canada, Australia, and New Zealand. (3) In the Nine Power Treaty, concluded by all participants of the Washington Conference, the Powers pledged to respect the independence and integrity of China and to refrain from seeking special rights in China that would curtail the rights of citizens of friendly states.

Japan, in addition to signing the three treaties, pledged at the

Washington Conference to evacuate Siberia and northern Sakhalin, a pledge made good in 1922 and 1925 respectively. Moreover, Japan restored Chinese sovereignty to the Shantung province by the Sino-Japanese treaty of February 4, 1922, without, however, relinquishing the Japanese economic advantage in Shantung.

On the surface, the Washington treaties of 1921/1922 appeared to have taken a major step towards naval disarmament and the peaceful settlement of Great Power conflict in Asia and the Pacific. The United States appeared to have reaped the greatest benefits since the Washington Conference established naval parity between the U. S. and Britain, abrogated the Anglo-Japanese alliance, and pledged all signatories to the observation of the Open Door principle for China. The fundamental weakness of the Washington treaties, like that of the Paris Peace Settlement of 1919, was the absence of any machinery for their enforcement or of provisions for penalties and sanctions against future violators. The effectiveness of the Washington treaties thus depended on the faithfulness and good will of their signatories and thus, ultimately, upon the observance of the sanctity of treaties among the Great Powers generally. The United States could have contributed significantly to the creation of a climate of international morality and treaty observation by its mere presence in the League. The American absence from the League raised the question, however, whether the weight of American moral persuasion could, by itself, produce the desired effect upon Japan over an extended period of time and in the face of renewed temptation to dismember China.

As for the technicalities of naval disarmament, the Washington treaties also achieved more in appearance than in substance. The limitations necessitated the scrapping of existing capital ships above the agreed-upon ratios, but in practice the naval powers confined destruction of existing capital ships to those vessels already earmarked for scrapping because of obsolete armaments or power plants. As the treaty limitations were confined to capital ships and carriers, the powers were free to increase the number of other vessels, such as cruisers, which proved far more useful in the fast movements of Pacific naval warfare of the Second World War than the slower and cumbersome battleships. Moreover, the lack of fortified American naval bases in the Philippines and on Guam gave Japan local superiority in the western Pacific over the United States, in spite of the inferior overall naval ratio accepted by Japan in the Five Power Treaty.

THE LACK OF ALLIED UNITY OF PURPOSE IN POSTWAR EUROPE; THE PRE-EMINENCE OF FRANCE, 1920/1924

After the peace settlement of 1919, France, in the words of Winston Churchill, "peered into the future in thankful wonder and haunting dread." The dread was occasioned not only by the American retreat into isolation but the lack of unity among the European Allies after 1919. The failure of France and Britain to coordinate the enforcement of the peace stemmed in part from their divergent national interests and in part from their fundamentally different interpretations of the postwar situation in Europe. Never having possessed such a vast army as she had assembled during the First World War, Britain was anxious to demobilize her land forces soon after the conclusion of hostilities. The demands of the Empire in India and the Middle East, as well as those imposed by the Irish crisis, absorbed most of the British ground forces that remained after demobilization. The British military presence on the European continent thus shrank to a very small contingent of 13,000 men stationed in the Rhineland, together with a few British regiments in the disputed areas of Upper Silesia and East Prussia. Although Great Britain was not insensitive to the unrelieved French anxiety over national security, she considered the provisions of the existing peace treaties as adequate insurance against war in themselves. Hence, the British were reluctant to subscribe to new guarantees or to follow the French example of forming new alliances. The most that Britain was willing to offer France by way of additional safeguards was a treaty to guarantee the eastern borders of France, which Lord Curzon proposed in 1922, along the lines of the abortive Anglo-American treaty of 1919. As the British offer did not include a military convention containing precise definitions of Britain's military contribution to French security, the French Prime Minister Poincaré rejected it.

ANGLO-FRENCH DISAGREEMENT OVER THE LEAGUE

Nor did Britain and France agree on the significance of the League of Nations as an effective instrument of peace. Based on the Anglo-American conception of the superior power of moral persuasion, the League, to France, seemed little more than a debating society without coercive powers against disturbers of the peace. It was precisely on the value of debate within a permanent international forum that France and Britain held divergent opinions. With the passions of war receding, the opinion became widespread in postwar Britain that the outbreak of war might have been prevented in 1914 if more time had been available for international discussion and mediation of the Austro-Serb controversy of June and July, 1914. Gaining time for discussion had, in fact, been the principal aim of the mediation policy of Sir Edward Grey, the British Foreign Secretary, in the July crisis of 1914. To Britain, the provisions of the League Covenant gave adequate assurance that efforts towards mediation in a new crisis would not be cut short again by events, as they had been when Grey proposed a compromise in the Austro-Serbian confrontation of 1914. The League of Nations, Lord Curzon stated in 1920, "provides the machinery by which practical effect may be given" to the principles of international friendship and good understanding. Such optimism was not shared by France, since several League members, such as Canada and the Scandinavian states, voiced objections and reservations at the very first meeting of the League Assembly at Geneva in November, 1920, regarding the obligations under Articles 10 and 16 of the Covenant.

ANGLO-FRENCH DISAGREEMENT OVER EASTERN EUROPE

A further point of fundamental disagreement in the British and French approach to postwar Europe arose over the Eastern settlement of 1919/1920. Britain regarded the eastern border of France, in Curzon's words, as her "outer frontier." The Rhine thus formed Britain's first line of defense on the European continent. France, by contrast, regarded the new and enlarged states of Eastern Europe as her "outer frontier" and the Vistula, rather than the Rhine, as the first line of French defense in Europe. Britain refused to undertake guarantees for the states of Eastern Europe in 1920 or any other year prior to 1939, both for reasons of strategic assessment and because of doubts about the justice and wisdom of some of the eastern arrangements. "The populations in that quarter of Europe," Lloyd George observed after the First World War, "were unstable and excitable; they might start fighting at any time, and the rights and wrongs of the dispute might be very hard to disentangle. . . ." Other British spokesmen, such as J. M. Keynes, the critic of Versailles, regarded the states of Eastern Europe as Germany's legitimate sphere of influence in the future. "Germany's future," Keynes observed in 1922, "now lies in the East."

Far from conceding the new states of Eastern Europe to German influence, France regarded them as essential links in a chain of alliances to contain German power and secure a new balance favorable to the perpetuation of French hegemony over continental Europe.

ITALIAN GRIEVANCES

Added to the lack of Anglo-French agreement on postwar strategy in Europe was the friction between Italy and her allies of the First World War. Although Italy withdrew from her exposed positions in Turkey and Albania in the immediate postwar period, she remained a dissatisfied power. Italy's dissatisfaction aggravated her relations with France more than they did those with Great Britain, as Italy had more and larger claims against the former than the latter.

In the division of German colonial spoils, Italy had been left empty-handed. From Britain Italy received Trans-Jubaland in 1924 by way of compensation, an area adjacent to Italian Somali-Land in East Africa. An Italian-Egyptian agreement of 1926 adjusted the Egyptian-Libyan frontier in Italy's favor. No similar colonial agreements were concluded between Italy and France. Not only did Italy ask for guarantees for the protection of the large Italian settlement in French Tunisia, but Italy desired an extension of Libya southward, all the way to Lake Chad. There remained, as a further point of French-Italian friction, the issue of naval rivalry, which the Washington agreements of 1921/1922 had failed to settle. Being both a Mediterranean and an Atlantic power, France claimed the right to a fleet larger than Italy's.

Mussolini's advent to power in 1922 sharpened existing Italian-French disagreements and added new ones when Italy resumed an active East European policy in 1923. Mussolini's initial steps in foreign policy were, to be sure, cautious, since he was more concerned with the dramatic effects they might have on the Italian public than with real and lasting gains in foreign affairs. Mussolini's carefully staged arrival at the Lausanne Conference in 1922, which prepared a new peace treaty for Turkey, was an early example of Fascist theatrics for Italian domestic consumption. Having obtained a French and British pledge of Italian "equality" among the Great Powers at the Lausanne Conference, Italy secured no greater advantages from the Treaty of Lausanne than she already enjoyed before the Lausanne Conference – the recognition of Italian claims to the Dodecanese islands. However, Italy's attack on the Greek island of Corfu, to be presently discussed, as well as her renewed pressure on Yugoslavia beginning in 1926, foreshadowed the course of Fascist foreign policy, disturbing France's goal of preserving the Eastern *status quo*.

With America withdrawn from Europe, with Britain professing aloofness and revealing irritation over French anxieties, with Italy determined to revise the *status quo* of 1919, France placed her reliance on a policy of force towards Germany and of alliances with the new states of Eastern Europe.

FRANCE, RUSSIA, ITALY, AND THE NEW STATES OF EASTERN EUROPE

Before the final victory of the Bolshevik regime in the Russian Civil War, France had supported both the new states of Eastern Europe and the anti-Bolshevik forces of Russia, which, if victorious, would in all likelihood have reclaimed the Baltic provinces and eastern Poland. Although the end of the Russian Civil War had freed France from the dilemma of supporting both Poland and the Whites, it raised the more important question of Soviet Russia's future relationship to the states of Eastern Europe and Europe generally. Of the vulnerability of the states of Eastern Europe to Soviet pressure, the westward surge of the Red Army towards Warsaw during the Russo-Polish War of 1920 had given a striking demonstration. Although the Soviet invasion was repulsed, the outcome of the Russo-Polish War was not indicative of the true measure of the relative strength of Soviet Russia and Poland. Moreover, with the exception of France, not a single power had aided Poland in her moment of crisis. Hungary, acting from sentiments of anti-Bolshevik solidarity as well as old ties of friendship to the Polish nation, had tried to send troops to the defense of Poland; but she was barred from doing so by a hostile Czechoslovakia.

The energies of Soviet Russia were, to be sure, turned inward after the Civil War, towards the dual task of economic reconstruction and political consolidation. World-revolutionary euphoria and expectations of imminent utopia had given way to the realities of a Communist Russia surrounded by a non-Communist world. Soviet Russia had become a state among states and needed, as such, a minimum of economic and political contact with the outside world in order to survive. Soviet foreign policy under Commissar for Foreign Affairs Chicherin thus aimed to secure recognition of the Soviet government by foreign powers and to establish normal trade relations. Britain had extended de facto recognition to the Soviet government through the conclusion of the Anglo-Soviet trade agreement of March 16, 1921, in which both powers agreed to resume trade and to bar blockades against each other. Soviet Russia attended the Genoa Conference for the economic reconstruction of Europe in April, 1922, at the invitation of Britain, France, Italy, and Belgium. At Genoa, Chicherin hoped to secure the western credits and investments which Russia desperately needed for her recovery from the devastations of war and civil war. As an economic venture, the Genoa Conference was a failure since negotiations with Russia became deadlocked over the issue of tsarist pre-war debts. The Genoa Conference produced other results for Soviet Russia, however, in the form of the Rapallo Treaty, concluded between Germany and Russia on April 16, 1922, during a recess of the conference.

THE RAPALLO TREATY

The Rapallo Treaty was in the nature of a separate peace treaty between the Weimar Republic and Soviet Russia. Both powers resumed full diplomatic relations and accorded each other the most-favored-nation principle in their trade relations. All mutual claims for damages, arising from the First World War or the confiscation of German property in Russia, were cancelled.

The Rapallo Treaty was as mutually advantageous to Germany and Russia as it was disquieting to France and the states of Eastern Europe. Though a "Capitalist" power, which had fought off internal Communist revolts since 1918, Germany was hostile to the West because of the Treaty of Versailles and the Franco-German reparations struggle. Consistent with Lenin's thesis of 1918 that Soviet Russia must take "advantage of the conflict and antagonisms among the imperialists" in order to escape the dangers of a capitalist encirclement, Soviet Russia hoped to deepen the gulf between Germany and the West through the agreement of April, 1922. Moreover, the Rapallo Treaty brought Soviet Russia additional benefits of trade and military collaboration with Germany, which, though not mentioned in the Treaty of Rapallo, developed on an extensive scale. By 1922 Germany, overtaking Britain, accounted for 32 per cent of Russia's total imports. Under the secret collaboration between the Red Army and the German *Reichswehr,* Germany aided in the training of Red Army officers—including the future Marshall of the Soviet Union Zhukov, the conqueror of Berlin in 1945—as well as the construction of armaments plants for the manufacture of military aircraft and poison gas in Russia. In return, Germany obtained training facilities in Russia for the development of those very weapons which the Treaty of Versailles had outlawed for Germany. The German political advantage, deriving from Rapallo, was the escape from Germany's postwar isolation in Europe and the hope that the Rapallo Treaty would point the way towards German-Soviet collaboration in a future dismemberment of Poland. The hope of dismembering Poland was widespread among the German military, whose principal spokesman, *Reichswehr*-chief von Seeckt, preached that "Poland will and must disappear through its own internal weakness and through Russia with German help."

THE COMINTERN

While Soviet Russia advanced along the conventional path of treaties and trade agreements in its dealings with the outside world, she continued to challenge the non-Communist world through the pronouncements and activities of the Communist International (Comintern), which were revolutionary and theoretically worldwide in their aspirations. Officially, the Soviet government maintained the fiction that the Comintern was a private agency unrelated to the Soviet government, its policies or foreign representatives. The Soviet government, in Chicherin's words, "is not responsible for the activities of the Comintern and has nothing in common with it." The fiction of the separation of Comintern and Soviet government, stubbornly maintained between the two world wars, was belied by the fact that Lenin and Trotsky, both members of the Soviet government, also happened to be members of the Comintern Executive. Ironically, the invitations to the founding congress of the Comintern in Moscow in 1919 were issued through the channels of the Soviet Commissiariat for Foreign Affairs. Moreover, the choice of Moscow as the seat of the Comintern, as well as the domination of the world's Communist parties by Lenin and the Bolshevik party from the inception of the Comintern, relegated the non-Russian Communist parties to mere appendages of the Bolshevik party. The trend towards Bolshevik domination of the Comintern was to increase after the death of Lenin in 1924 and with the advent of Stalinism, as will be seen later in the account of Russian internal affairs.

From the beginning of Soviet foreign policy, Russia thus acted within and without the rules of diplomatic custom, signing international agreements with one hand, fomenting internal revolution with the other, sometimes within the very power with which an agreement had been concluded. Such had been Soviet strategy at the time of the signing of the Treaty of Brest-Litovsk in 1918, when Soviet propaganda was used in an effort to incite the working classes of the Central Powers into revolution against their imperial governments. Such continued to be the practice in Soviet Russia's relations with Great Britain when Russia concluded a trade agreement in March, 1921, while carrying on an active anti-British propaganda campaign in Afghanistan, India, and the Middle East. Within little over a year after signing the Treaty of Rapallo with the German Weimar Republic, the Comintern launched its most determined revolutionary effort within Germany, in October, 1923.

On the whole, the ideological struggle of the Comintern produced no lasting gains for Soviet Russia in the 1920's. The Comintern-sponsored "meeting of the peoples of the East" at Baku in September, 1920, fell short of its goal of inciting the "peoples of the East" to liberate themselves "from the chains of servitude." The Soviet attempt to exploit anti-Western nationalism among the peoples of Turkey and the Middle East for an attack on British power failed, owing to the lack of cohesion and often contradictory objectives among the assembled delegates at Baku. Under the threat of severing trade relations with Soviet Russia, British Foreign Secretary Curzon forced Russia to curtail anti-British propaganda in an ultimatum in 1923. No more successful than the Baku Conference of 1920 was the Soviet-sponsored Peasant International of 1923, established for the purpose of exploiting peasant unrest in Eastern and South-Eastern Europe. The Comintern-inspired Bulgarian Communist uprising of 1923 was crushed, as was the German Communist revolt of "Red October" in the same year. The abortive Estonian Communist uprising in Reval in December, 1924, ended the series of foreign Communist uprisings which had begun under the initially promising conditions of ravaged postwar Germany and Hungary in 1918/1919.

For the time being, Russia was turned inward and Germany's hands were tied by the fetters of Versailles. Once these two nations had recovered from their temporary weakness, it was doubtful whether the states of Eastern Europe could fulfill the dual function of containing Germany while shielding Europe from Bolshevik influence. One would have to return to French diplomacy during the Age of Louis XIV in the latter 17th century or under Cardinal Fleury in the early 18th century, to find a parallel with France's effort in the 1920's to balance off German power in Central Europe through the states of Eastern Europe without the participation of Russia. French Eastern strategy in the 1920's, aimed as it was against both a unified Germany and a Russia capable of emulating Western industrial achievements, possessed far slimmer chances of working than did the policy of Bourbon France.

THE EAST EUROPEAN DEFENSE PACTS

Intramural strife among the states of Central-Eastern Europe, of which the Polish-Czechoslovak quarrel over Teschen was but one example, rendered the attainment of regional pact systems extremely difficult. The attempt to build a regional defensive system in the Baltic, between Finland, Estonia, Latvia, Lithuania, and Poland, failed in spite of several Baltic conferences held between January and August, 1920. Poland's seizure of Vilna caused Lithuania to withdraw from the negotiations for a Baltic Pact. An agreement of March 17, 1922, concluded among the remaining four Baltic states for common defense against Soviet Russia, failed to go into effect as a result of Finland's withdrawal. Fearful of being drawn into a Soviet-Polish conflict, in which her immediate interest was not involved, Finland refused to ratify the treaty of 1922. Estonia and Latvia, following the example of Finland, concluded a bilateral defensive alliance on November 1, 1923, whose deterrent power was doubtful in view of the limited resources of the signatories. The only regional Baltic Pact to materialize was the Helsinki Convention of Conciliation and Arbitration of 1925 between Poland, Latvia, Estonia, and Finland. Whatever else its merits, the Helsinki Convention did not add to the security of the Baltic states. Russia undermined Poland's claim to Baltic hegemony by concluding a nonaggression pact with Lithuania on September 28, 1926.

The common interest of Poland and Rumania, in defending their respective gains from Soviet Russia against future Soviet demands for revision, paved the way for the Polish-Rumanian military alliance of March, 1921. The Polish-Rumanian alliance was weakened, however, by Poland's refusal to apply its terms to a Rumanian-Hungarian conflict over Transylvania, the territory taken from Hungary in the Treaty of Trianon in 1920. Not only did Poland consider the Rumanian-Hungarian frontier unfair to Hungary, but she was generally inclined to espouse the Hungarian interest for reasons of traditional friendship towards Hungary.

Fear of Hungarian revisionism and of Habsburg restoration led Czechoslovakia, Yugoslavia, and Rumania to form the "Little Entente," implemented through a Czech-Yugoslav alliance of August, 1920, a Czech-Rumanian alliance of April, 1921, and a Yugoslav-Rumanian alliance of June, 1921. The latter alliance was also aimed against Bulgaria. Although the Little Entente had little to fear from Hungary by way of a military challenge, its members were afraid that a return of the

Habsburgs to Hungary might rekindle old dynastic loyalties within the Hungarian provinces seized by Czechoslovakia, Rumania, and Yugoslavia. Between 1919 and 1921 the Habsburgs had made two unsuccessful bids for a return to Hungary, Archduke Joseph in 1919 and the former Emperor Charles I in 1921. It was the latter incident which spurred the three neighbors of Hungary into concluding the above-mentioned alliances.

Since France was anxious to promote unity among the states of Eastern Europe, she hoped to combine the Polish-Rumanian with the Little Entente pact system. All such efforts failed in the 1920's, as they were to fail in the 1930's, because of the obstacle of Czechoslovak-Polish hostility. France bolstered the Eastern pact systems through alliances between herself and the members of the two Eastern blocs. A Franco-Polish alliance of 1921 was followed by a French-Czechoslovak alliance in 1924, a French-Rumanian alliance in 1926, and a French-Yugoslav alliance in 1927.

The French-Yugoslav alliance of 1927 was concluded in response to the renewed pressure which Italy began to exert on the Balkans soon after Mussolini's coming to power in 1922. The Treaty of Rapallo of November, 1920, in which Italy and Yugoslavia had reached a compromise on the Fiume dispute, appeared to have aligned Italy alongside the *status quo* powers of Eastern Europe. In addition to achieving a compromise on Fiume, the Rapallo Treaty had pledged both powers to uphold the peace treaties with Austria and Hungary and to take joint action against a Habsburg restoration in Hungary.

THE CORFU INCIDENT

The Corfu Incident of August, 1923, marked Italy's noisy return to a policy of aggrandizement in the Balkans. Following the murder of General Tellini on Greek soil, an Italian member of the Allied Commission entrusted with the drawing of the Greco-Albanian frontier, Italy retaliated with the bombardment and occupation of the Greek island of Corfu. Italy also demanded an indemnity from Greece. Greece, whose ties to Great Britain were far less secure since the fall of its own Prime Minister Venizelos and that of Lloyd George in October, 1922, appealed for help from the League. Since Mussolini refused to recognize League jurisdiction in the Corfu Incident, and since Britain and France were anxious to settle the conflict by compromise outside the League, Greece was prevailed upon to pay an indemnity of 50 million lire to Italy; Italy withdrew from Corfu. The lesson of the Corfu Incident appeared to be that small powers could not count on unqualified League assistance whenever the interests of a great power were involved. The fact that Britain and France had urged an Italian withdrawal from Corfu created, on the other hand, a feeling of lasting suspicion and resentment on Mussolini's part towards the Western democracies. To Mussolini, the League was henceforth "an Anglo-French duet." The Corfu Incident contained in miniature the issues that were to divide Italy from Britain and France in the Ethiopian crisis of 1935/1936.

THE EXTENSION OF ITALIAN CONTROL OVER ALBANIA

Having seized Fiume in October, 1923, and having obtained Yugoslavia's acquiescence in the Fiume annexation in the Pact of Rome in January, 1924, Mussolini extended Italian control over Albania. Taking advantage of Albania's internal political problems, which both Italy and Yugoslavia had promised not to interfere with, Italy secured financial and political control over Albania in quick order. In the Pact of Tirana of November, 1926, concluded between Italy and the Albanian government of Ahmed Bey Zogu, both powers pledged mutual support and cooperation. The Pact of Tirana was followed by an Italian-Albanian "Unalterable Defensive Alliance" of November, 1927, in which both powers promised to make available to each other all necessary financial and military resources. The assumption of the title of "King of the Albanians" by Zogu, with Italian blessing, was offensive to Yugoslavia, as it implied Zogu's claim over Albanians living in Yugoslavia.

Mussolini maintained pressure on Yugoslavia by encouraging the revisionist demands of both Hungary and Bulgaria against Yugoslavia. An Italian-Hungarian Treaty of Friendship and Cooperation of April, 1927, foreshadowed the more intimate Italian-Hungarian alignment of the 1930's. Moreover, Italy and Hungary granted refuge and training facilities to Croatian terrorists, whose aim was Croat secession and the break-up of the Yugoslav state.

Italy's East European policy of the 1920's did not yet constitute a serious challenge to French hegemony over the Eastern state system. The Italian pressure on Yugoslavia was counterbalanced by the French-Yugoslav alliance of 1927; Italy's flirtation with Czechoslovakia, although it produced a Czechoslovak-Italian treaty of July, 1924, failed to detach Czechoslovakia from either its French connection or that with the Little Entente partners, Yugoslavia and Rumania. On the contrary, the feeling of Yugoslav-Rumanian-Czechoslovak solidarity increased in proportion to Italy's mounting pressure on Yugoslavia and the advance of Italian policy into Hungary and eventually Austria. By 1929 the Little Entente Powers not only agreed that their mutual treaties would be renewed automatically at the end of each five-year period, but began to hold regular conferences among their military staffs.

By aligning Italy with the "loser states" of Eastern Europe, Hungary, Bulgaria, and, beginning in 1933, Austria, and by proclaiming that "treaties are not eternal," Mussolini introduced a disturbing note into the affairs of Eastern Europe which, under circumstances more favorable to revision, would upset the Eastern *status quo* in the 1930's.

THE ENFORCEMENT OF THE PEACE
AGAINST GERMANY

Although the Allies had given Germany an opportunity to propose a lump reparations sum before the Allied Reparations Commission fixed the amount in May, 1921, no agreement was reached between Germany and the Allies on a definitive reparations sum before that date. The Allied Conference at Spa of July, 1920, to which Germany was admitted, secured no agreements other than those pertaining to German coal deliveries and the ratio of Allied reparation shares. Under the threat of an Allied occupation of the Ruhr, the center of German mining and heavy industry, Germany agreed at Spa to the delivery of two million tons of coal per month for a six months period. Allied shares of future German reparation payments were fixed at 52 per cent for France, 22 per cent for Britain and the Dominions, 10 per cent for Italy, and 8 per cent for Belgium, the remainder to be divided among the lesser Allies.

At the beginning of 1921, Germany offered the Allies a lump sum of 50 billion marks from which 20 billion were to be deducted for German deliveries made between 1919 and 1921. The Allies not only considered the German offer far too low but charged Germany with defaulting on her current deliveries in kind. On March 8, 1921, the Allies launched a partial occupation of the Ruhr as a means of sanction, seizing the industrial cities of Düsseldorf, Ruhrort, and Duisburg. The Allies imposed tariffs on goods passing between Germany and the occupied area and levied a 26 per cent charge on all German goods imported into Allied nations. On April 27, 1921, the Allied Reparations Commission fixed the overall sum of German reparations at 132 billion marks ($33 billion), a figure considerably below the sum of 210 billion marks which France had demanded in January, 1921. On May 5, 1921, the Reparations Commission presented the London Ultimatum to the Weimar Republic, demanding acceptance of the $33 billion reparations debt together with a payment plan of 2 billion marks annually for 30 years. The Ultimatum also demanded German reparations in kind and 25 per cent of the proceeds of German exports. The London Ultimatum, enforced by an Allied threat to occupy the entire Ruhr, was accepted by Germany within the six-day time limit.

THE ECONOMICS AND POLITICS OF
REPARATIONS

Germany's acceptance of the London Ultimatum was as certain as her ratification of the Treaty of Versailles in 1919, since the alternatives to compliance in either case were political and economic ruin. It was less certain, however, whether the reparations settlement of 1921 was economically feasible and politically defensible.

Economically, the First World War had left all European belligerents, whether Allies or Central Powers, in the position of losers, since it had shifted world economic and financial primacy from Europe to the United States. The economic consequences of the war were obscured, however, by France's victorious pose on the Rhine, by Britain's satisfaction over the disappearance of German naval and colonial rivalry, and by the fact that the United States did not demand a role in the political and military affairs of postwar Europe commensurate with its vastly increased economic and financial power.

The impoverishment of Germany was more tangible than were the economic consequences of the war to France and Britain, for Germany had lost all her colonies, most of her merchant ships, and the industrial and mining assets of Lorraine and Upper Silesia. Britain, France, and Italy, together with the lesser Allies, had incurred huge foreign war debts, however, both mutually and with the United States. Whereas the United States had owed Europe nearly $4 billion before the outbreak of the First World War, the European Allies had incurred war debts in the United States of over $10 billion. The sale of European assets in the United States to help finance the war and the curtailment of European exports to the United States after the war through high tariffs, such as the Fordney-McCumber tariff of 1922, worsened Europe's chances to re-dress its financial imbalance with the United States. Given the adverse financial balance between the European Allies and the United States, it was difficult to see how they could repay their war debt. Britain's debt to the U. S. was over $4 billion, France's nearly $3 billion, and Italy's $1.6 billion. Moreover, the First World War had curtailed the earning power of Britain and France by reducing Britain's foreign markets and diminishing France's industrial production. Unlike the Napoleonic wars of a century before, which had vastly increased Britain's foreign trade, the First World War resulted in a 50 per cent drop in the value of British exports. The decline in British exports was due, in part, to increased output, spurred by the war, in the Dominions, Japan, and the United States. The dislocation and devastation suffered by wartime France resulted in a 34 per cent drop of her industrial output by 1920.

The cancellation of the Allied war debts to the United States, though economically desirable from the European standpoint, was po-litically inadmissable in postwar America and was, in fact, barred by American legislation. By Act of Congress in February, 1922, the United States government was not only barred from cancelling the Allied debts but prohibited from accepting reparations from the defeated enemy powers in lieu of Allied debt payments to the United States. At the Paris Peace Conference, President Wilson had rejected an offer from Britain to cancel her claims against her own war-time debtors if the United States cancelled its claims against the Allies. The British proposal was generous enough, since more money was owed to Britain than Britain owed to the

United States, although Britain had little hope of ever recovering her loans to Russia. To Allied disappointment over America's refusal to shoulder political responsibilities in postwar Europe was thus added European bitterness over American determination to regard the war loans as a strict business deal. To the European Allies, the cost of the First World War could not be measured in monetary terms alone but in the blood which the soldiers of the European Allies had shed in far greater profusion than the soldiers of the United States. President Coolidge's famous phrase that the Allies had "hired the money" added a realistic though jarring note to the idealistic aura with which Wilson had entered the war and concluded the peace.

Although the United States had refused in 1922 to recognize a link between Allied debts to America and German reparations to the Allies, that link remained a reality which Allied reparations policy towards Germany could not ignore. Only by drawing enough funds from Germany could the Allies hope to cover both their obligations to the United States and the cost of reconstructing their own economies. The question arose whether Germany, the ultimate link in the chain of debts and reparations, would be capable of satisfying Allied expectations.

The German government, subjected to a growing campaign of abuse from German nationalist opposition, pleaded inability to implement the London payments schedule. Having paid a billion marks in reparations in August, 1921, Germany declared her inability to meet the payments for 1922. The "policy of fulfillment," which the German chancellor Wirth had inaugurated in 1921 in the hope of demonstrating to the Allies the impossibility of their reparation demands by attempting to fulfill them in a spirit of honesty and cooperation, hardened in 1922 into a policy of "first bread, then reparations." As the mark fell to one tenth of its value under the German inflation between 1920 and 1922, the German government proposed a long-range solution to the reparations problem along the following lines: (1) An Allied loan should be issued to Germany for purposes of currency stabilization and economic recovery; (2) a moratorium on German reparations payments should be granted until the above purposes had been achieved; (3) impartial bankers and experts should reassess Germany's capacity to pay reparations; (4) a new reparations plan, based on the "experts'" findings, should replace the London Payments Plan of 1921.

As a further alternative to the London Payments Plan, Germany proposed to discharge her reparations obligation mainly through the delivery of goods. The Wiesbaden Agreement of October 7, 1921, concluded between the French and German ministers of reconstruction, Louis Loucheur and Walter Rathenau, marked such an attempt. The Wiesbaden agreement failed to point the way towards a solution of the Franco-German reparations deadlock, as French industry opposed the flooding of the French market with German reparation goods.

The German Offer of a Security Pact

Since Germany recognized that France's postwar policy was motivated as much by the desire for security as by economic need, Germany offered France, in December, 1922, a pact to guarantee the French-German border, to be joined by Italy and Great Britain. The German offer of a guarantee was significantly silent on the subject of Germany's eastern borders; it was, moreover, premised on the assumption that France would terminate the Rhineland occupation in the event of Franco-German agreement on a guarantee pact.

Raymond Poincaré, French Prime Minister since the beginning of 1922, rejected the German pact offer as a maneuver to distract Allied attention from the reparations issue. Why, Poincaré asked pointedly, did Germany's offer not include the Polish-German and Czechoslovak-German frontiers as well? The German plea of inability to pay reparations, Poincaré dismissed as a "policy of false bankruptcy, either out of weakness or duplicity." Better than most Allied statesmen, Poincaré knew how to differentiate between the wealth of German industry and the weakness of Germany's postwar democratic governments, which dared not mobilize the wealth of Germany for the purpose of reparations. Poincaré was correct in blaming the German inflation less on Allied reparation demands than on the easy credit policy of the German *Reichsbank,* which favored big business. As Allied dealings with the German government on reparations had been a long exercise in frustration and delay, Poincaré decided to seize the assets of German heavy industry and mining by occupying the Ruhr. The Ruhr accounted for 85 per cent of Germany's hard coal production, 90 per cent of German coke, 77 per cent of German pig iron, and 85 per cent of German steel. France would hold the industrial and mining assets as "productive guarantees" and appropriate their earnings as reparations.

Apart from its economic objectives, the French project of an indefinite occupation of the Ruhr had political goals as well, goals which the Anglo-American veto of 1919 had denied France at the Paris Peace Conference. The occupation of the Ruhr would favor the French design of separating the Rhineland from Germany and turning it into a buffer state between Germany and France. By exploiting the reparations crisis for the realization of the foremost foreign political objective of France, Poincaré hoped to obtain the lasting guarantees for French security which the peace settlement of 1919 had failed to provide. The occupation of the Ruhr and the separation of the Rhineland would postpone Germany's recovery as a Great Power more effectively than reparations and disarmament alone. Poincaré's design of 1923 was based, no doubt, on the lessons provided by the history of the Third French Republic after 1871. Although Bismarck had imposed a war indemnity of five billion francs on defeated France in the Peace of Frankfurt of May, 1871, an indemnity deemed exorbitant by the standards of 1871, France had managed to pay her debt to Germany by 1873. Once France had paid her debt, the token German occupation of northern France was ended and France regained her foreign political freedom of action. Just as France had tried to escape from the iron ring of Bismarck's policy of isolation, Weimar Germany strove to overcome her postwar isolation after 1919. The Treaty of Rapallo between Germany and Soviet Russia in 1922, mentioned previously, suggested Germany's opportunities to maneuver even in a disarmed and weakened condition.

Neither Britain nor the United States approved of France's decision to occupy the Ruhr, since both nations feared the economic and political consequences for Germany. King George V expressed the fear that France would "make Germany bankrupt and turn her Bolshevik and throw her into the arms of Russia." The U. S. State Department voiced similar anxieties, in addition to pointing out that France might combine the heavy industries of the Ruhr with those of France, thereby creating a "monster cartel" with a commanding position on the world's steel markets. The coal and steel industries of France and Germany were, indeed, complementary, as France possessed more iron ore than Germany and Germany more coal than France.

Whatever concern Britain and the United States might voice about the occupation of the Ruhr, neither power possessed the leverage with France in 1922 that both had enjoyed at the Paris Peace Conference. The fall of Prime Minister Lloyd George in October, 1922, had removed one of the most powerful restraints on French policy toward Germany. His colorless successor, the Conservative Prime Minister Bonar Law, possessed neither the prestige nor the persuasion to overpower as determined a leader as the French Premier Poincaré.

THE PROPOSAL OF CHARLES E. HUGHES

The United States had persistently rejected Germany's efforts, made since 1921, to involve the American government in the German-French reparations duel. A German appeal to President Harding in April, 1921, to act as arbiter in the reparations quarrel had been turned down. On December 29, 1922, speaking before the American Historical Association meeting at New Haven, Connecticut, U. S. Secretary of State Charles E. Hughes abandoned the American reserve by endorsing what was essentially the German and British position. While upholding Germany's liability, Hughes rejected force as the least suitable means of extracting reparations. Instead, impartial experts were to assess the extent and nature of the German payments, based on Germany's capacity to pay. American experts were to participate in a future assessment of Germany's capacity to pay.

The Hughes proposal of December 29, 1922, was an attempt to lift reparations from the arena of power politics and to find economic answers to an economic problem which concerned both Europe and the United States. As a deterrent to French invasion, it came too late. At the initiative of France and against the vote of Britain, the Reparations Commission declared Germany to be in voluntary default of reparations deliveries in December, 1922. The deliveries in question concerned a shipment of 100,000 German telegraph poles to France which had not arrived at the promised date. The verdict of the Reparations Commission provided France with a legal basis for the application of sanctions. On January 11, 1923, five French divisions, plus Belgian auxiliaries, invaded the Ruhr.

THE RUHR STRUGGLE

From the beginning, the Ruhr struggle was an uneven contest between French power and German stubbornness, in which both contestants hoped that time would aid their cause. France established a control commission, called Micum (*Mission Interalliée de controle des usines et des mines*), for the economic exploitation of the Ruhr and the collection of tariffs and taxes. The Ruhr was sealed off from the remainder of Germany by French tariffs. The German government responded to the Ruhr invasion by stopping all reparations deliveries and adopting a policy of passive resistance in the Ruhr. Passive resistance amounted to a general strike, since neither German officials, railroad personnel, nor the workers and miners of the Ruhr were willing to assist France in the exploitation of the region. The political strategy of the German government under Chancellor Wilhelm Cuno was to isolate France morally, deny her the fruits of occupation, and pressure her into withdrawing with the diplomatic support of Britain and the United States. The attitude of Soviet Russia was also encouraging to Germany in the initial stages of the Ruhr struggle. Soviet Russia welcomed the Franco-German confrontation in the Ruhr, as it promised to deepen the divisions among the capitalist powers of the West while increasing Germany's dependence on Soviet Russia. The Ruhr struggle thus represented in its initial stages one of the rare occasions in the 1920's when the aims of official Soviet foreign policy were identical with those of the Communist International. The propaganda apparatus of the Comintern duly denounced the invasion as the latest example of French imperialism; the German Communist Party, for once, supported the policy of the German government. Karl Radek, the ubiquitous Comintern emissary to Germany, even felt called upon to praise Albert Leo Schlageter, a German Free Corps veteran previously engaged in anti-Communist activities, for his terrorist exploits against the French in the Ruhr. The practical value of Soviet support to Germany was minimal, however, as it could do little to aid in the ouster of France from the occupied area. The Soviet government warned Poland, however, not to exploit the Ruhr struggle by undertaking forceful action of her own against Germany.

The support of Britain and the United States, upon which German strategy in the Ruhr struggle was based, did not materialize in time to prevent the collapse of Germany's policy of passive resistance. The British demarche in Paris, through the strongly worded Curzon note of August 11, 1923, which condemned the invasion, coincided with the fall of the Cuno government in Germany. The united front, ranging from Communists to nationalists, which the Ruhr invasion had established among the German political parties (only Hitler and the National Socialist Party were an exception, placing the overthrow of the German Republic before opposition to France) collapsed under the strain of the economic and fiscal consequences of the struggle. To support the striking population of the Ruhr, the German government resorted to printing ever larger amounts of paper money, with ruinous consequences to the German currency. The mark, exchanged in February, 1923, at 20,000 to the dollar, collapsed in October, 1923, at an exchange rate of 2.5 billion to the dollar. To keep up with the demand for paper money, the German government commissioned thirty paper factories and over 130 printing plants. The governments of the German federal states, especially the industrial states of Saxony and Prussia, warned the German federal government that hunger and despair among the urban population could lead to riots and a complete social collapse.

The newly formed German government of Gustav Stresemann recognized the need for abandoning the policy of passive resistance in the Ruhr. It hoped thereby not only to improve conditions for the population of the occupied area, of which France had deported some 100,000 in retaliation for passive resistance, but also to reopen the Franco-German dialogue on the reparations issue. On September 26, 1923, Stresemann proclaimed an end to German passive resistance. The change of policy was decried by die-hard German nationalists, who compared the abandonment of passive resistance in September, 1923, with the German request for an armistice in October, 1918.

The new course in German policy did not immediately yield the results which Stresemann had hoped for. Soviet Russia, for one, interpreted the cessation of the Ruhr struggle as the first sign of a settlement and possible reconciliation between Germany and the Western democracies. As Stresemann moved Germany from confrontation with France towards reconciliation, Russia changed its attitude towards Germany from one of support to one of subversion. The Comintern, taking advantage of the social and economic disorder of inflation-ridden Germany, launched a major Communist uprising in the German states of Saxony and Thuringia with the objective of overthrowing the government of Stresemann. Though crushed, the Communist uprising of "Red

October," 1923, encouraged political extremists of another kind to challenge the government. On November 9, 1923, Hitler and his hitherto little-known National Socialist Party launched their abortive coup in Munich, to be more fully discussed later.

THE MICUM TREATIES

France viewed the end of German passive resistance in September, 1923, not as an invitation to resume negotiations with the German government but rather as an opportunity to reach the economic and political objectives of the invasion. Before September, 1923, the costs of the Ruhr occupation to France had threatened to outweigh the meager economic benefits which France was able to derive from the stricken factories and mines. The steel industry of France, heavily dependent upon German reparations coal, was forced to bank 39 of its 116 blast furnaces, owing to the halt in German coal deliveries. After the end of German passive resistance, France concluded the so-called Micum treaties with the Ruhr industrialists, rather than with the German government. The Ruhr industrialists were to bear the cost of the French occupation, pay their taxes to France, and deliver one third of the Ruhr coal output to France.

RHINELAND SEPARATISM

The fall of 1923 also witnessed the flare-up of separatist movements in the Rhineland, which enjoyed the support of French military authorities, such as General De Metz and Paul Tirard, chairman of the Rhineland Commission. With Belgian and French support, the Rhineland separatists captured a number of Rhineland cities, including Aachen, Bonn, and Trier, and proclaimed separate republics in the Rhineland and the Palatinate. However, Poincaré's attempt to separate the Rhineland from Germany was no more successful in 1923 than Clemenceau's had been in 1919. The separation of the Rhineland was opposed by an overwhelming majority of the Rhineland population, which ignored the orders of the separatist governments and killed as many of the separatist leaders, such as Heinz-Orbis, as it could. More important, Great Britain protested France's political activities in the Rhineland, following a fact-finding British mission under the British Consul General in Munich, Clive. At the beginning of 1924 Poincaré quietly withdrew his separatist policy; the territorial integrity of the Weimar Republic was preserved, in large measure, by British intervention. Failing to achieve the political objectives of his Ruhr policy, Poincaré was forced to yield to Anglo-American pressure on the reparations question. Acting on a proposal from the U. S. Secretary of State in December, 1922, Britain and the United States secured the reluctant consent of France in November, 1923, to hold a conference of experts for the assessment of Germany's capacity to pay reparations. Poincaré's effort to enforce the Treaty of Versailles through unilateral French action had been defeated by the intervention of Britain and the United States. The lesson of the Ruhr invasion seemed to be that Western Europe and Germany might have been spared the postwar reparations crisis if Britain, France, and the United States had preserved a minimum of common outlook and action in enforcing the peace against Germany between 1919 and 1923. In France, the failure of the Ruhr action contributed to the fall of Poincaré's government, in May, 1924.

THE DAWES PLAN

When France consented to a conference of experts, she was concerned lest the experts by-pass the authority of the Allied Reparations Commission or lessen Germany's overall reparations debt. "The Treaty of Versailles," Louis Barthou, the French president of the Reparations Commission, advised the financial experts gathered in Paris, "is our charter as it will be yours, and it is within the framework of that treaty, that you will conduct your inquiry." The competence of the experts who met in Paris on January 15, 1924, was thus narrowly confined to an investigation of Germany's present capacity for payment. However, participation by the United States in the two experts' committees, as well as efforts to avoid the past mistakes of the Reparations Commission, resulted in the drafting of a full-blown reparations plan, named the Dawes Plan after the American banker Charles G. Dawes, who headed one of the experts committees.

The work of bankers and financial experts, the Dawes Plan proposed a reparations scheme based on economic realities rather than power politics. Whereas the London Payments Plan of 1921 had demanded reparations without considering the sources from which reparations might flow, the Dawes Plan identified the sources, in addition to proposing foreign aid for the stabilization of the German currency. The first annual reparations installment under the Dawes Plan was thus reduced to $50 million (200 million marks), while Germany was to receive a foreign loan of $200 million (800 million marks). On the assumption that the German economy would recover rapidly, once order and confidence had been restored, the annual installments were to rise between 1925 and 1928 from 1.22 billion marks to the standard payment of 2.5 billion.

One half of the standard annuity of 2.5 billion marks was to come from the regular German budget, in which the proceeds from certain taxes, such as those on beer, sugar, and tobacco, would serve as guarantees for reparations payments. The Dawes Plan did not regard the sum of 1.25 billion marks as beyond German budgetary capacity, as the inflation of 1923 had wiped out most of Germany's internal debt. The remaining half of the 2.5 billion mark annuity was to be raised from a transportation tax, the German railroads, and the dividends of industrial debentures. The German railroads, it should be noted, had yielded an annual surplus of 1 billion marks before the First World War. Both the German railroads and the *Reichsbank* were to be subjected, in part, to Allied supervision and control.

The Dawes Plan introduced another novel feature through the system of transfer protection. Previously, Germany had complained that she was unable to pay reparations in hard, convertible foreign currency, owing to the decline of German exports and the diminishing German gold reserve. Under the Dawes Plan, reparations obligations were fulfilled once the German government had deposited the payments in Germany currency with the newly installed American Reparations Agent, Parker Gilbert. The Reparations Agent could convert or transfer only such amounts into foreign currencies as would not endanger the German balance of payments and hence the stability of the German currency. If the German balance of payments was adverse, the mark account of reparations would increase in Germany; if it was favorable, the reparations annuity could be increased proportionately to a prosperity index.

That the Dawes Plan was not considered as a definitive solution to the reparations problem by its authors is evident from its silence on the remaining total of the German reparations debt. As an interim solution, the Plan was considered both fair and workable by the experts. Its fairness derived from the experts' principle of the "commensurate burden," meaning that German taxes should not be lower than those of any of the Allied nations. In the words of Owen D. Young, an American expert, "the German scheme of taxation must be fully as heavy proportionately as that of any of the Powers represented on the Commission." The Plan was deemed workable on the assumption of Germany's economic growth. "Germany's growing and industrious population," the experts report stated, "her great technical skill, the wealth of her material resources, the development of her agriculture on progressive lines, her eminence in industrial science, all these factors enable us to be hopeful with regard to her future production."

To Germany, the Dawes Plan offered the advantage of lower reparations payments for the immediate future and the psychological advantage of a return of international business confidence in the German economy. On the other hand, the Dawes Plan had extended new Allied economic controls over Germany through the foreign supervision of German railroads and the *Reichsbank*. The Dawes Plan thus appeared to some as an application to the entire German economy of Poincaré's principle of "productive guarantees." Whereas Poincaré had attempted to seize "productive guarantees" in the Ruhr by force, the Dawes Plan earmarked taxes and railroad earnings as guarantees for reparations in a peaceful manner. "Germany is to be taken over and administered," the *New York Commercial and Financial Chronicle* observed, "in the same way as a corporation no longer able to meet its obligations is taken over by the law and transferred to the hands of the bankruptcy commissioners. . . . Never before has it been proposed to take such complete possession of the wealth of a nation."

At the London Conference of July and August, 1924, the Dawes Plan was accepted by the Allies and Germany. The French Prime Minister, Edouard Herriot, who had succeeded Poincaré, liquidated the latter's Ruhr policy by promising to evacuate the Ruhr district within a year after the London Conference. The French evacuation was completed by July, 1925. The last hurdle to the enactment of the Dawes Plan was cleared when the German *Reichstag* ratified the Plan with the required two-thirds majority. A two-thirds majority was called for because the changeover of the German railroads from a public to a private corporation could be achieved through constitutional amendment only. For a while it was doubtful whether the *Reichstag* could muster a two-thirds majority for the crucial vote on the Plan, since both the Communists and the Nationalists opposed it. German Communists, echoing the Comintern position, denounced the Dawes Plan as a scheme of American Capitalism for the colonization of Germany. The Nationalists rejected the Dawes Plan on the grounds that it curtailed German sovereignty beyond the limitations imposed by the Treaty of Versailles. Moreover, the Nationalists had made an Allied renunciation of the "war guilt" clause of the Treaty of Versailles (Art. 231) a condition for their support of the Dawes Plan, a condition which the German Foreign Minister Stresemann wisely refrained from raising at the London Conference. The warning of the U. S. ambassador to Germany, Houghton, that a defeat of the Dawes Plan by the *Reichstag* would discourage American investment in the German economy influenced a sufficient number of Nationalists to support ratification of the Plan.

Although the American role in drafting the Dawes Plan was unofficial—the American experts acted as private individuals rather than representatives of the U. S. government—the Dawes Plan marked the first major American initiative in the affairs of postwar Europe since the retreat into isolation. The flow of American investments into Germany and Western Europe, beginning in 1924, was crucial not merely to the economic recovery of Europe but to the creation of an improved political climate in the relations between the former European enemies of the First World War.

7 | The Enforcement of the Peace II:
The Illusion of Stability

THE GENEVA PROTOCOL

The fair weather of Europe's economic recovery following the adoption of the Dawes Plan was conducive to a relaxation of the political tensions of postwar Europe as well. The Ruhr struggle, in a sense, had been a final battle in the war between Germany and France which the Treaty of Versailles had not really ended but merely cast in a different mold. Anglo-American intervention in the Ruhr crisis had jeopardized France's policy of unilateral treaty enforcement against Germany without, however, offering a new and satisfactory answer to the continued quest for French security. The newly formed French government of the Cartel of the Left under Prime Minister Herriot, though more conciliatory towards Germany than the previous government under Poincaré, thus conditioned the French evacuation of the Ruhr upon obtaining additional guarantees against aggression within the framework of the League.

An earlier attempt to fill the gaps against aggression which the League Covenant had failed to close had been made at the fourth League Assembly in 1923 in the form of the Draft Treaty of Mutual Assistance. Under its terms the League Council was to have identified an aggressor within four days after the outbreak of hostilities, whereupon all members of the League were to have rendered obligatory military assistance to the attacked party. The Draft Treaty, though eminently satisfactory to France and her Eastern European allies, was rejected by Great Britain, the British Dominions, and the Scandinavian states.

In opposing the Draft Treaty, the British Labor Government under Ramsay MacDonald was motivated by the same sentiments of pacifism which were to influence the foreign policy views of the British Labor Party well into the 1930's. The Labor Party believed in collective security under the League, but it also regarded armaments in themselves as a cause of war. In the view of the Labor Government, the Draft Treaty threatened to transform the League into an instrument of militarism that would promote, rather than lessen, the dangers of war.

In September, 1924, Ramsay MacDonald joined the French Prime Minister Herriot, however, at the fifth session of the League, in an effort to strengthen League safeguards against aggression, without subverting the original purpose of the League. The result was the Geneva Protocol (Protocol for the Pacific Settlement of International Disputes), adopted unanimously by the fifth League assembly of 1924.

Under the Covenant, the League Council was powerless to act when the subject of a dispute was ruled a matter of domestic jurisdiction or when the Council failed to reach a unanimous decision. To fill these gaps, the Geneva Protocol established compulsory arbitration for both political and legal disputes. In legal disputes the Permanent Court of International Justice would render binding decisions. Disputes in which the Council failed to reach a unanimous verdict would be referred to a committee of arbitrators. Refusal to accept arbitration or to abide by its decision would, in itself, constitute an act of aggression. In disputes concerning matters of domestic jurisdiction, a party would not be judged an aggressor if it submitted such a dispute to the conciliation procedure under Article ii of the Covenant.

The Geneva Protocol specifically exempted demands for the revision of the peace treaties of 1919/1920 from the category of "disputes" under its jurisdiction. Accordingly, Germany or any other of the defeated powers could not invoke the provisions of the Geneva Protocol in seeking to change the postwar settlement. The Geneva Protocol was thus devised as an instrument to uphold the *status quo*.

Although the British Labor government fully supported the Geneva Protocol, it was rejected by the Conservative government under Prime Minister Stanley Baldwin, which succeeded the Labor cabinet in November, 1924. To the Conservatives, the Geneva Protocol implied British commitments too numerous and too unspecified for comfort. Under its terms, Britain might be called upon to act in disputes which were not of immediate British concern, such as disputes in Eastern Europe, whose population Lloyd George had called "unstable and excitable."

Strong opposition also came from the Dominions, and it is difficult to say whether their veto was instrumental in Austen Chamberlain's rejection of the Geneva Protocol or whether the Conservatives used Dominion opposition as a convenient excuse for repudiating the Protocol. That the Dominions would play an important role in the formation of British foreign policy was acknowledged by Lord Curzon in 1921, who declared that British policy was not only the policy of "Downing Street" but "of the Empire." Austen Chamberlain, upon becoming Foreign Secretary in 1925, stressed that the interests of Britain and of the Dominions "were one" and that the Foreign Secretary must "preserve in word and act the diplomatic unity" of Empire.

Like Austen Chamberlain, the Dominions opposed the Geneva Protocol out of fear of foreign entanglements. The aversion of the Dominions to being drawn into remote disputes was succinctly expressed by the Canadian League delegate Dandurand, who stated that Canadians dwelt "in a fireproof house, far removed from easily inflammable materials."

The Dominions rejected the Geneva Protocol on the further grounds that it subjected disputes concerning matters of domestic jurisdiction to international investigation. As Japan had been the author of this particular feature of the Geneva Protocol, the Dominions rightly suspected that Japan wished to draw the issue of the Dominions' immigration policy before the League.

The United States, though not a member of the League, contributed to the failure of the Geneva Protocol by protesting its possible consequences to American interests in the Western Hemisphere. Were the United States to act unilaterally against a hemispheric power, the entire League might be arrayed against it under the provisions of the Geneva Protocol.

THE GERMAN INITIATIVE FOR A REGIONAL SECURITY PACT: THE BOLD COURSE OF BRIAND; STRESEMANN IN THE FOOTSTEPS OF METTERNICH; THE LOCARNO TREATIES

Austen Chamberlain's rejection of the Geneva Protocol at the League Assembly of March, 1925, provided the German Foreign Minister Stresemann with a favorable opportunity for submitting a German proposal for regional security in Western Europe. Reviving an earlier German pact offer which Prime Minister Poincaré had rejected in December, 1922, Stresemann offered to recognize the Versailles frontiers with France and Belgium as final and to accept the permanent demilitarization of the Rhineland. Britain and Italy were to act as the guaranteeing powers of the proposed security pact. Like the German offer of 1922, the pact proposed in 1925 did not contain a pledge to recognize Germany's eastern borders with Poland, Czechoslovakia, and Austria as final.

The German offer amounted to a renunciation of German claims on Alsace-Lorraine. Its significance derived from the fact that Germany accepted of her own free will the western borders of the Treaty of Versailles, whereas previously she had denounced the entire Treaty as dictated and imposed upon defeated Germany.

By offering security to France, which France had been seeking vainly within a strengthened League, Germany hoped to reap immediate and long-range benefits. The immediate benefit would be an end to German postwar isolation in Europe. A security pact without Germany, such as had been proposed in the Geneva Protocol, was interpreted in Berlin as a security pact against Germany. It was for this reason that

Germany had viewed the Geneva Protocol with apprehension and had been relieved over its failure.

The security pact offered Germany the further immediate advantage of preventing a repetition of the Ruhr invasion of 1923. The guarantee of the French-German borders by Britain and Italy would benefit Germany more than France, since disarmed Germany had neither the means nor the intention of invading France in the foreseeable future.

The principal long-range advantage to Germany would be Allied willingness to revise the peace settlement of 1919 in Germany's favor. Stresemann hoped to induce the victorious democracies into an overall revision of the Treaty of Versailles, once French anxieties were put to rest and Allied confidence in German good behavior had been restored. The ultimate objective of Stresemann's revisionism was the return of Germany to the status of a great European power. In the west, Stresemann hoped for an early return of the Saar territory and the evacuation of the Rhineland before 1935, the date stipulated in the Treaty of Versailles. In the east, he desired the return of Danzig, the elimination of the Polish corridor, and the eventual union of Germany and Austria.

The aims of Stresemann's eastern policy thus appear, at first sight, not far removed from those which Hitler was to seek between 1938 and 1939. The fundamental difference between the revisionism of Stresemann and that of Hitler consisted in the approach towards similar objectives, however, as well as in the sense of proportion which guided Stresemann but was lacking in Hitler. The aims of Stresemann were definable, limited, and compatible with traditional concepts of a European power balance. Those of Hitler would be neither limited nor definable, for German foreign policy ambitions under Hitler would increase in direct proportion to the Western Powers' willingness to make concessions. Stresemann chose negotiation and multilateral agreements as the means towards the goal of restoring German power. Hitler would divest himself of the multilateral agreements and commitments which Stresemann had assumed, as rapidly as possible, to set the stage for revision of the peace settlement of 1919 by force or the threat of force. Hitler's principal bargaining asset would be the threat of using Germany's military power, which had revived by the late 1930's; Stresemann's chief bargaining asset in the mid and late 1920's was the promise that Germany would not abuse her future power if the Allies showed willingness to redress her present grievances.

The model of Stresemann's diplomacy was thus not Bismarck, with whom Stresemann was frequently compared, but Prince Metternich of Austria. As Metternich had guided Austria from defeat at the hands of Napoleonic France to preeminence at the Congress of Vienna in 1814, not through the exploits of Austrian arms, but the skill of his diplomacy, Stresemann hoped to lead the German republic from a position of military impotence and economic crisis into a respected place among the victors of the First World War by peaceful means rather than war.

After some hesitation, Britain responded favorably to Stresemann's offer of a regional security pact for Western Europe. British hesitation was occasioned by memories of Stresemann's annexationist attitude during the First World War. During the war Stresemann had been among the most outspoken advocates of German territorial aggrandizement, as realized in the Treaty of Brest-Litovsk of March, 1918. Britain's war-time Prime Minister Asquith, for one, characterized Stresemann as a "real Junker." Stresemann's metamorphosis from annexationist to "good European" was thus, at first, disputed in the West, and it was not until after the foreign ministers of Britain and France, Austen Chamberlain and Aristide Briand, had met Stresemann face to face in the negotiations at Locarno in October, 1925, that a spirit of confidence and mutual trust developed between the western statesmen and their German counterpart.

Britain liked the pact offered by Stresemann because it limited British commitments to the Rhine, Britain's "outer frontier" in Curzon's definition, and because it promised to restore a European power balance, which many Britons had seen disturbed by the policy of postwar France. Britain also agreed in principle to a revision of Germany's eastern borders by peaceful means, which was implied in Stresemann's pact. Britain's refusal to guarantee the Polish-German borders as final and irrevocable was given new expression in Austen Chamberlain's celebrated statement that "no British government ever will or ever can risk the bones of a British grenadier" for the Polish corridor.

France and her Eastern European clients, Poland and Czechoslovakia, received the German pact offer with reserve because it was limited to western Europe. In the event of the pact being accepted by the Western powers, Poland demanded an identical guarantee for her frontiers with Germany. Czechoslovakia was concerned lest Germany be given a free hand in Eastern Europe and allowed to annex Austria. "To permit Austria's annexation," in the words of the Czechoslovak Foreign Minister Eduard Benes, "means war." Italy likewise entered reservations against the German pact offer, arguing that if the French-German border were to receive an international guarantee, the Brenner frontier between Italy and Austria must be similarly guaranteed.

Despite its eastern loopholes, France accepted the German offer of 1925. Both the circumstances and the leadership of French foreign policy had changed since 1922. Since the end of the First World War two schools of thought had developed in the making of French policy on the German question. Prime Minister Poincaré, as has been seen, represented those forces which relied on French military strength and an uncompromising policy of enforcement of the peace as the best guarantees of French security. By contrast, Aristide Briand, the French Foreign Minister from 1925 to 1932, though no less security-conscious than Poincaré, advocated a policy of reconciliation rather than of confrontation, as the most promising means of achieving lasting peace with Germany. Briand thus criticized Poincaré's policy of unilateral reprisal against Germany in the Ruhr invasion, on the grounds that it had alientated Britain from France, resulting in the isolation of France rather than that of Germany. Moreover, the Ruhr action had inflamed German nationalist passions and had identified the young German democracy once more with foreign political defeat and humiliation. It was, however, in the French national interest to foster German democracy, since the alternatives of either a nationalist or a Communist dictatorship in Germany would bode ill for French-German relations.

Briand's faith in the redeeming power of reconciliation was shared by the influential Secretary General of the French Foreign Office Philippe Berthelot, whose views were instrumental in shaping French foreign policy in the mid and late 1920's. Were France to fail in creating a German republic hostile to war, Berthelot had warned as early as 1922, France would be doomed. Postwar France, in Berthelot's view, was the strongest military power in Europe and would remain so for another dozen years; but fifty years hence, Berthelot argued, the weight of Germany's larger population and industrial power would "end up by being heavier" than the resources of France. Instead of "stirring up hatred," France should be generous with defeated Germany.

French foreign policy under the guidance of Briand and Berthelot was thus a blend of idealism and realism. Briand's policy was idealistic to the extent that it welcomed the opportunity of a new beginning in French-German relations; it remained realistic enough, however, not to accept Germany's word as a substitute for French safeguards in Eastern Europe. To fill the eastern gap in Stresemann's pact offer, France insisted on including treaties of mutual guarantee between herself, Poland, and Czechoslovakia as integral parts of the multilateral pact system, known as the Locarno Treaties. Signed by Britain, France, Germany, Poland and Czechoslovakia on October 16, 1925, in the Swiss town of Locarno, the multilateral pact contained the following agreements: (1) A treaty guaranteeing the German-French and German-Belgian borders as well as the demilitarized status of the Rhineland, with Britain and Italy acting as the guaranteeing powers. Germany, France, and Belgium pledged that they would "in no case attack or invade each other or resort to war against each other." In the event of a "flagrant violation" of the above pledge, the other treaty powers would immediately assist the party against whom a "flagrant violation" had been directed. (2) Arbitration treaties between Germany and her neighbors France, Belgium, Czechoslovakia, and Poland. (3) Treaties of mutual guarantee between France, Czechoslovakia, and Poland.

FIGURE 2   *Stresemann and the German delegation at Locarno.*

GERMAN ENTRY INTO THE LEAGUE

The effectiveness of the Locarno Treaty was made dependent upon German membership in the League, for which Germany had applied as early as September, 1924, after the adoption of the Dawes Plan. Not only was German League membership a natural corollary of the Locarno Treaty, as the latter had gone far in removing from Germany the stigma of moral outcast, but it was politically desirable from the Allied standpoint as well. As Ramsay MacDonald had pointed out to Herriot in 1924, a Germany inside the League was better than a Germany outside the League once Germany had regained her economic strength under the Dawes Plan. The obligations of the Covenant would limit German freedom of action and further the political integration of the German republic into the western system of states.

The Western powers agreed that Germany should be admitted to the League as a Great Power with a permanent seat on the League Council. Disagreement arose between France and Germany during the Locarno negotiations, however, concerning Germany's obligations under Article 16 of the Covenant, dealing with sanctions. Stresemann feared that Germany, as a League member, might be drawn into a Western-Soviet controversy if sanctions were voted by the League against Soviet Russia. The German reservations were more than academic, being based rather on the experience of the Russo-Polish war of 1920. Were Germany to act in concert with the Western powers in the event of a Soviet attack on Poland or any other of the states of Central-Eastern Europe, disarmed Germany might become the battleground in a Soviet-Western conflict. Austen Chamberlain's assurance that, in such an event, "those who had disarmed Germany would be the first to rearm Germany again," though comforting to Stresemann, did not provide sufficient safeguards to Germany against the dangers of a Soviet invasion. To allay German fears the Locarno powers granted Germany what amounted to a virtual exemption from participation in sanctions against Soviet Russia. In a protocol the Locarno powers recognized that German participation in League sanctions was limited by her military situation and geographic position.

Germany's entry into the League, originally scheduled to take place at a special session of the League Assembly in March, 1926, was delayed until September, 1926, owing to the demands of Poland, Brazil, and Spain for permanent Council seats also. Before 1926, the Council consisted of the four permanent members, Britain, France, Japan, and Italy, as well as six non-permanent members, chosen by majority vote of the Assembly. When Germany applied for League membership as a Great Power with a permanent Council seat, Poland feared that German equality with the established Great Powers of the League might result in a revision of the peace settlement at Poland's expense.

As Germany refused to compromise and as France supported Poland's claim, the League became deadlocked on the German application for membership. The impasse of March, 1926, was resolved by increasing the number of non-permanent members of the Council from six to nine and by permitting three of the nine non-permanent members to be reelected to their Council seats as semi-permanent members at the end of their three-year terms. The compromise was accepted by Germany and Poland. Poland was promised a Council seat as a semi-permanent member. Both Spain and Brazil withdrew from the League in protest in 1926, but Spain was to return in 1928.

On September 10, 1926, Germany entered the League amidst the applause of its members and to the accompaniment of Briand's optimistic oratory.

To Stresemann's pledge of assisting the League to become a true community of nations based on equality, Briand responded with a plea for Franco-German reconciliation and the attainment of European unity.

THE SPIRIT OF LOCARNO

The Treaty of Locarno and Germany's entry into the League were widely interpreted as the two events which had truly ended the conflict of 1914. Austen Chamberlain called the Locarno Treaty the "dividing line between the years of war and the years of peace." More important than the Locarno agreements in themselves, in Chamberlain's assessment, was "the spirit which produced them."

For the next half-decade the "spirit of Locarno" would be invoked with increasing frequency by a Europe rejoicing in its new prosperity and the belief that war was banished from its horizon. The church bells of Locarno, which had been rung on the occasion of the signing of the Treaty, and the splendid oratory of Briand, which had greeted the entry of the German delegation at Geneva, seemed to have opened a new chapter in the troubled history of 20th-century Europe. It seemed that confidence in the preeminence of Europe and the dream of the forward march of European civilization were about to be restored. The psychology of optimism, engendered by the favorable economic-political constellation of the mid-1920's, may well have wrought the miracle of pacifying Europe if Europe had been granted a longer spell of economic normalcy. The World Depression, coming within four years after the signing of the Locarno Treaty, abruptly ended the illusion of economic soundness. Resurgent nationalism, feeding on economic woes, thrust Europe back into the abyss from which the architects of reconciliation had hoped to rescue Europe in 1925.

In retrospect, the era of Locarno thus appears to have postponed, instead of solved, the fundamental economic and political problems of postwar Europe, which were to burst upon the European scene with new ferocity in the 1930's and 1940's. The era of Locarno has been justly called the Indian summer of Europe, in which the afterglow of pre-war Europe was mistaken for the dawn of a period of new stability. The fruits of Locarno, to be presently discussed, were too meager to provide the Old World with the resilience required to withstand the shocks of the Depression or the virulent nationalism which the Depression fostered in Germany and elsewhere. As Europe moved into the feverish decade of the 1930's, the work of Briand and Stresemann appeared an illusion and a failure. The failure of the policy of reconciliation should not obscure the effort, however, which was as admirable as it was difficult under the prevailing circumstances. Both Briand and Stresemann, as has been seen, acted from motives of national interest. The novelty of their approach, compared with Great Power diplomacy before the First World War, consisted in their willingness, however, to adjust national interest to the requirements of European peace. In so doing, both men had to contend with hostile and vociferous nationalist critics in their own par-

205

liaments, whose backing they required to stay in office. It took the lesson of the Second World War, which witnessed both the fall of France and the destruction of Germany, to pave the way for Franco-German reconciliation upon more lasting and substantial grounds.

THE FRUITS OF LOCARNO

Following the League session of September, 1926, Stresemann and Briand met at the village of Thoiry in an attempt to settle specific problems pending between France and Germany. Stressing the close cooperation between the heavy industries of France and Germany as well as the favorable turn in French-German political relations, Stresemann proposed an end to the Rhineland occupation on the grounds that it was no longer necessary. In addition to requesting an Allied withdrawal from the Rhineland by September, 1927, Stresemann asked for a border correction in the district of Eupen-Malmedy, the repurchasing of the Saar mines, and the withdrawal of the Allied disarmament commission from Germany.

In exchange for these concessions, Stresemann offered France substantial sums above the required reparations payments under the Dawes schedule. In addition to 300 million marks, which France would obtain for the Saar mines, Germany would raise capital through the sale of the industrial and railroad bonds deposited under the Dawes Plan. The German payments were to help France stabilize the franc, whose value had declined steadily since 1922, partly as a result of French expenditures in the Ruhr action of 1923.

Although the Thoiry communiqué, issued jointly by Briand and Stresemann, spoke optimistically of agreement on the general principles for the solution of pending Franco-German problems, the Thoiry meeting ended in failure and mutual disappointment. To Briand and Poincaré, who had meanwhile returned to the premiership of France, Stresemann's revisionist requests were too numerous and fast for comfort. Poincaré managed to halt the French inflation without the aid of additional German payments. As the Rhineland occupation remained the last tangible guarantee of German fulfillment of the disarmament provisions of Versailles, as well as of German reparations payments, France refused to consider an evacuation by the date suggested by Stresemann. Although the German army was reduced to 100,000 men, numerous private and paramilitary organizations, the *Wehrverbaende,* survived in disarmed Germany. Their numbers had been augmented through units of the *Black Reichswehr,* which were recruited with the blessing of the German government during the Ruhr crisis. Allied dissatisfaction over Germany's non-compliance with the disarmament provisions of Versailles was the cause for postponing the evacuation of the first Rhineland zone (the Bonn-Cologne area) until February, 1926. Stressing French fears of the German *Wehrverbaende,* Briand claimed that they constituted a potential reserve of a million trained men.

Stresemann's failure to reap immediate benefits at Thoiry resulted in the denunciation of his policy as the "Phantasy of Thoiry" by German nationalists. Although Britain and France did offer Germany tangible concessions, beginning in 1927, the German public responded less with gratitude than with a sullen mood of "too little and too late."

In January, 1927, the Allies withdrew the disarmament commission from Germany, although the secret military collaboration between Germany and Soviet Russia had recently been revealed through indiscretions of the German Social Democratic Party, as well as through reports of the *Manchester Guardian.* The Allies did not, however, consider the *Reichswehr*-Red Army contacts sufficiently dangerous to maintain their arms' inspection over Germany. Likewise, Allied forces in the Rhineland were reduced in 1927 to 10,000 men, while all French troops stationed in the Saar were withdrawn. If not invisible, the Rhineland occupation became as unobtrusive as possible.

GERMANY AND POLAND AFTER LOCARNO

Whereas French-German relations had been marked by definite improvements despite continued rumblings of nationalist discontent in both countries, those between Poland and Germany entered into a new phase of mutual distrust upon the signing of the Locarno Treaty. The immediate occasion of German-Polish friction was the expiration, in January, 1925, of the five-year period during which Poland, together with the other signatories of Versailles, enjoyed the advantage of the most-favored-nation principle in her trade relations with Germany. Polish-German negotiations for a new trade agreement remained deadlocked until 1927 owing to Germany's restriction of Polish agricultural and coal exports to Germany. Poland retaliated with a ban on German imports and a tariff war.

The quarrel over trade relations was symptomatic of the larger political conflicts that continued to divide Germany from Poland even in the most tranquil years of the Locarno era. Having forsaken force as a means of revising Germany's eastern frontiers, Stresemann hoped to exploit Poland's economic weakness for the attainment of his political aim. "A state of extreme economic and financial emergency" in Poland, according to Stresemann, was the condition necessary for the eventual restoration of Danzig, Upper Silesia, and the Polish corridor. Stating that "only an unlimited recovery of sovereignty over the territories in question can satisfy" Germany, Stresemann withheld German support from international measures to stabilize the Polish currency in 1926.

In the 1920's, the Polish economy did not reach the "state of extreme emergency" which Stresemann desired, nor is it likely that France would have permitted a decisive change in Germany's frontiers with Poland even if it had. In regard to the sanctity of her eastern and western borders, however, Germany was anxious in the late 1920's to preserve the double standard which Britain had observed when it limited its guarantee to Germany's western borders in the Locarno Treaty. Stresemann thus opposed the project of an "Eastern Locarno," which Briand advanced unsuccessfully before the League in 1927. Briand called for the conclusion of security pacts in Eastern Europe for Finland, Latvia, Estonia, Poland, and Rumania, to be guaranteed by Britain, France, and Russia. The project failed for the familiar reason of Britain's refusal to go beyond the limited guarantees under the Locarno Treaty.

Polish-German relations remained strained also over the issue of the German minority in Poland. The German minority, organized in the *Volksbund,* complained that Poland had failed to live up to the promises made in the Minority Treaty which Poland had signed on June 28, 1919. Before the League, Stresemann made himself the vigorous spokesman, not only of the German minority in Poland, but of German minorities elsewhere, including that of the South Tyrol. The Polish Foreign Minister August Zaleski countered German complaints before the League with the charge that the *Volksbund* was less interested in settling minority problems than in destroying the Polish state.

The disagreeable state of German-Polish relations suggested the limited and temporary nature of the peace achieved in the Locarno settlement. Like other problems whose solution Locarno had postponed, rather than solved, the German-Polish quarrel remained a charge against the future peace of Europe.

LEAGUE PRESTIGE AND THE
FAILURE OF DISARMAMENT

The threats to peace in Central-Eastern Europe were obscured in the half decade following the Treaty of Locarno by the illusion of a strengthened League. Germany's admission to the League had seemingly erased the division of Europe into victors and vanquished, conferring a new spirit of community upon the League such as the Great Powers had failed to achieve in the pre-war era of mutually hostile blocs and alignments. The personal appearances of Austen Chamberlain, Briand, and Stresemann at the League Assembly sessions between 1926 and 1929 heightened League prestige and upheld faith in the survival of the spirit of Locarno.

To be sure, the League remained, even at its zenith, an organization primarily oriented towards Europe since neither the United

States and Russia nor Brazil and Argentina were members. Though falling short of the original Wilsonian concept of a universal body, the League gave promise, in the mid and late 1920's, of becoming an effective guardian of world peace since Europe had been the place of origin for the world conflict of 1914. Moreover, the United States and Soviet Russia, despite the unchanged isolationism of the former and the ideological suspicion of the latter, participated in League affairs to a greater extent than previously. Russia and the United States joined the disarmament talks in the League-appointed Preparatory Commission for the Disarmament Conference, to be presently discussed. Brazil and the United States were members of the League-affiliated International Labor Organization.

Although the League's political importance had grown as a result of the Anglo-French-German understanding, its actual powers as mediator of Great Power disputes remained untried during the Locarno era. The Corfu incident, previously discussed, had suggested the limits of League authority in disputes involving the prestige and direct interests of a permanent member of the League Council. In the mid and late 1920's the League's arbitration machinery was successfully employed, to be sure, in the settlement of several international conflicts. The conflicts involved lesser powers only, however, or concerned issues too small to endanger the general peace. The League resolved, for instance, the Greek-Bulgarian conflict, which arose from the invasion of Bulgarian territory by Greek forces in October, 1925. Acting upon Bulgaria's appeal under Article 11 of the Covenant, the Council investigated the Bulgarian complaint, adjudged Greece guilty, and imposed an indemnity on Greece. The reaching of an impartial and swift verdict in the Greek-Bulgarian controversy was an easy task since both powers were small and neither enjoyed Great Power patronage.

In 1925 the Council, in conjunction with the Permanent Court of International Justice, settled the border dispute between Turkey and the British Mandate of Iraq concerning the Mosul district. Turkey's refusal to accept as binding the Council decision, awarding most of the Mosul territory to Iraq, resulted in the Council's seeking an advisory opinion of the Permanent Court. The Court's ruling, that under the Peace of Lausanne the consent of the parties to the border dispute was not required for the enforcement of the Council decision, resulted in Turkish compliance and the conclusion of an Anglo-Iraqi-Turkish border agreement in 1926.

In 1927, acting on an appeal of Lithuania under Article 11 of the Covenant, the Council prevented an open clash between Poland and Lithuania, arising from the Vilna issue. In response to frequent border incidents and the deportation of Lithuanian nationals from Poland, Lithuania appealed to the League in the hope of undoing Poland's forceful seizure of Vilna in 1920. Although the Council failed to enter into the substance of the dispute, neither recognizing nor condemning the incorporation of Vilna into Poland, it secured the adherence of both parties to a peace formula. The Council resolution declared the incompatibility of a state of war between two League members with the spirit and the letter of the Covenant. Open warfare between Poland and Lithuania was avoided, though diplomatic and trade relations between the contestants remained severed. Poland retained possession of Vilna, regardless of the means by which she had obtained it. Political expediency, rather than the precepts of international law, decided the Vilna question, as Poland, not Lithuania, constituted the keystone of the French alliance system in Eastern Europe.

MINORITY PROTECTION AND THE LEAGUE

The vested interest of France in upholding the sovereignty of her Eastern allies was instrumental also in minimizing the minority issue, which was being broached before the League in the late 1920's. The most frequent plaintiffs were the Hungarian minority in Rumania and the Ukrainian, Jewish, and German minorities of Poland. The minority complaints before the League and the publicity given them in the pages of the *Manchester Guardian* recall the observation of Winston Churchill that to be born in the middle of a continent can be a misfortune in itself. The Hungarian minority of Rumania complained that Rumanian land reform laws discriminated against Hungarian land owners. The Jews and Ukrainians of Poland charged job exclusion and the destruction of cultural facilities and schools.

The treaty guaranteeing minority rights in Poland of 1919 contained the pledge that "differences of religion, creed, or confession shall not prejudice any Polish national in matters relating to the enjoyment of civil or political rights, as for instance admission to public employments, functions and honors, or the exercise of professions and industries." The promise remained a dead letter for the sizeable Jewish minority of Poland, however, whose opportunities of education, employment, and residence remained severely limited as a result of official and private discrimination. In the Poland of the 1920's and 1930's, Jews remained barred from virtually all employment in government or municipally operated establishments. "The bias against Jews," the *Manchester Guardian* reported, "is everywhere. They feel it in the law courts and in the presence of the magistrates, they feel it in school, in politics, in business, and at the universities. . . ."

The minority treaty of 1919, likewise, had promised that "no restrictions shall be imposed on the free use by any Polish national of any language, in private intercourse, in commerce, in religion, in the press or in publications of any kind. . . ." Yet the Ukrainian minority of Poland remained subject to punitive raids by the Polish police, resulting, among other losses, in the destruction of the Ukrainian library at Tarnopol, containing some 40,000 volumes, and the uprooting of Ukrainian schools and institutions.

League procedure permitted complaints of national minorities to be submitted to a committee of three Council members in conjunction with the reply of the accused government. The procedure was not always satisfactory to the complaining minority since, unlike the accused government, it was barred from discussing minority grievances before the Council at large or the Committee of Three. The redress of minority grievances thus depended in the last resort upon the good will of the accused government in applying such improvements as the Council or the Committee might recommend. The League did not provide for direct Council action on behalf of national minorities and against governments accused of violating the minority treaties. A German initiative of 1929 for the creation of a permanent League commission for minority questions was rejected by the Council.

THE PERMANENT COURT OF INTERNATIONAL JUSTICE; HUMANITARIAN AND SOCIAL WORK OF THE LEAGUE

The peace-keeping role of the League Council was supplemented by the work of the Permanent Court of International Justice, whose decisions, like those of the Council itself, remained primarily concerned with minor issues. Composed of fifteen judges of different nationalities, elected by the League Assembly, the Court had been organized by the Statute of 1920 in pursuance of Article 14 of the Covenant. The Court's competency, under Article 14, was to "hear and determine any dispute of an international character which the parties thereto submit to it." In addition, the Court was to give "an advisory opinion upon any dispute or question" referred to it by the League Council or by the Assembly. The Court's jurisdiction was extended under the "optional clause" of the 1920 Statute to all international disputes of a legal nature between League members subscribing to the "optional clause." The number of League members who adopted the "optional clause" increased significantly in the late 1920's when the illusion of stability had reached its high point in postwar Europe.

The Court's decisions and opinions ranged over a wide field, including the interpretation of certain clauses of the treaties of Versailles and Lausanne, as well as a tariff dispute between France and Switzerland, rival claims of Norway and Denmark on East Greenland, the Mosul dispute, and border questions between Poland and Czechoslovakia and between Yugoslavia and Albania. The Court's most controversial decision—and the most explosive one politically—was on the Austro-German customs' union, to be described more fully in the context of the crisis of 1931/1932.

In the period of stability, the League continued the humanitarian and social enterprises that it had successfully begun in the immediate postwar era. In the early 1920's, the Norwegian explorer Fridtjof Nansen, as League High Commissioner for the repatriation of prisoners of war, had succeeded in obtaining the release of over 400,000 prisoners of war from Soviet Russia. Undertaking a similar task in the late 1920's for refugees who had been displaced by the Russian Revolution, the Turkish-Greek conflict, and the expulsion of Armenians from Turkey, Nansen, as High Commissioner for Refugees, aided in the resettlement and employment of hundreds of thousands of displaced persons. The so-called Nansen passport for refugees, adopted by fifty-one governments in 1929, eased the legal insecurity of homeless refugees.

The International Labor Organization, in addition to assisting Nansen's effort of resettling the displaced persons of the First World War, adopted a number of conventions dealing with labor questions. Established for the purpose of securing fair and humane labor conditions, as envisaged under Article 23 of the Covenant, the International Labor Organization was patterned after the structure of the League, with an Annual Conference, a Governing Body, and an Office. The delegations to the Annual Conference were formed by representatives of the member governments as well as representatives of workers' and employers' organizations.

THE FAILURE OF DISARMAMENT

The League had proven itself competent in settling small-power disputes and in promoting causes of social and humanitarian betterment. It was less successful in reaching an agreement on the limitation of armaments, however, as disarmament was a question affecting the vital interests of the Great Powers.

Disarmament was one of the purposes for which the League had been established. "The Members of the League recognize," Article 8 of the Covenant announced, "that the maintenance of peace requires the reduction of national armaments to the lowest point consistent with national safety and the enforcement by common action of international obligations." Moreover, the Treaty of Versailles had promised that the disarmament of Germany was to be only the first step towards "a general limitation of the armaments of all nations." The League Council appointed a Temporary Mixed Commission for the purpose of formulating disarmament plans, as stated in Article 8 of the Covenant, at the very first League session in November, 1920.

The Temporary Mixed Commission failed to produce a disarmament plan acceptable to all Great Powers in the League. The failure of the Temporary Mixed Commission reflected the larger failure of the two principal Allies, Britain and France, to develop a common policy in the enforcement of the peace in the early postwar period. Anglo-French disagreements on the subject of security, which had been evident in the drafting of the Treaty of Versailles as well as of the League Covenant in 1919, deadlocked the disarmament talks of the early 1920's. Unlike France, Britain approached the twin problems of security and disarmament from the standpoint of a sea power. Based on the experience of the successful Washington Conference, which had limited the number of capital ships of each major sea power through fixed ratios, Britain proposed a similar solution for the limitation of land armaments. According to the British plan, submitted to the Temporary Mixed Commission in 1922, land forces were to be divided into units of 30,000 men each; each power was to be assigned a fixed number of such units proportionate to its security requirements. The ratio suggested for Britain, Italy, and France was 3:4:6. The British plan was rejected by France as well as other continental powers on the grounds that the fighting strength of armies could not be measured in terms applicable to battleships since it depended on other variables such as training and equipment.

France opposed the British initiative on the more general grounds that the requirement of "national safety," which Article 8 of the Covenant had cited as a condition for disarmament, remained unfulfilled in a League incapable of swift retaliation against aggression. A reduction of armaments depended, in the French view of the early 1920's, on the complete fulfillment of the peace treaties, disarmaments control over the defeated nations, and the establishment of an effective control system for the armaments of League members. The two efforts of providing the League with increased retaliatory powers, made in the form of the Draft Treaty of Mutual Assistance of 1923 and the Geneva Protocol of 1924, ended in failure, as previously mentioned. The defeat of the Geneva Protocol marked a further setback for disarmament. The Disarmament Conference that was to have opened in June, 1925, on condition of the Geneva Protocol's ratification was not held when the Geneva Protocol was repudiated in early 1925.

The Locarno Treaty promised a fresh start in the disarmament question, in view of the Treaty's benevolent effect on French-German relations. In signing the Locarno Treaty, the signatories expressed the hope that the agreements reached would render possible the disarmament provided for in Article 8 of the Covenant. Accordingly, the League

Council appointed a Preparatory Commission for the Disarmament Conference, which opened in May, 1926. The Preparatory Commission consisted of the members of the League Council, six League members which were not represented on the Council, and the United States and Germany. Soviet Russia, invited in 1925, joined the Preparatory Commission in 1927. The Preparatory Commission was to prepare draft agreements on disarmament and to suggest ways for the international supervision of armaments.

Disarmament became the crucial test of the spirit of Locarno. It remained for the Preparatory Commission to show whether European tensions had relaxed sufficiently to permit a solution of the security problem through disarmament rather than armed alliances. After laboring five years, the Preparatory Commission achieved no results, however, other than recording the disagreements among the powers on the principles of disarmament. Whereas Germany wished any limitation of armaments to be expressed in numbers, such as the Treaty of Versailles had imposed, France desired a limitation of military budgets, the only type of limitation not imposed on Germany under the Treaty of Versailles. On the subject of naval disarmament, France and Italy pleaded for a limitation of the total tonnage of fleets, whereas Britain and the United States favored a limitation of each category of war ships. Soviet Russia exploited the Preparatory Commission chiefly as a propaganda forum, demanding total and universal disarmament for all nations. Although the Preparatory Commission had failed to reach agreements even on the general principles of disarmament, the League called for the convocation of a Disarmament Conference for February, 1932.

THE NAVAL CONFERENCES OF GENEVA AND LONDON; LIMITED AGREEMENT ON NAVAL ARMAMENTS

While the Preparatory Commission remained deadlocked over questions of principle, the United States invited the signatories of the Washington Five Power Treaty in June, 1927, to attend a separate naval conference at Geneva. The United States deemed a supplementary naval agreement among the signatories of the Five Power Treaty desirable and necessary, as the naval race had been shifted to those vessels, not covered by the Washington agreements of 1922. Neither France nor Italy accepted the American invitation, since both powers preferred a general disarmament agreement to one limited to naval forces. The Geneva Naval Conference, which opened in June, 1927, thus remained limited to the United States, Great Britain, and Japan.

Agreement on the limitation of cruisers, destroyers, and submarines proved to be impossible even among the three powers which attended the Geneva Naval Conference, however, owing to the poor preparations of the Conference and the resulting clash of British and American viewpoints. The United States proposed to extend the Washington ratio for battleships of 5:5:3 to cruisers, destroyers, and submarines. To this arrangement, Britain objected on the grounds that Britain's far-flung possessions required seventy cruisers for protection. Although willing to extend the Washington ratio to heavy cruisers of 10,000 tons, Britain refused to accept a similar limitation for small cruisers of up to 7500 tons, carrying an armament of six-inch guns. The United States suspected a British attempt to evade the principle of naval parity, which the Washington agreements had established for the battleship fleets of Britain and the United States. On August 20, 1927, the Geneva Naval Conference ended without agreement, the mediation efforts of Japan having failed. The failure of the Geneva Naval Conference embittered Anglo-American relations and buried, for the moment, the concept of Anglo-American naval cooperation in the Pacific.

The Anglo-American naval rift was healed at the London Naval Conference, which opened in January, 1930. The threat of another Anglo-American deadlock was removed in advance of the London Conference when Britain's Labor Prime Minister Ramsay MacDonald had reaffirmed the principle of Anglo-American naval parity on his visit with President Hoover in October, 1929. Whereas Anglo-American differences on cruiser strength were settled at the London Naval Conference, the United States and Britain agreeing on parity in that category of vessels, Japan, France, and Italy balked at extending the Washington ratio to non-capital ships. France demanded a larger cruiser force for the protection of her colonies and refused to accept parity with Italy in non-capital ships. Japan advanced her claim for naval parity with the United States and Britain for the first time, suggesting the adventurous course of Japanese policy in Asia and the Pacific in the coming decade.

Agreement was reached at the London Naval Conference between the United States, Britain, and Japan only, since neither France nor Italy ratified the London Naval Treaty of April 22, 1930. In addition to establishing the principle of parity for the cruiser forces of the United States and Britain, the London Naval Treaty assigned Japan a 60 per cent ratio for heavy cruisers, a 70 per cent ratio for light cruisers and destroyers, and parity in submarine strength. The Washington ratio for capital ships was extended for another five years. An "escalator clause" permitted naval construction beyond the agreed limits by any signatory if a signatory deemed itself threatened by the naval construction of an outside power.

The agreements reached on the limitation of naval armaments in the Washington Five Power Treaty and the London Naval Treaty did not survive the stormy 1930's. Japan gave the required two years' notice for withdrawal from the Five Power Treaty in December, 1934. On December, 1935, Japan walked out from another naval conference convened in London, when she failed to win parity with the United States and Britain. In the Three Power Naval Treaty of March, 1936, the United States, Britain, and France agreed to exchange advance information on their naval programs. The United States and Britain reaffirmed the principle of naval parity between them. Naval disarmament, the only form of disarmament in which limited progress had been achieved in the 1920's, was succeeded in the late 1930's by a new naval race with the approach of war in the Atlantic and the Pacific. In 1938 the United States launched a naval building program designed to create a two-ocean navy superior to the combined fleets of Japan, Italy, and Germany.

THE KELLOGG-BRIAND PACT

While the great powers failed to achieve progress towards disarmament, new pact schemes appeared within and without the League which seemingly enhanced the cause of peace. On April 6, 1927, at the behest of the prominent pacifist leader Professor James T. Shotwell of Columbia University, Briand addressed an appeal to the American people to outlaw war as an instrument of national policy between France and the United States. The Republican administration of President Coolidge at first ignored Briand's initiative because of its informal nature. More important, the United States suspected Briand's motive, fearing a trap to associate the United States indirectly with the French alliance system in Europe. Briand persisted, however, and submitted a formal draft of the proposed treaty to the United States in June, 1927. Although the U. S. Secretary of State Frank B. Kellogg declared the proposed treaty to be neither necessary nor desirable, the Republican administration could ill afford to ignore the growing popularity of the concept of outlawing war, since a presidential election was approaching in 1928. Rather than accept the French proposal in its original form of a bilateral American-French Treaty, Kellogg suggested, on December 28, 1927, the renunciation of war as an instrument of national policy by "all of the principal powers of the world." The idea of a multilateral declaration had been endorsed by a resolution of the Senate Foreign Relations Committee, introduced on December 27, 1927 by its chairman Senator William E. Borah.

On August 27, 1928, the Kellogg-Briand Pact, or Pact of Paris, was signed by the United States, Britain, France, Germany, Italy, and Japan as well as Belgium, Poland, Czechoslovakia, the Dominions, and India. The number of states which eventually adhered to the Paris Pact increased to sixty-five, exceeding the membership of the League. Soviet Russia at first interpreted the Pact of Paris as a sinister device for capitalist encirclement. In the words of Soviet Foreign Minister Chicherin, the Pact of Paris was "an organic part of the preparation for war against the USSR." Upon closer examination, however, Russia regarded the Pact of Paris as a possible aid to Soviet security in Eastern Europe. The Litvinov Protocol, signed in February, 1929, between Soviet Russia and most states of Eastern Europe bordering on Russia, put the Pact of Paris into regional effect in advance of its general ratification.

The Pact of Paris was as brief in its provisions as it was silent on the manner of their enforcement. The signatories pledged to renounce war "as an instrument of national policy" and to settle their disputes "by peaceful means." Like the Holy Alliance, concluded after the Congress of Vienna, the Pact of Paris announced pious principles without devising a machinery for their application. Moreover, the numerous interpretations, amounting to reservations, which the signatories gave to the Pact of Paris suggested that none would hesitate to use force if force were necessary to uphold vital national interests. The Treaty was not to impair the right of self-defense. Britain declared that self-defense included, in her case, the defense of "certain regions" whose welfare and integrity constituted "a special and vital interest" of British policy. The U. S. Senate, when ratifying the Pact of Paris in January, 1929, specifically exempted the Monroe Doctrine from its scope.

Isolationist opponents of the Pact of Paris, such as Henry Cabot Lodge, denounced the Pact as a "misconception," since the signatories appeared to have agreed never to go to war except in those cases where they were most likely to go to war. American isolationists criticized the Pact on the further grounds that it had raised European expectations of an increased American role in world affairs. Such was, in fact, the hope of Briand, who characterized the Pact of Paris as a new "moral association" of the nations of the world, which France and the United States had jointly sponsored.

To implement the promise of the Pact of Paris, Great Britain proposed an amendment of the League Covenant in 1929 that would extend the sanctions of Article 16 of the Covenant to all wars, outlawed by the Pact of Paris. The British initiative of 1929 was a significant departure from previous British efforts to limit, rather than expand, the obligations of collective security under the League. In 1929 Britain had formed its second Labor government, however, and the policy of Prime Minister Ramsay MacDonald and Foreign Secretary Arthur Henderson reflected the foreign policy platform of "Labour and Nation," the document adopted by the Labor Party Conference of Birmingham of 1928. "Labour and Nation" had called for a British foreign policy based on both collective security against aggression and collective renunciation of war as an instrument of national policy.

The British initiative, which was strongly supported by France, became the subject of extended debate in the League. In 1931, when the Assembly moved to a vote, the British government had changed once more and the general world situation had deteriorated to the point where unanimous approval by the Assembly was impossible. The ineffectiveness of the Pact of Paris was demonstrated as early as 1929, when Soviet Russia brusquely rejected an American proposal to solve a Soviet-Chinese dispute concerning Manchuria by invoking the Pact of Paris. Japan and Italy, both signatories of the Pact of Paris, would soon display a more overt contempt for the pledge of outlawing war, through the invasion of Manchuria and the attack on Ethiopia.

PROSPERITY AND THE SHADOWS OF DEPRESSION; THE YOUNG PLAN

The flow of American capital to Europe was essential to the regaining of Europe's economic health in the mid-1920's. Of the $11.4 billion in American foreign loans made between 1920 and 1931, Europe received the largest share of any region of the world, with 40 per cent. Germany alone obtained some two billion dollars in American loans during the five-year period following the adoption of the Dawes Plan, together with an equal amount from other sources, principally British and Dutch. During the economic boom of the mid and late 1920's, the industrial growth rate of Western Europe surpassed that of the United States. German industrial production, which had dropped to less than half the 1913 level under the impact of the Ruhr invasion, regained its pre-war level in some, though not all, areas by 1927.

Unlike the economic recovery of Western Europe after the Second World War, which was accomplished in large measure through the $13 billion Marshall Plan aid, the European boom of the 1920's was based on borrowed money. Unlike the Allies of the Second World War, whose war expenditures were covered to a substantial extent by the gift of American Lend Lease, the European Allies of the First World War had to repay their war debts to the United States. Between 1923 and 1926 the United States negotiated individual funding agreements with its debtors of the First World War, calling for the full repayment of the debt principals at varying interest rates over a sixty-two year period. The solution of the European debt problem was further aggravated by the neo-mercantilist tariff policy of the United States as reflected in the Fordney-McCumber tariff of September, 1922, and the Hawley-Smoot Act of June, 1930. The high protective tariffs virtually closed the American market to numerous articles of European export.

The cycle of German reparations payments to the Allies under the Dawes Plan and of the Allied debt payments to the U. S.

Treasury continued without difficulty, as long as the life blood of American loans kept flowing into Germany. Germany's foreign public debt, the reparations, was in fact financed by foreign private loans to Germany, as Germany's own export earnings remained inadequate to cover the reparations payments. Once American loans were stopped, as they would be in the aftermath of the 1929 depression, the structure of reparations payments and Allied debt payments was bound to collapse. Even before the crash of 1929, Germany began to experience foreign exchange difficulties, however, in part because of unsound borrowing practices. Only 35 per cent of the foreign loans went to German industry and business enterprises, which could repay the loans through foreign earnings. The largest share, 45 per cent, went to the government and municipalities, which spent the money on such projects as urban renewal and public works. As a result, it became difficult for Germany to maintain sufficient foreign currency reserves for the payment of reparations as well as the servicing of Germany's extravagant private debt.

The German government deemed the signing of the Kellogg-Briand Pact on August 27, 1928, a favorable moment for the reopening of talks on reparations and on early evacuation of the Rhineland, on which the Thoiry meeting of 1926 had failed to reach a settlement. The French Prime Minister Poincaré and Stresemann, the two opponents of the Ruhr crisis, met in the French Ministry of Finance on August 27, 1928. To Stresemann's observation that Germany's good credit rating in the United States was a better guarantee of German reparations payments than the Rhineland occupation, Poincaré replied that no final reparations settlement was possible without a solution of the inter-Allied debt problem. As Britain was anxious to end the Rhineland occupation, however, Germany succeeded on September 16, 1928, in obtaining a pledge from Britain, France, and Belgium to open negotiations on the Rhineland evacuation and on a final reparations settlement.

The Allied decision to reopen the reparations question was prompted, in part, by the recommendations of the Transfer Agent, Parker Gilbert, who had pointed to the growing indebtedness of Germany and the desirability of removing Allied controls, imposed by the Dawes Plan, on the German economy.

On June 7, 1929, a "committee of financial experts," which, unlike that of 1924, included German representatives, presented a new reparations plan named after its U. S. chairman, Owen Young. Unlike the Dawes Plan, the Young Plan of 1929 was conceived as a "complete and definite solution of the reparation problem." The Plan removed all foreign controls, established under the Dawes Plan, including the Allied Transfer Agent. The Reparations Commission was dissolved and replaced by a new Bank of International Settlements. For a period of thirty-seven years, German reparation annuities were to rise from 1.7 billion to a maximum of 2.5 billion marks, and decline thereafter to a final payment of 900 million marks in 1988. In the event of an American remission of Allied war debts, Germany was to benefit up to two thirds of the remission prior to 1965 and to its full extent afterwards. In the event of German exchange difficulties, two thirds of the reparations annuity (the "conditional" part) could be postponed for up to two years.

During the drafting of the Young Plan, the German "experts," headed by Hjalmar Schacht, had attempted to raise political conditions as a price for German acceptance of a new reparations settlement. These conditions, a frontier revision with Poland and the return of German colonies, were rejected by the Allies. Still, Stresemann achieved his major goal of securing an Allied promise for the evacuation of the Rhineland by June, 1930, five years ahead of the Versailles timetable. The promise, made at the Hague Conference on August 30, 1929, was to be Stresemann's last foreign policy triumph. Exhausted by partisan domestic strife, the German Foreign Minister died on October 3, 1929, amidst a violent campaign against the Young Plan, a campaign organized by the German Nationalist opposition and Hitler's rising Nazi party.

On June 30, 1930, the last foreign troops left the Rhineland. In the German celebrations which followed, no mention was made of Briand and Stresemann or the spirit of Locarno which both men had tried to implement with varying success. The moment of Stresemann's greatest foreign policy success also marked the return of suspicion and distrust to French-German relations. France watched in bewilderment as Germany responded to the Rhineland evacuation, not with a gesture of gratitude, but with the election of 107 Nazi deputies to the Reichstag in September, 1930.

BRIAND'S PROJECT OF A EUROPEAN FEDERAL UNION

The death of Stresemann in October, 1929, and the emergence of Hitler's Nazi party as a German mass movement in September, 1930, signalled the end of a liberal Germany in foreign and domestic affairs. As recently as September, 1929, Briand had submitted a project for a European Federal Union to the Tenth League Assembly in the hope of crowning his policy of international understanding with a system for the economic and political integration of Europe. Like the illusion of a Europe pacified, Briand's idea of a federal union vanished with the onset of the harsher climate of the 1930's.

The proposed European Federal Union was to have permanent supranational organs, such as a political committee and a secretariat. The Union was to promote the lowering of tariffs without, however, affecting the sovereignty and independence of its members. "Will not the very genius of each nation," Briand asked, "be able to assert itself more consciously in its individual cooperation in the collective work, under a system of federal union fully compatible with respect for traditions and for the characteristics peculiar to each people?"

Although Briand's proposal was received politely in 1929, the reservations and objections raised by the powers in the course of 1930 condemned the project to a quiet death in the League-appointed Commission of Inquiry for European Union. In opposing the European Federal Union, Britain advanced arguments similar to those which made her entry into the European Common Market difficult in the 1960's. Apart from expressing the fear that a Federal Union might become a rival of the League of Nations, Britain stressed her special relationship with the members of the Commonwealth as an obstacle to British membership in the projected European Federal Union. Italy objected on the grounds that an agreement on disarmament must precede the more ambitious project of a federal union. The small states of Eastern Europe were generally in favor of the French proposal. Germany opposed it on the grounds that the union project seemed to be another French attempt to assure the permanence of the European frontiers, especially those of Central-Eastern Europe, which Germany was anxious to revise.

In seeking a more positive approach to French security, Briand had based his foreign policy since 1924 upon four major principles: (1) the preservation of the French alliance system in Eastern Europe as a safeguard of immediate security; (2) the broadening of the base of European peace through the collective guarantees of the Locarno Treaty and the establishment of a European Federal Union; (3) the achievement of a moral and psychological solidarity of the nations of the world against war through the Kellogg-Briand Pact; and (4) the concentration on collective action in the event that "pressing risks" endangered the pacification of Europe. The recrudescence of German nationalism on a broad scale in 1930 represented the "pressing risk" of which Briand had spoken. In the period from 1930 to 1933, which shattered the illusion of stability, France was increasingly concerned with implementing the fourth of Briand's foreign policy principles.

SOVIET RUSSIA, THE WEST, AND ASIA IN THE ERA OF LOCARNO

By 1924 Soviet Russia had succeeded in establishing full diplomatic relations with every major European power as well as with many of the smaller nations. Following the *de jure* recognition of Soviet Russia by Ramsay MacDonald's Labor government on February 2, 1924, Fascist Italy followed suit on February 8, 1924, and Herriot's Cartel of the Left on October 28, 1924. The Weimar Republic had established full diplomatic relations with Soviet Russia in the Treaty of Rappalo of April 1922, as previously noted. Norway, Denmark, and Sweden, as well as Austria and Greece, likewise extended *de jure* recognition to the Soviet government in 1924, whereas Spain, Portugal, Holland, Belgium, Switzerland, Hungary, and Bulgaria, as well as the nations of the Little Entente, continued to withhold formal recognition. In the Western Hemisphere only Uruguay and Mexico had extended formal recognition to the Soviet regime. The United States, despite increased investments and business dealings by private American companies in Soviet Russia, rejected all Soviet overtures for formal diplomatic relations throughout the 1920's.

The establishment of formal relations with the Great Powers of the non-Communist world was essential to Soviet Russia, not only for reasons of national security, but also for the purpose of increased trade with the West. With the gradual termination of the N.E.P. in the late 1920's and the beginnings of Soviet Russia's industrial crash program under the first Five Year Plan, the Soviet need for Western machinery and technical assistance in the form of engineers and skilled workers rose sharply. Although overall Soviet foreign trade remained small relative to the total volume of world trade, accounting for only 1.3 per cent of world trade in 1929, Soviet imports from the industrial nations of the West, particularly Germany and the United States, rose sharply between 1924 and 1929. By the latter date, Germany supplied over 22 per cent of Russia's imports and the United States over 20 per cent, Britain and France following at a considerable distance with 6 per cent and 4 per cent respectively. The overall value of Soviet imports between 1926 and 1928 rose from $346 to $490 million, remaining, however, considerably below the pre-war level of Russian imports, which had climbed to $700 million in 1913.

While Soviet foreign policy aimed at the achievement of normal political and trade relations with the non-Communist world, it continued to view the major Western powers with profound suspicion, watching their every move for possible signs of a new coalition against Soviet Russia. Soviet talk about the imminence of another Western intervention, such as Britain, France, and the United States had launched during the Russian Civil War, did not always reflect the true Soviet estimate of Western intentions, to be sure. The war hysteria which the Soviet government stirred up in 1927 after the rupture of Anglo-Soviet relations served rather the needs of the domestic power struggle within the Politburo. It also served to create an atmosphere of fear and siege within Soviet Russia to justify the enormous demands which the Soviet regime was about to impose on its population to implement the first Five Year Plan.

The memory of foreign intervention remained alive, however, and the basic hostility of the Western powers, particularly Britain, continued to be taken for granted. The Manifesto of the Sixth Comintern Congress of 1928 thus charged that "despite all the contradictions and antagonisms which exist between the capitalist powers . . . they are preparing, with Great Britain at their head, a war against the Soviet Union."

The "contradictions and antagonisms" between the capitalist powers, which, in the Soviet view, had been so essential to the success of the Bolshevik Revolution and its survival in the Civil War, had been considerably lessened, however, in the Locarno era. Soviet Russia had thus followed with growing dismay the adoption of the Dawes Plan, the signing of the Locarno Treaty, and Germany's entry into the League, for the German-Allied rapprochement of the mid-1920's threatened to end the postwar divisions of Capitalist Europe and heightened the chances of concerted action against the Soviet Union.

Accordingly, Soviet Foreign Minister Chicherin had made strenuous efforts in 1925 to block Germany's political integration into the West. The Locarno Treaty, Chicherin threatened, would mean the end of the Rapallo Treaty; the road to Geneva (into the League), Chicherin warned, would become for Germany "a road to Canossa."

THE TREATY OF BERLIN

Chicherin's threats and warnings had limited success only. The main thrust of German foreign policy under Stresemann was pro-Western, as previously noted, since Stresemann had few illusions about the lasting value of Soviet friendship. During his brief tenure as German chancellor from August to November, 1923, Stresemann had had occasion to observe the difference between official Soviet friendship, as pledged under the Rapallo Treaty, and the revolutionary designs of the Communist International, as implemented in the German Communist uprising of "Red October" in 1923. "When the Russians will have reached Berlin," Stresemann observed, "and the Red Flag will wave from the Castle, they will be content to bolshevize Europe as far as the Elbe and will throw the rest of Germany to the French to devour." However, whereas Stresemann desired a rapprochement with the West, he did not wish to sever Germany's special relations with Soviet Russia under the Rapallo policy. Accordingly, Germany granted Soviet Russia a neutrality pact, for which Chicherin had been asking. On April 24, 1926, Chicherin and Stresemann signed the Treaty of Berlin, which pledged the neutrality of both powers in the event of an unprovoked attack upon either, as well as nonparticipation in economic boycotts directed against either power. Germany reaffirmed the limitations of her obligations under Article 16 of the Covenant, limitations to which the Locarno powers had agreed and which virtually ruled out German participation in League sanctions against Russia. The Berlin Treaty was followed by a Soviet-German treaty of conciliation in January, 1929. The Berlin Treaty, it should be noted, remained in effect also in the 1930's, upon its renewal by Hitler soon after the Nazi seizure of power in 1933.

The Berlin Treaty formed but one link in the chain of security pacts that Soviet Russia concluded in Europe to minimize the dangers of her new isolation in the wake of the Locarno Treaty. In December, 1925, Soviet Russia had concluded a neutrality treaty with Turkey, which was followed by a treaty between Soviet Russia and Afghanistan in August and a Soviet-Lithuanian non-aggression pact in September, 1926. In October, 1927, Russia concluded a non-aggression pact with Persia, in which both powers further agreed not to participate in boycotts or block-ades directed against either signatory. The Litvinov-Protocol of February 9, 1929, as previously noted, was an adroit Soviet move to turn the Kellogg-Briand Pact to Russia's advantage by using it as a regional secur-ity system in Eastern Europe. Signed by the USSR, Poland, Rumania, Latvia, and Estonia in February, the Litvinov Protocol was expanded to include Lithuania, Turkey, Persia, and the Free City of Danzig by July, 1929. With the exception of Finland, which was anxious to align itself with the Scandinavian states, all the border states of European Russia had thus joined in accepting the Litvinov Protocol.

Soviet relations with the Western democracies remained tense, however, partly because of the activities of the Comintern, partly because the Soviet government itself continued to heap scorn on Western efforts to pacify Europe through schemes such as Briand's Federal Union. The role of the Communist International had changed, to be sure, and even so optimistic a prophet of world revolution as Leon Trotsky had to admit, after the German Communist fiasco of 1923, that "Red October" was "the last card of an historic epoch." In the mid-1920's the relationship between Soviet Russia and the Comintern became reversed from what it had been in the immediate postwar period. Whereas previously Soviet Russia had seen its *raison d'être* as the promoter of world revolution through the in-strument of the Comintern, the Comintern increasingly assumed the task of protecting Soviet Russia against foreign dangers while socialism was being built in Russia. The total submission of foreign Communist parties to Moscow and the eradication of the last vestiges of an independent ap-proach to Communism, following the establishment of Stalinism in the late 1920's, were but two expressions of the Comintern's new role in the 1920's.

In China, as will be seen, Comintern efforts to promote revo-lution on a grand scale continued until 1927. In the Western democracies,

Comintern activity focused on sharpening the divisions of class, of nationality, and, in the case of the United States, of race.

GREAT BRITAIN AND THE COMINTERN

The prime target of Comintern propaganda remained Great Britain, however, which occupied a position in the Soviet mind of the 1920's that the United States would occupy in the period of the cold war during the late 1940's and the 1950's. The pre-war confrontation of tsarist Russia and the British Empire in Asia, briefly overcome after the Anglo-Russian entente of 1907, reappeared under the new guise of ideological conflict between imperialism and Comintern-supported national revolutions in China, Persia, and Turkey. Although Russia had promised to stop anti-British propaganda in Persia, India, and Afghanistan, following the Curzon ultimatum of May 8, 1923, Comintern agitation for the total independence of India, Egypt, and Ireland was resumed in 1924. In that year the British Secretary of State for India, Lord Birkenhead, charged that Soviet Russia aimed at the destruction of the British Empire. Sir Austen Chamberlain, the Foreign Secretary, sought common action with French Prime Minister Herriot to suppress Communist propaganda in the colonies.

The continuing attacks by the Comintern on the British Empire were bound to affect Anglo-Soviet political and trade relations. The Anglo-Soviet trade agreement, concluded on August 8, 1924, by the British Labor government, was denounced in November, 1924, by the Conservative government, which had succeeded Ramsay MacDonald following the incident of the "Zinoviev letter." In 1924, the British Foreign office claimed to have come into possession of Comintern instructions to the British Communist Party, drafted by Zinoviev, for the subversion of the British army and munitions workers, in order to paralyze Britain's future war efforts. Although denounced as a forgery by Zinoviev, the "Zinoviev letter" was instrumental in the defeat of the Labor Party in 1924. Anglo-Soviet relations declined rapidly under the Conservative government of Stanley Baldwin when Russian trade unions offered financial aid to British workers during the general strike of 1926. In 1927 the Conservatives severed diplomatic relations with Soviet Russia following the exposure of the Soviet trade mission in London, "Arcos," as a center of Soviet espionage and Comintern propaganda. Anglo-Soviet relations were not resumed until December, 1929, after Britain had formed its second Labor government.

Although Soviet Russia participated in the Preparatory Commission for the Disarmament Conference, she kept aloof from the League of Nations at large. Briand's project of a European Federal Union, Stalin denounced in June, 1930, in scathing terms as a camouflage for upholding the hegemony of France, "the most striking representative of the bourgeois movement towards intervention against the Soviet Union" and "the most aggressive and militaristic country among all aggressive and militaristic countries of the world," in Stalin's words.

SOVIET RUSSIA AND CHINA

Soviet policy in China in the late 1920's was equally unsettling to the Western powers when Russia appeared initially to succeed in exploiting the Chinese nationalist revolution for the larger Soviet aim of weakening Western influence in Asia. The prospects for collaboration between Communist Russia and Sun Yat-sen's nationalist Chinese Kuomintang seemed bright indeed in the early phase of Soviet foreign policy, as the Kuomintang, without being Communist, admired the Bolshevik mastery of the technique of political revolution. Moreover, the young Soviet regime had scored a major propaganda success in China when it renounced, in the so-called Kharakan declaration of July, 1919 (after Lev Kharakan, Soviet Deputy Foreign Commissar), the unequal treaties between tsarist Russia and China, as well as Russian rights over the Chinese Eastern Railroad. The early 1920's witnessed a return of Russian power politics to China, however, when Soviet Russia reclaimed control over the Chinese Eastern Railroad, established a protectorate over Outer Mongolia, and dealt with the several existing centers of Chinese political power.

With the official Chinese Republican government at Peking, Russia established diplomatic relations in 1924, while dealing separately with the Chinese war-lord Chang Tso-lin, who controlled Manchuria. To the Kuomintang, centered in Canton and South China, Soviet Russia furnished advice and military assistance, in the hope of using it for Bolshevik ends in China as the Kuomintang's political effectiveness and military power grew. Sun Yat-sen's military adviser, Chiang Kai-shek, was trained at the Moscow Military Academy. The Chinese Communist Party, only recently established in 1921, was ordered by Moscow to support the Kuomintang.

Soviet and Chinese Communist influence increased perceptibly in the Kuomintang following the death of Sun Yat-sen in 1925; in 1926 the Kuomintang was even admitted to the Communist International, despite its official non-Communist character. Soviet Russia seemed on the verge of a major victory in China, when Chiang Kai-shek spoiled the Russian game, beginning in 1926. Whereas Stalin had hoped to use the Kuomintang, it was Chiang Kai-shek who purged the Kuomintang of all Communist influence after accepting Soviet military assistance. Having advanced to Shanghai in early 1927, Chiang Kai-shek ordered a massacre of Chinese Communists on April 12, 1927.

Coming at a time when Soviet foreign policy faced a serious

crisis in Europe owing to the rupture of Anglo-Soviet relations, the Chinese crisis of 1927 preoccupied the Soviet leadership as few issues of Soviet foreign policy had since the controversy over the Treaty of Brest-Litovsk in 1918. As mentioned in the discussion of Soviet domestic affairs, the Chinese crisis of 1927 also had a direct bearing on the Trotsky-Stalin feud. Whereas Trotsky favored unleashing the Chinese Communists against the Kuomintang in 1927, Stalin postponed independent action by the Chinese Communists until 1928, when their forces were scattered and defeated.

The China debacle of 1927 pointed to the risks attendant upon an ambitious Comintern policy while Soviet Russia itself remained too weak militarily and industrially to withstand foreign attack. The revolutionary energy and dynamism of the Bolshevik party, which had failed to achieve a single lasting success abroad in the first decade of Soviet Russia's existence, was directed in the second decade of the history of Soviet Russia towards the massive industrialization and mechanization of Soviet society under the Stalinist Five Year Plans. It required the dual threat of German Nazism and Japanese imperialism in the 1930's to achieve a better coordination of Soviet foreign policy and Comintern behavior than had appeared possible under the often contradictory purposes of Soviet foreign policy and Comintern action in the 1920's.

8 | The End of the Illusion

THE DEPRESSION

The crash of the New York Stock Exchange in October, 1929, resulting in a drop of share values by $30 billion, set off a worldwide economic slump of unprecedented intensity and duration in the history of the modern world. The crisis in the American economy quickly spread to Europe, owing to the latter's dependence on American loan capital and the financial interdependence through Allied debt payments and German reparations.

Although the Depression affected the national economies of Europe in varying degrees and at different times, no European nation escaped its effects altogether. During its initial and most acute phase from 1929 to 1932, the Depression caused a drop in overall European industrial production by 30 per cent, excluding Russia. World trade similarly showed a decline by 20 per cent between 1929 and 1931, while unemployment figures in the industrial nations of the West climbed to catastrophic levels, reaching 12 million out of a total labor force of 48 million in the United States, 3 million in Great Britain and 6 million, or 43 per cent of the entire labor force, in Germany.

Not only did the Depression shatter the illusion of economic recovery held in the 1920's, but it assaulted the very foundations of democracy as well. The opening of a new decade in 1930 seemed to fulfill the prophecies of doom which Western intellectuals, such as Paul Valery, had issued at the conclusion of the First World War. Assessing the illusion of Europe's recovery in the 1920's more accurately than most statesmen of his time, Valery had warned that the end of the First World War was but a temporary passing of the storm which had engulfed the civilization of the West in 1914; Europe remained restless and uneasy, in Valery's observation, "as if the storm were about to break" again.

The "storm" or "economic blizzard," as Winston Churchill called it, was not met by concerted action of the powers principally affected by it. As has been seen, it had been difficult enough to achieve even a measure of political collaboration among the European powers in the apparently tranquil 1920's; no permanent organs of international economic cooperation had issued from the peace treaties of 1919, however, and, with the onset of the Depression, each power sought salvation and survival through a return to economic nationalism and a policy of autarky, or economic self-sufficiency. Such efforts at concerted action as were undertaken, were shortlived and barren of results. The World Economic Conference at London in June, 1933, attended by the representatives of sixty-four states, repeated vainly the call for lower tariffs which the Geneva World Economic Conference, held under League auspices in 1927, had issued. A British proposal for a "tariff truce," made in 1929, likewise had gone unheeded. The generalities of international economic cooperation faded before the concrete issues of economic nationalism: whereas Britain, the United States, and Japan had abandoned the gold standard by 1933 in an effort to stimulate their exports, France and other members of the "gold bloc," such as Italy and Switzerland, had not. At the London World Economic Conference, France thus demanded that currency stabilization precede any agreement on the reduction of tariffs and import quotas. By July, 1933, the World Economic Conference adjourned *sine die,* no significant agreement having been reached. The gold-bloc nations, in any event, soon abandoned the gold standard, Italy in 1935, France, Switzerland, and Holland in 1936. In 1937, France, Britain, and the United States concluded a Tripartite Agreement to maintain a fixed exchange rate between the franc, pound, and dollar, following devaluation.

Briand's project of a European Federal Union, proposed, in part, as a means of lowering tariffs, remained stillborn, as previously noted, because of the political reservations of Great Britain, Italy, and Germany. No more successful was an attempt at regional economic cooperation among the predominantly agricultural nations of Central-Eastern Europe and the Balkans, which were particularly hard hit by the fall of world timber prices since 1928 and the decline of wheat prices since 1929. The project of a Balkan federation, advanced by Greece in 1930, failed when Bulgaria injected the issue of minority rights into the discussion. Similarly fruitless were the economic conferences held in rapid succession throughout 1930 in Bucharest, Warsaw, and Athens between Poland, the Danubian states, and the Balkan states, for the purpose of devising economic remedies against the agricultural depression.

The Hoover Moratorium, announced on June 20, 1931, was a notable exception to the failure of international cooperation against the effects of the Depression. By waiving all intergovernmental payments for one year on condition that other governments would follow the American example, the Hoover Moratorium restored temporary confidence following the collapse of the Austrian and German banking systems, to be more fully discussed in the context of the Austro-German customs' union project of 1931. The beneficial effects of the Hoover Moratorium were considerably lessened, however, by the reluctance of France to accept the standstill agreement and the delay caused thereby. Since the Hoover Moratorium applied to government debts only, including reparations and Allied debts, but not to private loans, France suspected a move to protect private American loans in Europe at the expense of French reparation receipts under the Young Plan. Accordingly, France agreed to the Hoover Moratorium only after protracted negotiations with Britain and the United States and on condition that the principle of reparations be upheld. Whereas Germany was thus made to pay the "unconditional" part of her obligations under the Young Plan during the Hoover Moratorium, the payment was reissued as a loan to the German railroads.

Although the participants of the London World Economic Conference paid lip service to the reduction of tariffs as a remedial measure against the stagnation of world trade, the nations of depression-ridden Europe pursued, in fact, the opposite course. The United States, as previously mentioned, set the example of higher protective tariffs with the adoption of the Hawley-Smoot Tariff of 1930. To be sure, a Reciprocal Trade Agreement Amendment to the Hawley-Smoot Tariff in June, 1934, empowered the President of the United States to reduce American tariffs by as much as 50 per cent. Although the benefits of the Reciprocal Trade Agreement were extended eventually to twenty-one states, the Hawley-Smoot tariff rate was so high to begin with that even a cut of 50 per cent did not bring significant relief to foreign nations anxious to sell on the American market.

Britain followed the American example with the adoption of the Import Duties Bill of February 4, 1932, which imposed a general duty of 10 per cent on all imports, save those from the Empire. In addition Britain sought relief through preferential tariff agreements with the Dominions, concluded at the Imperial Conference at Ottawa in July and August, 1932. As a result of the Ottawa agreements, British imports from the Dominions, the British colonies, and India increased from 24 per cent of Britain's overseas trade in 1931 to 37 per cent in 1937, while British exports to these areas rose from 32 to 39 per cent. Germany, Italy, and the states of Eastern Europe all followed the pattern of protectionism; Germany, for example, raised the price of rye and wheat considerably above the world level at a time when starvation threatened the growing army of German unemployed.

In combatting the Depression, the governments of Europe and the United States employed the time-honored methods of cutting public expenditures, increasing taxes, and attempting to balance budgets. Government intervention in the economy reached, to be sure, unprecedented proportions, as under the New Deal of the United States, the economic program of Leon Blum's Popular Front government in France, and the corrective measures of the National Government of Britain. No Western government embarked on a deliberate policy of deficit spending, however, as a means of overcoming the Depression. Massive intervention notwithstanding, belief in the self-correcting mechanism of Capitalist economies, typical of 19th-century classic economic liberalism, was not abandoned.

By contrast, John Meynard Keynes, the noted British economist, advocated in his *General Theory of Employment, Interest, and Money,* in 1936, that depressions should not be left to work themselves out through the self-regulatory mechanisms of a free economy. Although Keynes never lost faith in Capitalism and although he did not question its ability to cure itself out of its own resources in the long run, he doubted the relevancy of classic economic liberal doctrine to the crisis in 20th-century Capitalism. In his view, the correctives of 19th-century Capitalism, such as price flexibility, no longer fully obtained in 20th-century Capitalism. As the experience of the Depression clearly showed, the decline in prices did not keep pace with diminishing demand, since consumption declined as a result of wage cuts and unemployment. The mechanism of supply and demand was disturbed by the power of organized business and organized labor or by government intervention through such devices as minimum wage standards. The way out of a depression, in Keynes's thesis, was not reduced spending, so characteristic of economic policy between 1930 and 32, but increased spending. As increased spending could not, under depressed conditions, come from the consuming public, and would not come from business, which lacked the confidence, it must come from governments by virtue of their greater borrowing power. As a necessary, short-term, remedial measure, Keynes thus proposed the creation of additional spending power through deficit financing. Deficit financing, according to Keynes, was sound economics if undertaken for limited periods, until the rate of savings had equalled the rate of new investments. In the long run, the Capitalist economy could recover from depressions without such remedial measures, according to Keynes, but the damage done would be too great; in the long run, Keynes observed, "we will all be dead."

Revolutionary at the time of its publication in 1936, the *General Theory of Employment, Interest, and Money* did not influence the economic policy of governments in the 1930's. The application of Keynes's theses awaited another generation, whose leaders had been exposed to the "new economics" of the late 1930's.

The Depression ran its full and lamentable course and, in the process, gnawed at the very roots of European democracy. The siege of European democracy through external pressure and internal doubt and alienation began with the Depression, as the young and inexperienced democratic regimes of Germany, Austria, and the successor states of Eastern Europe fell one by one under the weight of economic misery and despair. The Depression was the midwife of the totalitarianism of Hitler in Germany, of Dollfuss in Austria, and of the various forms of dictatorship which emerged in the early 1930's—in Hungary under Gömbös, in Bulgaria under King Boris, and in Rumania under King Carol. In the Far East, the drop of Japanese exports by nearly 50 per cent between 1929 and

1931 was a powerful incentive to Japanese aggression in Manchuria, as Japan sought self-sufficiency through the conquest of Manchurian natural resources. Although the political repercussions of the Depression were less severe in the established Western democracies, Western intellectuals, such as André Gide and André Malraux, looked to the Soviet example as an inspiration for the future. The failure of classical economic liberalism seemed to confirm the validity of classical Marxism, as Europe and the United States groped in the economic dark while Soviet Russia embarked on her bold new course of industrialization under Stalin's first Five Year Plan. The disillusionment of Western intellectuals with Stalinist Russia, more fully described in the discussion of Soviet Russia's domestic affairs, did not arrive until the late 1930's, following the display of Stalinist terror in the Great Purge and the cynical reversal of Soviet foreign policy in the Stalin-Hitler pact of 1939. Ideologically as well as politically, European democracy remained on the defensive throughout the decade of the 1930's, however, reaching its nadir at the end of the decade with the fall of the Third French Republic in 1940. By that time, every major power of continental Europe from the Urals to the Atlantic had adopted either Communist, Fascist, or related forms of government.

THE JAPANESE CONQUEST OF MANCHURIA

As the Depression shattered the illusion of European postwar prosperity, the Japanese conquest of Manchuria, beginning with the attack of September 18, 1931, near Mukden, revealed the hollowness of the Kellogg-Briand Pact as well as the inadequacy of the League in conciliating Great Power disputes.

Japanese interests in Manchuria, like those of Russia, dated from the beginning of the 20th century. Although Manchuria had nominally remained a part of China, Russia and Japan exercised virtual control over Manchurian rail communications, Russia through the Chinese Eastern Railway, Japan through the South Manchurian Railway. In addition, both Russia and Japan owned various commercial interests. Those of Japan extended to mining, forestry, cattle-raising, shipping, and steel industries, which together accounted for 40 per cent of Japanese foreign investments in 1931. The Treaty of Portsmouth of 1905, ending the Russo-Japanese war of 1904/1905, had given Japan the right to station troops in Manchuria, which numbered some 15,000 and which were supposed to be confined to the railway zone of the South Manchurian Railway. Soviet Russia, as has been seen, reclaimed its rights and interests in Manchuria through a treaty of May 31, 1924, with the Peking government as well as an agreement of September 20, 1924, with the Manchurian authorities at Mukden, following Soviet Russia's earlier repudiation of the "unequal treaties" with China.

The rise of Chinese nationalism and the successful Nationalist Chinese revolution of the late 1920's was bound to affect the position of both Russia and Japan in Manchuria. Not only did the Nationalists clamor for an end to the "unequal treaties" between China and the Western powers, which had limited Chinese sovereignty in such matters as the fixing of tariff rates and the extraterritorial status of foreign residents; they also aimed at control over Manchuria as North China was being brought under Nationalist power, following the capture of Peking in June, 1928.

By the late 1920's Britain and the United States attempted to come to terms with the Nationalist Chinese government, which had installed itself first at Hankow, then at Nanking. The Western powers' willingness to deal with Chiang Kai-shek increased when he purged the Kuomintang of its Communist influence in 1927. Britain extended *de facto* recognition to the Kuomintang as early as December, 1926, when it sent its ambassador to Hankow in order to propose negotiations for a revision of the "unequal treaties" and an increase of the Chinese tariff. The United States granted China full sovereignty in the tariff question through a treaty of July 25, 1928, thereby also extending recognition to the Chinese Nationalist government at Nanking. The development towards normal relations between the Chinese Nationalist government and the Western powers did not proceed without setbacks. The deep-seated Chinese aversion to all foreigners was vented in such explosions as the Nanking Incident. Upon entering Nanking in March, 1927, Nationalist Chinese troops as well as aroused private citizens attacked foreign residents and their property. Though threatening to retaliate with military force, the Western powers did not implement that threat when the United States broke the common Western front, seeking redress through negotiations instead. The Nanking Incident of 1927 thus did not result in common punitive action by foreign powers such as they took after the "Boxers" Rebellion of 1900, when an international force of American, British, French, German, Italian, Russian, and Japanese troops had been sent against Peking.

Emboldened by its growing success and recognition by the Western powers, the Nationalist Chinese government tried to oust Soviet Russian influence from Manchuria in 1929, as a prelude to forcing Japanese interests from Manchuria as well. Relations between Soviet Russia and the Nationalist Chinese had been severed since 1927, when Chiang Kai-shek purged the Kuomintang of Communists. Charging Soviet Russia with violation of the treaty of 1924, which had forbidden Communist propaganda in Manchuria, Manchurian authorities seized Soviet railway and consular personnel, beginning in May, 1929, and captured control over most of the Chinese Eastern Railway by July. In August, 1929, Russia responded with force, dispatching troops into Manchuria, which crushed resistance by November. The Protocol of Khabarovsk of December 22, 1929, between Russia and the Manchurian authorities at Mukden, restored Soviet control over the Chinese Eastern Railway, as well as Soviet commercial and consular rights in Manchuria.

The Soviet-Manchurian clash of 1929 marked the first test of the recently signed Kellogg-Briand Pact. In July, 1929, the United States invoked the Pact, which Russia had also signed, in an attempt to halt the fighting. The American initiative was joined in December by Britain, France, and Italy. Soviet Russia rejected the American appeal indignantly, arguing that Russia had acted in self-defense. Moreover, the Soviet government expressed its "astonishment" that the United States should find it possible to give "advice and directions" to Russia, while the American government persisted in its official non-recognition of the Soviet Union.

The lesson of the Soviet-Manchurian clash was that collective security against armed force in Asia was not likely to materialize. No nation recorded this fact with greater interest than Japan.

During the brief Soviet-Manchurian conflict, Japan had observed strict neutrality, refusing Chinese troops the use of the Japanese-controlled South Manchurian Railway. All the while, Japan had taken active steps to counter Chinese Nationalist incursions into Manchuria, however, and the Chinese defeat of 1929 emboldened Japan to seek the appropriation of all Manchuria. Baron Tanaka, the Japanese Prime Minister, had advocated a "Blood and Iron" solution of the Manchurian question as early as 1927, on the grounds that Manchuria alone could provide Japan with the necessary resources as well as an outlet for her annual population increase of 800,000.

Whereas the Western powers were content to protect their trading interests under the new Nationalist government of China, Japan remained intent on territorial conquest.

In 1927 Japan had moved troops into the Shantung province in response to the northward march of the Kuomintang. When the Manchurian war-lord Chang Tso lin showed signs of coming to terms with the Nationalist government of China, he was murdered in a bomb plot of presumed Japanese origin. As Chinese immigration into Manchuria mounted between 1929 and 1931, incidents of violence between Chinese peasants and Japanese authorities mounted. On September 18, 1931, Japanese troops went into action, following an explosion on the railtracks north of Mukden, which the Japanese authorities ascribed to Chinese sabotage but which was, in fact, staged by Japan. Under the guise of a "police action" undertaken for the ostensible purpose of restoring order in a bandit-ridden province, Japan swiftly conquered North Manchuria by mid-November, 1931, and completed the conquest of South Manchuria by early January, 1932. The conquest of Manchuria was followed by the seizure of the Chinese province of Jehol and the enforcement of a demilitarized zone upon China to the south of the Great Wall.

The timing of the Japanese conquest of Manchuria was well chosen, as the great Western powers were in the throes of the Depression and collective action against Japan was unlikely; the League was preoccupied with the problem of disarmament, about to be discussed at the Geneva Disarmament Conference. Britain was absorbed in a grave financial crisis, following massive gold withdrawals in the late summer of 1931; British elections were scheduled for October, 1931. Moreover, not all the leading men of British politics were convinced that the Japanese attack on Manchuria warranted a forceful Western response. "I do not think the League of Nations would be well-advised to quarrel with Japan," Winston Churchill announced to the House of Commons, "the League has a great work to do in Europe." In Churchill's words, there was no more use affronting Japan "than there would be in ordering the Swiss and Czechoslovak navies to the yellow sea. . . ." Never convinced of the wisdom of Britain's termination of the Anglo-Japanese alliance in 1922 under American pressure, Churchill was not unsympathetic to Japan's Manchurian enterprise, in view of Japan's being caught between what he termed "the dark menace of Soviet Russia" and "the chaos of China." In 1931 Churchill, to be sure, spoke for no one but himself. Although the policy of Britain's Foreign Secretary Simon was less accommodating to Japan than Churchill's views suggested, the British government at no time contemplated League sanctions against Japan in the Manchurian crisis. Nor did Japan have cause to fear any French action hostile to Japanese interests. Since the departure of Briand, apostle of collective security in Europe, from the French Foreign Office, France showed, on the contrary, a sympathetic attitude towards Japan. Rather than censure Japan, France was interested in improving commercial relations between French Indo-China and Japan, a wish Japan was happy to fulfill with the signing of a French-Japanese trade agreement on May 13, 1932. Moreover, Japan offered the inducement of French commercial gains in Manchuria.

Soviet Russia was the power whose interests, next to China's, were most immediately affected by the Japanese conquest of Manchuria, both for commercial reasons and for the sake of national security. In the Far East, Soviet Russia was isolated, however, enjoying diplomatic relations neither with Nationalist China nor with the United States. Nor was Russia strong enough militarily to challenge Japan in Manchuria in 1931. Moreover, Soviet Russia refused to collaborate with the League, as it neither belonged to that body nor trusted its policies in 1931. The Soviet attitude thus remained passive, even as Japan usurped the Chinese Eastern Railway for purposes of troop transport in the course of the Manchurian campaign. The principal aim of Soviet policy regarding Japan in the Manchurian crisis was to prevent Japan from following up the conquest of Manchuria with an invasion of Soviet territory in the Far East. *Izvestia,* the official organ of the Soviet government, thus warned on

March 4, 1932, that Russia will not "permit anyone to violate the security of Soviet frontiers . . . or to seize even the smallest portion of Soviet land." The message was repeated in the May Day speech of 1932 of the commander of Soviet Far Eastern defenses, General Bluecher, who pledged Red Army resistance to "any alien foot" trampling on the soil of Russia. When the Japanese government assured Soviet Russia in June, 1932, of its peaceful intentions, Soviet-Japanese tensions relaxed. Japan rejected a Soviet offer of a non-aggression pact in December, 1932, however. The Japanese rebuff prompted Russia to seek collective security in the Far East in conjunction with the United States, as will be seen in the discussion of Soviet Far Eastern policy of 1933. By 1935 the last vestiges of Soviet influence in Manchuria were withdrawn with the sale of Russian interests in the Chinese Eastern Railway to the Japanese puppet state of Manchukuo.

The League likewise proved to be no deterrent to the Japanese design in Manchuria. In response to Japan's military action of September, 1931, Nationalist China appealed both to the League, invoking the conciliation procedure under Article 11 of the Covenant, and to the United States as a signatory of the Kellogg-Briand Pact. Accepting Japanese assurances that the purpose of Japan's military action was not annexation but merely the protection of Japanese lives and property in Manchuria, the Council called for the "restoration of normal relations" on September 30, 1931. Japan was to withdraw her forces into the railway zone as the safety of Japanese lives and property was being secured. When the true purpose of the Japanese action became apparent, the League Council demanded, on October 24, 1931, that Japanese troops be withdrawn by November 16, the date of the next Council meeting. Since Japan vetoed the Council resolution of October 24, and since unanimous adoption was required for the conciliation procedure under Article 11, conciliation had failed. With Japan's consent, the League appointed an investigative commission, however, headed by Lord Lytton and consisting of representatives of France, Italy, Germany, and the United States. Participation by the United States in the Lytton Commission was testimony to American concern over Japan's actions, which were seen in the U. S. as a gross violation not only of the Kellogg-Briand Pact but of the Nine Power Treaty of 1922 as well, in which the signatories had pledged to respect the integrity of China. The Lytton Commission conducted its investigation in Manchuria and did not produce its report until September, 1932. In the meantime, Japan not only completed the conquest of Manchuria and Jehol but proclaimed the puppet state of Manchukuo on February 18, 1932. For good measure, Japan launched a punitive naval expedition against Shanghai in January, 1932, which was not withdrawn until May. The Shanghai expedition was undertaken in retaliation against the Chinese boycott of Japanese goods as well as Chinese violence against Japanese visitors to Shanghai. At the time of the Lytton Report's release, the Manchurian crisis, if not altogether forgotten in Europe, had receded behind the more immediate problems of disarmament and the end of German reparations.

Though recognizing the legitimacy of Japanese economic interest in Manchuria, the Lytton Report criticized the measures taken by Japan in advancing that interest. "About the feelings of the people of Manchuria towards the present regime (the puppet government of Manchukuo)," the Lytton Report stated, "there can really be no doubt." The Report took note of the fact that many Chinese witnesses were afraid to testify out of fear of Japanese retaliation. "After careful study of the evidence," the Report stated ". . . there is no general Chinese support for the 'Manchukuo' government, which is regarded by the local Chinese as an instrument of the Japanese." The Lytton Report concluded with an appeal to restore the principle of the Open Door to Manchuria.

The League did not resort to sanctions for the political reasons, previously mentioned, which influenced the attitude of France and Britain. The failure to apply sanctions could be justified on formal grounds, however, since the Manchurian case, in the wording of the Lytton Report, was not "a simple case of the violation of the frontier of one country by the armed forces of a neighboring country."

Having taken no action against the Japanese aggression, the League disengaged itself from the Manchurian affair by refusing to recognize the results of Japanese aggression. On February 24, 1933, the Assembly voted against the recognition of the Japanese puppet state of Manchukuo. The Japanese delegation responded with a walk-out. In March, 1933, Japan announced its withdrawal from the League.

The United States had displayed unusual interest in League affairs during the Manchurian crisis, to the extent of placing an American representative on the League Council on October 16, 1931. The United States had taken the lead in the policy of non-recognition of Japan's conquest with the Stimson Doctrine, announced by U. S. Secretary of State Stimson on January 7, 1932. The Stimson Doctrine proclaimed American non-recognition of any agreement or gains made in violation of the Kellogg-Briand Pact or impairing the policy of the Open Door. American efforts to enlist British support in invoking the Nine Power Treaty against Japan remained unsuccessful.

The damage done to League prestige and to the concept of collective security as a result of Japanese aggression was not as evident in 1933 as it would be only a few years later. Excuses for the League's failure in 1931 were not difficult to find, the most frequent arguments being that China's case was unique in view of her unsettled internal conditions and that Manchuria, at any rate, was far removed from Europe. Winston Churchill's observation that "the League has a great work to do in

Europe" was unquestionably true; the League's European task in the mid-1930's might well have been made easier, however, had it not failed before in Asia.

THE RETURN OF DISTRUST IN EUROPE

Stresemann's death in October, 1929, coinciding with the beginning of the Depression, ushered in a new phase in French-German relations, marked by impatient German demands for stepped-up revision of the Treaty of Versailles and a corresponding French distrust of German motives and actions. In name, the Weimar Republic outlived Stresemann by another four years, prior to Hitler's coming to power in January, 1933. In substance, German political behavior underwent a profound change between 1930 and 1933. The fundamental questions of Germany's domestic and foreign political orientation, apparently decided in favor of democracy and peaceful integration into the Western world in the late 1920's, came up for review once more at the beginning of the 1930's. The democratic system of the Weimar Republic was tried in the crucible of the Depression, and was found wanting by a growing number of extremists on the far left and right. Accordingly, Stresemann's concept of Treaty revision through well-timed and patient negotiation came under increasing nationalist attack. Beginning in 1930, a new nationalism was afoot in Germany, better organized than the anarchic outbursts of German nationalist opposition in the early twenties and made more militant and vociferous by the passionate oratory of Hitler. The new German nationalism reflected, in part, the frustrated energies of the postwar generation, coming of age in the early 1930's and excluded from a normal and productive role in society as a result of the Depression. The observation of Webster and Sydney Herbert, historians of the League, which summed up the League's role as keeper of the peace in the first postwar decade, was especially pertinent to the situation of Germany: "Peace has been preserved in Europe partly because the victors have had overwhelming force and the generation that fought is tired and worn out by war. There is no guarantee that peace can be maintained as a new generation grows up with its own ambitions, grievances, and unsatisfied energy."

France, a keen observer of the German national temper after the First World War, had registered three unmistakable signs in the radicalization of the German national spirit since 1929: (1) the campaign for a plebiscite against the Young Plan, jointly organized by Hitler's National Socialists and the conservative Nationalist Party; (2) the lack of German gratitude for French evacuation of the Rhineland in June, 1930; and (3) the increase in Nazi representation from 12 to 107 seats in the Reichstag in the German elections of September, 1930.

Although the last three chancellors of the Weimar Republic,

Brüning, Papen, and Schleicher, attempted, each in his own way, to contain the rising Nazi flood between 1930 and 1932, their foreign policy demands increased in proportion to the nationalist clamor of the Nazi opposition. By achieving swift and decisive results in foreign policy, the last governments of the Weimar Republic hoped to divert domestic attention from the economic crisis, which they failed to master, and to take the wind out of the sails of the Nazi opposition. Both in substance and tone German foreign policy became increasingly indistinguishable from Nazi pronouncements between 1930 and 1932, causing France and, to a lesser extent, Great Britain to pause in wonderment and alarm. The Western powers were not insensitive to the tremendous pressures to which Chancellor Brüning was subjected during his administration from March, 1930, to May, 1932, and they were well aware of the fact that Brüning's failure in Germany might well result in Hitler's coming to power. Though interested in helping save German democracy, they could not jeopardize their own national interests, which seemed endangered by the stepped-up tempo of German revisionism. The German demand for a speedy French evacuation of the Saar, which followed on the heels of the French withdrawal from the Rhineland, the renewed pleas to revise Germany's eastern borders with Poland, in order to end the "unnatural cutting-off of East Prussia" from Germany, and hints of the desirability of terminating the demilitarized status of the Rhineland, all voiced in 1930, were too sweeping and fast for French comfort. In the West, the uncomfortable feeling gained ground that Germany was using every new concession as a peg on which to hang fresh demands. Most alarming to France, however, was the project of an Austro-German customs union, which the German government announced in March, 1931, and which was widely interpreted as a preliminary step towards a full political union (Anschluss) between the two German states.

THE AUSTRO-GERMAN CUSTOMS UNION

After lengthy negotiations between Germany's Foreign Minister Curtius and Austria's Vice-Chancellor Schober, both governments announced on March 21, 1931 an agreement on the establishment of a German-Austrian customs union. Although the negotiations had been conducted in secrecy, the announcement did not come altogether as a surprise, owing to a Viennese press leak in the *Wiener Neue Freie Presse* of March 17, 1931, for which Austrian circles, hostile to the project, were responsible.

Germany's motives in seeking a customs union with Austria were both economic and political. As Austria's economy was in dire need of foreign assistance, Germany feared an Austrian appeal to Italy unless assistance were forthcoming from Germany. Although the German government stressed the purely economic purpose of the project, eventual political union was, in fact, the real German intention.

The news of the customs union project acted like a bombshell in Paris and the capitals of the Little Entente. France, supported by Italy, protested the undertaking on the grounds that it violated not only the Peace of St. Germain of 1919, safeguarding Austria's political independence, but the Austrian Reconstruction Protocol of 1922 as well. The latter, also referred to as the Geneva Protocol of 1922, had advanced French, British, Italian, and Czechoslovak loans to Austria on condition that Austria not endanger her independence directly or indirectly through economic or financial treaties.

Anticipating the French objections, Germany declared the customs union open to other states besides Germany and Austria, while stressing that the project was merely a local application of Briand's scheme for a European union. Far from accepting the German explanation, Briand regarded the incident as final proof that his policy of reconciliation with Germany had failed. France took it for granted that the customs union would inevitably lead to political union, if permitted to proceed, just as the German *Zollverein* had paved the way for German political unification under Prussian hegemony in the 19th century. Political union between Germany and Austria would mean a decisive shift in the European balance, however, which France had forestalled through her veto at the Peace Conference of Paris in 1919.

Although Britain did not object to the customs union in principle, she deplored the poisonous effect which it produced on the political climate of Europe generally. The worsening of French-German relations occurred at the very time when Britain's Labor Foreign Secretary Arthur Henderson was striving valiantly to lay the groundwork for a successful Disarmament Conference, due to begin in 1932. To save the Disarmament Conference from becoming a failure, Britain favored the abandonment of the Austro-German customs union. In order to spare German feelings, and to make Germany's withdrawal as painless as possible, Britain suggested adjudication of the Franco-German dispute by the Permanent Court of International Justice, rather than allow the quarrel to be aired before the League Council.

THE CRASH OF THE CREDITANSTALT

Before the Permanent Court handed down its advisory opinion on September 5, 1931, France employed other means, however, to defeat the customs union project. The most potent weapons of France were economic, as she, unlike Germany and Austria, had remained relatively unaffected by the Depression thus far. By withdrawing substantial funds from Austria's largest bank, the *Creditanstalt,* France caused its collapse on May 11, 1931. The collapse of the Austrian Creditanstalt had disastrous effects on the German banking system as well, resulting in the closing of some of Germany's largest banks on July 13, 1931. Both Austria and Germany were forced to turn to the Western powers for loans to overcome the banking crisis. Among the Western powers, France was in the strongest financial position in the summer of 1931, however, since both Great Britain and the United States were in the throes of a severe financial crisis of their own. France was willing to extend financial assistance to both Germany and Austria, provided that certain political conditions were met: the abandonment of the customs union and, in the case of Germany, a pledge not to demand further revisions of the Versailles Treaty for a period of several years.

Although Germany refused the French bargain, the governments of Austria and Germany announced the withdrawal of the customs union on September 3, 1931. On September 5, 1931, the Permanent Court declared in an 8:7 decision the incompatibility of the customs union project with the Austrian Reconstruction Protocol of 1922, though not with the Treaty of St. Germain. That the decision was influenced by considerations other than purely legal is evident from the nationality of the justices voting for or against the project. The justices voting in favor of the German position were those of Germany, the United States, Britain, Japan, China, Holland, and Belgium; those voting in favor of France represented France, Italy, Spain, Poland, Rumania, Cuba, San Salvador, and Colombia.

Following the collapse of the Austro-German customs union, France proposed a scheme for economic cooperation among the Danubian states, designed to consolidate the political influence of France as well as the Little Entente in the Danube area. The Tardieu Plan of March 5, 1932, named after the French Prime Minister André Tardieu, suggested an economic union with preferential tariffs between Austria, Hungary, Czechoslovakia, Rumania, and Yugoslavia. Italy opposed the Tardieu Plan because of its own aspirations to hegemony in the Danube Basin. As Britain failed to support it also, the Tardieu Plan was abandoned. Austria appealed to the League for financial assistance. In the Lausanne Agreement of July 19, 1932, Austria was granted an international loan on condition that she not seek again a customs union with Germany. Having launched an ambitious and ill-timed project, the German government emerged from the ensuing crisis with its prestige badly damaged at home and its relations with France seriously impaired.

THE END OF GERMAN REPARATIONS AND ALLIED WAR DEBT PAYMENTS

The worsening of the political climate in Germany, following the elections of September, 1930, together with the loss of confidence in

Germany's immediate economic future, resulted in a massive withdrawal of foreign capital. Between September, 1930, and July, 1931, nearly one billion dollars in short-term credits were recalled from Germany by foreign investors. Although the German government attempted to master the financial crisis through a strict austerity program, announced on June 6, 1931, as well as through a system of exchange controls, it was doubtful whether Germany could meet her commercial debts, much less the reparations payments under the Young Plan. As early as June 6, 1931, Chancellor Brüning, in announcing his domestic austerity program, called for an end to "unbearable reparations."

The Hoover Moratorium freed Germany from reparations payments for one year, beginning on July 1, 1931, subject to the exceptions insisted upon by France, as previously explained. A commercial debt agreement, also concluded in July, 1931, with various foreign creditors, likewise brought Germany temporary relief from the flight of foreign capital. As the Depression approached its depth in Germany, the Brüning government, both for economic and domestic political reasons, was determined that German reparations should not be resumed after the expiration of the Hoover Moratorium in 1932. In January, 1932, in the midst of the worst Depression winter, Brüning thus announced that Germany neither could nor would resume reparations payments in the future.

The German plea for an end to all reparations had been supported, in principle, by a committee of financial experts which had examined, on German request, the German financial situation in August, 1931. The committee's report of August 18, 1931, drafted by Walter Layton, the editor of the *Economist,* thus stated that no new loans could be granted Germany, if reparations were continued.

The Layton Report agreed with Britain's official position, though not with that of France. Whereas Britain showed far greater interest in the restoration of German commercial credit, France was anxious to salvage at least part of the defunct Young Plan. To France, Brüning's pleas of insolvency were not entirely convincing, as the German government persisted in its plans for the construction of a new pocket battleship at the very time when Germany suspended payment of her foreign obligations.

When Britain proposed a new conference for the settlement of reparations and Allied debts for January, 1932, to be convened at Lausanne, France first opposed the scheme and subsequently delayed the opening of the Lausanne Conference until June 16, 1932. The urgency of Britain's call for a new reparations conference was motivated both by political and economic reasons. The British ambassador to Germany, Sir H. Rumbold, had warned his government on January 29, 1932, that a postponement of the reparations conference could result in the overthrow of Brüning and the coming to power of Hitler. Moreover, the standstill agreement on German short-term loans of July, 1931, was due to expire in February, 1932. Rather than agree to a cancellation of German reparations, France advocated an extension of the Hoover Moratorium for another year in the hope that the recovery of German finances would permit the resumption of reparations payments at a later date.

While Britain remained adamant in its call for an end to reparations, the British government hoped to extract from Germany a political promise in return for the cancellation of reparations. Prior to the opening of the Lausanne Conference, Prime Minister Ramsay MacDonald thus proposed an agreement for a fifteen-year political truce in Europe, during which no further revisionist demands would be made by Germany. A political truce, the British Prime Minister argued, would lessen the tensions of Europe. It would not only enable France and Britain to reduce their armament expenditures and thereby compensate for the loss of reparations, but it would also make a good impression in the United States. Herriot, who had returned to the premiership of France in early June, 1932, rejected the British proposal on the grounds that enough political treaties existed for the preservation of the *status quo* and that a moratorium, such as Britain suggested, could only result in the weakening of existing treaties.

The British proposal having failed, Germany's newly appointed Chancellor, Franz von Papen, Brüning's successor, proposed a French-German entente to Prime Minister Herriot at Lausanne. In exchange for French willingness to cancel German reparations and as a price for French recognition of Germany's equality of rights in armaments, Papen suggested close economic, political, and military collaboration between France and Germany through a customs union, a pact of consultation, and a military accord. Papen's proposals reflected his strong dislike for Soviet Russia and his desire to reorient German foreign policy away from the Rapallo policy of the 1920's and towards a Franco-German military bloc against the Soviet Union.

For a favorable French response, the sweeping Papen proposals would have required a measure of mutual trust such as no longer existed between France and Germany in 1932 after the bitter experience of the Austro-German customs union. Also, far from enjoying the prestige of Stresemann, Papen was personally distrusted in France. A further reason for the fruitlessness of Papen's initiative at Lausanne was the suspicion shown by Great Britain. Britain resented the Papen proposals for their exclusion of British interests and the unbalancing effect which a French-German entente would produce on Western Europe. While Britain supported the German position on reparations, she opposed Papen's more ambitious political schemes. In effect, the Lausanne Conference thus cancelled German reparations, except for a remaining token sum of 3 billion marks. The final German payment of 3 billion marks was to be made in the form of interest-bearing bonds, to be deposited with the Bank of International Settlement. The German bonds were not to be placed on the market, however, for three years. A supplementary agreement between France, Britain, Italy, and Belgium made the ratification of the Lausanne agreement conditional upon a satisfactory solution to the inter-Allied debt problem.

The subject of German reparations inevitably raises the question of the total amount actually paid by Germany between the end of the First World War and the Hoover Moratorium of 1931. The answer depends on whether the records of the Reparations Commission or those of the German government are used as the source. According to the former, German reparations totalled 20.7 billion marks; according to the latter, the amount was 67.7 billion marks. The wide discrepancy is explained by the fact that part of the German reparations, especially during the pre-Dawes Plan period, consisted of deliveries in kind, upon which the Allies and Germany put differing values. Moreover, Germany included in the reparations sum the value of German property delivered to the Allies as war booty after the armistice of November 11, 1918, including the German fleet, as well as merchant vessels.

Having relieved Germany of her reparations burden, the European Allies of the First World War waited in vain for a remission of their war debts to the United States. Following the expiration of the Hoover Moratorium, Britain and Italy resumed payment of their war debts to the United States in 1932. In 1933 both nations made token payments which were discontinued thereafter. France and the remaining Allies never resumed payments after the end of the Hoover Moratorium. On April 13, 1934, Congress passed the Johnson Debt Default Act, which prohibited American loans to foreign governments in default of their debts to the United States.

THE FAILURE OF DISARMAMENT

On February 2, 1932, the Disarmament Conference opened at Geneva with all League members present, plus five non-members, including Soviet Russia and the United States. Arthur Henderson, Britain's Foreign Secretary until the resignation of the Labor government in 1931 and one of the most fervent advocates of disarmament, was elected President of the Conference.

Armaments, Henderson believed, were the cause of fear and disarmament thus the first necessary step towards greater security. "The pace is slow," Henderson warned, referring to the lack of progress in disarmament prior to the opening of the Geneva Disarmament Conference, "and the peoples of the world are growing impatient. . . ."

What had not been achieved in the more tranquil 1920's, however, was not likely to be accomplished under the changed circumstances of the early 1930's. The Manchurian crisis had revealed the ineffectiveness of the treaty guarantees of the 1920's in the face of the power politics of the early 1930's. The deterioration of French-German relations since 1930 also contributed to the atmosphere of unreality that attended the proceedings in Geneva. Hitler's coming to power in January, 1933, while the Disarmament Conference was still in session, buried whatever chances for agreement remained.

From the beginning of the Conference, Germany expected, in Chancellor Brüning's words, a solution of the disarmament problem "on the basis of equal rights and equal security for all peoples." As the other powers were not likely to disarm in the immediate future, the German claim to equality amounted to a demand for German rearmament above the level of the Treaty of Versailles. The response of the powers to the German demand was far from uniform, Soviet Russia voting with Germany on most important issues, at least before Hitler's appointment to the German chancellorship. After January, 1933, Russia increasingly sided with France in the disarmament question as part of the general French-Soviet rapprochement which began with the signing of the French-Soviet Non-Aggression Pact in December, 1932.

France presented a disarmament plan to the Conference on February 5, 1932, named after the French Minister of Defense André Tardieu. The Tardieu Disarmament Plan contained the familiar recommendations France had advanced unsuccessfully since the inception of the League in 1919: a convention for compulsory arbitration of international disputes with a clear-cut definition of aggression; and the creation of an international police force for the enforcement of League decisions. The Tardieu Disarmament Plan thus repeated the French contention that security had precedence over disarmament. Predictably, the Tardieu Disarmament Plan was not acceptable to either Britain or Germany. Soviet Russia opposed the French proposal on the grounds that Russia could not entrust its security to the League, "an international organization of states openly hostile" to the USSR.

Britain's Foreign Secretary John Simon submitted a proposal for qualitative, rather than quantitative, arms limitation. Disarmament was to be achieved through the abolition of offensive types of armaments. However appealing Simon's proposal appeared in principle, it proved impossible of practical realization, as the technical commissions of the Disarmament Conference failed to agree on what constituted offensive or defensive weapons. Whereas the great naval powers considered submarines offensive weapons and battleships defensive, the lesser naval powers took the opposite view. Whereas all tanks appeared to be offensive weapons to some, others included in that category only tanks above a certain weight. Germany classified as offensive all weapons which the Treaty of Versailles had denied her. President Hoover's appeal for a reduction of existing armaments by one third, though applauded by Germany, Russia, and Italy, was received cooly by Great Britain. Britain interpreted the Hoover proposal as a disguised attempt to cut down British cruiser strength.

After nearly five months of debate, the Disarmament Conference produced a meager resolution, submitted on July 20, 1932, by the Czechoslovak Foreign Minister Eduard Benes. The Benes Resolution, prohibiting aerial bombardment and chemical warfare and recommending limitations in the size of tanks, was adopted by forty-one states. Germany and Russia voted against it; eight powers, including Italy and China abstained.

Having failed to extract a clear promise of equality in arms, Germany threatened to boycott any further meetings of the Conference until recognition of German equality of rights in armaments had been achieved. Germany's virtual ultimatum did not result in a common Anglo-French response, as France had hoped. At the Lausanne Reparation Conference, which coincided with the Geneva Disarmament Conference, Britain and France had issued a joint declaration on July 13, 1932, pledging an exchange of views on any question "similar in origin" to the reparations issue. In a confidential interpretation of the Declaration of July 13, the British government had gone considerably further, assuring France of advance consultation before answering future German demands for the revision of the Treaty of Versailles. The German demand for equal rights in armaments clearly belonged in the above category. The Declaration of July 13, 1932, notwithstanding, however, Britain supported the position of Germany rather than that of France, since the British government was anxious to give Germany some satisfaction in the disarmament question. On December 11, 1932, after informal negotiations, Britain, France, Italy, and the United States agreed on a compromise formula with Germany, which seemed to satisfy both the German claim to equality and the French insistence upon security. The compromise recognized Germany's "equality of rights in a system which would provide security for all nations."

Before the formula of December 11, 1932, could be implemented, Hitler assumed power in Germany. Although Hitler maintained the pretense of serious armaments negotiations during the early part of 1933, the desire for unilateral and unrestricted German rearmament soon gained the upper hand. A comprehensive draft convention, submitted by Britain's Prime Minister MacDonald on March 16, 1933, which recommended an increase of German troop strength by 100,000, failed of acceptance after lengthy debate. Hitler's withdrawal from the Disarmament

Conference as well as the League on October 14, 1933, was foreshadowed by the statement of the German Foreign Minister Neurath that "what is right for others is right for Germany."

The dream of a world made safe through disarmament was shattered in the general disillusionment which had buried the hopes of the Locarno area. President Roosevelt's proposal of May, 1933, for an agreement on gradual reduction of armaments, coupled with a non-aggression pact between all nations willing to keep their forces within their national frontiers, belonged in spirit to another era and failed to halt the march of European nations towards a new armed confrontation.

THE BEGINNINGS OF GREAT POWER REALIGNMENT: THE SOVIET-FRENCH NON-AGGRESSION PACT

Growing French anxiety over the course of German policy between 1930 and 1932 prompted France to seek an improvement in her relations with Soviet Russia. The French-Soviet rapprochement proceeded at a slow pace, as the obstacles to improved relations were numerous. France, next to Great Britain, had been the chief target of Comintern propaganda in the 1920's, and the Bolshevik repudiation of the tsarist debt was not forgotten in the early 1930's. French-Soviet trade had sunk to its lowest level in years in 1930, owing to a tariff war and mutual boycott. In the Disarmament Conference Russia invariably sided with Germany, as previously noted, until the summer of 1932. Russia had opposed both the Tardieu Plan for a Danubian customs union and the Tardieu Disarmament Plan of February, 1932. The friendly attitude of France towards Japan during the Manchurian crisis likewise had added to French-Soviet tensions.

The first step towards improved relations was taken on July 15, 1931, when France and Russia ended the mutual boycott of goods while preparing a new trade agreement. Following the normalizing of trade relations, France and Russia opened negotiations for a non-agression pact in August, 1931. As a first condition for a non-aggression pact, France demanded that Russia conclude non-aggression pacts with Poland and Rumania also, the Eastern clients of France. Although Poland was willing to sign a non-aggression pact with Russia, as she shared the French anxiety over Germany's revisionist demands, a non-aggression pact between Rumania and Russia failed to materialize owing to the issue of Bessarabia. As in the past, Soviet Russia refused to recognize the Rumanian annexation of Bessarabia of 1918. While Soviet-Rumanian negotiations remained deadlocked throughout 1932, Russia had concluded non-aggression pacts with Finland, Latvia, and Estonia between January and May, 1932. The Soviet-Polish Non-Aggression Pact, though signed on July 25, 1932, was not ratified by Poland until November 26, 1932. The delay was due to Poland's promise not to ratify the pact until a similar pact had been concluded between Russia and Rumania. By November, 1932, both France and Poland were sufficiently alarmed by new signs of German militancy, however, to seek agreement with Soviet Russia without awaiting the outcome of the Soviet-Rumanian negotiations. In the German elections of July 31, 1932, the Nazi party had emerged as the strongest political party with 230 Reichstag seats. The German threat to boycott the Disarmament Conference unless equality in armaments was conceded acted as a further incentive for France to hasten the rapprochement with Russia. On November 29, 1932, the French-Soviet Non-Aggression Pact was signed in Paris.

France not only viewed the pact as a supplementary guarantee of her security but hoped that it would contribute to the loosening of German-Soviet economic and military ties. To Soviet Russia the non-aggesssion pact with France was an added guarantee that France would not support Poland in a Polish-Soviet conflict, as France had done in 1920. Soviet Russia was careful, however, not to allow its economic and political ties with Germany to be disturbed by the non-aggression pact with France. German trade and economic assistance remained important to the fulfillment of Stalin's Five Year Plan, since Germany had extended 300 million marks in credits to the Soviet Union in the trade agreement of April 14, 1931. The German-Soviet neutrality treaty of 1926 (Berlin Treaty) likewise was renewed in 1931. To allay German suspicions, the Soviet government declared, after the signing of the Soviet-French Non-Aggression Pact, that the latter need not disturb good German-Soviet relations any more than Germany's signing of the Locarno Treaty had affected friendly German-Soviet relations in 1925.

The French-Soviet Non-Aggression Pact was not a final option in the foreign policy of either country. It required the shock of Hitler's foreign policy after 1933 to draw France and Soviet Russia together more closely in the French-Soviet Pact of Mutual Assistance of 1935.

9 | The Victorious Democracies I:
Great Britain and Its Empire

Britain's victory in the First World War was due in no small measure to the contribution in men and materials made by the British Empire. The Dominions had sent a million volunteers to the European battlefields, and Indian divisions had played a key role in the British conquest of much of the Middle East. Moreover, India contributed a "gift" of £100 million to Britain's war effort in Europe. The Dominion governments of Canada, Australia, New Zealand, and South Africa shared in the direction of the British war effort in Europe through representation in the Imperial War Cabinet.

The war thus marked a high point in both the power and unity of the British Empire, and the peace settlement promised to strengthen the Empire further. In 1919 many would have agreed with Churchill's opinion that the First World War had raised Britain and the Empire to the highest position they had yet attained. The sea lanes between Britain and the Empire had been freed from the threat of German naval power; the disintegration of Imperial Russia had removed Russia as a rival in Persia and a threat to the buffer of Afghanistan and to British India itself; the collapse of the Turkish Empire opened up new possibilities for strategic control and economic exploitation of the Middle East; whereas Britain had been chronically short of troops to fulfill her worldwide Empire commitments before the First World War, the war had created a seasoned army of unprecedented size, British troops in the Middle East alone numbering 400,000 by the end of the war.

The favorable prospects of 1919 notwithstanding, the British Empire failed to preserve in peace the cohesion shown in war, nor did it develop towards the closely-knit organic world community which the common war effort suggested and which Britain's pre-war imperialist spokesmen had hopefully envisaged for the 20th century. Rather, the postwar years and indeed the entire period between the two world wars proved to be a transition period, during which the imperial concepts of the latter 19th century gradually gave way to more relaxed controls and freer association between the European center and the worldwide members of the British Empire. The areas thus affected did not include the British crown colonies and possessions in Black Africa, the West Indies, or the

Far East, where direct rule through the colonial office continued undisturbed between the two world wars. Rather they embraced those regions of the Empire where varying degrees of self-government or native participation in the exercise of power had been conceded before the First World War, such as the self-governing Dominions of Canada, Australia, New Zealand, and South Africa (the blacks of South Africa were specifically excluded from the franchise when Britain granted Dominion status to South Africa in 1909), the Empire of India, and those parts of the Middle East where British power was already established (Egypt) or being established after the First World War (Iraq, Palestine, Transjordan).

The circumstances chiefly responsible for recasting Imperial relations after the First World War may be summarized as: (1) the new international morality, as preached by the Allies and the United States during the First World War; (2) the rise of nationalism and the growth of political awareness in India and the Middle East; (3) the growth of democracy in postwar Britain and the resulting criticism of British autocratic rule in India; (4) the economic self-interest of the members of the Empire as distinct from that of Great Britain; and (5) a shift in Britain's own economic priorities towards increased domestic spending in the interwar period.

Before the First World War the justification of British imperialism had ranged from arguments of political and economic necessity to doctrines of racial superiority tempered by pleas of humanitarian mission. Joseph Chamberlain, Britain's Colonial Secretary at the turn of the century, argued that half of England would starve if the British Empire were reduced to the dimensions of the United Kingdom. Sir John Seeley, Cambridge historian and author of *The Expansion of England* (1883), warned that in the coming century Britain would be overshadowed by Russia and the United States, unless she developed the Dominions into an integral part of the United Kingdom. The conquerors and administrators of Empire, Cecil Rhodes, Viscount Milner, and Lord Curzon, shared a belief in the colonizing mission of the "Anglo-Saxon race," to which Milner attributed "something distinctive and priceless in the onward march of humanity." The theme of social Darwinism, as applied to whole nations and races, was echoed in the imperialist literature of the 1890's and early 1900's, in the works of Benjamin Kidd and Karl Pearson. Kidd attributed the success of the Empire to the superiority of the "Anglo-Saxon race," and Pearson even recommended its improvement through selective breeding among the physically and mentally strong. Race, in Pearson's view, was the key to Empire, hence his concern lest "the mentally and physically inferior" have a "dominant fertility." It was England's mission, Britain's Liberal Prime Minister Rosebery explained in the 1890's, to "take care that the world, as far as it can be molded, shall receive the Anglo-Saxon and not another character." Cecil Rhodes, Britain's empire-builder in Africa, added that "the English people intend to retain every inch of land they have got and perhaps intend to secure a few more inches."

The First World War, with its ideological overtones of a struggle between just democracy and oppressive autocracy as well as its projection of liberal ideas onto the international plane through Wilson's Fourteen Points, rendered the imperialist doctrines of the latter 19th century suspect and obsolete. The Allied message of democracy and self-determination was broadcast, to be sure, for European ears. The echo of the Allied message was audible around the world, however, providing the nationalist leaders of India and Egypt alike with a new moral weapon against their British masters. Henceforth, Britain, in her dealings with the peoples of India and the Middle East, would be increasingly judged by the standards which she herself had set in waging war in Europe, both by a more critical public at home and by the politically conscious masses of the East. Moreover, the League of Nations had set new standards of international behavior that had inescapable consequences for relations within the British Empire.

The surviving spokesmen of pre-war imperialism, such as Milner (Colonial Secretary after the First World War), Curzon (Foreign Secretary in the postwar coalition government), and Churchill (Secretary of War, Colonial Secretary after the war), thus were put increasingly on the defense, their message out of tune with the changed spirit of the times. The British Labor party and its leader Ramsay MacDonald were the first to recognize the postwar period as one of transition in the development of Empire between the old imperialism and the new conditions, which, in MacDonald's view, "were going to come before long." Winston Churchill, on the opposite end of the political spectrum, decried concessions to the nationalist forces in the Empire as the "sinking of the great ship in a calm sea." Deploring Britain's declining "faith in herself and her mission" in the mid-1930's, Churchill asked: "Are we to conclude that British administration in Oriental lands is no longer capable of facing a storm?" By the 1930's Churchill's views were those of a minority, even within his own Conservative party; the majority of Conservatives, including the party's leader Stanley Baldwin, had come to recognize the inevitability of change in Empire relations.

The question of Empire was also one of finance and economic interest, and it was in these areas that the First World War also marked a watershed in British imperial history. In the last decades before 1914, Britain had found it increasingly difficult to meet the rising expenditures for defense, social reform, and imperial expansion out of her own resources. In 1899 parliament had defeated an old-age pension plan because its projected cost of £20 million per year was deemed excessive. The Conservative government of the early 20th century, on the other hand, spent £250 million to wage the Boer war for the conquest of the Transvaal and Orange Free State.

The Conservatives viewed the problems of rising social cost and increased defense budgets in Britain, as well as Britain's financial burden of Empire, as interdependent parts of the larger imperial question. The ideal solution, in the Conservative view, was to adopt tariff protection, which all European industrial powers, save Britain, had instituted before the First World War. Protective tariffs would yield additional revenue, to cover the cost of social reform; they would also protect those British industries, such as iron and steel, which were hard pressed by German and American competition. Although protective tariffs would raise the price of some commodities, especially food, they would enhance the economic well-being of the nation at large and thereby strengthen the foundation of the Empire. Moreover, by exempting the Dominions from British tariffs, a stronger economic cohesion between Britain and her Empire would be achieved. Thus, the ultimate ideal aspired to by pre-war Conservatives was a self-sufficient Empire, protected by common external tariffs, with Britain as the chief supplier of manufactured articles and the Empire as the producer of raw materials and food.

Joseph Chamberlain failed to fulfill the ideal of an organic Empire before the First World War. The idea of tariff protection enjoyed strong support among a great many of Britain's leading economic historians, such as Halford J. Mackinder, William Cunningham, and William J. Ashley. Free trade was a tradition too deeply rooted, however, to succumb easily to arguments of imperial grandeur. It was partly over the issue of tariff protection that the Conservative party lost the elections of 1910 to the Liberals. Except for the iron and steel workers, who constituted a minority in the British labor force, labor rejected tariff protection as a "stomach tax." Ship-builders, ship-owners, the cotton industry, banks, and insurance and investment houses all continued to support free trade, upon which their fortunes had been made. Moreover, the trading and investment patterns of pre-war Britain did not exclusively, or even predominantly, follow the routes of Empire; more than half of Britain's pre-war overseas investments went to non-Empire areas, and the bulk of British exports were directed outside the Empire. Similarly, the economies of the Dominions were no longer solely oriented towards British markets. Since the attainment of self-government, the Dominions had begun to adopt protective tariffs of their own. Although the Dominions granted preferential tariffs to British imports, beginning with Canada in 1897, Canadian exports to the United States and Germany exceeded those to Britain before 1914. In India alone Britain continued to dominate both exports and imports by virtue of her commanding political and economic controls over the Empire of India. The trend towards economic nationalism in the Dominions was accelerated after the First World War, as their economies became more diversified and they began to produce manufactured articles themselves. After the First World War the Dominions would grant tariff preference to Great Britain only to the extent that they raised existing tariffs to higher levels against trading partners outside the Empire.

The First World War had brought both unprecedented expenditures and new expectations for social reform in Great Britain. The social legislation of the pre-war Liberal administrations between 1906 and 1914, although creating unemployment insurance, old-age pensions, and health and accident protection, had merely extended benefits considered long overdue in an advanced industrial society. The returning veterans demanded improvements in housing and education, and Prime Minister Lloyd George, running for reelection in December, 1918, had promised to make Britain a "home fit for heroes to live in." At the same time, the demands and opportunities of Empire imposed new charges upon the British Treasury. The new imperialist ventures in Iraq, Persia, Palestine, and Transjordan, together with the British military intervention in the Russian Civil War, consumed an estimated £300 million. India and Egypt were rife with national rebellion. Winston Churchill, as Secretary of War in Lloyd George's cabinet, proposed to meet the postwar challenge of Empire by maintaining a peace-time army, air force, and navy of 900,000 men. Churchill's bill of 1919 was defeated, as it no longer corresponded either to the means or to the mood of an exhausted postwar Britain. Compromise, accommodation, and disguised controls, rather than annexation and repression, became the characteristics of Britain's postwar imperialism.

THE CHALLENGE OF NATIONALISM:
IRELAND, INDIA, AND THE MIDDLE EAST

IRELAND

Although not, properly speaking, a member of the British Empire, Ireland had formed part of the United Kingdom since the Act of Union of 1801. Nevertheless, the Irish struggle for emancipation from British rule formed part of the larger challenge of nationalism which Great Britain encountered within the Empire after the First World War and it was interpreted as such both by the British opponents of Irish independence and the nationalists of India and Egypt.

The old Irish grievances of land tenure and religious discrimination had been largely settled by the beginning of the 20th century; the Protestant church had been disestablished, and tenant farming had given way to land ownership partly with the financial assistance of the British government. Still Ireland continued to be ruled by British-appointed officials, and it was against this form of British control that Irish nationalism turned, through the channels of parliamentary politics before the First World War, through revolutionary means during and after the First World War.

Irish home rule had become both a bitter partisan issue and an emotional controversy in prewar Britain. The Liberals supported limited home rule for Ireland, while the Conservatives frequently denied that a separate Irish nationality even existed. The very thought of an independent Ireland always seemed preposterous to Curzon. Joseph Chamberlain feared the loss of the Irish market. More generally, the Conservatives suspected that Irish home rule would act as the signal for the dissolution of Empire.

Two Irish Home Rule Bills, sponsored by the Liberal Prime Minister William Gladstone, had been defeated in 1886 and 1893 respectively. The Home Rule Bill of 1912, passed by the Liberal administration of Asquith, granted a separate Irish parliament in Dublin with limited jurisdiction, while reserving control over finance, defense, and external affairs to the government of Great Britain. Though limited in scope, the Home Rule Bill of 1912 came close to precipitating civil war in Ireland, as the six predominantly Protestant counties of Ulster in Northern Ireland refused association with the Catholic south under home rule. The suspension of the Home Rule Bill for the duration of the First World War in September, 1914, merely postponed, rather than solved, the problem of Ireland. The Easter Rebellion of 1916 and its suppression by Great Britain eclipsed the moderate Irish Nationalist party, whose leader John Redmond had sought redress of Irish political and constitutional grievances through parliamentary means. Leadership passed to the radical Sinn Fein. Arthur Griffith, founder of the Sinn Fein and historian of the Hungarian struggle for emancipation in the 1860's (*The Resurrection of Hungary,* 1904), molded his strategy after that of Hungary. As Hungary had succeeded in wresting home rule from Habsburg Austria in 1867 by ignoring the presence of Austrian courts and officials, Ireland would set up its own government without taking official notice of the British presence. The Sinn Fein tactics were first implemented in the British elections of December, 1918. Having captured all seventy-three Irish seats outside of Ulster, the Sinn Fein delegates refused to take up their seats in Westminster and set up the Dail, as the legal parliament of Ireland in Dublin. The Dail elected DeValera, veteran of the Easter Rebellion, president and Arthur Griffith vice-president. The Dail thereupon created a republican government, levied taxes, and transferred jurisdiction to Irish republican courts.

Although the Sinn Fein had originally planned to carry out its program through nonviolent means, violence inevitably followed as a result of clashes between the Royal Irish Constabulary and the "National

Volunteers," soon to become known as the Irish Republican Army. By May, 1919, when the Paris Peace Conference was in session, Ireland, north and south, was in the grip of full-scale civil war. Edward H. Carson, a fierce opponent of Irish Home Rule before 1914, fanned the flames of civil war against the Catholics of Ulster. In the south, the Irish Republican Army engaged in guerrilla warfare against the Royal Irish Constabulary and its British reinforcements, the Black and Tans. The latter, not far removed in spirit and behavior from the German free corps, which made its appearance at approximately the same time in Central Europe, were recruited from veterans of the British army, restless men who found readjustment to civilian life difficult. The discipline of the Black and Tans did not always conform to police standards. Altogether, the Irish civil war, known as the "troubles," claimed some 700 dead on either side.

The government of Britain faced the alternatives of full-scale repression—which, in the estimate of the Imperial General Staff would require an army of 100,000 men—or compromise with revolutionary Ireland. Lloyd George, following the advice of King George V, wanted compromise. The government of Ireland Act of 1920 proposed two separate Home Rule parliaments, one for the 26 Catholic counties of the south, the other for the six predominantly Protestant counties of Ulster. A Council of Ireland, to be formed from both Irish parliaments, was to adminster common affairs, such as railroads. Both parts of Ireland were to be represented in the British parliament.

The government of Ireland Act was rejected by the south, as it sanctioned partition. A settlement was reached with the Anglo-Irish treaty of December 6, 1921, signed in London. The London Treaty established the Irish Free State with complete autonomy over internal affairs; Ireland received Dominion status on the Canadian model; Britain retained three "treaty ports" (Cork Harbor, Berehaven, Lough Swilly) for the Royal Navy; Ulster was given the option of joining the Irish Free State, an option promptly rejected by plebiscite in Northern Ireland.

Ireland contributed to the fall of Lloyd George from power in 1922, as it had ruined the careers of previous Liberal statesmen; Lloyd George's own Liberal party was appalled by the terror of the Black and Tans, while the Conservatives were equally agitated over the concessions made to revolutionary Ireland. Nor did the Irish Treaty restore immediate peace to troubled Ireland. The Sinn Fein extremists, under DeValera's leadership, rejected the settlement of 1921 as insufficient and waged civil war against Griffith, the new president, and Collins, the Prime Minister of the Irish Free State. The second phase of the Irish Civil War, from April, 1922, to April, 1923, claimed more lives than had the first. Among its victims was Michael Collins, assassinated in August, 1922. Gradually, conditions in Ireland became stable during the long-term premiership of William Cosgrave from 1922 to 1932.

Anglo-Irish relations took a turn for the worse in 1932, when the election victory of the Sinn Fein extremists swept DeValera into power as Irish Prime Minister. In the previous year, the British parliament had enacted the Westminister Statute, to be described more fully in the context of Dominion developments. The Westminister Statute of 1931 had, in effect, bestowed unfettered sovereignty upon the Dominions by declaring that no law of the British parliament could be applied to any Dominion without the latter's express consent. Where other Dominions viewed the Westminster Statute as a legal definition of an otherwise sentimental union with Britain, DeValera made it the means of repudiating the Anglo-Irish Treaty of 1921. DeValera abolished the oath of allegiance to the British monarch, created a separate Irish citizenship, and stripped the British governor-general of his functions. Moreover, Ireland discontinued payment of the land annuities to Britain, the funds originally advanced by Britain to enable Irish tenant farmers to purchase land. Britain retaliated with stiff import duties on Irish products, but compromised in the end. In 1938 Prime Minister Neville Chamberlain ended the tariff war with Ireland, accepted a token payment of £10 million for the £100 million owed in land annuities, and relinquished control over the three Irish "treaty ports." Britain raised no objection to the new Irish constitution of 1937, which made southern Ireland (now styled Eire) for all practical purposes an independent state.

INDIA

While Britain witnessed the outbreak of revolution across the Irish Sea in 1919, violence had erupted in India at Amritsar in the Panjub, where some two thousand Indians were killed and wounded by order of General Dyer. The Amritsar massacre was precipitated by the slaying of five Englishmen and the beating of an English missionary. Indians wishing to pass the scene of the attack on the British missionary had to do so by crawling in the street, according to General Dyer's notorious "crawling order."

Amritsar signalled the opening of a new and painful chapter in India's long association with Great Britain. Since Britain's formal assumption of power over India from the East India Company in 1858, India had been governed by a highly centralized British bureaucracy. The administrative hierarchy extended from the provincial governors to the Viceroy and the Secretary of State for India, a member of the British cabinet. The Indian native states, some six hundred in number and comprising one third of India's area, were technically outside British India. The Hindu and Moslem princes were tied to Britain by treaties, however, which subjected their external affairs to British control under the British doctrine of "paramountcy."

Until the outbreak of the First World War, British concessions to growing Indian pressures for decentralization and native participation in government, had been minimal. The most notable change in the British government of India prior to the First World War had been the so-called Minto-Morley reforms (after the Viceroy and Secretary of State, respectively), which enlarged existing provincial councils. The reforms of 1909 merely grafted constitutional forms on the existing British autocracy, the powers of the Indian councils being advisory, elections being indirect and the suffrage severely limited. Self-government for India was neither the immediate nor the long-range intention of the Minto-Morley reforms. The East, noted Britain's Conservative leader Balfour, had a splendid history, but not one of self-government.

The British refusal to consider Dominion status for India before and after the First World War was rooted not only in the unspoken prejudice of color, but the fact that India was not a nation in any Western sense. India formed a geographic unit and had made great strides towards economic integration as a result of British-built roads and railroads. Within less than a century after the first opening of an Indian rail-line in 1852, India had developed the third largest railroad system in the world by the early 1930's.

Ethnically, linguistically, religiously, and culturally, India was the most diversified of British possessions, however. Two thirds of the population were counted as Hindu, subdivided into rigid castes; the remainder was predominantly Moslem, with a small Christian minority. The very diversity and friction of Indian society, especially between Hindus and Moslems, thus raised for Britain two fundamental questions: (1) Who, in India, could speak on behalf of all India, including the semi-independent princes? (2) Would the granting of Dominion status and the withdrawal of British authority not result in a sudden breakdown of the precarious peace, which Britain had maintained between quarreling factions?

The Indian National Congress, the largest and best organized among Indian political associations, claimed to speak for all India. The Congress had been founded in 1885 with the assistance of Allen O. Hume, a retired British colonial officer. Hume was motivated by compassion for the misery of India's masses, whose lot he described as "toil, toil, toil; hunger, hunger, hunger; sickness, suffering, sorrow."

Initially, the demands of Congress were modest, its attitude towards Britain almost servile. At its founding, Congress thanked Britain for having given India "order, railways, and above all the inestimable blessings of Western education." It was largely under the influence of Western education, however, with its messages of liberalism, constitutionalism, and nationalism, that Congress became a militant organization, which, by 1906, demanded *"Swaraj"* (self-government). Though Congress claimed to represent Indian national aspirations, it remained predominantly Hindu in composition and relegated the less articulate Moslem minority to an inferior position. The cry of Tilak, the militant Hindu leader, was not "India for the Indians" but "India for the Hindus." Accordingly, the Moslems founded their own All-Indian Moslem League in 1906 for the purpose of advancing the Moslem interest as distinct from that of the Hindu majority.

The First World War temporarily united Congress and the Moslem League in their common expectation of British concessions. Indian nationalism, both of the Hindu and Moslem variety, had become bolder after the Irish Easter Rebellion, an event which was followed with keen interest in India. Moreover, Indian nationalism had ceased to be the quiet preserve of a few intellectuals and had grown into a genuine mass phenomenon, with Mohandas Gandhi its new symbol and spokesman. Finally, India's transition from semi-feudalism to the threshold of an industrial society within little more than half a century highlighted the inadequancies of the British administration. The upholding of law and order had always been the chief argument with which Britain justified her Indian presence, and it was once said in India that a precipitous British withdrawal would not leave a single rupee or virgin in Bengal. In the early 20th century, India yearned for a government which could provide more than the maintenance of public order, however, as India's economic problems awaited solutions from imaginative and dedicated programs. Britain had instituted agricultural improvement programs through the Indian Department of Agriculture. The British civil service in India remained, on the whole, ill-equipped, however, to deal with the broader tasks of economic development. Britain, rather than India, determined the priorities of Indian spending, and the largest single item in the Indian budget remained military expenditures. By contrast, the illiteracy rate was over 90 per cent before 1914.

THE GOVERNMENT OF INDIA ACT OF 1920

Britain was willing to make concessions to India, but only of a kind that left the substance of British rule unaltered. E. J. Montagu, Secretary of State for India, promised in a declaration of August 2, 1917, an "increasing association of Indians in every branch of the administration and the gradual development of self-governing institutions. . . ." The implementation of Montagu's promise was the Government of India Act of 1920. The act established a system known as "diarchy," in which certain areas of administration on the provincial level were left to Indian ministers, while all important functions remained in the hands of the British provincial governors. Britain hoped that "diarchy" would provide India with parliamentary experience without endangering British rule. Democracy, Lloyd George observed, was a recent, Western experience, which could not be applied to India full-fledged. India might well question the sincerity of Britain's intentions when Birkenhead, the Secretary of State for India in the Conservative government of the mid-1920's declared that Britain did not hold India for the Indians, but as an outlet for British goods.

India rejected "diarchy" as an outmoded concept and responded with a boycott of British goods as well as Gandhi's campaign of civil disobedience. Although civil disobedience was conceived as a nonviolent undertaking, it greatly increased the level of violence. Unperturbed, Britain continued along the path of regulated political advance through the process of inquiry and dictation from above. In 1927 the Conservative government of Baldwin appointed the Simon Commission to examine the workings of the Government of India Act of 1920. The Commission, consisting solely of British members, was boycotted in India. The Commission's report of May 1930 remained still-born.

In 1929 Britain softened its tutelage over India by inviting Indian leaders to a Round Table Conference in London in order to devise a constitution for India. In the same year the British Viceroy in India, Lord Irwin (later to become Lord Halifax), promised Dominion status for India without, however, being authorized to do so by his government. Altogether three Round Table Conferences were held in London. Lord Irwin's hasty promise notwithstanding, Britain was not disposed to grant Dominion status to India. This was especially the case after the Conservative leader Stanley Baldwin returned to the prime ministership in 1935. Gandhi, having vainly demanded *"Purna Swaraj"* (complete independence) at the second Round Table Conference, departed empty-handed for India. The third Round Table Conference provided the basis of the Government of India Act of August 2, 1935.

THE GOVERNMENT OF INDIA ACT OF 1935

The Government of India Act of 1935 was a valiant British attempt at constitution making for all India—Hindu, Moslem, and Indian princes. The projected constitution was federal, with a federal legislature, composed of the elected representatives of the provinces (eleven in number) and the designated representatives of the princes. Although the act of 1935 went far to establish parliamentary government on the provincial level, it maintained the overriding British interest at the federal level by reserving such matters as the defense and the external affairs of India to the British governor-general. The 1935 constitution, in effect, applied the principle of "diarchy" to the federal level. Moreover, the provincial legislatures were barred from discriminating against British commercial interests.

The act of 1935 was careful to protect the interest of both the Moslem minority and the princes, as the India Congress party had displayed a growing Hindu militancy with the broadening of its national appeal. The Moslems had become wary of Congress as a result of the *Suddhi* and *Sangathan* movements. The former represented a Hindu effort to convert Moslems to Hinduism; the latter was an attempt to imbue Hindus with an aggressive and martial spirit.

The Hindu Congress rejected the Government of India Act in its entirety. In the tradition of Western nationalism, Congress demanded an all-Indian constituent assembly, which would draft its own constitution by virtue of its sovereign powers, rather than accept a constitution from British hands as a gift. The majority of the princes likewise rejected the 1935 constitution, mainly because they had second thoughts about living under a Congress-dominated, federated India. The Moslems increasingly spoke of partitioning India along religious lines and of setting up a separate Moslem state called *Pakistan*. (The word was formed out of the names of the predominantly Moslem provinces of the Punjab, Afghanistan, Kashmir, Sindh, and Baluchistan; *Pakistan,* in Arabic, also happened to mean "land of the pure.") "Moslems," the leader of the Moslem League Jinnah said in 1937, "can expect neither justice nor fair play under a Congress government."

The Government of India Act of 1935 was not without its critics in England. Its most outspoken British critic was Winston Churchill, who called the 1935 constitution voluminous but not luminous. In matters of imperialism, Churchill's had become a lonely and isolated voice in the House of Commons, however, and it required Hitler's challenge of the Second World War to change his fortunes from willful isolation into enduring national and international fame. Despite the opposition it encountered, the Government of India Act of 1935 went into effect in 1937 minus the provisions relating to the princely states. Congress leaders, torn between resentment of Britain and temptations of power, however limited, opted for power and formed governments in eight out of the eleven provinces. Relations between Congress leaders and the British authorities became, on the whole, remarkably harmonious. The 1935 constitution worked well until the outbreak of the Second World War. The outbreak of the Second World War sowed new discord between Britain and India, when the British governor-general declared war on Germany without consulting any of India's national leaders. Although he was within his constitutional rights in doing so, he needlessly offended Indian sensibilities. The Indian princes supported Britain without reservation. The Congress ministers in the provinces resigned in October, 1939, and Britain ruled by emergency decree. India, the Congress party declared in 1939, could not be expected to support a war of freedom and democracy in Europe, while the Indians' limited freedoms were being curtailed.

Not until much of Britain's empire in Asia had crumbled under the Japanese attack did Britain make a clear-cut promise of Dominion status to India in March, 1942. Both the circumstances and the timing of the British pledge deflated its appeal to India. In its "Quit India" resolution of August, 1942, the Congress party declared that "British rule in India must end immediately, not merely because foreign domination even at its best is an evil in itself . . . but because India in bondage can play no effective part in defending herself and in affecting the fortunes of the war. . . ." Britain outlawed the Congress party for the remainder of the war; but she could not banish its spirit, which drove irresistibly towards independence once the Second World War had ended.

THE MIDDLE EAST

In a military sense, the Middle East had been a British "sideshow" during the First World War, with only a fraction of British power having been committed to that theater. The British Empire, in Lloyd George's observation, had traditionally "done very well out of sideshows," however, and the collapse of Turkey opened up momentous possibilities for Britain in 1919.

The overall objective of Great Britain in the Arab Middle East was summarized by Britain's Foreign Secretary Balfour in 1919 as "supreme economic and political control, to be exercised . . . in friendly and unostentatious cooperation with the Arabs." The scope of British control extended from Persia to Aden and from the sheikdoms on the Persian Gulf to Iraq and Palestine, awarded to Great Britain as Mandates in the San Remo Conference of 1920, as well as Egypt and the Egyptian Sudan. British control did not take the form of outright annexation, but rather consisted of a network of treaties which safeguarded Britain's military, political, and economic interests.

PERSIA

Persia was vital to Great Britain both as a bridge to India and a source of oil, which had been discovered in Persia in 1908. In July, 1914, the British government had bought a controlling interest in the Anglo-Persian Oil Company. The collapse of tsarist Russia eliminated the Anglo-Russian agreement of 1907, which had divided Persia into a northern, Russian and southern, British sphere of influence. In 1919 Britain sought to bring all of Persia under her sway through the Anglo-Persian Treaty of August, 1919, subjecting Persia to extensive British military, financial, and political controls. The Shah of Persia was to draw an annual salary of £150,000 from the British treasury. The Anglo-Persian Treaty of August, 1919, failed to go into effect, however, owing to the resistance it encountered in the nationalist-minded Persian parliament (Majlis). A national revolution, spearheaded by Reza Khan, ousted Ahmad Shah in 1921. Like Kemal of Turkey, Reza Shah attempted to launch his nation on a path of foreign independence and domestic reform. A further cause of Britain's failure to turn Persia into a virtual Protectorate was the opposition which British policy in Persia aroused in both the United States and France. Though failing to maintain a military-political hold over Persia, Britain retained her Persian oil interests with the conclusion of the Anglo-Iranian oil agreement of May, 1933. The latter treaty superseded the original oil concession of 1901 and granted the Persian government a fixed royalty for each ton of oil produced during a sixty-year period.

EGYPT

Egypt, Britain's chief garrison in the Middle East during the First World War, remained the pivot of her Middle Eastern empire after the war. Before 1914 Britain's position in Egypt had been ill-defined. Nominally a part of the Ottoman Empire, Egypt had been under permanent British military occupation since July, 1882, despite Prime Minister Gladstone's assurance to the European powers that "of all the things in the world, permanent occupation is the thing we are not going to do." Britain retained the Egyptian monarch (Khedive) as well as the facade of a native government; real power rested with the British representative at Cairo, who determined the shape of Egypt's constitutions of 1883 and 1913. Lord Cromer, Britain's long-term representative in pre-war Egypt, was successful in restoring Egypt's solvency and promoting agricultural and irrigation programs. He was equally successful in arousing Egyptian national ire because of his demeanor, considered overbearing and patronizing by Egyptians. Egyptian domestic reforms, in Cromer's opinion, required "the singular political adaptability of Englishmen to execute. . . ."

With the outbreak of the First World War, Britain suspended the Egyptian constitution of 1913, declared Egypt a British Protectorate, and ruled by martial law. Britain assumed the direction of Egypt's foreign affairs and instituted compulsory labor for much of the Egyptian peasantry.

The end of the First World War brought violence to Egypt, as it did to India and Ireland. Egypt expected the British Protectorate to be ended with the conclusion of hostilities in Europe, and Saad Zaghlul, formerly Egyptian Minister of Education, headed a delegation (Al Wafd) to plead independence in London and Paris. To induce Britain into withdrawal, the Wafd pledged to uphold the Suez Canal Convention of 1888, assuring all ships free access to the canal in time of peace or war. Britain deported Zaghlul, first to Malta, later to more distant islands off East Africa. The Egyptian cabinet resigned in protest, and riots broke out in Cairo in March, 1919, almost at the same time as violence erupted at Amritsar in India.

Britain wavered between annexation of Egypt and ending the Protectorate. Following the recommendations of a commission of inquiry under Milner, Britain issued a Declaration of Policy on February 28, 1922, ending the Protectorate. Officially, Egypt became a sovereign nation; in fact, the Declaration altered the substance of British controls but slightly, as Britain "absolutely reserved" to herself the defense of Egypt, the security of imperial communications, the protection of foreign interests, and control over the affairs of the Egyptian Sudan. The Egyptian Sudan had been held as an Anglo-Egyptian condominium since 1899, although *de facto* rule was in the hands of a British governor-general.

Egypt adopted a new constitution in April, 1923, modelled after that of Belgium. Sultan Fuad assumed the title of King, and Saad Zaghlul, leader of the Wafd party and popular hero, became Prime Minister. Relations between the kingdom of Egypt and Britain remained tense as a result of continuing terrorism as well as the pressure of the Wafd. The Wafd sought emancipation through negotiation or, failing that, through the techniques employed by Ireland and India: non-cooperation, boycott, passive resistance. The assassination of Sir Lee Stack, on November 19, 1924, who was both the British governor-general of the Sudan and commander-in-chief of the Egyptian army, brought Anglo-Egyptian relations to a new low. Britain demanded an apology, as well as an indemnity of £500,000, and expelled Egyptian troops from the Sudan.

Anglo-Egyptian relations improved in the mid-1930's largely because of the ascendancy of Mussolini's Mediterranean imperialism. Though not reconciled to the imperialism of Great Britain, Egypt feared the prospects of Italian imperialism even more. It was thus on the Egyptian initiative that the Anglo-Egyptian Treaty of Alliance was concluded on August 26, 1936. The Alliance declared the British military occupation of Egypt ended and reopened the Sudan to Egyptian commerce and immigration. The Suez Canal, though termed an integral part of Egypt, was also recognized as an essential means of communication between the different parts of the Empire. All British troops remaining in Egypt were to be withdrawn to the Canal Zone, although some, in fact, continued to stay in Cairo. Both powers pledged mutual support in the event of war. Britain sponsored Egypt's entry into the League in 1937.

What continued to disturb Anglo-Egyptian relations was the emotional issue of Palestine, to be presently discussed, as well as Britain's interference in the internal affairs of Egypt during the Second World War. On February 4, 1942, the British ambassador to Egypt, Sir Miles Lampson, supported by British armor, forced King Faruk into dismissing Egyptian Prime Minister Ali Mahir, suspected of pro-Axis leanings. If worst came to worst, Foreign Secretary Balfour had said in 1919 with regard to Anglo-Arab relations, Britain's "advice" would have to be supported "by troops, aeroplanes, and tanks." Though a battlefield during the Second World War, Egypt did not declare war on Germany until February, 1945.

IRAQ, TRANSJORDAN, AND PALESTINE

Britain, as has been shown in the discussion of Allied war aims, had made promises of independence to the Arab provinces under

Ottoman rule. Addressing the British Trade Union Congress on January 5, 1918, Lloyd George had stated that Arabia, Mesopotamia, Syria, and Palestine were "in our judgement entitled to a recognition of their separate national condition." However, the frontiers drawn for the British and French mandates in the Middle East at the San Remo Conference of April, 1920, served the purpose of delimiting the respective spheres of influence of Britain and France, rather than that of setting up new Arab nation states.

The announcement of the British Mandate over Iraq (Mesopotamia) thus resulted in a fullblown revolt of Iraqi nationalists in June, 1920, for whose suppression Britain was forced to dispatch troops from India. In March, 1921, Winston Churchill, as Colonial Secretary, called together the Cairo Conference of British Middle East experts, in order to deal with Iraq as well as other British problems in the Middle East. The Cairo Conference installed Feisal, second son of the Sharif Husein of Mecca, as king of Iraq. The choice proved to be politically sound, as Feisal's prestige had grown in Arab eyes since his expulsion from Syria by the French. With Feisal, who drew a substantial British salary, cooperation proved possible as the forms of British control became less visible. Britain reduced her troop strength, while maintaining eight squadrons of the Royal Air Force — one third of the entire RAF in the 1920's — in Iraq. Having proven its worth in the conquest of Iraq during the war, British air power was equally valuable in the policing of Iraq in peace time. To lessen the impact of mandatory controls, Britain concluded the Anglo-Iraqi alliance of October 10, 1922, in which Britain promised to support Iraq's admission to the League. The League's award of the Mosul territory to Iraq in 1925 further enhanced British prestige. Although the principal beneficiaries of Iraq's oil riches were the foreign oil companies, which together formed the Iraq Petroleum Company, the government of Iraq shared in the profits under terms similar to those of the Anglo-Iranian oil agreement.

The Anglo-Iraq Treaty of January, 1931, ended the British Mandate over Iraq; in 1932 Iraq joined the League of Nations. Britain's interests remained, nevertheless, protected under the military and political provisions of the 1931 treaty: Britain retained control over the air bases of Habbaniya and Shaiba; all of Iraq's war material had to be purchased in Great Britain, and British military advisers stayed with the Iraqi forces. Moreover, the treaty provided for mutual assistance in war time.

Britain's relations with Iraq worsened after Feisal's death in 1933, as Feisal's son and successor, King Ghazi, increasingly fell under the influence of nationalist extremists. Under Ghazi the growing power of the Iraqi army over politics became a permanent feature of domestic developments, climaxing in the military revolt of April, 1941, to be discussed more fully in the context of the Second World War. Only after the revolt was crushed did Iraq return to the terms of the 1931 treaty and declare war on the Axis in January, 1943.

Palestine was important to Great Britain as a strategic buffer to Egypt. Included in the British Mandate of Palestine was originally the area of Transjordan, where Britain set up Abdullah, the elder brother of King Feisal, as Emir in March, 1921. In 1922 Transjordan was excluded by Britain from the area open to Jewish immigration and settlement. British control over Transjordan was exercised by a Resident Adviser, who was responsible to the British High Commissioner of Palestine. A Treaty of 1928 formally established British controls over Transjordan's finance and foreign and military affairs; the army of Transjordan was organized by British officers, whose best-known representative was General Glubb, the founder of the Arab Legion.

In Palestine proper, Britain, in due course, became confronted with two types of nationalism, Arab and Zionist, with adverse consequences to Britain's overall position in the Middle East. Britain's pledge to Zionism during the First World War through the Balfour Declaration was implemented in the terms of the British Mandate over Palestine, which called for the establishment of a Jewish National Home in Palestine. The Treaty of Sèvres of 1920 with Turkey likewise stipulated that the administration of Palestine would facilitate Jewish immigration under suitable conditions and would encourage Jewish settlement on the land. The British military in Palestine were unenthusiastic about the prospect of large-scale Jewish immigration, fearing its impact on Arab nationalism. Britain's Foreign Secretary Balfour favored the Zionist movement, as it would, in Balfour's opinion, bring a civilizing influence to the Middle East. Within the British government, the idea of an autonomous Jewish state in Palestine had been advanced as early as November, 1914, by the then Home Secretary Herbert Samuel, who was to become the first High Commissioner of Palestine after the First World War.

As British High Commissioner of Palestine, Herbert Samuel, a Zionist, worked hard to do justice to both native Arabs and immigrant Jews, his pledge to the Arabs being "to treat them with absolute justice and every consideration for their interests. . . ." With rising Jewish immigration, however, the fear of the Palestinian Arabs that they would eventually be outnumbered increased. Winston Churchill, as Colonial Secretary, had tried in vain to calm Arab fears with a memorandum of 1922, designed to explain the precise meaning of the Balfour Declaration of 1917. The Churchill Memorandum stressed that not all of Palestine was to be converted into a Jewish National Home but that such a home should rather be established in Palestine. Moreover, Churchill pledged that Britain did not contemplate the disappearance of the Arab population, language, or culture from Palestine. However, Jewish immigration, which had numbered 34,000 in 1925, sharply increased to 40,000 in 1933, following the beginning of Jewish persecution in Nazi Germany. Even prior to that date, Arab-Jewish tensions had led to violence, such as during the Wailing Wall Incident in Jerusalem in August, 1929.

Britain dispatched several commissions of inquiry to Palestine, as she had sought solutions to the problems of Egypt through the Milner Commission and those of India through the Simon Commission. Whatever the proposals of the British commissions to Palestine, they failed to bring the Arab-Jewish problem nearer solution, however, and ended up antagonizing both parties to the conflict. A White Paper on Palestine, issued by the British Colonial Secretary Lord Passfield in October, 1930, advising the curtailment of Jewish immigration, came under strong Zionist attack. The Peel Commission of 1936 recommended the end of the British Mandate over Palestine and the partitioning of Palestine into an Arab and a Jewish state. The Arab state was to be joined with Transjordan, while Britain would retain a mandate over Jerusalem, Bethlehem, and the port of Aqaba. The Peel Report's recommendations were unacceptable to both Arabs and Jews. Britain's last attempt to settle the problem of Palestine before the Second World War was the White Paper issued by the Colonial Secretary Malcolm MacDonald on May 17, 1939. It dropped the idea of partition and advised the establishment of an independent state of Palestine within a decade. The Jewish population was not to exceed one third of the Arab, however, and Jewish immigration was to be limited to 75,000 for the next five years. MacDonald's attempt at compromise was no more successful than earlier British efforts. The outbreak of the Second World War suspended the Palestine problem without a solution, acceptable to both Arabs and Jews, in sight. The emotional nature of the conflict obscured the many positive achievements of the British administration. Above all, Britain, though striving for a fair settlement for both sides, had, in Arab eyes, become identified with Zionist objectives in Palestine.

TOWARDS DOMINION INDEPENDENCE: THE WESTMINSTER STATUTE OF 1931

While Britain relaxed her controls over India, Ireland, and the Middle East during the inter-war period often reluctantly and under the pressure of revolutionary nationalism, she conceded equality and virtual independence to her Dominions of her own free will. Before the First World War, the privileged position of the Dominions had been reflected in the large measure of autonomy granted them and in their inclusion in periodic Imperial Conferences where the affairs of the Empire were discussed. It was in response to the Dominions' increased independence in foreign affairs, to which reference has been made in the discussion of British foreign policy of the 1920's, that Britain gave formal recognition to the changed status of the Dominions in the Imperial Conference of 1926. The resolution, drafted by Balfour and adopted by the 1926 conference, defined Great Britain and the Dominions as "autonomous communities within the British Empire, equal in status, in no way subordinate one to another in any aspect of their domestic or internal affairs, though united by a common allegiance to the Crown, and freely associated as members of the British Commonwealth of Nations." Moreover, every self-governing member of the Empire was declared "master of its destiny." "In fact, if not in form," the Balfour resolution concluded, "it is subject to no compulsion whatever."

As a practical consequence of this resolution, Britain ceased to handle Dominion affairs through the colonial office and established a separate department for Dominion relations. The British governor-generals in the Dominions henceforth were appointed upon the recommendation of the Dominion governments. The Westminster Statute, adopted by Parliament in 1931, gave legal form to the 1926 Resolution. The Westminster Statute recognized the legal equality of the Dominions with Great Britain, barred the application of British laws in the Dominions except through the latter's express consent, and made the alteration of laws concerning royal succession dependent on Dominion assent.

The Westminster Statute was an attempt to put into written form what was, to most Dominions, less a matter of law than of spirit and sentiment. Not all Dominions considered the attempt necessary or even wise, Australia postponing ratification of the Westminster Statute until after the Second World War. Ireland, by contrast, as previously noted, was quick to take advantage of the Westminster Statute to denounce the 1921 Anglo-Irish Treaty. Canada, at whose insistence the 1926 Imperial Conference had given definition of the Dominions' independence, maintained only three separate foreign embassies before the Second World War, in Washington, Paris, and Tokyo. Although the Dominions had made their point in cautioning Britain against hasty European commitments or entanglements during the inter-war period, they all responded, with the exception of Ireland, to Britain's call for help in 1939. At the beginning of the Second World War, the Royal Navy still proved to be the "Maypole" around which fluttered, in the words of a British historian, "the activities of Commonwealth, like so many ribbons."

BRITISH DOMESTIC DEVELOPMENTS, 1919 TO 1931

Politically, British democracy had evolved peacefully to as advanced a stage as anyone could wish by the end of the First World War. The Reform Bill of 1911 had drastically reduced the powers of the aristocratic upper chamber, the House of Lords, by abolishing its veto over finance bills and limiting its veto over other bills to a suspensive one. Since the enactment of the Reform Bill of 1911, the Commons could override the Lords' veto by passing the same bill three times over a two-year period. Women above the age of thirty were enfranchised in 1918, and the Equal Franchise Act of 1928 extended the vote to all women over twenty-one.

If Britain provided a model of political democracy and parliamentary rule, she remained, nonetheless, a thoroughly aristocratic society in an economic and social sense. In Britain one per cent of the population owned two thirds of the national wealth and 96 per cent of the land remained in the hands of some 30,000 individuals. The social barriers between the privileged few and the masses were reinforced through two unequal systems of education, which extended from the primary to the university level. Whereas ordinary children attended free day schools on the primary level and grammar schools on the secondary level, the wealthy passed from private boarding schools to the misnamed "public schools," which were, in fact, expensive private secondary institutions. From the "public schools" came most of the Oxford and Cambridge undergraduates, only one in a hundred of the latter being of working class origin. From the "public schools" and Britain's two leading universities came, in turn, the majority of Britain's political leaders, except those of the Labor party, as well as the administrators of the Empire. It was a rarity indeed to find a British cabinet between the two world wars whose members were not graduates of the privileged and private system of education. The Labor cabinets of the early and late 1920's provided the exception, signalling the beginning of a quiet social revolution in postwar Britain.

The First World War had made but a small dent in the class structure of Great Britain, and its levelling social effect remained much smaller than that of the Second World War a generation later. The war, demanding equal sacrifice without class distinction, had, nevertheless, heightened the expectation of the masses for better living conditions, and thus imposed a mandate for social action upon Britain's first postwar government under Lloyd George.

The social pressures of postwar Britain, it should be noted briefly, did not translate themselves into violent or extremist political action, such as was common in many continental European societies. The formation of soldiers' "soviets" by British troops, awaiting demobilization at Calais and in a number of camps in England, was a phenomenon without lasting political significance. The British Communist party, established in July, 1920, never exceeded 10,000 members at its peak between the wars and remained an oddity rather than becoming a serious factor in British politics. There was sympathy among British workers for Soviet Russia, and London dockers refused to load ammunition for Poland during the Russo-Polish war of 1920. The growing political and economic power of labor did not manifest itself outside the established system, however, but within the existing organizations of the unions, whose membership swelled to eight million, as well as through the Labor party.

The Conservative-Liberal coalition government under Prime Minister Lloyd George owed its return to power in the elections of December, 1918, as much to its promise of a strong peace as to its pledge of rewarding veterans for their service to king and country. Lloyd George had run on a platform of full employment for the veterans and "homes for heroes." Lloyd George's election promises had been made on the assumption of a postwar economic boom that would bring both full employment and increased revenue for social services. After a brief upswing, the expected boom failed to materialize, however, partly because of the changed conditions in the world market. Britain could export little to impoverished postwar Europe, while encountering the competition of Japan and the United States in her traditional overseas markets. Moreover, Britain's staple industries, which had assured her industrial leadership during the better part of the 19th century, such as textiles, coal, iron, and steel, were in urgent need of overhaul and modernization. Likewise, the British economy had failed to develop the newer, light industries, such as chemical and electrical industries, at the same rate as her competitors. These shortcomings of the British economy were not new; they had existed since before the First World War. Their effects had been less evident before the 1920's, however, since Britain's pre-war income from invisible exports, such as shipping, insurance, and banking revenue, had covered the deficit in British trade. This continued to be true for the first postwar decade, during which invisible exports helped maintain Britain's favorable balance of payments. In 1929 Britain still showed a favorable balance of payments of £103 million, whereas the balance of payments for 1931 turned unfavorable to the extent of £104 million under the impact of the Depression.

British exports in the old staple industries continued to decline after the First World War. The export of British coal declined from 82 to 70 million tons between 1907 and 1930, that of cotton goods from 105 to 86 million tons, despite a worldwide increase in the demand for cotton goods by 20 per cent over the same period. As India increased its output of cotton goods, the export of Lancashire cotton to India declined by 42 per cent in 1929 as compared with pre-war figures. The characterization of England by Friedrich List, the German economist, in the *System of Political Economy* of 1841, as "a cosmopolitan country supplying all nations with manufactured products, and asking in return from each country its raw materials and commodities," no longer applied to the conditions of the early 20th century.

In the immediate postwar period, British unemployment thus rose sharply, doubling between 1920 and 1921 and reaching two million in June, 1921. Unemployment remained a persistent and chronic feature of the British economy between the wars, the number of unemployed never falling below one million or ten per cent of the labor force. The unemployment problem was regional, rather than national, however, since it was most acute in the areas of concentration of the old staple industries – South Wales, Scotland, and the industrial region north of the river Trent. The centers of the newer industries, such as the automotive, chemical, and electrical industries, around London, Birmingham, and south-central England, enjoyed greater prosperity throughout the 1920's and 1930's.

Under the impact of the economic slump, the achievements of the Lloyd George government fell short of promises and expectations. Lloyd George's task as war-time prime minister had been simpler than his peace-time mandate, since war production had been expanded without concern over cost. The enormous industrial capacity displayed by war-time Britain could not easily be sustained in peace-time, however, when emergency war-time controls had been ended. In 1921 Lloyd George lifted the last controls of "war socialism" under pressure from the employers as well as the unions. The results were soaring prices and a return to the pre-war pattern of wage conflicts, especially in the coal mines and railroads. Lloyd George's promising programs in housing and education were cut short for lack of funds. Under the Addison Act of 1919, named after the Minister of Health, over 200,000 new homes were built between 1919 and 1922. The Fisher Act of 1918 had provided for significant improvements in public education that included raising the age for leaving school. The economy measures of 1922, known as the "Geddes axe" after their sponsor Sir Eric Geddes, thwarted the implementation of the Fisher Act while curtailing war pensions and the housing program. Addison, who together with Lloyd George had been instrumental in the spectacular expansion of the munitions program during the war, discovered that housing needs in peace-time could not be satisfied at public expense with the methods of war socialism. Stop-gap measures, such as the Unemployment Insurance Act of 1920, rather than long-range programs, thus became characteristic of the Lloyd George administration. Lloyd George lost the support of labor and of many veterans, to whom the promise of making Britain a "home for heroes" seemed cynical and empty by 1922.

Parliament had rewarded some of Britain's leading generals with substantial gifts of money, such as Field Marshal Douglas Haig, who received £100,000. General Dyer, forced to resign after the Amritsar affair, was given £26,000 by the Conservative newspaper *Morning Post.* The ordinary and anonymous veteran, by contrast, faced the hazards of unemployment, somewhat ameliorated by the Unemployment Insurance Act of 1920, which greatly broadened coverage compared with similar, pre-war legislation.

The economic and social failures of the Lloyd George cabinet thus stemmed in large measure from the dilemma posed by the widespread desire for a return to the pre-war pattern of *laissez-faire,* on the one hand, and the pressure for social services, including housing, on the other. The latter services required for their realization sweeping measures, which the British government had been able to adopt under conditions of "war socialism" but which it hesitated to repeat in peace-time. Politically, the position of Lloyd George had weakened as a result of the loss of labor sympathy and the declining support of his own Conservative coalition partners. Angered by the Irish settlement, the Conservatives also feared the loss of their identity as a political party if the coalition were maintained. More generally, Lloyd George had lost touch with parliament because of the demands of foreign affairs. The very dynamism of Lloyd George's personality, which had contributed to his war-time popularity, became a liability after the war, when the British public desired a return to "normalcy," whether "normalcy" in the pre-war sense was attainable or not. Following the Conservatives' withdrawal of support from the coalition, Lloyd George resigned as Prime Minister on October 19, 1922. Having held public office for sixteen years, he was not to do so again.

The fall of Lloyd George was symptomatic of the decline of his Liberal party. Having been badly split during the war, as a result of Lloyd George's easing Prime Minister Asquith out of office in 1916, the Liberal party lost influence among its traditional pre-war voters. Before 1914 the Liberal party had drawn a considerable portion of the labor vote because of its commitment to social reform between 1906 and 1914. At the same time, the Liberal party had continued to be the representative of well-to-do financial and industrial circles. The First World War had polarized property-holders and wage-earners, the former supporting the Conservatives, the latter increasingly moving towards the Labor party. In due course, the political battle was waged between Conservatives and Laborites, with the Liberals holding the balance, rather than between Liberals and Conservatives. The Liberal party continued to develop imaginative programs for the solution of Britain's economic and social ills, especially with the onset of the Great Depression in 1929. After the fall of Lloyd George, the party failed to produce a national leader of equal caliber, however, nor did it command the financial resources or the close-knit organization enjoyed by Conservatives and Laborites.

CONSERVATIVE GOVERNMENT AND THE LABOR INTERLUDE OF 1923/1924

The Conservative decision to end the coalition under Lloyd George appeared justified by the elections of November 15, 1922, which returned the Conservatives as the strongest party with 345 seats, enabling them to form a government under Bonar Law. Labor emerged as the second strongest party with 142 seats; the Liberals, split between the Asquith and Lloyd George factions, ended up last with 117 seats.

Law's retirement from office for reasons of health in May, 1923, resulted in a fight within the Conservative party for leadership between Curzon and Stanley Baldwin. By comparison with Baldwin's, Curzon's was an illustrious career, which included the post of British Viceroy of India. Although Curzon dismissed Baldwin as "a man of the utmost insignificance," the Conservative party preferred the latter as Prime Minister. Baldwin's unexciting personality appeared better suited to the prevailing trend towards "normalcy" than Curzon's imperious air.

Baldwin's chief asset, by all accounts, was his gift as a politician and manipulator of his party, although the wisdom of his first political decision as Prime Minister was open to question. Baldwin hoped to reduce unemployment through tariff protection, and called new elections for December, 1923, on this issue. Although Britain had introduced duties on certain imports since 1914, such as the McKenna tariff on luxury goods and the 1921 tariff for selected industries, the free trade principle, so hotly debated before 1914, was still firmly established in the public mind. The elections of December, 1923, were fought and lost by the Conservatives over the issue of tariff protection. Although the Conservatives remained the single largest party in the Commons with 258 seats, they were outnumbered by the combined strength of Labor (191) and the Liberals (159).

The formation of a new government proved difficult because the Liberals rejected a coalition with both the Conservatives and the Labor party, the obstacle being tariff protection in the one case, socialism in the other. Without joining Labor in government, however, the Liberals were willing to tolerate a minority Labor government. King George V concurred. Although the Labor leaders were, in the King's words, "all socialists, . . . they ought to be given a chance and ought to be treated fairly." On January 22, 1924, the twenty-third anniversary of Queen Victoria's death, Ramsay MacDonald formed the first Labor government of Britain.

Not a few Conservatives were horrified at the prospect of a Labor government. Winston Churchill had called Labor "unfit to govern," and the election campaigns of 1922 and 1923 had given an example of Conservative anxieties over Labor. The Conservative *Daily Mail* warned that Labor threatened "every man's house and furniture and every woman's clothes and jewelry." In 1923 the Conservatives had run under the slogan of "Baldwin for Britain — MacDonald for Moscow."

The first Labor government constituted a revolution of sorts for Britain, though not of the kind Conservatives had warned against. It was revolutionary to find men at the helm of the British government most of whom had not passed through the privileged "public schools." Politically, Labor governed by the rules of British parliamentary tradition; economically, Labor proceeded with caution, as its survival in office depended on Liberal benevolence in the Commons; Labor was in office, but not in power. The majority of the Ramsay MacDonald cabinet was drawn from the party's moderate wing. The radicals, the so-called "Clydesiders," were represented in Charles S. Wheatley, the Minister of Health. A coal miner at age eleven, Wheatley had risen in Glasgow politics largely through his efforts at self-education.

During its first brief tenure of office, Labor thus was more concerned with demonstrating its ability to govern than with proposals for radical change that had no chance of parliamentary approval. Ramsay MacDonald, a pacifist during the First World War, commissioned five new cruisers for the Royal Navy. The Labor budget, prepared by the Chancellor of the Exchequer, Philip Snowden, brought few surprises other than a reduction of duties on tea and sugar. The McKenna tariffs were abolished. When threatened by strikes in the transport industry, the Labor government invoked emergency powers against the very unions on whose financial contributions the Labor party was dependent. The most notable Labor achievements in social policy were the Wheatley Housing Act, for a long-range, low-income housing program, and improvements in secondary education instituted by the Minister of Education, Trevelyan. Unemployment persisted at well over a million. As noted elsewhere, neither in the affairs of Empire nor in the conduct of British foreign policy did Labor depart from the mainstream of British tradition, save for the formal recognition of Soviet Russia.

Soviet Russia proved to be MacDonald's undoing, as the Conservative opposition, together with a number of Liberals, seized upon incidents in 1924 to substantiate the charge of Labor's "pro-Moscow" orientation. On July 25, 1924, the radical *Workers' Weekly* appealed to British soldiers not to turn their guns on "fellow workers," either in a class war, or in a foreign war. Although the Labor party was in no way associated with the appeal, the Labor government was charged with complicity in the affair. Hastings, the British Attorney General, had dropped charges against the *Workers' Weekly* editor on the Prime Minister's advice. Conservatives and Liberals combined to bring the Labor government down by a vote of non-confidence.

The "red-scare" tactics which had overthrown the Labor government were instrumental also in securing a Conservative majority of 419 seats, over 151 Labor and 40 Liberal seats, in the election of October, 1924. The Conservative charge of Labor connections with the Communist International was reinforced by the "Zinoviev letter," discussed in the context of British foreign affairs. Though no original copy of the "Zinoviev letter" was ever produced and its authenticity remained in doubt, its effect on the elections of 1924 was strong. Well might the Labor party ask whether the fair play which the Liberals and the King had promised Labor in 1923 had, in fact, been observed during the brief Labor government.

THE BALDWIN YEARS;
THE RETURN TO STABILITY, 1925/1929
    The second Conservative government under the premiership of Baldwin included both able and colorful men, despite the Prime Minister's alleged mediocrity and laziness. Winston Churchill, as Conservative Chancellor of the Exchequer, returned the pound to the gold standard in 1925. Despite his brilliance, Churchill continued to meet with the distrust of the Conservative Old Guard, having switched his party allegiance from Conservative to Liberal before the First World War and back to Conservative after the war. Of Churchill's liberalism, it was said that it was tainted by the foreign accent common to men who have learned to speak a new language late in life. Labor feared and disliked Winston Churchill, especially after the General Strike of 1926, to be presently discussed. The most energetic member of Baldwin's cabinet was the Minister of Health, Neville Chamberlain, whose record of foreign appeasement in the 1930's has largely overshadowed and obscured his domestic achievements in social reform during the 1920's. Having sponsored the Housing Act of July, 1923, in the first Baldwin government, Chamberlain was responsible for new social legislation in the second Baldwin cabinet, such as the Widows, Orphans and Old Age Contributory Pensions Act and the creation of Public Assistance Committees; the Rating and Valuation Act supported farm prices through government subsidies.
    Economically, the mid-1920's witnessed Britain's recovery from the effects of the First World War, the industrial production of 1925 exceeding that of 1913 by ten per cent. The volume of imports had grown over the same period by 10 per cent, however, while that of exports had fallen by a quarter. The growing gap between imports and exports did not affect Britain's balance of payments, however, as the terms of trade were more favorable to Britain after the war than they had been before 1914. Whereas the price of imported primary goods had fallen, that of industrial exports had remained constant or had increased. With her exports, Britain could buy more abroad than before the First World War.
    The drop in British exports nevertheless continued to disturb the British government. To reduce the high price of British articles, the Conservatives proposed to cut industrial wages. The pressure for lower wages, officially sanctioned by the Prime Minister, precipitated the General Strike of 1926, Britain's worst labor crisis between the wars.
    The General Strike had its origins in Britain's ailing coal industry, which suffered once again from German competition after the

settlement of the Ruhr strike in 1923. Moreover, the British coal industry was run in a disorganized and inefficient manner without uniform wage standards. Miners' wages ranged from £2 to £4 weekly, depending on the yield of the coal seams. Altogether 1,500 separate companies operated some 3,000 mines, with over a million workers. After the First World War the coal miners had demanded nationalization of the mines, but the Labor government of 1923 had desisted from any nationalization schemes for the reasons stated previously. A call for reorganization of the entire coal industry, issued by the government-appointed Sankey Commission of 1919, had gone unheeded.

In 1925 the mine-owners wanted not only to slash wages by as much as 25 per cent, but to increase working hours at the same time. To cheapen the price of coal, the owners also recommended a cut in railroad workers' wages in order to reduce freight rates. Miners refusing to work at the revised rates were threatened with a lock-out. The miners answered with the slogan "not a penny off the pay, nor a minute on the day."

THE GENERAL STRIKE OF 1926   Baldwin prevented an immediate show-down in the coal industry by pledging to subsidize both wages and profits for a nine months' period, during which a Royal Commission under Sir Herbert Samuel was to propose ways of raising efficiency in the coal industry. The Commission's report of March, 1926, though rejecting most of the owners' arguments, upheld the recommendation for wage cuts. On May 4, 1926, the miners, supported by the unions of the railroads, transport workers, printers, construction and steel workers, and gas and electrical workers, commenced a general strike. A last-minute attempt at avoiding the general strike through an emergency meeting between Baldwin and Labor party leaders, including MacDonald, failed as a result of the printers' strike in the Conservative *Daily Mail.* Baldwin abruptly abandoned his mediation efforts when the *Daily Mail* printers refused to print an article calling the threatened strike a "revolutionary movement."

The general strike pursued no political objectives, its goal being the protection of miners' wages. The unions feared that a cut in miners' wages would act as the signal for wage cuts in other industries. The Conservative government, by contrast, regarded the general strike less as a contest between unions and employers than as a contest between unions and the government. Baldwin called the general strike an "attack on constitutional government" and "the road to anarchy and ruin."

The general strike was brief and overwhelmingly peaceful. The government, in anticipation of the strike, had divided England into ten districts, each under a civilian commissioner, to maintain vital transportation. Ex-officers and university students acted as volunteer drivers of trucks and railroad engines. With newspapers blacked out by the strike, the government issued its own newspaper, the *British Gazette,* under the editorship of Churchill, for the duration of the strike. Churchill's editorials were more pugnacious than seemed warranted by the nature of the strike, declaring the strikers the "enemy," on whose "unconditional surrender" the government must insist. The *British Gazette* stamped Churchill as an enemy of labor, a fact remembered by not a few as late as 1945, when Churchill was defeated in his bid for reelection as Prime Minister.

The general strike ended in mid-May, 1926, after union leaders, other than those of the miners, reached agreement with Herbert Samuel. The miners' strike continued, unaided, until the end of 1926, when funds ran out. Many strikers were victimized by their employers, being rehired at lower wages and longer hours.

Baldwin followed up the workers' defeat with the Trade Disputes and Trade Union Act of 1927, which outlawed sympathy strikes designed to "coerce the government." Civil servants were forbidden to join a union affiliated with the Trade Union Congress; union dues could no longer be deducted automatically for Labor party funds. The Conservative government had overplayed its hand, as public sympathy for the workers and miners in particular was widespread. Britain remained prosperous for the remainder of Conservative rule, to be sure, but hunger marches by the unemployed and the persistent problem of unemployment in the depressed areas foreshadowed the economic crisis that lay ahead.

THE SECOND LABOR GOVERNMENT;
THE FINANCIAL CRISIS OF 1931 AND THE
FORMATION OF THE FIRST NATIONAL GOVERNMENT

In the elections of May 30, 1929, the Labor party captured 288 seats, as against 260 for the Conservatives and 59 for the Liberals. The Liberals held the balance, as they had in 1923/24, and once again supported the formation of a Labor government under Ramsay MacDonald, on June 5, 1929. The second Labor government included Philip Snowden, who once again became Chancellor of the Exchequer, Arthur Henderson in the Foreign Office, and Sidney Webb, now Lord Passfield, in charge of Dominion and colonial affairs. Margaret Bondfield, as Minister of Labor, became the first woman to serve in a British cabinet.

In foreign and Imperial affairs, Labor policy differed little from Conservative attitudes, the Labor concessions to India being undertaken with the approval of the Conservative opposition, except for Winston Churchill. Angered over the promises made to India, Churchill resigned from the Conservative shadow cabinet, with few regrets from Baldwin.

Before the full impact of the Depression had reached the British economy, the Labor government enacted a moderate program of social reform, such as slum clearance under the Housing Act of 1930 and the reduction of working hours in the coal mines under the Coal Mines

Act of the same year. Labor's effort to repeal the 1927 Trade Disputes Act failed.

With the onset of the Depression and the increase in unemployment figures to 2½ million by December, 1930, the Labor government became deeply divided among its own ranks as to the best solution of the crisis. Among Britain's three political parties, the Liberals alone had produced novel economic concepts during the election campaign of 1929. Under the slogan "We can conquer unemployment," Lloyd George had presented an economic program which was based on industrial, agricultural, and urban surveys and to which economists, such as John M. Keynes, had contributed. The Liberal platform of 1929 anticipated the theories which J. M. Keynes was to develop in the mid-1930's in his *General Theory of Employment, Interest, and Money,* discussed in the context of the World Depression. Specifically, the Liberals of 1929 broke with the concepts of *laissez-faire* and balanced budgets and advocated public works on a large scale, financed by deficit spending.

MacDonald did not apply Keynesian cures to the British economy, since the theories of Keynes failed to win general acceptance, even in academic circles, for many years to come. Although MacDonald blamed the system under which Labor governed for the Depression, he limited his economic policy to measures approved by that system. Labor combatted the Depression with a policy of austerity and budget cuts, including cuts in unemployment benefits. Within the Labor party, Oswald Mosley proposed alternative solutions, which Labor refused to consider because of Mosley's increasingly anti-democratic and imperialist stance. Formerly a Conservative, Mosley had joined the Labor party in 1924, only to leave it again in 1931 to form his "New Party," which became the "British Union of Fascists." In substance, Mosley's economic and political ideas were a blend of pre-war British imperialist doctrine and postwar fascist ideology. Under the slogan of "Britain for the British," Mosley called for a self-contained and self-sufficient British Empire with controlled foreign trade and domestic economic expansion through government credits. Like the Communist party of Britain, the B.U.F. remained an oddity in British politics. In Britain, the Depression failed to spawn totalitarian mass movements, and Mosley was derided as a "pocket Mussolini" by his former Labor colleagues.

By August, 1931, Britain was in the grip of a severe financial crisis, owing to the mass withdrawal of foreign deposits from Britain while Britain's own loans to Germany remained frozen. The Bank of England advised the Labor government that the flight of foreign capital was due to a "complete want of confidence in His Majesty's government existing among foreigners." The bankers demanded a balanced budget to uphold international confidence in the pound and urged a reduction in unemployment benefits by 10 per cent. Although MacDonald agreed, his cabinet was split over the issue of reduced unemployment benefits, and resigned.

The King urged the formation of a National government under MacDonald, whose prestige went far beyond his own Labor party. On August 25, 1931, MacDonald formed such a government, consisting of four Labor, four Conservative, and two Liberal ministers. The declared purpose of the coalition was "to deal with the national emergency that now exists"; the political parties were to resume their "respective positions" once the purpose of the National government had been achieved. In fact, the practice of coalition replaced one-party government in Britain for the remainder of the 1930's.

The chief victim of the National government was the Labor party. Only a minority of Labor leaders, including Philip Snowden, supported MacDonald as leader of the National coalition. The majority of Labor, as well as the Trade Union Council, accused MacDonald of "treason" and opposed the National government. On September 28, 1931, the Labor party voted MacDonald, Snowden, and Thomas, who continued to serve in the National government, out of the party. As the First World War had split the Liberal party and left Lloyd George without a following, the Depression split Labor and isolated MacDonald.

The National government mastered the deficit in the British budget without being able to halt the run on the pound. Snowden, as Chancellor of the Exchequer in the National government, imposed a general cut on government salaries from cabinet members on down to policemen, teachers, and seamen. While taxes were raised by £76 million, government expenditures were cut by £70 million. The salary cuts in the Royal Navy produced a minor revolt among the sailors at the Atlantic Fleet base at Invergordon, who complained that the greatest reduction affected "the lowest paid men on the lowest deck." Whereas admirals' salaries were cut by 7 per cent, those of enlisted seamen were reduced by 15 per cent. The Invergordon mutiny was resolved by discharging the ringleaders and reducing the paycuts of sailors. The Invergordon incident increased Labor's animosity towards the National government while causing surprise abroad at what seemed to be an unprecedented crisis in Royal Navy morale.

On September 21, 1931, acting on the advice of the Bank of England, parliament suspended the gold standard with a resulting drop in the value of the pound from $4.86 to $3.80. The Conservatives pressed for new elections, though they wished to retain MacDonald as Prime Minister and head of a national coalition. On October 7, 1931, parliament was dissolved. The ensuing election campaign resembled that of December, 1918, in its atmosphere of urgency and crisis, with the Conservatives as the chief beneficiaries. Ramsay MacDonald, running for reelection as Prime Minister, asked the nation for a "doctor's mandate" to cure Britain's economic and fiscal woes. Running under the banner of "National Labor," MacDonald's followers elected a meager 35 members to the Commons. The "National Liberals" obtained 13 seats, while the Conservatives, the most successful in appropriating the national label, scored an overwhelming victory with 473 seats. The Labor opposition gained 52 seats. Neither the Communists nor Mosley's party gained a single seat, a striking contrast to the mushrooming of left- and right-wing extremists in the depression-ridden continental Europe of 1931. In Ramsay MacDonald's second National government, Conservative influence prevailed with eleven cabinet posts in Conservative hands as against five for the Liberals and four for "National Labor."

10 | The Victorious Democracies II:

The Third French Republic

In contrast to the stability of British democracy, France before the First World War often gave the appearance of a democracy in chaos, without firm executive leadership. The weakness of French governments under the Third Republic, exemplified by the brevity of French cabinets—altogether fifty between 1871 and 1914—was less a reflection of national temperament than the result of limited executive powers under the French constitution of 1875.

The Third Republic concentrated power in the bi-cameral legislature, the Chamber of Deputies, and the Senate. The executive was weak and overshadowed by the legislature; the president was chosen by the combined votes of Senate and Chamber, rather than by popular vote, and the prime minister was subject to a vote of non-confidence by either the Senate or the Chamber. The principle of ministerial responsibility, which functioned as a means of alternating power in the two-party system of Great Britain, became a means of executive disruption and a source of ministerial instability under the multi-party system of republican France.

The executive weakness of the Third Republic was intentional. It reflected the peculiar circumstances out of which the republic grew as well as the distrust of strong government after the experience of Bonapartism and royalist restoration during the first half of the 19th century. The system of limited executive powers was also geared to the preservation of the social *status quo,* which the majority of Frenchmen favored before the First World War.

The essence of French republican philosophy was explained in the writings of Emile Auguste Chartier, better known under his pseudonym Alain. Proceeding from the assumption that "power corrupts all those who exercise it," Alain viewed the chief task of the legislature as one of control and limitation of the executive and the bureaucracy. The citizen, according to Alain, should obey the law, and thereby uphold public order; he should, at the same time, resist the government, and thereby protect individual liberty against the power of the state. It was not the task of the state to enrich its citizens; it was enough if the state did not ruin them.

Behind the turbulent politics of republican France and the

frequent change in prime ministers, there existed a broad consensus between the republican parties on the principles of social conservatism and government by legislative restraint. The terms "Left," "Radical," and "Radical Socialist" in French politics did not connote a commitment to social or economic change but suggested rather the difference between democratic liberalism and conservative liberalism. Radical republicans and conservative republicans might disagree on the form, but not the substance, of the Third Republic. The French republic was, in the words of its critics, a "republic of pals."

The serious domestic political battles of pre-war France were not waged between republicans of different shades but between republicans and royalists over the issue of whether the republic was there to stay. The republican-royalist controversy, which filled the years of the Third Republic until the turn of the century, reflected the division of the French nation into "two Frances," a division going back to the French Revolution of 1789. Republican France claimed to uphold the ideals of the revolution of 1789; monarchist France, supported by the army and identified with the Catholic Church, represented the values of the Old Regime.

The Dreyfus case, involving a Jewish army officer falsely accused and convicted of espionage by the French army in 1894 and exonerated by the Republic in 1906, marked the climax of the royalist-republican feud. To consolidate its victory, the Republic struck at the Catholic Church, symbol of royalist opposition, with anti-clerical legislation and the abrogation of the Concordat of 1801. The Associations Act of 1901 aimed at minimizing the educational role of the Church by making the operation of religious orders in France depend upon government authorization.

Monarchism, though dead as a political force, continued to survive in the anti-semitic and anti-republican ideology of the *Action Française* of Charles Maurras. Although the *Action Française* never attracted a large following, its influence remained considerable even after the First World War, among army officers, high civil servants, and the well-to-do. The monarchy alone, in Maurras' words, could "reconcile all Frenchmen and unite them against their enemies both domestic and foreign." The domestic enemies, according to the *Action Française,* included "Jews, Protestant pedagogues, and Freemasons." Against the individualism of the liberal republic, Maurras preached "integral nationalism," which signified the subordination of individual and social interests to the national good. After the First World War, the *Action Française* became the prototype of the French fascist leagues.

The real left in French politics was represented by the Socialists, who achieved a unified national organization only by 1905 under the name of SFIO (*Section Française de l'Internationale Ouvrière*). The

French Socialist party, like socialist parties elsewhere before the First World War, was a blend of doctrinaire Marxism and gradualist reformism, Jules Guesde representing the former, Jean Jaurès the latter. Jean Jaurès and his disciple Léon Blum, who succeeded to the leadership of the SFIO after Jaurès' assassination on the eve of the First World War, symbolized the humanitarian dimension of French socialism, which regarded social revolution as the fulfillment of the uncompleted French revolution of 1789. In practice, the SFIO became a party of reform, which developed into the second largest political party in 1914.

The labor unions (*syndicats*), united in the CGT (*Confédération Générale du Travail*), represented the revolutionary element in the pre-war labor movement of France. Disillusioned with the parliamentary tactics of the Socialist party, the unions embraced the doctrine of direct action, or syndicalism, as advocated in George Sorel's *Reflections on Violence* (1906). Sorel dismissed parliamentary socialism as "noisy, garrulous, and lying" and advocated the "myth of the general strike" as an alternative. The adoption of Sorel's syndicalism by the CGT in the "Charter of Amiens" of 1906 was followed by a wave of strikes, which the government defeated by 1910. Although syndicalism failed, its impatient and revolutionary spirit reemerged after the First World War in the French Communist party.

Despite its inconspicuous beginning under the shadows of foreign defeat and the internal strife between royalists and republicans, the Third Republic, by 1914, had outlasted all previous French régimes since the French Revolution of 1789. The republic had lasted longest because it had divided Frenchmen least. With the First World War the Third Republic reached the high point of its prestige by the mere fact of its survival under the attack of the German Empire and by its recovery of the lost provinces of Alsace and Lorraine.

THE THIRD REPUBLIC AFTER THE FIRST WORLD WAR: THE END OF THE SACRED UNION

The outbreak of the First World War united all political parties of France in a "Sacred Union" (*union sacrée*), for which President Poincaré had called on August 2, 1914: "As of this moment, there are no more parties. There is eternal France, pacific and determined France." The French socialists followed the government's call to national defense and entered the government of the Sacred Union with Jules Guesde and Marcel Sembat.

The Sacred Union of August 2, 1914, did not survive the stresses of the First World War. By 1917, the year which marked a general crisis in European war morale, French socialism had split three ways, into war supporters, pacifists, and those inspired by Lenin and the successful Bolshevik revolution. The majority of the SFIO supported a compromise peace by 1917 and bitterly resented the French government's refusal to permit French socialists to attend the International Socialist Congress at Stockholm in 1917. During the final and most critical stage of the war, Georges Clemenceau, the veteran Radical Socialist leader, guided France from the moral crisis of November, 1917, to the triumph of 1919. "The winner is the one," Clemenceau told the Chamber of Deputies on March 8, 1918, "who believes, a quarter of an hour longer than his enemy, that he has not lost."

The Allied victory of 1918 failed to restore the political unity of France of August, 1914. Socialist France remained largely unaffected by the nationalist wave that swept over bourgeois France in the wake of the German defeat. To the Socialist leader Léon Blum, the First World War was "the great insomnia of the world, filled with the nightmare of hatred." Whereas the French nationalist right denounced the Treaty of Versailles as too lenient, the SFIO condemned it as punitive and vindictive and as a betrayal of Wilson's promises. Blum had expressed the hope that the First World War would differ from all previous wars in that "the peace would determine the nature of victory," rather than "the victory the shape of the peace."

Nor was the French Socialist repudiation of the 1919 peace settlement the only issue which widened the gulf between bourgeois and socialist France. The war had made the French industrial proletariat more demanding and rebellious, and the majority of French Socialists bitterly opposed French intervention in the Russian Civil War of 1919. Workers' riots in Paris on May 1, 1919, the rekindling of the syndicalist movement, and the sailors' mutiny of the French fleet in the Black Sea, incited by André Marty, were signs of the workers' unrest and opposition to Marshall Foch's Allied "crusade" against Bolshevik Russia.

On the morrow of its victory over Germany, the Third Republic was haunted by the specter of social revolution. In addition to the radicalization and alienation of the workers, postwar France was confronted with a multitude of new problems. These may be summarized as (1) the financial liquidation of the war, (2) the reconstruction of the devastated areas, (3) the adjustment of French society to growing industrialization, accelerated by the demands of war production, (4) the challenge of colonial nationalism, which France, though to a lesser degree than Great Britain, encountered in the 1920's and 1930's, and (5) the enforcement of the peace and the demands which the Great-Power position of postwar France made upon her human and material resources. This last challenge overshadowed all domestic problems.

The great number and magnitude of postwar problems raised

the fundamental question whether the governmental system of republican France, geared to weak executive leadership and the preservation of the social *status quo,* was equipped to cope with postwar reality. Léon Blum, for one, recognized the need for constitutional reform and made proposals towards that end in his *Lettres sur la Réforme Gouvernmentale* of 1918. Without constitutional reform, Blum warned, France, "worn out by parliamentary impotence," might fall under the power of the "captains of industry." Accordingly, Blum proposed that the Chamber of Deputies be not only a "strict controller" of the government, but also "the inspirer of executive action." To streamline the legislative process, Blum urged the curtailment of the parliamentary committees which often killed legislation, as well as a clear definition of the Senate's veto powers. In practice, the French Senate frequently stifled legislation merely by refusing to act on Chamber bills.

Blum's recommendations went unheeded; the Third Republic did not change. The political philosophy of Alain, as expressed in *Elements d'une Doctrine Radicale* (1925), rather than Blum's *Lettres sur la Réforme Gouvernmentale,* remained fundamental to the Third Republic after the First World War. "In a democracy," Alain asserted, "not only does no party have power, but even better, there is no power properly speaking."

The discrepancy between government without power and the need for powerful government cast its shadow over the two postwar decades of the Third Republic, which were also to be its last. During the first postwar decade the Republic succeeded, on the whole, in mastering its foreign and domestic tasks. During its second postwar decade, it faltered when confronted with the Depression at home and the fascist dictators abroad. The political suicide of the Third Republic at Vichy in 1940 may be attributed, in part, to its failure to adjust its system of government from the needs of the latter 19th century to the turbulent conditions of the post-World War I era.

THE NOSTALGIA OF VICTORY: THE ELECTIONS OF 1919

Although the first postwar elections of France were not held until November 16, 1919 — little over a year after the Armistice — the election results reflected more the heightened nationalism of the past victory than a sober appreciation of present and future difficulties. During the first year after the Armistice, the Republic had commemorated the heroism of war-time France with speeches, parades, the unveiling of plaques, and a triumphant military entry into reconquered Strasbourg and Metz. The national mood favored the political parties of the right and center, combined in the *Bloc National,* which gained 338 seats as against 197 for the parties of the left. Socialist strength declined to 55 seats, about half the number of Socialists elected in 1914.

The Socialist party was discredited both by its own pacifism and by the specter of Bolshevism, with which the SFIO was rightly or wrongly identified. The SFIO, as noted, had withdrawn from the *Union Sacrée* and criticized the Treaty of Versailles; Bolshevik Russia had deserted the Franco-Russian alliance in 1917 and wiped out the savings of thousands of Frenchmen by repudiating the tsarist debt. In 1919, while Marshal Foch attempted to organize a Western crusade against Bolshevik Russia among the Allies of the First World War, a growing number of French Socialists looked towards Moscow for inspiration and guidance in social revolution. The postwar dilemma of socialism in France was complete when the SFIO was split between a Communist majority and a moderate minority at the party congress at Tours in December, 1920, over the issue of joining the Third (Communist) International on Lenin's terms. The Communist majority, outnumbering the moderates by three to one, accepted Lenin's "21 conditions," which demanded the submission of foreign socialists to Moscow. The minority under Léon Blum, retaining the old party label of SFIO, rejected Lenin's conditions on the grounds that the Third International aspired to "uniformity" rather than "unity" of the world's socialist parties. To Blum, the "first of all Internationals" was the "International of the human heart and the human conscience." The split of the SFIO at the Tours Congress was followed by a similar division of the French unions at the Lille Congress of July, 1921, into the non-Communist CGT, representing 370,000 union members, and the Communist C.G.T.U. (*Confédération Générale du Travail Unitaire*), which included some 500,000 workers. The causes of the French socialist split in 1920 ran deeper than the issue of the Third International; they were rooted in the ideological differences between the democratic and humanitarian socialism of Blum and the Bolshevik concept of dictatorship, which Blum called "a dictatorship over, not of, the proletariat." Reconciliation between French socialists and Communists will become possible, Blum announced to the Tours Congress, "the day when Russian tyranny will exact no more victims from among the Socialists, the day when democratic liberties and universal suffrage will be re-established in Russia."

For the moment, the chief beneficiaries of the French socialist split of 1920 were the Communists, who, in addition to commanding the majority at Tours and Lille, aslo inherited the old Socialist paper *l'Humanité,* which henceforth appeared as a Communist newspaper. *Le Populaire,* edited by Blum and Jean Longuet, the grandson of Karl Marx, became the new organ of the SFIO. In the early 1920's the French left remained absorbed in mutual recrimination of Communists and

Socialists. Not until 1924 did the SFIO recover from the defeat of Tours, to become, once more, a factor in national politics.

THE REALITY OF POSTWAR POLITICS: THE GOVERNMENT OF THE NATIONAL BLOC

The first business before the "horizon-blue" Chamber of Deputies (the name derived from the color of the French officers' uniform and signified the large number of ex-officers elected in 1919) was the election of a new president of the republic upon the expiration of Poincaré's seven-year term in February, 1920. Of all candidates, Clemenceau seemed the most deserving in view of his war-time services. In fact, the Chamber and the Senate repudiated Clemenceau and chose the undistinguished Paul Deschanel instead. Clemenceau's defeat was chiefly due to republican fears of a strong man in peace time; it was also due to the many enemies that Clemenceau had made in a life-time of public activity: Catholics opposed Clemenceau for his pre-war anti-clericalism; the right blamed Clemenceau for not having secured a harsher peace against Germany in 1919; the left remembered Clemenceau's war-time censorship and tough policy against pacifists.

Deschanel's presidency was brief. After serving only seven months in office, Deschanel resigned, following a bizarre incident in which the President of the Republic vanished from the Paris-Marseilles night train and was found sitting on the railroad tracks in his pajamas. The National Assembly (the combined meeting of Senate and Chamber) thereupon elevated Alexandre Millerand, the Prime Minister of the National Bloc government, to the presidency. Having begun his political career on the far left as a Socialist, Millerand had made the transition to the right not uncommon in French politics. As president, Millerand sought to strengthen the powers of his office beyond its largely ceremonial functions by intervening in the policies of the prime minister. When Briand, Millerand's successor as prime minister, was suspected of compromising the reparations claims of France at the Cannes Conference in January, 1922, he was recalled by the President and forced to resign.

The National Bloc displayed more vigor in the conduct of foreign affairs than in the solution of domestic problems. The domestic policies of the National Bloc may be characterized as toughness against revolutionary threats from the far left, reconciliation with the Church, and the postponement of painful fiscal decisions. The general strike that miners, railroad men, and transportation workers had called for May 1, 1920, was crushed by the government's seizure of the CGT headquarters. The revolutionary ardor of the workers cooled, and CGT membership dropped from a postwar high of two million to 600,000. In its religious policy, the National Bloc broke with the anti-clerical tradition of pre-war

France, by resuming diplomatic relations with the Vatican in 1921 and exempting Alsace-Lorraine from the anti-clerical legislation of the 1880's and the early 1900's. The Napoleonic Concordat of 1801, revoked by France in 1905, remained in effect in the reconquered provinces.

The fiscal policy of the National Bloc was based on the assumption that German reparations would pay for the reconstruction of the devastated areas of northern France. The National Bloc had been swept into power in 1919 on the promise of "making Germany pay," and the opposition, shown by Britain and the United States, against the French policy of forceful collection of German reparations became a source of growing irritation in the France of the early 1920's. To France it seemed that, while her former enemies were massed against her frontiers, her former allies were massed against her finances. When German reparations failed to materialize in the expected amounts, the National Bloc financed the cost of reconstruction in the same manner in which France had financed the war. Rather than increase taxes, the National Bloc borrowed 17 billion francs. The French budget consisted of an "ordinary" budget, which was balanced, and a "German" budget to cover war pensions and reconstruction expenses. Until German reparations were received, the "German" budget was covered by loans.

The fiscal policy of the National Bloc thus led inevitably to the French invasion of the Ruhr in January, 1923. The Ruhr invasion provided the principal cause for Poincaré's downfall and the defeat of the National Bloc in the elections of May 11, 1924. Initially, Poincaré's policy of force enjoyed the full backing of the French Chamber except for the opposition of Socialists and Communists. The Communist-controlled C.G.T.U. organized an "action committee" against Poincaré's Ruhr policy and *l'Humanité* characterized the French action as an "operation of pillage and murder." The SFIO, though less violent in its opposition, denounced Poincaré as "Poincaruhr" and "Poincaré-La-Guerre" ("War-Poincaré"). More serious to the National Bloc was the growing disillusionment of the French public with the results of the Ruhr invasion, which isolated France and yielded few immediate economic gains. Worst of all, the government of Poincaré was forced to raise taxes by 20 per cent to cover the cost of military intervention in Germany, a measure which the Ruhr invasion had been designed to avoid. The rise in taxes was accompanied by austerity measures and the dismissal of civil servants. On March 27, 1924, the Poincaré government fell from power.

THE CARTEL OF THE LEFT

The elections of May 11, 1924, reflected disillusionment with the power politics of Poincaré and the growing trend towards pacifism.

The spirit of France had changed from the confident nationalism of 1919 into an awareness of the limited powers which France possessed even in victory. Blum's SFIO and the Radical Socialists joined together in an electoral alliance, the *Cartel des Gauches* (Cartel of the Left), which obtained 328 seats against 226 for the parties of the right and center.

Edouard Herriot, mayor of Lyon and long-time spokesman of the Radical Socialists, formed a government of the Cartel of the Left, which did not, however, include members of the SFIO. Whereas the Socialists supported the Herriot government in parliament, they refused to enter it. The SFIO would join a coalition only if it was the majority party, a condition not fulfilled until 1936. In 1924 the Socialists had captured 108 seats only.

Socialists and Radicals shared a common outlook on the past issue of anti-clericalism and were agreed on a more conciliatory attitude towards the Weimar Republic in foreign affairs. They remained divided, nevertheless, over fundamental questions of political philosophy. The Radicals stood for weak government, as advocated by Alain; the Socialists favored strong governmental action, as recommended in Blum's reform proposals of 1918. Most important, Socialists and Radicals disagreed on the method for solving the most pressing problem of the day, the halting of inflation and the restoration of fiscal soundness to the republic. The Socialist recipe for the financial liquidation of the First World War was not "let Germany pay," but rather "let the rich pay." In practice, this amounted to a capital levy and higher taxes on the wealthy, a solution frowned upon by the socially conservative Radicals.

Divided in principle, the government of the Cartel remained indecisive in action. The Cartel succeeded in forcing Alexandre Millerand to resign from the presidency on June 11, 1924. Millerand was equally disliked by Radicals and Socialists; the former objected to his exceeding his ceremonial powers, and the latter resented his political metamorphosis from Socialist to right-wing nationalist. Although the government lacked constitutional powers to remove the president, it achieved its end by "ministerial strike": Herriot refused to form a government, as long as Millerand remained in office. The Cartel failed to place its own favorite, Paul Painlevé, into the presidency, however, when Senate and Chamber elected the moderate Gaston Doumergue instead.

Following its victory over Millerand, the Cartel engaged in a policy of symbolic gestures rather than action. Herriot honored the memory of Jean Jaurès by transferring the ashes of the most famous French Socialist leader to the Pantheon. He revived the issue of anti-clericalism by demanding the recall of the French ambassador to the Vatican, recently installed by the *Bloc National*. Herriot threatened to extend the anti-clerical legislation of France to Alsace-Lorraine, thereby antagonizing the Catholic population of the reconquered provinces, whose enthusiasm for France had somewhat diminished by 1924 for other reasons as well.

Initially, the reunion with France had netted Alsace-Lorraine immediate and tangible economic benefits, both provinces being spared the hunger and inflation of postwar Germany. Moreover, respecting the autonomous traditions of Alsace, France had governed the province through a special High Commissioner at Strasbourg. By 1924 the High Commissioner was withdrawn, and the reconquered provinces were subjected to the centralized administration from Paris. Under the French republic, Alsace-Lorraine thus enjoyed less autonomy than had been granted by the German Empire in 1911, nor did the two provinces retain the advantages of Bismarck's comprehensive social legislation after 1918. The substitution of French for German on the primary school level further embittered the relationship between France and the predominantly German-speaking population of Alsace-Lorraine.

Meanwhile, inflation continued unabated. The franc, which had been traded at 13 to the U. S. dollar in November, 1922, declined from 28 to $1, to 50 to $1 in the course of 1924. The results of the unchecked inflation were the flight of French capital abroad, the inability of the government to find additional buyers of bonds, even at an interest rate above six per cent, and a sharp rise in the cost of living. The Cartel was not lacking in financial experts — Herriot's government was dubbed the "government of professors." What it lacked mostly was the confidence of the financial interests, including the Bank of France, that it could solve the financial crisis by means acceptable to business, investors, and savers. When Finance Minister De Monzie proposed a special tax on large properties, a measure which came close to the dreaded "capital levy" advocated by the Socialists, the government of Herriot was voted out of power in early 1925. Although the Cartel formed five more cabinets between 1925 and 1926, it failed to regain the confidence of the nation.

On July 13, 1926, Poincaré, recalled as Prime Minister, formed a government of National Union without new parliamentary elections. The government of National Union rested on a broader basis than the National Bloc of 1919, including all political parties except Socialists and Communists. Poincaré became both Prime Minister and Minister of Finance.

Poincaré's mandate was to "save the franc." In this task, he largely succeeded, though his methods differed little from those advocated vainly by the Cartel of the Left. What differed was Poincaré's style of government, which impressed the Chamber and inspired confidence among the powers of finance. Equipped with special powers, Poincaré raised taxes, improved tax collection, and created a sinking fund from the proceeds of the government's tobacco monopoly. The budget was unified, the special "German" budget being discontinued. In his fiscal policy Poincaré was aided by the prompt payment of German reparations, which had begun to flow regularly since the adoption of the Dawes Plan. The flight of French capital was ended, and the franc was stabilized at 20 to the U. S. dollar, one fifth of its pre-war value. In 1928 France returned to the gold standard. Poincaré was hailed as the "savior of the franc."

The elections of April, 1928, were an overwhelming vote of confidence for Poincaré, the parties of the right and center gaining 330 seats. With the support of the Radicals, Poincaré controlled 440 seats in the Chamber of Deputies out of a total of 607. The Radicals withdrew from Poincaré's government in October, 1928, largely over disagreements on educational policy. The new Chamber enacted a national insurance law, establishing a system of pensions for old age, sickness, and disability. It also repudiated four fifths of the national debt, thus depriving bondholders of 80 per cent of their investment. The financial liquidation of the war was accomplished neither at the expense of Germany exclusively nor at that of the wealthy classes, but mainly through the sacrifice of ordinary Frenchmen.

The remainder of Poincaré's administration, until his retirement in September, 1929, was a period of economic prosperity and political stability. The right-wing leagues, such as General Castelnau's *Federation Nationale Catholique,* Taittinger's *Jeunesses Patriotes,* and the *Faisceau des Combattants et Producteurs,* whose appearance in the mid-1920's signalled a new crisis of confidence in the parliamentary republic, lost in appeal once the republic had mastered inflation and restored prosperity. The papal condemnation of the Action Française in 1927 as "Catholic by calculation and not by conviction" lessened Maurras' influence among French Catholics. The leagues were to reappear in more militant fashion a decade later, when France faced a more serious crisis under the Depression.

By 1928 the Third Republic had also largely completed the reconstruction of the war-devastated areas, while at the same time increasing the level of industrial and agricultural production above that of 1913. Based on the production figures of 1913, the industrial production index of 1930 measured 140, that of agriculture 110. Hardest hit by the war had been the ten northern departments, whose population declined from nearly 5 to little over 2 million. Some 800,000 dwellings had been either totally destroyed or damaged, coal mines flooded, and tens of thousands of factories ruined. The devastation of farmland in the combat zone was so extensive as to render its restoration practically uneconomical. Only a fraction of the reconstruction cost of an estimated $3 billion was covered by reparations.

On the positive side, the war had netted France the rich mineral and industrial resources of Alsace-Lorraine. The economic assets of the reconquered provinces included the textile industries and potash deposits of Alsace as well as the extensive iron-ore fields of Lorraine. The latter enabled France to become both a major producer of steel and iron, with an annual output of fifty million tons in 1929, and an exporter of iron ore.

Unlike Great Britain, postwar France did not suffer an unemployment problem. The reconstruction of the devastated areas, the growth of large-scale industry and public works, such as the construction of hydro-electric power stations in the French south, and the expansion of the port facilities of Strasbourg, LeHavre, and Cherbourg, provided ample employment in the 1920's. Unemployment figures never rose above 100,000 before the Depression. The low birth rate—the population of France had increased between 1871 and 1914 from 36 to only 39½ million—and the manpower losses of the First World War compelled France to import labor from Poland, Italy, Spain, and Algeria to the extent of three million in the postwar period.

The demands of war production and the accumulation of war profits stimulated the growth of big business in postwar France, as evidenced by the mushrooming of great electrical, chemical, and automotive enterprises, such as the Compagnie Générale d'Électricité, Saint-Gobain, Péchiney, and Citroën. Despite increasing mass production, France remained predominantly a nation of small-scale manufacturers, however, with 1.4 million enterprises employing five workers or less and 1.3 million factories employing over 500 workers. Among the great industrial powers, France also remained the most rural, despite growing urbanization, with more than half the population being rural in the late 1920's. Her near self-sufficiency and the high rate of domestic consumption of her industrial output made France less vulnerable to the fluctuations of the world market than industrial Britain and Germany. Nevertheless, though the Depression was slower in coming to France, it proved more persistent than elsewhere once its effects took hold.

THE CHALLENGE OF COLONIAL NATIONALISM

"Europe has lost her hegemony," the French Socialist leader Léon Blum observed after the First World War. "Yesterday the metropolis of the world, she depends today upon the respect of her former colonies." If Blum's verdict appeared exaggerated for the period after the First World War and more appropriate to the process of decolonization which was to follow the Second World War, it nevertheless recognized the emergence of a new spirit of nationalism that confronted France in North Africa, the Middle East, and Vietnam during the inter-war period.

Under the Third Republic, France had amassed a worldwide

colonial empire of three and a quarter million square miles, which far exceeded the earlier colonial empire that France had gained and largely lost again in the course of the 18th century. In North Africa, the Republic had extended French rule from the established possession of Algeria into Tunisia (1881) and Morocco (1912) in the form of protectorates; in the partitioning of Black Africa, France had established colonies in West Africa, Equatorial Africa, French Somaliland, and Madagascar; in Southeast Asia she built an Indo-Chinese colonial empire between 1884 and 1889, which comprised Cochin China, Annam, Tonkin, Cambodia, and Laos. After the First World War France gained a foothold in the Middle East in the mandates of Syria and Lebanon.

The motivation of 19th-century French imperialism had been essentially the same as that of other European colonial powers: Jules Ferry, prime minister and chief empire-builder of the Third Republic in the 1880's, regarded colonies as an outlet for French industry, a source of raw materials, and a place for profitable investment. Moreover, colonial expansion, to Ferry, was necessary to the Great Power status of France; to abstain from colonialism was, in Ferry's words, "simply the highway to decadence." Like the imperialists of Britain, Ferry justified French imperialism on the grounds of its civilizing and humanitarian mission: the "superior races," Ferry announced to the French Chamber of Deputies in 1885, "have the duty to civilize the inferior races. . . . Can anyone deny that it was the good fortune of the unhappy peoples of equatorial Africa to fall under the protection of the French or English nations?"

The principal difference between French imperialism and that of others consisted in the fact that France was bent upon the cultural assimilation of her subject peoples. The school formed a far more important element in French colonial administration than it did elsewhere. Following the tradition of ancient Rome, which forever inspired French colonial administrators, France wished to spread her civilization through education.

The policy of colonial assimilation was further expressed in the fiction of colonial representation in the government of France. Certain French colonies, including those of Southeast Asia and Central Africa, were permitted to elect members to the French Senate or Chamber of Deputies, or both. The Protectorates of North Africa, Tunisia, and Morocco were administered through the French foreign office. Algeria, however, was simply treated as an extension of metropolitan France, and divided into the three administrative departments of Algiers, Oran, and Constantine.

There were definite limits to the social and political benefits which cultural assimilation bestowed upon the natives. Throughout her Empire, France maintained a division between rulers and ruled. The native, though French-educated, remained a second-class citizen. The impetus for colonial nationalism after the First World War thus came chiefly from assimilated natives who discovered that a French education was not a passport to political power or even to administrative participation in French colonial rule.

NATIONALISM IN NORTH AFRICA AND THE FRENCH MANDATES IN THE MIDDLE EAST

Although Algeria was technically a part of France, French citizenship was confined to the European settlers, numbering some 660,000, chiefly of French, Italian, Spanish, and Alsatian descent. Native Algerians, numbering about 2½ million, could be naturalized only if they renounced their Moslem status. As a reward for Algeria's contribution to the French war effort in the First World War—native Algerians had been drafted into the French army—Clemenceau wished to simplify the rules of naturalization and increase Arab participation in local Algerian government.

Clemenceau's liberal policy towards the Arabs of Algeria precipitated the first serious split between the European residents (colons) and the French government, which was to last throughout the inter-war period and which became the immediate cause of the fall of the Fourth French Republic after the Second World War. The French law of February 4, 1919, which implemented some of Clemenceau's promises, met with strong opposition from the colons, while being denounced as inadequate by Algerian nationalists such as Emir Khaled and Messali Hadj. Although the French Governor General of Algeria, Maurice Violette, attempted to improve the social conditions of the Arabs in the 1920's, the French governments of the 1920's increasingly shared the colons' viewpoint under the impact of Arab rebellion in adjacent Morocco. The espousal of the Algerian national cause by the French Communist party further dampened the reform policy of Paris in the 1920's. The Communist-sponsored newspaper *Le Paria* became the organ not only of Ho Chi Minh, of whom more will be said presently, but also of the Algerian nationalist Messali Hadj. Léon Blum, as Prime Minister of the Popular Front government of 1936, proposed a liberalization of French policy towards the Arabs of Algeria. Blum's government was too brief, however, to effect the desired change, and the proposed legislation on Algeria was rejected by the Chamber. Algerian nationalists, who had passed through the French educational system, had acquired a taste for independence. Only the Second World War and its aftermath would provide a new opportunity for native Algerians to attack a segregated, colonial society consisting of a privileged minority of colons and a second-class majority of Arabs.

Although French rule over the protectorates of Tunisia and Morocco differed from that in Algeria in form, it differed little in substance. The Treaty of Bardo of May 13, 1881, which had established the French protectorate, had left a native Tunisian government under the Bey of Tunis in being, while reserving foreign affairs and the maintenance of internal order to France. The example of Egyptian emancipation from a British protectorate stimulated Tunisian nationalism after the First World War. As a gesture, France broadened the Tunisian Consultative Conference into a "Grand Council," while, at the same time, expanding the authority of the French civil service in Tunisia. By the early 1930's Tunisian nationalism became organized around the newspaper *L'Action Tunisienne* and the Neo-Destour Party, both launched by a young Tunisian lawyer, Habib Bourguiba. Bourguiba wished to replace the Bardo Treaty with a "spontaneous entente" between the peoples of both nations, on an equal basis. France responded with the arrest of Bourguiba in 1934. After his release, Bourguiba sought, unsuccessfully before the Second World War, to achieve the goal of Tunisian independence by the method of civil disobedience.

Until the mid-1920's, French control over Morocco proceeded more smoothly than in other areas of North Africa, partly because the Convention of Fez, of March 30, 1912, which had established the French protectorate, left greater freedom to the Sultan of Morocco. In part, the successful French pacification of Morocco resulted from the tact and circumspection which General Lyautey, the French Resident, displayed in dealing with the Sultan. French-Moroccon relations were disturbed less by native Moroccon opposition than by the successful revolt of Abd el Krim, a chieftain of the Riff tribe, in Spanish Morocco. Krim had defeated the Spaniards at Aloual on July 21, 1921, whereupon he invaded French Morocco and threatened the capital of Fez. Marshal Pétain, hero and veteran of Verdun, had to be brought to Morocco, and, in conjunction with the Spaniards, defeated Krim on May 26, 1926. The French Communist party encouraged and aided Abd el Krim, Maurice Thorez, the French Communist leader, establishing a "Central Action Committee" to aid the Moroccon insurgents. Jacques Doriot, another French Communist, expressed the hope that, after his victory over the Spaniards, Krim would "continue, in league with the French and European proletariat, the struggle against all imperialists, including French, until Moroccon soil is set completely free." After the abortive Krim revolt, French-Moroccon relations deteriorated further when Mohammed V, the new Sultan, showed growing opposition to the French protectorate. In the 1930's, France tightened her controls under the Resident, General Noguès, who ignored a Reform Plan submitted by Moroccon nationalists, and imprisoned the nationalist leader Allal al-Fassi.

French rule in the mid-eastern mandates of Syria and Lebanon was, on the whole, less successful than British rule in Iraq and Trans-

Jordan. Whereas Britain exercised power with a minimum of staff and through the collaboration of Arab leaders, such as Feisal in Iraq, France ruled through a vast bureaucracy and against the chosen leaders of Arab nationalism. France began her rule as mandatory power over Syria by evicting Feisal from Damascus in July, 1920, following his election as King of Syria on March 8, 1920, by a Syrian national congress. The French position was rendered more difficult still by the religious friction between the Moslem majority and Christian minority of Syria, with France favoring the interests of the latter. In 1926 France had to resort to an artillery bombardment of Damascus to crush a Syrian rebellion, which had initially succeeded in inflicting a humiliating defeat upon a French force under General Michaud. Although France granted constitutions to both Syria and Lebanon in keeping with her obligation as a mandate power, the governments thus established fell short of nationalist expectations. Britain's ending of the mandate over Iraq led to increased pressure by Syria and Lebanon upon France to follow the British example. In response to the demand for independence, advanced by the Syrian National Party of Anton Saadah and the Lebanese Phalanges, the Popular Front Government of Léon Blum drafted treaties of friendship and alliance for the French mandates of the Middle East. Like Blum's reform proposals for Algeria, however, the friendship treaties with Syria and Lebanon were rejected by the French parliament. With the approach of the Second World War, French relations with Syria and Lebanon became more tense as French rule grew more repressive.

NATIONALISM IN FRENCH INDOCHINA

Vietnamese opposition to French colonial rule was not a post-World War I phenomenon, but as old as the French colonial presence in Southeast Asia itself. Following the naval expedition of Emperor Napoleon III against DaNang in 1857, France embarked upon a full-blown conquest of Vietnam which lasted twenty-six years. Vietnamese resistance continued even after the establishment of a French protectorate, both in the "scholars' revolt" and in guerrilla action by groups of bandits. The "scholars' revolt" was a resistance movement of the 1870's and 1880's, organized by mandarins who resented the treaties imposed by France upon the emperor of Annam. The guerrilla harassment of the French administration continued until the eve of the First World War, despite the "splash of oil" strategy devised by Colonel Galliéni. The "splash of oil" or "drop of oil" strategy was designed to pacify Vietnam in stages, by bringing stability and prosperity to individual villages and thereby wresting village allegiance from the guerrillas.

By the beginning of the 20th century, France had united Vietnam, Laos, and Cambodia into an economic union, administered by a highly centralized bureaucracy under a governor general who resided alternately in Saigon and Hanoi. French colonial rule was not without its fringe benefits to Indochina; the agricultural yield in the south of Vietnam increased fourfold and eventually France was to complete 1,800 miles of railroad and 12,000 miles of paved road. The tax burden upon the peasantry grew apace with French improvements, however, and the French bureaucracy continued to exploit the former royal monopolies on opium, alcohol, and salt.

Events in Asia immediately before and after the First World War provided a powerful external impetus to the further development of indigenous Vietnamese nationalism. The Japanese victory over Russia in the Russo-Japanese war of 1905 demonstrated the vulnerability of a European power in Asia; the Chinese revolution under Sun Yat-sen of 1911 provided an example of an Asian power striving towards colonial emancipation through the adoption of Western political forms; the Bolshevik revolution of 1917 appealed to smoldering colonial resentment against the West throughout Asia; the revolution of the Chinese Kuomintang under Chiang Kai-shek in the late 1920's revealed the power which nationalism in Asia had attained after the First World War.

The various nationalist movements of Vietnam between the two world wars thus largely mirrored the examples of Asian nationalism at large. The error in French policy consisted in the fact that it turned with equal force against revolutionary elements bent on evicting France from Indochina altogether and those which merely aimed at a reform and relaxation of French colonial rule. Foremost among the latter were the efforts of the French-educated puppet emperor Bao Dai and his reform-minded advisers Ngo Dinh Diem and Pham Quynh in the early 1930's. Although France initially supported Quynh, the opposition of the French civil service in Indochina to the reform zeal of Diem resulted in the latter's resignation and the abandonment of Bao Dai's policy of modernizing Vietnam under French protection.

Of the several revolutionary movements which emerged in Vietnam after the First World War, the most influential were the Vietnam Nationalist Party under Nguyen Thai Hoc, which was non-Communist and patterned after the Kuomintang, and the Indochinese Communist Party of Nguyen Ai Quoc, better known under his pseudonym Ho Chi Minh. The Vietnam Nationalist Party, which drew its support chiefly from among civil servants and teachers, launched an abortive uprising against the French in 1930, after which Hoc was executed. The Indochinese Communist Party developed out of the Association of Vietnamese Revolutionary Youth, whose headquarters were initially in Canton. Ho Chi Minh combined in his person the teachings of the Vietnamese scholar Phan Chu Trinh, who preached national revolution to Vietnamese exiles in Paris, and the revolutionary Marxism of the Third International. As the emissary of the latter, Ho Chi Minh was active in China, before becoming the architect of the Southeast Asian Communist movement in the 1920's.

The 1930's witnessed a decline in the Vietnamese Communist appeal to Indochinese nationalism, as Ho Chi Minh soft-pedalled the issue of national liberation on Moscow's orders, after Soviet Russia's alliance with France in 1936. The Vietnamese Communists resumed their struggle against France only after the outbreak of the Second World War in the wake of the Stalin-Hitler pact. When France attempted to seize the Vietnamese Communist leaders in 1939, the Central Committee of the party escaped to China, to await another day for the reopening of its assault on French Indochina.

11 | The Victorious Democracies III:
The Kingdom of Italy: The Rise of Fascism

The outbreak of the First World War, as has been seen, resulted in an unprecedented measure of national unity among all belligerents, as classes and parties rallied to the defense of their governments in a psychology of siege. The unifying force of fear was absent in the case of Italy, however, since Italy, alone among the Great Powers of Europe, entered the First World War in 1915 from calculation rather than necessity.

Italy's option for war on the Allied side divided her people between neutralists and interventionists. The division was never entirely erased during the war and reemerged in sharpened form after the war when Italy's gains at the peace conference of 1919 were measured against the human and material cost of the Italian war effort.

The interventionists were headed by the King, Victor Emmanuel III, and his Prime Minister, Antonio Salandra, who had secured the Allied promise of territorial gains in the secret treaty of London of April, 1915. The interventionists also included the nationalists and irredentists who were eager to wrest *Italia irredenta* (the Italian-speaking parts of Austria-Hungary) from the Habsburg Empire. The most vociferous interventionists were the eccentric Gabriele D'Annunzio, Italy's foremost nationalist poet, and Benito Mussolini. The latter, as will be discussed more fully in the context of postwar Italy, had changed from revolutionary Marxist in 1914 to ardent nationalist by 1915.

Against the interventionists was arrayed an impressive force of neutralists, which included the Socialists, Pope Benedict XV and the politically active Catholics, the majority of Liberal deputies in parliament, and Italy's most prominent elder statesman and pre-war Prime Minister, Giovanni Giolitti. Giolitti opposed intervention on the grounds of Italy's unpreparedness for war and the belief that Italy could extract territorial concessions from the Central Powers as a price for continued neutrality; the Pope and the Socialists shared the motive of pacifism. In addition to denouncing the World War as "senseless carnage," Pope Benedict XV also feared the destruction of Austria-Hungary and its Catholic Habsburg dynasty.

From the standpoint of the progressive weakening of Italy's

parliamentary institutions after the First World War, it was highly significant that neutralists outnumbered interventionists in 1915. Although the majority of the Italian parliament opposed intervention, it was driven into a declaration of war against Austria-Hungary on May 23, 1915, by the combined pressures of dynastic ambition and extra-parliamentary agitation of the nationalist press and nationalist spokesmen such as D'Annunzio and Mussolini. By equating intervention with patriotism and neutrality with treason, the interventionists discredited parliament. D'Annunzio denounced the "stink of treason" in the Italian parliament, while Mussolini threatened that the King of Italy would lose his crown unless Italy declared war "on the enemies of European civilization." By imposing its will on the neutralist majority, the interventionist minority had set a precedent in 1915 which the Fascists were to follow during their rise to power after the First World War. The events of "Glorious May" *(Maggio Glorioso),* 1915, as Italian nationalists called the month of Italy's entry into World War I, appeared to many after the First World War as the true beginning of Italian Fascism.

Once in the war, Italy's political parties united in support of the government's war effort, with the notable exception of the Socialists. Having voted against the war in May, 1915, the Socialists continued to oppose the war without openly sabotaging Italy's war effort. By August, 1917, the echoes of events in Russia, together with bread shortages, produced serious workers' riots in "red" Turin, in the course of which some fifty workers were killed by intervening troops.

The disaster of Caporetto of October, 1917, succeeded in establishing momentary unity when the survival of Italy itself appeared in question. The aftermath of the battle of Caporetto reemphasized old divisions, however, when the military and the government looked for scapegoats for Italy's greatest military defeat in the First World War and found them, not surprisingly, in the Socialist party and its "defeatist" stand.

THE PRICE OF VICTORY AND THE EXPECTATIONS OF PEACE

Giolitti's warnings of 1915 that Italy could ill afford to wage a major war were fully vindicated by Italy's economic plight of 1919 and after. The war had deprived Italy of her traditional export markets in central Europe while at the same time forcing a rise in imports to fill the demands of a rapidly expanding war economy. While the war lasted, the Italian economy was kept going through the financial and economic assistance of Britain and the United States. After the Armistice, Allied economic aid to Italy was sharply reduced, resulting in an acute shortage of coal and wheat. Since France and Belgium enjoyed priority in the delivery of German reparation coal, Italy's coal imports fell short by nearly

50 per cent as late as 1920, compared with 1913 coal imports of approximately 11 million tons. The war had raised the Italian cost of living index to higher levels than those of France, Britain, or Germany, while revenue covered less than a quarter of the Italian government's expenses. Not until 1921 was the Italian government able to balance the budget and to stop borrowing abroad. The postwar budget deficit was kept high by the government bread subsidy, which was maintained for political reasons.

The demands of war production had vastly increased the capacity of Italy's leading industrial enterprises, Ansaldo in shipping, Ilva in steel, Fiat in motor vehicles, and Breda in aircraft and armaments production. The return to peace found Italian big business expanded beyond the needs and purchasing power of the civilian market, with resulting bankruptcies and a rise in unemployment to two million by 1921.

To have mastered the economic problems that Italy inherited from the war would have constituted a formidable task in itself, even in an otherwise stable and ordered society. In Italy, the economic and fiscal liquidation of the war coincided, however, with the return of social and economic pressures, suspended by the war and sharpened by the expectation of immediate solution in the impatient climate of the postwar era. With the exception of Russia, no major European power inherited as vast a store of unsolved social and economic problems from the pre-1914 era as did Italy. These problems may be summarized as (1) the land question, (2) the integration of industrial labor into society, (3) the evolution of the Italian political system from oligarchy into parliamentary democracy.

Rural Italy, unlike rural France, did not possess a peasant democracy. With half the Italian peasant population consisting of landless laborers *(braccianti)*, the Italian countryside was marked by bitter class struggle before the First World War. Sharecroppers *(mezzadri)*, though better off than the mass of *braccianti*, added to rural instability with demands for larger shares than the customary 50 per cent of the crop. The gulf between proprietors and rural proletariat was widest in the Italian south, where the plantation-size farm *(latifondo)*, often owned by absentee landlords, prevailed. The poverty and backwardness of southern Italy was reflected in the high illiteracy rate, which reached 70 to 90 per cent in some parts of the south. Although Italy's pre-war governments, notably that of Prime Minister Giolitti, had launched a southern development program between 1903 and 1914, the overall results remained disappointing. Emigration, which reached over 870,000 in 1913, rather than industrial development, provided the chief cure for southern poverty. The establishment of U.S. immigration quotas in 1921 significantly reduced the number of Italian emigrants after the First World War. Rural poverty thus continued to pose a potential revolutionary threat to Italian society at large, the unemployment rate among northern *braccianti* running as high as 80 per cent before 1914. In the south, the *latifondi* system had preserved feudalism intact, the plantation owners *(latifondisti)* enjoying a virtual monopoly of economic, political, and social power.

The class struggle of rural Italy was matched by the frequently violent clashes between industrial labor and capital which marked the development of large-scale industry in Italy's "industrial triangle" of Milan, Genoa, and Turin before the First World War. The Italian Socialist Party (Partito Socialista Italiano), established in 1892, unlike the socialist parties of western and central Europe, acted as the spokesman of both the industrial and rural proletariat. In the pre-war struggle between the moderate reformist wing and Marxist revolutionary wing of the P.S.I., the latter gained the upper hand by 1912, largely because of the Italian Socialist uproar over the imperialist war of 1911/12, in which Italy conquered Libya from the Ottoman Empire. The general strikes of 1904 and 1914 were testimony to the revolutionary mood of industrial workers and rural *braccianti*. During so-called "red week" *(settimana rossa)* of June, 1914, entire regions of Italy were held under Socialist control with local "republics" being proclaimed, taxes abolished, and the red flag hoisted over city halls by the striking workers.

The radicalism of proletarian Italy was further suggested by the strength of syndicalism in the trade-union movement. Next to the moderate General Confederation of Labor (C.G.L.), established in 1906, the Italian Syndicalist Union (U.S.I.) of 1912 grew into a major labor organization of some 100,000 members, chiefly among seamen, railroad workers, and rural laborers. In response to the pressures of organized labor, Italian industrialists and landowners established organizations of their own, the *General Confederation of Industry (Confindustria)* and landowners' leagues for breaking strikes.

The chief victim of the polarization of Italy into mutually hostile social and economic blocs on the eve of the First World War was the liberal state. The Italian constitution of 1861 had established a constitutional monarchy with a bicameral legislature, consisting of a Senate, appointed by the crown, and a Chamber of Deputies, elected by limited suffrage. The administration was highly centralized through a system of prefects, appointed by the ministry of the interior, who governed the sixty-nine provinces of Italy. Between 1860 and 1882 the suffrage was broadened from 2 to 7 per cent of the population.

In 1911, amidst rising social tensions, Prime Minister Giolitti took the decisive step from oligarchy towards parliamentary democracy by granting universal manhood suffrage. Under the suffrage bill of 1911, all literate males above 21 and all illiterate males over 30 received the vote. Giolitti was confident of being able to integrate the radicalized masses into the liberal system of Italy by timely concessions to just social and economic demands.

The political system, which Giolitti had developed to a high degree of perfection by the early 1900's and which was variously described as *Giolittismo* or "parliamentary Tammany," rested on patronage, personal bargains between the Prime Minister and individual deputies, and the power of the prefects, who influenced voting by political pressure. Under the system of *Giolittismo,* parliamentary majorities were created by the governments rather than governments by parliamentary majorities. *Giolittismo* worked well enough under the restricted suffrage system before 1911, when Giolitti's political strength rested on the combined support of northern industrialists and southern *latifondisti.*

Giolitti's attempt to draw the Socialists into his system failed, despite the enactment of social legislation under Giolitti's "New Deal" of 1911. The moderate wing of Italian socialism under Filippo Turati, which was willing to collaborate with the government, was silenced and discredited at the Socialist party congress at Reggio Emilia in July, 1912. The Reggio Emilia congress condemned socialist collaboration with "bourgeois" parties. The issue that radicalized Italian socialism in 1912 was Giolitti's imperialist war for the conquest of Libya; the personality chiefly responsible for pushing the Socialist party further to the Left was the young revolutionary Marxist and rising star of pre-war Italian socialism, Benito Mussolini. As a socialist, Mussolini bore major responsibility for the weakening of the liberal state on the eve of the First World War; as a Fascist, he was to deal the liberal state its death blow after the First World War, under circumstances to be discussed presently.

While the Libyan war of 1912 alienated Socialist labor from bourgeois democracy, it also emboldened the imperialist and nationalist elements in Italian society. The Nationalists, headed by D'Annunzio and Enrico Corradini, the apostle of Italian colonial expansion, desired and welcomed war as a unifying national experience. When Italy hesitated in taking the plunge into the First World War in 1915, the nationalists grew contemptuous of the liberal state and thereby added their own hostility towards liberal Italy to that of the Socialists.

Whereas Giolitti's political strategy had aimed at uniting the diverse social and political forces of Italy under a common denominator of bourgeois democracy, the Italy of 1915 was fragmented into a diminishing liberal center, an intransigent left, and an irrational and boisterous nationalist right. The failure of *Giolittismo* foreshadowed the deep postwar divisions of Italy and the crisis and collapse of the liberal state.

THE SPIRIT OF *DICIANNOVISMO* AND *TRINCERISMO*

Diciannovismo ("1919-ism") and *Trincerismo* ("the spirit of the trenches") signified the widespread expectation of revolutionary change, which characterized the attitude of returning war veterans and of the industrial and rural proletariat of postwar Italy. Peasant soldiers, who had suffered a disproportionately large number of casualties, demanded land redistribution under the banner of "land to the peasants." In the interest of army morale, the war-time government of Prime Minister Orlando had promised land reform in 1918, to be implemented by the newly created National Veterans Organization. Impatient with slow legal procedures, the peasants in south and central Italy took matters into their own hands in 1919. Land was seized and mansions burned down; livestock was slaughtered whenever the hated *latifondisti* resisted. In the north, militant *braccianti,* organized in the Socialist Federation of Land Workers, imposed working agreements on frightened peasant proprietors under conditions frequently ruinous to the latter.

In the cities, the pressure for higher wages and union hatred for war-profiteers produced a wave of industrial strikes, culminating in the general strike of July, 1919, in protest against Italy's participation in the Allied intervention in Russia. To combat the high cost of living, workers resorted not infrequently to "self-help" by forcing store-owners to lower prices or simply by looting. By 1920 the strike movement spread to government workers in the railroads and postal services. A dispute between the metal workers' union (F.I.O.M.) and employers in Turin resulted in the seizure and occupation of hundreds of factories in the "industrial triangle" by revolutionary workers in August and September, 1920. Having ejected management and owners, the workers proceeded, without much success, to operate the factories on their own.

THE WEAKENING OF THE LIBERAL STATE, 1919 TO 1922

The functioning of Italian parliamentary democracy, challenged by Socialist intransigence and nationalist contempt before the war, was rendered more difficult in the postwar fever of anarchy and violence. Italy's first postwar elections of November 16, 1919, which were held under a system of proportional representation, marked the defeat of the old liberal-democratic majority which had governed Italy before the war. Out of 508 parliamentary seats, the Socialists captured 156, the newly-formed Catholic Popular Party *(Popolari)* gained 100. The liberal-democratic center was reduced to 252.

The *Popolari* party, founded in January, 1919, by the priest Luigi Sturzo and Alcide de Gasperi, was a new element in Italian politics, whose appearance complicated, rather than facilitated, the formation of a stable postwar government. The political-social outlook of the Popolari was moderately progressive, with emphasis on social legislation, land reform, and the decentralization of the liberal state. The political base of the Popular party was chiefly petty-bourgeois, rather than proletarian. Among rural voters, the Popolari attracted sharecroppers, rather than braccianti; among urban voters, it attracted the small shopkeeper, rather than the industrial worker. The political strength of the Popular party was augmented by the Catholic trade unions, grouped together in the Italian Confederation of Labor (CIL). Although the Popular party was conceived as a democratic reform party, it added little strength to the cause of parliamentary democracy. The chief weakness of the Popular party was its parliamentary inexperience and the resulting tendency to place the fulfillment of partisan demands above considerations of stable government.

Most detrimental to the parliamentary system was the attitude of the Socialist party, which emerged as Italy's largest political party in the elections of 1919. The Italian Socialist attitude of 1919 was strongly influenced by events in Russia. Italian Socialists felt a greater kinship with the Russian Bolsheviks than did Socialists in other western nations, largely because they, like the Bolsheviks, had never compromised their anti-war stand as had the Socialists of France or the S.P.D. of Germany. Although the Italian Socialists recoiled from imitating Lenin's example of a forceful seizure of power, they interpreted Italy's postwar chaos as a sure sign of the impending collapse of the capitalist-bourgeois order. Accordingly, the Socialist party congress at Bologna of 1919 adopted a "maximalist" program, which condemned collaboration with the bourgeois state. At the Bologna congress, the Italian Socialist party also declared its adherence to Lenin's Communist International.

Inside the Italian parliament, the Socialist party thus limited its role to militant obstruction. Outside parliament, the Socialist party, if not always actively encouraging the anarchic violence of strikes and factory occupations, condoned it. Whereas the Socialist party lacked the will to coordinate the scattered local violence into a nationwide revolutionary effort for the overthrow of the government, it nevertheless aroused deep-seated fears and the hatred among the Italian bourgeosie and thereby set the stage for a powerful nationalist-conservative reaction.

At the party congress of Leghorn of January, 1921, the extreme left wing of Italian socialism seceded from the Socialist party and constituted itself as the Italian Communist Party. The break-up of the Socialist party at Leghorn was occasioned by Lenin's twenty-one conditions for membership in the Third International. The majority of the Italian Socialist party under Serrati, its sympathy for Bolshevik Russia notwithstanding, refused to bow to Moscow's demand for the expulsion of the old reformist Turati and his followers from the party.

Italy's Communists under Antonio Gramsci's leadership, though anxious to take the step from economic chaos to political revolution, lacked the organization to carry out their plans. The same applied to the anarchists, whose leader, Malatesta, was prematurely hailed as "Italy's Lenin" upon his return from British exile after the war.

The net effect of Socialist, Communist, and anarchist action was to force a stalemate on the liberal state, depriving it of its ability to govern effectively without actually overthrowing it. The paralysis of liberal Italy opened the gate to the conservative-nationalist reaction and paved the way for the Fascist march to power.

THE FAILURE OF MODERATE GOVERNMENT: THE CONSERVATIVE-NATIONALIST REACTION

With the exception of the short-lived government of Ivanoe Bonomi (from July, 1921, to February, 1922), a reform-socialist expelled from the Socialist party in 1912, the postwar governments of Italy between 1919 and 1922 were headed by liberal politicians. The liberal prime ministers, Nitti (from June, 1919, to June, 1920), Giolitti (from July, 1920, to June, 1921), and Luigi Facta (from February, 1922, to October, 1922), though fully conscious of the social and national passions engendered by the First World War, hoped to resolve the postwar crisis with the methods of parliamentary compromise and within the liberal system of pre-war Italy.

Since the Socialists had forsaken a constructive role in Italian politics, the governments of Nitti, Giolitti, and Facta rested on the coalition of Liberals and Popolari. The Liberal-Popolari alignment remained fragile and unstable, however, because of political and personal differences between the two coalition partners. Whereas Sturzo insisted on coalition government based on the agreement of parties, Giolitti preferred deals with individual parliamentary deputies and dismissed Sturzo as an "intriguing little priest." Moreover, the Popolari remained resentful of the Liberals' reluctance to implement the basic features of the 1919 Popolari program on land reform and higher Catholic education.

During its one-year term of office, the Nitti government failed to solve Italy's most urgent domestic and foreign problems. At home Nitti succeeded in neither pacifying nor containing militant labor. The Socialists ignored the new social legislation of 1919/1920, providing improved unemployment and old-age and accident insurance. The newly created royal constabulatory force of 25,000 men was inadequate to restore law and order in town and country.

Most damaging to Nitti and the prestige of the liberal state was the occupation of Fiume by D'Annunzio and his legionaries in 1919. The occupation of Fiume placed the Nitti government squarely between the Allies, who condemned D'Annunzio's action, and the Italian nationalists, who hailed D'Annunzio as the head of Italy's "real government." Whereas Nitti's dependence on Allied economic and financial assistance forced him to side officially with the Allies, he dared not move against D'Annunzio for fear of precipitating a nationalist revolution. The government of Italy thus "blockaded" Fiume, while making sure that D'Annunzio and his black-shirted legionaries remained supplied through the Italian Red Cross. The Fiume incident might have been good theater, but for its tragic consequences for the liberal state. Not only did D'Annunzio's action divide the army and set the first example of open army disobedience after the war, but it provided the model for Italian Fascism in style, nationalist rhetoric, and contempt for the liberal government of Italy. D'Annunzio's occupation of Fiume in 1919 continued the tradition of May, 1915, when the nationalist minority had imposed its will on the neutralist majority.

Among the liberal postwar governments of Italy, Giolitti's appeared to hold the greatest promise of solving the postwar crisis by parliamentary means. By including an ex-syndicalist (Labriola) and a reform socialist (Bonomi) in his Liberal-Popolari coalition, Giolitti succeeded in creating the impression of a broad coalition government. Benedetto Croce, historian and philosopher, added prestige as Minister of Education.

Giolitti's principal political aim was to restore parliamentary prestige, undermined by war, postwar chaos, and the arrogant defiance of the *"Comandante"* of Fiume, D'Annunzio. Where Prime Minister Nitti had lacked the courage to arouse the ire of the nationalists, the 78-year-old Giolitti ordered the Italian navy to bombard D'Annunzio out of Fiume in December, 1920. The *Comandante* and his legionaries who had dazzled Italy and each other for fifteen months with sworn pledges of yielding to death only, hurriedly left Fiume after the first salvos from the batteries of the battleship *Andrea Doria*.

Opposition to Giolitti developed less from his forceful action against D'Annunzio than from his economic policy and reaction to the workers' seizure of the factories in Milan, Turin, and Genoa in 1920. Big business, suffering from the transition from a war economy to peace, resented Giolitti's refusal to aid bankrupt companies, such as the Ilva steel trust, with public funds. The middle class likewise opposed Giolitti's high taxes, particularly the steep inheritance tax designed to restore fiscal stability. The factory owners were exasperated over Giolitti's refusal to use troops or police to oust the workers who had seized the factories. The factory owners interpreted the workers' occupation of plants as the decisive step towards Socialist revolution. Giolitti correctly saw in the factory occupation the final spasm of Socialist violence and forced the employers to settle the dispute by granting wage increases and by recognizing the workers' factory councils.

On May 15, 1921, Giolitti held new parliamentary elections. On the assumption that militant socialism and the spirit of "1919-ism" had spent their force, Giolitti counted on a parliamentary majority favorable to himself. To assure unity among middle class voters, Giolitti formed a "National Bloc" *(blocco nazionale)* out of Liberals, Nationalists, Catholics, and even Fascists, whose numbers were small but whose influence over the middle class had increased in proportion to left-wing violence.

The election strategy of Giolitti resulted in a resounding defeat for liberalism. The *blocco nazionale* gained a mere 108 seats, 35 of which were Fascist. Although the Socialists dropped to 123, 15 Communists entered the Chamber of Deputies. The strength of the Popolari grew from 100 to 108. The parliament of 1921 was no more manageable than that of 1919 had been. On June 27, 1921, Giolitti resigned. A growing segment of the middle class—property owners large and small who had seen their property trespassed upon, seized, or destroyed—and leaders of big business and banking, threatened by bankruptcy, had lost faith in Giolitti and the pre-war liberal system that he embodied. The conservative reaction was augmented by outraged nationalism, which blamed the liberal postwar governments for having presented Italy with *vittoria mutilata* ("a mutilated victory") as a reward for her 600,000 war dead.

Frustrated by a lack of liberal vigor at home and abroad and angered by the humiliation and violence inflicted by anarchic socialism, the conservative-nationalist forces turned towards Fascism, which equated their aspirations with the national interest of Italy.

THE RISE OF FASCISM

Fascism had its origins in the personal transformation of Benito Mussolini from revolutionary Marxist to ardent nationalist and in the violent spirit of the restless ex-servicemen of 1919. As noted earlier, the young Mussolini had been the rising star of the militant left within the Italian Socialist party before August, 1914. In word and action Mussolini lived the part of Marxist revolutionary, as organizer of *braccianti,* as editor of the Socialist daily *Avanti!,* as vociferous critic of Italy's colonial war of 1912 against Turkey, as anti-militarist and internationalist who denounced nationalism and patriotism as "bourgeois tricks." Mussolini's extremism resulted less from a sober appreciation of Marxist doctrine, however, than from his revolutionary temper. To a degree, it also stemmed from the socialist influence of Mussolini's father Alessandro.

On November 15, 1914, Mussolini resigned as editor of *Avanti!* and founded his own newspaper *Il Popolo d'Italia,* which became one of the leading interventionist papers of Italy. The Socialists, who expelled Mussolini from the party on November 24, 1914, charged that he had been bribed by French money and the funds of Italian industrialists who were eager to enter the war on the Allied side.

Although it is certain that Mussolini's *Il Popolo d'Italia* was subsidized by the shipping and armaments enterprise, Ansaldo, it appears that Mussolini's conversion from anti-militarist socialism to militarist nationalism was motivated by reasons other than purely monetary. Mussolini shared the indignation of many Italians over Germany's aggression against Belgium and Austria's invasion of Serbia. Mussolini's Germanophobia eventually led him to conclude that the Second International, in which the German Social Democrats had been the most influential party, had been but another device of German inperialism before the First World War. Most important of all, it was Mussolini's thirst for action which caused him to break with the neutralist Socialist party and join the interventionists; he was true to his maxim, "To live is not to calculate, but to act." By December, 1914, Mussolini, together with a small following of ex-syndicalists and socialists, founded the *Fascio* (group) for Revolutionary Action, as a vehicle for intervention on the Allied side. The *Fascio* of 1914 has often been called the "germ cell of Italian Fascism."

On May 23, 1919, Mussolini founded the *Fasci Italiani di Combattimento* with a following of little over 100 members in a small building on the Piazza San Sepolcro in Milan. The group consisted mostly of veterans who shared a hatred of Socialists and Liberal neutralists. The *Fasci* were not satisfied with the social-political *status quo*, however, and their first program of June, 1919, very much revealed the influence of the spirit of *Diciannovismo* (1919-ism) upon the young Fascist movement. The first Fascist program of 1919, in addition to calling for a constituent assembly and the abolition of the Italian Senate, demanded land for the peasants, a workers' share in industrial management, the confiscation of church property, elected judges, and the decentralization of Italy's administration under the prefects. The overall outlook of early Fascism was republican, rather than monarchist, pro-labor, while at the same time anti-socialist, and pro-capital in the sense that Mussolini preached partnership, rather than class-war, between capital and labor.

From its inception, Fascism was marked by physical violence against political opponents. On April 15, 1919, Fascists sacked and burned the editorial office of *Avanti!* in Milan, the first organized political violence in postwar Italy, which aroused the sympathetic interest of the Milan middle class. It was to D'Annunzio, rather than Mussolini, that the nationalists looked for leadership in 1919, however, and Mussolini's movement did not gather strength until 1920. In the elections of November, 1919, the Fascists failed to conquer a single seat in parliament.

Mussolini's opportunity arrived with the failure of D'Annunzio's Fiume operation and the factory occupation of August, 1920. He became the new center of nationalist attention, inheriting from D'Annunzio his legionaries, his cause, and many of his followers. This same year also witnessed the birth of systematic Fascist *squadrismo*. Fascist squads, drawn mostly from veterans and *arditi* (commandos), but including also a growing number of middle-class students, developed the beating up of opponents and dissidents into a well organized system. The first victims of *squadrismo* were national minorities, the Slovenes of Triest and the German-Austrians in the Alto Adige (South Tyrol). After the Socialist factory occupation of August, 1920, the centers of Socialist strength—unions, cooperatives, party presses, and municipal governments—became the chief targets of *squadrismo*. The Fascists were to claim subsequently that the violence of *squadrismo* had saved Italy from Communist revolution in 1920. In fact, Fascist violence reached its greatest strength only after the socialist tide had passed its postwar peak, and the purpose of Fascist terror was not prevention but retaliation.

Fascist violence thus enjoyed the benevolent tolerance of many prefects and police officials as well as the blessing of industrialists and property owners. By December, 1921, Fascist strength had grown to nearly a quarter million members and Fascist squads had become the *de facto* police in many regions and cities of Italy. From the ranks of the squads emerged the future party bosses of Fascism, Dino Grandi of Bologna, Italo Balbo of Ferrara, and the fanatical Roberto Farinacci of Cremona. In November, 1921, Fascism, which up to then had been a loosely organized movement, constituted itself as a formal party at the Rome Congress. The Fascist party program adopted at the Rome Congress differed significantly from that of June, 1919. Mussolini, preparing the way for a legal seizure of power by Fascism, deleted the republican and social reform planks from the Fascist program. In foreign affairs, the Rome Program promised a nationalist policy; the economic plank was geared to please big business and private enterprise by calling for a ban on strikes, a balanced budget, and the reduction of the state's role in economic enterprises. The Church was promised freedom within the sovereign state. From 1921 onwards, *Confindustria,* the industrialists' association, and the banks contributed liberally to the Fascist cause.

By the summer of 1922 Mussolini had set the stage for a two-pronged attack on the liberal state. On the local and provincial levels, Fascists had begun to oust the legal authorities or were ruling in collusion with them. On the national, parliamentary level, Mussolini skillfully exploited the mutual distrust within the Liberal-Popolari-Socialist triangle to forestall a united anti-Fascist front.

A general strike, organized by the Socialists and Communists on July 31, 1922, in protest against a new wave of Fascist violence in Ravenna and Cremona, weakened, rather than strengthened, the Socialist-Communist opposition. Unlike previous Socialist strikes, that of July 31, 1922, was intended as a "strike for legality," to shake up the liberal government of Prime Minister Facta and remind it of its duty to uphold the law. While the government stood by idly, the Fascists crushed the general strike and thereby claimed to have protected Italy from further anarchy. The Communists, not unlike their German brothers on the eve of Hitler's seizure of power in Germany in 1933, viewed the prospect of a Fascist dictatorship with equanimity in the belief that Fascism represented the last stage in the collapse of the bourgeois-capitalist order.

The Liberals and Popolari were divided on the meaning of a Fascist conquest of power. Giolitti and Facta still hoped that violence and illegality were temporary and not essential to the Fascist party and that Fascism might well be turned into constructive channels within the framework of a Liberal-Fascist coalition. Sturzo deemed Fascism incompatible with the principles of Christian democracy as advocated by the Popolari. Pope Pius XI, the recently elected successor to Benedict XV, was a conservative, however, who preferred the inclusion of the Fascists in the government to a coalition of Popolari and reform-Socialists, such as Sturzo attempted to create.

In addition to the political parties, the crown and the army were important factors which Mussolini could ill afford to ignore. King

FIGURE 3 *Mussolini and D'Annunzio in 1925.*

Victor Emmanuel III, though not a friend of Fascism and its methods, had tired of the parliamentary crisis by 1922. Moreover, the King lacked the courage to defy the Fascists, fearing that Mussolini might oust him and install his cousin, the pro-Fascist Duke of Aosta, as regent. With the King intimidated, Mussolini had no cause to fear the army, which took its orders from Victor Emmanuel.

By September, 1922, Mussolini demanded power, not in the role of junior partner of a coalition government, but as Prime Minister. To put emphasis behind his demand, Mussolini threatened a coup d'état in the form of a "march on Rome" to coincide with the Fascist party congress at Naples in late October, 1922. Four Fascist leaders, the "quadrumvirs" Balbo, Bianchi, De Vecchi, and General De Bono, set up headquarters at Perugia to direct the planned Fascist operation. The "march on Rome," whose logistics were poor, could easily have been crushed by the army had the King ordered it. On October 28, 1922, Prime Minister Facta declared a state of siege, which the King refused to sign. Upon the advice of Italy's war-time Prime Minister, Salandra, the King appointed Mussolini Prime Minister on October 30, 1922. Only after Mussolini's appointment to the prime ministership did the hungry, ill-organized, rain-soaked, and poorly armed columns of the Fascist black shirts enter Rome. The "march on Rome" was not a conquest but a celebration.

FASCISM IN POWER; THE FIRST PHASE

Mussolini had come to power by constitutional means, though under the threat of a Fascist coup d'état, and his first government was a coalition, rather than an all-Fascist cabinet. The coalition included four Fascists, four Liberals, two Popolari, one Nationalist, and General Diaz of World War I fame. However, Mussolini accepted the non-Fascist members of his cabinet, not as representatives of their respective parties, but as individuals chosen on the basis of personal qualification.

Mussolini's government was greeted with a mixture of anxiety and hope. The Chamber of Deputies gave the new government a strong vote of confidence with 306 against 116 votes and granted it plenary powers for one year to carry out fiscal and administative reforms.

Mussolini had promised the King a "government," not just "another administration," which would attack Italy's problems with youthful vigor and in a spirit of unity. The new government, in Mussolini's words, "accelerated the whole rhythm of Italian life." Not a few outside the Fascist party would have agreed, in the first few months of Mussolini's government at any rate, with Mussolini's boast that he was the *"Salvatore D'Italia,"* the savior of Italy, who had ended class war and parliamentary paralysis. The number of strikes dropped significantly, a new calm seemed to have settled on strife-torn Italy.

Mussolini's early legislative program was designed to satisfy important interest groups. He paid his respects to the Catholic Church and paid off his debt to business. Giovanni Gentile, the Minister of Education and one-time friend of Benedetto Croce, restored compulsory religious instruction to public elementary schools and established equality between public and private (Catholic) secondary schools. The salaries of priests and bishops were increased; the crucifix, removed from classroom and law court, was restored.

To please business, Mussolini repealed Giolitti's legislation of 1920 concerning the steep inheritance tax and the compulsory registration of stocks and bonds. Consistent with the Fascist Rome Program of 1921, the government reduced the economic role of the state. The telephone system was turned over to private enterprise on lucrative terms, while the government subsidized the ailing Ansaldo company. The state monopoly on life insurance, established under Giolitti's "New Deal" of 1912, was abolished. Industrialists and businessmen hailed Mussolini as a true economic liberal in the Manchester tradition.

Fascism likewise promised labor peace and a privileged position for big business in the settlement of labor disputes. Mussolini recognized *Confindustria* as the sole representative of industry. An agreement, concluded with *Confindustria* in December, 1923, at the Palazzo Chigi, established a permanent commission of five employers' and five union representatives for the improvement of industrial-labor relations.

Fascism benefitted from the general prosperity which followed the postwar period of adjustment and economic crisis. The mid-1920's were prosperous years for Italy with a marked increase in steel production, ship construction, and the manufacture of synthetic fibers and chemicals. The workers' share in the prosperity of the mid-1920's was limited, the fighting spirit having gone out of the unions, which the régime would soon outlaw. Likewise, the social legislation of early Fascism was modest. In March, 1923, the government enacted the 8-hour day.

While Mussolini claimed credit for restoring order and promoting prosperity, he laid the groundwork for the gradual transformation of liberal Italy into a single-party dictatorship. Upon becoming Prime Minister, Mussolini did not formally abolish the constitution of 1861. Rather, it was through a slow process, both legal and illegal, that the political liberties and civil rights of Italy became eroded and extinct under the rule of Fascism.

The electoral law of July 15, 1923 (Acerbo Law), named after the Fascist Under-Secretary of State Giacomo Acerbo, was an ingenious device for assuring the Fascist party a parliamentary majority in the elections of April 6, 1924. The Acerbo Law combined all of Italy into a single constituency and stipulated that the party which obtained a relative majority would receive two thirds of the seats in parliament, provided the relative majority exceeded twenty-five per cent. The remaining third of the parliamentary seats would be divided among the other parties by proportional representation. In the elections of April, 1924, the government entered a single list of candidates, two thirds of whom were Fascists. The government secured 374 seats (of which 275 were Fascist), as against 39 for the Popolari, 46 for the Socialists, 19 for the Communists, and 30 for Liberal Democrats.

The functions and power of the cabinet had been altered as early as December, 1922, through the establishment of the Fascist Grand Council. Presided over by Mussolini and composed of the Fascist cabinet members, the leaders of the Fascist militia, Fascist party executives, and the police chief, the Fascist Grand Council became the *de facto* government, by which all political decisions were made. The regular cabinet was relegated to routine administrative tasks. The creation of a permanent Fascist militia of 300,000, maintained at public expense, marked a further step towards the gradual identification of Fascist party and state.

Since coming to power in October, 1922, Fascism had not abandoned its earlier lawlessness and violence. Although mass violence abated, selective terror against opposition deputies, critics of Fascism, and subscribers of anti-Fascist newspapers developed into a regular feature of Fascist rule. It was in protest against continuing lawlessness that the Popolari members of Mussolini's coalition cabinet withdrew from the government in April, 1923. For the same reason, some of Italy's distinguished diplomats, such as the ambassadors to Germany and France, Frassati and Sforza, resigned. Fascist violence had reached a new peak during the elections of April, 1924. On May 30, 1924, the Socialist deputy Giacomo Matteotti attacked Mussolini in a speech before the newly elected Chamber of Deputies, demanding that the election results of April 6, 1924, be invalidated on the grounds of Fascist violence and coercion. On June 10, 1924, Matteotti was kidnapped, stabbed, and buried in the woods outside of Rome by Fascist *squadristi*.

The murder of Matteotti created the most serious crisis for Mussolini since coming to power and might well have toppled his régime had King Victor Emmanuel rallied the opposition around his person. Amidst a nationwide uproar, the anti-Fascist deputies of parliament, Popolari, Socialists, Communists, and the liberal followers of Giovanni Amendola, one of Mussolini's most outspoken critics, left parliament and staged the "Aventine secession." (The exodus was named after the secession of the plebeians to the Aventine in ancient Republican Rome). The anti-Fascist deputies swore not to return to parliament until the Fascist militia had been abolished, the rule of law restored, and a new government installed. The publication of the so-called Rossi Memorandum in December, 1924 (named after Mussolini's former press secretary, Cesare Rossi), by the opposition press seriously endangered the régime. The

Rossi Memorandum charged that many acts of Fascist terror had been committed on Mussolini's personal order.

At first, Mussolini had tried to dismiss the Matteotti murder as the deed of an *agent provocateur.* After publication of the Rossi Memorandum, he assumed full responsibility: "If Fascism has been a criminal organization," Mussolini announced to parliament on January 3, 1925, "I am the head of that organization."

The Aventine secession had been intended to stir the king and the army into action while the Popolari looked towards the Church for a moral condemnation of Fascism. Victor Emmanuel did not move, however, and leading industrialists came to Mussolini's defense. Pope Pius XI, regarding the Popolari as an embarrassment and obstacle to good state-Church relations, likewise abstained from encouraging the Aventine secession. Luigi Sturzo went into exile in October, 1924.

Mussolini thus turned the uproar over Matteotti's murder into an excuse for rooting out the opposition. January, 1925, marks the beginning of the dictatorial phase of Italian Fascism, as the remnants of the liberal society were being dismantled in rapid order. The dissolution of all political parties, other than the Fascist, between November, 1925, and October, 1926, was followed by the outlawing of the Socialist and Catholic unions. When the deputies of the Aventine secession attempted to take up their seats in parliament in November, 1926, they were expelled. A series of laws, entitled the Fascist Laws of 1925 and 1926, expanded Fascist control over the judiciary, the civil service, and the executive. In February, 1927, a special tribunal was established for trying "crimes against the state" in secrecy. The creation of a Fascist secret police (Ovra) followed. The abrogation of Article 10 of the Italian constitution permanently transferred the power of legislative initiative from parliament to the executive. The laws of December, 1928, and December, 1929, legalized the dictatorship by conferring constitutional powers upon the Fascist Grand Council, hitherto a party organ. Henceforth, the Grand Council had to be consulted in matters of royal succession. Mussolini was no longer responsible to parliament but to the Grand Council. In April, 1926, Mussolini had laid the groundwork for the social transformation of Italy into a corporate society with the promulgation of the Labor Charter *(Carta del Lavoro),* to be discussed more fully in the context of Italian Fascism in the 1930's.

By the late 1920's Mussolini had moved Italy far along the road of *fascistizzazione,* the identification of party and state, under the motto: "Everything inside the state, nothing outside the state, nothing against the state." At home, the opposition was, for the most part, silenced or broken. The few opposition leaders, such as ex-prime minister Nitti, who had managed to escape abroad and who attempted to alarm the liberal conscience of the West evoked only a feeble echo in the 1920's. In the 1920's Fascist Italy was not ostracized by the governments of the Western democracies, partly because Italian foreign policy had not yet challenged vital interests of France and Britain. The violent course of Italian Fascist foreign policy was suggested, however, by the temper of Mussolini and his observation that "perpetual peace" was "degrading and negative toward the fundamental virtues of man." Most ominously, Mussolini had set a successful example of the piecemeal destruction of a liberal-democratic society, beset by poverty, social tension, and national frustration, through the violence and determination of a reactionary minority. In his mastery of the techniques of power, Mussolini owed a great debt to Lenin and the Bolsheviks, a debt he readily conceded when addressing the Italian parliament after the Matteotti murder: "We have admirable teachers in Russia. We have but to imitate what is being done in Russia . . . they are admirable masters. We are wrong not to follow their example completely." Mussolini was the first successful imitator of the Bolshevik technique in the destruction of liberal democracy. With the onset of the Depression, the example was to find many more imitators, from the Rhine to the Pyrenees, the Danube, and the Vistula.

12 | The Democratic Experiment in Central Europe:
The Weimar Republic and Austria

THE WEIMAR CONSTITUENT ASSEMBLY

After its convocation at Weimar, the Constituent Assembly elected Frederich Ebert as President of the Weimar Republic. The choice was politically sound, for Ebert had won the respect of a large segment of the German public, ranging from labor to the middle class and even to some of the military, through his proven leadership during the revolutionary events of November, 1918. Opposition to Ebert was strong only among the Communists and Nationalists; the former denouncing him for crushing the Spartacist uprising, while the latter falsely identified him with the "Marxist revolution" of November, 1918.

As President, Ebert appointed the first cabinet of the Weimar Republic, a coalition of Social Democrats, Democrats, and Catholic Center ministers under the chancellorship of the Social Democrat Philip Scheidemann. The "Weimar coalition," as the SPD-Center-Democratic coalition came to be known, was a continuation of the political alliance which had supported the Reichstag Peace Resolution of 1917 and which had made up the cabinet of Prince Max of Baden in October, 1918. Although disagreements existed within the coalition, notably between the Center and the SPD on religious issues, the common republican outlook among the three coalition partners outweighed their differences.

The chief tasks before the Constituent Assembly were the drafting of a constitution and the ratification of a peace treaty with the Allies. A constitutional draft had been prepared on Ebert's orders by Hugo Preuss, a liberal constitutional expert who also headed the Ministry of the Interior in the Scheidemann cabinet. The Preuss draft was inspired by both the German revolutionary experience of 1848/1849 and the models of the American, Swiss, and French republican constitutions. In several significant points, the draft of the Weimar Constitution marked a radical departure from the German Imperial Constitution of 1871. Whereas the Imperial Constitution had resulted from the agreement among the German princes and kings without popular participation, the Weimar Constitution stressed the principle of popular sovereignty in its preamble. "The German people," the preamble stated, "united in all their branches . . . have adopted the following constitution." To overcome the old dualism of Prussia and Germany, Preuss proposed to replace the federal system of the Empire with a unitary state. This demand had been raised repeatedly during the German revolution of 1918/1919 and seemed indeed a logical solution after the abdication of the German dynasties. In its final shape the Weimar Constitution retained the federal system, however, because of opposition from the states. Moreover, the Social Democrats came to regard Prussia as the bulwark of their own strength in the Republic, after the introduction of universal suffrage, just as the Conservatives had considered Prussia their stronghold in the Empire under the old three-class suffrage.

Although the federal system was retained, the Weimar Constitution favored the federal over the state governments in the distribution of powers and shifted the emphasis from the executive to the legislative branch. Not only did the Weimar Constitution grant much broader taxing powers to the federal government, but it eliminated special states' rights, such as Bavaria's separate postal administration and independent foreign service. Whereas the federal government under the Empire had depended primarily on indirect taxes for its revenue, the Weimar Constitution reserved the most lucrative direct taxes—income, corporate, and inheritances taxes—to the federal government. Whereas the individual states had subsidized the federal government under the Empire through annual contributions, in the Weimar Republic the federal government subsidized state and municipal governments, through revenue sharing. The shift of taxing powers from the states to the federal government was essential under the prevailing conditions of the postwar period, the financial burdens of the federal government having vastly increased as a result of the First World War and the German defeat of 1918. Added to the internal debt of 161 billion marks, incurred through the sale of war bonds, was the reparations debt, fixed at $33 billion by the Allies in 1921. The Reichstag, powerless to remove the chancellor under the Empire, became the central organ of federal power under the Republic. Elected by universal suffrage with one deputy for every 60,000 voters, the Reichstag could remove a chancellor from office through vote of non-confidence.

The Upper House (Reichsrat), consisting of the appointed representatives of the state governments, was reduced to an advisory body of the federal government, its chief power being the suspensive veto over Reichstag acts. To forestall Prussian domination of the Upper House, Prussia's representation was limited to two-fifths of the Reichsrat seats.

To counterbalance the broad powers of the Reichstag, the Weimar Constitution provided for a popularly elected president rather than imitate the example of the French president, elected by both chambers of the legislature. Although the president's powers were mostly ceremonial, he was commander-in-chief of the armed forces and possessed special emergency powers under Article 48 of the Constitution. Subject to the Reichstag's approval, the president could enforce federal law against states by force of arms and suspend the fundamental rights of the Constitution in times of national emergency.

The Weimar Constitution, unlike its predecessor, contained a lengthy Bill of Rights, which attempted to synthesize 19th-century liberal principles with socialist aspirations. In addition to granting the traditional liberal rights of free assembly, speech, and press, the Constitution declared the establishment of homesteads for landless peasants to be a goal of the republic. The socialization of industries, one of the chief demands of revolutionary workers in November, 1918, was declared permissible, though not stated as a desirable goal. The Bill of Rights further promised an elaborate system of economic councils, crowned by a *Reich* Economic Council, to aid in the drafting of social and economic legislation. On July 31, 1919, the Weimar Constitution was adopted against the votes of the Nationalists, the People's Party, and the Independent Social Democrats.

The Weimar Constitution would have been an admirable instrument of self-government in a politically mature society accustomed to the give-and-take of parliamentary compromise. There was doubt, however, from the start whether the German political parties, accustomed to the role of opposition in the Empire, would exercise their new freedoms with sufficient restraint to make the Constitution work. Hugo Preuss, the father of the Weimar Constitution, complained that the members of the Weimar Constituent Assembly did not seem to understand that the new government must be "blood of their blood and flesh of their flesh." Ernst Troeltsch, the noted German historian, added the pessimistic note that "many of us in Germany regard 'compromise' as the lowest and most despicable means which a thinker can have resort to. We are asked to recognize a radical disjunction here, and to choose either for or against." The election returns of January, 1919, were, on the other hand, an encouraging sign that parliamentary democracy suited the temper of the majority of German voters. Nor was the new Republic devoid of political talent, in spite of the many years of semi-autocratic government under the Empire. The German municipalities provided an ample reservoir of gifted political leaders, and men from the business world, such as Walther Rathenau, enriched political life with novel ideas on social and economic reform. Moreover, men such as Gustav Stresemann, associated with the Pan-German dreams of empire, managed to become loyal and outstanding republican leaders after a period of adjustment.

To succeed, the democratic experiment of Weimar needed above all a period of stability, in which the new Republic could take roots. A further prerequisite of a working democracy was attainment of the social progress that the Constitution had promised. Aside from modest gains in the field of social reform, the revolution of November, 1918, had left the economic structure of Imperial society intact. The laws passed in early 1920 for the implementation of economic councils, promised in the Bill of Rights, fell short of workers' expectations. The National Economic Council, representing workers and employers from numerous branches of the economy, remained a short-lived experiment without consequence. The constitutional promise of land reform was realized only to a very limited extent by the early 1930's, with only one ninth of the arable land affected by land reform. The large estates east of the Elbe remained for the most part intact, and the Weimar Republic fell far short of the extensive land reforms carried out in most of the new states of central-eastern Europe between the two world wars. Nor did the enactment of the Constitution make republican converts among the judiciary, the army, or the civil service, which remained largely attached in sentiment to the Hohenzollern Empire. In the long run, their attitude towards the Republic depended on the peace settlement which the Republican regime would obtain from the Allies.

THE NATIONALIST REACTION: THE KAPP-LÜTTWITZ *PUTSCH*

Widespread anger over the Treaty of Versailles combined with several other factors at the turn of 1919/1920 to produce a powerful shift to the right, setting the stage for the first attack on the Republic by disgruntled officers of the new army, the Reichswehr. Field Marshall Hindenburg lent his prestige to the "stab-in-the-back" legend when he testified before a Reichstag Committee, which was investigating the causes of the German collapse of 1918, that the German army, having done its duty in the field, was deserted in the decisive hour by a defeatist home front. Matthias Erzberger, the Center Party Minister of Finance, angered the well-to-do by his announced policy of "taxing the rich" to help pay German reparations to the Allies. The German middle class, barely recovered from the shock of the Spartacist revolt and the Bavarian Soviet Republic, was disturbed by the outbreak of new Communist riots in Berlin in January, 1920, during the Reichstag debate on the law establishing factory councils. Most important of all, the army bitterly resented Allied demands for the immediate German evacuation of the Baltic states and the reduction of the army to 200,000 men. Beginning with 1920 the Weimar governments were to be caught increasingly between the hammer of Allied demands and the anvil of German military and nationalist opposition.

The army's opposition to cuts in German troop strength was spearheaded by General Walther von Lüttwitz, the commander of an army group. On March 12, 1920, General Lüttwitz and Wolfgang Kapp, a Prussian reactionary, staged a coup against the Republican government by occupying Berlin with the forces of the Ehrhardt Marine Brigade.

Lüttwitz hoped to draw the entire army as well as the right-wing parties to his side, once the Republican government had been overthrown. The bulk of the German army assumed a wait-and-see attitude, neither supporting General Lüttwitz nor answering the government's call for help. Active army support of Lüttwitz was confined to Silesia and a few isolated garrisons in northern Germany. General Hans von Seeckt, soon to assume command of the Reichswehr, excused the army's inactivity with the laconic remark that German troops did not fire upon their own. In desperation, the government hurriedly left Berlin, seeking safety in Dresden and later Stuttgart. Kapp declared himself Chancellor in Berlin and announced a government of "freedom and order."

Although deserted by the army, the Republican government was not defenseless. Before departing from Berlin, it had appealed to the trade unions to paralyze the military insurgents through a general strike. When the banks and the civil servants also refused to collaborate, the *putsch* collapsed, and Kapp, the self-appointed chancellor, "resigned" on March 17, 1920.

On the surface, the collapse of the Kapp-Lüttwitz *putsch* signified a decisive Republican victory over the forces of militarist reaction. In truth, the victory was Pyrrhic, for it led neither to the establishment of firm Republican controls over the army nor to the eradication of the Free Corps menace. The Free Corps leaders continued to lead an underground existence in Bavaria, the hospitable haven to all nationalist leagues. Soon the veterans of the Ehrhardt Brigade would plot the assassination of prominent Republican figures, such as Matthias Erzberger, the former Minister of Finance, and Walther Rathenau, Foreign Minister of the Weimar Republic in early 1922. Erzberger was assassinated by two ex-members of the Ehrhardt Brigade on August 26, 1921, Rathenau by veterans of the same organization on June 14, 1922.

The labor unions, not satisfied with the mere collapse of the militarist coup, demanded firm guarantees against its recurrence. Not until after Chancellor Bauer had granted a Nine Point Program which promised a union voice in the selection of coalition governments did the general strike end on March 23, 1920. The Communists, who had been slow in supporting the government during the Kapp *putsch,* urged a continuation of the strike and organized armed bands in the Ruhr. The government sent troops to crush the "Red Army" in the Ruhr. In so doing it violated the demilitarized zone, inviting a French retaliation in the form of a temporary occupation of Frankfurt, Darmstadt, and other German cities. The Kapp-Lüttwitz *putsch* also marked the end of collaboration between the Social Democrats and the German army, which Ebert and General Gröner had initiated during the revolution of November, 1918. Noske, the Social Democratic Minister of Defense, and General Reinhardt, the Chief of the Army, resigned in the wake of the Kapp affair. Both men had continued the tradition of collaboration between army and SPD and lost support among their following for that reason during the abortive military coup of March, 1920.

General Hans von Seeckt, Reinhardt's successor, supposedly kept the German army out of politics. In fact, the army became a state within the state of Weimar under Seeckt's direction, its loyalty belonging to the abstract ideal of the German *Reich,* not the transient Weimar Republic. Seeckt purged the army of suspected Republican loyalists, barred Socialists from enlistment, and rendered the officers' corps more aristocratic than it had been even under the Hohenzollern Empire. The reactionary trend in the army was matched by similar developments in the navy, whose officers suffered continued embarrassment over the fact that the "Red" revolution of 1918 had originated in the German navy.

Whereas Seeckt refused to identify the Reichswehr with the Weimar Republic, he maintained close contacts with right-wing paramilitary and veterans organizations, such as the *Stahlhelm* (steel helmet) and the anti-Republican organization *Oberland.* Along the troubled German-Polish frontier, Seeckt maintained an irregular border guard, recruited from among Free Corps veterans and supplied by the regular army. In times of national emergency, Seeckt hoped to double or treble the strength of the regular army through the inclusion of the frontier guards.

As mentioned in the discussion on the enforcement of the peace, Seeckt also held very definite views on German foreign policy and the role which the Reichswehr was to play in its development. An early advocate of rapprochement with Soviet Russia, Seeckt was among the German sponsors of the Rapallo Treaty of 1922, which paved the way for secret German-Soviet military collaboration. As the ultimate aim of the Rapallo policy, Seeckt viewed the elimination of an independent Poland and the restoration of the German-Russian border of 1914. A Germany rearmed and strong, Seeckt believed, would also raise its value as a potential ally of Great Britain.

THE REICHSTAG ELECTIONS OF JUNE 6, 1920

On May 21, 1920, the Weimar Constituent Assembly dissolved itself to make way for the first Reichstag under the Republic. The elections of June 6, 1920, reflected the disillusionment over the peace and its turbulent aftermath. The parties of the Weimar coalition, which had obtained over 75 per cent of the vote in 1919, sank to less than half the Reichstag seats. In 1920 Germany had seemingly become a "Republic without Republicans." As the Social Democrats and Democrats lost heavily, the parties of the right—the Nationalists and the People's Party —registered significant gains. The Independent Social Democrats, a mere 22 seats strong in 1919, jumped to 81 seats in 1920. In October,

1920, the greater part of the Independents joined with the Communists, at the Halle Congress, to form the United Communist Party. The minority of the USPD eventually rejoined the SPD at the Nuremberg Party Congress in 1922.

With the decline of the parties of the Weimar Coalition, the formation of a new coalition became exceedingly difficult, since the other parties lacked a political consensus. The Social Democrats, fearful of losing more labor support, refused to join Stresemann's People's Party in a coalition. The government formed in June, 1920, under Chancellor Konstantine Fehrenbach was thus a minority government, drawn from the Catholic Center, the Democrats, and the People's Party. When presented with the Allied reparations demand of 132 billion gold marks in April, 1921, the Fehrenbach government, evading responsibility, resigned. Since the Allied London Ultimatum had given Germany but six days to accept the decision of the Reparations Commission or face the consequences of an Allied occupation of the industrial Ruhr district, little time could be wasted on bringing together a new coalition government. Once more, the parties of the Weimar Coalition took responsibility for what was unpopular but inevitable, as they had done in 1919 when faced with the Treaty of Versailles. On May 10, 1921, the Center Party leader Joseph Wirth formed a coalition cabinet of Social Democrats, Democrats, and Center, which accepted the London Ultimatum.

THE RUHR CRISIS

Between May, 1921, and November, 1922, the Wirth government was confronted with an ever-deepening crisis in foreign and domestic affairs, which foreshadowed the near-collapse of the Weimar Republic in the ensuing Ruhr crisis of 1923. In the field of foreign affairs, the Weimar Republic faced the Allies in the reparations struggle in virtually total isolation. The Rapallo Treaty with Russia, which Wirth's foreign minister Walther Rathenau had signed in April, 1922, was a spectacular, though at the time ineffective, German attempt to escape from the isolation of 1922. The partitioning of Upper Silesia by the League Council in October, 1921, not only undermined German faith in the League but seriously impaired the prestige of the Wirth government at home. The nationalist critics denounced Wirth and Rathenau as *"Erfüllungspolitiker"* ("politicians of fulfillment"), who sold out German national interests to the victorious Allies.

The assassinations of Erzberger and Rathenau, previously mentioned, were the result of nationalist agitation, grown increasingly reckless and contemptuous of the Republic. That Walther Rathenau had rendered distinguished service to the Hohenzollern Empire during the First World War as chief of the war materials board did not raise him in the esteem of his young nationalist assassins. Rathenau was a German Jew and, as such, a particularly inviting target of nationalist assassins, who attributed Germany's defeat, the German revolution, and the postwar crisis to "Jewish influence."

The murder of Rathenau on June 14, 1922, stung the Republican parties into action. On July 18, 1922, the Reichstag adopted a law for the protection of the Republic that made the subversion of the Republic in word or deed a treasonable crime. Stresemann's People's party, whose loyalties to the Republic had been doubtful before, voted for the measure. The effectiveness of the law of July 18 remained in doubt because of the anti-republican attitude of many judges who had to enforce it. Significantly, the state of Bavaria, a hotbed of reaction, refused to recognize the law of July 18 as binding upon itself on the grounds that it exceeded federal powers. Soon Bavaria would flaunt federal authority more openly, as the Weimar Republic drifted towards political and economic disintegration in the Ruhr crisis.

With France poised to strike at the Ruhr, Germany's most important industrial district, and domestic concern in the wake of the Rathenau murder, Chancellor Wirth attempted to strengthen his government by including the People's Party in the Weimar coalition of Social Democrats, Center Party, and Democrats. The attempt to forge a "great Weimar coalition" in the face of approaching disaster failed, largely because of basic disagreements between the Social Democrats and the People's Party. Although the latter was willing to accept Wirth's invitation, the Social Democrats objected because of the People's Party's social and economic views. As the representative of industrial interests, the People's Party favored the abandonment of the eight-hour day in industry, which the SPD regarded as one of the major social gains of the German revolution of 1918. Runaway inflation provided a further source of disagreement between the two parties. Whereas the Social Democrats demanded an immediate halt to inflation through currency reform, the industrialists, standing to profit from its continuation, opposed immediate currency reform. The inability of Social Democrats and the People's Party to reconcile narrow interests of social class for the sake of the national interest in times of emergency pointed to a fundamental weakness in the party system of the Weimar Republic. In 1930 another confrontation between Social Democrats and the People's Party, similar to that of 1922, was to pave the way for the end of German parliamentary government. Unable to rally the Republican parties into the projected "great Weimar coalition," Chancellor Wirth resigned on November 14, 1922.

The task of coping with the French-Belgian military invasion of the Ruhr, which began on January 11, 1923, fell to Wirth's successor, Chancellor Wilhelm Cuno. As has been shown in the discussion of the reparations conflict, Cuno's policy of passive resistance in the Ruhr resulted in the ruin of the currency and the economic disintegration of Germany without achieving the desired goal of timely British intervention on the German side. On August 11, 1923, Gustav Stresemann, the head of the People's Party, succeeded Cuno as head of a "great Weimar coalition" consisting of Social Democrats, Center Party, Democrats, and representatives of Stresemann's own party.

STRESEMANN, THE "CHANCELLOR OF THE HUNDRED DAYS"; THE DOMESTIC CRISIS OF 1923

Gustav Stresemann's political background in the German Empire did not suggest his future role as one of Germany's most constructive Republican leaders. As leader of the National Liberal Party during the First World War, Stresemann had been an ardent annexationist who adjusted to the Weimar Republic only gradually and with difficulty after the defeat of 1918.

In foreign affairs, Stresemann's chancellorship marked a decisive change from the immediate postwar phase of confrontation with the Allies to that of accommodation and reconciliation, as exemplified in the new reparations settlement under the Dawes Plan in 1924 and the multilateral security pact of Locarno of 1925.

In domestic affairs Stresemann recognized the German preference for opposition over responsible political leadership as the chief woe of Republican politics. Asserting his faith in the Republican institutions of Germany, Stresemann claimed that they could have accomplished far more but for the repeated attacks upon them from within since 1919. As an eventual cure for Germany's parliamentary instability, he hoped to achieve a renewal of the party system through the establishment of a broad Republican party of the middle. Unlike the existing political parties of the Republic, which were, for the most part, carry-overs from the Empire, a new Republican party might unite all those who placed faith in the Weimar Republic above social or religious considerations. Stresemann's tenure as Chancellor, lasting from August to November, 1923, was too brief, however, to effect such fundamental changes in the party system. Stresemann nevertheless continued to exert a beneficial influence on German domestic politics in his capacity as Foreign Minister between 1923 and 1929, the year of his death. But for the prestige and success of his foreign policy in the mid and late 1920's, Stresemann's own People's Party and the powerful industrial interests which it represented might not have played the constructive role they did in domestic political affairs. Significantly, the end of parliamentary government in March, 1930, followed closely on the heels of Stresemann's death in October, 1929.

The immediate domestic tasks which confronted Stresemann

as Chancellor in 1923 were to stabilize the currency and to contain revolutionary threats from the extreme left and right in October and November, 1923. In dealing with the extraordinary financial and political crisis of 1923, Stresemann relied frequently on the presidential emergency powers under Article 48 of the Weimar Constitution. Although the special circumstances of 1923 no doubt warranted the use of special powers, the frequent use of Article 48 set a dangerous precedent for neutralizing the Reichstag in times of crisis.

THE STABILIZATION OF THE CURRENCY

The fact that no government prior to Stresemann's had seriously attempted to halt the runaway inflation was rooted in the German assumption that reparations were its main cause. Before there was hope of gaining a revision of the reparations settlement favorable to Germany, no German government was prepared to take decisive action in the fiscal crisis.

In fact, German reparation payments for the fiscal years from 1920 to 1923 accounted for only part of the annual budget deficits. The government's financing of passive resistance in the Ruhr in 1923 dealt the German currency its final blow. The Ruhr struggle was only the last in a series of developments, however, which had progressively weakened the German currency since the First World War. The value of the mark began to decline during the war because Germany, like France and unlike Britain, favored borrowing over taxation as a method of financing the war. After the war, it continued to decline as a result of speculation, imbalanced budgets, and the easy credit policy of the Reichsbank. German big business in particular benefited from the policy of Reichsbank president Rudolf Havenstein, who loaned ever larger amounts to German industry at interest rates below the inflationary rate. From a pre-war exchange rate of 4.2 marks to the U. S. dollar, the mark declined to 8.9 in 1919 and reached the extraordinary exchange rate of 4.2 billion marks to one U. S. dollar in November, 1923. The extent of the German monetary chaos may be measured from the interest rate of 22 per cent per diem in 1923 and the fact that private, gold-backed currencies had appeared for business transactions next to the worthless official money.

Stresemann entrusted the task of currency stabilization to the energetic Minister of Finance Hans Luther and Hjalmar Schacht, who was appointed special Currency Commissioner with broad powers in November, 1923. On November 15, 1923, Schacht issued a new currency, the *Rentenmark,* at the exchange rate of one *Rentenmark* for 1 billion inflation marks. The stability of the new currency was due mainly to psychological factors and the policy of severe credit restrictions which Schacht imposed upon both private business and the federal government. The virtual credit stop forced the former to draw upon its own hidden foreign currency reserves, and the latter to balance its budget. Although the *Rentenmark* was issued without any gold backing—German gold reserves having dipped to a mere $125 million by the end of 1923—German economic recovery under the Dawes Plan permitted the return to the gold standard in 1924. Interest rates, still as high as 100 per cent a year in early 1924, sank to 6 per cent in 1926.

The German inflation of 1923 left deep social and economic scars upon the working class as well as the bourgeoisie, which the economic boom of the mid-1920's obscured rather than healed. Though proletarianized in an economic sense, the middle class did not turn socialist or Communist. On the contrary, it became more receptive to extreme right-wing influences than ever, blaming the Republic for the loss of its savings. Big business, on the other hand, often benefited from the inflation of 1923, converting Reichsbank loans into real assets and repaying only a fraction of the actual value of loans as the inflation progressed. The inflation accelerated industrial concentration and stimulated the growth of monster cartels, of which the Hugo Stinnes enterprises were the most notorious. Upon the governments of Germany, during the Weimar Republic and after, the inflation of 1923 left its permanent mark, making German fiscal policy after 1923 one of the most conservative in Europe.

THE CONTAINMENT OF REVOLUTION ON THE LEFT AND RIGHT: "RED OCTOBER" AND THE "BEER HALL *PUTSCH*"

While the Stresemann government was laying the groundwork for currency reform, it was threatened with political insurrection, from the Communist side in October and from the extreme right in November, 1923.

Until August 1923 Soviet Russia had supported the German struggle against France in the Ruhr, largely because of the devisive effect upon the capitalist West. When Stresemann took the initiative in ending the Ruhr struggle by terminating German passive resistance on September 26, 1923, the Communist International directed the German Communists to overthrow the Stresemann government.

Proceeding from the states of Saxony and Thuringia, where the German Communists had entered into coalition governments with left-wing Social Democrats, Communist "Red Hundreds" were to march on Munich and Berlin. To assure the success of the German Communist uprising, Moscow sent arms, money, and military advisers. Coming on the heels of the Bulgarian Communist uprising under Georgi Dimitrov, Germany's "Red October" of 1923 marked the most ambitious Soviet attempt to export Communist revolution since 1919. It proved to be, in

Trotsky's words, "the last card of an historical epoch," however, for the German army crushed the insurrection before it gained momentum. By mid-November, 1923, both Saxony and Thuringia were under federal control, its Communist–Social Democratic coalitions ousted. The Communist uprising in Hamburg of October 22, 1923, was crushed by local police after two days of fighting.

As Stresemann was moving with speed and purpose against the Communists, a right-wing coup had been brewing in reactionary Bavaria, seething with discontented nationalist and monarchist forces.

Although united in their hatred of the Republican government in Berlin, the rightist forces in Bavaria showed little unity of purpose otherwise. Whereas the monarchists aspired to restore the Wittelsbach dynasty to the Bavarian throne, Hitler, allied with General Ludendorff, wished to stage a march on Berlin in imitation of Mussolini's march on Rome of October, 1922. The Bavarian army command, under General Lossow, sympathetic to both causes, stood undecided in the middle. Fearful lest the abandonment of passive resistance on the Ruhr should provoke Hitler and Ludendorff into premature action, the monarchist state commissioner Gustav von Kahr proclaimed a Bavarian state of emergency on September 26, 1923. Stresemann countered by declaring a national state of emergency, which placed executive power temporarily in the hands of the army. Its chief, General Seeckt, after briefly contemplating an army coup against Stresemann, remained loyal in the end. A local revolt by the army garrison of Kuestrin under Major Buchrucker was crushed on October 1, 1923, and General Lossow, the head of the Bavarian army command, was dismissed when he failed to carry out federal orders. The final reckoning between Munich and Berlin was delayed by the Communist insurrection in Saxony.

Although Stresemann's swift action against the Communists considerably cooled the revolutionary ardor of the Bavarian monarchists, Hitler forced Kahr and Lossow at gun point to join him in his proposed march on Berlin. Proclaiming the outbreak of a "national revolution," Hitler declared the government in Berlin overthrown. General Lossow was to become military dictator of Germany and Ludendorff chief of the army, while Hitler himself would be in charge of "political direction." The Monarchist-Nazi alliance, conceived under duress on November 8, 1923, in the Munich beer hall *"Bürgerbräu,"* collapsed as soon as Kahr and Lossow had regained their freedom. Instead of joining Hitler, Kahr declared the Nazi party outlawed and ordered the Nazi demonstration of November 9, 1923 crushed by armed force. Sixteen of Hitler's followers were killed in the fire of Bavarian police and army units, Hitler escaped, and General Ludendorff marched in solitary procession through the firing line without harm.

Under the laws of the Republic, Hitler, still an Austrian citizen in 1923, should have been deported as an undesirable alien. Such was the political climate in Bavaria and the mood of the Bavarian judiciary, however, that he was given the minimum sentence of five years' imprisonment in his trial for treason in February, 1924. Paroled after serving eight and a half months at the Landsberg prison, Hitler was free to resume his political activities in Bavaria. His trial before the Bavarian People's Court had given his cause excellent publicity. Unknown to most outside Bavaria before the *"Beer Hall putsch,"* Hitler turned the courtroom into a propaganda sounding board against the Republic.

Stresemann's Great Weimar Coalition of Social Democrats, Democrats, Center Party, and People's Party had not withstood the shocks of Communist and Nazi insurrection. The Social Democrats, angered that Stresemann had dealt swiftly with the Communist threat but tardily with reactionary Bavaria, withdrew from the government on November 2, 1923. On November 23, they joined with the Nationalists to bring down the Stresemann government in a vote of no confidence. President Ebert, more statesmanlike than most of his Social Democratic colleagues, warned: "What caused you to overthrow the chancellor will be forgotten in six weeks, but the results of your folly you will feel for ten years." Not until 1928 did the Social Democrats join another coalition government.

THE GERMAN ECONOMY
UNDER THE DAWES PLAN

During the five years following the adoption of the Dawes Plan, the German economy experienced a remarkable boom, comparable to that of the 1870's and 1880's under the Hohenzollern Empire. The recovery was due partly to the massive inflow of foreign capital and partly to the modernization and rationalization of German industry. As the confidence of foreign bankers in the German economy returned, an estimated 20 billion marks in foreign short- and long-term loans were invested in Germany between 1924 and 1930. During the same period, German investments abroad totaled approximately 5 billion marks.

As foreign investments in Germany came chiefly from the United States, German industry patterned its modernization after the American example. Increased mechanization brought sharp rises in productivity. In the coal industry 90 per cent of the German output was mechanized by 1928, as against 2 per cent in 1913. Although the number of German blast furnaces had declined by 20 per cent between 1913 and 1927, owing to the losses under the treaty of Versailles, the output per blast furnace was raised by as much as 99 per cent due to improved production methods. The German chemical industry, hard hit by the loss of German patent rights after the war, recaptured its pre-war share of 28 per cent of world exports by 1928. The German merchant fleet, which had dropped from five million tons in 1913 to less than 700,000 tons after the war, climbed to over 4 million tons in 1930. As the sister ships *Bremen* and *Europa* symbolized Germany's comeback as a merchant sea power, the flight around the world of the dirigible *Count Zeppelin* in 1929 marked the recovery of German civil aviation. The German gross national product, estimated at 45 billion marks in 1913, rose to over 76 billion by 1929, though the purchasing power of the mark in the late 1920's was below that of the pre-war mark.

The economic boom of the 1920's accelerated the process of industrial concentration, a development characteristic of the German pre-war economy and emphasized under the conditions of the war-time economy. In the Republic, industrial cartels were not considered inimical to the public interest but an asset to the efficient organization of the economy. In the coal and potash industries, the government itself aided in the formation of cartels. By 1925 the Weimar Republic counted no fewer than 2,500 cartels. The process of concentration was most marked in the steel, electrical, and chemical industries where a few giants, such as United Steel, Siemens, and the I. G. Farben trusts dominated their fields. The German monster cartels, in turn, entered into cartel agreements with foreign producers for the division of markets. The Continental Dye Cartel, established in 1929 between the I. G. Farben, French, and Swiss chemical industries allocated 75 per cent of exports to the German producers. Despite its spectacular recovery after the Dawes Plan, Germany, like Britain in the 1920's, continued to suffer from unemployment. Unemployment figures, which stood above two million in the winter of 1925/1926, fell to 1.5 million in the winter of 1927/1928, only to rise again to 2.6 million at the turn of 1928/1929. On July 16, 1927, the Weimar Republic established a *Reich*-institute for unemployment insurance, providing unemployment benefits for a maximum of six months. The funds for unemployment insurance, raised through workers' and employers' contributions, were projected to cover 600,000 unemployed. The unemployment insurance system of 1927, barely adequate for the needs of the late 1920's, was to break down entirely under depression conditions.

The German economic boom concealed serious flaws not readily discernible until the onset of the World Depression. Leading among these were (1) the large-scale use of foreign loans for non-productive purposes, and (2) the payment of German reparations out of foreign loans. German state and municipal governments borrowed heavily abroad to finance urban renewal and recreational facilities, without possessing the means of repaying foreign loans in foreign currency. German reparations, on the other hand, were largely paid from the proceeds of foreign loans rather than the earnings of German exports. With the withdrawal of foreign loans from Germany for economic and political reasons after 1930, the Weimar Republic faced once again a serious dilemma in meeting both its reparations payments and its private foreign debts. The relative prosperity which the Weimar Republic had at last achieved in 1928 proved to be short-lived and only an interval between inflation and Depression.

THE SEARCH FOR DOMESTIC STABILITY,
1924/1930

The return to economic prosperity and foreign policy stability did not lessen the sharp domestic political conflicts of the mid and late 1920's. The Reichstag elections of May, 1924, reflecting the turmoil of 1923, led to a significant weakening of the Social Democrats, the Democrats, and the People's Party, which had shared government responsibility in 1923. By contrast, the Nationalists and Communists increased their strength, the former gaining 95, the latter 62 Reichstag seats.

Chancellor Wilhelm Marx of the Catholic Center, who had followed Stresemann in December, 1923, strove valiantly to forge a new coalition, which, in addition to the parties of the Great Weimar Coalition, was to include the Nationalists. Marx's project of a government of national concentration (*Volksgemeinschaft*) collapsed, since neither the Social Democrats nor the Nationalists were willing to serve as coalition partners in the same government. Hoping to obtain a clearer parliamentary picture, Marx dissolved the "Inflation-Reichstag" of May, 1924, and ordered new elections. The Reichstag elected in December, 1924, enlarged the Nationalist delegation to 103. The Nationalists faced a serious dilemma: should they continue to oppose the hated Weimar Republic or attempt to influence its policy by joining the federal government? In early 1925 the Nationalists opted in favor of the latter and entered, for the first time, a coalition government under Chancellor Hans Luther, the former Minister of Finance. The Nationalists' entry into the government did not result in their permanent reconciliation with the Republic. Dissatisfied with Stresemann's Locarno policy, they withdrew into their role of opposition in late 1925. Nor was Nationalist hostility to the Republic changed by the election of the 78-year-old ex-Field Marshal Paul von Hindenburg as President of the Republic in April, 1925. Friedrich Ebert had died on February 28, 1925. His death was a serious blow to the Republic for none had better represented its spirit or purpose since its founding.

Hindenburg had been elected over the votes of the parties of the Weimar coalition—Social Democrats, Democrats, and Center Party. Wilhelm Marx, the candidate of the Weimar coalition, owed his defeat largely to the wasting of 1.9 million votes on the Communist candidate Ernst Thälmann, who had earned national notoriety during the events of "Red October" in 1923.

As President of the Republic, Hindenburg was pledged by

oath to uphold its Constitution. Neither by upbringing nor personal inclination was Hindenburg destined to become its faithful servant, however, for he regarded it as second best to the monarchy. "The German," Hindenburg had said at the outset of the revolution of 1918, "will always look foolish in a Jacobin hat." Thus, the new President did not lend the moral weight of his office to calm the bitter parliamentary clashes of the late 1920's over such issues as the adoption of a new flag, the disposition of the property of the former German princes, or school and federal reforms, behind which often loomed the larger question of acceptance or repudiation of the Republic.

The flag law of May, 1926, permitting the flying of the old Imperial colors of black, white, and red in German overseas embassies, infuriated the Social Democrats and led to the downfall of Chancellor Luther. On the other hand, the joint sponsorship by the Social Democrats and Communists of a plebiscite for the expropriation of the princes' property outraged Hindenburg. The exposure of the supposedly secret collaboration between the German and Soviet armies by the Social Democrats in January, 1927, likewise enraged the President and led to fresh charges against the Social Democrats as "scoundrels without a fatherland."

The quarrel over school and federal reform added religious and regional divisions to the partisan strife. The Catholic Center demanded publicly supported denominational schools; the Social Democrats and People's Party, both believers in the separation of church and state, opposed them. The parties of the Weimar coalition urged reforms to strengthen the federal government; the Nationalists and the Bavarian People's Party, both supporters of the loose federal system under the Empire, rejected it. The parliamentary deadlock resulting from these issues led to new Reichstag elections in May, 1928, in which the Social Democratic Party scored an impressive victory with 153 seats. Hermann Müller, the first Social Democratic chancellor in eight years, formed a government of the Great Weimar Coalition.

The Social Democratic return to power in 1928, together with Stresemann's successful foreign policy, gave a false impression of Republican stability. "The foundations of the German Republic," Chancellor Müller announced to the newly elected Reichstag, "are sound and unshakable." The Social Democratic Party, for one, seemed stronger in 1928 than at any other time since the beginning of the Republic. Not only did the SPD control the chancellorship and the premiership of Prussia with Hermann Müller and Otto Braun, but it possessed a vast newspaper empire, a party-financed bank, and a trade union movement of nearly 5 million members, which, though not formally affiliated with the SPD, was politically close to it. Moreover, the SPD-sponsored paramilitary group, *Reichsbanner* Black-Red-Gold, organized for the protection of the

Republic, was larger, with three million men, than either Hitler's Storm Troopers or the Communist Red Front Fighters' League.

For all its organizational prowess, however, the Social Democratic Party had failed to change its image from a labor party with Marxist overtones into a broad Republican party with an appeal transcending class. Rather, by its continued lip service to Marxist ideology in the Heidelberg and Kiel programs of 1925 and 1927 respectively, the SPD preserved the contradiction between its words and actions, so harmful to itself and the development of parliamentary traditions in the Empire. Moreover, the party retained its pacifist stance, widely regarded as anti-national in middle-class circles. Not only did the party vote against the construction of a 10,000-ton pocket battleship in the 1928 Reichstag, but the SPD resolution of the Magdeburg Party Conference of 1929 threatened revolutionary action against any German government which went to war in violation of an arbitration decision. The Magdeburg Resolution was reminiscent of the revolutionary threats issued by the Second International before the First World War. As the outbreak of the First World War had unmasked the hollowness of Social Democratic militancy, the rise of Hitler would soon call the Social Democratic bluff in the final years of the Republic.

Because of the barriers which continued to divide German Social Democracy from the rest of German society, Social Democratic strength in 1928 was not identical with Republican stability. This fact, obscured during the remaining months of tranquility, became painfully evident with the advent of a new, sharp economic crisis in 1929. The Depression, eating away at the strength of the middle-class parties, opened the path to political extremism on the Right and Left.

THE END OF PARLIAMENTARY DEMOCRACY; THE FALL OF THE GREAT WEIMAR COALITION

By 1930 the Weimar Republic had had fifteen governments under ten different chancellors over a twelve-year period. Many of the short-lived coalition governments had fallen from power through party whims or over trivial issues. On March 27, 1930, the Great Weimar Coalition under Chancellor Hermann Müller also fell over what appeared to be a trivial issue: the failure of the Social Democrats and the People's Party to agree on an increase in the unemployment insurance contributions of workers and employers, to cover the rising deficit in federal unemployment funds.

The deeper cause of the fall of the last parliamentary government of the Republic was the growing lack of confidence in the parliamentary system, as the economic crisis worsened in the Depression. Although the Depression led to political crises and the adoption of emergency measures even in successful and established democracies, such as Great Britain, in Germany it became the occasion for an all-out attack on the very concept of parliamentary democracy. This attack was strengthened by the resurgence of militant German nationalism, beginning with the Nationalists' campaign against the Young Plan in 1929, and by the emergence of the German army as a key factor in domestic politics in 1930.

The German payments schedule under the Young Plan, running in theory until 1988, easily lent itself to demagogic exploitation by rightist forces, as the German economy was heading towards disaster. Thus, Alfred Hugenberg, the recently elected chairman of the Nationalist Party, together with Hitler and the nationalist veterans' organization *Stahlhelm* (Steel Helmet), organized a Committee for the Plebiscite against the Young Plan. It proposed a law to indict any German government for treason if it took on further reparations obligations. Although the petition for a plebiscite failed to win the required majority, Hugenberg's campaign against the Young Plan succeeded in inflaming nationalist passions even in formerly moderate circles. It also marked the first alliance between the Nationalist Party, Hitler's National Socialists, and the veterans' organization *Stahlhelm,* an alliance which, after reappearing in the "Harzburg Front" of 1931, ultimately destroyed the Republic in January, 1933.

Whereas the former Reichswehr chief Seeckt had established the policy of a "non-political" army after the abortive Kapp-Lüttwitz *putsch* of 1920, General Kurt Von Schleicher was determined to throw the full weight of the army into the political balance of 1930. General Schleicher's official position was Chief of the "Minister's Office" *(Ministeramt),* a section of the defense ministry established for purposes of political coordination with the government. With the army's help, Schleicher wished to abolish the pluralist democracy of Weimar and replace it with a more authoritarian regime along Bismarckian lines. By 1930 such a political program was attractive not only to the Nationalists but to a growing number of leaders of the Center Party and the People's Party as well, who were disillusioned with parliamentary government. Though not formally in charge of the Reichswehr, General Schleicher exerted powerful pressure on German domestic politics after 1930 through his influence over the aged and increasingly senile President Hindenburg. Schleicher became the "field-grey eminence" behind Hindenburg's "throne," who made and unmade chancellors between 1930 and 1932.

The chancellor picked by Schleicher to succeed Hermann Müller was the 46-year-old Center Party leader Heinrich Brüning. Like Schleicher, Brüning, a decorated veteran of the First World War, favored a return to more authoritarian forms of government and even considered the restoration of the monarchy after an interim regency under Hindenburg. With Brüning's appointment to the chancellorship, the "presidential cabinet" became the rule, depending less on the support of a Reichstag majority than on the confidence of Hindenburg—and General Schleicher.

Both in his foreign and domestic policies, Brüning wished to obtain quick results, but it was doubtful whether his personality or tactics were conducive to success in either field.

In domestic politics Brüning projected the image of a pedantic financial expert rather than that of a popular leader who inspired confidence and raised hope. His answer to the Depression was a policy of deflation through wage cutting and strict government austerity. A mild inflationary policy, such as might have absorbed the urban unemployed in public works projects, the Chancellor rejected because of the memory of the disastrous German inflation of 1923. The number of unemployed, which had stood at 2.7 million in April, 1930, increased to 5.7 million shortly before Brüning's fall from office in May, 1932. Brüning's policy was all the more unpopular with the urban working class because it protected the agrarian interests through higher import tariffs. Although Soviet grain sold for 60 marks per ton on the world market, Brüning increased German rye tariffs to 200 marks per ton. Among the unemployed, Brüning came to be known as the "hunger chancellor." Nor did he bother to consult the Reichstag in the formulation of his policies. As in his foreign policy, the Chancellor presented the Reichstag with accomplished facts, leaving it the choice of accepting his policy or risking its dissolution by Presidential decree. When the Reichstag withheld its approval of Brüning's legislative program, the Chancellor dissolved it and ordered new elections for September 14, 1930.

The dissolution of the Reichstag, whose normal legislative term would not have expired until 1932, was a major political blunder, for it opened the doors to extremist mass movements on the left and right. The Communists, strengthened by the vote of the unemployed, increased their representation from 54 to 77 seats. The real shock of the election was the growth of Nazi strength from 12 Reichstag seats to 107. The significance of the Nazi election victory was summed up in the words of Joseph Goebbels, chief Nazi propagandist: "We come as enemies! As the wolf breaks into the sheepfold, so we come. . . ." By rejecting the possibility of compromise with the old Reichstag, in spite of Social Democratic overtures to the Chancellor, Brüning had intensified the German political crisis with dire consequences to himself and the entire Republic.

THE PHENOMENON OF NATIONAL SOCIALISM

After the startling election results of September, 1930, National Socialist strength continued to soar in virtually every national and state election until the Nazi party became the strongest German political

FIGURE 4 *Hitler and followers in the Munich Bürgerbräu, the scene of the 1923 beer-hall putsch.*

party in the Reichstag elections of July, 1932, with 230 seats or slightly more than 37 per cent of the German vote. In the elections to the Prussian state diet of April, 1932, Nazi strength increased from 6 to 162 seats.

The sharp increase in Nazi strength was gained primarily at the expense of the middle-class parties, especially the People's Party, and the Democrats, whose share in the popular vote declined from 25 per cent in 1928 to 5 per cent in 1932. At the same time, Nazi influence in the armed forces had grown, mostly among young officers, as evidenced in the treason trial of Reichswehr officers in September, 1930, for the dissemination of Nazi propaganda.

By contrast the Social Democrats and the Catholic Center remained largely immune to Nazi penetration, the SPD obtaining 133 seats in the elections of July, 1932, the Center increasing its strength to 97.

The Nazi conquest of the middle-class vote was chiefly due to the fact that Nazi slogans and Nazi ideology were particularly well attuned to the fears, prejudices, and hopes of the German middle class after a decade of parliamentary feebleness and national frustration.

THE IDEOLOGY OF NATIONAL SOCIALISM; THE MIDDLE CLASS RESPONSE

Unlike its ideological opponent Marxism, National Socialism was not an intellectual movement; its founders and early propagators, Hitler, Gottfried Feder, the amateur economist, and Dietrich Eckart, the anti-semitic poet-journalist, were not intellectuals. The roots of National Socialism were embedded in Hitler's Austrian background and his experience as a soldier in the German army of the First World War. In *Mein Kampf,* a mixture of autobiography and political manifesto, Hitler faithfully recorded the impact which the Austrian environment of his youth had upon his adult views: the nationality strife of the Dual Monarchy and the pan-German agitation of Georg von Schoenerer, which bred Hitler's contempt for the Slavs; the petty-bourgeois anti-semitism of Vienna, Austria's cosmopolitan capital, exemplified in the Viennese lord mayor Karl Lueger, whom Hitler called the "greatest German mayor of all times"; the parliamentary stagnation of the Austrian Reichsrat, rendered impotent by the quarreling and fighting among the nationalities; the poverty of the Viennese proletariat and its indifference to national questions, ascribed by Hitler to Marxist influence.

To the impressions of a society torn by hatreds of class and nationality was added the experience of personal failure, which left permanent scars on Hitler's embittered character, shaping his vision of the world as a place of ruthless struggle, without charity or compassion. Rejected as a student at the Vienna Academy of Fine Arts because of his incomplete secondary education, Hitler found neither roots nor regular employment in pre-war Vienna. The boarding house of the poor became his social environment, the crude anti-semitic pamphlets of Adolf Lanz his inspiration, the flotsam of the Viennese netherworld his first audience.

The First World War, the catalyst of political upheaval in other parts of Europe, plucked Hitler from an aimless and anonymous existence and launched him on the road to national notoriety. Having moved to Munich before the war, Hitler volunteered for the German army. His comrades remembered him as a withdrawn and somewhat odd companion, who gave a good account of himself as a soldier, however, earning the war-time decoration of the Iron Cross.

The war had lent purpose to Hitler's existence for the first time in his life; the German defeat of 1918, which shattered his nationalist euphoria, sent him scurrying after the internal enemy whom he held responsible for Germany's collapse. The experience of the German revolution of 1918 and of the short-lived Bavarian Soviet Republic of 1919 convinced Hitler that Germany's internal enemy was identical with the forces he had come to hate in his Vienna days: Marxism, the Jews, and parliamentary government. Dietrich Eckart, the anti-semitic journalist with whom Hitler established a close friendship in postwar Munich, related in his *Bolshevism from Moses to Lenin: A Dialogue Between Adolf Hitler and Myself* how Hitler's anti-semitism had hardened into a doctrine that ascribed the fall of empires from Roman times to the 20th century to the influence of a "Jewish conspiracy."

What might have remained the rantings of an unbalanced fanatic took root in the fertile soil of turbulent postwar Bavaria. In Munich Hitler joined, and soon headed, Anton Drexler's German Workers' Party, which he elevated from a back-room club to an effective party through his gifts of oratory and political propaganda.

Renamed the National Socialist German Workers' Party (NSDAP in its German initials), the party adopted a formal program in February, 1920, which, in itself, did not suggest the vehemence or mass appeal of the party in the final years of the Republic. The party program of 1920 demanded the restoration of German power through the breaking of the Treaty of Versailles, the elimination of all Jews from German national life, and the "breaking of the yoke of interest capital." The vague anti-capitalist note suggested in Gottfried Feder's utopian formula was soon forgotten. Those among Hitler's associates who took the socialist label in the party's name too literally, such as Otto Strasser, were driven from the party in the mid-1920's.

Of greater impact than the obscure program of 1920 was Hitler's tireless repetition of the themes of anti-liberalism, anti-westernism, anti-Marxism, and anti-semitism and the promise of national rebirth through the reconciliation of classes and the abolition of parties. The German soldier, Hitler was fond of saying, had not charged into battle with the words "long live universal, secret and equal suffrage" but "Germany above all." It was the Nazi promise to recapture the fleeting moment of national unity of August 4, 1914, remembered with nostalgia in divided Weimar Germany, and the Nazi pledge to recast German society in the image of the military comradeship of the First World War, that endeared Hitler, not only to military men like General Seeckt, but also to an ever growing bourgeois following.

The German bourgeoisie perceived in Hitler's raucous phrases an echo of the more refined, though equally destructive gospel that the German middle class intellectuals Paul de Lagarde, Julius Langbehn, and Moeller van den Bruck had been proclaiming during the half century preceding Hitler. De Lagarde and Langbehn had severely criticized the Hohenzollern Empire for its failure to follow up the political unification of Germany with a reconciliation among its divided classes and for not creating a distinctly Germanic culture. Moeller van den Bruck, writing in the early years of the Weimar Republic, had coined the phrase "Third Reich," soon to be appropriated by the Nazi movement, a Reich that would fulfill Germany's destiny by reconciling all its past divisions, regional, religious, political, and social. Common to all three prophets of a new German nationalism was their bitter anti-westernism, their vehement anti-semitism, often indistinguishable from Hitler's in its language, and their call for a reconciliation between nationalism and socialism. All three had called for a new German "Fuehrer" as the embodiment of German national unity and purpose. Although Moeller van den Bruck never became an active collaborator of Hitler before his death in 1924 — Moeller denounced Hitler's National Socialism as being totally devoid of any intellectual basis — his anti-liberal and totalitarian message helped pave the way for Hitler's acceptance by the German middle class. The Nazis, rather than the Nationalists of Hugenberg with their nostalgia for Wilhelmian society, seemed to answer the call for the conservative revolution, a revolution not against but for greater authority, which Moeller, Langbehn, and de Lagarde had issued. Alfred Rosenberg, Hitler's chief party ideologue, proudly acknowledged the Nazis' ideological debt to de Lagarde and Langbehn.

THE FAILURE OF CONTAINMENT

After the failure of his Munich putsch of 1923, Hitler had vowed never to seek power again by means other than constitutional. The Nazi victory at the polls in September, 1930, though stunning, had given Hitler no more than 18 per cent of the total vote, however, and it was difficult to see how he would realize his aim of capturing the chancellorship by constitutional means. His chance lay in the continued division of the non-Nazi Reichstag majority as well as in the opening which Article 48 of the Weimar Constitution could provide in the hands of an unscrupulous president.

The German left remained divided between Communists and Social Democrats in the final years of Weimar, as it had been in the moment of its birth. A Social Democratic offer of forming a united anti-Nazi front was rejected by the Communists in 1931. Confident that a Hitler dictatorship would form but a brief, final chapter in the collapse of German bourgeois society, the Communists viewed the prospects of a Nazi seizure of power with equanimity. At times they even collaborated with the Nazis in organizing strikes and disrupting Reichstag procedure to hasten the collapse of Weimar democracy. "Brüning's facism," the KPD organ *Rote Fahne* intoned, "is not better than Hitlerite fascism by a hair's breadth. We strike the main blow against the SPD."

The conservative coalition of Schleicher, Brüning, and Hindenburg, formed prior to the Nazi election success of 1930, likewise crumbled over General Schleicher's disagreement with the chancellor on how to deal with the Nazi movement. Both Brüning and the Reichswehr minister General Gröner were confident that the Nazi flood could be contained if the government remained firm. Gröner, who had supported the Provisional Government against all Communist attacks during the revolution of 1918/1919, was determined to uphold Brüning against similar attacks of the Nazis after 1930. To Gröner the Nazis seemed infinitely more dangerous, however, because, unlike the Communists, they had made significant headway among the officers of the Reichswehr. Not only had the former Reichswehr chief Seeckt swung over to Hitler's side, but the Crown Prince openly supported Hitler in the presidential elections of April, 1932.

The Brüning-Gröner policy of Nazi containment might have succeeded if given the continued support of Hindenburg. The Reichstag had resigned itself to the passive role of endorsing the chancellor's emergency decrees, and Gröner issued a ban on Hitler's paramilitary formations, the SA and SS. General Schleicher, on the other hand, wished to achieve his goal of authoritarian revolution not against but with the support of the Nazi movement. Like the Bavarian Conservatives of 1923, Schleicher wished to use Hitler as the "drummer" of the conservative revolution without, however, conceding supreme power to him.

The Hugenberg-Hitler alliance of 1929 against the Young Plan suggested the Nationalist-Nazi front that Schleicher hoped to achieve. The so-called "Harzburg Front" of October, 1931, between Nationalists, Nazis, and the *Stahlhelm* seemed a further step in the same direction. In either alliance Hitler had been careful, however, to retain his independence, and it was the Nazi tail that wagged the Nationalist dog, rather than the opposite.

To Schleicher, Brüning's anti-Nazi policy threatened to disrupt the precarious Nationalist-Nazi alliance. By relying on the tacit support of the Social Democrats in the Reichstag, Brüning had, in Schleicher's eyes, moved too far to the left. The presidential elections of March and April, 1932, revealed the split among the right-wing parties. In the first contest of March, 1932, in which none of the candidates obtained a plurality, the Nationalists and Nazis ran separate candidates in Duesterberg (the deputy *Stahlhelm* leader) and Hitler, against Hindenburg. In the run-off elections of April, 1932, Hindenburg was re-elected with the support of the parties of the Weimar coalition. Far from appreciating Brüning's efforts on behalf of his re-election, Hindenburg blamed the Chancellor for having alienated his conservative friends, who had helped elect him in 1925 but had turned against him in 1932. The whisper in the President's entourage that Brüning was an "agrarian Bolshevik," because of his modest land reform program, provided the final push for Brüning's curt dismissal on May 30, 1932.

The man whom Schleicher had groomed for the succession was Franz von Papen, a wealthy, conservative Center Party politician of little national renown. The new Papen government, soon dubbed the "baron's cabinet," included, next to Schleicher as Reichswehr minister, six aristocrats and one director of the I. G. Farben trust as minister of economics. Papen's opening statement that the former Weimar governments had weakened the moral fiber of the nation by turning the Republic into a welfare state was provocative to nearly six million German unemployed. Nor was the winning of labor support Papen's political purpose. From the beginning he strove towards an accommodation with the Nazis. As a down payment for Nazi support, Papen fulfilled three Nazi demands: (1) the lifting of Brüning's ban on the SA and SS, (2) the ouster of the Prussian state government under the SPD premier Braun, and (3) the holding of new Reichstag elections.

Each of these steps represented a further blow against the tottering structure of Weimar democracy. The lifting of the ban on the SA unleashed Hitler's storm troopers once more, creating conditions of near civil war, especially in Prussia. On the pretext that the Prussian state government under SPD premier Otto Braun was unable to maintain law and order, Papen removed it on July 20 under threat of armed force and installed himself as federal commissioner. The Social Democratic leadership, which had boasted of its militancy in the Magdeburg Resolution of 1929, surrendered meekly to Papen's Prussian *coup d'etat* when faced with the alternative of civil war. The same party which had defeated the militarist putsch of Kapp and Lüttwitz in 1920 through a general strike had cause to doubt the wisdom of armed resistance in 1932, however, when the Reichswehr had openly shifted to the anti-republican forces. The Reichstag election of July 31, 1932, gave Hitler the opportunity of scoring another national election victory, making his party the largest in the Reichstag with 230 seats.

Far from accepting the subordinate role of vice chancellor, which Papen was prepared to offer, Hitler now demanded the chancellorship. President Hindenburg, who felt a strong personal aversion towards the "Austrian corporal" Hitler, denied it. Having failed to achieve a Nazi-Nationalist coalition, Papen, like Brüning before him, had lost his usefulness in Schleicher's view. Unlike Brüning, Papen refused to step down from the chancellorship, however, nor could he be removed as easily as Brüning, for Papen had replaced General Schleicher in the favor of the senile President. After August, 1932, the political fate of Germany was decided increasingly by the personal rivalry and power-struggle between Papen and Schleicher, who, scheming and intriguing against one another, performed a frivolous dance of death upon the ruins of republican Germany.

Papen's answer to the deadlock was the dissolution of the newly elected Reichstag, in which the Nazis had obtained 230 seats, before it could express its lack of confidence in the Chancellor. By ordering new Reichstag elections for November, 1932, Papen hoped to exploit the disillusionment which had gripped Nazi voters over Hitler's inability to secure the chancellorship. Although the Nazi vote dropped to 196 seats, the Reichstag of November 6, 1932, was no more manageable than that of July, for Communist strength had risen to 100. In a Reichstag of 584 deputies, Papen could count only on the support of the 52 Nationalist deputies. As a last resort, he suggested to the President a military *coup d'état* and the adoption of an authoritarian constitution.

Papen's project of a military dictatorship was vetoed by Schleicher on the grounds that it would provoke both a Nazi and Communist insurrection, which the armed forces were not prepared to control. Moreover, Schleicher warned, a German civil war might tempt Poland into an external attack on East Prussia. Reluctantly, Hindenburg parted company with Papen and entrusted Schleicher with the chancellorship on December 2, 1932.

Consistent with his past practice of intrigue, General Schleicher hoped to win majority support for his government by splitting the mass parties of the left and right from within and alienating the rank and file from their uncompromising leadership. On the right, Schleicher appealed to those Nazis who feared that Hitler's all-or-nothing stand would ruin the party, a trend indicated by the drop in Nazi strength from 230 to 196 seats. Gregor Strasser, the brother of Otto Strasser, accepted Schleicher's promise of the vice chancellorship. Hitler faced a serious challenge from within his party that threatened to break it apart. For the benefit of the left, Schleicher assumed the role of the "social general," hoping to woo the trade unions with generous promises of social reform and a new land settlement program for poor peasants. All the while, Schleicher hoped to cut across established party lines by appealing directly to the public in "fireside chats" over the radio.

Schleicher's brief excursion into the limelight of open politics ended in quick disaster. Hitler crushed the Strasser rebellion in his own party in December, 1932, before it could spread to the rank and file. The Social Democrats, mindful of the army's role in the Prussian *coup d'état* of July, 1932, distrusted Schleicher and denied him their support. The Junker lobby, small in numbers but influential with the President, himself the owner of an East Elbian estate purchased out of public donations, was up in arms over the prospect of land reform.

As Schleicher surveyed the wreckage of his policy, Papen, eager to take revenge against the General, was preparing Hitler's appointment to the chancellorship. In early January, 1933, Papen proposed to Hitler the renewal of the Harzburg front of 1931 with the altered condition, however, of recognizing Hitler's leadership over the Nationalist-Nazi alliance. For himself Papen proposed the vice-chancellorship. Papen regarded his own special relationship of personal confidence with Hindenburg as a sufficient safeguard against a full-blown Nazi dictatorship, especially since the Nationalists were to outnumber the Nazis in the proposed Hitler cabinet. So confident was Papen of his ability to control Hitler that he predicted privately that he would have him "squeaking in a corner" within two months of his appointment to the chancellorship.

Papen's plan enjoyed the support of powerful German industrialists, many of whom had been won over by Hitler after the latter's appearance before the Rhine-Ruhr Club of German industry in January, 1932. In a speech which lasted several hours, Hitler had skillfully appealed to the fears and ambitions of his audience, calling the Nazi party the last German bulwark against Marxism and equating the leadership principle in politics with the Social-Darwinist notion of "survival of the fittest." Impatient with the Papen-Schleicher feud, the industrialists had petitioned Hindenburg as early as November, 1932, to appoint Hitler to the chancellorship. Hindenburg would have preferred the reappointment of Papen to the chancellorship after Schleicher's failure, asserting as late as January 26, 1933, that he had no intention of making "that Austrian corporal either Minister of Defense or Chancellor." In the end, both Schleicher and Papen, ironically, urged the President to appoint Hitler to the chancellorship, Schleicher's preference for Hitler being motivated by his hatred for Papen and the fear that a new Papen government would face an overwhelming opposition inside and outside the Reichstag. On January 30, 1933, Hitler was sworn in as the nineteenth and last chancellor of the Weimar Republic. To many of Hitler's supporters, his triumph seemed to promise a new beginning in German political life. Soon the Hitler dictatorship was to reveal itself as the beginning of something altogether new, such as had not been experienced before in modern German history.

THE REPUBLIC OF AUSTRIA

The Republic of German-Austria, renamed "Republic of Austria" under the Peace of St. Germain in 1919, began its existence seemingly without national purpose or prospect of economic survival. Since Austria attained nationhood by default rather than design, most of the German-speaking population of Austria, numbering some 6.5 million, desired union with the German republic. The wish for union, expressed in the unanimous vote of Austria's first parliament on November 12, 1918, was vetoed by both the treaties of St. Germain and Versailles, as previously noted. The impression of an artificial state, created mainly by the will of the victors, rather than the desire of the people of Austria, continued to stifle the development of Austrian nationhood, at least until Hitler came to power in 1933.

The economic prospects of republican Austria were grim, considerations of economic viability having been largely absent when Austria's frontiers were drawn in the peace settlement of 1919. Although possessing considerable natural resources in timber, water power, iron ore, oil, and natural gas, much of Austria's natural wealth remained underdeveloped until the latter 1930's or, in the case of oil and gas, was not discovered in its full extent until the Second World War and after. Foreign capital, first Italian, later German, remained in control of Austria's iron ore, while water power was not developed on a large scale until 1937. The most immediate economic problem was that of assuring an adequate food supply, especially for the capital city of Vienna, cut off from its traditional markets and sources of supply by the new frontiers. Conditions of near-starvation persisted until 1921 and self-sufficiency in food up to 81 per cent was not attained until 1937. Vienna, the financial and administrative center of the former Austrian half of the Dual-Monarchy of 28.5 million inhabitants, was altogether too large a city for a nation of 6.5 million, nearly one third of whom resided in the Austrian capital. Unable to provide for its overgrown staff of civil servants or to feed its restless proletariat, Vienna threatened to become a mere fossil of its once great imperial past. Austria's currency was ruined by war and postwar inflation, the Austrian crown dropping to one fifteen-thousandth of its pre-war value by 1922. The World Depression destroyed much of what little economic progress had been achieved in the 1920's. Austrian unemployment remained exceptionally high, the unemployment figure being 480,000 for 1933 and still 398,000 for 1937. Added to these were an additional 300,000 unemployed who had exhausted benefits. Rather surprisingly, the level of Austrian scientific and cultural achievement remained high under the Republic, as evidenced by the large number of Austrian Nobel Prize recipients in the 1920's and 1930's, such as Wagner-Jauregg, Karl Landsteiner, and Otto Löwi in medicine, Franz Victor Hess in physics, and Fritz Pregl in chemistry.

The political and social fabric of republican Austria, reflecting the conditions of persistent national poverty between the two world wars, was ill-suited to liberal democracy. Unlike most of the other successor states of Austria-Hungary, Austria was fortunate in not having a serious land problem; small and medium-size farms prevailed over large estates. In Austria, the social and political battle lines were drawn, rather, between the predominantly Socialist urban proletariat, on the one side, and the conservative Catholic bourgeoisie and class of peasant proprietors, on the other. The latter two were chiefly represented by the Christian Social party, which remained strongly monarchist and which retained some of the anti-semitic prejudices of its founder Karl Lueger. Cooperation between the Austrian Socialists and the Christian Social party proved far more difficult than between the related German Social Democrats and the Catholic Center party in the Weimar Republic, because of the more doctrinaire and inflexible positions of both antagonists in Austria. The German Nationalists or Pan-Germans constituted the third major Austrian political party. Of middle-class background like the members of the Christian Social party, the German Nationalists included more Protestants and continued to clamor for union with Germany when that objective had ceased to be popular with Austrian Socialists and the Christian Social party after Hitler came to power in Germany. The Austrian Communists, though vociferous and active in the spring of 1919 during the Communist disturbances in neighboring Hungary and Bavaria, never elected a single deputy to the Austrian parliament in the First Republic.

The elections to the Austrian constituent assembly of February 16, 1919, returned the two leading political parties, Socialists and the Christian Social party, in almost equal strength, with 72 and 69 seats respectively, whereas the Pan-Germans obtained 26. Despite their mutual distrust, Socialists and the Christian Social party formed a coalition government under the Socialist Chancellor Karl Renner, largely because of common concern over Austria's economic and foreign political problems.

The constitution, adopted on October 1, 1920, organized Austria as a federal republic with a weak executive and a bicameral legislature, chosen on the basis of proportional representation. In 1929 the constitution was amended to strengthen the executive, the president being elected by popular vote rather than by both houses of the legislature.

The year 1920 also marked the end of the precarious coalition of Socialists and the Christian Social party with the latter emerging as the strongest party in the elections of October, 1920. Henceforth, the Socialists were excluded from national power; the governments of Austria between 1920 and 1934 were formed by the Christian Social party either alone or in coalition with the German Nationalists. The capital of Vienna, whose municipal government the Socialists controlled, remained, however, a bastion of Socialist strength until the Civil War of February, 1934. In Vienna the Socialists launched an extensive public housing program, building 64,000 apartment units between 1923 and 1934, chiefly for the benefit of Socialist party members and their families. The cost of Socialist housing, such as the "Karl Marx" complex, was covered by a steep municipal tax on private home ownership.

The most forceful political personality to emerge from the Christian Social party in the 1920's was Monsignor Ignaz Seipel, professor of Catholic theology and Chancellor of Austria from 1922 to 1924 and again from 1926 to 1929. Dubbed the "Austrian Richelieu," Seipel was somewhat of an anachronism in the political climate of the 1920's, being the only clergyman in Europe to head a government. In 1922 Seipel stabilized the currency with the aid of foreign loans under the Geneva Protocols of October 4, 1922. This agreement, concluded between Great Britain, France, Italy, and Czechoslovakia on the one hand and Austria on the other, conditioned foreign loans on Austria's pledge not to seek political union with Germany for twenty years. The schilling became Austria's new currency, at a rate of 1:10,000 in relation to the old Austrian crown. Until 1926 Austrian finances remained under League supervision.

Though instrumental in achieving financial stability for the Republic, Seipel failed to accomplish similar results in the political field. During the Seipel era the conflict between the Socialists and the Christian Social party worsened, in part because of the stepped-up activities of the armed leagues, whose total strength exceeded the size of the regular Austrian army of 30,000 men. The Socialists had formed a paramilitary organization in 1924 with the *Republikanischer Schutzbund* (league for the protection of the republic), which was matched on the right by the *Heimwehren* (home guards). Under their leaders Starhemberg, Fey, Pfrimer, and Steidle the *Heimwehren* became increasingly Fascist-oriented. In the so-called Korneuburg Oath of May 18, 1930, the *Heimwehren* openly endorsed the principles of Fascism while rejecting "democracy and the parliamentary system." The *Heimwehren* maintained close contact with Austrian industrialists and frequently intervened on the latter's behalf in labor disputes by force of arms. Seipel's own attitude towards the parliamentary system was at best equivocal, especially after the first armed conflict between the government and the Socialist opposition in 1927.

On July 15, 1927, a Socialist mob burned down the Ministry of Justice in Vienna, following a clash between the *Schutzbund* and the rightist leagues, in which several Socialists were killed. Seipel called out the army, the police, and the irregular *Heimwehren* to crush the Socialist riots of July 15, 1927, and the Socialist-led general strike which followed. The events of July, 1927, dealt Austrian democracy a blow from which it failed to recover and which set the stage for the Civil War in 1934.

THE DOLLFUSS DICTATORSHIP

Events in Germany and the economic crisis following the collapse of the Austrian *Creditanstalt* in 1931 hastened the end of Austrian parliamentary democracy. In March, 1933, Engelbert Dollfuss, the Christian Social Chancellor, dissolved the deadlocked Austrian parliament and instituted a thinly disguised dictatorship based on the dubious legal grounds of a war-time emergency decree of 1917. On May 1, 1934, Dollfuss issued a new constitution, patterned after the Italian Fascist model.

The "May constitution" supposedly established an Austrian corporate state although few of the projected corporations were, in fact, ever created. Meanwhile, the Socialist opposition had been eliminated through a series of measures which began with the outlawing of the *Schutzbund* in March, 1933, and culminated in the Civil War of February, 1934. Fighting between government forces and Socialists began on February 12, 1934, spreading from the Upper Austrian capital of Linz to Vienna and throughout the provinces. The struggle was particularly severe in Vienna, where government troops opened fire with artillery against the municipal workers' flats at close range and with devastating results. The Socialist party was outlawed, only a few of its leaders escaping to safety in Czechoslovakia.

The forceful suppression of Austrian Socialism in 1934 seemed particularly ill-advised from the standpoint of the Austrian government, as it coincided with the rapid growth of Austrian Nazi strength at home and rising German pressure from without. Together, Socialists and the Christian Social party, commanding about 80 per cent of the total vote, could have formed an effective front against internal and external Nazi threats. Moderate Socialist leaders, such as ex-Chancellor Renner, had approached Dollfuss before February, 1934, in an attempt to unite the anti-Nazi majority. However, Renner's proposal to recognize the special powers of the Dollfuss government for a five-year period on condition that the parliament be reopened was rejected by Dollfuss. In pushing Austria towards Civil War in 1934, Dollfuss followed not only the dictates of his Fascist *Heimwehr* allies at home but the wishes of his powerful foreign protector Mussolini as well. At the Riccione meeting of August 18/19, 1933, between Dollfuss and Mussolini, the Austrian Chancellor had committed himself to the corporate reorganization of Austria and the crushing of the Austrian Socialists. The Rome Protocols, signed with Mussolini on March 17, 1934, after the Austrian Socialists had been crushed, tied the Austria of Dollfuss even closer to Fascist Italy through economic and political agreements.

On July 25, 1934, Dollfuss himself fell victim to the bullets of Austrian Nazi assassins, an event that will be discussed more fully in the context of foreign policy. In July, 1934, Mussolini's intervention saved Austrian independence but the value of Italian protection declined in proportion to the growing Italian-German rapprochement after 1935. The attempt of Chancellor Kurt Schuschnigg, Dollfuss' sucessor, to strengthen Austria's position through a Habsburg restoration in 1936 had to be abandoned in the face of strong opposition by Austria's neighbors, Czechoslovakia and Yugoslavia. The German military occupation of Austria on March 13, 1938, proceeded with ease, as Hitler reaped the benefits of Austria's internal divisions and the division of Europe at large at the height of appeasement.

13 | Nationalism, Democracy and Dictatorship in the Small States of Eastern Europe

In the broad, ethnically mixed region of Eastern Europe between the Baltic and the Aegean Sea, altogether eleven states emerged after 1918, newly independent or with their frontiers changed by the peace settlement after the First World War. In addition to the Austrian republic, the mosaic of the East European nation states comprised Poland, Czechoslovakia, Hungary, the Baltic states of Estonia, Latvia, and Lithuania, and the Balkan nations of Yugoslavia, Rumania, Bulgaria, Albania, and Greece.

The task of nation-building in Eastern Europe between the two world wars was made difficult enough by the overlapping of nationalities. It was rendered more difficult still by the poverty, backwardness, and wartime devastation characteristic of much of Eastern Europe. Poland, Rumania, and Serbia had suffered extensive damage during the First World War, and the Baltic area had been fought over not only during the First World War but during the Russian Civil War as well.

With the exception of Czechoslovakia, whose special political and economic conditions will be described presently, the East European nations were predominantly rural, their social and economic structures frequently pre-industrial and feudal. With the exception of Poland and Hungary, the East European states carried out extensive land reforms soon after their national revolutions had been completed in 1919. Although politically necessary and socially desirable in the interest of stable conditions, the change-over from large-scale farming to small and medium-size farms often lowered the agricultural yield, which remained, on the average, far below that of Western Europe. The new peasant proprietors were too poor to afford modern machinery or chemical fertilizer, agricultural methods remained primitive, and the use of the wooden plough was still widespread. With the Depression, many peasants sold out their newly acquired plots to former landlords. Nor did the farm economies of Eastern Europe develop a successful cooperative movement, which made small-scale farming efficient and successful in the Scandinavian countries. The Baltic states alone, possessing a cooperative tradition which preceded the

351

First World War, succeeded in imitating the Danish example with the development of a highly successful dairy economy.

The land reform programs likewise failed to solve the problem of rural overpopulation, the birth rate of Eastern Europe being among the highest in postwar Europe; the average number of yearly births in Poland alone was 450,000 between the two world wars. After the United States had closed its doors to unlimited European immigration, France alone continued to absorb a number of Eastern, particularly Polish, immigrants. The industrialization of Eastern Europe, on the other hand, failed to reach a level prior to the Second World War where it could readily accommodate the surplus rural population.

Educational facilities remained poor in many of the Eastern European states, especially the Balkans: Yugoslavia's illiteracy rate was over 50 per cent, Greece's 25 per cent, and Albania's 85 per cent. Industrially and culturally advanced Czechoslovakia was again the exception, as were the Baltic states. With 30 out of every 1,000 inhabitants university-trained, Latvia was among the best educated nations of Europe.

The refugee problem represented both a severe economic strain and a political danger to some of the East European states, notably Greece, Bulgaria, and Hungary. Greece, as noted previously in the discussion of the Greek-Turkish war of 1920/1922, ultimately absorbed 1.2 million refugees from Turkey, a figure nearly equal to a quarter of the total Greek population. Bulgaria was flooded with some 200,000 refugees from the provinces acquired by Yugoslavia, Greece, and Rumania in the peace settlement. Hungarian civil servants and members of the professional classes likewise returned to Hungary in large numbers after 1918 from adjacent Slovakia, Croatia, and Transylvania, victims of discrimination or outright persecution. Both in Bulgaria and Hungary the refugees provided a fertile recruiting ground for nationalist and extremist organizations, of which the Bulgarian I.M.R.O. was to become the most notorious.

Despite the crying need for economic and social development, the underdeveloped nations of Eastern Europe devoted a disproportionally large share of their revenue to the maintenance of expensive military establishments, both for reasons of national security and as a badge of newly gained independence. The military budget of Rumania for 1932, for example, represented no less than 75 per cent of the total budget. The purchase of foreign armaments, added to foreign loans for currency stabilization and refugee settlement, thus increased the foreign indebtedness of the underdeveloped Eastern states to the point where interest payments alone constituted a crushing burden on their national economies. By the early 1930's interest payments on foreign debts thus equalled nearly half the value of the total exports of Greece and Hungary, nearly a third of those of Yugoslavia and Rumania, and a quarter of those of Poland. The foreign debt problem of Eastern Europe did not become critical as long as the price of agricultural exports remained high and as long as foreign loan capital remained available. The drop in world agricultural prices and the drying up of loan capital during the World Depression plunged Eastern Europe into default and utter poverty.

Upon completion of their respective national revolutions, virtually all East European states, with the possible exception of Hungary, adopted parliamentary forms of government, with France providing the chief constitutional model. The democratic experiment broke down by the latter 1920's and early 1930's, as a result of political inexperience, the strife of nationalities, and the failure of the agrarian economies. With the exception of Czechoslovakia, all East European states from the Baltic to the Aegean abandoned representative government in favor of dictatorship, both open and disguised.

THE BALTIC STATES: ESTONIA, LATVIA, AND LITHUANIA

All three Baltic states adopted ultra-liberal constitutions, beginning with Estonia in 1920, Latvia and Lithuania following suit in 1922. The three Baltic states likewise enacted land reforms, which chiefly affected the German "Baltic barons," such as the Stackelbergs and Ungern-Sternbergs, whose estates covered over half the territories of Estonia and Latvia. In Lithuania, land reform was mainly carried out at the expense of Polish landlords and estates owned by the Russian Orthodox Church. The Baltic land reforms created a new class of small peasant proprietors, whose Agrarian and Peasant parties dominated the political scene after 1918. The influence of the Socialist parties, strong at the beginning of Baltic independence, declined, as did that of the Communists, owing to the proximity of Soviet Russia and the memories of the Bolshevik terror of 1919. Among the Baltic states, Estonia alone experienced a Communist uprising in 1924, which was quickly crushed.

The parliamentary governments which the Baltic states had modelled after the examples of France, Switzerland, and the Weimar Republic, soon resulted in political paralysis and deadlock, the reasons being both external and internal. The establishment of a disguised military dictatorship under Marshal Josef Pilsudski in neighboring Poland in 1926, of which more will be said presently, exerted a powerful influence on Lithuanian politics. The system of proportional representation produced an excessive number of political parties—fourteen in Estonia, twenty-five in Latvia—as well as a frequent overthrow of governments by negative parliamentary majorities. Between 1920 and 1934 Estonia had eighteen governments, Latvia sixteen.

Lithuania was the first to establish a dictatorship after a *coup d'état* of Voldemaras and Smetona, the leaders of the Lithuanian Nationalist party, on December 16, 1926. Following the suppression of the Lithuanian parliament *(Seimas)*, Voldemaras proclaimed a constitution in 1928, while organizing a semi-Fascist militia out of various nationalist societies, such as the "Iron Wolfs" and the "Sharp Shooters." In 1938 Lithuania returned to more democratic forms, following the adoption of a new constitution under the regime of President Smetona.

In Latvia, where the early 1930's had witnessed the growth of various Fascist organizations, such as the National Socialist party and the Pehr Konkrusts Society, Ulmanis established a dictatorship on May 15, 1934. After the dissolution of the Latvian parliament *(Saeima)*, Ulmanis reorganized the political and economic life of Latvia along Fascist-corporate lines and adopted the title "leader" (Vadonis). Until February, 1938, Latvia was ruled by martial law.

Estonia moved towards a presidential dictatorship in January, 1934, under Paets, whose "Patriotic Front" replaced all other parties in the Estonian parliament *(Riigikogu)*. Although the Paets dictatorship too adopted corporate ideas, its chief purpose had been the prevention of a take-over by the semi-Fascist Estonian "Freedom Fighters" (VAPS) in 1934.

Despite their disappointing political record, the Baltic states developed prosperous economies. The Baltic farm economies, which had been oriented towards the Russian market before 1914, found new outlets for their dairy products in Britain, Germany, and the United States. Latvia and Estonia were in the process of developing their water-power resources with Swedish help when the Soviet annexation of 1940 put an end to national independence. All Baltic states were highly successful in the establishment of an excellent school system, which, despite its late start after the First World War, ranked among Europe's finest. The treatment of national minorities in Estonia, mostly German and Russian, was exemplary, less so in Lithuania and Latvia, where discrimination against Russians, Poles, Jews, and Germans persisted.

The Baltic states vainly attempted to stay out of Great Power conflict, as will be shown in the discussion of the Second World War. As late as October, 1939, the Soviet Foreign Minister Molotov dismissed the charge of impending Soviet annexation of the Baltic states as "foolish prattle" and the talk of "anti-Soviet provocateurs." By June, 1940, all Baltic states were invaded by Soviet troops, and by August, 1940, fully absorbed in the Soviet Union. The political leaders of the Baltic states, Ulmanis, Voldemaras, and Paets, vanished into the interior of Russia, as did some 150,000 of their fellow citizens between 1940 and 1941. How many more Lithuanians, Letts, and Estonians shared their fate after the Soviet reconquest of the Baltic states in 1944 must remain a matter of conjecture.

POLAND

On the surface, the new Poland which emerged from the First World War was an impressive nation with a population of twenty-seven million and an area larger than that of Italy. From the beginning, however, Poland was plagued with national tension and economic difficulties, to which was added the partisan strife in Poland's parliament, the *Sejm*. Fewer than eighteen million of Poland's inhabitants were of Polish nationality, the remainder consisting of nearly four million Ukrainians, two million Jews, one million White Russians, one million Germans, and a quarter million Czechs and Lithuanians. Although its economy was predominantly rural, Poland possessed valuable industrial and mining assets centered around Warsaw and Polish Upper Silesia. Its industries, having been geared to the German, Austrian, and Russian markets, lacked rail communications and cohesion, however. Inflation and industrial unemployment remained a serious problem until the currency stabilization of 1925 and the issuing of a new Polish currency, the *zloty*. Although the need for land reform was recognized by the *Sejm* in principle as early as February, 1919, the actual implementation of land reform was delayed until 1925. Even afterwards, large estates, such as those of the Radziwills and Potockis, continued to survive, with feudal conditions remaining largely intact in Eastern Poland.

The Polish constitution of March 17, 1921, created a parliamentary regime with a weak executive, the powers of the president being ceremonial rather than political. The large number of political parties, fifteen as of 1921, of which the Peasant party, the Nationalists, the National Democrats, and the Socialists were the most important, contributed to instability and frequent changes of government. Poland's democratic experiment ended on May 12, 1926, with the military *coup d'état* of Marshal Pilsudski in Warsaw. Pilsudski had served as Poland's first head of state from 1918 to 1922, but had subsequently withdrawn from public life, largely because of his disapproval of the ultra-liberal constitution of 1921. Having watched the parliamentary paralysis between 1922 and 1926 from his estate at Sulejowek, Pilsudski established a military dictatorship after the forced resignation of Prime Minister Witos and President Wojciechowski in May, 1926.

Although the military dictatorship retained the outward forms of the Polish constitution between 1926 and 1935, Pilsudski, in effect, ruled Poland until his death on May 12, 1935. In addition to being Inspector General of the Polish armed forces, he held the prime ministership between 1926 and 1928. Poland's new president Ignatius Moscicki was Pilsudski's personal choice and friend. The new Polish constitution of 1935, adopted shortly before Pilsudski's death, severely restricted the

FIGURE 5 *Marshal Joseph Pilsudski.*

suffrage while concentrating power in the hands of the President and of the Supreme Commander of the armed forces.

On the economic side, the Pilsudski dictatorship could claim a number of achievements. The *zloty* finally became stable, industry recovered, and Polish coal exports, especially to Scandinavia, increased. The national minorities continued to give trouble, the "Ukrainian Liberation Organization" (UWO) staging a rebellion in Eastern Poland in 1930, which was ruthlessly suppressed. The German minority, as stated elsewhere, had found a new spokesman before the League in German Foreign Minister Stresemann. In 1934 Poland repudiated the Minorities Treaty of 1919. Pilsudski eased somewhat the plight of Poland's Jews, repealing the anti-semitic legislation of tsarist Russia in 1931, which up to that point was still applied in Poland.

Pilsudski's dictatorship survived the death of its author until the destruction of Poland in September, 1939. Marshal Rydz-Smigly, Pilsudski's successor, governed Poland through the Polish National Movement (O.Z.N.), known popularly as the "Colonels' party." Moscicki, Pilsudski's puppet, remained President. The election victory of the O.Z.N. in Poland's last election before the Second World War in November, 1938, by no means reflected its real strength nor the mood of the country. The "government of the colonels" had done little to relieve the economic plight of town and country under the Depression. What saved Poland from domestic upheaval in the latter 1930's was the tense international situation, rather than popular support for the Pilsudski system.

CZECHOSLOVAKIA

Economically, the Czechoslovak Republic was the most viable of the new states of Eastern Europe, its territory having been the center of much of the industry of the old Austro-Hungarian Empire. In Bohemia and southern Slovakia, the Czechoslovak Republic possessed ample and rich farm land. Leading among Czechoslovak industries were textile and glass works, the great armaments factory of Skoda, and the paper industry of Slovakia. The thrift and devotion to work among Czechs had been proverbial in the Austro-Hungarian Empire. Czechoslovakia likewise enjoyed an advanced system of social legislation, some of it inherited from Austria-Hungary, some newly adopted after the First World War.

As against its economic and social blessings, Czechoslovakia was burdened with nationality strife throughout its existence between the two world wars, being the least homogeneous state nationally among the Eastern European states. Out of a total population of 13.4 million, only 8.75 million were counted as Czech and Slovak, the balance consisting of a German minority of over three million, a Hungarian minority of over one million, and a Ukrainian (Ruthene) minority of nearly half a million. The minority problem might have been less severe had Czechs and Slovaks formed a harmonious majority. This, as has been shown elsewhere, was not the case; the economically and culturally more advanced Czechs, numbering some 6.8 million, claimed a leadership role over the predominantly rural and more backward Slovaks.

Czech political predominance in the new republic manifested itself from the outset in the Constituent National Assembly, which was in session from 1918 to 1920. In addition to producing a constitution on February 1, 1920, the Assembly enacted social legislation and a land reform program that affected chiefly the estates of the Hungarian and German minorities. The national minorities were not represented in the Constituent Assembly and thus played no part in shaping Czechoslovakia's institutions.

The Czechoslovak constitution was both democratic and strongly centralist. The constitution abolished the old historic divisions and created, instead, twenty-six districts with very limited local autonomy. Largely in response to minority pressure, the constitution was decentralized in 1927, the old historic "lands" of Bohemia, Moravia, Slovakia, and Ruthenia being restored as administrative units, each with a provincial diet and governor. The 1920 constitution declared "Czechoslovak" as the official language but allowed national minorities the use of their languages in courts and schools in areas where national minorities constituted at least 20 per cent of the population. Ruthenia was promised a special statute of autonomy, which was, in fact, never granted.

The governments of Czechoslovakia were, for the most part, coalitions of the five leading Czech political parties, of which the Agrarians and Social Democrats were the most important. The Sudeten-Germans were not represented in the national government until 1926. The attitude of the Slovaks towards the Czechoslovak Republic changed from indifference to hostility with the growing Czech influence over the civil service and the school system of Slovakia. Slovak opposition found expression in Father Hlinka's "Slovak People's Party," which became the largest of all Slovak political parties and which received support and encouragement from neighboring Hungary and Poland.

The widespread hostility of the national minorities towards the Czechoslovak Republic notwithstanding, there were hopeful signs by the late 1920's that the minorities might be reconciled and integrated into the state. The Sudeten-German entry into the government in 1926, as well as the decentralization of the constitution in 1927, suggested a trend towards peaceful co-existence, and Czechoslovakia might yet have attained her announced goal of becoming an "eastern Switzerland." Such hopes were destroyed by the mid-1930's, owing to the militant nationalism of the Sudeten-German party of Conrad Henlein, whose rise and destructive influence over the Republic will be discussed more fully in the context of the Munich crisis of September, 1938. Henlein's attacks acted as the signal for the other minorities to increase their opposition and join in the eventual dismemberment of Czechoslovakia between September, 1938, and March, 1939.

HUNGARY

The promise of democratic government, never strong in the Hungary of the Habsburgs before 1918, suffered a severe setback in postwar Hungary as a result of the brief Communist dictatorship under Bela Kun in 1919. The Communist reign of terror, which lasted until Kun's departure from Hungary on August 1, 1919, discredited not only socialism but, in the minds of the Hungarian bourgeoisie and land-owning class, the cause of liberal government as well.

In reaction to Kun's dictatorship, a Hungarian "national government" under army captain Gyula Gömbös and Admiral Horthy, the last commander of the Austro-Hungarian navy, had installed itself at Szeged on the Yugoslav border as early as May, 1919. At Szeged was born what came to be known as the "Szeged idea," which connoted anti-Communism, anti-semitism, anti-liberalism, militant nationalism, and the resolve to regain the provinces lost in the peace settlement. Implicit in the "Szeged idea" was the origin of Hungarian Fascism, of which Gömbös himself was to become a leading exponent in the 1930's.

In 1920 the newly elected Hungarian parliament gave post-Communist Hungary its final constitutional form. Although the powers of the Habsburg crown were declared ended, the institution of monarchy as such was not abolished. Admiral Horthy was elected Regent, exercising the powers of the crown as provisional head of state. Hungary thus remained a kingdom without a king under an admiral without a navy. Two brief attempts of the ex-emperor-king Charles I to reclaim the Hungarian crown in March and October, 1921, failed, as Horthy opposed Habsburg restoration. Moreover, as mentioned in the context of the Little Entente, Hungary's neighbors, Czechoslovakia, Yugoslavia, and Rumania would not have permitted a Habsburg restoration even if Horthy had favored it.

Next to Horthy, Hungary's dominant political figure during the decade from 1921 to 1931 was Prime Minister Istvan Bethlen. The Bethlen regime was politically reactionary and socially conservative. Bethlen curtailed the suffrage and formed a new political party, the Party of Unity, out of the agrarian Smallholders' party and the conservative Christian National Union. The Party of Unity won all Hungarian elections until the Soviet conquest of Hungary in 1944/1945. Among all East European nations, Hungary made the least progress towards land reform, with one third of the arable land remaining in possession of estate owners.

The economic achievement of Hungary during the Bethlen era was considerable; the currency was stabilized in 1924 with the financial assistance of the League, industrial and mining output increased, and foreign markets for Hungarian agricultural exports were re-established. In foreign policy the over-riding aim of Hungary remained the revision of the Peace Treaty of Trianon.

Under the impact of the World Depression and the rise of the Fascist dictators, Hungarian politics moved further to the right with the return of Gömbös to the government in 1932. The "Szeged idea," which Gömbös had sponsored in 1919 found a new and more extreme exponent in the Hungarian Arrow Cross Party, established in the mid-1930's by another ex-army officer, Ferencz Szalasi. Szalasi advocated the creation of a new Hungarian empire from Ruthenia to the Adriatic, based on the concepts of "Soil, Blood, and Work." The Arrow Cross Party was a rival, rather than a supporter, of the ruling Party of Unity, gaining no less than 750,000 out of two million votes cast in the elections of 1939. The anti-semitic legislation of 1938, excluding Hungarian Jews from many professions, reflected the views and prejudices of Szalasi's Arrow Cross. In October, 1944, shortly before the Soviet conquest of Hungary, Szalasi replaced Horthy as chief of state.

YUGOSLAVIA

The chief domestic problem of Yugoslavia, like that of Czechoslovakia, was the strife between its nationalities. Although the three South (Yugo) Slav nationalities — Serbs, Croats, and Slovenes — were ethnically and linguistically kindred, no Yugoslav nationality as such existed. Until 1929 the official title of Yugoslavia was, in fact, "Kingdom of the Serbs, Croats, and Slovenes." Of the three South Slav nationalities, the Serbs were the largest with 5.9 million, followed by the Croats with 3.2 million, and the Slovenes with 1.1 million. The differences among Serb, Croat, and Slovene were religious, cultural, and economic. Most of the Serbs were Greek Orthodox; most of the Croats were Roman Catholic. Among Serbs, a sizable Moslem minority existed, amounting to 11 per cent of the total population. Belgrade and Zagreb, the respective capital cities of Serbia and Croatia, were commercial rivals.

Like the Czechs of Czechoslovakia, the Serbs of Yugoslavia claimed and maintained a leadership role, dominating the political life and controlling both the armed forces and the foreign service of Yugoslavia. All Yugoslav prime ministers between 1919 and 1941 were Serbs, with one single exception in 1928 when Korosec, a Slovene, was Prime Minister. Until his death in 1926, Serbia's pre-war Prime Minister Pasič remained Prime Minister of Yugoslavia with the Serbian Radical party the chief force in Yugoslav politics. To the Serbs, the new Yugoslav state was thus essentially an enlarged Serbia.

The first serious clash between Serbs, Croats, and Slovenes was occasioned by the Yugoslav constitution of June 28, 1921. Whereas Croats and Slovenes demanded a federated Yugoslavia with maximum autonomy for each national region, the 1921 constitution created a highly centralized state, controlled from Belgrade. Although the Serb-Slovene conflict subsided somewhat after 1921, the Slovenes being granted limited autonomy, the majority of the Croats remained unreconciled and hostile to the Yugoslav state.

Croat opposition crystallized in the Croatian Peasant party under the leadership of Stjepan Radič. The Croatian Peasant party frequently boycotted the Yugoslav parliament *(Skupsina),* and Radič declared the laws of the *Skupsina* void in Croatia. In seeking foreign support for the Croatian national cause, Radič even joined briefly the Communist International in 1924. Moscow welcomed the Croatian Peasant party, consistent with the policy of the Communist International of allying national with Communist causes for the larger purpose of dividing and weakening the non-Communist West.

The climax to the Croat-Serb conflict was reached with the assassination of Croat Peasant party deputies in the Belgrade parliament on June 20, 1928. Radić, wounded in the shooting, died shortly afterwards. In the ensuing upheaval, King Alexander vainly negotiated with Radić's successor, Vladko Macek, to reach a compromise between Croat nationalism and the interests of the Yugoslav state. Alexander rejected Macek's demand for federation, however, fearing the break-up of Yugoslavia if it were granted. On a smaller scale, Yugoslovia thus experienced the same dilemma which had paralyzed the Austro-Hungarian Empire, from whose territory Yugoslavia herself had emerged in part in 1918.

King Alexander attempted to resolve the Serb-Croat dilemma with the establishment of a royal dictatorship on January 6, 1929. In order to weaken local nationalism, Yugoslavia was reorganized into nine provinces, whose borders cut across areas of national settlement. As of October, 1929, the "Kingdom of the Serbs, Croats, and Slovenes" was officially renamed the "Kingdom of Yugoslavia." In September, 1931, Alexander proclaimed a new constitution, which changed the franchise from secret to public and limited the voters' choice to government-approved lists. The only form of opposition thus remaining was the boycott of elections. Croat nationalism, banished from the public scene, reappeared in underground and more extreme fashion in the form of Ante Pavelić's *Ustase* (Rebels). The *Ustase* group was a terrorist organization, which sought and received foreign aid from Hungary and Fascist Italy. Together with the Bulgarian terrorist organization I.M.R.O., to be discussed presently, the *Ustase* was responsible for the assassination of King Alexander in Marseilles in October, 1934.

During the regency of Prince Paul on behalf of the young King Peter, Yugoslav politics increasingly assumed Fascist forms under Prime Minister Jan Stojadinović. Stojadinović assumed the title *"Vodja"* (leader) and organized the green-shirted Yugoslav Radical Union. Prince Paul, disturbed by the pro-Axis leanings of Stojadinović's foreign policy, replaced the self-styled *Fuehrer* of the Yugoslav Radical Union with Prime Minister Dragisa Cvetković in February, 1939. The Cvetković government was notable for its attempt of bridging at last the old Serb-Croat differences by concluding an agreement with the Croatian leader Macek on August 23, 1939. The agreement gave full autonomy to Croatia, Croatia being granted its own assembly and administration. Foreign affairs, national defence, and communications remained under the control of Belgrade. Before the beneficial effects of the agreement of August, 1939, could make themselves felt, Yugoslavia was overrun by German troops in early April, 1941.

BULGARIA

Bulgaria, like Hungary a "loser state" in Eastern Europe, developed a political and social system in the early postwar period that was unique among the Balkan states. The prestige of the monarchy had suffered greatly as a result of Bulgaria's joining the Central Powers and her defeat in 1918. King Ferdinand abdicated on October 6, 1918, in favor of his son Boris III, who, until 1923, remained largely in the political background.

The dominant force and personality in Bulgarian politics between 1919 and 1923 were the Agrarian party and its leader, Prime Minister Alexander Stambolisky. Stambolisky's views on foreign and domestic questions differed markedly from those of the establishment that had ruled Bulgaria before 1918. Opposed to Bulgaria's entry into the First World War, Stambolisky was not a revisionist but rather favored reconciliation with neighboring Yugoslavia. His ultimate vision was a greater South-Slav federation, to consist of both Yugoslavia and Bulgaria, which would render the Yugoslav-Bulgarian border dispute over Macedonia irrelevant. Accordingly, Stambolisky denied support to the Bulgarian terrorist organization, I.M.R.O. (Internal Macedonian Revolutionary Organization), which challenged Yugoslav possession of Macedonia with acts of violence and murder. In May, 1923, Stambolisky concluded the Convention of Niš with the Yugoslav government for the joint combatting of I.M.R.O. terrorism.

At home, Stambolisky established a "dictatorship of the village" over the towns, which was anti-bourgeois, anti-urban, and chiefly concerned with the economic well-being of the peasantry. A rigorous land reform abolished large estates, and the land thus gained was used to resettle Bulgarian refugees from Yugoslavia and Greece. Stambolisky shifted the tax burden from the peasantry to the urban population and subsidized farm prices while keeping the price of industrial goods down. The so-called "Pioneer Law" of 1920, which particularly outraged the upper classes, introduced a system of compulsory labor for all adult Bulgarians. Men and women between the ages of twenty and fifty had to perform physical labor for the state, six months for men, four months for women, during the first year, and ten days for every following year. The compulsory labor service, while it lasted, was instrumental in land reclamation and the construction of several hundred miles of new railroads and numerous bridges.

The Stambolisky regime was denounced as "Bolshevik" by disaffected army officers and middle-class opponents, many of whom Stambolisky imprisoned. Yet Stambolisky was not a Communist; the Communist party of Bulgaria, the second strongest party after the Agrarians, was, in fact, his opponent. Stambolisky's aim was to establish a prosperous class of peasant proprietors who, unlike the peasants of Soviet Russia, would remain masters of their own land. Stambolisky compared the peasantry to an "old tree"; whereas the Bolsheviks, in his view, wished to cut it down, he merely wished to prune its "excess branches, which kept the sun away." By specializing in fruit and vegetable growing, Bulgaria, according to Stambolisky's vision, was to become the "California of Europe."

By 1923 the Agrarian dictatorship of Stambolisky had aroused widespread opposition, ranging from the Communists on the left to the urban middle class, I.M.R.O. terrorists, and army officers on the right. That same year, Stambolisky's hint of abolishing the monarchy added the crown to the anti-Agrarian forces.

On June 9, 1923, Colonel Volkov, the head of the Officers' League, staged a *coup d'état* in the Bulgarian capital of Sofia that ousted the Stambolisky government. Stambolisky, having been ordered to dig his own grave, was executed by the I.M.R.O. The overthrow of the Agrarian dictatorship encouraged the Communists to stage an uprising of their own in September, 1923, which was put down.

The newly installed government under Prime Minister Alexander Tsankov repealed Stambolisky's legislation but failed to develop a constructive policy of its own. For the remainder of the 1920's and during the early 1930's, Bulgaria continued to be plagued by recurring waves of terrorism, perpetrated by both the Communists and I.M.R.O. The climax of Communist terror was reached on April 16, 1925, with the bombing of Sveta Nedelja Cathedral in Sofia, in which 120 people were killed. Although Communist terrorism abated thereafter as a result of wholesale persecution of Bulgarian Communists by the government, I.M.R.O. terrorism continued. In 1933 Yugoslavia retaliated by halting the transit of Bulgarian exports over Yugoslav territory.

Order of sorts was restored to chaotic Bulgaria after another military coup of May 19, 1934, carried out by Colonel Damian Velchev. The Velchev coup was supported by the recently formed *Zveno* (chain) movement under Khimon Georghiev, which was both authoritarian and anti-I.M.R.O. The newly formed government under Georghiev at last succeeded in uprooting I.M.R.O. and ending its terror. Otherwise, Bulgaria moved towards a royal dictatorship under King Boris, following the dissolution of all political parties and the confinement of the Bulgarian parliament (*Sobranje*) to a consultative role.

RUMANIA

The new Rumania which emerged from the peace settlement of 1919 was, as previously noted, more than twice the size of the pre-war kingdom of Rumania, known as the "Regat." Four and a half million of

Rumania's total population of eighteen million were national minorities, consisting mainly of Hungarians, Jews, Germans, Ukrainians, and Bulgarians in the order of their numerical strength. Rumania faced the double task of assimilating its minorities and integrating the "new Rumanians." The latter were people of Rumanian nationality who were previously under foreign rule and, in the case of the Rumanians of Transylvania, accustomed to considerable autonomy.

In 1917, when the Rumanian government was fighting for survival under the German onslaught, King Ferdinand of Rumania had promised both an extensive land reform and a democratizing of the constitution, as a reward for the valor of the Rumanian peasant soldier during the war. Accordingly, Rumania's first postwar elections of November 8, 1919, were held under a new, democratic franchise. The chief beneficiaries of the liberal franchise were the newly constituted Peasant party and the Transylvania party, which together formed a coalition government under Prime Minister Vaida-Voevod. Rumania's leading pre-war political parties, the Conservatives and the Liberals, emerged as a minority, the Conservatives being discredited by their past German sympathies, the Liberals being essentially confined to the Rumanian capital of Bucharest.

The rise of the agrarian parties alarmed King Ferdinand and the old political bosses of the Regat, who regarded Stambolisky's Agrarian dictatorship in neighboring Bulgaria as a grim warning. The King thus dismissed the agrarian government of Prime Minister Vaida-Voevod in March, 1920, and appointed Marshal Averscu, the former chief of staff, Prime Minister. Averscu was loyal to the crown and possessed the additional advantage of lowly origin and popularity among the veteran peasant soldiers.

Although reactionary in other respects, the Averscu government enacted a sweeping land reform on July 21, 1921, affecting one third of all arable land and turning the small peasant proprietors into the largest single class. The land reform was applied with special vigor against the remaining Hungarian estates in Transylvania. Although the Liberal urban establishment was content enough with the break-up of the large estates, it balked when Averscu threatened its own interests with a property tax. The King, siding with the Liberals, dismissed Averscu in December, 1921.

The Rumanian constitution of March, 1923, was largely the work of the Liberal party under Bratianu, which returned to power after Averscu's fall. The constitution was nationalist and centralist and left vast powers in the hands of the King. The King was free to appoint and dismiss cabinets at will and retained an absolute veto over legislation. The era of Liberal rule, which ended with the death of King Ferdinand in 1927, was characterized by increased suppression of the national minorities and growing economic nationalism. A series of nationalization laws of 1924 placed foreign-owned companies under Rumanian control.

After the death of King Ferdinand, a Council of Regency was

established on behalf of the King's grandson, Michael, the King's son Carol having been barred from succession because of his scandalous private life. The Council of Regency permitted free elections to be held in 1928, in which the two leading parties of 1919, the Transylvania party and the Peasant party, emerged once more as winners. Together, both parties formed the National Peasant party under Juliu Maniu, who headed a National Peasant government between 1928 and 1930.

The Maniu government, by all accounts, was the least corrupt, most popular, and efficient Rumanian government between the two world wars. Maniu stabilized the currency, granted greater autonomy to the minorities, and succeeded in attracting foreign capital for industrial development. Maniu's chief political blunder was his consent to the return of Carol from exile in June, 1930. As king, Carol dominated and manipulated Rumania's political parties in the tradition of his father Ferdinand. The popularity and integrity of the royal regime were not enhanced by the intrigues of the King's long-time mistress Magda Lupescu, who dispensed patronage and political favors in the manner of a Balkan Pompadour. In February, 1938, King Carol formally abolished the constitution of 1923 and established a royal dictatorship.

The year 1938 also witnessed the showdown between the King and Corneliu Codreanu's semi-Fascist Iron Guard, whose origins date back to Codreanu's student days at the University of Jassy in 1923. The Iron Guard proclaimed itself a movement for the "moral regeneration" of Rumania on the basis of anti-liberalism. The Iron Guard failed to produce a concrete economic or political program of its own, however, Codreanu's creed being that Rumania was "dying for lack of men, not programs." Codreanu's anti-semitism was, in part, the result of the teachings of Professor A. C. Cuza of the University of Jassy, himself a disciple of Charles Maurras and the *Action Française*.

By the latter part of the 1930's, the Iron Guard had grown into Rumania's most formidable political movement. King Carol, though himself an admirer of Italian Fascism and Mussolini, was jealous of Codreanu's mounting influence. In 1938 Codreanu was imprisoned and killed "while trying to escape" from prison.

GREECE

Questions of foreign policy overshadowed and deeply influenced the course of Greek domestic politics in the early postwar years. The First World War, as noted earlier, had divided the Greek nation between interventionists under the pro-Allied Prime Minister Venizelos and neutralists under King Constantine, the latter being forced to abdicate in favor of his younger son, Alexander, in 1917. By 1920 Greece had tired of war and Venizelos, the author of the Greek policy of expansion into western Turkey after the First World War. In November, 1920, Venizelos fell from power and King Constantine returned from exile, following the death of his son Alexander.

The Greek military debacle at the hands of Nationalist Turkey under Mustafa Kemal in 1922 reopened the divisions between Constantine's supporters and opponents, the King being blamed, rightly or wrongly, for the Greek military defeat. A colonels' mutiny of 1922 forced Constantine to abdicate for the second time, the crown passing to Constantine's elder son, George II. The colonels' government likewise imposed the death penalty on several leading politicians, including two former prime ministers, charged with responsibility for the military defeat in Turkey.

In 1924, following Venizelos' return to power, the Greek parliament deposed King George II and declared a Greek Republic. Greece assumed the appearance of a revolving-door monarchy, as kings exited and entered with disconcerting frequency. Between 1924 and 1935 Greece remained a republic. Despite continuing political turmoil, the republican era was a time of economic progress. Greece absorbed and resettled the enormous flood of refugees, which had arrived from Asia Minor. With the financial assistance of the League, entire new villages were built and farms prepared, permitting refugee families and whole communities, which had left Turkey en masse, to stay together in their new homeland. Although a poor country otherwise, Greece steadily expanded her merchant fleet and replaced the shipping losses of the First World War. The Greek merchant fleet, which had declined from 900,000 tons to 126,000 tons by 1918, reached 1.87 million tons in 1938, thus becoming the tenth largest merchant fleet in the world. Piraeus, the port of Athens, was the third busiest Mediterranean port after Marseilles and Genoa.

In November, 1935, the newly elected parliament declared Greece a monarchy once more, with King George II assuming the crown for the second time. In August, 1936, General Metaxas established a military dictatorship with the King's blessing. The Metaxas dictatorship exiled opposition leaders to the Greek islands and imposed a rigorous press censorship. Anticipating the style of Greek military government in the late 1960's and early 1970's, the Mataxas dictatorship even banned Greek classical drama, such as Sophocles' *Antigone,* on the grounds that it might undermine Greek respect for "authority."

On the positive side, Metaxas strengthened Greek national defenses, building a formidable line of fortifications along the Bulgarian frontier that bore his name and that the Germans found difficult to breach during the invasion of April, 1941. Although the Metaxas dictatorship bore many Fascist features, the General refrained from personal emulation of Mussolini, remaining rather a modest and inconspicuous figure until his death in 1941.

Islands of Peace and Stability:

Scandinavia and Switzerland

THE SCANDINAVIAN STATES

The political order of Scandinavia that the European Great Powers had established at the Congress of Vienna in 1815 endured throughout the 19th century. The union of Norway and Sweden under the Swedish dynasty persisted until 1905, despite its unpopularity among Norwegians. Finland, established as a Grand Duchy of Russia under the tsars following the Russian conquest of Finland from Sweden in 1809, remained under Russian rule until the collapse of the tsarist empire in 1917. Denmark alone among the Scandinavian nations experienced a change in frontiers when it lost Schleswig and Holstein to Germany after the Danish war of 1864.

Apart from the Danish war, Scandinavia had been at peace throughout the 19th century, thanks to its geographic isolation from Great Power conflict. Though large in area—five times the size of the United Kingdom, more than double the size of France—Scandinavia was sparsely populated. By 1900 Sweden numbered 5.1 million people, Denmark 2.4 million, Finland 2.6 million, and Norway 2.2 million. Although rich in natural resources, especially timber and iron ore, Scandinavia was little affected by the Industrial Revolution until the early 20th century, largely because of the absence of coal, the chief source of energy for Europe's 19th-century industrial revolution. The economies of Norway and Sweden underwent industrialization on a large scale only with the development of hydroelectric power along the abundant streams and waterfalls of Norway and Sweden by the early 1900's.

The First World War at once shattered Scandinavian tranquility by focusing Great Power attention on the strategic and economic significance of the Scandinavian nations. Norway, Sweden, and Denmark depended on foreign trade not only for profit but for survival, since none of the Scandinavian economies attained self-sufficiency before 1914. Norway and Sweden were heavily dependent on food imports, since Norway's arable land was limited to 3 per cent of its territory and Sweden's to 10 per cent. Denmark, although an agricultural surplus area and one of the chief exporters of dairy products and bacon, relied on coal and oil imports, as did Sweden and Norway.

The Scandinavian nations declared their neutrality at an early stage of the First World War, with Norway and Sweden taking the lead on August 8, 1914. In December, 1914, the kings of all three Scandinavian states issued a joint declaration of neutrality at Malmö, Sweden, which was reaffirmed at a second royal gathering at Oslo in November, 1917. However, the belligerents respected Scandinavian neutrality only to the extent that it suited their own objectives. Britain imposed restrictions on Scandinavian trade lest Germany find a loophole in the British blockade, and forbade Norway to export fish to Germany. Britain also put pressure on Sweden to collaborate in the opening of a direct sea route to Russia, just as Britain would exert pressure on Norway and Sweden at the beginning of the Second World War to secure passage for Allied troops to Finland in early 1940. Germany, on the other hand, tried to pressure Sweden into joining the war against Russia in 1916, a danger which Sweden escaped by the timely collapse of Russia in March, 1917.

Caught between the British blockade and German submarine warfare, the Scandinavian economies suffered serious shortages in food and industrial raw materials. Sweden witnessed food riots in 1917, and both Sweden and Norway were forced to introduce food rationing. British import restrictions for Sweden and Denmark were lifted only after both nations consented to the lease of part of their merchant fleets to Britain for the duration of the war. The Norwegian merchant fleet, the fourth largest in the world, had been employed in Allied service from the outset of the war. All three Scandinavian nations suffered serious losses in vessels and men due to German submarine action and mining. Norway's losses were 2,000 sailors and 1.18 million tons, nearly half the entire Norwegian merchant fleet; Sweden's were 201,000 tons of shipping and 1,150 sailors, and Denmark's were 240,000 tons and 670 men.

The end of the First World War brought few territorial changes to Scandinavia save for the emergence of an independent Finnish Republic in 1919. Denmark, as noted in the context of the Paris peace settlement of 1919, obtained northern Schleswig from Germany, following the plebiscite of February, 1920. In 1918 Denmark granted independence to Iceland through the Danish-Icelandic Act of Union of December 1, 1918. Iceland and Denmark retained a common sovereign, however, in the person of the Danish king, and Denmark continued to represent Iceland in foreign affairs. The island of Spitsbergen (Svalbard) was awarded to Norway by the Allies in the Treaty of Sèvres of February 9, 1920, and formally incorporated into Norway in 1925. The gain was of economic significance owing to the Spitsbergen coal deposits.

Finland, as noted in the account of the Russian Revolution, declared its independence on December 16, 1917, a few weeks after the Bolshevik seizure of power in Petrograd. Although Bolshevik Russia recognized Finnish independence on January 4, 1918, the ultimate success or failure of Finnish emancipation depended on the imponderables of the

First World War in east and west during its final stage in 1918. Moreover, Finland started independence as a nation divided internally between the so-called White Guards and Red Guards. The former, representing chiefly the middle class and peasant proprietors and headed by Finland's Prime Minister P. E. Svinhufvud, looked towards Imperial Germany as a prop to Finnish independence. The Red Guards, composed of Finnish Social Democrats and Communists, headed by Kullervo Manner, preferred association with Soviet Russia.

Civil War between the White and Red Guards erupted on January 28, 1918, when the Red Guards seized control of the capital of Helsinki and proclaimed Finland a Socialist Workers' Republic. The White Guard forces, commanded by Baron Gustav Mannerheim, a former tsarist cavalry corps commander, ousted the remaining Russian troops from Finland and crushed the Red Guard strongholds of Viborg and Tampere by April, 1918. On April 14, 1918, Helsinki was captured by German troops under General von der Goltz, which the German Empire had dispatched to the aid of the White Guards. After the White Guard victory, Prime Minister Svinhufvud and the Finnish parliament, minus the discredited Social Democrats, proposed to establish a Finnish monarchy under a German prince, preferably a son of the German Emperor William II. Prince Friedrich Karl of Hesse, William II's brother-in-law and choice for the Finnish throne, never assumed power in Finland, however, because of the German collapse in November, 1918.

The monarchist scheme having failed, Finland declared itself a republic on June 17, 1919. The eastern frontiers of Finland were not definitively drawn until the conclusion of the Peace of Dorpat with Soviet Russia in October, 1920. Finland pledged to demilitarize its islands in the Gulf of Finland; Finland obtained the Petsamo district while failing to make good its claim on Eastern Karelia, an area of mixed Finnish-Russian population. Soviet Russia was determined to hold on to Eastern Karelia, over whose territory passed the Murmansk-Petrograd (Leningrad) railroad. The Soviet promise of autonomy for Eastern Karelia, made in the Peace of Dorpat, was not fulfilled.

Throughout the disturbances which had accompanied the establishment of Finnish independence, Sweden had carefully avoided any involvement despite Finnish appeals for help. Such Swedish aid as was provided to the cause of the Finnish White Guards under Mannerheim, in the form of volunteers and arms, was of a strictly private nature. The establishment of an independent Finland raised the question of ownership of the Aland Islands and thus precipitated the most serious territorial dispute to arise among Scandinavian nations from the First World War.

The Aland Islands, some 300 in number with a predominantly Swedish population of 30,000, had been part of Finland during the latter's association with Russia until 1917. Before the First World War the islands were demilitarized as a result of the Paris Peace Settlement of 1856 which had ended the Crimean War. During the First World War Russia had fortified the islands once again, thereby arousing the concern of Sweden. After 1917 both Sweden and Finland laid claim to the Aland Islands, Sweden on the grounds of nationality, Finland on the basis of historic association. The dispute was referred to the League of Nations, which ruled in Finland's favor in 1921. The Aland Islands remained part of Finland as an autonomous region with Swedish as the official language.

The peaceful solution of the Aland Islands dispute reflected the great faith which Scandinavia placed in the League and was suggestive of the spirit of cooperation that the common trials of the First World War had engendered among the Scandinavian states. The sentiment of "Scandinavism," connoting a common outlook and a policy of mutual support, which had been little more than a phrase in the 19th century, acquired substance after the experience of the First World War. Between 1919 and 1939 the Scandinavian nations developed a growing measure of cooperation in cultural, economic, and political questions.

All Scandinavian nations staunchly supported the League and its affiliate organs as the most promising guarantee of small power survival through the rule of international law. The Danish-Norwegian dispute over East Greenland was solved through a decision of the International Court of Justice at the Hague in 1933, which confirmed Denmark's possession of Greenland while upholding Norwegian fishing rights in Greenland waters. The Scandinavian nations strongly condemned Mussolini's bombardment of Corfu Island in 1923 before the League of Nations, precisely because it involved the intimidation of a small power, Greece, by a great power, Italy. The failure of the League's sanctions policy against Italian aggression in Ethiopia in 1935 prompted the Scandinavian nations to issue a joint declaration in July, 1936, announcing strict Scandinavian neutrality in any future sanctions which the League might impose. Outside the League, the Scandinavian powers moved towards coordination of their foreign policies with the inauguration of foreign ministers' conferences, the first of which was held at Copenhagen in January, 1932. With the exception of Denmark, which concluded a non-aggression pact with Nazi Germany on May 31, 1939, the Scandinavian states rejected Hitler's offers of non-aggression agreements on the eve of the Second World War.

In the economic field, Scandinavia attempted to counter the trend towards economic nationalism and tariff protection of the early 1930's by establishing the Oslo Convention for economic cooperation in December, 1930, which, in addition to the Scandinavian states, also included Belgium, Holland, and Luxembourg. In the area of social policy, Scandinavia established the principle of reciprocity in the receipt of social benefits, such as old-age pensions, for any Scandinavian citizen in any one of the Scandinavian countries.

ECONOMIC DEVELOPMENTS AND POLITICAL AND
SOCIAL DEMOCRACY IN SCANDINAVIA BETWEEN THE
TWO WORLD WARS

As the Scandinavian states set an example in the peaceful settlement of international controversies after the First World War, they also provided a model of political democracy and social progress in the 1920's and 1930's. From an underdeveloped and relatively poor area in the latter 19th century, Scandinavia turned into one of the most prosperous regions of Europe between the two world wars, one whose standard of living was equalled by few other European nations. Scandinavia's economic and social progress was due, in part, to the absence of huge internal and external war debts, which mortgaged the national wealth of the great European powers after the First World War. In part, it was also due to the small defense outlays, the average armed strength of Sweden between 1919 and 1939 being 27,000 men, that of Norway 12,000, of Denmark 14,000, and of Finland 30,000. Added to the economic advantages derived from neutrality was the initiative of private enterprise in the development and expansion of the industrial resources of Norway and Sweden and of agricultural production in Denmark. The growth of cooperative organizations in farming, marketing, and even manufacturing became a distinct characteristic of the Scandinavian economic and social scene, as did the enactment of pioneering social legislation, particularly during the decade of the 1930's. Being a late-comer to the industrial revolution, Scandinavia appeared to have found a "middle way," avoiding the excesses of both unfettered 19th-century economic liberalism and 20th-century state capitalism, whether in Communist or Fascist form.

Among the Scandanivian states, Sweden became the industrial leader by virtue of her larger population, her more abundant resources, and the advanced stage of her technology. The development of hydroelectric power, beginning on a large scale in 1906 with the opening of the Trollhätten Falls works, provided the energy basis for a growing iron and steel industry as well as a mechanized wood and pulp industry. The rich deposits of iron ore in the older mining center of Bergslagen and the newly opened mines at Kiruna in the Swedish north enabled Sweden to become both a producer of finished steel and an exporter of ore. Shipbuilding centered in the ports of Göteborg, Malmö, and Hälsingborg, electrical appliances and heavy equipment produced by the Swedish General Electric Company (A.S.E.A.), and ball bearings manufactured by the Göteborg-based company of S.K.F. became the main staples of Sweden's newer industries. The Bofors Company at Bergslagen, dating back to the mid-17th century, became an important armaments manufacturer in the 20th century. The electrification of the Swedish railroad system was inaugurated in 1926 with the opening of an electrified line between Stockholm and Göteborg. The Swedish merchant fleet, amounting to 940,000 tons at the beginning of the 20th century, reached 1.62 million tons on the eve of the Second World War.

Norway's economy, less industrialized than Sweden's, relied to a large extent on fishing and shipping. By 1939 the Norwegian merchant fleet had more than made good the losses of the First World War, increasing its size to 4.8 million tons. The development of Norwegian water power, beginning on a large scale in 1905 with the establishment of the Norsk Hydro Company, made Norway a leader in the electro-chemical industry for the manufacture of chemical fertilizer as well as in the field of electro-metallurgy, chiefly in the production of aluminum. In the 1920's Norwegian aluminum output accounted for 12 per cent of world production.

The economy of Denmark remained predominantly rural until the Second World War, with three-fourths of Danish exports being agricultural during the 1930's. Denmark's rural economy became a model of high intensity, scientific farming following the change-over from grain farming to dairy farming and animal husbandry in the latter 19th century. By the early 1930's Denmark produced three million hogs per year, a figure nearly equal to the Danish population of that period. Danish farming likewise pioneered in the development of cooperative organizations for the production and distribution of milk, butter, and eggs. By 1933 cooperatives accounted for 90 per cent of the Danish milk industry.

THE COOPERATIVE MOVEMENT

The cooperative movement, as suggested earlier, became a characteristic feature of the Scandinavian economies generally, including farm cooperatives, consumer cooperatives, and even cooperative enterprises in industry. Together the cooperatives formed national organizations, such as the Cooperative Union (K.F.) of Sweden, the Norwegian Cooperative Union, and the Finnish Cooperative Wholesale (SOK). The Scandinavian Cooperative Wholesale (NAF), established in 1918, combined cooperatives for all four Scandinavian states. The Scandinavian cooperatives were privately operated and jointly owned enterprises, which competed, often fiercely, with conventional capitalist businesses. As a successful measure of economic self-help, benevolently supported by government, the cooperatives developed into pillars of democratic strength in Scandinavia.

Closely related to the farm cooperative movement was the system of adult education, in which Denmark pioneered with the establishment of the so-called "folk high schools" in the latter 19th century under the supervision of bishop Grundtvig and the educator Kristen Kold. Adult education was instrumental in raising social and economic standards and thus helpful in the popularization of scientific farm methods.

All Scandinavian states shared a tradition of representative government, which had progressed towards political democracy by the early 20th century through peaceful evolutionary change. The Norwegian "Eidsvoll Constitution" of 1814, so-called after its place of adoption, belonged to the most liberal documents of its time, providing for a bill of rights and a single-chamber legislature, the *Storting*. During the course of the 19th century, the Eidsvoll Constitution evolved into a fully democratic system of government more rapidly than did the constitution of Sweden, with which Norway was united since 1815. Norway adopted universal manhood suffrage in 1898 and enfranchised women in 1913.

On June 7, 1905, Norway declared the union with Sweden terminated, a decision ratified by Sweden in the Karlstad Convention of September 23, 1905. The immediate cause of Norwegian secession was Sweden's refusal to grant Norway separate consular representation abroad. The deeper reason was Norway's resentment of Swedish domination. Although the union had left Norway free to manage her internal affairs, friction between the Norwegian *Storting* and the Swedish kings had been frequent and mounting. Upon emancipation, Norway invited Prince Charles, the second son of the Danish king, to become the new ruler of Norway. Charles adopted the name of Haakon VII.

The Swedish constitution dated back to 1809, a bicameral legislature, the *Riksdag*, being created only in 1865. Universal manhood suffrage for the lower house was introduced in 1907, for the upper chamber in 1918. Women were enfranchised in 1921.

The Danish "June Constitution" of 1849 established a bicameral legislature, the *Rigsdag*, both houses being elected by universal manhood suffrage as of 1915. All three Scandinavian monarchies had adopted parliamentary government by the early 20th century, with executive power vested in the prime minister and his cabinet under parliamentary control. The Scandinavian monarchs, like the monarch of Great Britain, were figureheads and historic symbols.

The republican constitution of Finland of 1919 was essentially an adaptation of the Finnish constitutional change of 1906. In 1906 Finland, while still associated with Russia, had created a single-chamber Diet of 200 members, elected by universal male and female suffrage.

The Scandinavian democracies proved singularly impervious to political extremism of the Communist or Fascist variety during the entire inter-war period, despite the economic impact of the Depression, which was severe in Scandinavia. By 1932 Swedish unemployment alone had climbed to 160,000. In escaping the adverse political effects which the Depression caused in other parts of Europe, the Scandinavian societies were no doubt aided by the social alertness of their governments.

In Norway, Quisling's *Nasjonal Samling* (National Union), a right-wing movement chiefly supported by depressed farmers, attracted but a small following in the 1930's. Discontented Danish farmers also formed the bulk of Fritz Clausen's Danish Nazi party, which captured three seats in the Danish parliament in 1939.

The most significant semi-Fascist movement to develop in Scandinavia in the 1930's was the so-called Lapuan movement of Finland. The Lapuan movement originated in the town of Lapua among Finnish farmers in 1929 and grew into a nationwide anti-Communist force under the name of *Suomen Lukko*. The growth of the Lapuan movement coincided with a renewed outburst of Finnish Russophobia—a sentiment deeply rooted in the civil war experience of 1918—as a result of keen competition with Soviet Russia in timber exports on the world market in the early 1930's.

The Finnish government, under Prime Minister Svinhufvud, at first gave in to Lapuan pressure when it outlawed the Finnish Communist party in 1930. The Lapuans became an embarrassment to Finnish foreign policy when they demanded the extension of Finland's eastern frontiers all the way to the Ural Mountains. Soviet Russian concern over Lapuan chauvinism became the more pronounced as Finnish army circles were known to be sympathetic to a Finnish-Estonian-Polish military alliance against the Soviet Union.

In early 1932 the Lapuan movement staged a "march on Helsinki," which marked both its climax and collapse. Following Svinhufvud's appeal, the Finnish nation rallied to the defense of its parliamentary institutions and traditions. The "march on Helsinki" failed in its purpose of establishing a right-wing dictatorship, and General Wallenius, the Lapuan leader, was imprisoned. In March, 1932, the Finnish Diet outlawed all Lapuan organizations. Democracy prevailed in Finland at a time when it collapsed in other parts of Europe under the impact of economic depression and nationalist reaction.

Communism was no more successful than Fascism in winning popular support in Scandinavia. Communist strength in the Swedish *Riksdag* never exceeded eleven seats out of a total of 230 before 1939; Danish Communists captured three seats in the 1939 elections. Norway's Social Democrats stood further to the left than did those of the other Scandinavian states after the First World War. The Norwegian Socialists joined the Communist International in 1920. The association proved only temporary, however, since the Norwegian Social Democratic party split as a result of it. The Communist minority, continuing its affiliation with the Third International, failed to gain representation in the Norwegian *Storting*.

SCANDINAVIAN SOCIAL DEMOCRACY

Common to the political development of all the Scandinavian states after the First World War was the emergence of the Social Democratic parties from opposition to governing parties, either alone or in coalition with farm and liberal groups. Socialist governments were formed for the first time in Sweden in 1920, in Denmark in 1924, in Finland in 1926, and in Norway in 1928. On the eve of the Second World War, the governments of Norway, Denmark, and Sweden were all under Social Democratic prime ministers—Johan Dygaardsvold, Thorvald Stauning, and Per Albin Hansson, respectively.

Scandinavian Social Democracy was pragmatic rather than doctrinaire, a fact accounting for the ease with which coalition governments with non-Socialist parties could be formed. The Social Democratic parties were instrumental in enacting comprehensive social legislation that made the Scandinavian states pioneers in the development of the welfare state in the 1930's. In the mid-1930's Norway's labor government under Prime Minister Nygaardsvold instituted annual paid vacations and enacted a Workers' Protection Act, which gave labor a voice in the determination of employment rules. Sweden pioneered in the development of unemployment relief with a system of "reserve work," administered by the National Unemployment Commission since 1914. "Reserve work" consisted of public works projects, mostly in the construction of highways, bridges, and railroads, activated by the government in times of economic recession. Wages paid on public "reserve work" projects were equal to unskilled wages in private enterprise. When the "reserve work" system proved inadequate to the demands of the Depression, the Social Democratic government of Per Albin Hansson introduced a scheme to stimulate national purchasing power. Purchasing power was to be restored through the employment of all unemployed at union wage rates either in public works or private enterprise, subsidized by government. The cost of the program was to be covered by a sharply raised inheritance tax. Hansson's drastic cure for the Depression, though not actually implemented because of the Swedish economic recovery of 1934, suggested nevertheless the inventiveness and boldness of Swedish social policy during the 1930's.

Both Norway and Sweden experimented with prohibition after the First World War. Norway lifted prohibition in 1927, partly because of its adverse social effects and the increase in crime, partly because of the economic retaliation of Spain and Portugal, the traditional suppliers of wine to Norway. Sweden adopted a system of alcohol control, named the Bratt system after its author Ivan Bratt. The system confined the distribution of alcoholic beverages to specified chartered companies and limited the consumer to a fixed quantity of spirits, an average of four quarts per month. Consumers had to be registered and in possession of a passbook *(motbok)* for recording purchases.

Scrupulous neutrality, respect for international law, and the dedication of national resources to the peaceful development and betterment of their societies failed to protect the Scandinavian states from the holocaust of the Second World War. Finland, as will be shown in the discussion of the Second World War, was the first to suffer Great Power aggression, at the hands of Soviet Russia in 1939, to be followed shortly afterwards by Nazi aggression against Denmark and Norway in April, 1940. Sweden alone narrowly escaped involvement in the Second World War, partly because of her greatly augmented defense preparations after April, 1940.

SWITZERLAND

Neutrality was an essential ingredient in Swiss national life to an even greater extent than in the Scandinavian states. Swiss neutrality had been internationally recognized by the Congress of Vienna in 1815. "The neutraility and inviolability of Switzerland, and its independence from all foreign influence," the Congress of Vienna Declaration of November 20, 1815, stated, "are in the true interests of the policy of the whole of Europe."

The Great Powers had respected Swiss neutrality throughout the 19th century; only Bismarck threatened to abrogate German recognition of Swiss neutrality in 1889, following the expulsion of a German police agent from Switzerland who had spied on German political emigrés.

At the outset of the First World War, Switzerland invoked the Declaration of 1815, at the same time mobilizing her army of some 220,000 men for the protection of her neutrality. The Great Powers respected Swiss neutrality during the First World War, largely because they found it expedient for political, military, and economic reasons. As a neutral, Switzerland assumed the diplomatic representation of virtually every belligerent power in enemy nations at one time or another in the course of the war. Moreover, Swiss neutrality shortened the front lines of both France and Germany, while Switzerland supplied both sides with much needed consumer goods. In 1917 Germany exempted Switzerland from unrestricted submarine warfare by allowing overseas imports, chiefly grain, to proceed from the French Mediterranean port of Séte to Switzerland. As a service to all belligerents, Switzerland provided facilities for 68,000 wounded prisoners of war, 1,500 of whom were placed as students at Swiss universities during the war.

The First World War nevertheless imposed a severe strain on Switzerland, largely because of its psychological impact on the multinational Swiss Confederation. The German-Swiss element, accounting for approximately 73 per cent of the population, had long been under the cultural influence of the German Empire before the war and thus sympathized with the German cause during the war. The French-Swiss, representing about 21 per cent of the population, were, by contrast, deeply shocked by the German violation of Belgian neutrality in August, 1914, and remained fiercely loyal to the French cause for the remainder of the war. The propaganda war between the Allies and the Central Powers was thus reflected in the attitude of the German-Swiss and French-Swiss press, and it appeared as though the centuries-old co-existence of Germans, Frenchmen, and Italians within the Swiss Confederation might be destroyed under the nationalist impact of the war.

Added to the national recriminations was the social tension between workers and middle class, which resulted both from war-related economic hardships, such as price increases, and from the presence of foreign revolutionaries, chiefly Lenin and his Bolshevik followers, on Swiss soil. The Swiss Social Democrats, radicalized by the Bolsheviks since 1917, gave Switzerland a brief taste of social revolution with the general strike of November 11, 1918. The principal demands of the strikers included the 8-hour day in industry, a capital levy on the bourgeoisie to pay off the national debt, and proportional representation for elections to the National Council, the lower house of the Swiss federal parliament.

Although the Swiss government succeeded in crushing the general strike, it fulfilled some of its conditions, including the demand for an 8-hour day and for proportional representation. Otherwise, the Swiss system of government, as established by the constitution of 1848, remained unaffected by the crisis of November, 1918. The Swiss federal constitution provided for a bicameral legislature (the Federal Assembly), consisting of the National Council, which represented the people at large, and the Council of the States, which represented each of the twenty-two cantons. The executive of the Swiss federal government, called the Federal Council, consisted of seven men, elected by the Federal Assembly. In Switzerland even the commander-in-chief of the armed forces, the "General," was elected by the Federal Assembly, the General's command being limited to the duration of foreign wars.

The end of the First World War affected Swiss foreign rights and interests only to a small extent. The Treaty of Versailles reaffirmed the neutrality declaration of 1815. The Treaty of Versailles abrogated, however, the Mannheim Convention of 1868 pertaining to free navigation on the Rhine from Basle to the North Sea, conferring instead special shipping privileges on France. The Treaty of Versailles likewise abolished the Gotthard Treaty of 1913, which had given Germany and Italy preferential tariffs on Swiss railroads, and lifted the Swiss customs zone on French territory adjacent to Geneva.

Vorarlberg, the westernmost province of the newly constituted Republic of Austria, posed somewhat of a problem and embarrassment to Switzerland in 1919. Invoking the right of national self-determination, the people of Vorarlberg, anxious to join prosperous and neutral Switzerland, voted for union with Switzerland in a plebiscite of 1919 with a four-fifths majority. Swiss enthusiasm for territorial expansion at Austria's expense was muted by fear of international complications and by reservations about admitting impoverished Vorarlberg to Swiss affluence. Moreover, the Protestants of Switzerland, accounting for nearly 58 per cent of the population, opposed union with Catholic Vorarlberg on religious grounds. Despite the plebiscite of 1919, Vorarlberg thus remained Austrian. The tiny principality of Liechtenstein, on the other hand, previously tied to Austria-Hungary, entered into economic and administrative union with Switzerland on March 29, 1923.

The most serious foreign policy issue confronting postwar Switzerland was the League of Nations. Switzerland, which considered herself to be somewhat of a league of nations in miniature, wished to join the League without jeopardizing her traditional neutrality. The principal obstacle to Swiss League membership was Article 16 of the Covenant, pertaining to League sanctions. In the Declaration of London of February 13, 1920, the League Council offered to reconcile Swiss neutrality with the obligation to impose sanctions against an aggressor, by exempting Switzerland from military, though not economic, sanctions. Switzerland thereupon joined the League, following a popular referendum on May 16, 1920, in which 416,870 voted for, 323,719 against, Swiss membership in the League. Until 1938, when Switzerland withdrew from all sanctions obligations, Swiss neutrality changed from total, or integral, to partial neutrality. Switzerland's long-time Foreign Minister, Guiseppe Motta, who continued to hold office from 1920 to 1940, subsequently became one of the most influential and respected figures in League affairs, referred to by French Foreign Minister Briand as the *"Talleyrand montagnard."*

The rise of the Fascist dictatorships and the beginning of Fascist aggression placed Swiss democracy into an increasingly precarious position. The crisis in Swiss democracy during the 1930's resulted less from the economic impact of the Depression than from the stepped-up propaganda campaign of Nazi Germany. Economically, Switzerland actually benefitted to a certain extent from the economic and fiscal crisis of the Great Powers during the 1930's, as a result of the increased flow of foreign "flight capital" into Switzerland. Swiss gold reserves, which had stood at 500 million francs in 1929, increased to 2.5 billion in 1932 and reached 5 billion by the end of the Second World War.

As Europe approached the Second World War, the threat to Switzerland was political and ultimately military, rather than economic. Switzerland had carefully avoided offending Mussolini during the Ethiopian crisis of 1935/1936, by including Ethiopia in the Swiss arms embargo against Fascist Italy. After Hitler's annexation of Austria in March, 1938, Switzerland reverted to total neutrality by withdrawing from all League sanctions obligations in May, 1938. Still, the mere existence of a liberal, German-language press in Switzerland, such as the venerable *Neue Zuericher Zeitung* and the biting *Nebelspalter* with its irreverent cartoons by the internationally famous cartoonist Carl Boeckli, continued to annoy and outrage Nazi Germany.

Hitler's attempt to create a Swiss "fifth column" was unsuccessful. Although a number of right-wing leagues developed in Switzerland during the 1930's, such as the pro-Nazi "National Front," neither the leagues nor their anti-semitic newspapers, such as the *Iron Broom,* succeeded in attracting a large Swiss following.

The approach of the Second World War found Switzerland more united politically, better prepared economically, and better armed, than she had been before the First World War. Beginning in the mid-1930's, when the great democracies, Britain and France, still placed their faith in appeasement, Switzerland inaugurated a vast program of stockpiling raw materials and food stuffs in expectation of another world war. The tensions between capital and labor, which had contributed to the Swiss general strike of 1918, were largely overcome as a result of a comprehensive "labor-peace" agreement of 1937 between unions and employers in the Swiss watch and metals industries. Under the direction of the agronomist Wahlen, Switzerland nearly doubled its arable land, in order to lessen Swiss dependence on foreign food imports.

At the outbreak of the Second World War, Switzerland mobilized an army of 400,000 men, commanded by the popular General Henri Guisan. Guisan upheld Swiss determination to remain neutral even in the darkest days of 1940 when Switzerland was completely surrounded by Axis powers following the collapse of France. Hitler called Switzerland "a small abscess on the face of Europe" during the Second World War; however, except for one brief moment in March, 1944, when Nazi Germany seriously contemplated a military invasion, Switzerland remained free from direct military threats. On April 1, 1944, Switzerland experienced its one major air raid, when the U.S. air force mistakenly bombed the city of Schaffhausen, killing forty inhabitants.

Total Swiss neutrality during the Second World War did not preclude a brisk trade with both sides. Two-hundred million francs worth of Swiss anti-aircraft guns, originally destined for France, were sold to Germany when France had ceased to be a customer after her defeat in June, 1940. Altogether, Switzerland exported 4.4 billion francs worth of goods to the Axis powers during the Second World War, as against exports of 3.4 billion francs to non-Axis nations. That a substantial portion of Swiss exports to war-time Germany was delivered on credit, rather than for cash, may help explain the survival of Swiss independence in Axis-dominated Europe during the Second World War.

15 | The Triumph of Dictatorship I:

Soviet Russia

FROM THE TREATY OF BREST-LITOVSK TO THE COLLAPSE OF THE CENTRAL POWERS

The Treaty of Brest-Litovsk had freed Bolshevik Russia from the immediate threat of a German invasion, which the Bolshevik regime could not have resisted with any chance of success. Potentially, the German Empire remained a grave threat to Lenin, however, for there was little doubt that Germany would eliminate the Bolshevik government in Moscow should she succeed in winning the war against the Allies in the west. For Germany, the Treaty of Brest-Litovsk was an expedient to heighten German chances of victory in the west by permitting large-scale troop transfers to the western front. The ultimate design of Germany's eastern policy was suggested, however, by the swift economic, military, and political penetration of those borderlands which Soviet Russia was compelled to surrender to the German Empire under the Brest-Litovsk settlement. These included the Baltic provinces, the Ukraine, and even a part of the Caucasus. In the Ukraine, Germany installed a puppet government under the hetman Paul Skoropadsky, with whom it concluded an alliance and with whose help it laid the groundwork for the exploitation of the Ukraine's mineral resources. The Caucasus was divided between the German Empire and Turkey, the former extending its power over Georgia, the latter over Armenia and Azerbaidjan.

Although the German military authorities in the east urged their government to oust the Bolshevik regime in the summer of 1918, the German Empire preferred to keep the bargain of Brest-Litovsk until a military decision had been reached in the west. This decision was not altered even after the assassination of Count Mirbach, the German ambassador to Soviet Russia, on July 6, 1918, in Moscow. Germany accepted the Bolshevik explanation that the assassination had been prompted by the Left Social Revolutionaries, who were intent on wrecking the Peace of Brest-Litovsk by provoking a new conflict with Germany. In August, 1918, the Bolshevik government signed an additional agreement to the Treaty of Brest-Litovsk, for the delivery of Russian oil and the payment of a six billion mark indemnity. Although Germany turned down Bolshevik appeals for help in the unfolding Civil War, it did not give aid to the anti-Bolshevik forces. The preoccupation of Germany and the Western powers with the World War in the west until November, 1918, thus rendered the Bolshevik regime an inestimable service during the first phase of the Russian Civil War, when Bolshevik defenses were still weak and in the process of mobilization.

The first serious challenge to Bolshevik rule came from within Russia. In January, 1918, after dispersing the Constituent Assembly, Lenin had dismissed the opposition to the Bolshevik dictatorship as "idle talkers," who would, in the manner of the 19th-century Russian intelligentsia, "soon fall asleep after drinking a lot of tea." The forceful dissolution of the Constituent Assembly by Bolshevik rifles was not the end of organized opposition, however, but merely the first act in the unfolding drama of the Russian Civil War. In this drama, the enemies, rivals, and even temporary allies of the Bolsheviks made their re-appearance in an attempt to reverse the political decision of November 7, 1917.

The Right Social Revolutionaries, who had emerged as the largest party in the elections to the Constituent Assembly, openly called for the overthrow of the Bolshevik dictatorship at their party conference in Moscow in May, 1918. Most serious to the Bolsheviks was the opposition of the Left Social Revolutionaries, who had initially supported the Bolsheviks during the Revolution of November, 1917, and had briefly formed a coalition with the Bolsheviks, from which they withdrew on March 15, 1918, over the treaty of Brest-Litovsk. The opposition of the Left Social Revolutionaries was prompted both by their rejection of the Peace of Brest-Litovsk and by the increasingly coercive measures of the Bolsheviks against the peasantry in the requisitioning of grain. Unlike the Right Social Revolutionaries, the Left Social Revolutionaries did not hesitate to use terror and assassination, their time-proven weapons against tsarism, against their former Bolshevik allies. The Left Social Revolutionary insurrection, whose beginning coincided with the session of the Fifth All-Russian Soviet Congress, in Moscow in early July, 1918, took the form of a far-flung and organized campaign of terror, which spread from Moscow and Petrograd into some twenty towns of Central Russia and the provinces. On July 6, 1918, von Mirbach, the German ambassador to Russia, was killed by two Left Social Revolutionaries in an attempt to provoke German reprisals and the resumption of war between Germany and Russia. On August 30, 1918, the Chief of the Petrograd Cheka Michael S. Uritsky, was assassinated and Lenin seriously wounded by the Left Social Revolutionary terrorist Dora Kaplan.

The Bolsheviks, answering terror with counter-terror, crushed the Left Social Revolutionary uprising but not until after bitter and prolonged fighting, especially in the city of Yaroslavl.

As the Bolsheviks were fighting off the Left Social Revolutionary attack, new centers of opposition had crystallized on the periphery of European Russia, beyond the reach of Soviet power. The resistance groups which formed on the soil of the Ukraine, the Caucasus, and western Siberia consisted of the scattered political leadership of the Cadet Party, Mensheviks, Right Social Revolutionaries, and even some Octobrists, together with former tsarist army and naval officers. Paul Miliukov of 1917 fame joined Generals Alexeyev and Kornilov in the so-called "Don Republic," which had been set up by Don Cossacks under their hetman Alexey M. Kaledin. Following the death of Kornilov and the suicide of Kaledin, the leadership of the Don Republic passed to General Anton Denikin and Peter N. Krasnov, the new hetman of the Don Cossacks.

In the east, Victor Chernov, leader of the Right Social Revolutionaries and former Minister of Agriculture in the Provisional Government of 1917, had launched a movement for the restoration of the Constituent Assembly at Samara. At Omsk in western Siberia, Admiral Alexander V. Kolchak, former commander of the Black Sea Fleet, had set up a predominantly conservative opposition government. In an effort to combine the opposition forces at Samara and Omsk into a united anti-Bolshevik front, an All-Russian National Conference was held at Ufa in September, 1918. The Conference paved the way for an anti-Bolshevik coalition established at Omsk in October, 1918, under the title "Directory."

The chief flaw in the emerging opposition forces, generally called the "Whites" as opposed to the Bolsheviks (Reds), was their lack of common purpose and inspiring leadership. To be sure, the "Whites" were agreed on the objective of eliminating the Bolsheviks from power, and by 1918 even the Left Social Revolutionaries had come to regard Bolshevik rule as a disaster for Russia. But even after the lessons of November, 1917, the opposition failed to reach a consensus on the all-important questions of land reform, representative government, and the freedom of the non-Russian nationalities within a reconstructed Russia. The military leadership of the "Whites" was in the hands of former tsarist generals and admirals, whose understanding of the underlying social and national causes of the March, 1917, revolution had improved little since the fall of the Russian monarchy. At best, the White generals were willing to consider land reform as an objective of the future, to be realized by a new Constituent Assembly. General Peter Wrangel, Denikin's successor in the last stages of the Civil War, was an exception and had a detailed program for land reform drawn up by the former tsarist Minister of Agriculture, Krivoshein, in June, 1920.

Better than most of his White comrades-in-arms, Wrangel realized that military strength alone would not decide the issue of the Civil War but that it was equally important to offer acceptable political and social alternatives to Bolshevik rule. The Whites produced neither a program nor a personality capable of capturing the imagination of the majority and galvanizing its power into moral and material resistance to Bolshevik dictatorship.

In the battle of ideas, the Whites could not hope to match the militant optimism of Lenin, who justified the terror and the violence of revolution as the inevitable birth pangs of a new and just social order, one which would eliminate the very principles for which the Whites seemed to be fighting. That the Bolsheviks' announced purpose of achieving social justice did not remain without effect on foreign statesmen is indicated by President Wilson's attitude on the moral side of foreign intervention: "to try to stop a revolutionary movement by the use of armies in battle order," Wilson observed in 1919, "is like using a broom to stop a tidal wave." In the battle for the allegiance of the peasants, the Whites made few converts, for the peasant, though resisting with all his strength the forceful seizure of his grain by the Bolsheviks, preferred *de facto* possession of the land to the restoration of old-regime landlordism. Nor did the Whites exploit discontent among the nationalities over the cynical nationality policy which the Bolsheviks had demonstrated in ample measure before the Treaty of Brest-Litovsk. Steeped in the Great Russian traditions of tsarism, the White generals vowed to restore Russia "one and indivisible," an aim which implied a return to Russification and Great Russian domination of the non-Russian nationalities. The Whites suffered a further psychological disadvantage through their growing dependence on Allied support, especially after the German collapse in November, 1918. Their dependence gave the White cause an appearance of foreign intervention that was harmful not only to the gains of the Russian Revolution but to Russian national interests as well.

The lack of a common purpose and political consensus among the anti-Bolshevik forces was evident from the start of the Civil War. The "Directory" formed in October, 1918, at Omsk dissolved almost as quickly as it had been formed. The conservatives, unable to reach agreement with the Right Social Revolutionaries on the land question, ousted the latter from the Directory in November, 1918, and formed a government of their own under Admiral Kolchak as "Supreme Ruler." The Social Revolutionaries responded with a call to fight Kolchak. The Bolsheviks, having climbed to power in 1917 over the backs of mutually hostile opponents, continued to profit from the division of their enemies. Disunity among the anti-Bolshevik opposition in western Siberia and Kolchak's indecisive leadership also prevented the full exploitation of the startling victories of the so-called Czechoslovak Legion.

The Legion, under the command of General Stefanik and numbering eventually some 60,000 men, had been formed out of prisoners and deserters of Czechoslovak nationality from the Austro-Hungarian army. Before the revolution of 1917, the Legion was to have fought alongside the Russian army. After the Bolshevik revolution, its leaders asked to join the Allied armies in France. On March 26, 1918, the French government secured permission from the Bolshevik government for the Legion's transport across the trans-Siberian railroad to Vladivostok, whence it was to return to Europe by sea. After it clashed with Soviet authorities in early May, 1918, however, Trotsky, as Commissar for War, ordered the Legion disarmed. In the ensuing clash, the Czechoslovaks soon captured not only the principal railroad junctions between the Urals and Lake Baikal but numerous cities in western Siberia as well. It was in the course of the Legion's Siberian campaign that the Bolsheviks ordered the execution of tsar Nicholas II and his family on July 16, 1918, lest the tsar be freed from his prison in Ekaterinburg.

The Czechoslovak military exploits revealed the precariousness of Bolshevik control beyond the Urals and suggested the power of a small but well-armed and disciplined force in the Civil War. More immediately, the Czechoslovak victories influenced the Allied decision to broaden the scope of military intervention in Russia.

Allied intervention had begun in March, 1918, when British troops landed at Murmansk and later at Archangelsk for the ostensible purpose of securing the vast stores of supplies and ammunitions shipped to Russia before the Bolshevik seizure of power in 1917. Another British force proceeded from Persia into the Transcaucasus in August, 1918, to deny Germany the exploitation of Russia's oil. In the Far East Japan had landed troops at Vladivostok during the summer of 1918 under the pretext of protecting Allied supplies but actually to further Japanese interests in Siberia and with an eye to possible annexations. The true purpose of the Japanese intervention was suggested by the Japanese occupation of Northern Sakhalin in 1918, which Japan had failed to secure in the Russo-Japanese war of 1904/1905. In August, 1918, American troops also landed at Vladivostok, chiefly to keep an eye on Japanese designs in Siberia.

The Czechoslovak victories in Siberia broadened the Allies' aim beyond that of protecting supplies in Russia against German seizure. Acting on the Czechoslovak Legion's message that it was "extremely desirable and also possible to reestablish a Russo-German front in the east," the Allies decided to make the Czechoslovak Legion the nucleus of a new Allied front in Russia in order to force Germany into transferring some of her troops to the east. An Allied military mission under French General Janin was dispatched to Siberia on August 30, 1918, with the objective "to establish, against the Austrians and the Germans, a line of resistance running from the White Sea to the Black Sea." To fulfill this ambitious goal, the French government counted on the support of White forces in Russia, on the British forces in Murmansk, and on the Japanese, whose operations Prime Minister Clemenceau would have liked to see extended as far west as the Urals.

The goal of resurrecting an anti-German front in Russia was never realized. Janin did not arrive in Siberia until November 16, 1918, by which time the armistice of November 11, 1918, had ended the World War. After the collapse of Germany, the Allied presence in Russia assumed a new, political significance in the Civil War between Bolsheviks and Whites, for it could no longer be justified on military grounds alone.

At the close of 1918, the Bolshevik government had weathered all challenges from within and without. The attempt of the Whites to seize the strategically important city of Tsaritsyn on the Volga had been beaten off in October, 1918. Owing to Stalin's presence on the Tsaritsyn front, the city was renamed Stalingrad in 1926. Among the distinguished Bolshevik defenders of Tsaritsyn were Klimenti E. Voroshilov and Semyon M. Budyenny, both men of humble origin who were able to rise to the highest rank of Marshal in the Red Army of the 1930's.

THE EMERGENCE OF THE RED ARMY

Of decisive importance to Bolshevik fortunes in the Civil War was the development of the Red Army from an ill-organized volunteer force at the beginning of 1918 into an effective army of over 800,000 men by December, 1918. The achievement was largely Trotsky's, who, as Commissar for War reorganized the Red Army from top to bottom. Trotsky eliminated the egalitarian trappings of the "Socialist Army of Peasants and Workers," such as the election of commanders and the abolition of military ranks. The Red Army was put on a conscript basis and advised that the "cleaning of rifles and greasing of boots" were more important than holding political debates; military ranks and discipline were restored, and thousands of former tsarist officers drafted as "military specialists" to offset the shortage of qualified leaders of trustworthy proletarian origin. The latter expedient involved serious risks for the Bolshevik regime and initially encountered strong opposition among Party leaders. At the Eighth Party Congress in March, 1919, Lenin, upholding Trotsky's decision to employ tsarist officers, defeated the so-called "Military Opposition." Trostsky's experiment was, by and large, successful. Towards the end of the Civil War some 50,000 former tsarist officers served in the Red Army, including Vatsetis, a former staff officer placed in command of all field units in July, 1918. In the later stages of the Civil War, particularly after the Polish attack on the Ukraine in 1920, many former tsarist officers volunteered for the Red Army in the belief that they were defending the integrity of Russia against foreign dismemberment. Among those who placed patriotism above ideological scruples was one of the Tsar's most successful generals of the First World War, Brusilov, who issued an appeal for the defense of Russia during the Russo-Polish War of 1920. Not counting on the loyalty of all former tsarist officers, Trotsky devised special safeguards against treason and desertion: the officers' families were held as hostages, and political commissars were attached to the Red Army for the dual purpose of control and political indoctrination. The political commissar was to remain a permanent Red Army institution, withdrawn only in periods of relaxation or when the regime had to depend on the army's good will.

Many future Marshals of the Soviet Union, among them Tukhashevsky, Budyenny, and Voroshilov rose from the ranks of former tsarist non-commissioned and commissioned officers. Of these some were to fall victim to the Stalinist purge of the Red Army in 1937/1938, together with numerous other high-ranking Red Army officers who gave distinguished service to the Bolshevik regime during the Civil War.

As Trotsky improved the fighting efficiency of the army in the field, new high-level agencies were established in 1918 to coordinate the defense: the Operations Division in March, 1918, the Revolutionary War Council under Trotsky's chairmanship in September, 1918, and the Council of Defence in November, 1918.

Superior organization and discipline, together with the zeal of Communist cadres—all factors in the Bolshevik march to power in 1917—also contributed to the Bolshevik victory in the Civil War. However, these factors were, as Soviet historians of the 1920's readily admitted, not the only keys to Soviet success. Equally important factors, such as a lack of Allied unity on the question of intervention or the political ineptitude of the Whites, were discounted only with the officially inspired rewriting of Civil War history under Stalin in the 1930's. The official *History of the Communist Party of the Soviet Union (Bolsheviks)* of 1938 portrayed the Civil War as an early example of Stalin's brilliant generalship and Trotsky's treason. Written in the final stages of the Stalinist purge of the 1930's, it served the dual purpose of strengthening the Stalinist dictatorship and identifying the people with the Soviet regime as World War II approached. The *History* thus attributed the victory chiefly to the "correctness" of the Soviet government's policy and the "faithfulness" of the Red Army, which displayed "unexampled mass heroism" as the "true son" of Mother Russia. The political commissars, the regime's watchdogs over the Red Army, likewise were given credit for their role "under the guidance of Lenin and Stalin."

FROM THE COLLAPSE OF THE CENTRAL POWERS TO THE JAPANESE EVACUATION OF SIBERIA

The collapse of the Central Powers in October and November, 1918, presented the Bolshevik regime with new opportunities and new hazards. The most immediate advantages were the removal, once and for all, of the danger of a renewed German advance on Russia and the opportunity of regaining the borderlands lost in the Treaty of Brest-Litovsk. The German-Allied armistice of November 11, 1918, specifically demanded the evacuation of German troops in the east. The Bolshevik government, having declared the Treaty of Brest-Litovsk null and void on its part two days later, sent the Red Army into the Ukraine and the Baltic provinces of Latvia, Estonia, and Lithuania. As the German troops withdrew from the Baltic, the Red Army ousted the newly established governments of Ulmanis in Latvia, of Paets in Estonia, and of Voldemaras in Lithuania. By the end of 1918 the Red Army had advanced as far as the border of East Prussia.

However, Lenin's ambition went beyond the mere recovery of the tsarist patrimony. The collapse of the Hohenzollern and Habsburg empires, together with the exhausted state of the Allied countries at the end of the First World War, seemed to presage the collapse of Western imperialism in general, as Lenin understood it, and to set the stage for the proletarian world revolution. "The conflagration of the workers' revolution," Lenin wrote optimistically at the beginning of 1919, "has overtaken a number of countries. . . . We were never so close to an international proletarian revolution as at this very moment." With the same sense of urgency with which he had driven his Bolshevik associates towards the armed uprising of November 7, 1917, Lenin wished to assist and direct the Western proletariat in its historic revolutionary task at a moment which he regarded as uniquely favorable.

The revolutions in Germany and within the former Habsburg Empire in the aftermath of defeat seemed to justify his hopes. The German revolution of November 9, 1918, in particular, evoked, in Lenin's words, "rapture and attention" in Soviet Russia. A Communist triumph in the socially and economically advanced German Empire would not only vindicate Lenin's seizure of power in backward Russia, but would act as the spark and catalyst of the proletarian revolution in the West. The Bolsheviks had thus done their best to hasten the revolution in Germany by spreading propaganda among German troops in the east and financing and arming German left-wing radicals through the Soviet embassy in Berlin. The spontaneous formation of German soldiers', sailors', and workers' councils (soviets) at the outset of the German revolution was seen in Moscow as a sure sign that the Germany of 1918 would follow the Russian example of 1917. In the enthusiasm of the hour, the Bolsheviks showered the German revolutionary government of Ebert with congratulatory messages and pledged two trainloads of Russian grain as a token of socialist solidarity.

However, the German revolution, though soviet in form, was essentially liberal-democratic in substance. The majority of German workers remained loyal to the moderate Social Democrats when they crushed the first armed bid for power by the German Communists during the

Spartacus rebellion of January, 1919. The second German Communist uprising of 1919 suffered a similar fate when the short-lived Bavarian Soviet Republic was crushed in May.

THE THIRD INTERNATIONAL

The repeated setbacks of German Communism did not shake Lenin's confidence in the ultimate success of Communism abroad. Viewing Germany from the vantage point of Bolshevik experience, he equated the defeat of the German Spartacus uprising of January, 1919, with the "July days" of 1917 in Russia. For its ultimate success, however, the Western proletariat would need the organizational and political experience of the Bolshevik Party. In order to provide both, Lenin launched the Third (Communist) International in Moscow in March, 1919. In addition to providing leadership to the Communist parties abroad, the Third International was designed to prevent the revival of the pre-war, Social Democratic Second International and to counter the League of Nations. The League of Nations, in the Bolshevik definition, was but an "anti-revolutionary league of capitalist states" intent on halting "the tremendously swift pace of world revolution."

The founding congress of the Third International held in Moscow on March 2, 1919, was a small and unimpressive gathering of only 39 delegates, who were later joined by a few more Communist representatives from abroad. The membership of the Congress was overwhelmingly Russian; the German Communist party, which Lenin regarded as the most important next to his own, was represented by only one delegate. Nor was the small gathering agreed on the aims of the Third International or even on the need for such an organization at the present time. The German representative, H. Eberlein, whose German comrades had just suffered a resounding defeat in the Spartacus uprising, argued that the founding of a Communist International was premature in view of the small number of Communist parties outside Russia and their failure thus far to attract a mass following.

The viewpoint that majority support was essential to Communist action and success had never been popular in Bolshevik circles, however, and the Russian-controlled congress quickly silenced Eberlein's objections. Zinoviev, the newly elected Comintern chairman, boasted that soon the Third International would be based, not only on the "three Soviet Republics of Russia, Hungary, and Bavaria, but on six or more Soviet Republics. Europe is hurrying toward the proletarian revolution at breakneck speed."

In fact, the Bavarian Soviet Republic disappeared by early May, 1919. The Hungarian Soviet Republic, launched in March, 1919, by Bela Kun, did not survive the onslaught of Rumanian troops, which invaded Hungary in August, 1919. The revolutionary tide that had en-

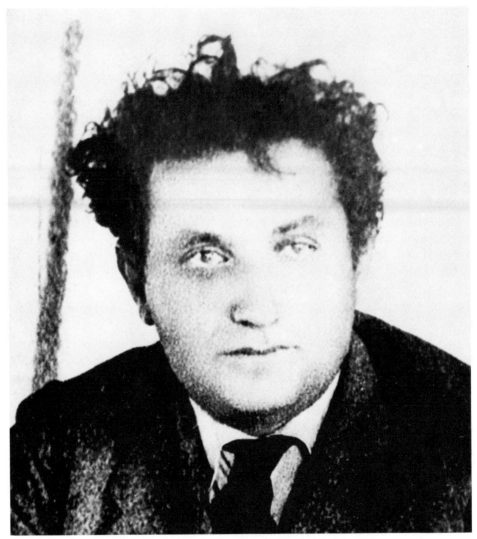

FIGURE 6   *Gregory Zinoviev.*

gulfed the former Central Powers in the immediate postwar period began to subside for lack of Communist support among the masses. In Germany a deep suspicion of Bolshevik tactics and violence was evident not only among the moderate majority of workers but even among the leaders of the newly formed German Communist party. Rosa Luxemburg, the chief theorist of the extreme German left, though fervently believing in the ultimate triumph of Communism, had rejected the Bolshevik tactic of violence and minority rule before her own violent death in the Spartacus uprising of January, 1919.

Within the former Austro-Hungarian Empire, nationalism, rather than socialism, proved to be the most potent revolutionary force, and the establishment of nation states, not soviet republics, was the end product of the revolutionary upheavals of 1918/1919 in the Danubian area.

Instead of witnessing a victorious march of proletarian revolutions from the borders of Russia to the shores of the Atlantic, the Bolshevik leaders faced the prospect of a greater challenge to their own rule inside Russia. In 1919 Russian Communism was too weak to influence materially the course of social revolutions in Europe. It remained to be seen whether the Allied powers, victorious in their struggle against German imperialism, would be able and willing to muster the necessary strength to influence the course of social revolution in Russia.

THE ALLIED INTERVENTION IN THE RUSSIAN CIVIL WAR

The German collapse had deprived the Allied presence in Russia of its original *raison d' etre,* but the Bolshevik government had, in effect, hurled an ideological declaration of war against the Western powers by promoting Communist revolution abroad and launching the Third International. The declared purpose of the latter was "the overthrow of capitalism, the establishment of the dictatorship of the proletariat and the International Soviet Republic for the complete abolition of classes, and the realization of socialism."

Although the meaning of the Bolshevik challenge was generally understood among Allied statesmen and although it was within their military power to destroy the Bolshevik regime in 1919, important psychological and political factors militated against a clear-cut policy of military intervention. The mobilization of Allied resources for another and probably prolonged conflict in faraway Russia on the heels of Europe's most expensive war would have required a degree of public support and enthusiasm that could no longer be mustered in the exhausted Allied nations of 1919. There was, to be sure, a strong desire among French military and political leaders as well as British cabinet members, including Secretary of War Lord Milner and Winston Churchill, to "strangle the Soviet regime" at its birth.

Prime Minister Lloyd George was sufficiently afraid of a Communist take-over in Germany in 1919 to urge moderation in the drafting of the Allied peace terms for Germany, lest a desperate German government form a united anti-Western front with Bolshevik Russia. Marshal Foch, the French Supreme Commander, disquieted by the impact of Communist propaganda on the morale of French soldiers and workers, urged that Communism be crushed, not only on the periphery, in Germany and Hungary, but at the center in Moscow. The first steps towards a full-fledged Allied involvement in the Russian Civil War were thus taken on November 13, 1918, the day that Russia denounced the Treaty of Brest-Litovsk. On that date, Britain and France agreed to divide southern Russia into operational spheres on either side of the River Don.

Shortly afterwards British and French naval forces entered the Black Sea, the French landing an expeditionary force of some 6,000 men under Marshal Franchet d'Esperey at Odessa with some Polish and Greek supporting units.

The French expedition was both short and unsuccessful. Marshal d'Esperey failed to develop a working relationship with General Denikin's army, whose obvious lack of order and discipline exasperated the French. Moreover, French sailors and soldiers were not immune to Bolshevik propaganda, as evidenced by the outbreak of a mutiny in the French Black Sea fleet.

While Britain and France were taking the first steps towards intervention, President Wilson cast his decisive vote against a policy of intervention at the Paris Peace Conference. Wilson opposed intervention on both political and moral grounds. An extension of the Russian Civil War, he feared, would strengthen Japan's hold on eastern Siberia, a development wholly undesirable from the American viewpoint. Wilson's moral objections to intervention stemmed from his assessment of the Russian Civil War as a social revolution which could not and should not be decided by the presence of foreign troops. The best way to fight Bolshevism, Wilson argued, was to "eliminate its cause," but he added significantly that "we are not even entirely sure what the causes are. Besides," the President mused, "the armies might be affected by the Bolshevism they would be required to fight. A grain of sympathy exists between the forces supposed to be fighting each other." Wilson wished to limit the role of the Western powers to mediation between the opposing factions in the Russian Civil War. Accordingly, an invitation was sent to the Bolsheviks and the Whites to begin negotiations towards a compromise on the Turkish island of Prinkipo. On February 4, 1919, the Bolshevik government responded favorably, whereas the Whites rejected the proposal. The plan of Marshal Foch, to use Poland and Rumania as the springboard of Allied intervention, was rejected by the Allied governments on March 27, 1919, largely because of an American veto. In defining Allied policy towards Soviet Russia, the governments of France and Britain thus had to consider, not only the moral and material resources of their own nations, but the wishes of the United States as well, whose collaboration was essential in fashioning a successful peace with defeated Germany. Clemenceau and Lloyd George could ill-afford to antagonize President Wilson over Russia if they expected him to compromise on the peace settlement with the defeated Central Powers.

The French military, in particular, were bitterly disappointed over what they considered to be the irresolution of Allied political leaders. They would have preferred an energetic and consistent campaign to defeat Communism wherever it gained a foothold. Instead, the French expeditionary forces were withdrawn from the Black Sea on April 5, 1919. The

French military mission in Siberia under General Janin remained for the time being. Of Marshal Foch's grand design for a crusade against Communist Russia there remained the limited French objective of supporting Poland and the other newly independent border states of Eastern Europe against Soviet incursions. The French military mission under General Weygand, which aided Poland in its defense against the Red Army invasion of 1920, was a visible expression of the French policy of the Cordon-Sanitaire, designed to keep Communist Russia in political and ideological quarantine from Europe.

The British military withdrawal from Russia, though less precipitous than that of France, had the same effect of leaving the White forces in the Civil War to fend for themselves. Ironically, the Allied military withdrawal from Russia coincided with the period when the White offensives held out the greatest promise of success. However, the Allies continued to equip the White armies, maintained their naval blockade against Soviet Russia, and recognized Admiral Kolchak's government, after the latter had given assurances regarding the independence of Poland and Finland and the goal of a new Constituent Assembly for Russia.

THE SEE-SAW BATTLES OF REDS AND WHITES, 1919/1920

The military initiative belonged to the Whites in the spring and early summer of 1919. In the south General Denikin had assembled three armies, the Army of the Don, the Army of Volunteers, and the Army of the Caucasus. Their aim was to conquer the Ukraine and link up with Kolchak's forces at Saratov. Kolchak's forces consisted of four armies, the Army of Siberia, the Western Army, the Southern Army, and a Corps of Volunteers. Kolchak's aim was to force a crossing of the Volga and to march on Moscow. In the west, General Nicolai N. Yudenich had raised an army of 20,000 in the Baltic provinces, equipped largely by Britain, which was to attack Petrograd from its Estonian base. If Yudenich captured Petrograd, he was to link up with the White forces marching south from Archangel. Though impressive in numbers and re-equipped with Allied arms, the White armies lacked the close coordination and communication necessary to offset the Bolshevik advantage of interior lines. Until October, 1919, Bolshevik forces were on the defensive, however, fighting off the White attacks from the south, east, and west.

Having taken Kharkov in June, 1919, Denikin conquered most of the Ukraine, including its capital Kiev and Odessa, which the Bolsheviks had captured after the French withdrawal. On the Volga, strategic Tsaritsyn (later Stalingrad) fell to the Whites on July 1, 1919. More ominous still to Bolshevik fortunes was Denikin's capture of Kursk and Orel in September and October of 1919. Both cities were vital to the defense of the Bolshevik capital, Moscow.

In the Baltic Yudenich's first dash from Estonia to Petrograd

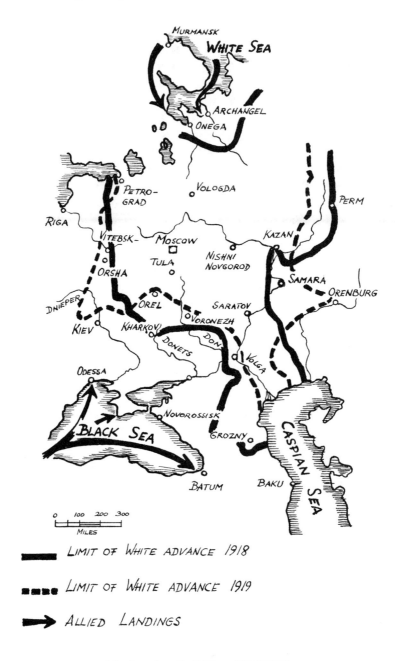

The Russian Civil War, 1918/1919.

was checked in May, 1919, by the superior artillery of Kronstadt. On October 13, 1919, the day of Denikin's entry into Orel, Yudenich, counting on the support of British naval gunfire, mounted his second assault on Petrograd. This assault brought him to the gates of the old Russian capital, but no further. Trotsky hurried to the scene, whipped up morale, and reinforced the garrison over the Moscow-Petrograd rail link, which the Whites had failed to snap. The Bolshevik counterattack of October 21, 1919, threw Yudenich back into Estonia, where his army was soon disarmed by the Estonian government. On February 1, 1920, Estonia signed the Peace of Dorpat with Soviet Russia. Petrograd and the Baltic front had ceased to be a matter of serious Bolshevik concern.

October, 1919, also witnessed the turning of the tide before Moscow. Ousted from Orel by a Bolshevik counterattack, Denikin was harassed in retreat by the swift and legendary cavalry under Budyenny's command as well as Ukrainian peasant uprisings. The peasants, organized by Nestor Makhno, fought both the Bolsheviks and the Whites, with little prospect of thereby advancing the Ukrainian goal of independence. By the end of 1919 Denikin had been ousted from the Ukraine altogether and had found shelter on the Crimean Peninsula. In April, 1920, he surrendered his command to General Peter N. Wrangel, one of the most gifted leaders of the Whites.

Kolchak's offensive of March, 1919, shared the fate of Yudenich's and Denikin's advances. After initial successes, he was forced to yield the strategic Ural passes, which Tukhashevsky captured for the Reds. From the Urals Kolchak retreated into Siberia, leaving behind vast stores of grain and ammunition which could have kept his army fighting for a long time. At Ufa the Red Army captured 230,000 carbines, 96,000 tons of wheat, and 64,000 tons of oats. Omsk, the seat of Kolchak's government, surrendered on November 15, 1919. In defeat, Kolchak was beset by Siberian peasant uprisings and the indifference of his supposed allies, the Czechoslovak troops and the French military mission under Janin. Never having had a high regard for Kolchak's leadership qualities — Janin called Kolchak a "reed," "too nervous to be a statesman" — the French did not prevent Kolchak's capture and his subsequent execution on February 7, 1920.

THE RUSSO-POLISH WAR OF 1920

The last challenge to Bolshevik power in the Civil War came with the dual attack of Poland's and Wrangel's army on the Ukraine in 1920. Poland, not content with the ethnic frontier proposed by the Allied Supreme Council on December 8, 1919, subsequently known as the Curzon line, invaded the Ukraine on April 25, 1920. The ultimate objective was to create a Polish-Ukrainian-Belo-Russian federation under Polish leadership. Lenin, aware that Russia was rapidly approaching economic chaos after years of civil war, had vainly proposed a compromise in the Soviet-Polish border dispute. By May, 1920, Poland had captured the Ukrainian capital of Kiev. The success of the Polish invasion prompted

Wrangel to break out from his Crimean sanctuary with an army of 70,000 men. As Wrangel crossed the Dneper to join hands with the Poles, the Ukraine seemed to be slipping from Bolshevik control once more.

By June, 1920, however, the Polish attack turned into headlong retreat as the Red Army counterattacked. As in previous Civil War campaigns, the Whites failed to win peasant support in spite of Wrangel's proclamation of a land reform law. As for the Poles, their invasion aroused the fury of many former tsarist officers, such as General Brusilov, who gladly offered their services to the Red Army to oust the hated foreign invader.

With the Poles in headlong retreat, Lord Curzon, the British Foreign Secretary, offered mediation on the basis of the Curzon line on July 12, 1920. Lenin, convinced that the joint attack by Poland and Wrangel represented the latest scheme of Western intervention, now rejected a compromise. Instead, he perceived in the Polish rout an opportunity to rekindle the flame of revolution in the West. Against the advice of Trotsky and the Bolshevik leaders of Polish background, such as Karl Radek and Dzerzhinsky, who argued that Poland was not "ripe" for a soviet-style revolution, Lenin established Polish soviets in the conquered areas. The prospect of carrying revolution into Germany, once Poland was sovietized, obscured Lenin's appreciation of the military realities. Having arrived at the gates of Warsaw, the Red Army was turned back in the "miracle on the Vistula" on August 14, 1920. One reason for the Red Army defeat at Warsaw was the scattering of Soviet forces in the Polish theater. Tukhashevsky, eager to reach the German border at East Prussia, had outrun his supplies and split the Soviet forces. On October 12, 1920, a Polish-Russian armistice was signed, followed by the Peace of Riga of March 18, 1921. The settlement was favorable to Poland, leaving over five million Ukrainians and Belo-Russians under Polish rule.

The Russo-Polish armistice had rendered Wrangel's position untenable. After retreating into the Crimea, Wrangel's army and numerous civilians left Russia on Allied ships in November, 1920.

THE BOLSHEVIK RECONQUEST OF THE CAUCASUS AND SIBERIA

With peace restored in European Russia, the Bolsheviks proceeded with the reconquest of the Transcaucasus and eastern Siberia. Following the British withdrawal from the area in 1920, anti-Bolshevik governments had maintained themselves in the three Transcaucasian republics of Armenia, Azerbaidjan, and Georgia. While the war against Poland was still in progress, the Bolshevik government refrained from a direct assault on the Transcaucasian republics. With Georgia, the Soviet government signed a peace treaty in May, 1920, which expressly and "unconditionally" recognized "the existence and independence of the

Georgian state." In all three republics the Bolsheviks masterminded insurrections by local Communists, however, who subsequently appealed for the assistance of the Red Army. In this manner, Azerbaidjan, Armenia, and lastly Georgia were overrun and organized as Soviet Socialist Republics. Thus, the independence which Latvia, Estonia, and Lithuania had achieved on the western periphery of Bolshevik Russia was denied to the Transcaucasian republics on Russia's southern borders.

The Soviet reconquest of Siberia east of Lake Baikal was delayed until October, 1922, when Japan withdrew her forces under Anglo-American pressure. Following the Japanese withdrawal, the Soviet government quickly put an end to the Far Eastern Republic and the White government at Vladivostok, which had survived through the support of the Japanese occupation until 1922. With the Japanese withdrawal from northern Sakhalin in 1925, the Bolshevik government, after nearly seven years of civil war and foreign intervention, had regained the tsarist patrimony, save for Finland, the Baltic provinces, Russian Poland, and the territories lost to Rumania and Turkey.

To the Soviet leadership, the conclusion of the Civil War represented only a pause in their ideological confrontation with the bourgeois West. "The existence of the Soviet Republic," Lenin observed, "side by side with imperialist states for a protracted period of time is unthinkable. In the end, one or the other will be victorious. Until that end is at hand, a series of most frightful clashes between the Soviet Republic and the bourgeois states is inevitable." Of the twin objectives of defending Bolshevik power in Russia and promoting world revolution, Lenin had attained only the former. World revolution had not followed the world war, as so many Bolshevik leaders had presumed at the time of Germany's collapse in 1918. The social and economic structure of Europe had shown greater resilience than Lenin had initially believed possible. "The first wave of world revolution," Lenin observed in 1921, "has spent itself—the second has not yet risen." The hope of future waves remained, however, and Lenin was determined to give the Communist International the form he considered essential to future victory. Far from becoming an association of equal partners, the Comintern was, from its inception, dominated by Russia, bearing the imprint of Bolshevik organization and tactics and becoming, in fact, an enlarged Bolshevik party. Lenin defined the conditions under which foreign parties would gain admission to the Communist International. The Leninist criteria, set forth in the so-called twenty-one conditions, were adopted by the Second Congress of the Communist International at Moscow in July and August, 1920. The conditions demanded a complete break with "Socialist reformists and centrists" (the current Bolshevik name for Social Democrats), periodic purgings of Communist parties, unconditional acceptance of Comintern decisions, and the rendering of "unconditional support" to any Soviet Republic.

WAR COMMUNISM

"War Communism" embraced two aspects of Soviet policy during the Civil War. To assure the adequate feeding of the Red Army and the urban masses the Bolshevik regime increasingly resorted to coercive measures in the requisitioning of food from the peasantry. No other recourse seemed open to the regime, since the peasantry refused to part with its surplus grain in exchange for useless paper money and since the chief grain-producing areas of pre-war Russia, the Ukraine, the Caucasus, and western Siberia, were lost for the better part of the Civil War. However, the violence of the Food Requisitioning Detachments organized by the Bolshevik authorities served a political and social purpose as well. The Bolshevik party wished to promote class war among the peasantry by inciting the rural proletariat, organized into Committees of the Village Poor, against the wealthy peasants, or Kulaks. The policy of requisitioning food by force, though successful enough in feeding the army and preventing starvation in the cities, had disastrous consequences otherwise. The enraged peasantry responded by not working the fields and refusing to plant new crops. The implementation of War Communism in rural areas thus led to the starvation of an estimated five million people between 1920 and 1922. The famine of 1921 seemed, in Lenin's words, "only a little less severe than the disaster of 1891." The Bolshevik government swallowed its pride and sent an appeal to all "honest European and American people for prompt aid to the Russian people" through the Patriarch Tikhon and the writer Maxim Gorky. The United States answered the Soviet cry for help through the generous aid of the Hoover relief mission.

"War Communism" or "militant communism" also represented the effort of the Soviet government, almost from the first day of its existence, to implement Communism by decree. The boldness of the Bolshevik-inspired social and economic revolution of Russia had no parallel among Western socialists at the time. By contrast, the German Socialists, renowned for their pre-war revolutionary rhetoric at international congresses, recoiled from implementing their economic program when political power fell into their laps in November, 1918. The socialist consensus in the West was that the World War had so exhausted the economy that social experimentation might result in a total collapse of economic life. The Bolsheviks, however, attacked the existing social and economic order of Russia with a zeal that often impressed foreign visitors and attracted the sympathetic attention of Western intellectuals. André Gide, before his disillusionment with the Soviet experiment in the 1930's, wrote that he would gladly give his life "to assure the success of Soviet Russia."

The Bolshevik party program of March, 1919, outlined the social and economic goals of the promised future society: free education; the emancipation of women from the "material burdens" of housekeeping;

communal kitchens and nurseries; a leading role for the trade unions in running the economy; the recognition of small peasant holdings for the present but the elimination of the rich peasants (Kulaks) in the future; the six-hour working day for labor (plus two hours spent daily for military and technical training); and the eventual abolition of money and abundant production of goods in a planned economy.

Beginning in December, 1917, the Bolshevik regime showered decrees upon war-torn and exhausted Russia to eradicate the remnants of the old social and economic order and to establish the foundations of the new. Nationalization of the banks was followed by progressive expropriation of the means of production and exchange: mines, factories, business enterprises (except for small businesses of under ten workers), and retail and wholesale trading. For the overall direction of the economy, a Supreme Economic Council was established in December, 1917. A State Planning Commission (Gosplan), created in February, 1922, did not assume an important role until after the end of the New Economic Policy. On the lowest level, factory committees, established in November, 1917, were to assist in the management of the nationalized plants.

The Bolshevik sweep was equally broad and revolutionary in the social and educational field. The Bolsheviks regarded the family as an outmoded and potentially dangerous social unit, in which parental authority might perpetuate religious and counterrevolutionary traditions. The family, as defined by War Communism, was an expression of "Anarcho-Individualistic Disorganization." Soviet legislation thus aimed at loosening family ties and traditions. The right of property inheritance was abolished, as was the principle of community property for husband and wife. The legal requirements for marriage were reduced to mutual consent, and divorce was declared effective by the withdrawal of either spouse. Married women no longer had to follow their husbands if residence was changed, nor did they have to assume their husband's surname. Children, in the words of one prominent female Bolshevik, were to be rescued from the "nefarious influence" of family life, to be reared by the state. Abortion was legalized. Madame A. Kollontai, Bolshevik high priestess of free love, A. V. Lunacharsky, Commissar of Education, and E. A. Preobrazhenski, Bolshevik economist, were all essentially agreed that the family, in its traditional form, was destined to die out in a socialist society.

Religion was an object of special scorn and vituperation in the early period of unfettered Bolshevik experimentation. In the streets of Moscow, huge posters echoed the Marxist slogan that religion was the "opiate of the people," and the Russian Orthodox Church became the target of widespread persecution. The land of the church was confiscated, and an estimated 6,700 priests and twenty-eight bishops and archbishops were executed. Tikhon, the Metropolitan of Moscow, defied the Bolshevik government in word and deed. In a letter of November 7, 1918, the first anniversary of the Bolshevik seizure of power, Tikhon accused the Soviet government of abusing its power by persecuting its neighbors and destroying the innocent: "You have given the people a stone instead of bread and a serpent instead of fish." "The blood of our brothers." Tikhon added, "has formed rivers and cries out to heaven." The Bolshevik government responded by depriving the clergy of civil rights and outlawing all religious instruction in the schools. The "Association of Militant Atheists," first under Trotsky's direction, later under E. M. Yaroslavsky, became the spearhead of Bolshevik anti-religious propaganda with its journal *Bezbozhnik.*

The effect of official anti-religious propaganda was slight among the peasants. Amidst the turmoil of Civil War and War Communism, many villagers journeyed to Moscow to reclaim the church bells at the Commissariat of the Interior, which had been seized during the war because of the metal shortage. Nor were all Bolshevik leaders insensitive to the strong influence which the Orthodox Church still exercised upon the peasantry. "The Bolsheviks hailed freedom," Angelica Balabanoff, Secretary of the Communist International, observed, "and spread obscurantism at the same time, applauding insults against religion and then going to confession to be absolved by those who had been publicly denounced as the worst exploiters of the poor."

The rash and speedy revolution of War Communism brought Russia to the point of economic disintegration and social chaos. The Bolsheviks learned by painful experience that an overwhelmingly peasant society could not be changed overnight and under conditions of civil war into a classless society by decree. The practical effects of nationalization and bureaucratic management were an industrial standstill and labor anarchy. The Bolsheviks had drastically altered the social and economic base of Russian society without providing instruments for the enforcement of the revolutionary changes. In the factories the workers had either brought production to a standstill by interfering with management or deserted their place of work for the country in search of food. Whole cities were depopulated at the end of the Civil War, Moscow dropping to one half its pre-war population. Overall production in industry had fallen to one seventh of the pre-war output.

The loosening of family ties, together with the vicissitudes of civil war, resulted in millions of homeless children, the *Bezprisornye,* who roamed the countryside in armed bands. "Borne along on the crest of the wave of enthusiasm," Lenin admitted in 1921, "we reckoned on being able to organize the state production and the state distribution of products on communist lines in a small peasant country. . . . Experience has proved that we were wrong."

The most serious by-product of War Communism, from the Bolshevik standpoint, was the growing alienation of industrial labor from the Bolshevik party and of the party rank and file from its top leaders. War Communism, for all its sweeping decrees, had brought neither prosperity nor power to the industrial proletariat. Contrary to the promises made, the unions were denied a leading role in the management of the economy; strikes were outlawed, and workers were forced to stay at their place of employment. The syndicalism of the factory committees gave way to one-man management and close supervision by the Supreme Economic Council. By 1920 the regime had virtually introduced compulsory labor when the Soviet government decreed universal labor service. The resulting low morale of factory workers prompted Lenin to observe that since the war Russian factories were not staffed by the working class but "malingerers."

Morale among the mass of party members declined in proportion to the workers' disillusionment. The party rank and file decried the increasing bureaucratization of the party machine and the exclusion of ordinary party members from the decision-making process at the highest levels. Under the exigencies of civil war, power had, in fact, been concentrated in the hands of fewer and fewer men as the Central Committee lost more and more of its power to the revived Politburo (originally created in 1917 to direct the revolution), the newly created Organization Buro (Orgburo), and the Party Secretariat. Although the Bolsheviks had denied political dissent and democratic freedoms to others, they counted on a free discussion of the issues within their party. Such freedom rapidly declined under War Communism. In the words of Alexander Shlyapnikov, the first Soviet Commissar for Labor, the "former fusion between party members and leaders" no longer existed.

THE WORKER'S OPPOSITION
AND THE KRONSTADT REBELLION

The grievances of the trade unions, disillusioned party members, and ordinary workers found expression in the so-called Workers' Opposition and the Democratic Centralists. Attacking the Bolshevik élite at the Ninth Party Congress in 1920, the Democratic Centralists assailed the yielding of party leadership to the party bureaucracy. The Central Committee's intolerance towards dissent at lower party levels was castigated by the Democratic Centralists with the remark that the "head of the fish begins to smell first." At the Tenth Party Congress in 1921, the Workers' Opposition, headed by Madame Kollontai and Alexander Shlyapnikov, demanded a division of power in Soviet society between labor unions, soviets, and the Bolshevik party. The unions were to exercise economic leadership, the soviets, whom the Bolshevik leaders had relegated to executive organs of the party's will, were to have genuine political authority, and the Bolshevik party was to be confined to mapping overall policy.

As the Workers' Opposition clashed with Lenin at the Tenth Party Congress, Soviet Russia was being severely shaken by the Kronstadt rebellion. The Kronstadt rebellion had its origin in food strikes among the workers of Petrograd, who protested the cutting of rations. From the dissatisfied workers the protest spread to sailors at the Kronstadt naval base, many of whom had been drafted from among the peasantry. The Kronstadt sailors turned the protest into a political revolt against the Bolshevik regime when they organized a "Provisional Revolutionary Committee" on March 2, 1921, and issued a call for a third Russian revolution. Under the slogan of "soviets without Bolsheviks," the revolutionary sailors demanded new elections to the soviets, an end to the privileged position of the Bolshevik party, and freedom of speech, assembly, and press. The spectacle of a workers' and sailors' rebellion, denouncing Bolshevik rule as "three years of bloody destruction" in the very city where the Bolsheviks had taken power with the promise of emancipating the working class of the world, was deeply embarrassing to Lenin. Publicly, he characterized the Kronstadt rebellion as another attempt of the Whites and counter-revolutionaries to overthrow his government. Privately, he conceded that the rebellion was the outcry of an exhausted and disillusioned populace.

Lenin met the dual challenge from within and without his party with the pragmatism characteristic of his march to power in 1917 and his confrontation with German imperialism at Brest-Litovsk in 1918. Openly admitting the failure of War Communism, he promised a redress of economic grievances through a "New Economic Policy." Communism, Lenin preached, could not be built by order of the proletarian state in a small-peasant country; a number of "transitional stages" were necessary—state capitalism and socialism—to prepare by "many years of effort for the transition to communism." The Bolsheviks, ruling over a small-peasant country, would first have to build "solid little gangways to socialism."

The first step of the New Economic Policy (NEP), adopted by the Tenth Party Congress in 1921, was to liberalize the regime's policy towards the peasantry. By decree of March, 1921, the forceful requisitioning of food was ended, and the hated Food Requisitioning Detachments disbanded. A new, progressive tax in kind was levied, depending on the harvest and the size of the farm. Poor peasants were exempted from the tax in kind. To stimulate production, the regime granted further concessions that amounted to a virtual recognition of the peasant's ownership of the land. The new Agrarian Code of December, 1922, permitted the lease of farmland and the hiring of rural labor.

The liberal peasant policy led logically to a relaxation of other economic controls. The return of private enterprise in trade and small-scale manufacturing was followed by the leasing of state-owned industries to private enterpreneurs, often the former plant-owners. Large industries and mining, the so-called "commanding heights" of the economy, accounting for 80 per cent of the industrial labor force, remained in the hands of the state. Banking likewise remained a state monopoly, and money, the discredited agent of bourgeois capitalism, became respectable once more. In 1924 the currency was stabilized and put back on the gold standard.

The NEP was designed as a temporary retreat, not a lasting compromise with Capitalism. Precisely because it was a retreat, Lenin was determined to keep the reins of party discipline tighter than ever and to destroy dissent within and without the Bolshevik party. The launching of a new, liberal economic policy thus coincided with the ruthless crushing of the Kronstadt rebellion, the suppression of dissent within the Bolshevik party, and the purging of the party ranks of wavering, dissident, or opportunist members. The threat of a workers' and peasants' revolution against the Bolshevik regime, which emanated from the Kronstadt uprising, was overcome by a swift and ruthless application of force. After Mikhail S. Kalinin, the Chairman of the Soviet Executive Committee, had failed to persuade the rebels into peaceful surrender, the Red Army, commanded by Tukhashevsky and exhorted by Trotsky, stormed Kronstadt on March 18, 1921. In vain the Kronstadt garrison had appealed to the workers and peasants to join the rebels: "the dawn which rose in Kronstadt," the radio appeal pleaded, "will become the light of day for the whole of Russia." The call remained unanswered among the mute masses of Russia, who lacked instruments to express their will.

THE RESOLUTION ON PARTY UNITY

The challenge, mounted by the Workers' Opposition, to the concept of a Bolshevik élite was effectively disposed of by the Tenth Party Congress. Although the leaders of the Workers' Opposition, Madame Kollontai and Shlyapnikov, spoke for the majority of trade union members, Lenin controlled the votes of the Bolshevik party congress. After denouncing the views of the Workers' Opposition as "syndicalist," "anarchist," and "incompatible with membership in the Russian Communist Party," the Tenth Party Congress adopted two resolutions, one on the Workers' Opposition and one on party unity. The resolution on party unity restricted criticism of the party line to the party congress as a whole and forbade the discussion of opposition views within party groups between the annual congresses. A violation of the ban on "factionalism" entailed the risk of expulsion from the party. The sanction of expulsion could be invoked even against members of the Central Committee by a two-thirds vote of the Central Committee and the Party Control Commission.

The resolution on party unity was fraught with grave consequences for the future of the Bolshevik party. By banning the development of "platforms" within groups between the annual party congresses, Lenin reduced the party congress to the role of propaganda sounding board of the party élite, which drafted and executed policy without the benefit of meaningful discussion by the elected party congress. The concentration of power in the highest party organs—Central Committee, Politburo, Orgburo, and Secretariat—pointed to the establishment of a dictatorship by the few or even by a single individual. During the power struggle for Lenin's succession after his death in 1924, the Tenth Party Congress resolution on party unity could easily be turned into a formidable weapon between rivals vying for personal power. By equating dissent within the Bolshevik party with treason against the Bolshevik party, the resolution on unity had laid a cornerstone to the edifice of Stalinism.

A further means of tightening political controls during the era of economic liberalization was the mass purge of the Bolshevik party in 1921. The purge of 1921, in Lenin's words, was to rid the party of "rascals, bureaucrats, dishonest or wavering communists" as well as former Mensheviks turned Bolshevik since the revolution. Bolshevik party membership had increased sharply between January, 1917, and January, 1921, from fewer than 24,000 to nearly 580,000, with an attendant decline in the urban-proletarian membership and an increase in the peasant element. Fearful lest the Bolshevik party lose its pre-revolutionary discipline, esprit de corps, and proletarian thrust through the influence of opportunists and peasants, Lenin purged 175,000 party members in 1921. Under the purge each party member's ideological fitness was examined. Those who were found wanting in the necessary qualifications lost no more than their membership cards, however, or, at the worst, an opportunity for advancement in soviet society. After Lenin's death in 1924, expulsion from the Bolshevik party entailed considerably graver risks for those affected.

THE NEP: A PAUSE BETWEEN TWO BATTLES

As an emergency measure to prevent economic disaster, the NEP was a qualified success. The industrial recovery proceeded at a much slower rate than did the restoration of the farm economy. The greatest gains in the industrial sector were made in the coal industry, which returned to the pre-war output by 1926. Industry as a whole reached only one fourth of its pre-war output in 1922, whereas farm production equalled three quarters of the pre-war level in the same year. Such gains as were made in industry occurred mainly in the light and consumer goods industry. Heavy industry, remaining under government management and ownership, did not keep pace. The Soviet government lacked the necessary capital for the revival of heavy industry, much less its expansion. The hoped-for capital investments from the capitalist West, which Lenin had attempted to attract with liberal concessions under the NEP, did not materialize. Nor did Lenin think much of large-scale planning for the future industrialization of Russia. While conceding the urgent need for heavy industry in the future, Lenin dismissed a comprehensive development plan as "bureaucratic Utopia" as long as the people of Russia were "starving, destitute paupers." Only in the field of electrification did Lenin wish to make an immediate start under the slogan of "Soviets plus electrification equal Socialism."

One of the most striking results of the NEP—and, from the standpoint of Bolshevik morale, one of the most distressing—was the sharpening of class divisions between city and countryside and between the urban poor and the newly emerging tradesmen. The return of private enterprise to the retail and wholesale business produced the new class of "NEP-men," who amassed quick fortunes in the exchange of goods. Shop windows, empty since the Revolution, filled overnight with consumer goods and luxury items as if by magic. Moscow under the NEP developed many characteristics typical of the inflation-ridden capitals of postwar central Europe, where misery and hunger dwelt side by side with the ostentatious wealth of the *nouveaux riches.*

The spectacle of a new class of private profiteers, which flaunted its wealth in Moscow nightclubs and gambling casinos and which hired and fired workers as in pre-revolutionary days, had a demoralizing effect on both workers and dedicated Bolsheviks. In the early 1920's many party leaders were still abiding by the rule of accepting no larger salaries than those of skilled factory workers. The NEP seemed to have rendered such Spartan habits obsolescent and many party members, certified as ideologically pure in the purge of 1921, resigned from the party in disgust. To many workers, NEP came to symbolize "New Exploitation of the Proletariat." After the exhilerating experience of having fought for and won a revolution of worldwide, historic importance, many workers and party members felt that Lenin's advice to Russian Communists in 1922 to learn the business of trading "from ordinary salesmen" had an anticlimactic and disenchanting ring.

The chief beneficiary of the NEP was the peasant. By the sheer weight of his numbers, he had compelled the soviet government to recognize his interests and grant a "peasant Brest-Litovsk." For the first time since the Bolshevik revolution, the peasant could enjoy the fruits of *de facto* land-ownership without disturbance. But even among the peasantry the NEP was not regarded as a satisfactory long-range solution to economic problems. Because Russia's industry had not fully recovered from the effects of war and revolution, its articles were both expensive and insufficient to meet the demands of the huge rural market. As industrial prices outdistanced agricultural prices, the peasant obtained fewer goods for the same amount of produce than before the war. To meet the demand, industry had to expand. In a backward country short of investment capital, industrial expansion could be financed only by increased sacrifices from the people. The question raised but left un-answered by the NEP was: at whose expense was capital to be accumu-lated — the urban minority through low industrial wages or the peasant ma-jority through low agricultural prices or even the confiscation of the land? It was a question of growing concern to Lenin's presumptive heirs, as failing health removed him from the center of the political stage prior to his death in January, 1924.

The NEP was a stopgap, a pause between the past battles of the Civil War and the future struggle for the ultimate shape of Soviet Russia's political forms, economic priorities, and social environment.

THE ESTABLISHMENT OF THE SOVIET UNION: THE CONSTITUTION OF 1924

Drafting a formal constitution to define governmental powers and individual freedoms was not a chief concern of the Bolsheviks after they seized power in 1917. Reasons of expediency and propaganda made it appear advantageous, nevertheless, to proclaim a constitution at an early stage of Bolshevik rule. Such a document would give the soviets official status, mask the Bolshevik monopoly of political power behind the soviet hierarchy, and define the relationship between Russian and non-Russian nationalities within soviet society.

The Constitution of the Russian Socialist Federated Soviet Republic, RSFSR, adopted on July 10, 1918, by the Fifth All-Russian Congress of Soviets, was the first Bolshevik attempt at constitution-making. The constitution of 1918 applied only to Russia proper, not to the border regions detached under the Treaty of Brest-Litovsk in March, 1918. As suggested by its title, the constitution was conceived as a federal structure. Regions with "distinctive customs and national characteristics" could unite into "autonomous regional unions" and enter the RSFSR on a federal basis. Since the RSFSR was itself a multinational state with nearly half its population not Great-Russian, some of the national minor-ities were organized as autonomous republics, such as the Volga German Republic, others as "autonomous regions," such as the Tartar and Karelian regions. The repression of national minorities and the limitation of their rights in any way was declared "contrary to the fundamental laws of the Republic."

The constitution conferred supreme power upon the All-Russian Congress of Soviets, to be elected by a suffrage which excluded members of the "exploiting classes," including businessmen and the clergy. To offset the great preponderance of the peasant over the urban population, the franchise favored the latter. The urban soviets were represented by one deputy for every 25,000 voters, the provincial soviets by one deputy for every 125,000 inhabitants. Between sessions of the All-Russian Congress of Soviets, supreme power was vested in the Central Executive Committee (VTSIK) of no more than two hundred members, chosen by the All-Russian Congress of Soviets. The Central Executive Committee, in turn, appointed the members of the cabinet, the Council of Peoples' Commissars (Sovnarkom).

Below the highest soviet organs, a system of regional, provincial, county, district, and village soviets was established, each with an elected executive committee. The problem of the division of power between the higher and lower soviet organs was solved by the simple formula that the All-Russian Congress of Soviets and its Central Executive Committee could decide on any question which they deemed "within their jurisdiction."

The constitutionally guaranteed rights contained in a Bill of Rights, including freedom of speech, press, and association, were confined to the working class. The constitution failed to mention the role of the Bolshevik party and its leading organs, such as the party Central Committee, which ruled, in fact, through the soviets.

In the course of the Civil War, the soviet government promoted the education and cultural advancement of national minorities in the areas reconquered by the Red Army, while extending the control of the Russian Communist Party. The control of Moscow over the reconquered areas was assured by the dual policy of setting up sister parties, such as the Ukrainian and Belorussian Communist parties, and signing treaties of alliance with the nominally independent Soviet Socialist Republics of the Ukraine, Belorussia, and the Transcaucasus. As the Communist sister parties were but an extension of the Russian Communist Party, treaties of alliance subjected all vital functions of government, such as trade, finance and defense to the Russian government in Moscow. The nationality policy of Moscow thus followed the slogan of "proletarian in content and national in form." By encouraging the non-Russian nationalities to participate in all Soviet organs established in the border regions, Moscow strengthened its hold over the national minorities. The right to secede from Russia, though recognized in theory, was condemned in practice as being "profoundly counter-revolutionary."

The constitution of the Union of Soviet Socialist Republics (USSR), adopted in January, 1924, was designed to replace the makeshift solution of the Civil War period by a formal merger of the four Soviet Socialist Republics into a permanent union. In its original form, the Soviet Union consisted of the Russian, Ukrainian, Belo-Russian, and Transcaucasian republics. The latter had been formed out of the three separate Transcaucasian republics of Georgia, Armenia, and Azerbaidjan in 1922 under Stalin's pressure and against the strong opposition of the Georgian Communist leader Budu Mdivani.

The central government organs of the USSR were patterned after the example of the Russian Constitution of 1918. Supreme power was vested in the Congress of Soviets, elected in the same manner as the All-Russian Congress of Soviets under the 1918 constitution, with one deputy for every 25,000 urban voters and one for every 125,000 rural inhabitants. The Congress of Soviets elected a Central Executive Committee (VTSIK), which was divided into a Soviet of the Union and a Soviet of Nationalities, the latter a representative organ of the union republics and autonomous regions.

The division of power between the central government and the union republics clearly favored the former. Foreign affairs, foreign trade, the armed forces, the direction of the economy, and questions of war and peace were reserved to the central government.

The 1924 constitution provided for three types of People's Commissars: all-union Commissars who formed the Council of People's Commissars (Sovnarkom), union-republic or unified commissariats, which existed on both the central and the union republic level, and republic commissariats, which had no counterpart in the central government. The decentralization in the executive branch was more apparent than real, however, for the Sovnarkom could issue regulations binding on all types of commissariats.

Like its predecessor of 1918, the constitution of 1924 did not identify the real seat of power, the Bolshevik party and its highest organs, the Central Committee, the Politbureau, the Orgburo, and the Secretariat. It was in the organs of the party, however, rather than the organs established under the constitution, that all-important decisions continued to be made. Lenin himself complained that "everything that comes up at the Council of People's Commissars is dragged before the Politburo."

Although highly centralized, the Constitution of 1924 appeared to give the nationalities equal participation with the Great Russians. This was of particular importance in Soviet Asia, where new union republics were formed and admitted to the USSR in the mid and late 1920's. In 1925 Turkmenistan and Uzbekistan were added as union republics; in 1929 Tadjikistan followed. The Constitution of 1924 did not, however, provide the framework for the advancement of genuine national autonomy among the various union republics. Tendencies towards autonomy among Ukrainian Communists in the late 1920's were ruthlessly suppressed by Stalin and ended with the purge of the Ukrainian leaders, such as the Ukrainian Commissar of Education, Shumsky. Stalin increasingly identified Communist orthodoxy with Great Russian chauvinism and denounced the advancement of non-Russian nationalism as "un-Marxist." "Leninism," Stalin observed in 1926, was the "supreme achievement of Russian culture."

THE DEATH OF LENIN;
THE FOUNDATIONS OF THE
STALINIST MACHINE

After suffering four strokes in less than two years, Lenin died on January 21, 1924. In theory, his death ought not to have precipitated a major political crisis in the Soviet Union, since Bolshevik party rule supposedly rested on the principle of collective leadership. However, Lenin had set the example of one-man rule, though tempered by his tact and official modesty. Nor had he designated an heir or established rules of succession. His memorandum of December 25, 1922, subsequently called his "testament," as well as the postscript of January 4, 1923, did not express a clear preference for any of his associates. Though critical of Stalin, whose ouster from the post of party General Secretary Lenin urged because of Stalin's "rudeness," the testament also pointed out the shortcomings of others. Trotsky was lauded as the most able leader in the Central Committee but criticized for his individualism and tendency to place himself above party discipline. Bukharin, though acknowledged as one of the party's most popular men, was found wanting in his basic grasp of Marxist theory.

The appearance of collective leadership among Lenin's colleagues in the Politburo was shattered, even before Lenin's death, in an unfolding power struggle in which personal ambitions played as much a part as fundamental policy differences.

After Lenin's death the Politburo consisted of seven men: Zinoviev, Kamenev, Trotsky, Bukharin, Rykov, Tomsky, and Stalin, each of whom enjoyed the support of a specific domain within either party or state. Zinoviev was chairman of the Communist International and head of the powerful Leningrad party organization. Kamenev had taken Lenin's post as chairman of the Politburo and was chairman of the Moscow party organization. Trotsky had declined Lenin's repeated invitation to become vice-premier, but was still Commissar for War. Bukharin was the party's chief theorist and generally popular with the old party leadership. Rykov had succeeded Lenin as chairman of the Sovnarkom, and Tomsky was the head of the trade unions.

Stalin enjoyed neither the popularity of Bukharin, the fame of Trotsky, nor the eloquence of Zinoviev. Characterized by Trotsky as a "mediocrity" but not a "nonentity," Stalin was the archetype of the pre-revolutionary underground organizer, the committeeman or *komitetchik,* who had turned professional party bureaucrat, or *apparatchik,* since the revolution. Contemptuous of the "literati," the party intellectuals who wrote articles and split ideological hairs, Stalin had amassed great power through his attention to administrative detail and the holding of key offices. He was a member of the Central Committee, the Politburo, and the Orgburo, in addition to becoming General Secretary of the party in 1922. His former position as chief of the Workers' and Peasants' Inspectorate (Rabkrin) had enabled him to place friends and allies in important positions by turning the Inspectorate into a private police force. Similarly, the party's Central Control Commission, established in 1920 for the purpose of hearing complaints from below, was turned into an instrument of Stalinist control over the party apparatus.

The post of General Secretary gave Stalin broad powers of patronage. Although party functionaries on the lower levels were supposedly elected, they were, in practice, appointed by the Secretariat. In 1922 alone, the Secretariat made some 10,000 appointments. Appointments at the highest party level fell into the province of the Orgburo, which acted, however, on the advice of the Secretariat.

Having gained considerable control over the lower party echelons before Lenin's death, Stalin gradually captured control over the highest party organs after Lenin's death by enlarging the membership of the Central Committee, the Politburo, and the Party Control Commission. On the surface, the increase in membership in the highest organs served the cause of intra-party democracy. In reality, it strengthened Stalin's control since the new appointees were invariably Stalinists. Thus the size of the Central Control Commission was expanded from 50 to 151 in 1924, that of the Central Committee from 25 to 40 in 1923 and again to 53 in 1924. Moreover, the overall size of the party was expanded by the admission of 250,000 new members in 1925. The increase in party membership was advertised as a "Lenin levy" to honor the dead leader. In effect, it served Stalin's purpose since many of the newcomers looked to him as the rising star in the Bolshevik firmament and the dispenser of future favors.

Thus, whatever the fame or popularity of other Bolshevik leaders, none could match Stalin in organizational power. Control over the party apparatus, was, in the nature of Bolshevik politics, the decisive factor, for no other channels existed for the expression of views or the formation of policy.

THE "TROIKA" OF ZINOVIEV, KAMENEV, AND STALIN

The concentration of power in Stalin's hands did not, as might have been expected, result in a common front among the remaining Politburo leaders against the General Secretary. Zinoviev and Kamenev, though somewhat apprehensive of Stalin's power, feared the establishment of a dictatorship under Trotsky far more. The fear of Trotsky was inspired not only by his control over the armed forces but by Trotsky's manner, which had grown more imperious with success. Whatever

Trotsky's contribution to the Bolshevik cause—as organizer of the Petrograd uprising of November 7, 1917, or as the architect of victory in the Civil War—he had essentially remained a stranger among Bolshevik veterans. This estrangement stemmed partly from the fact that he had not joined the party until 1917 and partly from the exuberance and sarcastic wit of his intellect, which had left scars on the pride of many less articulate Old Bolsheviks. Behind Trotsky's passionate appeals to the downtrodden of Russia and the world the Old Bolsheviks suspected a vaulting personal ambition dangerous to themselves and harmful to the Bolshevik cause.

To contain Trotsky, Zinoviev and Kamenev allied themselves with Stalin in a "troika." The political alignment against Trotsky in the Politburo did not correspond to the division of views on major policy issues, however. On the two most important issues confronting Lenin's successors—Russia's economic priorities and its relationship to the outside world—the Politburo was divided into a Left and Right faction. The Left, whose views were shared in all essentials by Trotsky, Kamenev, and Zinoviev, was impatient to end the tactical retreat of the NEP and to launch a major industrial program. Adopting the views of the economist E. Preobrazhensky as expressed in the *New Economics* of 1924, the Left urged rapid industrialization at the expense of the Russian peasantry. Preobrazhensky's thesis of "primitive socialist accumulation" called for the exploitation and even the expropriation of the peasantry to raise the capital necessary for industrialization.

While advocating rapid industrialization at home, the Left continued to espouse the cause of world revolution abroad. In its view, the ultimate success of the Russian revolution depended on the triumph of the world revolution. Consistent with the internationalist outlook of the Left, Zinoviev, as chairman of the Communist International, had launched the abortive German Communist uprising of October, 1923.

The Right, headed by Bukharin, believed neither in the imminence nor in the necessity of world revolution at the present time, nor in the wisdom of an industrial crash program at the peasantry's expense. Bukharin favored a continuation of the basic NEP pattern, issuing the call "enrich yourselves" to the peasantry. According to Bukharin, Russia's peasant economy allowed only for very slow progress towards industrialization, "by tiny, tiny steps," with Russia's "large peasant cart" being pulled slowly behind.

At first Stalin avoided clear identification with the views of either the Left or the Right, except for his early endorsement of the thesis of "Socialism in one country." After arguing in favor of world revolution immediately after Lenin's death, Stalin changed his position in his article "The October Revolution and the Tactics of the Russian Communists" of December, 1924. Stalin's thesis of "Socialism in one country" was particularly appealing to soviet youth, as well as Russian nationalism, since it implied the building of a socialist society without outside aid. That Stalin did not, however, share initially the Left's impatient urging for immediate industrialization is indicated by his remark in 1926 that the Dnieprostroi hydroelectric plant, proposed by Trotsky, would have the same value to Russia as a gramophone to a Russian peasant without a cow.

Before announcing an economic platform of his own, Stalin utilized the personal feud among his colleagues and the policy disagreements within the Politburo to consolidate his own power. As Zinoviev, Kamenev, and Trotsky traded insults and exhumed each others' past political sins, Stalin affected the role of guardian of party unity while urging moderation in his comrades' feud. In his funeral oration for Lenin of January 28, 1924, he had stressed the theme of party unity and had sworn to guard the unity of the party "like the apple of our eye." The theme of party unity was repeated in Stalin's *Foundations of Leninism,* which appeared soon after Lenin's death. By contrast, Trotsky's *Lessons of October,* also appearing in 1924, seemed divisive in its revelation of Kamenev's and Zinoviev's efforts to prevent Lenin from launching the Bolshevik uprising in Petrograd in November, 1917. Though Stalin himself joined in the attack on Trotsky, he did not support Kamenev's and Zinoviev's extreme demand for Trotsky's expulsion from the Bolshevik party. For the moment, Stalin was satisfied to have Trotsky removed from the Commissariat for War. The method of "chopping off heads," Stalin warned in 1925, was "infectious. . . . Today you chop off one head, tomorrow another, the day after a third—what in the end will be left of the Party?" Ten years later many party members may have asked themselves the same question, when the "chopping off of heads" had become an everyday occurrence in the Stalinist Purge.

THE DEFEAT OF THE LEFT

By 1925 the feud between Trotsky, on the one hand, and Kamenev and Zinoviev, on the other, had sufficiently weakened the latter to enable Stalin to jettison his allies of the troika. At the Fourteenth Party Congress of December, 1925, he allied himself with the leaders of the Right, Bukharin, Rykov, and Tomsky, when he endorsed the Bukharin platform of gradual evolution from agricultural to industrial society. Stalin did not thereby become the prisoner of the Right, however. While demoting Kamenev to candidate member of the Politburo, the Fourteenth Party Congress added Molotov, Kalinin, and Voroshilov, all trusted Stalinists, to the Politburo. At the same time the Stalinist base in the Central Committee was enlarged through the addition of ten new Central Committee members. To add insult to Kamenev's injury, Stalin appointed his former ally Soviet ambassador to Fascist Italy.

The proceedings at the Fourteenth Party Congress revealed the extent of Stalin's control over the party apparatus. Kamenev's and Zinoviev's angry charges of treason and betrayal by Stalin were drowned out in shouts of "Stalin, Stalin" from the congress floor. The Fourteenth Party Congress launched, in fact, the Stalin cult.

Outvoted in the highest party organs and outmaneuvered at the party congress, the Left combatted Stalin ineffectually for another two years before its ultimate defeat and disappearance at the Fifteenth Party Congress of December, 1927. In vain did Kamenev, Zinoviev, and Trotsky bury their personal differences in 1926 in a belated discovery of their past folly. Stalin could easily discredit the newly formed opposition "bloc" of Kamenev, Zinoviev, and Trotsky by quoting from their past recriminations and ridiculing the alliance as "mutual amnesty." The party organs, high and low, were under Stalin's firm control, and there remained few other avenues of opposition. Trotsky still had many sympathizers in the Red Army, but the "bloc" recoiled from a military *coup d'état* for fear of wrecking the entire Communist regime. The "bloc" toyed with the idea of launching another political party, but the thought of splitting the working class was anathema to even the most disillusioned Bolshevik. "The Party," Trotsky had said in 1924, "in the last analysis is always right because the Party is the single historic instrument given to the proletariat for the solution of its fundamental problems. I know that one must not be right against the Party. One can be right only with the Party, and through the Party, for history had created no other road for the realization of what is right." In 1927, Kamenev added that the road of a second party "under the conditions of the dictatorship of the proletariat would be fatal for the revolution."

There remained a direct appeal to the masses, but under the increasingly totalitarian atmosphere of the late 1920's, the "bloc" could not make its voice heard any better than the sailors and workers of the Kronstadt uprising of 1921. The press was in Stalin's hands, and when Trotsky tried to speak to the masses in Moscow, and Zinoviev to those in Leningrad, on the tenth anniversary of the Bolshevik revolution on November 7, 1927, they were harassed by Stalin's police and found no echo among the bewildered masses.

By contrast, Stalin had stripped his rivals of their high offices with majority approval of the Politburo and the Central Committee. In 1926 Trotsky was expelled from the Central Committee, and Zinoviev was ousted from his post as chairman of the Communist International and the Leningrad party organization. Zinoviev's post in the powerful Leningrad organization was filled by Sergej M. Kirov, the former Party Secretary of Baku and a trusted Stalinist. In 1927 both Trotsky and Zinoviev were expelled from the Central Committee after Trotsky's so-called "Clemenceau statement." The statement was made in the context of the war scare which followed the severing of diplomatic relations by Great Britain. Should it come to war, Trotsky asserted, he would act with the same decision which Clemenceau had shown in 1917 in the face of the German danger. Stalin branded the "Clemenceau statement" as a thinly disguised threat of an impending *coup d'état* by the "bloc." On November 14, 1927, the Central Committee expelled both Trotsky and Zinoviev from the party. The Fifteenth Party Congress of December, 1927, expelled altogether seventy-five opposition leaders from the party and demanded that those expelled fully recant as a condition for their readmission. Kamenev and Zinoviev recanted, Trotsky did not. Having stood for ten years in the front ranks of the Bolshevik party, Zinoviev and Kamenev were permitted another ten years of anonymity before Stalin demanded their lives in the show-trials of the Great Purge.

In January, 1928, Trotsky was deported to Alma Ata in Kazakhstan. It was to be only the first leg in a long journey of exile, leading from Soviet Asia to Turkey and on to France, Norway, and Mexico. Exile neither silenced Trotsky nor dimmed his hopes for the coming of world revolution. After the Third (Communist) International, which he had helped establish in 1919, had failed to give support to the German Social Democrats on the eve of Hitler's seizure of power in Germany, Trotsky called for a Fourth International. In his *The Revolution Betrayed* of 1937, Trotsky condemned Stalin for having distorted the original aims of the Bolshevik party by creating a privileged class of party bureaucrats and technocrats which exploited the workers of Russia in the same manner as the capitalist bourgeoisie. Trotsky's *The Revolution Betrayed* foreshadowed much of the criticism of 20th-century Communist society which the Yugoslav author Milovan Djilas expressed in his *The New Class* a generation later.

Except for a handful of admirers in Western Europe and the United States, Trotsky failed to win a following in exile. The Fourth International did not materialize. Western intellectual sympathizers of the soviet experiment continued to look to Stalin, by and large, as the successful leader of Russia's social and economic revolution of the 1930's. In the words of André Malraux, the French author, Trotsky was "a great moral force, but Stalin has lent dignity to mankind." To Stalin Trotsky may have seemed dangerous even in exile, however. On August 20, 1940, when the attention of the world was focused on Britain's battle against Hitler, Trotsky was assassinated in his Mexican exile.

THE DESTRUCTION OF THE RIGHT

The Fifteenth Party Congress of December, 1927, which witnessed the end of the Left opposition, also marked the beginning of Stalin's break with Bukharin and the Right. The Stalin platform, submitted to the Fifteenth Party Congress, marked the end of the NEP. The platform called for the launching of a massive industrialization program and the establishment of collective farms. The State Planning Commission (Gosplan) was directed to prepare the first Five Year Plan. The announcement was followed by coercive measures against the wealthy peasants (kulaks), on the grounds that the government was short of two million tons of grain.

The battle between Stalin and the Right, provoked by his change of course in 1928, followed the pattern of Stalin's defeat of the Left. In 1928 it was Bukharin's turn to be outraged at Stalin's turnabout and to search in vain for allies. As Trotsky had forged a belated alliance with Zinoviev and Kamenev in 1926, Bukharin approached the fallen leaders of the Left opposition in 1928. To Kamenev Bukharin confided that Stalin was the "new Genghiz Khan," an "unprincipled intriguer" who will subordinate everything to his lust for power. "He will slay us, he will strangle us," Bukharin cried in prophetic despair.

Bukharin's plan of uniting the leaders of the Right with those of the Left failed, since the Left itself was without power. Moreover, many supporters of the Left, flattered by Stalin's apparent adoption of their industrialization program, counted on a reconciliation with him.

The Politburo had long ceased to be a source of power for the Right. Stalin had replaced the ousted Left leaders with his own men. In Voroshilov, Kalinin, Molotov, Kuibyshev, and Rudzutak, the leaders of the Right, Bukharin, Rykov and Tomsky, faced a solid Stalinist phalanx. With Politburo support, Stalin ousted Bukharin from the chairmanship of the Communist International, to which Bukharin had succeeded after Zinoviev's fall, and from the Politburo itself in November, 1929. Tomsky was ousted as chief of the trade unions in 1929 and expelled from the Politburo in 1930. In 1930 Rykov was dismissed as chairman of the Sovnarkom and ousted from the Politburo.

On his fiftieth birthday on December 21, 1929, Stalin could survey the field of political battle with confidence. The Old Bolsheviks, more famous and brilliant but less ruthless than he, were exiled, silenced, or discredited. Portraits and busts of Stalin began to fill the public places, and Tsaritsyn had been renamed Stalingrad. From his foreign exile, Trotsky had called for a new revolution in Russia. A new revolution was, in fact, in the making, in which Stalin would apply the proven methods of his power struggle within the Bolshevik party to the whole of Russia.

THE STALIN ERA

The consolidation of Stalin's power in 1929 heralded the beginning of an economic, social, and political revolution more sweeping in its effects than the two previous Russian revolutions of March and

November, 1917. Within a decade after crushing the Left and the Right, Stalin would change Russia into one of the leading industrial nations of the world, uproot millions of peasants, and leave his personal imprint upon virtually every phase of Russian cultural, scientific, and social life.

However great the changes wrought by Stalin, the roots of the Stalinist revolution were deeply embedded in past Bolshevik theory and practice. In method, the Stalinist revolution of the 1930's followed the example of War Communism; in its aim it appropriated many of the ideas espoused by Lenin before the compromise of the NEP and taken up again by the Left during the ideological debate of the late 1920's. Stalin appropriated the program of the Left, but he did so with a difference in emphasis and timing which gave his revolution a character all its own.

The Left had wanted industrialization, but it had hoped that labor would be permitted to share its fruits, both through increased material benefits and through a larger role in management. Under Stalin labor would lose its last vestige of independence from the bureaucracy, and industrialization would aim primarily at the creation of a huge defense establishment. Soviet defense industry in the late 1930's would expand two and a half times as fast as Soviet industry as a whole.

The Left had denounced the kulak as a parasite who fattened on the freedoms of the NEP, but the rural revolution it had in mind fell far short of Stalin's physical destruction of the entire kulak class. The Left, above all, had hoped that the human cost of revolution could be kept within tolerable bounds. The human cost of the rural and industrial revolution of the 1930's was largely a matter of indifference to Stalin as long as the cost did not impair ultimate success.

The most significant departure under Stalin from Bolshevik tradition would be the unprecedented expansion of terror and its direction against the Bolshevik party itself. Terror had not been an unknown weapon in the Bolshevik arsenal, but under Lenin it had been used mainly against the "class enemy"—i.e., external foes or competing political parties. Under Stalin, terror would become an expedient to punish scapegoats for industrial failures of the regime, or a personal weapon to settle accounts with enemies of the past and suspected enemies of the present. Eventually, the terror of the 1930's would debase all of Soviet society to a chanting chorus of frightened worshippers of Stalin's infallibility.

THE REVOLUTION IN AGRICULTURE

The peasantry, by far the most numerous class in Russia, was the first to feel the impact of Stalinist rule. The strength of the peasant population relative to the urban population had actually increased between 1913 and 1928 from 65 to 72 per cent. The number of individual peasant households had increased from 16.5 million in 1918 to nearly 26 million in 1929. Considerable differences in wealth existed among the 26 million households. Some two million were classified as kulaks, fifteen million as middle income, and nine million as poor peasants.

The growth of a class of peasant proprietors in the midst of the Bolshevik citadel had been a source of concern to most Bolshevik leaders from the beginning of their rule. Small-scale production on the farms, Lenin had warned, would give "birth to capitalism and the bourgeoisie constantly, daily, hourly with elemental force."

To Stalin the most compelling reason for collectivization was economic. Since the Five Year Plan had to be financed primarily from rural surpluses, it was far simpler for the government to draw its grain supply for exports from a quarter million collective farms than twenty-six million individual households. By reclaiming title to the land—in theory the Bolshevik regime had never abandoned it—the government itself became the chief agricultural producer and did not have to haggle over farm prices. Large-scale farming, as envisaged by Stalin, also promised to raise farm efficiency. Under the NEP, grain surpluses had actually declined, owing to increased peasant consumption and inefficient farming methods on small plots. Since the supply of consumer goods would predictably decline under the Five Year Plan, its emphasis being on the expansion of heavy industry, the government could expect a new wave of passive resistance if the peasantry were allowed to keep its farms. The political and social consequences of collectivization were equally desirable from the Bolshevik standpoint. The abolition of capitalist modes of production on the farm would atomize the peasant class into a rural proletariat whose individual members were equally dependent on the regime and hence more easily controllable politically.

Originally two types of farms were contemplated as a replacement for private farms—the collective (kolkhoz), to be formed out of several private farms, and the state farm (sovkhoz), run directly by the government. By 1934 Stalin shifted the emphasis to the collective farms, owing to the poor yield on the state farms in spite of heavy investments and preferential assignment of mechanical equipment.

THE POLICY OF FORCED COLLECTIVIZATION   Stalin's appeal for a voluntary merger of private farms into collectives brought little result since only 4 per cent of the peasant households had responded favorably by October, 1929. Coercion followed on an ever larger scale as the secret police (OGPU, NKVD since July, 1934) launched a full-scale attack on the kulak class. The casualties among the kulaks may have run as high as one million. Those who survived were driven off the land, forming the first huge installment of a vast and growing army of forced labor. Surviving children of kulaks, who escaped imprisonment, were marked as class enemies and denied a higher education in the cities or advancement in the urban economy.

The policy of forced collectivization heavily depleted the rural wealth of Russia. An estimated 30 million head of cattle, 100 million sheep, and 17 million horses were slaughtered by the enraged peasantry. As late as 1941 Russian livestock figures had not returned to their pre-collectivization level. The burning of crops and the refusal to plant seeds resulted in a new famine in 1931 and 1932, which exceeded that of 1920 and 1921. Estimates of deaths due to starvation in the early 1930's have run as high as ten million. Although Stalin could boast in 1930 that 58 per cent of all farm land had been collectivized, his rural policy threatened to become self-defeating. In March, 1930, the regime beat a temporary and tactical retreat. Under the headline of "Dizziness with success," *Pravda* called a halt to the violence and blamed the excesses on over-zealous subordinates. The method was altered, but not the aim. Violence was replaced by a policy which favored collective farms with preferential assignment of seed grain and tractors and discriminated against the remaining private farms with a crushing tax burden. The number of collective farms steadily increased thereafter, reaching over 90 per cent in 1936 and nearly 100 per cent in 1940.

As collectivization took root, the Soviet government perfected its controls while offering modest concessions to the new class of peasant proletarians. As an inducement, the regime permitted each family a small garden plot of its own with a limited number of cattle, sheep, and goats and an unlimited number of fowl and rabbits. Proceeds from the garden plots could be sold for personal profit. Likewise, surpluses achieved above the assigned quotas by the kolkhoz could be sold on the open market.

THE COLLECTIVE FARM CHARTER   The Collective Farm Charter of 1935 provided the structure of kolkhoz administration. All working members above the age of 16 formed a "general meeting," which elected a chairman. In practice the chairman was designated by the local party organization. The "general meeting" could not veto the government quotas, which were often fixed without considerations of weather or soil conditions. As many kolkhoz members preferred to devote their energies to their private garden plots, the regime decreed in May, 1939, minimum work norms for the kolkhoz. Depending on location, a minimum of 100, 80, or 60 work-days per year was prescribed for the kolkhoz and loss of garden plots threatened in the event of noncompliance.

The Machine Tractor Stations (MTS) served as an ingenious device both for the mechanization of collectives and the extension of party controls into rural areas. The MTS were government-owned and operated on a contract basis, payment being made by the collective in kind. Attached to each MTS was an assistant director for political affairs for purposes of indoctrination and control.

In spite of the chaos which collectivization initially caused, the total grain output of the late 1930's exceeded that of the NEP. Collective farming did not, for that reason, become more popular among the rural population. Those possessing skills and freedom of movement migrated to the cities in search of better living conditions. Rural labor continued to form the bottom of the social and economic pyramid of Soviet society.

THE REVOLUTION IN INDUSTRY

Having once denounced the leaders of the left opposition as "super industrializers," Stalin launched Russia's most ambitious industrial expansion to date in the decade following the announcement of the first Five Year Plan in 1928. National defense was the primary concern. "One feature of the history of the old Russia," Stalin observed in 1931, "was the continual beating she suffered because of her backwardness." In the past, Stalin added, Tatars, Khans, Turks, Swedes, Poles, and Anglo-French capitalists had beaten Russia. In the past the word was: "Thou art poor, Mother Russia, but thou art helpless, Mother Russia!" In Stalin's view, unless Russia caught up with the more advanced west in ten years, she would be crushed. Stalin thus stated the overall purpose of the first Five Year Plan as providing "all the necessary technical and economic prerequisites for increasing to the utmost the defense capacity of the country."

By the end of the first Five Year Plan, Soviet Russia claimed to have achieved a fourfold increase in the output of machinery and a doubling of its oil production. At Stalingrad Europe's largest tractor plant had been established, and at Dnieprostroi Europe's largest electrical power station was erected, with an output of 650,000 kilowatts. Between 1928 and 1937, steel production was said to have increased from four to eighteen million tons per year, that of hard coal from 36 to 128 million tons. Entire industrial cities had been built in the Urals and Siberia close to ore and coal deposits, and new rail and water communications had been developed. After the completion of the "Turksib," the rail link connecting Siberia with Turkestan, new inland waterways were opened with the White Sea and Moscow-Volga canals.

The great enterprise in industrial and communications expansion was launched to the applause of enthusiastic young Communists, especially since it coincided with the Great Depression in the West. In time, the pace of Stalin's industrial revolution could not be sustained by enthusiasm alone, however, and force became an essential ingredient in the urban revolution, as it had in the rural. Bukharin's forecast of 1928 that Stalin's socialism would necessarily lead to a police state, because of the resistance it would provoke and the coercion it would require, was confirmed by events.

THE SOCIAL COST OF INDUSTRIAL PROGRESS   The regime made few provisions for the large population influx into the cities which increased the industrial labor force from six to eight million between 1932 and 1940. By contrast, a smaller percentage of the total capital investment went into housing after 1929 than during the preceding decade. The result was over-crowding to the point where whole families shared a single room and indi-viduals lived in stairways or cellars. The regime claimed to have doubled the real wages of industrial workers under the second Five Year Plan, but real wages, in Western estimates, declined by as much as 43 per cent in non-agricultural jobs between 1928 and 1940. The unions were largely reduced to the task of "stimulating productive initiative," and labor in-creasingly lost its freedom of movement through the issuing of internal passports and "labor books." With the approach of Russia's entry into the Second World War, labor discipline was tightened further. By decree of June, 1940, lateness by twenty minutes or sickness on the job were punishable by loss of one fourth of wages, and imprisonment of up to six months. Beginning in 1936, workers in industry were urged to emulate the example of Alexei Stakhanov, a Donets Basin coal miner, who had ex-ceeded his work norm by 1300 per cent by allegedly mining 102 tons of coal in a single shift. The shortage of labor, particularly in such areas as canal building, prompted the regime's ever wider use of forced labor. At the peak of the Stalinist purge, the size of the forced labor army was vari-ously estimated as between seven and fourteen million, declining to an estimated three and a half million on the eve of Russia's entry into the Second World War. Certain industries, such as gold mining, were the ex-clusive domain of the NKVD, which employed forced labor or hired it out to other industries on a contract basis. The extensive use of forced labor under Stalin suggested the contrast between the announced goals of the Bolshevik revolution in its early stages and the reality of Soviet life in the 1930's. "The exploitation of prison labor, . . ." the first Soviet penal code stated, "in places of confinement which, while profitable from a commer-cial view, is fundamentally lacking in corrective significance and entirely inadmissable in Soviet places of confinement."

THE SHOW TRIALS OF "WRECKERS" AND "SABOTEURS" Nor was the coercive trend confined to industrial labor. Engineers and managers, who formed a privileged élite by virtue of high salaries and preferential hous-ing, were subjected to periodic persecution as a warning and as an in-centive. "Bourgeois specialists," including foreign engineers who filled the gaps in the Communist technological establishment, were singled out as scapegoats for industrial failures in a number of show trials, beginning with the Shakty trial of 1928 and continuing with the trial of the so-called Industrial Party of Professor Ramzin in 1930 and the trial of Professor Groman in 1931. When "engineer baiting" seemed to demoralize too many specialists—one oil engineer took up taxi driving in Moscow for fear of reprisals if his test drillings yielded no results—Stalin called a temporary halt in June, 1931. The identification of all Old Regime engineers as "criminals and wreckers" was then officially termed "stupid and unwise." The practice of charging engineers, managers, and eventually government officials with sabotage continued, nonetheless, with the show trial of six British Metro-Vickers engineers in 1933 and reached its climax during the Stalinist Purge of the late 1930's. To remove all blemishes of bureaucratic bungling from the regime, agricultural failures were variously ascribed to the deliberate wrecking of machinery, willful distribution of bad seed grain, misbreeding of cattle, and sabotage against the Turkestan cotton crop. The availability of winter clothing at the peak of summer and of summer clothing in the depths of winter in Moscow stores was explained as a well planned conspiracy of the soviet head of cooperative stores, Zelensky.

The leap from rural backwardness to industrial society within the short span of one decade would have demanded a supreme human sacrifice under any circumstances. The tasks of accumulating investment capital without any assistance from the established industrial nations of the West, training hundreds of thousands of skilled workers among a semi-literate peasantry, and producing a new generation of competent engineers would have taxed the resources of any society to their utmost limits. It may be questioned, therefore, whether the Stalinist preference for terror as an incentive to plan fulfillment did not needlessly increase the human cost of industrialization. The industrial revolution of the 1930's provided Soviet Russia with modern armaments whose quantity and quality astounded the world when the necessity for their use arose in 1941. The dispirited use of these armaments by many soldiers of the Red Army, especially those who were not of Great Russian nationality, in the initial stages of the Russo-German war would suggest that many soviet citizens did not consider Stalin's Russia worth saving.

THE STALIN CONSTITUTION OF 1936

On December 5, 1936, the Soviet Union adopted a new constitution, hailed by Stalin as the "only thoroughly democratic constitution in the world." The Stalin Constitution served the dual purpose of proclaiming the establishment of a new society at home and of advertising the Soviet Union as an essentially democratic nation abroad. The liquidation of the kulaks and of the NEP merchants had, in Stalin's words, ended the class struggle in the Soviet Union and laid the foundations of a new society in which only two friendly classes, workers and peasants, lived side by side in harmony. The new constitution thus abolished the discrimination between urban and rural voters and substituted direct for indirect elections. With an eye to the Western democracies, with whom Stalin was seeking an accommodation against Hitler's Germany at the time, the Stalin Constitution guaranteed the right of personal property to the Soviet citizen and added an elaborate bill of "Fundamental Rights and Duties." The constitution also established an independent judiciary "subject only to the law."

The Stalin Constitution retained the federal structure of 1924, adding only a few changes to established federal organs. The number of union republics was gradually increased to sixteen by 1940 as a result of the division of the Transcaucasian Republic into its original components, Armenia, Georgia, and Azerbaidjan, the creation of the new Kazakh and Kirghiz republics, and the establishment of the Karelo-Finnish, Moldavian, Estonian, Latvian, and Lithuanian republics after the Soviet annexations of 1940.

The union republics retained the theoretical right of secession and were even authorized, by constitutional amendment of 1944, to maintain separate foreign diplomatic representation. The true purpose of the 1944 amendment was to justify the Soviet demand for more than one seat in the projected United Nations.

The bicameral Supreme Soviet, the highest organ of state, consisted of the Soviet of the Union, with one deputy elected by every 300,000 inhabitants, and the Soviet of Nationalities, with 25 deputies elected in each union republic, 11 deputies in each autonomous republic, 5 deputies in each autonomous region, and one deputy in each national area. In joint session, both chambers elected a Presidium, which acted as a collegial presidency and was empowered to appoint or dismiss the members of the cabinet, called Peoples' Commissars and renamed Ministers in 1946.

The Stalin Constitution departed from earlier Soviet constitutional practice in that it mentioned the Communist party by name and recognized its overriding role in Soviet politics. Article 141 of the Stalin Constitution listed the Communist party as one of the organizations entitled to the nomination of candidates for elective office. Article 126 identified the party as "the leading core of all organizations of the working people, both public and state."

As a propaganda venture for the benefit of Western liberal opinion, the Stalin Constitution was a limited success only, for its promulgation coincided with the beginning of the Stalinist Purge. The constitutionally guaranteed protection of the individual from arbitrary arrest and search as well as the right of the accused to defense counsel do not seem to have appreciably affected NKVD methods of arrest and interrogation or the carefully rehearsed proceedings at the show trials. Bukharin and Radek, who had participated in the drafting of the Stalin Constitution, were among the early victims of the Purge.

SOCIAL CHANGE AND THE REVIVAL
OF NATIONALISM

As previously noted, the permissive and experimental social climate of the 1920's had loosened family ties and created roaming bands of homeless children. By the mid-1930's one out of every two marriages in Moscow ended in divorce. This social climate was ill suited to the discipline and regimentation demanded during the era of the Five Year Plans. Stalin thus repudiated the social ethics of Kollontai, Preobrazhensky and Lunacharsky, and embraced the more conservative teachings of Anton S. Marenko, an educator experienced in the rehabilitation of homeless children. Marenko praised the family as a collective in miniature, in which parents could impart the values of duty, discipline, and hard work.

Reflecting Marenko's social ethics, Soviet social legislation of the 1930's outlawed abortion and imposed heavy penalties on divorced fathers for non support of children. Childbearing was officially encouraged through the granting of awards and titles to prolific mothers. Divorce was made more expensive, if not more difficult, under the divorce law of June 1936, which charged 50 rubles for the first, 150 rubles for the second, and 300 rubles for the third or subsequent divorces. Stalin contributed personally to the new cult of the family by a much publicized journey to his mother in Georgia in 1934, of whom little had been heard previously. The return to traditional social mores coincided with an official campaign to revive interest in pre-revolutionary Russian heroes and to foster a rebirth of traditional nationalism. In the Red Army, service ranks were restored and the saluting of officers made mandatory by decree of September, 1935. In 1936 the title "Hero of the Soviet Union" was introduced and officers' pay significantly increased. Under the new oath of 1939, the soldier no longer swore allegiance to the "international proletariat" but to his "homeland, the Union of Soviet Socialist Republics." The official campaign to restore Russia's pre-revolutionary heroes inevitably led to changes in the writing and interpretation of Russian history. The Central Committee and the Sovnarkom thus decreed by joint resolution of May, 1934, that secondary school history textbooks be rewritten with more emphasis on the "greatness and dignity of the national past of the peoples of the Soviet Union." M. N. Pokrovsky, the dean of soviet historians until his death in 1931, was now criticized for his predominantly Marxist interpretation of history and his failure to pay sufficient attention to the "role of genius in history." The soviet film industry and soviet literature were given similar assignments for the rehabilitation of past heroes, such as the tsarist generals Suvorov and Kutuzov and even the tsars themselves.

The revival of nationalism was intended to unite the Russian people against the growing danger from Japan and Germany in the 1930's and to exalt Stalin's role as the prime mover of Russia's progress in the present by identifying him with historic figures in Russia's past. In Sergej Eisenstein's sympathetic film portrayal of Ivan the Terrible, fighting rebellious and scheming Boyars, or Alexander Nevsky, defeating the Teutonic Knights, the viewer could detect without much difficulty the heroic traits of Russia's current leader.

The creative artist, apart from being obliged to glorify the leader *(vozhd)*, was called upon to promote official policy within narrowly defined and often changing limits. The writer became the "engineer of the human soul," encouraged to express "social realism" by portraying the world, not as it was, but as it should and will be in a perfect socialist society.

The heavy hand of party censorship also fell on the Soviet scientific community. Einstein's theory of relativity, Norbert Wiener's cybernetics and Gregor Mendel's genetics were officially condemned as incompatible with dialectical materialism. Stalin intervened personally in the debate between Professor N. J. Vavilov, the Russian geneticist of world renown, and Trofym D. Lysenko, a charlatan by all professional accounts, and upheld Lysenko's thesis of environmental influence on plant heredity. In 1938 Lysenko advanced to the presidency of the Soviet Academy of Agricultural Sciences, and Vavilov vanished into Siberia. Those who belonged to the Vavilov school of Soviet genetics were denounced as "unpatriotic fly-breeders."

THE STALINIST PURGE

On December 1, 1934 Sergej M. Kirov, Stalin's protegé, member of the Politburo, and party secretary of Leningrad, was assassinated by Leonid V. Nikolaev, an obscure party member who was frustrated by his failure to advance in the party. On December 1, 1934, the Central Committee promulgated a decree directing the NKVD to carry out death sentences against terrorists without appeal to higher party organs. On December 27, 1934, Nikolaev and several other party members were tried in secrecy for the murder of Kirov and executed shortly afterwards.

Kirov's assassination touched off a purge *(tshistka)* of unparalleled dimensions. Whereas previous purges or show trials had served the intelligible purpose of cleansing the party of suspected opportunists or of finding scapegoats, the Stalinist Purge affected, in stages, the party, the armed forces, and eventually the entire population in a seemingly irrational holocaust of arrests, deportations, and executions. The original purpose of the Stalinist Purge appears to have been to eliminate surviving members of the Left and Right opposition of the 1920's and their sympathizers. In its later stages, the purge seems to have been prompted by Stalin's fear of a military revolt, as Red Army generals complained about sagging troop morale in the wake of forced collectivization. In its final stage, the purge seems simply to have gotten out of control before Stalin called a sudden halt in December, 1938, lest it devour the entire party and jeopardize the hard-won gains of industrialization. The secrecy of Nikolaev's trial, the Central Committee order for prompt executions on the day of Kirov's murder, and hints by Khrushchev at the Twentieth Party Congress in 1956 suggest that Kirov's assassination was arranged by Stalin and that Nikolaev was an unwitting tool of the regime who merely provided a pretext for the purge.

The purge began with a screening of party members in 1935 and a subsequent reduction in party membership from 2.8 million to little over two million in 1936. The mass expulsion of party members was followed by the show trial of the former Left Opposition leaders Zinoviev and Kamenev as well as fourteen other Old Bolsheviks in August, 1936.

Zinoviev, Kamenev, and their co-defendants were charged with conspiring with Trotsky to murder Kirov. All accused confessed and all were executed. During the trial, the accused styled themselves "bandits, assassins, fascists, and agents of the Gestapo." One accused thanked the prosecutor for having demanded the "only penalty we deserve." Tomsky committed suicide on August 23, 1936.

The second show trial against seventeen Old Bolsheviks, including Karl Radek and G. Sokolnikov, Lenin's trusted companion, opened in January, 1937. The charge was conspiracy with Trotsky to overthrow the Soviet regime and restore capitalism to Russia with the aid of Germany and Japan. Fourteen of the accused were executed. Radek, though given only a ten year prison sentence, was never heard of again. On June 12, 1937, the execution of Marshal Tukhashevsky, hero of the Civil War and organizer of the Red Army in the early 1930's, was announced. Tukhashevsky's execution was followed by the death of other leading Red Army officers, among them General Uborevich, the victor over Denikin in the Civil War. The military purge claimed the lives of three Marshals out of five, thirteen out of fifteen army commanders, sixty-two out of eighty-five corps commanders, 110 out of 195 divisional commanders, and 220 out of 406 brigade commanders. As hundreds of the Red Army's top commanders were slain, Communist party control over the army was increased by decree of August 15, 1937, which declared political commissars equal to army officers. Some of the arrested officers were rehabilitated in 1938, Tolbukhin and Rokossovsky among them, who served Stalin with distinction in the Second World War.

The show trials continued in March 1938 with the Trial of the Twenty-one, which settled accounts with the former Right opposition. In addition to Bukharin and Rykov, the prisoners included the former Commissars of Foreign Trade and Finance, Rosengoltz and Grinko, as well as the former NKVD chief, Yagoda. The charge was secret collaboration with Nazi Germany and Japan, sabotage, and intent to kill Stalin

FIGURE 7 *Three victims of the tshistka: Tomsky, Rykov, Bukharin.*

and other members of the Politburo. Yagoda, NKVD chief at the time of Kirov's murder, was accused of having facilitated Kirov's assassination, which may indeed have been the case after Stalin had ordered it.

The trial of the twenty-one did not go as well for the regime as the earlier show trials, owing to Bukharin's irrepressible sense of humor in the face of certain death and the unscheduled withdrawal of a confession by one of the accused, the former Party Secretary and one-time Soviet ambassador to Germany, Krestinsky. Krestinsky's deviation was corrected after a court recess, but Bukharin continued to confound Andrej Vishinsky, Stalin's star accuser in the show trials, by his injections of Hegelian philosophy into the testimony. In the end, Bukharin confessed, however, and the words of his confession suggest that an enduring faith in the cause of his youth, rather than hopes for personal survival, motivated his surrender. Against "everything positive that glistens in the Soviet Union," Bukharin concluded his testimony, "all the personal incrustation, all the rancor, pride and a number of other things, fall away and disappear."

Before the purge ground to a halt at the turn of 1938/1939, it had destroyed not only Stalin's old opponents but many who had actively supported his rise to power, such as I. E. Rudzutak, S. V. Kossior, and Sergej Ordjonikidze. Of the 71 members of the Central Committee elected at the Seventeenth Party Congress in 1934, 55 had been purged. The victims of the purge also included many foreign Communists, such as Bela Kun of 1919 fame, who had sought asylum in the Soviet Union. It seemed as though Stalin was bent on exterminating all Bolshevik leaders who had achieved fame before he came to power and on replacing them with younger men who had joined the party after Lenin's death in 1924. From his distant exile, a saddened and resigned Trotsky delivered the eulogy for a fallen generation of Old Bolsheviks as though accompanied by the sound of muffled drums: "The old generation with whom we once embarked upon the road of revolution has been swept off the stage. What Tsarist deportations, prisons and katorga (concentration camp), what the privations of life in exile, what civil war, and what illness had not done, Stalin, the worst scourge of the revolution, has accomplished in these last few years."

The end of the purge was heralded by the dismissal of N. I. Yezhov, Yagoda's successor in the NKVD, in December, 1938. Soon afterwards Yezhov, after whose name the final stage of the purge has been called "Yezhovshchina," disappeared without trial unmourned. The purgers were being purged. A report in the soviet press of December, 1938, of the arrest of a Moldavian NKVD official for the extortion of false testimony from innocent prisoners was a further hint of impending change. At the Eighteenth Party Congress of March, 1939, Zhdanov noted a "lack of concern" for the people among party leaders and demanded better protection of party members. Stalin had silenced his real and imagined foes; the purge was ended. Silenced too was the spirit of enthusiasm and genuine dedication with which the young had once mounted

FIGURE 8 *Stalin attending session of Supreme Soviet in 1937. With Stalin (left to right): Bulganin, Zhdanov, Voroshilov, and Khrushchev.*

the new barricades of the industrial revolution. The packed suitcase, held in readiness for the expected pre-dawn arrest by the men of the NKVD, epitomized the spirit of Stalinist Russia in the 1930's more eloquently than all statistics of the Five Year Plans.

The Stalinist Purge disillusioned many of Soviet Russia's Western intellectual friends. Their disillusionment was invariably a shocking experience and often a traumatic one, if only because Stalinism before the purge seemed to be offering rational answers to the material needs of man when Western liberalism appeared to have failed in the social and economic catastrophe of the Great Depression. To Arthur Koestler, whose novel *Darkness at Noon* gave a fictional account of the Stalinist terror, the break with his Communist past seemed like the falling from a tightrope into a net full of "veteran acrobats who had lost their dialectical balance." Those who had rationalized the Stalinist terror as an ugly but inevitable aspect of Soviet Russia's preparations for war with Nazi Germany suffered their ultimate disillusionment with the conclusion of the Stalin-Hitler Pact of August, 1939.

16 | The Triumph of Dictatorship II:
Nazi Germany

THE NAZI CONQUEST OF THE STATE

Like Mussolini in 1922, Hitler came to power by legal means and as the head of a coalition government. In Germany, the Nazi members of the coalition were outnumbered by their conservative partners eight to three. Like Italian Fascism after 1922, German National Socialism accepted the coalition government of January 30, 1933, as a temporary arrangement only, imposed by political necessity and useful as a screen for the implementation of a single party dictatorship in the guise of national revolution. The Nazi conquest of the machinery of the state proceeded, however, at much greater speed and produced more thorough-going results than had been the case in Fascist Italy.

THE EMERGENCY DECREES OF FEBRUARY 1933

Hitler's first assault on the constitutional barriers against dictatorship came with the emergency decrees of February 4 and 28, 1933, issued on the basis of Article 48 of the Weimar constitution. The decree of February 4 empowered the government to ban newspapers and public assemblies; the decree of February 28 entitled "Ordinance for the Protection of the Nation and State," suspended the constitutionally guaranteed civil liberties for an indefinite period.

The emergency decree of February 28, 1933, though less publicized than subsequent Nazi measures, marked nonetheless the decisive step in the transformation of Germany from liberal democracy to police state. By suspending the civil liberties of Weimar Germany, Hitler ended not only individual freedoms but the chance for the free manifestation of political forces other than his own. As one of the cornerstones of the Nazi political edifice, the decree of February 28, 1933, remained in force until the end of Hitler Germany in 1945.

President Hindenburg sanctioned the sweeping measures of February 28, 1933, on the strength of Nazi allegations that the burning of the Reichstag building on February 27, 1933, was engineered by the Communist party and was to have served as the signal for a nationwide Communist uprising. Although the Nazi party itself was widely credited by its opponents with having started the Reichstag fire, as a pretext for

Communist persecution, the origins of the fire have remained obscure to the present day. The only person actually seized in the Reichstag during the fire and subsequently executed for the crime, the Dutch ex-Communist Martinus van der Lubbe, steadfastly denied any connection with German Communists during his trial. Whatever the origins, Hitler exploited the Reichstag fire, not only as a justification of the suspension of civil liberties, but as an issue in the forthcoming Reichstag elections of March 5, 1933.

THE ELECTIONS OF MARCH 1933

The elections of March 5, 1933, did not produce the Nazi landslide that Hitler had expected. Despite a virtual Nazi monopoly over the means of mass communication and political propaganda, thanks to the emergency decree of February 4, Socialist, Communist, and Catholic Center party voters showed themselves surprisingly impervious to Nazi threats and blandishments. As against the elections of November, 1932, SPD strength declined from 20.7 to 18.3 per cent and KPD strength from 16.9 to 12.3 per cent, while the Center party vote decreased from 15 to 14 per cent. The increase in Nazi strength from 33.1 to 43.9 per cent was due less to voter defection from other parties than to the support of newly registered voters, as well as previous non-voters. With 89 per cent, voter participation was unusually high. Though falling short of a simple majority, the Nazi party nonetheless secured control over the new Reichstag with the support of its Nationalist allies, who polled 8 per cent of the vote. For the first time since 1930, Germany had a government supported by a parliamentary majority, making Hitler less dependent on Hindenburg's confidence than Brüning, Papen, or Schleicher had ever been.

The opening of the newly elected Reichstag on March 21, 1933, was a grand ceremony, carefully staged by Hitler in the Potsdam garrison church over the tombs of Frederick William I and Frederick the Great. The bringing together of Hindenburg, the crown prince, the army leadership, the Nazi bosses, and the Reichstag in a shrine of Prussian history was designed to symbolize the union between aristocratic Prussia and dynamic Nazism. The speeches and ceremonies of the "Day of Potsdam" thus served the Nazi purpose of claiming the succession to the grandeur of Imperial Germany and of attaching the Hindenburg mystique to the Nazi course of action.

THE ENABLING ACT

The rites of Potsdam successfully concluded, Hitler proceeded to eliminate the second major obstacle on his path towards personal dictatorship by depriving the Reichstag of its legislative function. The enabling act ("law for terminating the suffering of people and nation"), enacted by the Reichstag on March 24, 1933, conferred the legislative powers of the Reichstag upon the government for a four-year period. Since the enabling act was not a simple law but a constitutional change, it required a two-thirds majority for passage.

Through threats and false promises—the Catholic Center was promised revocation of the emergency decree of February 4, 1933, in return for its vote—Hitler secured the support of all parties except that of the Social Democrats. The Communists posed no problem since their deputies had not been seated in the new Reichstag. Social Democratic opposition to the enabling act, though politically futile, was nevertheless a demonstration of moral and physical courage, all the more so because

FIGURE 9   *Hitler and Hindenburg in May Day Parade, 1933.*

Nazi storm troopers were placed conspicuously between the aisles of voting deputies.

THE HITLER-WELS EXCHANGE

Otto Wels, the SPD spokesman and himself a veteran of many a battle with the Communists during the German revolution of 1918/1919, attacked Hitler in a bold speech for the lawlessness, persecution, suppression of criticism, and dictatorial designs of the Hitler government. Wels, who might be called the Matteotti of the Nazi revolution, concluded his accusations against Hitler with the remark: "No enabling act empowers you to remove ideas which are eternal and indestructible." The Wels speech prompted the first and last parliamentary debate to which Hitler was a party. In his response, Hitler accused the SPD for its failure to turn the German revolution of 1918 into a national uprising as republican France had done after the defeat of the Napoleonic Empire in 1870. To the Social Democratic charge that his government had silenced criticism, Hitler replied; "He who loves Germany may criticize us; he who worships the International, may not."

THE DISSOLUTION OF THE POLITICAL PARTIES

The dissolution of the political parties, either by their own decision or the order of the government, followed the self-immolation of the Reichstag as a natural corollary. After the banning of the SPD on June 22, 1933, the other political parties announced their dissolution in July. The law against the formation of new parties of July 14, 1933, declared the Nazi party the sole political party of Germany.

After 1933 Reichstag elections were limited to Nazi candidates. The Reichstag became a rubber stamp legislature which periodically renewed the special legislation of 1933, including the enabling act, upon its expiration. Otherwise, the Reichstag served as a propaganda sounding board and also as a fashion show in which the Reichstag members could display a wide array of Nazi uniforms, identifying the wearer as a member of the party, the SA, the SS, or any of the numerous affiliate organizations of the party.

Having eliminated the civil liberties of the Weimar constitution and destroyed the powers of the Reichstag, Hitler proceeded to dismantle the federal structure of Germany. The first step towards that end was the emergency decree of February 28, 1933, which authorized the national government to take over the police powers of the federal states. After the enabling act, Hitler dissolved all state legislatures and reorganized them on the basis of the national election results of March 5. In April, 1933, Nazi governors were appointed to all federal states, and in January, 1934, the state legislatures were dissolved. In February,

1934, the Reichsrat, the upper chamber and representative body of the states, was abolished. Germany had become a unitary state; the Nazi governors were responsible to the ministry of the interior, the federal states were reduced to administrative districts.

The abolition of the federal structure of Germany, it should be noted, had been a goal strongly advocated by many German Social Democrats during the revolution of 1918/1919. What the socialist revolution of 1918 had failed to accomplish for lack of determination the Nazi revolution achieved in short order without encountering opposition.

THE CIVIL SERVICE AND THE COURTS

Nazi control over the civil service was established by law of April 7, 1933, "for the restoration of the career civil service," empowering the regime to dismiss civil servants for reasons of past political activity or racial origin. The integration of the judicial branch of government into the Nazi system proved a more difficult task. Although Nazi Germany did not formally abolish the independence of judges, it brought great pressure to bear on the law courts to render decisions consistent with the Nazi slogan "law is what is useful to the German people." Despite the creation of a Reich Commissioner for justice for "the renewal of the legal system," the coordination of the judiciary never quite succeeded. Hitler's distrust of the legal profession in general and judges in particular persisted to the end of Nazi days. The extent of his personal interference in the judiciary may be gleaned from an incident which occurred during the Second World War. When informed through a newspaper article about a court sentence against a defendant in a manslaughter case, Hitler telephoned the ministry of justice and demanded a retrial with a stiffer penalty. The case was duly reopened, and the defendant was sentenced to death. Following this incident, Hitler announced to the Reichstag, on April 26, 1942, that henceforth judges would be dismissed if their decisions were not consistent with the seriousness of the times.

Within a year of his coming to power, Hitler had removed all obstacles to dictatorship save the institution of the presidency and the armed forces. Hitler's conservative coalition partners, pinning their hopes on Hindenburg as the last bulwark against a full-blown Nazi dictatorship, attempted to persuade the President to appeal for the restoration of the monarchy. Before his death on August 2, 1934, Hindenburg indeed expressed his wish for a restoration of the monarchy to Hitler, although in private only. Hitler ignored the wish. Apart from his refusal to share power with anyone, Hitler regarded the example of Fascist Italy, where the crown continued to enjoy a certain prestige and power independent of Mussolini, as a warning to himself. Following Hindenburg's death, he united the offices of president and chancellor in his own person, assuming the title "Fuehrer and Reich-Chancellor." In a new and personal oath of loyalty, the army swore "unconditional obedience to the Fuehrer of the German Reich and people."

HITLER, THE WEHRMACHT, AND THE SA

The armed forces posed a special problem to the young Nazi regime in view of the mounting tension between the regular army and Hitler's SA formations. Though largely of aristocratic background and disdainful of the proletarian element in the Nazi movement, the army leadership generally welcomed Hitler's chancellorship as an end to the political bickering of Weimar and a beginning to rearmament. The younger, more technologically minded officers, eager to mechanize the German army, were particularly impressed with the personal interest which Hitler displayed in such matters at an early stage. Shortly after becoming chancellor, Hitler paid a visit to the army's weapons research and development center at Kummersdorf—the first German chancellor to do so since Bismarck. General Werner von Blomberg, the Minister of War, was anxious to serve the new regime.

As a condition for its service to Hitler, however, the army demanded the elimination of the SA as a rival and recognition of the German army as the "sole bearer of arms." By 1933 SA membership had grown to nearly a million and Ernst Roehm, the SA chief of staff, favored the merger of his own forces with the Reichswehr. By 1934 Roehm and the SA had thus become a liability to Hitler, not only because of Roehm's military ambitions but for political reasons as well. Impatient with Hitler's "legal" revolution for the conquest of the state apparatus, the radical elements in the SA demanded a second, social, revolution. Towards the end of 1933 the remark, "Adolf will have to be taught a lesson," could be heard in gatherings of SA leaders.

On June 30, 1934, Hitler resolved the SA dilemma in a surprise attack upon the SA throughout Germany, in which hundreds of SA leaders, as well as ordinary members, were executed by the SS, Hitler's elite guard. The victims of the Blood Purge included individuals unrelated to Hitler's quarrel with the SA, such as Gregor Strasser, ex-chancellor General Schleicher and his wife, General von Bredow, Gustav Kahr, who had thwarted Hitler's beer-hall putsch of 1923, and others who had crossed Hitler's will. Hitler justified the murders as an act of emergency to protect the state against a treasonable conspiracy. The law of July 3, 1934, sanctioned Hitler's action.

On the surface, Hitler appeared to have paid his price to the German army. In truth, the events of June 30, 1934, marked the beginning of the army's submission to Hitler, outwardly symbolized by the new loyalty oath as well as the appearance of the swastika eagle on the German army uniform. The opposition of the army leadership to Hitler's

FIGURE 10 *Victim of Hitler's Blood Purge of 1934:*
Captain Ernst Roehm.

foreign policy designs in 1938 enabled him to tighten his control over the armed forces through the abolition of the war ministry and its replacement by a new agency, the High Command of the Armed Forces (OKW).

The German army retained, nevertheless, a larger measure of independence opposite the Nazi regime than did the Red Army opposite the Bolshevik regime of Soviet Russia, there being no political commissars in the German army. Only after the army officers' abortive plot to assassinate Hitler on July 20, 1944, were so-called "political guidance officers" introduced and the regular army salute replaced by the Nazi salute.

The true winner of the contest between army and the SA in 1934 was the SS, since 1929 under the command of Heinrich Himmler. After July 30, 1934, the disorganized violence which the SA had perpetrated, much in the manner of the Fascist *squadristi,* gave way to a system of SS terror, more centralized, institutionalized, and disciplined to Hitler's will. In due course, the SS developed into a state within the Nazi empire. In 1936 Himmler became chief of all German police and in 1943 minister of the interior. The SS provided Hitler's personal guard with the *Leibstandarte A.H.* and administered and guarded the Nazi concentration camps through its deathhead formations. With the establishment of armed SS divisions *(Waffen-SS)*, Hitler broke his promise to the army that it alone would be the bearer of arms in Nazi Germany.

On the surface the Nazi system of government, based on the principles of "coordination" *(Gleichschaltung)* and leadership, effected an appearance of great efficiency. The air of dynamism and efficiency was enhanced by the tangible economic gains of Nazi Germany before the war, by the multitude of public projects, and of endeavors launched, and by the disciplined grandeur of mass party rallies, dramatically staged by Hitler's chief architect, Albert Speer. The official image of smooth and responsive government belied the reality of inefficiency, rivalry, and duplication of effort on the part of Nazi governors, SS empire builders, and governmental agencies. On the highest level, Hitler soon discontinued the practice of regular cabinet meetings and issued orders and directives without the knowledge of the minister in charge. During the Second World War, it was not uncommon for a minister of the Nazi government to learn of the existence of a new decree from the newspapers. Setting up rival agencies for an identical task became one of Hitler's favorite administrative devices for reserving ultimate decisions to himself and preventing any individual from amassing too much power. The absence of a free and critical press did not remove corruption from public life in Nazi Germany but merely made it more invisible.

Corruption luxuriated in high places more abundantly in Nazi Germany than ever was the case in the Weimar Republic, whose petty scandals Goebbels had delighted in castigating in his paper *Der Angriff*. As though obsessed with a desire to crowd as much high living and plunder as possible into the twelve years of Hitler's thousand-year empire, the high dignitaries of Nazism outdid one another in the construction of palatial homes, the sequestration of art treasures, or, in the case of Goering, the collection of precious stones. Even the Fuehrer, spartan in his personal needs, found ways of supplementing his income by claiming royalties from the sale of postage stamps which bore his image.

THE CHURCHES AND THE NAZI STATE

Hitler opened his chancellorship with reassuring words for the Christian churches of Germany. In his first government address, broadcast over the radio on February 1, 1933, Hitler told his listeners that the new government would "protect Christianity as the foundation of our entire morality." Some years later, Hitler would privately term Christianity "a fairy tale invented by the Jews" and express the hope that the Christian churches would "rot away like a gangrened member."

The Christian churches were a reality, however, which Hitler could neither integrate into the Nazi state nor afford to antagonize too openly for fear of adverse public repercussions. Hitler's initial attempt to draw a substantial majority of German Protestants into the Nazi system through the so-called "German Christian" church under Reichsbishop Ludwig Mueller was abandoned in the face of strong opposition by such Protestant clergymen as Pastor Martin Niemoeller. Among Niemoeller's followers, who organized the "Confessional Church" in protest against Hitler's "German Christians," was Dietrich Bonhoeffer, who died a martyr of German resistance against Hitler during the Second World War.

The Catholic Church, acting upon the advice of former Center Party chairman Kaas, concluded a concordat with Hitler on July 20, 1933. As in the case of Fascist Italy in 1929, the Catholic Church renounced all political activities and political organizations in Germany in exchange for liberal concessions, including the right to maintain Catholic schools in Germany. The concordat raised Hitler's international respectability but failed to secure a lasting peace between the regime and the Church. Individual Catholic clergymen, such as Cardinal Faulhaber of Munich and Bishop Galen of Muenster, spoke out publicly against the pagan attitudes and racist policies of Nazi Germany. Among the victims of Hitler's Blood Purge of June 30, 1934, was Erich Klausener, the head of Catholic Action in Berlin. On March 14, 1937, Pius XI attacked the fundamental tenets of Nazism in the encyclical *Mit Brennender Sorge* (with burning anxiety). In 1938 Monsignor Bernhard Lichtenberg of St. Hedwig's cathedral in Berlin called on his congregation in a public sermon to pray for "Jews and inmates of concentration camps."

On the eve of the Second World War, Nazi Germany and the Christian churches maintained an uneasy truce, which Hitler, judging from numerous private statements recorded during the war, had every intention of ending with a wholesale assault once he had won the war.

THE ECONOMIC AND SOCIAL POLICY OF NATIONAL SOCIALISM

The promise to end unemployment and restore a healthy economy was among the chief weapons in the Nazi propaganda arsenal. German unemployment stood at 30 per cent towards the end of 1932 with no immediate relief in sight. By 1936 the unemployment rate had fallen to 2 per cent, and by 1938 unemployment was virtually nonexistent.

Although there existed a scarcity of certain consumer goods, owing to import restrictions and the tight rationing of foreign exchange, the economic situation seemed, on the whole, more encouraging to the German public under Hitler than it had appeared in the final years of Weimar Germany.

The economic upswing of Nazi Germany may be attributed to

a variety of factors, not all of which were due to Nazi initiative or planning. To begin with, the World Depression was at the point of levelling off at the time of Hitler's advent to power, and public works projects, funded by Hitler's predecessors, reached the stage of practical implementation only after January, 1933. The Nazi regime added public works projects of its own with the launching of the four-lane super-highways *(Autobahnen)* in September, 1933. The beginning of rearmament in 1935, as well as the inauguration of the Four Year Plan in 1936, added new stimuli to the German economy. The objective of the Four Year Plan was the attainment of self-sufficiency in strategic raw materials as a prelude to war. By developing the low-yield ore fields of Salzgitter in central Germany, the regime hoped to reduce significantly the size of German ore imports. The latter, due to Germany's loss of Lorraine and parts of Upper Silesia after the First World War, accounted for 80 per cent of German consumption. Even after the acquisition of the rich Austrian ore deposits of the *Erzberg* in Styria, following the *Anschluss* of 1938, Germany still depended on imports for two thirds of its ore needs on the eve of the Second World War. In the manufacture of synthetic rubber *(Buna)*, the Four Year Plan not only achieved self-sufficiency, but produced surpluses for exports. The production of synthetic gasoline and lubricants, on the other hand, remained far below needs and planning targets at the beginning of the Second World War.

The scope of Germany's armaments production was far greater in official Nazi propaganda than in actual fact, as will be shown in the discussion of the Second World War. The total impact of public spending upon the German economy through armaments, public works, and the projects of the Four Year Plan was nonetheless considerable, one third of the national income depending on government investment and spending.

The farm program of the Nazi regime reflected the "blood and soil" mentality of Nazi ideology, which idealized the German peasantry as the foundation of racial strength. The peasant inheritance law *(Reichserbhofgesetz)* of September, 1933, declared medium-sized farms of up to twenty-four acres indivisible and prohibited such farms from sale or mortgaging. The intention was to preserve a debt-free class of peasant proprietors and combat rural migration to the cities. The latter aim was only partially fulfilled, as the needs of German industry drew several hundred thousand farm laborers into the towns between 1933 and 1939. Nazi policy did not provide for land reform through the break-up of large estates and the resettlement of small farmers, such as the Weimar Republic had contemplated under Chancellor Brüning in 1932. Only with the conquest of Poland and the Ukraine during the war did Hitler initiate a resettlement program at the expense of subjugated peoples. The scope and duration of the resettlement program remained necessarily small owing to the short period of German occupation.

The financing of Nazi economic policy was based on large-scale borrowing and deficit spending. Hjalmar Schacht, the wizard of the *Rentenmark* of 1923, advanced twelve billion marks to Hitler between 1933 and 1939, in his capacity as president of the Reichsbank. Afterwards, the Nazi government resorted to forced loans from private banks and financial institutions to cover the rising cost of war and armaments.

Nazi economic policy was pragmatic rather than doctrinaire, bearing little resemblance to the economic tenets of the early Nazi party program. The class of petty-bourgeois shopkeepers and craftsmen, which had supported Nazism on the strength of its economic promises, lost out to big business once Hitler was in power. The Nazi regime respected private ownership of the means of production, though it imposed a growing number of restraints through wage-price controls and the allocation of raw materials. Whenever big business was found wanting in effort or enthusiasm, the government launched enterprises of its own, such as the Salzgitter steel works or the Volkswagen plant at Wolfsburg.

Though borrowing some of the terminology of the Fascist corporate state, the Nazi economy was not truly organized along corporate lines. Farmers were organized in the so-called Reich Food Estate, industry and trade in the Reich Estate of German Industry. All trade unions were abolished as early as May, 1933. The Nazi Labor Front (DAF) and its affiliate *Kaft durch Freude* (KdF), a workers' leisure organization under the name "Strength through Joy," became the sole organs of labor. KdF organized extensive cultural and recreational activities, including ocean cruises on its own vessels. In 1938 KdF also launched the Volkswagen, initially called the "KdF-car," under the slogan "a car for every German." The Volkswagen plant was built by the state against considerable opposition from privately owned automobile factories, which feared the competition of a vehicle officially priced at less than $250. In any event, few Volkswagens reached the private consumer before the war, the Wolfsburg factory becoming the supplier of the military version of the Volkswagen to the German army in the Second World War.

To meet the demand for labor, the Nazi regime instituted a compulsory national labor service (RAD) by law of 1935, which drafted all German youth above eighteen for a six-month period. RAD men were used extensively in the construction of super-highways as well as in the building of military fortifications. Women were mostly assigned as farm labor.

NAZI CULTURAL AND EDUCATIONAL POLICY

The book-burning ceremony of May 10, 1933, in front of the Berlin opera, in which students consigned the works of Jewish and other "undesirable" authors to the flames, was a fitting overture to the cultural policy of National Socialism. On March 15, 1933, Hitler had established the Ministry for Popular Enlightenment and Propaganda under Joseph Goebbels for the control of press, literature, and motion pictures. The radio, previously under the administration of the postal ministry, likewise was seized by Goebbels. In due course, Goebbels established professional chambers for the arts, the theater, literature, the news media, and the movie industry. The chambers were combined to form the Reich Chamber of Culture under Goebbels' presidency. Exclusion or expulsion from the Chamber of Culture spelled the end of any professional career in the above-mentioned fields.

The editors' law of October, 1933, empowered the regime to remove newspaper editors on the grounds of political unreliability, and editors were exhorted to present the news, not in "suicidal objectivity," but in a "positive" manner. As Minister of Propaganda, Goebbels kept a watchful eye over new publications, issuing weekly lists of "undesirable" or "forbidden" books. Paintings deemed "degenerate" were removed from public galleries, though not from the private collections of Nazi dignitaries, such as Goering's. The movie industry stressed the themes of antisemitism ("Jew Suess"), the Nazi struggle against Communism before 1933 ("Hitlerjunge Quex"), or the excesses of 19th-century British imperialism ("Ohm Krueger"). Amidst the mass of Nazi propaganda films, German movie directors succeeded, on occasion, in disguising a ringing indictment of Nazi dictatorship and censorship in the context of historical subjects. In the motion picture *"Die Entlassung"* (the dismissal), which dealt with Bismarck's career, the German Social Democratic leader August Bebel was shown delivering a stinging attack against Bismarck's policy of Social Democratic persecution in words which the viewer could easily apply to the political conditions of Nazi Germany. The device of attacking the present regime through historical parallels or Aesopian parables was also employed in the writing of fiction and even in historical scholarship.

In architecture, Nazi Germany produced its own style of grandiose proportions, designed to bear witness to the Hitler era for future generations. Hitler, himself a frustrated architect who had failed to gain entrance to the Vienna Academy of Fine Arts as a youth, took a personal hand in determining architectural style and city planning. Albert Speer, Hitler's favorite architect and "Inspector General of Buildings," translated Hitler's sketches, some of which dated back to the 1920's, into reality. During the short period from 1933 to 1939, when Nazi Germany was still at peace, only a few of the planned buildings were actually completed. Among these were the House of German Art in Munich, the vast Nuremberg Zeppelin Field for party rallies, and the new Reich Chancellery, completed in 1939. The latter, bombed out during the war, served as a stone quarry for the huge Soviet war memorial in East Berlin after

1945. Paris and Vienna were the European cities whose architecture Hitler most admired. Nazi plans for the redevelopment of Berlin, scheduled to be completed by 1950, were to outdistance either city, however, at least in the dimensions of the projected public buildings and avenues. Berlin's "Grand Boulevard," more than twice the length of the Champs Elysee of Paris, was to be flanked by a Soldiers' Hall as burial place of German field marshals, an arch of triumph, over 500 feet wide and 386 feet high, and a domed hall with a cupola sixteen times the size of St. Peter's in Rome, reaching nearly a thousand feet into the sky. Berlin, Hitler predicted, would be "changed beyond recognition," a forecast which proved to be accurate though not in the sense intended. Among other cities favored by Nazi town planning were Nuremberg, to receive a stadium large enough for 400,000 people, and Linz, the capital of Upper Austria and place of Hitler's boyhood. The criteria of Nazi architecture were not only unprecedented dimensions of public buildings but the safety of their occupants from riot and mob violence. Hitler's palace on the Grand Boulevard of Berlin was to be equipped with bullet-proof steel shutters for doors and windows. The masses, which Hitler's oratory whipped into frenzies of emotional abandon, it appears, continued to inspire fear in Germany's most powerful dictator.

German youth was subjected to Nazi propaganda and ideology from an early age, not only through the Hitler Youth organization under Baldur von Schirach, but in the textbooks for primary and secondary education. Sometimes the party line in textbooks for secondary schools could not keep pace with the rapid shifts in Hitler's foreign policy. History textbooks, for example, which had been revised after the conclusion of the Stalin-Hitler pact of 1939 were sympathetic in their treatment of Soviet Russia and praised the discipline and conduct of Red Army troops in the Russo-Polish war of 1920. This interpretation was in striking contrast to the new image of Soviet man, which Nazi propaganda invented after Hitler's attack on the Soviet Union on June 22, 1941, depicting the people of Russia as *"Untermenschen"* (sub-humans).

The coordination of the universities proceeded with relative ease, and instances of open student or faculty rebellion against the regime were few. In February, 1943, Hans and Sophie Scholl, two students at the University of Munich, together with Professor Kurt Huber, were seized and executed when attempting to distribute anti-Nazi leaflets on the Munich campus. The old student fraternities were dissolved at an early stage, and the universities lost their autonomous status, with deans and presidents appointed by the state rather than elected by the faculties, as had been customary. For the training of the future party élite, the régime instituted special National Political Education Institutes (Napola), renowned more for their emphasis on ideology than scholarship.

ANTI-SEMITISM:
THE NUREMBERG RACIAL LAWS

Nazi persecution of the German Jews began with an official boycott of Jewish businesses and shops on March 28, 1933. The boycott was organized throughout Germany by local "action committees" of the SA and was justified by the régime as a retaliation against foreign press reports, unfavorable to the Nazi government and attributed by Hitler to Jewish influence. The Jews of Germany were thus held hostage for the good behavior of the foreign press. The civil service law of 1933, previously mentioned, marked a further step along the path of Jewish persecution, removing Jews from German public life. President Hindenburg vainly protested these measures, especially where they involved German Jewish veterans of the First World War or Jewish war orphans. "If they were worthy of fighting and bleeding for Germany," Hindenburg wrote to Hitler, "they must be considered worthy of continuing to serve the fatherland in their professions."

Within a year of Hindenburg's death Hitler issued the Nuremberg racial laws ("Law for the Protection of German Blood and German Honor") of September 1935, which deprived German Jews of the rights of citizenship. The racial laws and subsequent implementing decrees outlawed mixed marriages, prohibited Jews from employing non-Jewish female domestics below age 45 and excluded Jews from virtually all professions. Jewish children were forbidden to have Christian surnames and had to be given first names authorized by the ministry of the interior.

The policy of humiliation and chicanery of the Nuremberg laws was followed by mass violence during the events of November 9, 10, 1938, known as *"Kristallnacht"* (literally: "crystal night" — night of broken glass). Following the assassination of the German embassy counselor Ernst von Rath in Paris by a young Jew, Herschel Grynspan, Goebbels unleashed the SA on synagogues, Jewish businesses and homes. The SA carried out its mission without wearing uniforms in order to give the violence the appearance of a spontaneous popular uprising. The pogrom of November 1938 marked the transition of Nazi policy from legalized discrimination to wholesale physical extermination of the Jews, which the Hitler regime commenced soon after the outbreak of the Second World War.

17 | The Triumph of Dictatorship III:
Fascist Italy

FASCIST DOCTRINE

Having secured a monopoly of political power through the Fascist Laws of the 1920's, Fascism proceeded to recast the social, economic, cultural, and educational life of Italy in a totalitarian mold. In its march towards full-blown dictatorship, Italian Fascism followed less the dictates of a preconceived ideology than pragmatic considerations of power. The ideological underpinnings of Italian Fascism had always been slight, in part because of Mussolini's own intellectual vacillations from Marx to Nietzsche to Sorel, in part because action, rather than thought, had formed the essence of Fascism from its beginnings. Philosophy, Mussolini once confessed, was "an impediment to freedom of action."

By the early 1930's Fascism represented, nevertheless, more than the sum total of its individual actions. Rather, it proclaimed itself as a new political philosophy, whose general validity was confirmed by the course of European history since the First World War. The official statement of Italian Fascist doctrine was contained in the *Fundamental Ideas* and the *Political and Social Doctrine,* both published in volume XIV of the *Enciclopedia Italiana* in June, 1932, and written by Giovanni Gentile, Mussolini's first Minister of Education and by Mussolini himself. Henceforth, the *Fundamental Ideas* and the *Political and Social Doctrine* were quoted under the title of *Fascist Doctrine (Dottrina Fascisma).*

The *Fascist Doctrine* attributed the origin and rise of Fascism to the failure of liberal democracy, both in Italy, as well as on the broader plane of early 20th-century European civilization. Liberalism, according to Mussolini, had failed in the solution of Italy's foremost national problem, that of economic development. Fascism alone, in Mussolini's view, could "regain in a few years the time lost in half a century" through a government based on the principles of *credere, obbedire, combattere* (to believe, to obey, to fight).

As for Europe at large, Italian Fascism pointed to the First World War as the most damning failure of 19th-century liberalism. "The liberal century," Mussolini stated in the *Fascist Doctrine,* "after piling up innumerable Gordian knots, tried to cut them with the sword of the world war. Never has any religion claimed so cruel a sacrifice."

The *Fascist Doctrine* denounced Marxian socialism together with the entire concept of historical materialism. Likewise, it rejected democracy as an "absurd conventional lie of political egalitarianism" and as a "kingless regime infested by many kings." By contrast, it defined "Fascist democracy" as rule of the most qualified, rather than rule by the sheer majority of numbers. The *Fascist Doctrine* credited Fascism with having found a unique solution to the problem of capital-labor relations in the form of the "corporate system." The corporate system, whose structure and actual workings will be discussed more fully in the context of Fascist economic and social policy, was defined as a new partnership of capital and labor under state guidance, avoiding both the chaos of unfettered liberalism and the extreme measure of expropriation of the means of production, adopted under Communism. Lastly, on the subject of religion, the *Fascist Doctrine* professed not only respect, but a desire to "defend and protect" religion. Fascism vowed that it would neither set up its own "god" nor seek to efface God from the soul of the masses, as the Bolsheviks had attempted to do in Russia.

Except for the novel concept of the corporate system, the *Fascist Doctrine* was essentially a restatement of conservative principles, which did not adequately explain the Italian Fascist phenomenon of the 1930's. Though extolling the all-powerful "Fascist state," the doctrine failed to suggest the emotional and irrational dimensions of Fascist mass-psychology, the militarization of public utterances and events, and the choreography of public rallies, from the smallest village piazza to the grand setting of the Piazza Venezia of Rome under Mussolini's balcony. Ritual was as important to Fascism as were its stated goals, for it was in the rites of uniformed and chanting masses that Fascism aspired to attain its myth and grandeur. The *Fascist Doctrine,* although devised as the political creed of Italy, also addressed itself to Europe at large. The Great Depression of 1929, and the increased role which democratic governments of the West were forced to play in economic and social affairs under its impact, appeared to Mussolini as evidence that Fascism, or something closely resembling it, was evolving in the Western world as well. To Mussolini, Fascism thus appeared as the ideology of the future, which would leave its imprint on 20th-century Europe in much the same way that liberalism and individualism had shaped the course of 19th-century European civilization. "Never before," Mussolini wrote in the *Fascist Doctrine,* "have the peoples thirsted for authority, direction, order, as they do now. If each age has its doctrine, then innumerable symptoms indicate that the doctrine of our age is the Fascist. . . ." When Communist Russia entered the Stalinist decade of the 1930's with a public display of inner conflicts and suicidal purges, Mussolini became more firmly convinced than ever that Fascist Rome, rather than Communist Moscow, was des-

FIGURE 11 *King Victor Emanuel and the Duce during Italian army maneuvers in 1938.*

tined to preside over the political and ideological renewal of 20th-century Europe.

The Fascist presumption of moral leadership may help explain Mussolini's diminishing sense of proportion and realism in the conduct of Italian foreign affairs of the 1930's, which will be discussed elsewhere. It was not as the leader of a medium-sized European nation without adequate resources that Mussolini played his role on the diplomatic and military stage of the 1930's; rather, he acted as the herald of a new political faith, soon to affect European civilization at large and expressing the hidden desires of the European bourgeoisie everywhere.

THE ECONOMIC AND SOCIAL POLICY OF FASCISM

During the early period of Fascist rule, Mussolini, as has been shown, was content to minimize the economic and social role of his regime. The policy of laissez-faire gave way to ever increasing intervention of the state in economic and social matters, however, as soon as Fascist rule had been consolidated.

The stated objective of Fascist social policy was, in Mussolini's words, "the realization of a higher social justice for the entire Italian people." In fact, the regimentation and political indoctrination of labor became the practical outcome of Fascist social policy. The economic policy of Fascism aimed primarily at self-sufficiency, or autarchy, especially after the Italian invasion of Ethiopia and the imposition of economic sanctions against Italy by the League.

The promulgation of the Labor Charter *(Carta del Lavoro)* by the Fascist Grand Council on April 21, 1927, was hailed by the Fascist regime as the beginning of a new, Fascist social order through the creation of the corporate system. The corporations were bodies consisting of representatives of the employers and employees of a given industry or economic branch, as well as of three representatives of the Fascist party. In theory, the corporations were public organs with power to enforce labor agreements achieved by compromise. The Labor Charter did not affect private ownership of the means of production, stating rather that private enterprise in the domain of production was "the most efficient method and the most advantageous to the interests of the nation."

Eventually, by law of February, 1934, altogether twenty-two corporations were established, sixteen for various branches of industry and agriculture, commerce and transportation, six for the arts and professions. The corporate structure was crowned by a National Council of Corporations, a General Assembly of Corporations, and the Ministry of Corporations.

At the time of its creation, the corporate system evoked lively interest in Italy and abroad, since it appeared to hold out the promise of economic democracy, exercised through autonomous and representative economic institutions. The practice of corporatism did not fulfill this expectation, however. Far from becoming an autonomous entity, the corporate structure became an adjunct of the Fascist dictatorship, providing it with new opportunities for patronage and corruption. The members of the corporations were appointed, rather than elected as originally promised, and Mussolini himself filled the post of Minister of Corporations for several years. Nor did the corporate system achieve the promised equality of capital and labor, favoring rather employers over workers and workers who belonged to the Fascist party over those who did not.

The Fascist regime, to be sure, claimed special concern for the welfare of labor through the organization *Dopolavoro,* established on May 1, 1925. The official purpose of *Dopolavoro* was the development of the workers' "physical, intellectual and moral capacity" through organized sports, adult education courses, and inexpensive vacations. Whatever social services *Dopolavoro* actually provided after political indoctrination, however, could not offset the decline in real wages which Italian labor suffered during the decade of the 1930's.

The chief beneficiaries of Fascist economic policy continued to be big business and the large landowners. Under the corporate system, the trend toward industrial concentration and the growth of big business continued at an accelerated rate to the detriment of both the consumer and the small businessman. As for rural Italy, Fascism did little to reform its social structure, which remained sharply divided between landless laborers, tenants, and proprietors. In 1930 one half of one per cent of Italy's rural population still owned nearly 42 per cent of the land. Not unlike Prime Minister Giolitti at the beginning of the 20th century, Mussolini ruled with the consent and in the interests of northern industrialists and southern landowners. The one important difference between Giolitti's oligarchy and Mussolini's Fascism, however, was that the latter had eliminated the political voice and economic organizations of labor.

Although the corporate system remained a façade, it served as a convenient excuse for abolishing the remnants of Italy's representative electoral system. Under the electoral law of March 16, 1928, which superseded the Acerbo Law, the corporations and professional organizations submitted a list of candidates for national elections, from which the Grand Council selected 400 names. The voters' choice was limited to approval or rejection of the candidates endorsed by the Grand Council, in the manner of a plebiscite. In the two elections held under the electoral law of 1928, only 136,000 ballots were cast against the government list in 1929, and 15,000 in 1934. The logical consequence was the abolition of the Chamber of Deputies, long since a Fascist propaganda sounding board, and its replacement by a Chamber of Fasces and Corporations in 1939.

The Fascist drive toward economic self-sufficiency was opened in 1925 with the "battle for wheat" *(battaglia del grano)*. By increasing the yield per acre and through an extended program of land reclamation in the Pontine marshes, Mussolini hoped to free Italy from dependence on foreign wheat imports, which exceeded two million tons in 1925. The establishment of 3,000 new farms and the launching of an entire new city (Littoria) on the former wasteland of the Pontine marshes belonged to the proudest economic achievements of Italian Fascism, duly celebrated by official propaganda. Whereas Italians had previously been forced to cross the Alps or the ocean to find work, Mussolini commented, they were now able to find employment on land reclaimed within one half hour's distance from Rome. To spur wheat production, Mussolini joined the peasants of his native Romagna, performing the labors and accepting the wages of humble *braccianti* and having himself photographed harvesting wheat, not unlike a more recent Latin dictator in the Caribbean, pictured in the act of cutting sugar cane.

The Fascist goal of self-sufficiency in wheat was not attained on the eve of the Second World War, when only 85 per cent of wheat consumption was covered by native production.

The opening of the "battle for wheat" was followed by similar "battles" for the stabilization of the lira during the World Depression and the development of Italy's transportation system. In October, 1932, on the tenth anniversary of the Fascist march to power, Mussolini inaugurated the superhighway from Turin to Milan and opened the *Foro Mussolini* in Rome. The latter served as a new stadium, surrounded by sixty marble statues and an obelisk that, to this day, bears the inscription "Mussolini Dux." Projects of urban renewal in Rome, such as the half-mile Via dell' Imperio between the Coliseum and the monument of Victor Emmanuel, served the purpose of Fascist pomp rather than the social needs of Romans.

Beginning in the late 1920's, a distinctive element was added to Fascist social policy with the official promotion and encouragement of large families. Prior to Mussolini, Italy's high birthrate had posed a serious dilemma for Italian governments, which was only partially resolved through emigration. For Mussolini, a growing population was a prerequisite to the Great Power status of Italy. Deploring the fact that the population of Italy numbered only forty million as against "ninety million Germans and two-hundred million Slavs," Mussolini launched a "demographic" campaign in 1927 designed to raise the population of Italy to sixty million by the middle of the 20th century. To achieve his goal, Mussolini banned Italian emigration (already reduced through the American quota system) and devised incentives and penalties to reward large families and punish bachelors. Mussolini himself set an example of the demographic policy espoused by the regime with a family of five children, in addition to one illegitimate son. The regime outlawed birth control and imposed a heavy tax on bachelors (though not on unmarried women) between the ages of 25 and 65. The proceeds of the "bachelors' tax" went to support the National Organization for the Protection of Mothers and Children. Childbearing was termed a "gift" to the Fascist state, and prolific mothers were honored with medals, prizes, and an audience with Mussolini in the Duce's office at the Palazzo Venezia. Women introduced to Mussolini at social events would often not only give their names but state the number of their children as well. On occasion, the government staged mass weddings in Rome, with as many as 2,600 couples united in marriage in a single ceremony.

Mussolini's demographic policy was pursued without regard to Italy's capacity to absorb or feed the surplus millions, since the projected sixty million were not thought of solely as the future inhabitants of the Italian Peninsula, but as the masters of a new Roman Empire in the Mediterranean area. In any event, the population of Italy reached only forty-four million shortly before Mussolini's own downfall in 1943, the increase being due more to a lowering of the death rate than to a surge in the birthrate.

THE CHURCH AND FASCISM;
FASCIST CULTURAL AND
EDUCATIONAL POLICY

Both as a Socialist before the First World War and as a leader of the young Fascist movement after the war, Mussolini had been noted for his strong anti-clerical stand. In his Socialist days, Mussolini had once called the priesthood "black germs," as harmful to mankind "as the germs of tuberculosis." The first Fascist program of 1919, it will be recalled, had demanded the confiscation of church property by the state.

Since coming to power in 1922, Mussolini had found it politically expedient, however, to seek a reconciliation with the Vatican and to resolve the "Roman question," which had disturbed state-church relations in Italy ever since the seizure of Rome by the Italian kingdom in 1870. Mussolini's overtures to the Vatican were well received by the politically conservative Pope Pius XI, who, as Cardinal Achille Ratti and papal nuncio to Poland, had witnessed the Bolshevik onslaught on Warsaw in 1920.

The Lateran Agreements and the Concordat

After lengthy negotiations over a three-year period, the Vatican and the Fascist government concluded the Lateran Agreements of February 11, 1929, consisting of a Treaty of Conciliation and a concordat. In the Treaty of Conciliation, the Fascist government recognized Vatican city, comprising an area of 109 acres, as a sovereign, independent state and paid an indemnity of 1.75 billion lire (one billion in government bonds, the balance in cash) to the Vatican for the loss of Rome in 1870.

The concordat confirmed Roman Catholicism as the religion of the Italian state, extended the rules of canon law to marriage questions and eliminated civil marriage as a legal requirement. Catholic religious instruction was made compulsory in secondary public schools, and the Italian state recognized the organizations of Catholic Action *(Azione Cattolica),* provided their activities were non-political.

The settlement of the "Roman question" and the conclusion of the concordat with the Vatican raised Mussolini's national and international prestige to new heights, a fact which Mussolini exploited promptly by holding new national elections on March 24, 1929.

No liberal government of Italy, bound by the principle of separation of state and church, would have cared or dared to resolve the conflict between state and church on terms as favorable to the latter as those granted by the Fascist government in the Lateran Agreements. Giolitti, Italy's foremost liberal statesman before the First World War, for one, once remarked that state and church were two parallels which ought never to meet.

CONTINUING FRICTION BETWEEN STATE AND CHURCH

The happy resolution of the state-church conflict notwith-standing, tensions between the Fascist government and Pius XI arose almost as soon as the Lateran Agreements had been signed. The deeper cause of Fascist-Catholic friction was Fascism's totalitarian claim not only on the social, economic, or political dimensions of man but on the spiritual dimension as well. Mussolini's public utterances concerning church affairs showed a new truculence designed to demonstrate the primacy of state over church. The Christian religion, Mussolini observed, in a public speech of May, 1929, "was born in Palestine, but became Catholic in Rome." Had it remained in Palestine, it would, in all proba-bility, have remained an obscure sect or perished altogether without a trace, the Duce concluded.

The concrete issue over which state and church began to quarrel openly in Fascist Italy was the education of the young, a subject not defined in the Lateran Agreements. In the encyclical *Rappresentante in terra* of 1929, Pius XI stressed the educational mission of the Church as well as its right to judge secular education on its beneficial or harmful effects on Christian teaching. The activities of Catholic Action, a Catholic lay organization with social and educational functions, provided further cause for friction between state and church. The Fascist government de-clared the activities of Catholic Action incompatible with the tasks of the state and applied pressure, including violence, against its members. In 1931 Pius XI answered with another encyclical *Non abbiamo bisogno,* which condemned the Fascist theory of the all-powerful state.

Although the Fascist regime compromised on the issue of Catholic Action, it renounced none of its claims in the field of education and Fascist indoctrination of the young. Italian youth was organized, according to age groups, into paramilitary units—the *Balilla* for young-sters between 8 and 14, the *Avanguardisti* for those between 14 and 18, and the *Giovani Fascisti* for those between 18 and 21. In 1937 all Fascist youth groups were united in a single organization, *Gioventu Italiana del Littorio* (GIL). The Fascist School Charter of 1939 decreed compulsory membership in the GIL. Textbooks for primary and secondary education duly reflected the party line, portraying Mussolini as a new Caesar, who had saved Italian honor in the First World War by leading Italy into the war and who had rescued his nation from chaos in 1922. The educational slogan of Fascism became *"Libro e moschetto, fascista perfetto"* (a book and a rifle make a perfect Fascist). On the university level, the Fascist regime demanded an oath of allegiance from all professors. The oath of allegiance demanded loyalty not only to the king, but to the Fascist gov-ernment as well and exhorted faculties to aid in the development of citi-zens who were "industrious, honest and devoted to the Fatherland and the Fascist regime." Except for eleven dissenters, all professors took the

Fascist loyalty oath. Among the few academic figures who could afford to oppose Fascism publicly without penalty was the philosopher and historian Benedetto Croce, whose literary review *La Critica* continued to appear undisturbed. Croce's international fame as well as Mussolini's attempt to demonstrate a nonexistent academic freedom may help explain the uniqueness of Croce's position. Content to leave Croce in olympian isolation, the Fascist regime wooed successfully other internationally renowned figures of Italian science and culture. Among the latter were the playwright Luigi Pirandello, the composer Giacomo Puccini, and the physicist Guglielmo Marconi, all of whom endorsed Fascism with varying degrees of enthusiasm or accepted its honors. Arturo Toscanini, who acquired a reputation both as a great conductor and as an anti-Fascist had been a Fascist in his own right after the First World War.

As the 1930's drew to a close, Fascist Italy, which once had inspired and provided the model for Nazi Germany, increasingly copied the style and legislation of its former disciple, Hitler. The Italian imitation of Hitler Germany grew more pronounced, the more Mussolini changed his role from partner to satellite of Nazi Germany in foreign affairs. In 1937 Mussolini created a Ministry of Popular Culture (Minculpop), in imitation of Goebbels' Ministry of Propaganda, for the supervision of books, motion pictures, radio, and theater productions. Italian cultural and intellectual life, already subjected to Fascist controls through the Fascist Institute of Culture and the Italian Academy, thus approached the level of censorship instituted by Nazi Germany in 1933.

THE FASCIST RACE MANIFESTO

On July 14, 1938, the Fascist government launched a campaign of anti-semitism with the publication of a so-called "Race Manifesto" (*Manifesto della Razza*), drafted largely by Mussolini himself. The "Race Manifesto" asserted the existence of a "pure Italian race," to which Italian Jews did not belong. In October, 1938, Mussolini proclaimed that the Italians were "neither Hamites, Semites nor Mongols," but "evidently Aryans of Mediterranean type." In September and November, 1938, he issued a number of anti-Jewish laws, patterned after the Nuremberg racial laws of 1935, purging the civil service, the corporations, public schools, and universities of Jews and prohibiting foreign Jews from settling in Italy. Exempted from the Fascist racial laws of 1938 were Jewish war veterans and Italian Jews who had fought for Fascism or in D'Annunzio's legion.

Mussolini's anti-semitic policy shocked and surprised not a few Italians in view of Mussolini's own past statements on the subject as well as the advanced degree of assimilation of Italy's tiny Jewish minority of some 50,000. In 1932 Mussolini had denied the existence of anti-semitism in Fascist Italy and proclaimed that "Italians of Jewish birth have shown themselves good citizens" who had "fought bravely in the war." In 1934 Mussolini specifically attacked German Nazism on the issue of anti-semitism, denouncing Hitler's National Socialism as "one hundred per cent racism." In the early days of Italian Fascism, Jews had occupied prominent positions in the Fascist movement, such as Gino Arias, the theorist on corporations, and Enrico Rocca, the organizer of early Fascism in Rome. Mussolini's intellectual development as a Socialist before the First World War owed much to the guidance of his Russian Jewish friend, Angelica Balabanoff, the co-editor of *Avanti* and the future secretary of the Communist International.

Mussolini justified the racial laws on the ground that Italy needed a "racial consciousness . . . based not only on difference, but on the most definite superiority." To many Italians, Fascists included, the racial laws of 1938 were an unnecessary emulation of Nazi Germany, an emulation which Mussolini carried to the point of introducing the German goose step into the Italian army.

With the Munich Conference of September, 1938, Mussolini enjoyed one last upsurge of popularity among the Italian people, precisely because the conference had saved the peace and Mussolini had appeared as arbiter among the Great Powers. His aping of the Nazi style in domestic policy and his chaining Italy to Nazi Germany in the Pact of Steel in May, 1939, increasingly isolated the star performer of Italian Fascism among his own people, who had tired of perfunctory applause. When Mussolini led Italy into the Second World War in June, 1940, he repeated, in essence, though on a grander and more deadly scale, the folly of D'Annunzio's occupation of Fiume in 1919. Like D'Annunzio, Mussolini had been the best audience of his own nationalist rhetoric, which, after almost twenty years of power, blurred his vision to the military and political reality of his time. As D'Annunzio's legionaries had dispersed at the first sound of gunfire in 1920, Fascist Italy, unprepared for serious war in 1940, staggered from one military defeat to the next. The Fiume occupation had ended on a tragi-comic note; but the inflated nationalism of D'Annunzio, which had inspired it, survived in the Fascism that led all Italy to national disaster during the Second World War.

18 | The Failure of Democracy in Spain and Portugal

The constitutional monarchy of Spain, instituted in 1876 after the brief and turbulent first Spanish republic of 1874/1875, had largely failed to solve the foremost foreign and domestic problems confronting early 20th-century Spain. The loss of Spain's remaining colonial empire in the Pacific and the American hemisphere as a result of the Spanish-American war of 1898 had highlighted the decline of Spanish power and prestige. The inability of the Spanish army to thwart rebellion in Spanish Morocco demoralized and discredited the Spanish monarchy in the early 20th century.

More serious than the decline of foreign prestige were the accumulated domestic economic, social, and political problems of early 20th-century Spain, which resembled in many ways those of Italy. With a population of 18.6 million in 1900, abundant water power, and rich mineral deposits, Spain was potentially a wealthy nation. The natural wealth had remained largely undeveloped, however, because of backward social conditions and a political system unresponsive to the needs of a changing society.

Like early 20th-century Italy, Spain faced a serious land problem, land-ownership being limited to less than half the rural population. Like the Italian *braccianti,* the landless rural laborers of Spain, the *braceros,* formed a restless and potentially revolutionary element, especially in Andalusia and Estremadura, where absentee ownership of large estates prevailed. Rural poverty remained the most urgent social problem of early 20th-century Spain.

Spanish industry and mining had developed chiefly in the mineral-rich Basque provinces of the north—Guipúzcoa, Vizcaya, Alava, and Navarre, as well as in Catalonia in the northeast. Both the Basque provinces of the north and Catalonia aspired to regional autonomy for historic and economic reasons. The regional nationalism of both areas was rooted in linguistic differences and, in the case of the Basques, also in ethnic differences. The growth of industry spurred Catalan and Basque nationalism, the two areas being the most advanced economically and contributing a disproportionately large share to the overall wealth of Spain. The Catalan statute of autonomy of 1914, which granted limited home rule, fell short of Catalan expectations.

The political system of Spain under the constitutional monarchy was liberal and democratic in theory, with universal manhood suffrage granted as early as 1889. In practice, political democracy remained an abstract promise under conditions of widespread illiteracy. The illiteracy rate of Spain, estimated at 50 per cent in 1900, was still 25 per cent in the early 1930's. The politics of the constitutional monarchy remained under the control of a small oligarchy, which rigged elections through the pressure of political bosses, the *caciques*. The two leading political parties, Liberals and Liberal Conservatives, remained unrepresentative of the rural and urban proletariat and even of most of the new industrial middle class.

Spanish society, in the words of the Spanish intellectual leader Ortega y Gasset, consisted of separate, "water-tight compartments," each social-economic bloc pursuing its specific class interest without a unifying national purpose. The Catholic Church, once the common denominator of Spanish national life, had ceased to exercise its unifying function by the early 20th century, because of its identification with the interests of the possessing classes. The rural and urban proletariat rather looked towards the Socialists and Anarchists for leadership and deliverance from poverty. Of the two movements, the Anarchists, imbued with syndicalist ideas and organized since 1910 in the CNT (Confederación Nacional del Trabajo), were the more numerous and active, especially among the braceros of Andalusia and the industrial workers of Catalonia. With its simplistic appeal for direct and immediate action on behalf of social justice, anarcho-syndicalism had become a substitute religion for many of Spain's illiterate poor.

Spanish neutrality during the First World War had benefitted the Spanish economy and multiplied the Spanish gold reserves nearly fourfold, from 567 million to 2.2 billion gold pesetos. The war-related prosperity failed to extend to all social classes, however, remaining largely confined to the industrial employers. With the return of peace, Spain thus experienced social and economic turmoil not unlike that which swept the belligerent nations at the end of the First World War. CNT-inspired terror struck at employers, dissenting workers, and members of the Catholic hierarchy, including the Cardinal-Archbishop of Zaragoza, Soldevila, who was assassinated by anarchists. Between 1918 and 1923, Spain had ten short-lived governments, none of which succeeded in restoring a semblance of political order and economic stability.

THE DICTATORSHIP OF
MIGUEL PRIMO DE RIVERA

On September 12, 1923, General Primo de Rivera, the Captain General of Catalonia, ended parliamentary government with a military coup. Primo's manifesto, which announced the establishment of a military dictatorship, denounced the constitutional government as moribund and promised the reorganization and modernization of Spain.

The opponents of Primo de Rivera were quick to denounce the military dictatorship as a Spanish version of Mussolini's Fascism, and King Alfonso XIII himself occasionally referred to Primo de Rivera as "his Mussolini." In fact, the Primo de Rivera dictatorship was more in the 19th-century tradition of the *Pronunciamento,* the Spanish version of a military *coup d'état.*

The military dictatorship of 1923 was lacking in both an ideology and a political mass movement, as Primo's Patriotic Union (*Unión Patriótica*) failed to develop into a fascist-type political party. Moreover, the dictatorship was conceived as an interim measure only for the "renewal of public morals and the healing of the country from the disease of politics" in Primo de Rivera's definition. Although the dictatorship dissolved the political parties, it left the Socialist-directed trade unions unmolested. Largo Caballero, the Socialist leader, actively collaborated with the military dictatorship.

Primo de Rivera succeeded in ending the frustrating colonial war in Spanish Morocco while eliminating anarchist terror in Spain. Likewise, the military dictatorship suppressed Catalan and Basque nationalism, the Catalan statute of autonomy of 1914 being revoked. In the economic sphere, the military dictatorship launched a series of development projects, including the construction of highways and hydroelectric works. The land reform measure of January 7, 1929, which provided state loans to landless peasants for the purchase of farms, was too limited to attack the problem of rural poverty at its root. Until the onset of the Depression in 1929, the Spanish economy benefitted generally from the prosperity of Western Europe.

By 1930 support for the military dictatorship was dwindling rapidly. Initially, support was widespread if only because Primo de Rivera seemed to hold out the sole constructive alternative to the collapse of Spanish parliamentary government in 1923. The opposition, spearheaded by Spain's leading intellectuals, such as Miguel de Unamuno, included eventually not only the universities but the business community as well. The latter identified its own declining economic fortunes after 1929 with the dictator. On January 28, 1930, Primo de Rivera resigned, to die shortly afterwards in French exile.

The end of the military dictatorship brought down the monarchy as well within little more than a year, since Alfonso XIII was identified with the failure of the military dictatorship. Ortega y Gasset raised the cry *"delenda est monarchia,"* and Socialists, Republicans, and Catalan nationalists had concluded the "Pact of San Sebastian" in September, 1930, on the principles of a democratic Spanish Republic. On April 14, 1931, Alfonso XIII left Spain without a formal abdication, following the municipal elections of April 12, in which Republicans and Socialists had gained a majority in the large towns. The collapse of the Spanish monarchy resulted less from an overt attack than from its own lack of confidence. Not a few Republicans were surprised at the ease of their victory.

THE SECOND SPANISH REPUBLIC, 1931/1936

The birth of the Second Spanish Republic coincided, to its great misfortune, with the larger crisis and failure of European democracy under the impact of the World Depression. The prospects of a functioning Spanish democracy were slim enough owing to the passions and divisions of Spanish politics and the political inexperience of the newly elected constituent *cortes* of June, 1931. The drama of Republican Spain was also acted out, however, against the background of triumphant totalitarianism in Germany, Italy, and Russia, which overshadowed and deeply influenced the course of Spanish politics. It was thus largely the coincidence of the Second Spanish Republic with the greater disaster of European democracy in the feverish 1930's that gave the Spanish democratic experiment its heroic and tragic qualities.

Between 1931 and 1933 the Republican government was in the hands of a coalition of Socialists and Left Republicans, whose leader, Manuel Azaña, became prime minister in October, 1931. Azaña, a doctrinaire liberal, attacked the long neglected problems of rural poverty and illiteracy with zest, enacting a sweeping land reform on September 15, 1931, and launching an ambitious school-building program. Catalan nationalism, which had found a new spokesman in the *Esquerra Catalana* (the Catalan Left), was satisfied with a new statute of autonomy on September 9, 1932, establishing an autonomous Catalan government called the *Generalitat*. The Basque provinces were granted autonomy only on October 6, 1936, after the outbreak of the Spanish Civil War, in an attempt to ensure their loyalty to the Republican cause.

While tending to long overdue social and educational reforms, the Azaña government needlessly antagonized the Catholic establishment of Spain. The constitution of 1931, which declared Spain a "Republic of Workers of all classes," empowered the state to dissolve religious orders and virtually banned Catholic education. Azaña's claim of October 31, 1931, that "Spain has ceased to be Catholic" alienated Catholic Spain from the Republic and evoked a powerful reaction on the Right. The land reform measure added new opposition to the regime as it struck not only at absentee landlords of large estates but medium-sized farms as well. Above all, the Azaña government became discredited by its inability to curb anarchist violence, which had reappeared after the fall of the Primo de Rivera dictatorship. The growing opposition of the Right to Azaña revealed itself in the formation of the Falange Española, founded in

1933 by Jose Antonio Primo de Rivera, the son of the dictator, as well as the CEDA party. Whereas the Falange was patterned after the example of Italian Fascism, the CEDA (Conference of Autonomous Rightists) was a Catholic mass party conceived in imitation of Dollfuss' Austrian clerical Fatherland Front and concerned with the protection of Catholic interests.

In the parliamentary elections of November, 1933, the parties of the Left, which had held power since 1931, were thoroughly defeated by the parties of the Right, with CEDA emerging as the largest single party. The newly formed government of Prime Minister Alejandro Lerroux was met with strong opposition from the defeated parties of the Left, which exceeded the customary limits of a working parliamentary democracy. Fearful lest the Republic be destroyed by CEDA, the Socialists instigated a series of violent strikes which culminated in the mass uprising of Asturian miners on October 5, 1934, claiming the lives of 900 workers as well as 300 soldiers and policemen. Lerroux proved no more capable of reaching a national consensus than had his predecessors between 1931 and 1933. Attacked for its repeal of the land reform, for the suspension of Catalan autonomy, and the failure to counter rising unemployment, the Lerroux government exited in 1935 under a cloud of financial scandals.

The elections of February 16, 1936, the last elections to be held in Republican Spain, witnessed the return to power of the Left in the form of the Popular Front, consisting of Azaña's Left Republicans, Socialists, Communists, and the Catalan *Esquerra*. The victory of the Popular Front aggravated, rather than healed, the political divisions of Spain. The spring of 1936 witnessed the gradual disintegration of the Spanish body politic, with forceful land seizures proceeding on a massive scale in Andalusia and industrial strikes paralyzing the cities. Emboldened by victory, the parties of the Popular Front demanded the outlawing of all opposition parties and newspapers. On April 7, 1936, the parties of the Left deposed Alcala Zamora, the moderate President of the Republic, on dubious constitutional grounds and put Azaña in his place. Parliamentary deputies attended the *cortes* sessions armed, while Falangists and Communists fought pitched battles in the streets. The murder of Calvo Sotelo, the leader of the conservative *cortes* opposition on July 13, 1936, climaxed the violent confrontation between Left and Right and touched off the military insurrection against the Republic on July 17, 1936.

THE SPANISH CIVIL WAR

After a turbulent existence of fifty-seven months, the Second Spanish Republic had completed the full circle from high expectations of political and social betterment to the challenge of a military dictatorship. To many Spaniards dictatorship in one form or another, either military-fascist or Socialist-Communist, appeared indeed the only answer to the Iberian dilemma of 1936. The worsening of the Spanish political crisis since November, 1933, had radicalized the Socialists to the point where Largo Caballero, the once moderate Socialist leader, cried for the establishment of the dictatorship of the proletariat and was hailed by young Socialists as the "Spanish Lenin." The Communists, whose strength had been insignificant at the beginning of the Republic, had grown by leaps and bounds since 1931, claiming as many followers as the Socialists by May, 1936. Although allied with Azaña's Left Republicans in the Popular Front, neither the Communists nor the Socialists actually joined the Popular Front government prior to the outbreak of the Spanish Civil War, their ultimate intention being to use the Popular Front as a springboard for a future "workers' and peasants' government."

The military insurrection of July 17, 1936, spearheaded by General Emilio Mola of the Pomplona garrison, wished to restore "order" and establish strong government. Azaña's last-minute attempt to avoid civil war by offering a ceasefire to the military and by proposing a political compromise through new elections and the formation of an all-party "national government" without Communists, was rejected by General Mola.

On July 18, 1936, the 44-year-old Francisco Franco, former chief of staff and most prestigious officer of the Spanish army, joined the insurrection upon Mola's urgent pleas. Although close to CEDA in his sympathies, the withdrawn and devoutly Catholic Franco had stayed out of Spanish politics before 1936. His national reputation, rather, was based on a brilliant military career which included the command of the élite Spanish Legion in Morocco and direction of the Spanish military Academy in Zaragoza. In 1934 Franco was instrumental in crushing the Asturian miners' uprising. Azaña and the Left Republicans had considered Franco sufficiently dangerous to have him removed as chief of staff in 1935 and virtually exiled to the small island of Tenerife in the Canaries.

Franco quickly assumed both the military and political leadership of the insurrection. Having flown from the Canaries to Tetuan, the capital of Spanish Morocco, on July 18, 1936, Franco airlifted the crack Spanish Army of Morocco to metropolitan Spain with the aid of German transport aircraft at the end of July. On October 1, 1936, General Mola's military junta at Burgos proclaimed Franco Chief of the Nationalist State and Generalissimo of the Armed Forces.

The political creed of Nationalist Spain remained necessarily vague, owing to the wide discrepancy of views among its supporters, ranging from monarchist to fascist to Catholic. The common political denominators of Nationalist Spain were the hatred of the Republic in its present form and the desire to restore strong government and order. In

April, 1937, Franco merged the Falangists and the monarchists into the Falange Española Tradicionalista (FET), which was proclaimed the sole and official political movement of the state. The political forms of Nationalist Spain remained rudimentary during the Civil War, the emphasis being on the more immediate goal of military victory.

THE DIVISIONS OF REPUBLICAN SPAIN

As against the unity of Nationalist Spain, Republican Spain displayed disunity and internal bickering throughout the Civil War, a fact which contributed to the ultimate Republican defeat in March, 1939. During the short-lived Republican government of Jose Giral between July and September, 1936, the Republic appeared more concerned with immediate social revolution than the organization of its defense. The social revolution proceeded amidst a wave of "Red Terror" while authority slipped from Giral's hands to a number of local Left regimes. On September 4, 1936, the Socialist leader Largo Caballero replaced Giral as head of a Popular Front Government, composed of Communists, Socialists, and Left Republicans.

FIGURE 12   *British, French, and German members of the International Brigade during the defense of Madrid in 1937.*

459

The Caballero government gave Republican defense priority over social revolution, but in so doing it became deeply divided between its Socialist and Communist members. The Socialists resented the growing usurpation of Republican military affairs by the Spanish Communists, which was facilitated both by Soviet Russian military aid to the Republic and by the strength of the Spanish Communist Militia, called MOAC. Communist influence manifested itself not only in the disproportionately large number of Communist officers and the creation of political commissars, but in the adoption of the Red Star as the insignia of the Republican army and the introduction of the clenched fist salute. Moreover, the International Brigades, composed of foreign Communists and Republican sympathizers, remained under Communist control. The execution of Spanish left-wing dissenters within the Republic, such as anarchists and the followers of the Trotskyite POUM party, by Russian NKVD men in Barcelona suggested the growing political influence of foreign Communism over internal Spanish Republican affairs.

On May 15, 1937, Caballero resigned as Prime Minister largely over the issue of excessive Communist influence, to be succeeded by Juan Negrin, another Socialist. Although Negrin placed considerations of Republican military victory above all else, he too ended up quarreling with his Communist allies in the Popular Front because of Socialist opposition to Communist schemes for a Socialist-Communist party merger. In its final stage prior to Franco's entry into Madrid in March, 1939, Communists and non-Communist Republicans waged a virtual civil war within the larger Civil War of Spain, as Juan Negrin vainly attempted to achieve a negotiated end to the Civil War with Franco.

Among the military factors responsible for both the long duration and the final outcome of the Spanish Civil War, foreign arms aid and intervention were the most crucial. As will be shown at greater length in the discussion of the Spanish Civil War in its larger European setting, the Nationalist insurrection owed as much to German and Italian aid for its initial gains as the successful Republican defense of Madrid in 1936/1937 owed to Soviet military support. Otherwise, the Nationalists enjoyed the advantage of a more professional army, new junior officers being regularly supplied by Nationalist officer-training schools. Until 1937 the Republican forces enjoyed superior numbers, whose enthusiasm for the cause failed to compensate for their lack of military training. At the beginning of the Civil War, the Republicans controlled most of industrial Spain, including the munitions plants. Most of the Spanish air force and the navy remained loyal to the Republic. The Republican army showed its greatest strength in defense, as shown in Franco's first unsuccessful assault upon Madrid in late 1936.

Having captured nearly half of Spain by the end of 1936, the Nationalists mounted a second unsuccessful assault on Madrid with the support of the Italian volunteer corps, the *Corpo di Truppe Volontarie* in March, 1937. The Italian volunteers, many of whom were recruited from the Fascist militia rather than the regular Italian army, suffered a humiliating defeat at the hands of the Republicans in the battle of Guadalajara in March, 1937. Franco thereupon concentrated on the conquest of the northern zone, including Asturias and the Basque provinces, which was completed by October, 1937. The Republican offensive at Brunete, launched with great valor and enthusiasm to the northwest of Madrid, was defeated in July, 1937. By mid-April, 1938, the Republican zone was split in half, following a Nationalist offensive from Aragon to the sea. The Republican counterattack across the Ebro River, beginning in the summer of 1938 and lasting for three months, merely delayed Franco's final victory. By the end of 1938 all of Catalonia was under Nationalist control and the remaining Republican stronghold in and around Madrid was reduced by March, 1939. On April 1, 1939, the Spanish Civil War ended.

The Spanish Civil War was fought with even greater passion and ferocity than most civil wars. Nationalist military casualties may have run as high as 70,000 killed, and Republican casualties may have been as high as 100,000 killed. Nearly 300,000 Republicans fled Spain at the end of the Civil War, mostly for France. French reception and care of the Spanish Civil War refugees was less than enthusiastic, as evidenced by the death of some 70,000 Spanish refugees in French camps between 1939 and 1942. The question of which side killed the larger number of civilians seems moot, atrocities and mass executions having been common and widespread on both sides.

Perhaps the main distinction between the Nationalist "White Terror" and the Republican "Red Terror" consisted in the fact that the former continued well into the Second World War, long after the end of the Spanish Civil War, with executions of political prisoners persisting into 1943, and the number of political prisoners still being estimated at well over 200,000 during the Second World War.

The economic cost of the Spanish Civil War was also severe and sustained. Although agricultural output suffered relatively little from the war, industrial production did not regain the pre-Civil War level until 1950. Madrid and Barcelona, together with many smaller towns such as Guernica, bore the scars of aerial bombing, a grim warning of the destructiveness which air power was to wreak upon Europe at large within a short time after the Spanish Civil War.

PORTUGAL

The Portuguese Republic, established in October, 1910, after the overthrow of King Manuel II, developed during its sixteen years many of the same problems that plagued Republican Spain between 1931 and 1936. Inspired by the examples of Republican France and Brazil, the Portuguese Republic started out on an anti-clerical course, the Catholic Church being disestablished by the Law of Separation of April, 1911. The Portuguese Republican constitution of the same year, which established a democratic, parliamentary system, failed to provide a stable basis for political development. Between 1911 and 1926, there were altogether 44 Portuguese governments, 8 presidents, and 20 major political upheavals.

The political instability of Republican Portugal worsened under the impact of the First World War and the social and fiscal crisis of postwar Portugal. Unlike Spain, Portugal entered the First World War on the Allied side in 1916 and dispatched an expeditionary force of 40,000 men to France the following year. The war-time government of "sacred union" under Prime Minister Almeida failed to keep the nation united as opposition to the war and its cost mounted in 1917. In December, 1917, Major Sidonio Pais seized power in a coup in Lisbon, which aimed at strengthening the authority of the Republican government. Pais united the office of President and Prime Minister in his own person. The attempt at strong Republican government under Pais was short-lived, Pais being assassinated on December 14, 1918.

In 1919 Portugal returned to the "old republican system" of 1911, which proved inadequate to the social and economic pressures of the postwar years. Throughout the early and mid-1920's, Portugal was plagued by chronic financial deficits, incurred both by the cost of the First World War and the expenditures of colonial government in Portuguese Africa. The whole Republican regime became discredited in 1925 as a result of financial scandals involving Republican politicians and the Banco de Angola e Metrópole.

On May 28, 1926, the government was overthrown by a military coup of General Gomes da Costa, Portugal's war hero of the First World War. The leading figure to emerge from the military triumvirate installed by Gomes da Costa was General Oscar de Fragoso Carmona. In November, 1926, Carmona became acting president of Portugal, to be elected president in March, 1928, and re-elected in all subsequent Portuguese presidential elections during the remainder of his lifetime, in 1935, 1942, and 1949. Carmona's government of "national revolution" succeeded in solving Portugal's financial crisis, largely through the efforts of Dr. Antonio de Oliveira Salazar, the Minister of Finance and long-time economic theorist of the Portuguese Catholic Center. The Portuguese deficit, which had risen under the Republic from 300,000 escudos in 1911 to 642 million in 1926, was turned into a surplus by Salazar within a year of assuming office as Minister of Finance in 1928. In contrast to the lesser states of central-eastern and eastern Europe, Portugal succeeded in stabilizing her finances in the latter 1920's without assistance from abroad.

Financial success propelled Salazar into political prominence.

In November, 1932, he became Prime Minister under the regime of President Carmona with a decisive voice in both general economic policy and the drafting of the Portuguese constitution in 1933. Salazar appropriated the budget surpluses to various economic projects, including the development of communications and industry. Portugal attained self-sufficiency in wheat and remained relatively unaffected by the economic slump of 1929/1931.

The constitution of 1933, which established the "New State" (*esado novo*), was authoritarian and corporate and partly modelled after the Italian Fascist example. The chief difference between the Portuguese corporations, which were represented in the Corporate Chamber, the upper house of the bicameral legislature, and the Italian corporations was the voluntary nature of their association. Both strikes and lock-outs were outlawed, and the National Unity movement (*uniao nacional*) became the sole political party. The 1933 constitution emphasized the determination of the Portuguese state not to relinquish its sovereignty over any Portuguese colonial territory.

The political developments in neighboring Spain after 1931 affected Portugal only indirectly. A few Portuguese Democrats, encouraged by the fall of the Spanish monarchy in 1931, launched an abortive revolution in the Azores and Madeira, which produced a short-lived "Atlantis Republic" on the islands but which failed otherwise to make a lasting impression. After the outbreak of the Spanish Civil War, Portugal concluded a treaty of friendship with Nationalist Spain on March 17, 1939. The friendship treaty pledged mutual respect of territorial integrity and a policy of non-alliance with third powers directed against the other party. With the outbreak of the Second World War, Portugal declared her neutrality although her sympathies were largely on the British side. While supplying Nazi Germany with strategic materials, such as wolfram ore, Portugal acquiesced in the Allied military occupation of the Azores in 1943.

19 | The Democracies on the Eve of the Second World War

GREAT BRITAIN UNDER THE NATIONAL GOVERNMENT, 1931-1939

The first National Government under Ramsay MacDonald, it will be recalled, had been conceived in August, 1931, as a temporary emergency measure to solve the crisis of the British pound. Although the National Government had failed in its announced aim of "saving the pound," it stayed in office, becoming the second National Government after its endorsement by an overwhelming popular majority in the parliamentary elections of October 27, 1931.

Ramsay MacDonald's government was "national" in name, but predominantly Conservative in fact. The Conservatives prevailed in parliament with 473 seats and provided eleven out of twenty cabinet members. The withdrawal of the National Liberals from the cabinet in 1932 over the issue of tariff protection further increased the Conservative influence in the National Government. MacDonald, deserted by the majority of his own Labor party, continued to hold the office of prime minister until his retirement on June 7, 1935, for reasons of health. The Labor Opposition in parliament of 52 seats was headed by George Lansbury until 1935, and thereafter by Clement Attlee.

The second National Government assumed power at a time of mounting international crisis and growing nationalist pressures within the British Commonwealth, as has been explained more fully in the chapter covering the British Empire during the 1930's. Of the many tasks confronting the British government of 1931, none seemed more urgent, however, than the restoration of stable economic conditions at home.

Relative to the nations of continental Europe, Britain enjoyed the advantage of political tranquility in dealing with the Depression and its effects, there being no extremist forces of the far Left or Right of any consequence. The Opposition Labor party and especially its leader George Lansbury, to be sure, blamed the economic system of Britain for the Depression, which, in Lansbury's opinion, marked the collapse of capitalism. The Labor party veered to the Left ideologically, becoming more Marxist under the influence of middle-class intellectuals and the Socialist League, a radical organization affiliated with the Labor party.

The Labor Opposition continued to abide by the rules of parliamentary democracy, however, and incidents of violence by those hardest hit by the Depression remained few and far between. The British Communist party, numbering some seven thousand at its peak, had failed to win a single parliamentary seat in the elections of October, 1931, and succeeded in electing only one member of parliament, William Gallacher, in the elections of November 14, 1935. The National Unemployed Workers' Movement (NUWM), a left-wing organization, staged "hunger marches" on a large scale in 1934 and 1935 as well as sit-down demonstrations in the London business district as late as Christmas, 1938. The demonstrations evoked sympathy, however, from the general public, if not always from the police. The most violent clash between police and NUWM demonstrators occurred in London in 1932 during a rally against the "Means Test." Among the most unpopular economy measures of the National Government of 1931, the Means Test denied public assistance to those unemployed who possessed either savings of their own or well-to-do relatives.

On the far Right, Sir Oswald Mosley's British Union of Fascists, established in 1932, never exceeded 20,000 members. In imitation of continental Fascist dictators, the British Fascists wore black-shirted uniforms and held rallies against English Jews. Though they were never more than a noisy minority, the British government considered the Union of Fascists sufficiently dangerous to enact the Public Order Act of 1936. The latter prohibited political uniforms as well as insulting rhetoric and behavior in public gatherings. As a precautionary measure against Communist subversion, the government had enacted the Incitement to Disaffection Act (Sedition Act) in 1934. The Sedition Act was designed especially as a means of keeping subversive literature from the armed forces, and conferred powers of search and seizure on the police with proper judicial authorization.

THE ECONOMIC POLICY OF THE NATIONAL GOVERNMENT

In its economic policy, the National Government relied on a program of austerity, tariff protection, and limited state intervention as cures against the effects of the Depression. The chief architect of the government's economic and fiscal policy of the early and mid-1930's was Neville Chamberlain as Chancellor of the Exchequer. Chamberlain lowered the interest rate on Britain's internal war debt of £2 billion from five to three and a half per cent, thus achieving an immediate saving of £23 million to the government at the expense of war-bond holders. With the Import Duties Act of March 1, 1932, the National Government inaugurated a policy of tariff protection, ending the old and emotional issue of tariff protection versus free trade once and for all. The Import Duties Act imposed a general tariff of 10 per cent on all imports except most raw materials and food stuffs, such as meat and wheat. Empire goods were likewise exempted, largely as a result of Dominion pressure. Chamberlain hoped to follow up the tariff legislation of March, 1932, with a general tariff agreement between Britain and the Dominions, in order to realize the goal of a British Empire protected by common external tariffs, long cherished by Conservatives. The Imperial Conference at Ottawa of July/August, 1932, called for the purpose of Empire tariff negotiations, produced limited results only, however. Having developed industries of their own, the Dominions, foremost among them Canada, were as anxious as Great Britain to protect domestic manufacturers from foreign competition. At Ottawa, Britain and the Dominions concluded twelve tariff agreements, which fell short of Chamberlain's goal. Canada granted preference to British imports only to the extent of charging higher tariffs for non-British imports.

Nor was the National Government willing to neglect the interests of Britain's own agricultural producers. The farm policy of the British government rather aimed at bringing Britain closer to the goal of self-sufficiency in food stuffs. Domestic agriculture was stimulated through farm subsidies, through the encouragement of sugar beet growing and the institution of a wheat quota, which required a fixed percentage of all wheat consumed in Britain to be of domestic origin. Despite government incentives, Britain's agricultural output failed to reach the 1913 level before the outbreak of the Second World War.

Industry had largely recovered from the Depression by 1935, industrial production for 1935 exceeding that of 1929. The recovery was due chiefly to the rise in domestic consumption, rather than to an expansion of exports. The low interest rate of 2 per cent, adopted in June, 1932, contributed to a boom in the construction business; 2.7 million new homes were built between 1930 and 1940, nearly 350,000 in 1936 alone.

The unemployment rate, which had exceeded 22 per cent for the whole United Kingdom in 1932 — nearly three million — dropped below 2 million in July, 1935, and 1.6 million the following year. National unemployment figures did not accurately reflect economic conditions in all parts of Britain, however, since unemployment persisted in the so-called "depressed areas" even after the general economic upswing of the mid-1930's. Least affected by the Depression were London and the English South, where 13.7 per cent were unemployed in 1932, as against unemployment rates of 20.1 per cent for the Midlands, 27.1 per cent for Northern England, 27 per cent for Scotland and Northern Ireland, and 36.5 per cent for Wales. The depressed areas were the centers of the old staple industries of pre-war Britain, coal in South Wales and West Cumberland, cotton in Lancashire, and shipbuilding in parts of Scotland. Scotland, in particular, felt neglected by the government in Westminster, and some Scots went so far as to demand home rule similar to that of

Northern Ireland, through the Scottish Nationalist Party under the Duke of Montrose.

THE DEPRESSED AREAS

The National Government provided little more than minimal relief for the depressed areas, in part, no doubt, because their misery appeared to be less a national than a local problem, of which the more prosperous regions were not fully aware. The Special Areas Act of 1934 designated Scotland, South Wales, West Cumberland, and Tyneside "Special areas," earmarked for economic development and aid. Two commissioners each were appointed for Scotland, Wales, and England to facilitate the transfer of workers to more prosperous regions, to set up new industries, and to launch public works and land reclamation projects. The results of the Special Areas Act were disappointing, partly because of the very limited appropriations, partly because of the resistance which the commissioners encountered from local government and industry. The Special Areas Act had provided £2 million for relief and development purposes, a small sum if compared with the £1.5 billion that Britain was to spend annually by the late 1930's on rearmament. For the depressed or "special areas," unemployment thus often remained a form of life throughout the 1930's, unemployment running as high as 68-70 per cent in such places as Jarrow in Lancashire or the miners' town of Crook in South Wales.

With the Unemployment Act of 1934, Neville Chamberlain introduced improvements for those still dependent on the "dole." The administration of unemployment became centralized in the Unemployment Assistance Board and the hated "Means Test," introduced in 1931, was discontinued. The newly created unemployment fund was based on an estimated national unemployment rate of 17 per cent.

The rearmament of Britain brought tangible relief to the depressed areas, though not until the latter 1930's. The British defense budget of 1932 was the lowest between the two world wars. British rearmament did not begin in earnest until after the publication of the government's White Paper on rearmament (Statement Relating to Defense) of March 4, 1935. Chamberlain's original estimates for additional arms spending did not exceed £120 million in 1935, a low figure by the standards of 1937 when estimates had grown to annual expenditures of £1.5 billion.

THE GENERAL ELECTIONS OF 1935;
THE ABDICATION CRISIS OF 1936

During the Depression the institution of the monarchy, personified in the popular George V, had served as a reassuring rallying point to many Britons. The festivities surrounding George V's 25th anniversary

FIGURE 13 *Neville Chamberlain and Stanley Baldwin.*

of accession to the throne on May 6, 1935, were thus as much a personal tribute to King George V as a national celebration of Britain's recovery from the darkest days of the Depression. Stanley Baldwin, the Conservative leader who had replaced MacDonald as prime minister in June, 1935, was quick to capitalize on the optimistic and patriotic mood of Jubilee Day and scheduled general elections for November, 1935, a year in advance of the required election date.

Although the foreign policy issues of collective security and rearmament loomed large in the wake of Mussolini's Ethiopian invasion, the election campaign of November, 1935, was fought primarily over the domestic record of the National Government. National Labor candidates and some Conservatives were given rough treatment in industrial districts with high unemployment, but the Conservatives emerged triumphant with 432 over 154 Labor Opposition seats. Liberal strength declined from 33 to 20 seats, and the Communists, as previously noted, elected one member from West Fife.

The death of King George V on January 20, 1936, and the succession of his son, Edward VIII, plunged Britain into a major constitutional crisis because of the marital plans of the new monarch. The life-style of Edward VIII differed markedly from the conservative and stolid example set by his father, and there were expressions of concern that the 41-year-old bachelor king "ought to settle down." The private affairs of Edward VIII would not, in themselves, have constituted a political problem, there being ample royal precedents at the beginning of the century which the press had refrained from publicizing by custom. The liaison between Edward VIII and Mrs. Wallis Simpson, a twice-divorced

American, became a public issue only when the King proposed to marry her. The attack on the King's marriage plans was opened by the Church of England through Bishop Blunt of Bradford and Lang, the Archbishop of Canterbury. The press thereupon broke its silence, taking positions for or against the King, depending on editorial preference. The National Government, and Prime Minister Baldwin in particular, feared lest the royal controversy add a new divisive element to British politics, already strained by mounting differences over Britain's handling of the Ethiopian crisis in the League of Nations. Baldwin rejected as unconstitutional Edward's proposal to marry Mrs. Simpson without making her Queen and without claiming succession rights for any offspring, suggesting instead the alternatives of abdication or renunciation of Mrs. Simpson. The Dominion governments likewise opposed the marriage on the grounds that it would impair the prestige of the British crown — the only constitutional link between themselves and the United Kingdom since the Westminster Statute. Despite growing support for Edward, expressed in the popular phrase "God save the King from Mr. Baldwin," and Winston Churchill's words of encouragement, Edward VIII abdicated on December 11, 1936. Baldwin and the conservative social establishment of Great Britain, which still frowned upon divorce among public figures, were greatly relieved by the King's decision. Apart from his marriage plans, Edward VIII had given offense to many Conservatives by touring the depressed areas and expressing public horror at living conditions among the perpetually unemployed.

Edward VIII was succeeded by his brother Albert, who assumed the title of George VI. George VI, according to a British newspaper commentary of 1937, was made of the same "steady, sterling stuff," which had endeared his father to the British public and which gave promise of a noncontroversial reign. George VI's coronation of May 12, 1937, at Westminster Abbey surpassed in pageantry the celebration of George V's Jubilee Day, thus erasing the memory of Edward VIII's brief and unhappy reign.

Prime Minister Stanley Baldwin, known to his Conservative party comrades as "Honest Stan," resigned soon after George VI's coronation, his political prestige enhanced by the outcome of the abdication crisis of 1936. His successor became Neville Chamberlain, in many respects the most active and energetic member of Baldwin's cabinets, both in his capacity as Minister of Health in the 1920's and as Chancellor of the Exchequer in the 1930's. During the remaining years of peace, Neville Chamberlain, as Prime Minister, sponsored social legislation, such as a new Factory Act and Housing Act, in the tradition of his high principles of social betterment. The gathering storm of the Second World War largely overshadowed Chamberlain's domestic achievements, as the last prime minister of the National Government vainly attempted to avert a new war through the policy of appeasement.

THE THIRD FRENCH REPUBLIC

The external peace and domestic stability which France had at last attained under Poincaré's government of national union in the late 1920's did not extend into the early 1930's. As Briand's foreign policy of conciliation towards Germany shattered under the impact of German revisionist demands between 1930 and 1932 and Hitler's advent to power in 1933, the Depression cast its first shadows over the economic and political scene of the French Republic.

Poincaré's successor, Prime Minster André Tardieu, proposed to meet the challenge of the Depression with a bold program of economic and political reforms. Although a conservative, Tardieu called for a Five Year Plan, with increased government spending for housing, hospitals, transportation, plant modernization, social security, and rural electrification. The political corollary of Tardieu's reform scheme was a simplification of the republican system of France, which had been traditionally geared to social and economic inaction. Above all, Tardieu hoped to change the multi-party system of France into a two-party system with the Radicals, the Center, and the Right merging into a single group.

In 1930, Tardieu's reform plans had as little chance of being adopted as Léon Blum's proposals for governmental reforms, previously discussed, had had in 1919. The parties of the Right repudiated Tardieu's Five Year Plan for its economic unorthodoxy. The parties of the Left, particularly the SFIO, accused the conservative Tardieu of having stolen their own program. Tardieu's proposal for ending the proliferation of political parties prompted the charge of "authoritarian tendencies." Tardieu's successor, Pierre Laval, an ex-Socialist turned conservative, who was prime minister from January, 1931, to February, 1932, calmed conservative fears of a political and economic renewal of stagnant France by an orthodox policy of balanced budgets and austerity in government spending.

The parliamentary elections of May, 1932, revealed the public discontent with government inaction in the face of the Depression. The effects of the World Depression, as noted earlier, were slower in reaching France, but more persistent once established. By 1932 the French production index had declined by 34 points from the 1928 level, while unemployment climbed to 1.3 million in 1933. "Ships left unfitted in silent ports, no plume of smoke from the factory chimneys, long lines of unemployed in the towns, indigents in the countryside"—thus Paul Reynaud, the future prime minister, described the Depression in France.

As in 1924, the Radicals and the SFIO formed a Cartel of the Left in the elections of 1932 against the National Union, which combined the parties of the Center and the Right. The Cartel of the Left gained 344 seats over 259 for the National Union. The Communists remained an insignificant force with ten seats.

Between June, 1932, and February, 1934, the Cartel of the Left formed altogether six governments, the first of which was headed once again by the Radical Edouard Herriot. Herriot was quickly ousted as Prime Minister when he proposed continuing France's war debt payments to the United States after Germany terminated reparations payments to the Allies in 1932. The patterns and problems of the Cartel governments between 1932 and 1934 were similar to those of the first Cartel of the Left between 1924 and 1926.

Although supporting the Radicals in power, the SFIO refused to join the government, as Herriot considered most of the Socialist conditions for coalition government unacceptable. Among the SFIO demands were the nationalization of insurance companies and of the transport industry, a national insurance scheme against unemployment, the reduction of military expenditures to the 1928 level, and a forty-hour work week without wage reductions. Blum's conditions for coalition government with the Radicals exasperated some of his own SFIO followers, who, under the leadership of Marcel Déat and Adrien Marquet, seceded from the party and constituted themselves as "Neo-Socialists." Significantly, both Déat and Marquet concluded their political careers as members of Pétain's Vichy government during the Second World War.

From the disagreement between Radicals and Socialists on economic principles followed their inability to concur on practical economic and fiscal measures of the Cartel. The Socialists wanted to tax the rich to combat the Depression, just as they had demanded higher taxes in the 1920's for the financial liquidation of the First World War. The Radicals, mindful of the power of French financial interests, declined new taxes and practiced a policy of deflation, including a cut in civil service salaries by 6 per cent.

THE STAVISKY SCANDAL

To the record of discord and inaction, the Cartel of the Left added the odium of corruption in high places with the Stavisky scandal. Serge Alexandre Stavisky was a shady financier, whose long police record was matched by his connections to parliamentary deputies, who shielded him from prosecution. Stavisky's sale of fraudulent stock, based on the municipal credit of the city of Bayonne, touched off a major scandal at the turn of 1933/1934 that implicated Left parliamentary deputies and possibly members of Prime Minister Chautemps' government. Stavisky's death, officially ruled a suicide, added to public indignation because of the suspicion that he had been murdered by police officials to prevent him from exposing his political connections in public testimony. Prime Minister Chautemps resigned in the wake of the scandal, to be succeeded by the Radical Edouard Daladier, the last head of the Cartel of the Left.

Daladier hoped to restore the shaken prestige of the government with a promise of firm action, the first example of which was the dismissal of the Paris Police Prefect Chiappe. Chiappe's dismissal was Daladier's price for retaining Socialist support of his government, since Chiappe had antagonized the Socialists by his connections with the militant Fascist leagues.

The Stavisky scandal provided the French political Right, within and without the Chamber of Deputies, with a splendid opportunity to discredit the Cartel of the Left and the liberal Republic in general. Charles Maurras, the veteran champion of French anti-semitism, anti-republicanism, and conservatism, spearheaded the attack in his paper *Action Française*. The attack was all the more effective as public anger at republican politicians was by no means confined to the extreme Right. The firing of Chiappe acted as a final provocation of the Fascist leagues, which staged a violent demonstration on the night of February 6, 1934.

THE RIOTS OF FEBRUARY, 1934

From the Champs Elysees, the Boulevard Saint Michel, and the Esplanade des Invalides, the right-wing leagues of the *Union National des Combattants,* the *Action Française,* the *Croix de Feu,* and *Jeunesses Patriotes* converged upon the Place de la Concorde, threatening to storm the frightened Chamber of Deputies with shouts of "down with the thieves." The police drove the demonstrators away, killing fourteen and wounding over two hundred in the clash. Deputies, scurrying to safety, narrowly escaped bodily harm, and Prime Minister Daladier promptly resigned on February 7, 1934. For the first time in the history of the Third Republic, a government had been overthrown by the pressure of mob violence.

The riots of February 6, 1934, inspired widespread fears among the parties of the Left of a well organized Fascist *coup d'état.* The Fascist leagues of France, some of which dated back to the 1920's, had indeed grown in size and multiplied in number with the enfeeblement of republican politics since 1930. In addition to the older *Action Française* and Colonel de la Rocque's *Croix de Feu,* there existed the Young Patriots (*Jeunesses Patriotes*), the *Francistes,* the *Solidarité Française,* and "*La Cagoule*" (the hood), an underground organization for fighting Communism. La Cagoule counted a number of high ranking army officers on active duty among its members. A formal Fascist party was established only in 1936 with the French Popular Party under the ex-Communist Jacques Doriot.

The leaders of the French Fascist leagues echoed Mussolini's creed of "credere, obbedire, combattare" in their demand for "order, discipline, and a hierarchy of values." Moreover, the principal financial contributors to French Fascism, the perfumer Coty and the champagne producer Pierre Taittinger, openly advocated collaboration with Hitler against Communist Russia.

However, French Fascism remained, above all, French, in that it reflected the national passion for individualism in politics and the trend towards organizational proliferation: no single Fascist movement developed from the multitude of leagues; no Hitler or Mussolini emerged from among their leaders. Nor could French Fascism count on mobilizing the millions of followers who had hoisted the Italian and German dictators into power. The raw material of Italian and German Fascism was lacking in France: the middle class, though dispirited, was not proletarianized by the Depression, and France was free from the massive national inferiority complex which the "mutilated victory" of 1919 had engendered in Italy and which the defeat of 1918 had implanted in the German mind.

The riots of February 6, 1934, were thus not a plot but an explosion of anger which subsided when ex-president Gaston Doumergue succeeded Daladier as prime minister and formed a "national union" government in February, 1934. The national union government was center-right and the inclusion of Marshal Pétain, the hero of Verdun, as minister of defense, appeased the nationalist leagues. Doumergue cast himself in the role of Poincaré, pledging strong government in the tradition of the "savior of the franc." Following the ideas of Tardieu, who served in his government, Doumergue proposed constitutional reforms. Observing that "in our country governments do not last long . . . they can be overthrown for the slightest reason and nothing ever happens to those who participate in such assassinations," Doumergue called for strengthening the executive and curtailing parliamentary powers. Specifically, the president of the Republic was to be empowered to dissolve the Chamber of Deputies upon the advice of the prime minister without the approval of the Senate.

Doumergue's proposals for constitutional reform were unusual not only in their substance but the manner of their delivery, Doumergue making use of the radio to appeal directly to the public over the heads of parliament. This tactic helped to deprive him of majority support in the Chamber of Deputies, and the second conservative attempt at constitutional reform, after Tardieu's of 1930, ended in failure. The government of national union remained in power until early 1936 under prime ministers Flandin and Laval, the parties of the Left displaying mounting anger over Laval's deflationary policy and toleration of the Fascist leagues.

THE POPULAR FRONT

The approach of the parliamentary elections of May, 1936, was marked by the growing polarization of political and ideological forces under the double impact of foreign crisis and the domestic pressure for social change. Socialists and Communists, the most bitter of enemies since the Communist schism of 1920, had begun to draw together again under the impact of the Fascist riots of February 6, 1934. The first manifestation of a Socialist-Communist rapprochement was the joint strike of February 12, 1934, in protest against the Fascist "plot" of February 6, 1934. On July 27, 1934, the SFIO and the Communist party concluded a "unity of action" pact which committed both to a joint campaign against "Fascist organizations" and the defense of "democratic liberties." Both parties promised to refrain from attacks on each other.

The Socialist-Communist rapprochement of 1934 reflected the common fear in both parties of the rising power of Fascism, both at home and abroad. Nineteen thirty-four, the year of the Fascist riots in Paris, was also the year when Chancellor Dollfuss of Austria dealt Austrian Social Democracy its death blow during the civil war of 1934. The death of Austrian Social Democracy deeply touched Léon Blum, a close personal friend of some of Austria's Socialist leaders. "Let no one speak to us again of the independence of Austria," Blum declared after Dollfuss had crushed the Austrian Social Democrats, "it is henceforth the affair of governments, not of ours, not of the working people, not of international Socialism." The French Communists, on their part, had learned their lesson from the collapse of the Weimar Republic of 1933, a collapse hastened by the German Communists' refusal to form a common anti-Nazi front with the Social Democrats. The about-face of French Communism from denunciation to enthusiastic support of the Third Republic was motivated also, as shown in the chapter on French foreign policy, by Soviet Russia's alliance with France in 1935.

The Radicals, despite their economic disagreements with the Socialists and their enduring suspicion of the Communists, joined the Socialist-Communist alignment, to form the Popular Front. For the moment, the Radicals subordinated all other considerations to the safety and protection of the Republic, which they regarded as seriously endangered by the Fascist mob violence of 1934 and the continued growth of the Fascist leagues.

Socialists, Communists, and Radicals together drafted a common program for the Popular Front, or, as Léon Blum preferred to call it, *Rassemblement Populaire,* on January 11, 1936. The program was necessarily vague because of the social and economic differences among the three parties of the Popular Front. The program called for world peace and the combatting of Fascism at home. Among its economic demands were the creation of a national unemployment fund, the reduction of the

FIGURE 14   *Léon Blum.*

work week, and the establishment of a central wheat office to eliminate price speculation in wheat. The formation of the Popular Front was followed by the merger of the Socialist and Communist labor unions, the CGT and the CGTU respectively, which had been rivals since 1920. To the rank and file of labor, the Popular Front appeared as a new promise of social reform and political renewal in the stagnant and divisive world of republican politics. Not since 1919 had there been a like feeling of comradery and optimism in the ranks of French labor. The Popular Front seemed to usher in a new spring and a new liberation of energies after the long winter of social discontent. The Socialist and Radical leaders were less sanguine. Only the exercise of power by the Popular Front would show whether it possessed a common program of action in addition to common enemies.

The parliamentary elections of 1936 were fought in a climate of unprecedented bitterness and violence, the Socialist leader Léon Blum being dragged from his car and beaten by members of the Fascist leagues early in 1936. With 378 seats, the Popular Front scored an impressive victory over the parties of the Center and Right, which obtained 236 seats. Within the Popular Front, the chief beneficiaries of the electoral alliance were the Communists, whose strength increased from 10 to 72 seats. The SFIO, gaining 15 seats, emerged as the strongest of all parties with 146 seats. The Radicals, suffering a loss of 43 seats, declined to 115 seats in the Chamber of Deputies.

On June 4, 1936, Léon Blum became the first Socialist prime minister of the Third Republic as head of the Popular Front government. The Communists, repeating the Socialist tactics in the Cartel of the Left governments of the 1920's and early 1930's, supported Blum's government without joining it. While sharing the credit for Blum's achievements, the Communists thus reserved the liberty to denounce him should his policy run contrary to Communist interests.

Blum assumed power amidst widespread fears of social revolution, some two million factory workers having staged a sit-down strike in Paris since May 26, 1936. To the right-wing press, the mere fact of a Socialist prime minister, who happened to be a Jew as well, was proof of impending revolution and possibly civil war. The right-wing periodical *Gringoire* characterized the Popular Front as an "immense flood of Neapolitan filth . . . dismal Slavic stenches . . . the seeds of Abraham and the bitumen of Judea . . . the dregs of the ghettoes, . . . preceded by their smell and accompanied by their bugs." The outbreak of the Spanish Civil War in the summer of 1936 heightened the apprehension of French conservatives by raising the possibility that France would follow the example of Spain.

Blum settled the wildcat strikes by arbitrating a settlement between union and employer representatives in the Matignon Accord of June 7, 1936, so-called after the Hôtel Matignon, the Prime Minister's official residence. The Matignon Accord granted labor the right of collective bargaining, in addition to wage increases ranging from 7 to 15 per cent. All enterprises employing more than ten workers had to permit the election of shop stewards. Subsequent legislation provided for annual paid vacations and established the forty hour work week. In other areas, the Popular Front government established a Wheat Office (*Office du Blé*), composed of representatives of producers, consumers, and the government, for the setting of wheat prices. The Bank of France, previously a private corporation, was placed under state control through a newly established Board of Regents and a state-appointed Governor. The Blum government realized a favorite Socialist demand with legislation that nationalized the armaments industry. Except for the military aviation industry, the law was applied to a limited extent only, however. Lastly, the Popular Front outlawed the Fascist leagues, a measure only partially successful because some of the leagues reconstituted themselves as political parties. Colonel de la Rocque's *Croix de Feu* reappeared in the guise of the French Social Party (*Parti Social Française*).

Blum's social legislation, which some labeled the French version of the New Deal, had been swallowed by employers and the conservative Senate largely out of fear that resistance would result in larger disorders than the wildcat strikes of May and June, 1936. As fear of revolution receded in the fall of 1936, conservative opposition to the Popular Front mounted. Industrialists balked at concluding collective bargaining agreements with the unions; financiers and investors shifted funds abroad or exchanged francs into dollars and pounds in expectation of a franc devaluation. As labor had brought capital to terms in June, 1936, by massive strikes, capital confronted Blum with a strike of its own; twenty billion francs in gold—one fourth of the entire French gold reserve—left France between May and September, 1936. It was capital's way of showing its displeasure over Blum's social policy and his fiscal policy of deficit spending. Blum's budget for 1937 anticipated a deficit of 4.5 billion francs. Not included in the deficit were the expenditures for armaments and public works, amounting to an additional sixteen billion francs, which Blum proposed to raise through loans. The confidence of the financial establishment in the Popular Front government was lacking all the more because the key economic positions in the government—finance, public works, and agriculture—were all held by Socialists—Vincent Auriol, Charles Spinasse, and George Monnet, respectively.

On September 25, 1936, Blum was forced to devalue the franc. On February 24, 1937, he announced a "pause" in the Popular Front social and economic policy which, in reality, marked its end. When the announcement of the "pause" failed to halt the flight of French capital abroad, Blum asked the Senate for special decree powers in June, 1937, to deal with the financial crisis, presumably through the institution of exchange controls. When the Senate refused, Blum resigned as prime minister.

While fighting and losing his battles with French finance, Blum had come under increasing attack from both his Communist and Radical allies. Thorez, the Communist leader, criticized the failure of the Popular Front government to openly aid the Republicans in the Spanish Civil War. The Radicals discreetly withdrew their support from Blum, blaming him for continuing labor unrest and economic crisis. A man more ruthless than Blum might have accepted the challenge of the French Senate and his detractors among Communists and Radicals and appealed directly to the people for support in saving the Popular Front, which had inspired so much hope and optimism at the moment of its birth. From the beginning, Blum had been plagued by self-doubt, however, confessing to his own party, upon becoming prime minister: "I do not know if I have the qualities of a leader, in this so difficult struggle . . ."

Blum had wished to carry out long overdue social reforms while at the same time preserving the traditional forms and liberties of the Third French Republic. When confronted with the alternatives of abdicating from power or risking possible civil conflict in order to break the opposition of vested economic and financial interests, he did not hesitate in his choice. Although a Socialist, he did not act from the narrow interest of a single class, but the national interest of the Republic. In the troubled world of the mid-1930's, the spectacle of France paralyzed by civil war could only have acted as an encouragement to those foreign predatory powers that were already probing the national resolve of France along the Rhine and in the Mediterranean.

In name, the Popular Front government survived Blum's resignation until 1938. Camille Chautemps succeeded as prime minister with Blum as vice-premier. After Hitler's *Anschluss* of March, 1938, Blum returned as prime minister for a brief second term of office to be succeeded by Daladier. The formal end of the Popular Front came after the Munich conference of September, 1938. In spirit, the Popular Front had died in 1937 with the abandonment of its progressive social program. Under Daladier, many of the social gains of 1936 were overthrown, the application of the forty-hour work week limited. A general strike called by the CGT for November 30, 1938, in protest against Daladier's economic and social policy collapsed under the vigorous countermeasures of the government. Daladier's toughness opposite labor revived the confidence of French business and financial circles, and capital shipped out of France in 1936/1937 returned. The twin problems of national security and domestic political and social renewal, which had confronted France in 1919, were no closer to solution on the eve of the Second World War than they had been in the hour of republican triumph after the First World War.

20 | The Lesser States of Western Europe:

Holland, Belgium and Luxembourg

THE NETHERLANDS

Like Switzerland and the Scandinavian states, the Netherlands were among the few smaller powers of Europe whom the Great Power conflict of 1914-1918 had by-passed and left intact. Dutch neutrality, which was self-proclaimed rather than internationally guaranteed like that of Switzerland and Belgium, remained inviolate throughout the First World War, largely because Germany, needing a commercial outlet, had stricken the invasion of Holland from the Schlieffen plan. Similarly, Great Britain favored Dutch neutrality since the alternative of military action in Holland might have brought the Dutch North Sea coast under German control. Thus, despite the hardships and losses imposed by the Allied blockade and German unrestricted submarine warfare, the wealth of Holland emerged essentially unimpaired from the holocaust of the First World War.

With a population of some nine million before 1939, crowded together in an area of 13,000 square miles—one and a half times the size of Massachusetts—Holland was the most densely populated nation of Europe after Belgium. Despite its population density and the virtual absence of mineral resources, save for the coal deposits of Limburg, Holland was among the most prosperous nations of Europe. The sources of Dutch wealth in the 20th century were still essentially the same as those which had projected the Netherlands into commercial pre-eminence during the 16th and 17th centuries: a flourishing trade, thriving on Holland's ideal location as a transit point between the sea lanes of the Atlantic and the inland waterway of the Rhine; a large merchant fleet, reaching 2.9 million tons after the First World War and ranking eighth among the world's merchant fleets; and the excellent harbor of Rotterdam, which, by 1935, handled more cargo than any other European port. Added to the advantages of location was the aggressive and resourceful spirit of the Dutch commercial middle class, whose essence King Albert of Belgium once described as "love of liberty, zealous labor, and commercial honesty." Dutch industry, though less extensive than that of Belgium, had developed major enterprises in textiles, the Philips electrical industry, and the Royal

481

Dutch oil company, whose capital grew from five million guilders in 1890, the year of its establishment, to five hundred million guilders in 1930.

In the accumulation of Dutch national wealth throughout the 19th century and the 20th century up to the German invasion of Holland in 1940, the Netherlands' colonial empire of Curacao, Surinam (Dutch Guiana), and the East Indies played a major role. Following the restoration of the East Indies to Holland in 1816 after the Napoleonic wars, Holland was able to develop and exploit its most important colony during a century of peace, undisturbed by Great Power pressure or interference. The Japanese incursion into Indonesia, first commercial, later political and military, did not begin until after the First World War.

In the island empire of Indonesia, 250,000 Dutch nationals ruled over a native population which had grown to 70 million by 1939. Before the Second World War, Indonesia produced 3 per cent of the world's oil and 17 per cent of the world's tin, while Indonesian exports of rubber, tea, and sugar accounted respectively for 37, 19, and 11 per cent of world exports. In 1940 the value of Indonesian exports reached $493 million. The methods of Dutch colonial policy, both economic and administrative, changed over the years, without a corresponding change in basic purpose. Of Dutch rule in Indonesia, it was said that the Dutch grew in wealth, the Indonesians in number. For the better part of the 19th century, the so-called "culture system" or "Bosch system" of compulsory native labor, named after the Minister of Colonies Johannes van den Bosch, was applied, and the Dutch government exercised a monopoly of economic activity. By 1870 the government monopoly gave way to exploitation by private enterprise. The plight of Indonesia's population under Dutch colonial rule was first brought to public attention in Holland in the 1860's through the literary works of Edward Douwes Dekker. Himself a former Indies official who wrote under the pseudonym "Muetatuli," Dekker was instrumental in setting the Dutch government on a new "ethical course" in its dealings with Indonesia. Having recognized a "moral duty towards the Indonesian people" in 1901, the Dutch government instituted a "People's Council" (*Volksraad*) for Indonesia in 1916. Far from being a genuine Indonesian parliament, the *Volksraad* was an advisory body to the Dutch Governor General only, its membership being also predominantly European. Although the powers of the *Volksraad* were gradually broadened and Indonesian representation enlarged, Dutch concessions fell far short of Indonesian nationalist expectations. The disturbances of the 1920's and 1930's, touched off by the Indonesian nationalist organization *Sarekat Islam* as well as by Indonesian Communists in West Java and West Sumatra, served notice of the approaching end of Dutch colonial rule during the 1940's.

In Dutch domestic developments between the two world wars, few serious political issues arose, the evolution of parliamentary democracy from the 1848 constitution having been completed by the end of the First World War. The institution of the monarchy, represented by the popular and enduring Queen Wilhelmina, whose reign lasted from 1898 to 1948, was not an issue. The agitation of Dutch Socialists in 1918 for its abolition, inspired by the German revolution of November, 1918, failed to gain popular support. The most serious pre-war political issue, public support to denominational schools, was settled with the De Visser Law of 1917, which granted equal support to public and Church schools, both Catholic and Protestant. The Dutch franchise for the bicameral States General, still limited to 50 per cent of adult males at the beginning of the 20th century, was broadened to universal manhood suffrage in 1917. In 1919 women were enfranchised also and parliamentary elections based on proportional representation.

The introduction of proportional representation greatly increased the number of political parties and groups in a nation of highly individualistic political traditions. The large number of political parties, 54 by 1933, did not, however, detract from the political stability of Holland; there were only three prime ministers and eight cabinets between the wars. Governments were formed by coalitions of the mass parties, of which the Roman Catholic State party was the largest, followed by the Calvinist Anti-Revolutionary party and the Liberals. The Socialist Workers' party (SDAP), the second largest political party, did not enter the national government until 1939. Neither the Communists nor Anton Mussert's Dutch Nazi party (*National Socialistische Beweging*) attracted a large following, both parties obtaining four seats each in the States General before the Second World War.

The Depression affected Holland more severely than many of the great industrial powers; the impact of protectionism and preferential tariffs, such as under the Ottawa Agreements, was especially hard on a free-trade nation such as Holland. Public works projects, such as land reclamation in the Zuiderzee, which yielded 500,000 acres of arable land, though spectacular in themselves, failed to absorb the large number of unemployed. At the depth of the Depression, Dutch unemployment reached 400,000. The Oslo Pact of 1930 between Holland, Belgium, Luxembourg, and the Scandinavian nations as well as the Ouchy Convention of 1932 between Holland, Belgium, and Luxembourg were two, not entirely successful, attempts to combat the Depression through regional tariff agreements. Rearmament, which stimulated the economies of other Depression-ridden nations in the mid-1930's, did not get under way in Holland until shortly before the outbreak of the Second World War, largely because of opposition by both the Catholic State party and the Socialists.

With the approach of the Second World War, Holland, in conjunction with the other members of the Oslo Pact, vainly appealed to the

Great Powers on August 23, 1939, for the preservation of peace. A Dutch-Belgian proposal for mediation, launched after the outbreak of the Second World War in November, 1939, was similarly unsuccessful. On May 10, 1940, Holland, as scrupulously neutral in the Second World War as in the First, was overrun by German troops during the German spring offensive in the west. Within less than two years, Japan followed Germany's example in South Asia with the conquest of Dutch Indonesia.

BELGIUM AND LUXEMBOURG

Belgian neutrality, "perpetual and guaranteed" under the Treaty of 1831, fell victim to the German invasion of August 4, 1914, as previously discussed in the chapter on the First World War. Only the southwest corner of Belgium at the Yser remained free, defended successfully by the small Belgain army under King Albert, the symbol of Belgain resistance. Among the heavy costs imposed on Belgium by the First World War were 40,000 soldiers killed, some 120,000 civilians forcibly removed to Germany as labor, the reduction of Belgain livestock to one half its pre-war amount, and the dismantling of numerous industrial plants by Germany.

The experience of the First World War led Belgium to abandon her traditional neutrality in 1919. Belgium shared in German reparations under the Treaty of Versailles and obtained the territory of Eupen-Malmédy on the Rhine as well as Ruanda-Urundi in Africa. In 1920 Belgium formed a military alliance with France. The Belgian army was reorganized along French lines, and the newly built fortresses along the Meuse and the Albert Canal were designed to serve as an extension of the French Maginot line. Belgian troops participated in the Rhineland occupation as well as in the French invasion of the Ruhr in 1923. An additional safeguard to Belgium's eastern borders was seemingly obtained under the Locarno Treaty of 1925, with Germany confirming the demilitarization of the Rhineland and the Versailles frontiers with Belgium. In 1936 King Leopold III, who had succeeded Albert in 1934, reverted to a policy of Belgian neutrality under the impact of Hitler's remilitarization of the Rhineland and the enfeeblement of the League in the Ethiopian crisis.

Belgian relations with neighboring Holland were somewhat strained in the 1920's, owing to Belgian territorial claims on Dutch Flanders and Limburg at the Peace Conference of 1919, which were, however, not fulfilled. The common trials of the World Depression and the return of the German military threat in the 1930's restored close Belgian-Dutch relations, as evidenced by the Oslo Pact and the Ouchy Convention. With the Grand Duchy of Luxembourg, Belgium formed an economic union as early as 1922.

The economic reconstruction and recovery of Belgium was

completed by the mid-1920's, the Belgian franc being stabilized in 1926. Before 1929 Belgium manufactured one fourth of the world's zinc and ranked second in world glass production. With 75 per cent of Belgian iron and steel production going for exports, Belgian foreign trade was particularly hard hit by the Depression, declining to 47 per cent of the 1928 level in 1932. The devaluation of the Belgian franc in 1935 aided economic recovery, and unemployment was cut by two thirds in the mid-1930's.

The national wealth of Belgium, like that of Holland, derived in part from overseas colonial possessions. Under the motto "Belgium must have a colony," King Leopold II (1865-1909) had acquired the huge Congo colony of 920,000 square miles in 1884, almost singlehandedly and amidst Belgian national indifference and frequent opposition to imperialist ventures. Starting out with the *Association Internationale Africaine* in 1876, a private organization ostensibly formed for humanitarian and exploratory purposes in Central Africa, King Leopold secured Great Power recognition of the Congo Association as a state under his personal rule at the Berlin Congo Conference of 1884.

Between 1884 and 1908, the Congo remained the private domain of the Belgian crown. Having proclaimed himself "Sovereign of the Independent State of the Congo" on August 1, 1885, Leopold applied increasingly ruthless measures in the economic exploitation of the Congo, partly in order to redeem his personal fortune, which was heavily committed to the development of the colony. As Dekker's literary works had awakened the Dutch public in the 1860's to colonial abuses in Indonesia, the attention of Belgium, and indeed of much of the world, was directed to abuses in the Congo by the works of the journalist Edmund D. Morel, *King Leopold's Rule in Africa* and *Red Rubber*. Responding to worldwide criticism, which included Mark Twain's denunciation of the Belgian king as a "piety-mouthing hypocrite" and "bloody monster," Leopold II instituted reforms recommended by a Commission of Inquiry in 1904. The emphasis remained on colonial profit, however, the Congo having yielded $15 million between 1896 and 1906 and giving promise of yielding far more in the future. To the exports of rubber were added copper, uranium, and diamonds in later stages of the Congo's exploitation.

On November 15, 1908, the Belgian parliament annexed the Congo, turning it into a Belgian colony much to the annoyance of King Leopold, who distrusted the competency of the Belgian government in colonial matters. In annexing the Congo, the Belgian government acted out of fear lest continued international outrage at Leopold's administration of the Congo result in Great Power intervention in the Congo. It was perhaps fortunate for Belgium that Leopold's other imperialist schemes for colonial acquisition of the Philippines and Morocco never materialized.

Apart from the Depression, the key issues which overshadowed Belgian domestic politics between the two world wars were the school question and the nationality strife between the French-speaking Walloons and the Flemings. Political democracy in Belgium was fully realized in 1919 with the granting of universal and equal manhood suffrage and the enfranchisement of women in 1921. Although ministerial changes were frequent, political stability was assured by coalitions formed alternately between two of Belgium's three major political parties, the Catholics, Socialists, and Liberals. Prime Minister Van Zeeland was instrumental in the enactment of extensive social legislation in the 1930's, which, like that of France, established the forty-hour week in certain industries.

The school issue, stemming from the separation of state and church affairs in the 1870's, was largely settled in 1920 with equal support being granted to public and Catholic elementary education. The Flemish question, which had grown in the early 20th century from a cultural into a political issue, proved far more difficult, without a lasting settlement being achieved before the Second World War. Although the Flemish-speaking population actually outnumbered the Walloons, Walloon-French influence continued to prevail in education, politics, and the armed forces.

Equality of the two languages, French and Flemish, in all public institutions, education, and the army was granted by law in 1921, and the University of Ghent became an all-Flemish institution. The Walloon-Flemish controversy persisted, however, in part because of the memory of Flemish nationalist collaboration with the German occupation authorities during the First World War, in part because of the extremist demands of Flemish nationalism for the division of Belgium into two separate, autonomous regions. The most extreme spokesman of Flemish nationalism became the *Vlaamsch Nationaal Verbond* (VNV), imbued with Nazi ideology and destined to become a collaborator of Nazi Germany during the Second World War. During the 1930's, Fascist ideas spread among the Depression-ridden Walloon middle class as well, as evidenced by the decline of the Liberal party and the corresponding growth of Leon Degrelle's Rexist movement after 1935. Before the German invasion of Belgium in May, 1940, neither the VNV nor the Rexists attracted a sufficiently large following, however, to threaten Belgian democracy.

The small Grand Duchy of Luxembourg, to all intents and purposes, was part of Belgium in an economic sense, since the formation of the abovementioned economic union of 1922. Politically, the Grand Duchy, ruled by the dynasty of Nassau-Weilburg, a side line of the Dutch Orange family, remained an independent entity, however. In January, 1919, Grand Duchess Maria-Adelheid, once popular but compromised by her pro-German sympathies during the First World War, abdicated in favor of her sister Charlotte. Socialist attempts to overthrow the monarchy in Luxembourg in 1918 failed over the opposition of the Catholic Conservative majority. Despite its small size, Luxembourg ranked among

Europe's leading steel producers, the Luxembourg steel industry attracting a large number of foreign workers from Italy and Germany. By 1930 foreign workers, numbering 55,000, accounted for nearly one fifth of the total population of the Grand Duchy. German rule in occupied Luxembourg during the Second World War was particularly severe; the French language was forbidden and the young men were drafted into the German army.

21 | The Challenge to the Peace of 1919:
Prologue to the Second World War

THE SIGNIFICANCE OF *MEIN KAMPF;* THE NEW METHODS OF GERMAN FOREIGN POLICY

That Hitler's advent to power in Germany in January, 1933, signified more than an internal German revolution was widely understood in Europe, for National Socialism had denounced the peace settlement of 1919 from its earliest days and had marched to power largely on the strength of its promise to repudiate the Treaty of Versailles.

Hitler possessed neither experience in the field of foreign policy nor even a firsthand knowledge of the world outside Germany. With the exception of his war-time service in France, he had never set foot outside his native Austria or his adopted homeland Germany before 1933. Yet he considered foreign policy his very personal domain and area of special inspiration. After 1933 German foreign policy became increasingly the personal policy of Hitler, relying less and less on the advice of the professional diplomats and ambassadors whom Hitler had inherited from the Weimar Republic. The retirement of Constantin von Neurath as German Foreign Minister in 1938 and his succession by Joachim von Ribbentrop, a close personal follower of Hitler's, formalized Nazi domination of the German foreign service.

Nearly a decade before coming to power, Hitler had given a frank exposition of his foreign policy views in *Mein Kampf.* The foreign policy aims of *Mein Kampf* reflected his view of history as an unending struggle between unequal races for the possession of land, or "living space" (*Lebensraum*). Germany's "living space," in Hitler's view, was too confined to assure the attainment of world power. Thus, the stated objective of a National Socialist foreign policy was not the return of Germany to a Great Power position in Europe, as under Bismarck, nor even the resumption of William II's "world policy," with its emphasis on overseas colonies, naval power, and expanded foreign trade. The mere regaining of Germany's frontiers of 1914 Hitler dismissed as a "political absurdity of such proportions as to make it a crime." The reconquest of Germany's lost colonial empire he likewise regarded as unsatisfactory, since overseas colonial empires were "pyramids stood on their heads" with only the summit in Europe and the base "in the whole world." The

United States alone, Hitler observed in 1924, had secured a "base in its own continent," a fact which accounted for its "immense inner strength."

To become a world power, Germany must expand its land base on the Eurasian continent. National Socialist foreign policy must seek to obtain "boundaries of eternal justice," leading the German people from their "present restricted living space to new land and soil" and thereby freeing them "from the danger of vanishing from the earth or serving others as a slave nation."

The object of Hitler's expansionist dreams was Soviet Russia. Russia seemed the ideal German colony of the future because of its limitless expanse and its Slavic population, deemed racially inferior by Hitler. Moreover, the German conquest of Russia would destroy the center of world communism.

Hitler's eastern imperialism revived the imperialism of Ludendorff and the German High Command of 1918, which had achieved its temporary fulfillment in the annexationist Peace of Brest-Litovsk.

As the experience of the Second World War was to demonstrate, Hitler's eastern imperialism exceeded Ludendorff's, however, in its total lack of restraint and naked colonizing purpose. To achieve German domination of Russia, Hitler proposed in *Mein Kampf* a German alliance with Italy and Great Britain. The Germany of William II, in Hitler's view, had chosen the worst possible course of foreign policy by tying itself to "ancient states," "pensioned off by world history," such as Austria-Hungary, and by needlessly antagonizing Great Britain through naval ambitions and competition for world trade. By voluntarily restricting German sea power, Hitler hoped to obtain an agreement with Great Britain, whose Empire seemed to him living proof of the superior state-building powers of the "Nordic race."

Hitler's infatuation with Italy was rooted in the ideological affinity between Italian Fascism and German National Socialism and the great personal admiration, which Hitler admitted in *Mein Kampf,* for the "man south of the Alps." To obtain Mussolini's friendship, Hitler was willing to renounce once and for all any claims to German-speaking South Tyrol (Alto Adige), which Italy had taken from Austria in the peace settlement of 1919. The abandonment of South Tyrol was to Hitler a small price for Mussolini's friendship. Those who would not agree, Hitler dismissed as "hypocritical rabble."

Whether Hitler's foreign policy views and aims, as expressed in *Mein Kampf,* were the ravings of a frustrated politician out of power or represented the hard core of Hitler's unchanging ambitions has been a subject of debate among historians since the end of the Second World War. That Hitler had no intention of seeking the immediate fulfillment of his aims of *Mein Kampf* after coming to power in 1933 is clear from the early course of Nazi foreign policy.

When in possession of vast military power before the turning of the tide of the Second World War in 1943, Hitler's eastern policy suggested, however, that he had every intention of building the colossal German Empire, from the Rhine to the Urals, first mentioned in the pages of *Mein Kampf.* Consistency of aim was among Hitler's foremost characteristics; with the same singlemindedness with which in 1925 he drew sketches of an imaginary arch of triumph, to be erected in Berlin as a future monument to his victories, he penned the outlines, in 1924, of a future Germany of "250 million inhabitants." The limits of Hitler's foreign policy ambitions were not to be found in the traditional concept of a balanced system of European powers, nor in an awareness of the values of European civilization, but only in the resistance which his designs encountered in the world. Therein lay the revolutionary content of Nazi foreign policy that distinguished it from the policy of Stresemann or Brüning. Although both these statesmen of the Weimar Republic desired a revision of the Versailles system as keenly as did Hitler, the aims of their revisionism were not incompatible with the preservation of a balanced European state system.

Not to have recognized the fundamental difference between German revisionist policy under the Weimar Republic and under Hitler was among the chief faults of the Western statesmen who dealt with Hitler between 1933 and 1939. Inasmuch as Hitler's partners in negotiation were familiar with the utterances of *Mein Kampf,* they preferred to view the Führer as a statesman whose collaboration in the peaceful revision of the political settlement of 1919 could be obtained. In this they were as much the victims of their own illusions as of Hitler's deception. To visiting British statesmen, Hitler variously appeared as a "visionary rather than a gangster," a man "fond of children and dogs," or a statesman who "inculcated in his people the desire for equality with other nations in their rights and responsibilities." At worst, Hitler seemed a "superlatively exotic foreigner," or a German version of Mrs. Aimeé Macpherson, the American revivalist preacher of the 1920's. To Neville Henderson, the last British ambassador to Germany before the outbreak of the Second World War, Hitler was neither a "madman, paranoic or Austrian housepainter" but "one of those extraordinary individuals whom the world throws up from time to time."

This last characterization fully agreed with Hitler's own estimation of his place in history. Convinced of the uniqueness of his role, Hitler impatiently pressed for the fulfillment of his dream of German hegemony before time or accident removed him from the scene. In his foreign policy struggle, he saw a parallel to his rise in German domestic politics from obscurity and anonymity to dictatorship. As he had outmaneuvered the German Nationalists and ultimately chained them to his side by playing on their fear of Communism, he would captivate conservative Great Britain; as he had smashed the German Communists by brutal force, he would destroy Communist Russia when the time was right.

After coming to power in 1933, Hitler never again publicized his true foreign policy intentions with the same frankness he had shown in *Mein Kampf*. To his listeners abroad and audiences at home, he found moving words of peace. It was only to a select few in Germany and on rare occasions that he stated his true aims. The meeting of November 5, 1937, with the heads of the military services, recorded in the "Hossbach document," in which Hitler revealed his intention of annexing Austria and Czechoslovakia was one such occasion. Hitler's secret address of November 10, 1938, to German newspaper editors was another. On this occassion, he confessed that "circumstances have compelled me to speak for years of peace. . . . It is self-evident that such peace propaganda has its dangerous sides; it could lead to the opinion that the present regime itself was identical with the decision and the will to preserve peace under all circumstances." It had become necessary, however, Hitler concluded, "to change the psychology of the German people and to explain to it that there are things which must be obtained by forceful means . . . in such a manner that the inner voice of the people itself slowly begins to shout for force."

By his own admission to the German generals, Hitler had contemplated the use of force from the beginning of his regime in 1933. Before striking in September, 1939, he was to dismantle the safeguards of the peace settlement of 1919 in carefully timed stages. In this process, he was greatly abetted by the rivalry and selfishness of the victorious allies of the First World War and by their illusion that Europe could be spared another war by appeasing Nazi Germany.

THE FIRST PHASE IN NAZI FOREIGN POLICY: THE WITHDRAWAL FROM MULTILATERAL ENGAGEMENTS

In his first secret address to German army commanders after becoming chancellor, Hitler stated on February 3, 1933, that, once Germany had rearmed, her new might should be employed in the conquest of new "living space" in the east and its "ruthless Germanization." Publicly, Hitler took great pains to assure the world of the peaceful intentions of the new German regime. The Nazi regime still needed time to consolidate its power at home. Moreover, the military and diplomatic realities of 1933 were such as to invite speedy disaster for Germany should Hitler display a rash or aggressive policy. While he was taking the first steps toward the clandestine rearmament of Germany, France still possessed the most powerful army in Europe, and the eastern allies of France, Poland and Czechoslovakia, were, by comparison with Germany, great military powers in their own right. The ratification of the Franco-Soviet Non-Aggression Pact of 1932 by the French parliament on May 19, 1933, suggested the possibilities of even stronger Franco-Soviet collaboration in the future. In order not to provoke Poland, Hitler called the Nazis of Danzig to order. Moreover, he renewed the German-Soviet neutrality treaty (Berlin Treaty) of 1926 on May 5, 1933.

In his "peace speech" of May 17, 1933, favorably received in the West, Hitler expressed his "earnest desire" to avoid war. A new war, in his words, would amount to "infinite madness," causing "the collapse of the present social and political order" of Europe and benefitting Communism only. To obtain international respectability, the Nazi government pressed for and obtained a Concordat with the Vatican on July 20, 1933. His emphatic assurances of peace notwithstanding, Hitler refused to be drawn into new multi-power agreements. German foreign policy of the mid-1920's under Gustav Stresemann had coveted multilateral agreements and associations, such as the Locarno Pact and membership in the League of Nations, in order to escape from Germany's postwar isolation to find a measure of security for a disarmed Germany. Hitler, by contrast, was anxious to shed the multilateral agreements of the Weimar Republic and refused to accept new agreements of this kind in order to facilitate his policy of revision backed by armed might. Bilateral, rather than multilateral, agreements became the style of German foreign policy between 1933 and 1939, to achieve the isolation of Hitler's intended victims.

THE FOUR POWER PACT

The German government thus gave only lukewarm support to Mussolini's initiative of a Four Power Pact of March 18, 1933. The Italian proposal amounted, in effect, to a four-power directorate of Britain, France, Germany, and Italy that could impose its will upon the lesser European powers, including the eastern allies of France — Poland and the Little Entente. The four powers were to coordinate their policy in the revision of peace treaties, including the question of disarmament still pending before the Geneva Disarmament Conference, as well as in the colonial question.

Italy's motive in proposing the Four Power Pact was her desire to achieve equal status with France, particularly in eastern Europe where French influence predominated over that of Italy, and to satisfy Italy's colonial ambitions, unfulfilled in the peace settlement of 1919. The proposal was Mussolini's attempt to include Italy in any future revision of the European status quo which a militant Germany under Hitler might demand.

Whereas Britain responded to the Italian proposal with guarded interest, the Eastern European allies of France, opposed to revision in principle and resentful of being excluded from the Great Power concert, protested vehemently. France, though not rejecting the proposal outright, accepted it only under conditions which deprived it of its original purpose. Germany, together with the other three Great Powers, signed a watered-down version of the Four Power Pact in Rome on June 7, 1933. Since neither Germany nor France ratified the pact, however, it remained a dead letter.

THE GERMAN WITHDRAWAL FROM THE LEAGUE

The issue of disarmament gave Hitler the desired pretext for leaving the League of Nations and thereby repudiating Germany's multilateral obligations under the League Covenant. On December 11, 1932, at the Geneva Disarmament Conference, Britain, France, and Italy had conceded to Germany the principle of equality of right in armaments within "a system providing security for all nations." Alarmed by Hitler's coming to power a few weeks later, France insisted on a trial period of four years before a limitation of armaments by the other powers began. When Britain and Italy accepted the French condition, Germany withdrew both from the Disarmament Conference and the League of Nations on October 14, 1933. A German plebiscite, organized by Hitler, endorsed withdrawal from the League by a 95 per cent majority.

THE GERMAN-POLISH NON-AGGRESSION PACT

After withdrawing from the League, Hitler gave the first startling demonstration of his policy of bilateralism by signing a non-aggression pact with Poland on January 26, 1934. Concluded for a ten-year period, the pact promised to settle all mutual problems on a bilateral basis without resort to force. The German-Polish Non-Aggression pact came as an unpleasant surprise to France, as German-Polish relations had never been friendly even in the most peaceful years of the Weimar Republic owing to the refusal of all German governments between 1919 and 1933 to accept the eastern borders as final. After Hitler came to power, the Polish government contemplated preventive military action, such as a partial occupation of East Prussia, as guarantee that Germany would continue to observe the Treaty of Versailles.

Far from provoking Poland, Hitler wooed it. Having restrained his Nazi followers in Danzig, he emphasized to Poland the common danger of Soviet Russia while affirming Poland's "right to exist." Calling Poland an "outpost against Asia," Hitler excluded the very idea of the possibility of war from Polish-German relations. As a further inducement, he held out the promise of improved trade relations.

In courting Poland in 1933, Hitler did not abandon his intention of an eventual revision of the German-Polish border. Rather, the Non-Aggression Pact served the tactical purpose of protecting Germany's flank in the immediate years ahead, so as to facilitate the destruction of Austria and Czechoslovakia while weakening the Franco-Polish alliance. "My pact with Poland," Hitler was to confess to his generals on the eve of the German invasion of Poland in September, 1939, "was only meant to stall for time." If Poland's willingness to sign with Hitler in 1934 appears foolhardy and indeed suicidal in retrospect, it must be understood that the Poland of the 1930's regarded itself as a Great Power or, at any rate, as the greatest among the small European powers. Because of this self-image, Poland was deeply offended when France accepted the Four Power Pact, albeit in a watered-down version, in June, 1933. In Poland's view, the Four Power Pact not only implied revision at the expense of the East European "successor states" but divided Europe into great and small powers, Poland being counted among the latter. Chagrined over its role as junior partner in the Franco-Polish alliance and confident of being able to deal with Hitler on an equal basis, Poland even thought in terms of a common German-Polish front against Czechoslovakia. A rapprochement with Germany might offer the chance of obtaining the *Teschen* district, claimed by Poland but awarded to Czechoslovakia in 1919.

THE AUSTRIAN NAZI UPRISING OF JULY, 1934

The month of March, 1933, in which the last Reichstag elections took place in Germany in an atmosphere of Nazi terror, also witnessed the end of Austrian parliamentary democracy. Following the deadlock between the Austrian Social Democratic and Christian Social parties on March 4, 1933, in the Austrian parliament, Chancellor Engelbert Dollfuss suspended Austria's parliamentary constitution of 1919 and replaced it with an authoritarian regime. By February, 1934, the last vestige of Austrian democracy was extinguished when the opposing Social Democrats were wiped out in a brief but violent civil war. Though anti-Socialist, corporate, and authoritarian, the regime of Dollfuss was at odds with Hitler's Germany from the beginning. In *Mein Kampf* Hitler had demanded the union of his native Austria and Germany. In November, 1918, at the time of the founding of the Austrian Republic, both the people and the provisional government of Austria expressed with overwhelming majority the desire for union with Germany. This sentiment was expressed not only in the unanimous resolution of Austria's parliament of November 11, 1918, but in subsequent plebiscites in Austria's provinces in 1919. In his youth, Dollfuss shared these sentiments.

Hitler's advent to power in Germany appreciably cooled the Austrian desire for union with Germany. Though contemptuous of parliamentary democracy, Dollfuss was also a devout Catholic in the tradition of Austria's priest-chancellor, Ignaz Seipel. As a Catholic, Dollfuss shared the revulsions of many of his countrymen against the anti-Christian aspects of Hitler's National Socialism.

Soon after coming to power, Hitler brought pressure to bear on Austria from without and within. As the Austrian Nazis stepped up their terrorist attacks inside Austria, Hitler dealt the Austrian economy a crippling blow by levying a 1,000 mark fee for each German tourist crossing into Austria on May 27, 1933. Dollfuss responded by banning the Austrian Nazi party in June, 1933, and by rallying his countrymen under the slogan "Austria awake." Austria, in Dollfuss' words, would not "sell her freedom for a couple of tourist seasons."

Dollfuss could hope to defy Hitler only if supported by a Great Power. Before 1933 France had been the jealous guardian of Austrian independence and had balked at even such limited Austro-German contacts as Brüning's project of an Austro-German customs union of 1931. Beginning with 1933, Fascist Italy emerged as Austria's chief protector as Dollfuss patterned the Austrian government after the Italian Fascist model. Anxious to keep Germany at arms' length and out of the Danubian Basin, Mussolini strove toward the establishment of an Italian protectorate over both Hungary and Austria. The Rome Protocols of March 17, 1934, signed by Mussolini, Dollfuss, and Gömbös, the Hungarian premier, thus pledged to coordinate the policy of the three signatories.

Hitler's effort to enlist Mussolini's support for a gradual German takeover of Austria failed when the two dictators had their first face-to-face meeting in Venice on June 14, 1934. The meeting was a disappointment to Hitler. Mussolini did not respond to Hitler's plea that all matters relating to Austria be decided by mutual agreement between Italy and Germany.

On July 25, 1934, the Austrian Nazis staged an armed uprising in Vienna and a few scattered places in the provinces, in the course of which Chancellor Dollfuss was murdered. Mussolini's response was immediate and unmistakable. While Austria's police crushed the Nazi uprising in Vienna, Italy moved troops to both the Austrian and Yugoslav frontiers. Abandoning the Austrian Nazi cause, Hitler disclaimed any part in the July uprising of Vienna and sought to reestablish normal relations with Austria by dispatching the wily Franz von Papen as ambassador to Austria. In March, 1935, Hitler publicly announced a German policy of nonintervention in Austria's internal affairs and pledged to seek no annexations at Austria's expense.

Hitler's first overt act of foreign aggression had been thwarted by Mussolini's resolute response. Coming on the heels of Hitler's blood purge of June 30, 1934, in which hundreds of Hitler's own followers were executed without trial, the brutal murder of Dollfuss by Austrian Nazis led to Hitler's moral and political isolation in 1934. When Britain, France, and Italy reaffirmed their common interest in Austrian independence on September 27, 1934, a promising start towards the containment of Hitler's Germany seemed to have been made. Indignant at Hitler's intrusion into Austria, in 1934 Mussolini abandoned the idea of revising the status quo in league with Germany in favor of maintaining the status quo in central Europe with the support of the democracies.

THE SAAR PLEBISCITE;
THE REARMAMENT OF GERMANY

Hitler's international prestige, shaken by the Austrian Nazi coup of 1934, was somewhat repaired by the outcome of the Saar plebiscite of January 13, 1935. Consistent with the Treaty of Versailles, which had promised a plebiscite to the German population of the Saar at the end of a fifteen-year period, the people of the Saar were given a choice between joining France, rejoining Germany, or maintaining the League of Nations regime which had governed the Saar since 1920. The voters opted for a return to Germany with a 90 per cent majority, only 9 per cent favoring the continued administration of the League.

Having proclaimed Germany's intention to create an air force on March 10, 1935 — a force already in being at the time of the announcement — Hitler announced the introduction of universal military training on March 16, 1935. The stated aim of German rearmament was a peacetime army of thirty-six divisions or 550,000 men. As was Hitler's wont in subsequent violations of international agreements, the announcement of German rearmament in open violation of the Treaty of Versailles was accompanied by German protests against the actions of other powers that were not, in fact, treaty violations. Hitler thus timed German rearmament to coincide with the extension of the French term of service in the armed forces from twelve to twenty-four months and justified his action by pointing to the failure of others to disarm as well as the rearmament of Soviet Russia.

THE OPPORTUNITY OF CONTAINMENT:
THE FRANCO-SOVIET RAPPROCHEMENT

If France had statesmen, Hitler had confided to his generals soon after coming to power, she would not give Germany time to rearm but fall upon her together with her eastern allies. Although France did not contemplate a preventive war — her military and foreign policy outlook remaining defensive throughout the 1930's — she was sufficiently alarmed by Germany's withdrawal from the League in October, 1933, to seek the active collaboration of Soviet Russia.

The French desire for alliance with Soviet Russia proceeded

from the realization that the French postwar alliance system, adequate for the containment of Weimar Germany, was inadequate as a bulwark against Hitler. As Germany became stronger, Belgium indicated her desire to withdraw from the Franco-Belgian Military Convention of 1920. Poland, the principal eastern ally of France since 1920, no longer followed France blindly, as evidenced by the conclusion of the German-Polish Non-Aggression Pact of January, 1934. Of the members of the Little Entente, Czechoslovakia alone could be regarded as a staunch ally of France, as Yugoslavia and Rumania became increasingly dependent upon German economic strength, following the conclusion of trade agreements between Germany and Yugoslavia in 1934 and Germany and Rumania in 1935.

A further persuasive argument in favor of alliance with Russia was the memory of Russia's contribution to French survival in 1914 and the knowledge that France could not match Germany either in manpower or in military-industrial capacity, once German rearmament had begun. "For every Frenchman between the ages of twenty and thirty," Charles de Gaulle warned in his *The Army of the Future* in 1934, "there are two Germans. We could never surpass the mass production of German heavy industry." The years 1936 to 1940, the "hollow years," would be especially critical for the French army, when the number of annual draftees would fall from an average of 230,000 to 118,000 owing to the lower French birth rate during the First World War. Russia's growing industrial potential and Russia's manpower could fill the French gap. Before the Stalinist purge of the late 1930's had wrought havoc with the Red Army leadership, French estimates of Red Army capabilities were uniformly high. General Loiseau, a French witness to Red Army maneuvers, praised the "superiority" of the Red Army over all other European armies. Pierre Cot, the French Air Minister, regarded Russia's bomber force the strongest in Europe and Russia's industrial potential equal to that of Germany and double that of France.

Against the advantages of a Soviet-French alliance, the risks which collaboration with Communist Russia implied seemed tolerable. The Communist International, to be sure, had fomented national unrest in the French colonies throughout the 1920's, and the French Communist Party paper *l'Humanite* had denounced "French imperialism" as "the bloody tormentor of sixty million colonial slaves" as recently as 1932. The French Communist Party, holding only 10 seats in the French Chamber of Deputies before the elections of May, 1936, represented a minority, however, which Stalin, hopefully, would soon call to order.

The French Foreign Minister Joseph Paul-Boncour, who initiated negotiations for an alliance with Russia in 1933, dispelled the ideological scruples of his conservative countrymen by pointing out that France could not ignore a country of 165 million inhabitants. Louis

Barthou, Paul-Boncour's successor and the most vigorous advocate of a Franco-Russian alliance before his assassination in October, 1934, at Marseilles, argued that the ideological differences between France and Communist Russia should no more prevent the conclusion of an alliance than had the difference between Republican France and Tsarist Russia in 1894: "Geography commands history" was Barthou's thesis.

Though France might be willing to subordinate ideological differences to the needs of foreign policy, the situation of the early 1930's differed from that of the 1890's in essential points because of the existence of the East European "successor states" between Russia and central Europe. Having depended for their security chiefly on France since their inception, the "successor states" were vitally concerned lest a Franco-Soviet alliance be ultimately made at their expense. Anxious to reconcile the security of the successor states with her own policy of rapprochement with Soviet Russia, France had thus insisted on non-aggression pacts between Russia and her immediate neighbors to the west before signing the Franco-Soviet Non-Aggression Pact of November, 1932. Accordingly, Russia had signed non-aggression pacts with Finland, Poland, Latvia, and Estonia in 1932. The Soviet-Lithuanian Non-Aggression Pact of 1926 had been renewed in 1931. Rumania had remained the only exception to the pattern of Soviet non-aggression pacts of 1932 owing to the Soviet refusal to recognize Rumania's seizure of Bessarabia in 1918.

"EASTERN LOCARNO"

It was more difficult to reconcile an outright Franco-Soviet alliance with the security of Russia's western border states, however. A Franco-Soviet alliance directed against Germany would, of necessity, raise the question of Red Army passage across Poland and Rumania, as Germany and Russia shared no common borders. Polish fears that the presence of Soviet troops on Polish territory, under whatever pretext, would ultimately result in another Polish partition were no less pronounced in 1933, however, than they would be in 1939. To resolve the dilemma, France proposed in 1934 a multilateral security pact for Eastern Europe, analogous to the regional security pact concluded for Western Europe at Locarno in 1925. At Britain's insistence, Germany was included in the "Eastern Locarno" pact proposal, as Britain opposed any scheme directed chiefly against Germany. Moreover, the effectiveness of "Eastern Locarno" was made dependent on Russia's entry into the League. In addition to having symbolic value, Russian League membership might resolve the vexing problem of troop passage through Poland and Rumania. Under Article 16 of the League Covenant, League members pledged to "take the necessary steps to afford passage through their territory to the forces of any Members of the League which are cooperating to protect the covenants of the League."

"Eastern Locarno" consisted of two parts. First, a treaty of Regional Assistance between Russia, Germany, Poland, Czechoslovakia, the Baltic States, and Finland pledged the signatories to lend assistance to one another if attacked by another contracting state. Secondly, an Agreement between France and Russia pledged France to assume towards Russia, but none other, the obligations of a signatory of the treaty of Regional Assistance and pledged Russia to assume towards France, but none other, the obligations of a signatory of the Locarno Treaty.

Britain insisted that the Franco-Soviet guarantee be extended to include Germany in order to make "Eastern Locarno" reciprocal. Only after the pact was amended accordingly did Britain urge Germany to accept it. Eastern Locarno, in its amended form, was accepted by France, Russia, and Czechoslovakia and rejected by Germany and Poland. Hitler rejected the Eastern Locarno Pact as "impractical, illogical and hypocritical," as he could not envisage the defense of German territory against a French attack by Russian troops or against a Russian attack by French troops. The true reason for Germany's negative reply was Hitler's aversion to multilateral security pacts which would block his future aggressions in Eastern Europe. Poland rejected Eastern Locarno because of her undiminished fear of a Soviet military presence on her territory in a future war between Germany, Russia, and France.

THE FRENCH-SOVIET PACT OF MUTUAL ASSISTANCE

The repudiation of Eastern Locarno opened up the path to a bilateral Franco-Soviet alliance, which Russia had desired all along since the beginning of the Franco-Soviet negotiations in 1933. After Russia's entry into the League of Nations in September, 1934, Hitler's announcement of German rearmament on March 16, 1935, provided the final impetus for the signing of the Franco-Soviet Pact of Mutual Assistance on May 2, 1935.

The Pact of Mutual Assistance, concluded for a five-year period, pledged France and Russia to notify the League Council if a threat or danger of attack existed. In the event of an actual attack, both powers would render assistance to one another, if the League Council failed to reach a decision. The pact was limited to Europe and directed against Germany.

The Franco-Soviet Pact of Mutual Assistance was followed by a Czechoslovak-Soviet Pact of Mutual Assistance on May 16, 1935. The latter was identical with the former except for the provision that its effectiveness depended on France rendering assistance to the country attacked.

The French-Russian-Czechoslovak pact system of May, 1935, appeared a far more effective instrument for the containment of Nazi Germany than the unwieldy Eastern Locarno Pact. Moreover, France succeeded in obtaining Britain's tacit consent to the Pact of Mutual Assistance. The statement of Britain's Foreign Secretary Sir John Simon that Britain's guarantee to Germany under the Locarno Pact of 1925 would not apply in case of a French attack on Germany provoked by a German attack on Russia, put the newly assumed obligations of France towards Russia into harmony with French security under the Locarno Pact. Hitler's charge of May, 1935, that the Franco-Soviet alliance had brought an "element of legal insecurity" into the Locarno Pact was rejected jointly by Britain, Italy, and Belgium.

In spite of its deterrent appearance, the Franco-Soviet alliance suffered from serious flaws, which were to render it a worthless instrument when the occasion for its use arose in the late 1930's. The Pact of Mutual Assistance, unlike the Franco-Russian alliance of 1894, did not contain a military convention. Although Stalin proposed a supplementary military agreement, no such agreement materialized between France and Russia. French-Soviet staff conversations, begun in January, 1937, were discontinued after a few meetings for want of French enthusiasm. Nor did the French army fill the place of joint military training and research vacated by the German *Reichswehr* after Hitler's coming to power. No intimate Franco-Soviet military collaboration developed after 1935 such as had characterized the contacts between *Reichswehr* and Red Army during the "Rapallo period" from 1922 to 1933.

The absence of a military convention and the unsolved problem of Red Army passage over Poland rendered the military effectiveness of the Pact of Mutual Assistance dubious.

The credibility of the Franco-Soviet alliance was further undermined by the delay in its ratification by France until February, 1936, and the resurgence of French ideological scruples in the wake of the increase of French Communist strength from 10 to 72 deputies in the elections of May, 1936. In 1935 Stalin had directed the French Communists to desist from further attacks on French defensive power, and the Seventh Congress of the Communist International of 1935 had similarly instructed its adherents to end their sabotage of the armed forces in the democracies. The Comintern-approved strategy of the Popular Front, the alliance of Communist with democratic parties in the West, caused alarm rather than comfort in conservative France when it contributed to the Communist success in the French elections of 1936. Instead of being a bulwark against Nazi Germany, the Popular Front, in French conservative opinion, might become the springboard for an eventual Communist takeover.

Not the least important factor in the enfeeblement of the Franco-Soviet alliance after 1935 was the death of Foreign Minister Louis Barthou, on October 9, 1934. Barthou had read *Mein Kampf* and believed its message. Resolute towards Germany in the tradition of Clemenceau and Poincaré and pragmatic on the question of Communism, Barthou's policy during his brief tenure of office in 1934 suggested that a Franco-Soviet alliance under his guidance might have become an effective deterrent to Nazi aggression. Anthony Eden, Britain's Foreign Secretary in the 1930's, listed Barthou's death in 1934 as among the principal causes of the Second World War, when asked to comment on its origins in 1969, the thirtieth anniversary of the outbreak of the war.

THE SOVIET MOTIVE FOR
COLLECTIVE SECURITY

In a foreign policy address of December, 1933, the Soviet Foreign Minister Maxim Litvinov referred to the year 1933 as a "junction of two eras." The observation applied not only to German-Western relations but the attitude of Soviet Russia towards the non-Communist world. Before 1933 Stalin had interpreted German National Socialism as the death pangs of German capitalism which would open the path to a German Communist victory; Social Democracy was regarded not as the enemy but as the twin brother of Nazism. As late as June, 1933, the Communist International spoke out against an alliance of Soviet Russia with the Western democracies to fight Fascism.

The Hitler regime proved to be more than a brief episode, however, and soon displayed the very aggressiveness and lack of scruple which Soviet propaganda had previously ascribed to all "bourgeois" governments. The threat of Nazi Germany appeared doubly dangerous to Soviet Russia because it coincided with Japan's aggressive attitude towards Russia after the Japanese conquest of Manchuria.

Under the double impact of Japanese imperialism and Nazi hostility, Soviet Russia changed from a power which had promoted revolutionary change in the West and the colonial world through the instrument of the Comintern into a status-quo power seeking the collaboration of others equally desirous of maintaining the status quo in Asia and Europe. All references to class war and the inevitability of a Soviet-Western clash disappeared from Soviet rhetoric. In contrast to the intolerance and aggressiveness of the Fascist regimes, Russia advertised herself as a peaceful nation, one that did not persecute her racial minorites. The Stalin Constitution of 1936, in addition to serving certain purposes of Soviet domestic policy, was part of the overall Soviet propaganda effort to portray Russia as a quasi-liberal power.

To contain Japan and Germany, Stalin desired a "scheme of pacts." Of the two powers, Japan represented the more immediate danger, for, unlike Nazi Germany, Japan was not in the process of rearming, but fully armed and shared a common border with Soviet Russia. Russia's establishment of formal diplomatic relations with the United States in November, 1933, was intended as a first step towards a Far Eastern system of collective security. American policy in the Far East had, in fact, been beneficial to Soviet interests, even before U.S. recognition of Soviet Russia in 1933. Not only had American pressure been instrumental in the

Japanese troop withdrawal from eastern Siberia at the end of the Russian Civil War, but the United States had condemned Japanese action in Manchuria in 1931, and withheld recognition of the Japanese puppet state of Manchukuo. In 1934 Soviet Russia hoped to draw the United States into a regional non-aggression pact for the Far East, to be formed by the United States, Russia, China, and Japan. When the United States declined the Soviet invitation, Russia endeavored to deflect Japan from her Far Eastern borders by keeping the conflict between Japan and the Chinese Nationalist government alive. Towards this end, the Chinese Communists, previously engaged in war against the Nationalist Chinese government of Chiang Kai-shek, were ordered to form a common front against Japan. In the language of the Seventh Comintern Congress of 1935, the Chinese Communists were to repulse the "Japanese robber campaign" in alliance with the Chinese Nationalists. In August, 1937, Soviet Russia signed a pact of non-aggression and friendship with the government of Chiang Kai-shek, which was followed by Soviet military and economic aid. The full-scale resumption of the Sino-Japanese conflict in 1937 thus suited the purpose of Soviet Far Eastern policy, as it promised to preoccupy Japan and lessened the likelihood of a Japanese attack on Russia.

As Russia had hoped to counterbalance the power of Japan with the aid of the United States in the Far East, she aimed to counterbalance the power of Nazi Germany with the support of France in Europe. To Anthony Eden, Stalin stated in 1935 that "Germany must be made to realize that if she attacked any other nation she would have Europe against her." Although the Franco-Czechoslovak-Soviet pact system of May, 1935, fell short of Stalin's aim of European collective security, it lessened the likelihood of Franco-German accommodation as the prelude to a Nazi attack on Russia. While anxious to contain Nazi Germany, Stalin did not wish to provoke Hitler. Thus, the Franco-Soviet Pact of Mutual Assistance served a defensive purpose only and was not intended as the overture to a European-wide crusade against Fascism. Moreover, even when mutual recrimination was strongest between the Nazi and Soviet regimes, the door to a German-Russian understanding was never fully shut by Stalin. After 1933, the Soviet Union repeatedly asserted that ideological differences were not an insurmountable obstacle to improved German-Soviet relations.

THE ROME ACCORDS; THE DECLARATION OF FEBRUARY, 1935; THE STRESA FRONT

As France and Russia were moving towards an alliance in early 1935, Britain, France, and Italy took steps towards a common policy in response to the German threat to Austrian independence in July, 1934, and Hitler's proclamation of German rearmament in March, 1935. Although in 1935 Italian Fascism was not regarded as an obstacle to a common British-French-Italian front against Hitler, the elimination of certain national rivalries among the three powers was a necessary first to achieving an effective Western concert against Hitler.

The so-called Rome Accords of January 7, 1935, between Mussolini and French Foreign Minister Pierre Laval were an attempt to settle issues which had divided France from Italy. Apart from naval rivalry and Yugoslavia, Italy's colonial ambitions in Africa constituted the most sensitive issue in Franco-Italian relations at the turn of 1934/ 1935. The clash between Italian and Ethiopian forces at Wal-Wal in southeastern Ethiopia on December 5, 1934, was Mussolini's first warning of Italy's imminent aggression against all of Ethiopia. Under the Rome Accords, France ceded to Italy a desert area adjacent to southeastern Libya and a small coastal strip at Eritrea as well as 2,500 shares of stock in the Djibouti to Addis-Ababa railroad. More significantly, Laval promised to give Mussolini "a free hand" in Ethiopia. Mussolini, in turn, renounced Italian claims in Tunisia. Whereas Laval insisted that the promise of a "free hand" pertained only to peaceful, economic penetration of Ethiopia, Mussolini was to claim subsequently that the French promise had been unconditional and with the understanding of an eventual Italian conquest of Ethiopia.

With the colonial question seemingly resolved to Italy's satisfaction, Italy and France further agreed in the Rome Accords to take joint countermeasures against a renewed German threat to Austria. To put force behind this pledge, France and Italy concluded a military accord for the defense of Austria in June, 1935. As a permanent guarantee to Austrian independence, the Rome Accords proposed a multilateral "Danubian Pact," open to Germany, Austria, Italy, France, Czechoslovakia, Poland, Hungary, and Rumania.

Following the Rome Accords between Italy and France, France and Great Britain issued a Joint Declaration on February 3, 1935, for a "general settlement freely negotiated between Germany and the other Powers." Specifically, the Joint Declaration proposed: (1) the organization of security in Europe through the conclusion of pacts, such as the above mentioned Danubian Pact and a mutual assistance pact for Eastern Europe, which Hitler had recently turned down with his repudiation of an "Eastern Locarno"; (2) an arms convention with Germany, consistent with the principle of "equality of rights in a system of security" and Germany's return to the League; (3) an Air Pact for Western Europe, including Britain, France, Italy, Belgium, and Germany. Under the Air Pact, the powers mentioned would assist one another with their air forces if any one of them were attacked by "unprovoked aerial aggression." As an attempt to achieve the containment of Nazi Germany with Hitler's consent, the Joint Declaration was doomed to failure, since Hitler had already demonstrated his aversion to multilateral security pacts. Hitler's answer to the Joint Declaration was to announce German rearmament on March 16, 1935, unilaterally and without agreed limitations.

Of the Western powers, Italy and France showed the greatest alarm over the proclamation of German rearmament, Italy announcing her "most comprehensive reservations" and France clamoring for an anti-German front from Russia to Britain. As Britain had come to regard German rearmament as inevitable, she was more concerned with the form than the substance of the German move. However, Britain joined with France and Italy in the Stresa Declaration of April 11, 1935, the most forceful example of Anglo-French-Italian solidarity since Hitler came to power. Mussolini, British Prime Minister MacDonald, and Pièrre Flandin, the French Premier, declared their opposition "by all practicable means" to any unilateral repudiation of treaties which might endanger the peace *of Europe*. Britain and Italy warned Hitler by reaffirming their obligations to France arising from the Locarno Treaty; all three powers restated the necessity of maintaining the independence and integrity of Austria and invited Germany once again to negotiate an Air Pact and an Eastern Pact. The League Council, acting on the initiative of the Stresa powers, unanimously condemned German rearmament as a "threat to European security" and threatened to impose sanctions in the event of new German breaches of the Versailles Treaty.

ANGLO-GERMAN NAVAL ACCORD

Hitler responded to the Stresa front and the Franco-Soviet alliance with another "peace speech" on May 21, 1935, denying any German expansionist aims, including those against Austria, and asserting Germany's intention to keep all treaties she had signed of her own free will. In addition, Hitler offered to sign non-aggression pacts with Germany's neighbors.

The "peace speech" of May 21, 1935, was not without effect on England, where the hope for a negotiated revision of the Treaty of Versailles competed with the desire for containment. Although Hitler had proclaimed an expansion of the German army, he might be persuaded to accept treaty limitations on German naval armaments. Acting on a German initiative of March 25, 1935, which Hitler launched on the occasion of the visit of Foreign Secretary Sir John Simon to Berlin, Britain signed an Anglo-German naval accord on June 18, 1935. The accord permitted the expansion of the German navy up to 35 per cent of British naval strength and the creation of a German submarine force equal to that of Great Britain.

The Anglo-German naval accord seemed to hold definite advantages for Britain as it promised to prevent the repetition of the costly Anglo-German naval race of the decade preceding the First World War. When Britain had attempted to reach agreement on the limitation of German naval armaments in the Haldane mission of 1912, the attempt had failed because of the excessive political price which Emperor William II and Admiral Tirpitz had demanded in the form of a binding British neutrality pledge towards Germany. In June, 1935, Hitler consented to limit German naval armaments seemingly without any price in return. In fact, the price for Hitler's "concession" on naval armaments was Britain's tacit agreement that the disarmament provisions of the Treaty of Versailles no longer applied. Having scrapped one of the most important aspects of the Versailles Treaty by her own consent, Britain would find it difficult to uphold other provisions. Moreover, the Anglo-German naval accord could not help but create the impression of British selfishness and duplicity since neither France nor Italy had been consulted. The Anglo-German naval accord was a bilateral breach in the multilateral system of collective security which the status quo powers had been laboring so hard to achieve since 1934. Britain had acted not only against the spirit of the Stresa front but against that of the Anglo-French Joint Declaration of February 3, 1935, in which both governments had agreed to treat the questions of security and armaments as an indivisible whole. The Anglo-German naval accord thus set a dangerous precedent. If Britain made exceptions to the principle of concerted action when it suited her national interest, what was to prevent others from doing likewise under similar circumstances? The Ethiopian crisis, soon to burst upon Europe and the League of Nations, was to bring the dilemma of national interest versus collective security into full focus. As for the ultimate fate of the Anglo-German naval accord, Hitler renounced it less than four years after its conclusion, when it suited his ends.

THE ETHIOPIAN CRISIS

Although willing to uphold the European status quo against Hitler, Mussolini had been planning the conquest of Ethiopia since 1933. Wedged between Eritrea and French Somali in the north, Italian and British Somali in the south, Ethiopia had been an object of Italian colonial ambitions since the 1890's. Italy's first attempt to seize Ethiopia had failed when a native army routed the Italian would-be conquerors in the battle of Adowa in 1896. Subsequent Italian efforts to establish a protectorate over Ethiopia failed after Italy, together with France, sponsored the admission of Ethiopia to the League in 1923 and concluded a treaty of Friendship and Arbitration with Ethiopia in 1928.

The defeat of Adowa left a deep wound on Italian national pride which was aggravated by the Allied refusal to share the former

German colonial empire in Africa with Italy in 1919. If only the Italians had had 3,000 more fighting men at Adowa, the Duce complained in 1935, Adowa would have been an Italian victory. The conquest of Ethiopia would not only "wash out in blood" the memory of Adowa, in the phrase of the Italian diplomat Baron Aloisi, but bring Italy one step closer to Mussolini's stated goal, that "Italy's historic objectives lie in Asia and Africa." The conquest of Ethiopia would at last make Italy, in Mussolini's mind, a truly Great Power by virtue of her own strength and not by invitation of the Western democracies. The dream of an Italian Empire in Africa was not confined to Mussolini or the Fascist regime but enjoyed wide popular support in Italy, a fact which helps explain the tenacity of Mussolini when Ethiopia threatened to become an issue of war between Italy and Great Britain in October, 1935.

In anticipation of his attack on Ethiopia, Mussolini had made what appeared to him adequate diplomatic preparations. The tacit consent of France seemed to have been obtained in the Rome Accords of January, 1935, that of Britain in the Stresa Declaration of April, 1935. The latter, it will be recalled, had confined the condemnation of unilateral treaty revisions *to Europe,* at the Italian request. Moreover, Mussolini counted on the Manchurian precedent, in which the League had shown less vigor than it might have mustered in a case of aggression in Europe. Though a full member of the League, Ethiopia was an African state and as such, in the Italian view of 1935, not entitled to all its benefits. Throughout the Ethiopian crisis, Italy's Fascist-controlled press portrayed Ethiopia, in word and picture, as a savage state beyond the pale of European civilization.

Far from acquiescing in Italy's design for Ethiopian conquest, Britain opposed it, out of concern for League prestige and resentment over Italy's incursion into East Africa. The integrity of the League became the central theme of British policy in the Ethiopian crisis. In the words of Sir Austen Chamberlain, the former British Foreign Secretary, Ethiopia was a test case which would show whether the League "does mean anything for any one or nothing for any one." "If the League does fail," the British Foreign Secretary Sir Samuel Hoare added on October 22, 1935, "the world at large, and Europe in particular will be faced with a period of almost unrelieved danger and gloom." The sentiments expressed by Chamberlain and Hoare were fully shared by the vast majority of the British public, faith in the League being particularly strong among many veterans of the First World War and among the postwar generation.

Though anxious to uphold the reputation of the League, the British government was equally anxious to keep Italy as a partner of European collective security. Throughout the spring and summer of 1935, British diplomacy made a strong effort to achieve a compromise acceptable to Italy and compatible with the League covenant. Britain wished to avoid a confrontation with Italy in the League which would compel Britain to make a choice between the League and Italian friendship. The British aim was to achieve a compromise before Italy had actually mounted an attack. Thus, the League did not act immediately on the Ethiopian complaint after the incidents between Italian and Ethiopian troops at Wal-Wal in December, 1934, and at Gerlogubi at the turn of 1934/35, in the hope that Mussolini could be persuaded to accept a compromise settlement.

The British search for compromise was fully supported by France, which, depending more on Italian support for her security in Europe than did Britain, tried to avoid a clash with Italy at virtually any cost. Unlike Great Britain, France did not invoke the moral and legal principles of the covenent but the demands of her own security in Europe. France suspected, as did Mussolini, that Britain used the League covenant as a moralistic cloak for the protection of her colonial interests in East Africa. Would the enthusiasm, France asked, with which the British public seemed to endorse the League in the Ethiopian crisis apply equally against German aggressions in Europe?

Compromise was offered to Mussolini in three ways. In June, 1935, Anthony Eden, as British Minister for League of Nations Affairs, proposed to Mussolini a partial dismemberment of Ethiopia. Ethiopia was to cede the Ogaden Province, adjacent to Italian Somaliland, to Italy; Britain would cede the port of Zeila on the Gulf of Aden to Ethiopia as a compensation. Britain would support Italian economic penetration of rump-Ethiopia as well as the settlement of Italian colonists.

Pierre Laval, forever resourceful in finding solutions which kept up an appearance of legality, proposed an Italian protectorate over Ethiopia similar to that of France over Morocco. An Italian protectorate would make League involvement unnecessary, keep Emperor Haile Selassie on the throne, and surrender *de facto* control to Italy.

A third compromise proposal, submitted jointly by France and Britain in the fall of 1935, offered Italy economic concessions, the right of settlement of Italian colonists, and the participation of Italian advisers in the reorganization of the Ethiopian government.

Mussolini rejected all offers of compromise on the grounds that they would rob him of the prestige of a military victory. On June 8, 1935, the Duce announced that Italy had "old and new accounts to settle." A man like Signor Mussolini, Baron Aloisi, the Italian League representative added, cannot be expected to spend 600 million lire "in order to change his mind at the request of the League of Nations."

When the attempt at mediation failed, Britain hoped to deter Italy from attacking Ethiopia by a show of resolution. In September, 1935, Britain moved her Mediterranean fleet from Malta to the Levant and reinforced her Gibraltar squadron with two of the strongest ships of her Home Fleet, *Hood* and *Renown*. The show of British naval power was accompanied by a strongly worded address of Sir Samuel Hoare at the opening of the League Assembly in September, 1935, in which the Foreign Secretary proclaimed Britain's stand "for steady and collective resistance to all acts of unprovoked aggression."

Britain's resolute stand of September, 1935, drew the enthusiastic applause of virtually all the small powers represented in the League, which identified a strong League with their own survival. Soviet Foreign Minister Litvinov interpreted the British attitude of September, 1935, as a new manifestation of British world power which would sweep Mussolini and the Fascist regime from Italy.

On October 3, 1935, Mussolini invaded Ethiopia. On October 7, 1935, the League Council condemned Italy for having committed an act of aggression not only against Ethiopia but against all other members of the League. With the exception of Austria and Hungary, tied to Italy under the Rome Protocols of 1934, all League members endorsed sanctions against Italy, consistent with Article 16 of the League covenant. The League devised four types of sanctions against Italy: (1) a ban on the export of arms to Italy, (2) a ban on loans or credits, (3) a ban on all imports of Italian origin, and (4) a ban on the export to Italy of selected goods. The ban on exports included strategic materials deemed significant to Italy's war effort in Ethiopia, such as rubber and minerals, as well as horses and mules. The ban did not include, however, such vital strategic materials as oil, cotton, copper, coal, and iron. Lastly, the League proposed a system of mutual economic assistance for League members to minimize the effect of sanctions on those League states heavily dependent on trade with Italy.

THE FAILURE OF SANCTIONS

The sanctions policy, applied between November, 1935, and March, 1936 (officially, the policy of sanctions did not end until July 15, 1936), suffered from serious flaws which minimized its impact. Foremost among these was the loophole of evasion through triangular trade as well as direct trade with non-members of the League, especially the United States and Germany, which together accounted for over 23 per cent of all Italian exports in 1934. The Congress of the United States, in anticipation of war between Italy and Ethiopia, had adopted the Neutrality Resolution of August, 1935, which banned the export of "arms, ammunition and implements of war" to all belligerents upon the President's finding that a state of war existed. Although the American Neutrality resolution went into effect in October, 1935, it did not prevent a sharp increase in American sales to Italy, particularly oil deliveries. Accordingly, total American trade with Italy and her colonies was greater in 1935 than in either the year previous or the year following. American sales of oil to Italy during the three-month period from October to December, 1935, were equal to the total American oil exports to Italy for the entire year 1934.

The increased flow of American exports to Italy during the sanctions period reflected the great caution of American policy in the Ethiopian crisis. Uncertain about the determination of the League, the United States was afraid lest an embargo of American exports to Italy would leave the United States in the embarrassing position of being the only power to apply effective measures against Italian aggression. Although the United States rebuked Italy privately for spending vast sums of money in the pursuit of a new war without having paid its debts to the United States, incurred in the First World War, American policy statements were confined to generalities, urging the nations of the world to support economic and world peace. An inquiry of the League of October 22, 1935, as to American intentions was answered with the statement that the United States neither wished to be drawn into the Ethiopian war nor desired to contribute to its prolongation.

More detrimental to an effective League policy against Italy than American isolationism was the continued hesitation of France. When Mussolini threatened to withdraw his troops from the Austrian frontier in retaliation for League sanctions, France redoubled her efforts to settle the Ethiopian conflict by a compromise acceptable to Mussolini. When Britain asked for French assurances of full military and naval support in the event of an Italian attack on Britain's Mediterranean positions, France gave an evasive reply and refused to open staff conversations with Britain for naval coordination in the Mediterranean. The lukewarm support of France deflated Britain's resolute position of September, 1935, as the British government was not at all certain that Mussolini would not provoke an Anglo-Italian war through what the British government called a "mad dog act." Though Britain enjoyed the support of the small League members, she did not consider that support as adequate without the cooperation of France, the only other Great Power in the League besides Britain and Italy. Although the British government of Prime Minister Baldwin had won reelection in November, 1935, largely on the strength of its campaign pledge to uphold its firm League policy, Foreign Secretary Hoare betrayed that pledge by signing away the independence of Ethiopia in the so-called Hoare-Laval Agreement of December 7, 1935.

The Hoare-Laval Agreement

The Hoare-Laval Agreement, concluded hastily in Paris by the British Foreign Secretary on his way to a skating holiday in Switzerland, proposed to surrender approximately half of Ethiopia to Mussolini, including the Tigre province in the north as well as eastern and southeastern Ethiopia. In the remaining half of Ethiopia, Italy was to be given exclusive rights of economic development. Ethiopia was to be compensated by receiving either the port of Zeila or Assab together with an access corridor but without the right of building a connecting railroad.

The Hoare-Laval Agreement, leaked to the press before its official announcement, caused a storm of indignation in the British public, whose strong feelings on the Ethiopian issue the Foreign Secretary had misjudged. The agreement was denounced as a reward to aggression, and the London *Times* derided the proposed Ethiopian corridor to the sea as a "corridor for camels." The Agreement evoked equal, if not greater, anger among those small League powers which had loyally followed Britain's lead at considerable economic sacrifice to themselves. The British dominions, anxious to stop Italy from becoming a great colonial power, responded with surprise that their opinion had not been consulted in concluding the Agreement.

The Baldwin government repudiated the Hoare-Laval Agreement under public pressure and sacrificed the Foreign Secretary as a face-saving gesture. Anthony Eden, formerly Minister for League Affairs and an advocate of a firm policy towards Italy, succeeded as Foreign Secretary. Though keeping up appearances of a strong League policy, beating a respectable retreat was all that the youthful Anthony Eden could achieve in the Anglo-Italian confrontation. On February 26, 1936, the British government announced its decision to impose oil sanctions against Italy if other League members followed suit. The latter was most unlikely in view of Britain's own past vaccilations and the sentiments of France. By February, 1936, France, possessing reliable information about Hitler's impending remilitarization of the Rhineland, was more anxious than before to keep Italian friendship, lest Italy withdraw her guarantee to France under the Locarno Pact. As Europe became embroiled in the Rhineland crisis, of which more will be said presently, Mussolini completed his conquest of Ethiopia through the use of poison gas and air power. When Ethiopia protested against the use of poison gas, France blocked a League investigation into the matter. The fall of the Ethiopian capital of Addis Ababa at the beginning of May, 1936, marked the end of the war. On May 1, 1936, Emperor Haile Selassie departed from his capital, and on May 9, 1936, the King of Italy assumed the title of Emperor of Ethiopia. To Neville Chamberlain, Chancellor of the Exchequer in the Baldwin government and soon to succeed as Prime Minister, the continuation of the policy of sanctions against Italy seemed to be "the very midsummer of madness." If Britain were to pursue the policy of sanctions, Chamberlain added, "it would lead only to further misfortune which would divert our minds as practical men from seeking other and better solutions." League sanctions against Italy ended on July 15, 1936.

Mussolini emerged triumphant from the Ethiopian crisis less because of his own fortitude than because of the timidity of his irresolute opponents. Had the League imposed oil sanctions, Mussolini confided to

Hitler in 1938, Italy would have had to withdraw from Ethiopia within a week. But even without oil sanctions, the sanctions actually imposed might have been effective if maintained over an extended period of time, as evidenced by the decrease in Italian exports by 40 per cent and the drop in Italian imports by over 50 per cent during the sanctions period. At no time did Britain close the Suez Canal to Italian troop transports, nor did she respond to Ethiopia's urgent pleas for arms.

The long-range effects of the Ethiopian war on Europe were incalculable. The Stresa front was shattered beyond repair, as was the credibility of the League as an effective deterrent to aggression. The opposition of France and Britain to Italy had been sufficiently vexing to Mussolini to alienate him but not powerful enough to convince him of their strength and his weakness. Ethiopia prompted a realignment of Britain, France, Italy, and Germany, as Mussolini, both angry and contemptuous of Britain and France, began to look to Germany as a partner in aggression. Implicit in the realignment was the Rome-Berlin Axis and the withdrawal of the Italian guarantee to Austrian independence. The conquest of Addis Ababa in May, 1936, foreshadowed Hitler's seizure of Vienna less than two years later.

The policy of Britain in the Ethiopian crisis also led to a reassessment of Soviet Russia's views from the optimistic forecasts of Soviet Foreign Minister Litvinov in September, 1935, to a more guarded estimate of Britain's strength and reliability. The most immediate impact of the Ethiopian war was upon Germany. In September, 1935, Germany had followed Britain's initiative in the League with respectful interest. In March, 1936, after the fiasco of the Hoare-Laval agreement, Hitler, against the advice of all his generals, felt certain that the risk of occupying the Rhineland could be taken.

THE OCCUPATION OF THE RHINELAND

On March 7, 1936, German troops marched into the demilitarized zone of the Rhineland as aircraft of Hitler's new air force thundered across the Rhine. The Rhineland occupation constituted a violation not only of the Treaty of Versailles but of the Locarno Treaty of 1925 as well. Hitler thus violated his own pledge of 1935, of abiding by all international agreements signed by Germany of her own free will. The Locarno Treaty, in Hitler's words, had lost its "inner meaning," however, after France had ratified the Franco-Soviet Pact of Mutual Assistance in February, 1936.

From a military standpoint the Rhineland occupation was a reckless gamble, since the military power of France, together with that of her eastern allies, Poland and Czechoslovakia, could have crushed Germany in 1936. Having observed the lack of resolution and coordination in Anglo-French policy during the Ethiopian crisis, Hitler counted on psychological rather than purely military factors in estimating the response of the Western democracies.

As Britain had invoked the League against Mussolini, France proposed to invoke it against Hitler in the Rhineland crisis. According to the French plan, the Locarno Powers, Britain, France, and Italy, were to initiate League action against Germany by securing condemnation of the occupation on the grounds that it violated the Versailles Treaty. Moreover, the League was to demand German withdrawal from the Rhineland and impose sanctions of an economic, financial, and even military nature in the event of German non-compliance. Mussolini withheld support of the French plan on the grounds that Italy was still being subjected to League sanctions. Likewise, Britain refused to endorse the French proposal but for different reasons. The British public, in Eden's words, had been united in its condemnation of Italian aggression against Ethiopia "from the king on down"; the Rhineland occupation, by contrast, seemed "a much more doubtful cause." "There was," in Eden's assessment of British public opinion of 1936, "not one man in a thousand in the country at that time prepared to take physical action with France against a German reoccupation of the Rhineland nearly twenty years after the end of the War." The widespread British interpretation that Hitler had simply moved into his "own backyard" was not far removed from Hitler's own assertion that he had merely invoked the "fundamental right of a nation to secure its frontiers and ensure its possibilities of defense." As Germany gave no indication of following up the Rhineland occupation with an attack on Belgium or France, it did not, in the British view, constitute an act of aggression and was not liable to League retaliation through sanctions.

THE REASONS FOR FRENCH INACTION

For France, the remilitarization of the Rhineland was a far more serious matter than Hitler's walking into his "own backyard." It meant not only that German troops would be stationed along the Franco-German frontiers but that German fortifications would probably be built opposite the Maginot line, such as Hitler actually constructed in his *Westwall* between 1936 and 1939. Once fortified, the German border would be difficult for the French army to pierce should it be called upon to defend Austria or the eastern allies of France, Poland and Czechoslovakia, against a German attack. Behind the protective shield of his border fortifications in the west, Hitler could dismantle the East European state system by force or even the mere threat of force. The remilitarization of the Rhineland placed the eastern alliance system of France in jeopardy and thereby challenged the larger concept of French hegemony on the European continent. The question may be asked, therefore, why France, in full knowledge of the implications of the Rhineland occupation, did not act alone to enforce existing treaties that affected the most vital aspects of her national security. Militarily, France stood every chance of defeating Hitler by unilateral action, as Hitler well knew. It was for this reason that he had given orders to his troops to withdraw immediately if France invaded the Rhineland. Nor need France have felt restrained by moral scruples, since Great Britain had acted without consulting France in the Anglo-German naval accord of 1935.

In 1936 France failed to act against Hitler because she feared isolation and underestimated her own military strength. Having lost Italy's support, France was afraid of losing Britain's also if she invaded the Rhineland. A French invasion of the Rhineland in 1936 would, in all probability, have been condemned by Great Britain as Britain had condemned the French Ruhr invasion in 1923, and France, rather than Germany, would have appeared as the disturber of the European peace. Failing to secure Britain's support, France found other excuses for her inaction. The French government of Premier Sarraut and Foreign Minister Flandin hesitated to order general mobilization in March, 1936, with general elections less than three months away. When Sarraut asked General Gamelin, Chief of the French Army, about French military prospects in an isolated Franco-German war, the answer was equivocal. Initially, Gamelin stated, France would enjoy a military advantage; in a prolonged war, superior German manpower and industrial capacity would tip the scales in Germany's favor. Gamelin's assessment did not include the military power of the eastern allies. Its Non-Aggression Pact with Germany notwithstanding, Poland pledged to honor its alliance with France "under conditions conformable to the spirit of the alliance."

As Hitler had predicted, the Western response to the Rhineland occupation remained limited to verbal protest and condemnation. Referring to Hitler's promise of 1935, Anthony Eden observed that "the myth is now exploded that Herr Hitler only repudiates treaties imposed on Germany by force. We must be prepared for him to repudiate any treaty even if freely negotiated (a) when it becomes inconvenient and (b) when Germany is sufficiently strong and the circumstances are otherwise favorable for doing so." The League Council likewise condemned the Rhineland occupation without proposing penalties. Surprisingly, the Western powers agreed to consider new proposals which Hitler had advanced in conjunction with the Rhineland occupation: (1) a non-aggression pact for 25 years between Germany, France, and Belgium, (2) an Air Pact between Germany and Britain, (3) the creation of a demilitarized zone on *both* sides of the French-German border (the proposal implied the destruction of existing French fortifications in the Maginot line before any German fortifications had been built), and (4) a German offer to re-enter the League of Nations since Germany had now "regained full sovereignty." The offer of Germany's re-entry into the League was conditioned on the settlement of Germany's colonial grievances.

On the military side, France, Belgium, and Britain opened staff conversations on April 15, 1936, in London, a move designed more to reassure themselves than to frighten Hitler. In October, 1936, Belgium reverted to a policy of complete neutrality; though willing to accept aid in support of her independence, she would give none to others. France sought reassurance also in a sharply expanded armaments program that provided for the creation of two new armored divisions and three infantry divisions and for the mechanization of ten existing infantry divisions. Tanks and ammunition were to be manufactured at a "war tempo." A more determined policy in March, 1936, might well have saved France the additional cost of 31 billion francs incurred by the rearmament program of 1936. The small East European powers, whose security had been gravely undermined by French inaction of March, 1936, also sought reassurance in word and deed. In their meeting of May, 1936, the members of the Little Entente stressed their solidarity "with all the European forces of international law and order against all the European forces of international anarchy." In August, 1936, on the occasion of General Gamelin's visit to Warsaw, Poland reaffirmed its commitment to the Franco-Polish alliance of 1921. In May, 1936, Czechoslovakia had issued new laws conferring upon the government extensive powers in an emergency. The French attempt to strengthen the defense of the Eastern powers by effecting a Polish-Czechoslovak reconciliation and by persuading Poland to permit Soviet troop passage in the event of war, failed. Poland refused to sign a friendship pact with Czechoslovakia, sponsored by France in September, 1936, and declined to promise aid to Czechoslovakia in the event of a German attack upon the latter. The lack of concert among the great Western democracies, which had provided Mussolini and Hitler with the opportunity of aggression in 1935 and 1936, was duplicated in Eastern Europe by the continuing divisions between Russia and the "successor states" as well as among the successor states themselves.

THE SPANISH CIVIL WAR

The chances of collective security against Hitler, seriously weakened by the Ethiopian and Rhineland crises, were dealt a further blow by the Spanish Civil War. The elements which had facilitated Mussolini's aggression in Africa and Hitler's move into the Rhineland—the lack of Anglo-French coordination, the aloofness of the United States, and the incapacity of the League for action—reappeared in sharpened form in the prolonged carnage of the Spanish Civil War between July, 1936, and February, 1939. Added to these factors was distrust between the Western democracies and Soviet Russia, which increased in proportion to Russia's involvement in Spain.

The Spanish Civil War quickly developed into a European problem as the warring factions—the Spanish Popular Front government of Premier José Giral and the Nationalist insurgents under General Francisco Franco—appealed for outside help almost from the first day of the conflict. On July 19, 1936, Giral appealed to the French Popular Front government under Premier Léon Blum for arms and aircraft; shortly afterwards, Franco appealed to both Italy and Germany for armed aid, particularly transport aircraft to carry his troops from Spanish Morocco to Spain proper.

THE WESTERN REACTION TO THE SPANISH CIVIL WAR

The cause of Republican Spain enjoyed great sympathy among the workers and intellectuals of the Western democracies, since it appeared not only as a struggle against reactionary forces in Spain but as a symbol of European democracy beleaguered by Fascism. Republican Spain was the Popular Front in action, uniting, it appeared, all enemies of Fascism, including the Communists, in a noble cause.

The Popular Front government of France under Léon Blum was inclined to aid the Republican cause for reasons of both ideological compassion and national security. After forming the Popular Front government, Blum had been anxious to erase the impression of indecision and weakness created by the government of Premier Sarraut and Foreign Minister Flandin in the Rhineland crisis of March, 1936. He assured his Eastern allies that France would never again act as weakly as she had in March, 1936, and that her policy towards Germany would be "strong and firm." The Spanish Civil War thus afforded an early opportunity for a demonstration of French strength. Were Franco and the Nationalists to succeed, France would be flanked by three Fascist powers: Germany on the Rhine, Italy in the Alps, and Spain along the Pyrenees. As of July, 1936, Blum favored French intervention in the Spanish Civil War through armed aid to the Republican government.

Although public sympathy for the Republic was widespread in Great Britain also—especially in intellectual circles close to the "Left Book Club" of Victor Gollancz—the Baldwin government did not view the Spanish Civil War in terms of a clear-cut ideological confrontation between Democracy and Fascism. Apart from the fact that Franco too enjoyed support in Britain, notably in the British Admiralty, the Baldwin government rather considered the Spanish Civil War a nuisance and a disturbing interruption in the process of reorganizing Europe with the collaboration of Italy and Germany. Hoping for an early end of the Civil War, the British government wanted to observe strict neutrality and hoped to persuade the other Great Powers of Europe to follow its example. Above all else, Britain wished to keep the Civil War localized lest Great Power intervention result in a general European war between the democracies and the dictatorships. Britain thus warned Léon Blum to be "prudent" in the delivery of French arms to Spain and threatened not to support France if her intervention in Spain resulted in a Franco-German war.

American reaction to the outbreak of the Spanish Civil War followed the isolationist pattern of American policy in the Ethiopian War. In the words of the U. S. Secretary of State, American policy in the Spanish Civil War would be one of "moral aloofness." Resisting the pressures of American public opinion, the U. S. government thus forbade the sale of American arms to the Republican government of Spain. Since American Neutrality legislation of 1935 did not apply to the Spanish conflict because it was a civil war, the United States Congress Resolution of January 6, 1937, banned shipments of all American arms to either side in the Spanish Civil War. Moreover, the United States rejected an initiative of Uruguay to end the Spanish Civil War through mediation of the American Republics.

THE SOVIET REACTION TO THE SPANISH CIVIL WAR

For Soviet Russia, the Spanish Civil War posed a vexing problem as Soviet ideological ambitions and Russian foreign policy objectives in the Spanish crisis were not complementary but contradictory. As previously noted, the overall design of Soviet foreign policy after 1933 was the achievement of a "scheme of pacts" with the democracies against Hitler. Soviet foreign policy interests thus dictated the defeat of Franco, as a Nationalist victory in Spain would endanger the security and strength of France. The growing influence of the Spanish Communists in the Republican Popular Front government offered the temptation, however, of establishing a Spanish Communist regime. A Communist triumph in Spain, on the other hand, would wreck Litvinov's policy of collective security by alienating the democracies. The establishment of an openly or predominantly Communist government in Spain might even frighten the democracies into an accommodation with Hitler at Soviet Russia's expense. It has been suggested even that Stalin may have wished to expand the Spanish Civil War into a European war between the democracies and the dictatorships in order to facilitate Soviet domination of an exhausted Europe after a general war. Although such motives may have influenced Soviet foreign policy in 1939, it is doubtful that they were present in 1936, as evidenced by the cautious and gradual involvement of Russia in the Spanish Civil War. Initially, Soviet involvement was confined to financial aid to the Republican side via the Communist International, and the establishment of full diplomatic relations with Spain for the first time since 1917. A larger Soviet role in the affairs of Spain was suggested, however, by the arrival of a Soviet military mission in Madrid in August, 1936, together with the new Soviet ambassador, Marcel Rosenberg.

THE ITALIAN AND GERMAN REACTION
TO THE SPANISH CIVIL WAR

The response of Fascist Italy to Franco's appeal for aid in July, 1936, was neither cautious nor concealed. Fresh from his victory in Ethiopia, Mussolini welcomed the opportunity to intervene in Spain, since it promised to expand Italian power in the western Mediterranean and add to Italian prestige. Ethiopia had whetted Mussolini's appetite for aggression and robbed him of much of his sense of proportion. His over-confidence and militancy were reflected, not only in his immediate dis-patch of aircraft to the Nationalist side, but in his public pronouncements. The Italian army, in Mussolini's words, was an "immense forest of eight million bayonets well sharpened and wielded by young intrepid hearts." Italy would not "tolerate a Communist or Communist-influenced Spain."

Germany, like Fascist Italy, had a vested ideological interest in Franco's victory. Hitler's response to Franco's call for help was less overt than Mussolini's, however, as Hitler feared the prospect of a gen-eral European war over Spain. A European war over Spain in 1936 would be, in Hitler's estimation, the wrong war at the wrong time and place, for Germany was not yet fully armed and had no territorial ambitions in Spain. It was, however, very much to Germany's advantage to keep the Spanish Civil War alive and thus to aid Franco to the extent necessary for his survival. A long war in Spain would preoccupy the Western powers, sharpen Anglo-Italian friction, and generally divert Great Power attention from central eastern Europe, where Hitler planned his next moves; thus the War could help Germany annex Austria and dismember Czechoslo-vakia. Moreover, the Spanish Civil War offered certain economic and military opportunities to Germany: Germany demanded payment for its armed aid to Franco in the form of Spanish mining concessions, and the war afforded the German Air Force an opportunity to test its new equip-ment under combat conditions. By November, 1936, the German Condor Legion, 6,500 men strong, was established at Seville. Among its veterans was Adolf Galland, the chief of German fighter defenses in the Second World War. The temptation to treat the Spanish Civil War as a "war game" led other powers, principally France and Russia, to test their latest equipment also. Many of the aircraft of the Second World War, the Soviet *Polikarpov* fighter, better known under its Spanish nickname *Rata* ("Rat"), and the German *Messerschmitt,* fought their first duels in Spanish skies. The Spanish Civil War also provided the first examples of indis-criminate area bombing of civilian population centers, which the Italian air strategist Giulio Douhet had forecast in his theory of strategic bombing in the 1920's. The Italian air raid on Barcelona of March 16, 1938, killing 1,300 civilians, and the Condor Legion raid on Guernica of April 26, 1937, claiming over 1,600 civilian lives, were grim forewarnings of the destruc-tion of Warsaw and Rotterdam and of the area bombing of London, Hamburg, and Dresden in the Second World War.

THE FICTION OF NON-INTERVENTION

It was mainly out of fear of antagonizing Great Britain that the French Popular Front government of Blum decided against open intervention on the Republican side and proposed instead a nonintervention agreement among the Powers. With Britain's encouragement, such an agreement was signed in August, 1936, by France, Britain, Italy, Germany, and Russia. In September, 1936, the Powers installed a Non-Intervention Committee for the enforcement of the policy of nonintervention by outside powers in the Spanish Civil War. The British government was hopeful that the Non-Intervention Committee would keep the Spanish conflict localized by functioning in the tradition of the London Ambassadors' Conference, which had succeeded in localizing the Balkan wars of 1913.

Although the Great Powers paid lip service to nonintervention, all but Britain violated the Non-Intervention Agreement. After Stalin had called for the "liberation of Spain from Fascism" in October, 1936, the Communist International launched the International Brigades with recruiting offices in Paris. The membership rolls of the International Brigades resembled a Who's Who of European Communism, including many prominent Communists of the postwar era and those who were to acquire Communist fame after the Second World War. In addition to Tito, who recruited in Paris, the Brigades included Togliatti, Thorez, Klement Gottwald, the future Communist leader of Czechoslovakia, and Walter Ulbricht, the future Communist boss of East Germany. André Marty, famed for his instigation of the French Black Sea fleet mutiny of 1919, was the first commander of the Brigades' base at Albacete in Spain. Though the Brigades did not include Russian volunteers, they were advised by Soviet officers, among them Malinovsky, Konev, and Rokossovsky, future Marshals and heroes of the Soviet Union. Beginning in October, 1936, Russia also sent hundreds of aircraft and tanks to Spain, for which the Republican government paid with the Spanish gold reserve.

As Hitler dispatched the Condor Legion to Seville, Mussolini sent the largest ground forces of any foreign power, whose peak strength has been estimated as ranging from 50,000 to 70,000 men. On November 18, 1936, Germany and Italy extended full diplomatic recognition to the Nationalist government of Franco. In protest against the German and Italian action, the Republican government appealed to the League in December, 1936. True to its past record, the League Council condemned foreign intervention and demanded observance of the Non-Intervention Agreement but took no action.

As the pledge of nonintervention was being patently ignored, the British government proposed in December, 1936, to end the Spanish Civil War by the joint intervention of all Great Powers. The Powers were to arrange for an armistice, organize a free plebiscite, and aid in the establishment of a new Spanish government to be drawn from men previously not involved in the Civil War.

Although the British initiative was not acted upon, Germany and Italy decided on a genuine policy of nonintervention control in early

1937, since they intended to send little further aid to Franco by this time and since their forces in Spain outnumbered those of Russia. Beginning in April, 1937, German and Italian warships joined those of France and Britain in the Mediterranean Non-Intervention Control. The participation of the dictators was short-lived, however, as Republican forces attacked the German vessels in May, 1937. In retaliation, German naval forces bombarded the Republican port of Almeria on May 31, 1937; on June 15, 1937, Italy and Germany withdrew from the naval control. When Italian submarines began to attack freighters bound for Republican ports, including British vessels, the democracies at last appeared to have been stung into action. At the Noyon conference of September, 1937, Britain and France decided to attack any suspicious submarine, surface vessel, or aircraft in the western Mediterranean. The Noyon decision was rendered meaningless, however, through the readmission of Italy to the joint naval control. No sooner had Italy joined the Noyon front than her submarines resumed their practice of attacking neutral freighters. Between April and June, 1938, no fewer than eleven British freighters were either sunk or damaged by Italian submarines.

The British government under Neville Chamberlain preferred to ignore Mussolini's provocations as it was mainly interested in securing a negotiated Italian withdrawal from Spain and the restoration of the Mediterranean status quo. As early as January 2, 1937, Britain and Italy had concluded a so-called "Gentlemen's Agreement," in which both powers recognized the freedom of entry, transit, and exit in the Mediterranean and confirmed the Mediterranean status quo. On April 16, 1938, Britain concluded a further agreement with Italy, in which Britain promised to recognize the Italian conquest of Ethiopia in exchange for Italian troop withdrawal from Spain. British recognition would not take effect, however, until the Italian withdrawal had been completed.

The Agreement of April 16, 1938, was Britain's tacit recognition of a Nationalist victory in the Spanish Civil War as well as an admission that the policy of nonintervention was a dead letter. The Agreement was doubly injurious to the cause of the democracies since French Premier Blum had advocated a tougher policy towards Franco in order to repair the damage done to Western prestige in the Austrian crisis of March, 1938, to be presently discussed. Moreover, Neville Chamberlain's agreement with Mussolini had prompted the resignation of Foreign Secretary Anthony Eden. The resignation of Eden was greeted with undisguised joy in Rome and Berlin because he was widely considered the symbol of opposition to appeasement.

The last phase of the Spanish Civil War was fought in the shadow of the approaching Second World War as the Great Powers focused their attention once again on Germany in the Czechoslovak crisis of 1938. After the Munich Conference of September, 1938, Soviet Russia began to disengage itself from the Spanish embroglio. On November 2, 1938, Britain put into effect the Anglo-Italian Agreement of April, 1938, although the Italian troop withdrawal from Spain was far from complete. On February 27, 1939, France and Britain recognized the government of Franco; on April 1, 1939, the United States followed suit. By spring, 1939, all German and Italian troops were withdrawn from Spain.

THE ROME-BERLIN AXIS;
THE ANTI-COMINTERN PACT

The Spanish Civil War moved Germany and Italy, in Hitler's words, from a "community of views" to a "community of action." Although German and Italian policy in Spain pursued a parallel course, the Rome-Berlin Axis did not follow automatically, for a number of issues continued to divide Italy and Germany. Foremost among these issues were (1) mutual suspicion that the other power might seek an accord with Great Britain as an alternative solution to an Italian-German entente and (2) the question of Austrian independence, since Mussolini was not yet prepared in 1936 to leave Austria to Germany. On March 23, 1936, Mussolini had, in fact, reaffirmed his interest in Austrian independence by concluding an additional pact with Austria and Hungary. Under the Italian-Austrian-Hungarian Agreement of March 23, 1936, the foreign ministers of the three powers would hold periodic consultations; none would negotiate with a fourth power on the Danubian question without prior consultation with the other two members. Coming on the heels of the Rhineland occupation, the Agreement of March, 1936, was a confirmation of the Italian pledge to Austria under the Rome Protocols of 1934.

The initiative for the Rome-Berlin Axis came from Germany, rather than Italy, as Hitler needed Italy's blessing to fulfill his designs in central-eastern Europe. In his approach to Rome, Hitler assumed very much the role of deferential suitor, referring to Mussolini as the "leading statesman of the world" and "maker of history." To dispel Italian suspicions regarding Austria, Germany had concluded an Agreement with Austria on July 11, 1936. In the July Agreement, Germany recognized Austrian sovereignty and promised non-interference in Austria's internal affairs. Although the July Agreement stipulated that Austria's policy towards Germany would be guided by the fact that Austria was a "German state," it qualified that obligation by the recognition of Austria's "special relationship" with Italy and Hungary under the Rome Protocols of February, 1934.

As a further inducement to Italy, Hitler promised to recognize the Italian conquest of Ethiopia and also to recognize the Mediterranean as a "purely Italian sea." In October, 1936, Italy and Germany signed the "October Protocols," in which both powers agreed to cooperate on questions of common concern, such as Spain, Austria, the Danubian states, Ethiopia, and recognition of the Japanese puppet state of Manchukuo. It was Mussolini who termed the Italian-German agreement the "Rome-Berlin Axis," on November 1, 1936—an axis around which, in the Duce's words, all European states anxious for peace may work together.

The Rome-Berlin Axis marked the first concrete breach in the Rome-Vienna-Budapest axis, established under the Rome Protocols of 1934 and the March Agreement of 1936. As Mussolini became increasingly absorbed in African and Mediterranean pursuits, he slackened the Italian vigil on the Brenner. Significantly, the foreign ministers of Italy, Austria, and Hungary did not hold a single joint conference between November, 1936, and January, 1938, contrary to the March Agreement of 1936. By November, 1937, Mussolini was content "to let events take their natural course" in the question of Austrian independence. All that remained of Italy's vigorous defense in 1934 of Austrian independence was Mussolini's wish to be consulted in advance of an Austro-German union.

As Hitler had exploited the ideological affinity between Germany and Italy for the coordination of their foreign policy objectives under the Rome-Berlin Axis, he invoked anti-Communism as the common basis for agreement between Germany and Japan. In the Anti-Comintern Pact of November 25, 1936, Germany and Japan promised to consult each other in all matters pertaining to the activities of the Communist International. In the secret clauses of the Anti-Comintern Pact, Germany and Japan pledged neutrality in the event that either should be involved in a conflict with the Soviet Union. Moreover, neither Power would conclude political treaties with the Soviet Union which were not compatible with the spirit of the Anti-Comintern Pact.

On November 6, 1937, Italy joined the German-Japanese Anti-Comintern Pact, following Mussolini's state visit to Germany in September, 1937. Hitler's spectacular display of German military and industrial power, carefully arranged for Mussolini's benefit, deeply impressed the Duce and increased his appreciation of the German-Italian partnership. As a symbolic repudiation of Italy's past ties to the West, Mussolini left the League of Nations on December 11, 1937.

The Anti-Comintern Pact, though not a formal military alliance, was intended by its German instigators as the beginning of such. The pact was open to all desiring membership and was advertised as a bulwark against international Communism. Hitler pointed to Russia's involvement in the Spanish Civil War as proof of the worldwide ambitions of international Communism. Europe would soon realize, Hitler argued, that National Socialist Germany was "the strongest safeguard of a truly European, a truly human, culture and civilization." The "Bolshevik pesti-

FIGURE 15   *The architects of the Rome-Berlin Axis: Hitler receiving Mussolini in Germany in 1938.*

lence," Joachim von Ribbentrop, Hitler's Foreign Minister to be, added in 1937, would be contained by Germany in central Europe, by Italy in southern Europe, and by Japan in the Far East.

The German-Japanese-Italian alignment, first accomplished under the Anti-Comintern Pact in 1936/1937, was to reappear in altered circumstances in the Tripartite Pact of September, 1940. Although Hitler was to conclude the German-Soviet Non-Aggression Pact of August, 1939, without prior consultation with Japan, Japan maintained the German connection as a support to her own expansionist designs in Asia and the Pacific.

APPEASEMENT AND AGGRESSION

By the late 1930's, the leadership in the concert of the Western democracies had decidedly passed to Great Britain, as France had shied away time and again from unilateral action against Germany for fear of displeasing Great Britain. Similarly, the leadership of the Rome-Berlin Axis was rapidly passing from Italy to Germany, as Hitler's role toward Mussolini changed from deferential suitor to master. The crisis of Europe thus increasingly assumed the character of an Anglo-German confrontation, with France a resigned ally of Britain and Italy a weary partner of Nazi Germany.

Under the leadership of Prime Minister Baldwin between June, 1935, and May, 1937, the National Government of Great Britain had failed to take a resolute stand against Nazi Germany, partly because of Britain's preoccupation with problems of economic recovery and the reorganization of Empire, partly because of Baldwin's disinterest in foreign affairs and lack of appreciation of Nazi goals. In Churchill's words, Baldwin knew little of Europe and disliked what he knew. The Prime Minister did not wish to be troubled "too much with foreign affairs just now." While conceding that "with two lunatics like Mussolini and Hitler you can never be sure of anything," Baldwin was determined to keep Britain out of war. To the National Government and many Britons, the Unemployment Act of 1934 seemed a more important issue than the Austrian Nazi coup of the same year, the government of India Act of 1935 more significant than German rearmament. Why, in the words of a British humorist of the 1930's, would Britain want to roam, when she had got enough misfortunes at home? Why, indeed, not scrap the Foreign Office altogether?

Added to the preoccupation with domestic affairs was the memory of the First World War, which had consumed the blood and treasure of Britain as no previous British engagement on the European continent. The memory was kept alive in Britain by pacifist literature, such as the works of R. C. Sheriff and Edmund Blunden, depicting the War as senseless carnage. By contrast, the German war literature of the mid-1930's extolled the First World War as the noblest and most heroic struggle in German history. In Hitler's Germany, both the novel and the film *All Quiet on the Western Front,* by Erich Maria Remarque, were banned because of their alleged defeatism; instead, the Nazi regime promoted such war novels as Hans Zöberlein's *Glaube an Deutschland (Faith in Germany),* which attributed the German defeat of 1918 to a weak-kneed and Marxist-infected home front.

Where Baldwin had been content to let matters drift in foreign affairs, his successor, Prime Minister Neville Chamberlain, hoped to find a lasting solution to the problem that Germany posed for the peace of Europe by an active policy of appeasement. Chamberlain's policy of appeasement sprang from his profound abhorrence of war, his basic assessment of the peace settlement of 1919 as unjust, or at any rate unrealistic, and his deep-seated aversion to Communism and Soviet Russia. "In war," the Prime Minister observed, "there are no winners, but all are losers." Chamberlain remembered the "seven million young men who were cut off in their prime" during the First World War. Once Germany's grievances had been satisfied by a negotiated comprehensive revision of the peace of 1919, Neville Chamberlain hoped, the governments of Europe could devote themselves to the building of a new "Golden Age" of peace, of which Sir Samuel Hoare still dreamed in March, 1939. A negotiated revision of the peace of 1919, in Chamberlain's view, would have to include the recognition of German preeminence in central-eastern Europe and the Balkans as well as a solution to the problems of Austria, Czechoslovakia, and Danzig satisfactory to Hitler. Moreover, Chamberlain was willing to return the former German colonies.

The alternatives to appeasement, in Chamberlain's view, were either war or a British alliance with Soviet Russia. The latter solution was almost as distasteful to the Prime Minister as war itself. Russia, to Chamberlain, was a nation "half European and half Asiatic," whose motives and actions he viewed with "the most profound distrust." Since 1933 the animosity of Conservative Britain towards Stalinist Russia had grown with the show trial of British Metro-Vickers engineers in Soviet Russia in April, 1933, and the Stalinist Purge of the late 1930's. The Stalinist Purge not only diminished the military value of Russia in British eyes, but raised questions about the stability of the Soviet regime. "Personalities changed rather rapidly" in Soviet Russia, Chamberlain quipped in an obvious reference to the disappearance of the Old Bolsheviks in the Stalinist Purge. With whom in Russia was Britain to negotiate?

For all its violence and the unleashing of new pogroms against the German Jews in November, 1938, the Nazi regime appeared to Chamberlain and Lord Halifax as a positive force, if only because of its pronounced anti-Communism. Chamberlain could easily envisage the reorganization of the European state system with the collaboration of Hitler but not with the help of Stalin. Gaining time to catch up with the German lead in armaments has frequently been suggested as among Chamberlain's foremost motives of appeasement. The state of Britain's armaments, particularly in the air, was indeed a source of anxiety to the National Government of Britain at the time of Chamberlain's assumption of power in May, 1937. As Britain and Imperial Germany had engaged in a race for naval armaments before 1914, the late 1930's turned into a race between British and German air power. The air race of the 1930's differed from the naval race, however, in that Britain had yet to expand her production facilities for aircraft, whereas British shipyards before the First World War had enjoyed the advantage of superior building capacity over Germany. Britain's increased expenditures for air armaments of 1936/1937 did not result in an appreciable increase in air power before 1939, when the monthly output of aircraft was raised from an average of 240 for the year 1938 to an average of 660. The British early warning system of Radar, based on the invention of Watson Watts in 1935, barely covered the Thames Estuary in 1938. By September, 1939, the Radar warning system covered the air approaches from the Orkneys to the Isle of Wight. Before 1939 Britain's foreign policy was, in the words of British Minister of Defense Hoare-Belisha, "dominated in any crisis by the fear of the effects of London being bombed." The fear of German air raids on London was heightened by the assumption that Hitler would not hesitate to use gas against civilian population centers. In 1938 London found itself in the awkward position of having fewer fighter aircraft for its defense than at the height of the German air raids in the First World War. Whereas German bomber formations in 1917 had rarely exceeded forty aircraft in any one raid, British estimates of attacking German aircraft in the 1930's ranged into the hundreds. In 1938 it was estimated that as many as 600,000 civilians might be killed in German air raids and a further million and a half civilians wounded. The British military were thus anxious to postpone war with Germany as long as possible, as they did not expect completion of Britain's rearmament until 1942. In the words of Sir Edward Ellington, the British Chief of the Air Staff in 1937, "There cannot be war until 1942."

Gaining time for rearmament, though undoubtedly an important factor in the strategy of appeasement, did not constitute its foremost objective. Armed preparedness, rather, was a necessary precaution and insurance against the possibility that Chamberlain's peace overtures to Germany would fail.

Though Neville Chamberlain was the instigator and principal architect of appeasement, his policy enjoyed the solid support of his colleagues in government, especially of the "inner cabinet" consisting of the former Foreign Secretaries Sir John Simon, Sir Samuel Hoare, and Lord Halifax, who succeeded Anthony Eden as Foreign Secretary in February, 1938. The influential advocates of appeasement included also Geoffrey Dawson, Editor of the London *Times,* Horace Wilson, whose influence on British foreign policy far exceeded his official role as Chamberlain's Industrial Adviser, and Neville Henderson, the last British ambassador to Germany before the outbreak of the Second World War.

Equally important was the attitude of the British Dominions. Always concerned about the dangers of a new war in Europe which might claim their manpower and resources as the First World War had done, Australia and New Zealand were especially interested in preserving the European peace after 1937 in order to better withstand the rising power of Japan.

THE HOSSBACH MINUTES

The year 1937, which marked the beginning of the British policy of appeasement, also witnessed the maturing of Hitler's plans for a forceful revision of Germany's eastern frontier. Before 1937 Hitler had succeeded in dismantling the most essential safeguards of the Treaty of Versailles without possessing appreciable military power of his own. As German rearmament placed armored divisions, infantry, and a modern air force at his disposal towards the end of 1937, Hitler's impatience to use his newly gained might grew. In a secret meeting in the Reich-Chancellery with the chiefs of the three armed services, Hermann Göring, Erich Raeder, and Werner von Fritsch, as well as Minister of War Blomberg and Foreign Minister Neurath, Hitler outlined his foreign policy objectives for the immediate future. His remarks were recorded by his military aide, Colonel Hossbach.

After repeating the familiar arguments, first stated in *Mein Kampf,* that neither foreign trade nor economic self-sufficiency could solve the problem of German overpopulation, Hitler announced his intention to seize Austria and Czechoslovakia no later than 1943/45, but possibly as early as 1938. His timing was based on the assumption that the foreign political constellation of Europe was favorable to German aggression in Eastern Europe: the British Empire was challenged by the rise of Japan and weakened by the awakening nationalism of the colonial peoples; France was weakened by inner social and political strife; Britain was preoccupied with Italy in the Mediterranean; and Russia was involved in border tensions with Japan in the Far East. The use of force by Germany, Hitler admitted, involved risks, which could be minimized by speedy action. As an analogy to the situation of the 1930's, Hitler cited the speedy and successful action of Frederick the Great against Austria in the 18th century and that of Bismarck against France in the Franco-Prussian war of 1870/71.

Hitler's statements of November 5, 1937, as recorded in the Hossbach minutes, have been the subject of considerable controversy since the Second World War. Whereas some consider Hitler's address of November 5, 1937, as an unalterable decision to plunge Europe into war, others have interpreted his speech merely as an exhortation to the German generals to maintain the hectic pace of armaments. In support of the latter interpretation, the fact of opposition to overly hasty rearmament has been cited, which did exist among such leaders as Fritsch and Blomberg. Both Fritsch and Blomberg, together with numerous other high-ranking officers of like mind, were purged in 1938.

Regardless of the interpretation given to Hitler's secret address of November 5, 1937—whether it constituted a hypothesis, an exhortation, or a concrete plan of action—Hitler's intention to use force, his fear of missing a favorable opportunity not likely to recur, and his decision to strike at the vulnerable state system of Eastern Europe, emerge as recognizable motives for his subsequent actions.

The overriding impression of the Hossbach minutes is the element of impatience in Hitler's attitude and the repeatedly expressed fear that he might not live to see the execution of his foreign policy design. Significantly, Hitler opened his address with the remark that his words should be considered as his testament in the event of his early death.

THE VULNERABILITY OF EASTERN EUROPE

Although the Hossbach minutes mentioned Austria and Czechoslovakia as the only specific objectives of future German aggression, Hitler's announcement raised the larger question of the integrity of the entire East European state system, wedged between Germany, Russia, and Italy's ambitions in the Balkans. The small states of Eastern Europe, sometimes referred to as *Saisonstaaten* (states for a season) by German diplomats, had grown more vulnerable to Great Power pressure because of the divisions among themselves and the waning influence of France. Of the various projects for regional security pacts in Eastern Europe, none had materialized. The project of an Eastern Locarno had collapsed in 1934 over German and Polish obstruction; that of a Danubian Pact, tentatively agreed upon between France and Italy in 1935, had become a victim of the Ethiopian war. The Franco-Soviet-Czechoslovak alliance system of 1935 had lost much of its deterrent force since the remilitarization of the Rhineland. The Baltic states — Finland, Latvia, Estonia, and Lithuania — had failed to form a regional pact system with Poland, owing to the Polish-Lithuanian controversy over Vilna and Finland's fear of being drawn into a Russo-Polish quarrel. Poland had contributed to her own isolation from her principal ally, France, through the Non-Aggression Pact with Germany of 1934 and her obstinate refusal to improve relations with Czechoslovakia because of the controversy over *Teschen*. At the beginning of 1938, Poland was less concerned with possible danger from Germany than with the realization of a grand design for the establishment of a Polish "sphere of influence" from the Baltic to the Black Sea, which implied the dismemberment of Czechoslovakia. Similarly, Hungary did not view the prospect of German power in the Danube Basin with alarm, since it offered the opportunity of regaining Slovakia, which had seceded from the Kingdom of Hungary in 1918.

The Little Entente between Czechoslovakia, Yugoslavia, and Rumania had lost much of its former strength through the gradual withdrawal of Yugoslavia, following the assassination of King Alexander in 1934 and the establishment of a new government under the regent Prince Paul and Prime Minister Stojadinović. With the coming of age of Archduke Otto, the eldest son of the last Habsburg Emperor Charles I, Yugoslavia was less concerned with a German occupation of Austria than the possibility of a Habsburg restoration to Austria. In the latter event, Yugoslavia feared the loss of its national unity, as Croatia might gravitate towards a Habsburg Austria.

In the Balkans, Greece, Yugoslavia, Turkey, and Rumania had formed the Balkan Pact of February, 1934, at the instigation of Rumania's pro-Western Foreign Minister Titulescu. As Turkey had herself become a status-quo power and entered the League of Nations in 1932, the Balkan

Pact was initially conceived as a deterrent against Bulgarian revisionist demands. The members of the Balkan Pact had loyally followed Britain's lead in the sanctions policy of the League of Nations against Italy, and Greece, Yugoslavia, and Turkey, in particular, feared Italian retaliation. Mussolini's statement of March 18, 1934, that "Italy's historic objectives lie in Asia and Africa" was interpreted by Turkey as a threat. The Balkan Pact powers thus appealed to Britain for help at the height of the Ethiopian crisis. Turkey asked for a revision of the demilitarized status of the Straits under the Lausanne Agreement of 1923 to better withstand an Italian attack. Although Britain promised to support the Balkan Pact powers under the specific threat existing in 1936, she refused to undertake permanent treaty obligations towards any Balkan power. With British help, Turkey succeeded in revising the demilitarized status of the Straits in the Montreux Convention of June, 1936, to which Italy was not a party. Under the revised Straits settlement, Turkey was authorized to prevent the passage of foreign war ships in time of war only if the ships involved were not acting under a treaty concluded under League auspices, to which Turkey was also a member. Although Britain played a major role in financing Turkish economic recovery under the Turkish Five Year Plan, she declined all Turkish requests for an alliance, for fear of provoking Mussolini.

The signing of the Yugoslav-Italian treaty of March 25, 1937, weakened the Balkan Pact and the Little Entente, to both of which Yugoslavia belonged. Under the agreement, Yugoslavia and Italy promised to respect their common frontiers and to solve their differences by peaceful means. The main issue dividing Italy and Yugoslavia—Mussolini's harboring of the Croat nationalists *(Ustashi)*—was to be settled by the pledge that neither party would tolerate terrorist activities on its territory directed against the other. The impact of the Yugoslav-Italian treaty of 1937 upon the Little Entente was soon felt in the German-Czechoslovak crisis of 1938. As Hitler prepared the dismemberment of Czechoslovakia, Yugoslavia gave explicit assurances to Italy that she would not attack Hungary should the latter join Germany in the destruction of Czechoslovakia.

Apart from the political realignment in Eastern Europe in the late 1930's, the foreign policy freedom of action of the Balkan powers became increasingly limited through the latter's growing economic dependence upon Germany. Germany, rather than the Western democracies, became the chief buyer of the agricultural surplus of the Balkan states. By 1938 German purchases accounted for 40 per cent of Hungary's exports, 25 per cent of Rumania's, 42 per cent of Yugoslavia's, 59 per cent of Bulgaria's, 40 per cent of Greece's and 43 per cent of Turkey's. Moreover, Germany became an important supplier of arms to the Balkan states, especially Yugoslavia, Turkey, and Rumania.

It was the absence of effective regional security pacts in Eastern Europe, together with the apparent lack of British interest, that encouraged Hitler to take risks in the east. As recorded in the Hossbach minutes, he believed that Britain had quietly "written off" Czechoslovakia. The calculation proved correct for 1938; it proved fatal when repeated in the German-Polish confrontation of 1939.

THE ANNEXATION OF AUSTRIA

In January, 1938, Hitler decided, by his subsequent admission, to achieve Austrian "self-determination" one way or another. Austrian "self-determination" in the Nazi vocabulary meant annexation by Germany. Initially, Hitler did not intend to accomplish Austria's *Anschluss* (union) with Germany by military invasion, but preferred the "evolutionary" process of a gradual Nazi takeover from within. Towards this end, the Austrian chancellor Schuschnigg was summoned to Berchtesgaden on February 12, 1938, and presented with an ultimatum: Hitler demanded the inclusion of prominent Austrian Nazi sympathizers into the Austrian cabinet; the Austrian Ministry of the Interior was to be entrusted to Seyss-Inquart, the Austrian Ministry of War to Glaise-Horstenau.

Although Chancellor Schuschnigg was well aware that Mussolini was not likely to defend Austrian independence any more and that no help could be expected from the Western democracies, he defied Hitler's plan of quiet annexation by ordering an Austrian plebiscite for March 13, 1938. The people of Austria were asked to cast their vote for or against a "free and independent, German and Christian" Austria.

Schuschnigg's initiative set Hitler's plan for the military occupation of Austria in motion, as he could ill afford the free expression of Austrian opinion less than four years after the Nazi murder of Dollfuss. Before sending the German army across the Austrian frontier on March 12, 1938, Hitler did Mussolini the courtesy of announcing his intention and asking for his understanding in a letter of March 10, 1938. Hitler's appeal was coupled with the emphatic assurance that Germany would never raise the issue of the return of German-speaking South Tyrol. Mussolini gave his approval on March 11, 1938, for which Hitler promised to "stick to" Mussolini, "even if the whole world were against him." On March 14, 1938, Hitler joined his German troops in Vienna, the city of the failure of his youth. Those lining the streets of Vienna gave him a cheering welcome, partly as a release from the tensions of the past weeks, partly out of hope that Hitler's *Anschluss* would bring employment to depression-ridden Austria. Among those who did not cheer were the tens of thousands arrested by the Gestapo in Vienna from the first day of the German arrival. From the hostels of the Viennese working-class district of *Ottakring,* Hitler had arrived at the luxuries of Vienna's Imperial Hotel on the Ringstrasse. Speaking from the balcony of Franz Joseph's castle, a balcony that would be destroyed in an Allied air raid on Vienna during the Second World War, Hitler announced himself as the Man of Destiny, who had accomplished what no German statesman had achieved before him. The day before Hitler's arrival in Vienna, Seyss-Inquart had prepared a law proclaiming Austria a German province; Austria had become the *Ostmark.* In honor of the assassins of Dollfuss of July, 1934, a prominent business street in Vienna was renamed "Street of the July fighters." A plebiscite, organized in both Germany and Austria on the question of the *Anschluss,* registered approval by over 99 per cent.

After the annexation of Austria, the Western Powers refrained even from the ritual of seeking to condemn Germany's treaty violations by the League Council. Soviet Russia, at the time of the *Anschluss,* was absorbed in the show trials of Bukharin, Rykov, and Krestinsky. On March 17, 1938, Litvinov nevertheless warned the Western Powers that "tomorrow may be too late." Foreseeing Hitler's move against Czecho-slovakia, Litvinov proposed a conference to devise means of checking further aggressions in Europe. The Soviet proposal was rejected by Great Britain on the grounds that it would contribute to the division of Europe into two hostile camps. Chamberlain answered the Soviet appeal on April 4, 1938, with the remark that "so far from making a contribution to peace, I say that it would inevitably plunge us into war."

THE CZECHOSLOVAK CRISIS;
THE MUNICH CONFERENCE

At the time of Hitler's invasion of Austria, Göring, speaking in the name of the German government, had given his "word of honor" to the Czechoslovak government "that Czechoslovakia has nothing to fear from the Reich." The assurance was prompted by Germany's respect for the Czech army and the fear that it might move in defense of Austrian independence. No sooner had Austria been digested, however, than Hitler stepped up the campaign of the Sudeten German party against the Czecho-slovak government. The Czechoslovak Republic, like the Austro-Hungarian empire from which it had emerged in 1918, was a multinational state. In a total population of over thirteen million, 46 per cent were Czechs, 13 per cent Slovaks, 28 per cent ethnic (Sudeten) Germans, 3 per cent Ukrainians, and the remainder Poles. Of the non-Czech minorities, the German was not only the most numerous but also the most difficult to integrate into the Czechoslovak Republic. By 1935 the overwhelming majority of the Sudeten German minority supported Konrad Henlein's militant Sudeten German Party, which demanded, as early as 1937, the reorganization of Czechoslovakia into "national groups," each enjoying local autonomy. Although the German press had supported Henlein's demands before 1938, Hitler had not made the Sudeten question an issue between Germany and Czechoslovakia.

Beginning with March, 1938, Hitler decided to use the Sudeten German issue as a means of destroying the entire Czechoslovak Republic. The ultimate objective of German policy in the ensuing crisis was the dismemberment of Czechoslovakia. In seeking the destruction of Czechoslovakia Hitler was motivated both by his contempt for the Slavic Czechs and by his wrath over the Czech alliance with France and Russia. Accordingly, the Sudeten German party was instructed from Berlin in late March, 1938, to present unacceptable demands to the Czechoslovak government and to raise fresh demands if the "unacceptable" ones were fulfilled.

The Czechoslovak government of President Benes, unlike that of Austria, was willing to risk war in defense of its independence, however. In response to Hitler's threats, Czechoslovakia ordered a partial mobilization on May 18, 1938. The Czech mobilization was followed by French and British warnings that a German attack on Czechoslovakia would lead to a general war. Hitler's diplomatic defeat, which was given broad publicity in the Western press, together with the defiant gesture of the Czechs, prompted him to issue a new directive to his armed forces. On May 30, 1938, Hitler announced his "unalterable decision" to smash Czechoslovakia in the near future and fixed October 1, 1938, as the probable date of the German attack.

Throughout the summer of 1938, as the German press campaign against Czechoslovakia reached fever pitch, Britain was groping for a compromise. As Konrad Henlein journeyed to London in the summer of 1938 to popularize the Sudeten German cause, Neville Chamberlain dispatched Lord Runciman on a "fact-finding" mission to Czechoslovakia in July, 1938. Runciman's mission boosted, in fact, the Sudeten cause because he made little effort to acquaint himself with the Czech side of the controversy. On the mistaken assumption that self-determination for the Sudeten-Germans was Hitler's only objective, the British government cautiously spoke out in favor of the surrender of the Sudeten provinces to Germany. On September 7, 1938, the London *Times,* acting as a semi-official spokesman of the British government, recommended the cession of the Sudeten provinces to Germany.

THE BERCHTESGADEN AND GODESBERG MEETINGS

As Hitler showed no sign of compromise but increased his attack on Czechoslovakia in a violent speech of September 13, 1938, at the Nürnberg party rally, Neville Chamberlain flew to Germany on September 15, 1938, to arrange a peaceful compromise of the Czechoslovak crisis. At the Berchtesgaden meeting with Hitler, Chamberlain promised to secure the surrender of the Sudeten provinces to Germany. Having obtained the support of his own government as well as that of France and having also compelled Czechoslovakia to accept the arrangement, Chamberlain returned to Germany on September 22, 1938, in the hope of a final, peaceful settlement. In his second meeting with Hitler at Godesberg on September 22, 1938, Chamberlain offered the further concession of dissolving the Czech alliances with France and Russia. All cause for war seemed removed, since Germany would not only receive the Sudeten provinces, but the neutralization of rump-Czechoslovakia as well. To the consternation of the 69-year-old Prime Minister, who had staked his political career on a peaceful settlement, Hitler rejected the offers made at Berchtesgaden as no longer satisfactory. He insisted on an immediate military occupation of the Sudeten provinces and the fulfillment of Polish and Hungarian territorial claims against Czechoslovakia as well. The new German demands were presented in the form of an ultimatum, though Hitler affixed the innocuous title of "Memorandum" to his Godesberg demands.

After Godesberg, France and Britain reluctantly prepared for war, as even Chamberlain was not prepared to swallow the humiliation of September 22. Another public outburst by Hitler against Czechoslovakia in his Berlin *Sportpalast* speech of September 26, 1938, seemed to make war a certainty. Peace was saved, to the chagrin of Hitler, by Mussolini's last-minute initiative for a Four Power Conference of Britain, France, Germany, and Italy at Munich. The Munich Agreement of September 29, 1938, essentially fulfilled the conditions of Hitler's Godesberg "Memorandum." On October 1, 1938, German troops moved into the Sudeten provinces. Although the Munich Agreement had provided for plebiscites in areas of mixed population, no such plebiscites were held, resulting in the inclusion of 800,000 Czechs into the area annexed by Germany. On September 30, 1938, on Chamberlain's initiative, Hitler signed a German-British declaration. The German-British declaration cited the Munich Agreement and the Anglo-German Naval Accord of 1935 as symbolic of the desire of both peoples "never again to wage war against one another." Both powers pledged to solve other questions of mutual concern through consultation and thereby to strengthen the peace of Europe. A similar declaration was signed between France and Germany on December 6, 1938, in which both powers guaranteed their existing frontiers and promised to consult on questions of mutual concern.

The Munich Agreement, and the false spirit of relaxed tensions which it created, marked the high point of appeasement. To Neville Chamberlain, the Munich agreement signified "peace with honor" in the tradition of the Congress of Berlin of 1878, in which Bismarck and the British Prime Minister Disraeli had collaborated in the preservation of the European peace. The analogy was apparently accepted by the cheering multitudes which greeted Chamberlain on his return from Germany.

Similarly, the people of Paris welcomed the returning French Prime Minister Daladier with an outpouring of joy such as the French capital had not experienced since the announcement of the armistice of November 11, 1918.

The effect of Munich was more sobering on Soviet Russia. When Czechoslovakia had appealed for help at the height of the September crisis, Russia replied on September 21, 1938, that she intended to fulfill her obligations under the alliance of 1935 and to give assistance *together with France* by *the ways open to her*. When Poland assumed a threatening attitude towards Czechoslovakia, Russia issued a warning on September 23, 1938, that Soviet Russia would renounce the Polish-Soviet Non-Aggression Pact of 1932 if Polish troops crossed into Czechoslovakia.

At the Munich Conference, Soviet Russia was among the uninvited, however, and the Western surrender to Hitler must have appeared to Stalin as an attempt to exclude Russia from the affairs of Europe. That impression may have been confirmed by the Chamberlain-Hitler declaration of September 30, 1938, and the French-German statement of December 6, 1938.

FIGURE 16 *The illusion of peace: Chamberlain and Hitler after the Munich Conference, September 1938.*

To Hitler, Munich was a half victory at best, as it had robbed him of the chance of dismembering Czechoslovakia immediately. The ultimate disappearance of Czechoslovakia was only a question of time, however, since Poland had seized the Teschen district on October 3, 1938, and since Hungary's territorial claims against Czechoslovakia were fulfilled in part in the Vienna Award of November 2, 1938, by Italy and Germany. Moreover, Munich had loosened the bonds between Czechs, Slovaks, and Ukrainians in rump-Czechoslovakia. On November 22, 1938, Slovakia and the Carpatho-Ukraine constituted themselves as autonomous regions within the CSR, whose official name was altered from Czechoslovak Republic to Czecho-Slovak Republic. Czechs, Slovaks, and Ukrainians henceforth enjoyed their own regional governments under the new President Emil Hacha. Friction between the Czechs and Slovaks enabled Hitler to complete the dismemberment of Czecho-Slovakia. When the Diet of Slovakia declared its independence on March 14, 1939, President Hacha was prevailed upon to place "the fate of the Czech people in the hands of the Führer." As an alternative, Göring threatened to launch an air raid against Prague. On March 15, 1939, Hitler entered Prague. On March 16, 1939, Bohemia-Moravia was pronounced a protectorate of the German Reich. On March 18, 1939, Hitler took the nominally independent Slovak Republic under the government of Monsignor Tiso under his "protection." Among the prizes of the dismemberment of Czechoslovakia were the Skoda armaments works and the equipment of the Czech army. The German armored divisions which were to roll into France little more than a year after the fall of Prague included many Skoda tanks.

THE AFTERMATH OF PRAGUE

Western illusions about the stability of peace in Europe after Munich had been challenged even before the fall of Prague by Hitler's utterances throughout the autumn of 1938. "Today, France and Britain are governed by men who want peace," Hitler stated in his Munich speech of November 8, 1938; "other men, however, do not conceal the fact that they want war against Germany . . . tomorrow Mr. Churchill may be Prime Minister." The "British gentlemen," Hitler continued, might know their way about the British Empire, but they knew nothing of Central Europe. In a reference to the Arab-Jewish conflict in the British Mandate of Palestine, Hitler advised "these British gentlemen" to "concentrate their enormous knowledge on Palestine. They could offer great blessings there, for what is going on in Palestine smells of violence, not of democracy."

Faith in a peaceful Germany was shattered also by the officially inspired pogroms of November 9 and 10, 1938, when synagogues and Jewish shops were destroyed throughout Germany in retaliation for the assassination of Ernst von Rath, an official of the German embassy in

Paris, by Herschel Grynspan. The question asked in Paris and London throughout the winter of 1938/1939 was: Where will Hitler strike next?

Hitler's march into Prague on March 15, 1939, shattered his credibility in Britain beyond repair, as Hitler had given emphatic assurances in 1938 that he wanted "no Czechs" and that the Sudeten provinces represented his "last territorial demand." The feeling that German aggression acknowledged no bounds was heightened by the German ultimatum to Lithuania for the return of Memel, delivered on March 16 and accepted by Lithuania on March 19, 1939. The British public, the press, the House of Commons, and the Conservative Party angrily demanded that Neville Chamberlain change his attitude towards Germany. It was more in response to public pressure than out of a conviction of the failure of appeasement that Neville Chamberlain issued the warning in his Birmingham speech of March 17: "Any demand to dominate the world by force was one which the democracies must resist." On March 16, 1939, rumors of an impending German attack on Rumania had reached London; on March 29, 1939, the British government first learned of the extent of German pressure on the Polish government. Although Hitler had no designs on Rumania and although a German attack on Poland was not imminent, Hitler's action against Czechoslovakia in March, 1939, had made a German attack on the entire East European state system appear probable in the spring of 1939. It was from such fears that Neville Chamberlain issued a unilateral guarantee to Poland on March 31, 1939, pledging both Britain and France to lend all support in their power if the Polish government felt compelled to resist aggression. Poland accepted the offer at once.

THE GERMAN-POLISH CONFRONTATION

At the time of the signing of the German-Polish minority treaty on November 5, 1937, Hitler assured the Polish ambassador Lipski that Germany intended no change in the position of Danzig. Göring had given similar assurances when he asserted that Germany neither "wanted nor needed" the Polish Corridor. Less than a month after the Munich Agreement, the German government proposed a "general settlement" of pending German-Polish issues on the following terms: (1) Danzig was to be returned to Germany, (2) an extraterritorial rail and road corridor was to be built from Germany to East Prussia across the Polish corridor, (3) Poland was to retain a free zone in Danzig with free access rights, (4) the German-Polish Non-Aggression Pact of 1934 was to be extended by another ten or twenty-five years, and (5) Poland was to join the Anti-Comintern Pact.

The German terms, repeated after October, 1938, without a positive Polish response, were presented in sharper form after the liquidation of Czechoslovakia on March 21, 1939. When the terms were rejected again, the German press unleashed a propaganda offensive against Poland similar to its attacks on Czechoslovakia before Munich. On April 3, 1939, the German armed forces were ordered to be prepared for an invasion of Poland on September 1, 1939. On April 28, Hitler denounced the German-Polish Non-Aggression Pact of 1934 as well as the Anglo-German Naval Accord of 1935. On May 23, 1939, he announced his decision to "attack Poland at the first suitable opportunity" to a secret gathering of military leaders. Hitler defined as the objective of the attack not the city of Danzig but the gaining of *Lebensraum*.

THE BELATED ATTEMPT AT COLLECTIVE SECURITY IN EASTERN EUROPE

On April 7, 1939, Mussolini invaded Albania, in collusion with Yugoslavia, which had been promised a share in the Albanian spoils. A hastily constituted Albanian assembly offered the Albanian crown to the King of Italy on April 12, 1939. The Western powers, though helpless to uphold the independence of Albania, responded with guarantees designed to discourage further German and Italian aggression in Eastern Europe. On April 13, a French-British guarantee was issued to Rumania and Greece. The guarantee applied not only to an attack by the Axis Powers but to a Hungarian attack on Rumania as well. On May 12, 1939, Britain and Turkey issued a joint declaration for mutual aid in the event of aggression leading to war in the Mediterranean. The Anglo-Turkish declaration was followed by a similar Franco-Turkish declaration on June 23, 1939. By early summer of 1939, Western guarantees had been issued to all East European states from Poland to the Balkans, save for Hungary, Bulgaria, and Yugoslavia. Hungary was firmly tied to the Axis after joining the Anti-Comintern Pact on February 26, 1939; Bulgaria expected to profit from an Axis domination of the Balkans by recovering its losses to Greece and Yugoslavia of 1919; Yugoslavia, hoping to survive the Western confrontation with the Axis by a careful balancing act, had declined a British guarantee in April, 1939, and announced a policy of "absolute neutrality in an eventual conflict."

As a deterrent to Axis aggression, the hastily devised system of Western guarantees was lacking in persuasive power, since the Western powers had no military presence in Eastern Europe. Britain adopted military conscription on April 27, 1939, the first such measure undertaken in peace time. The immediate military value of conscription was doubtful, however, because Britain lacked the facilities for training. Of the 200,000 eligible for the draft, only 30,000 were inducted in June, 1939, and their training was not begun until July 15. The only power capable of providing effective military backing to the Western guarantees in Eastern Europe was Soviet Russia. For months, Lloyd George shouted in the House of

Commons that Britain had been "staring this powerful gift horse in the mouth." The British guarantees, Lloyd George asserted, were "demented pledges" if not sustained by an agreement with Russia.

SOVIET RUSSIA BETWEEN THE DEMOCRACIES AND HITLER

Russia had responded to the first signs of German pressure on Poland by joining in a Soviet-Polish declaration of November 26, 1938, in which both governments pledged to continue their relations on the basis of the Polish-Soviet Non-Aggression Pact of 1932. However, at the Eighteenth Congress of the Russian Communist Party in March, 1939, which coincided with the German occupation of Prague, Stalin had avoided an identification of Soviet with Western foreign policy aims. The Western powers were accused of spreading rumors in order to provoke a conflict between Germany and Russia, for which there existed "no visible reasons." Russia would not "pull somebody else's chestnuts out of the fire."

Russia's chief concern was either to compel or to persuade Hitler into delivering his major blow against the West should war break out in 1939. Hitler could be compelled to take that course by a Soviet-Western military alliance with ironclad guarantees of Western support; he could be persuaded to take it by a diplomatic revolution in Soviet-German relations and an agreement with Hitler. Throughout the spring and summer of 1939, Russia explored both possibilities. To the West, Russia made concrete offers on April 18, 1939: (1) the Western powers and Russia would guarantee militarily all East European states between the Baltic and the Black Sea, bordering on Russia; (2) Russia and the Western powers would open military conversations and pledge not to conclude a separate peace following the outbreak of war; and (3) the British guarantee to Poland would apply to German aggression against Poland only.

In the ensuing Western-Soviet negotiations, which were conducted on the Western side at a slow pace and by officials of low rank, Russia insisted on specific Western military guarantees. Russia demanded that Britain and France commit 70 per cent of their forces in an offensive against Germany if Germany attacked Poland.

On April 17, 1939, Russia took the first step towards a possible rapprochement with Germany with the statement that nothing precluded German-Soviet relations from being placed "on a normal footing" and from becoming "better and better" afterwards. On March 3, 1939, Litvinov, the symbol of Soviet policy of collective security, was replaced by Molotov as Soviet Foreign Minister. Hitler did not respond to the Soviet overtures until the end of May. On May 22, Hitler strengthened his ties with Italy by concluding the "Pact of Steel," in which Italy and Germany pledged mutual assistance in the event of war. By July 27, 1939, Germany and Russia had reached tentative agreement on a division of Eastern Europe into spheres of influence. Anxious to reach agreement with Russia before August 26, 1939, the date set for the German invasion of Poland, Hitler sent an urgent message to Stalin on August 21, 1939, to receive the German Foreign Minister in Moscow for the conclusion of a German-Soviet Non-Aggression Pact. On August 23, 1939, the Stalin-Hitler Pact was signed in Moscow. Hitler's price for Soviet neutrality was contained in the secret protocol affixed to the published Non-Aggression Pact. The German price for Russian neutrality on the eve of the Second World War was no less than the destruction of the states of the *Cordon Sanitaire*. By recognizing Finland, Latvia, Estonia, Eastern Poland, and Rumanian Bessarabia as being within the Soviet sphere of influence, Hitler, in effect, offered Stalin the restoration of the frontiers of Tsarist Russia of 1914. Poland was to be divided between Russia and Germany along the Narev, Vistula, and San rivers. Lithuania and Vilna were to form Germany's sphere of influence. The German Foreign Minister Ribbentrop had been authorized by Hitler even to concede the Dardanelles to Russia if Stalin asked for them.

EDWARD GREY AND NEVILLE CHAMBERLAIN

Hitler had hoped that the German-Soviet Non-Aggression Pact would act as the final deterrent to Britain's intervention in Eastern Europe. Instead, Britain concluded a formal treaty of alliance with Poland on August 25, 1939, the day of the announcement of the Stalin-Hitler pact. In a personal letter of August 25, 1939, Chamberlain warned Hitler not to repeat the German mistake of 1914 by misreading the intentions of Britain. Conscious of the German charge, made after the First World War, that the British Foreign Secretary Sir Edward Grey had deliberately misled Germany in the diplomatic crisis of July, 1914, by assuming the role of mediator while secretly encouraging France and Russia to prepare for war against Germany, Neville Chamberlain issued a clear warning to Hitler. It has been alleged, the Prime Minister stated, that the catastrophe of 1914 would not have occurred had Britain made her position clearer in 1914. "His Majesty's government are resolved that on this occasion there shall be no such tragic misunderstanding." No clearer statement of intent could have been issued; it differed markedly from the words of Edward Grey to the German ambassador Lichnowsky in July, 1914, that "Britain's hands were free" and that Britain had undertaken no formal obligations towards any European power.

Chamberlain's warning, which coincided with Mussolini's communication to Berlin that Italy was not ready for war, caused Hitler to falter for a few days, but no more. The German attack on Poland, scheduled for August 26, was postponed until September 1, 1939. In the last resort, Chamberlain's warning failed of its purpose, since Hitler clung to his own estimation of the Western statesmen as "little worms." The question of British rearmament, Hitler had stated in 1936, was not only one of "producing ships, guns and aeroplanes, but also of undertaking psychological rearmament which is much longer and more difficult." The Western surrender at Munich had convinced Hitler of the democracies' incapacity for "psychological rearmament."

The history of Hitler's aggressions in Eastern Europe from 1938 to 1939 had fulfilled the prophetic warning which James Headlam-Morley, the historical adviser of the British Foreign Office, had issued in 1925. Headlam-Morley had warned against the catastrophic consequences to all Europe, if Czechoslovakia were to be dismembered or Poland partitioned anew. Though Britain might be driven to interfere, her intervention would probably come too late. Until the dramatic reversal of Britain's eastern policy through the issuing of the British guarantee to Poland in March 1939, Britain had regarded the Rhine and not the Vistula as her first line of defense on the European continent. "The British people," Lloyd George had stated in 1921, ". . . would not be ready to be involved in quarrels which might arise regarding Poland or Danzig. . . ." Sir Austen Chamberlain, the British Foreign Secretary of the mid-1920's and half-brother of Neville Chamberlain, in paraphrasing Bismarck's famous statement of 1876 concerning Germany's lack of interest in the Balkans, had observed that the Polish corridor was not "worth the bones of a single British grenadier."

On September 3, 1939, Britain, and a reluctant France, declared war on Germany in response to the German invasion of Poland.

Reviewing the twenty years of diplomatic failure to reach a lasting European peace between 1919 and 1939, Winston Churchill observed in his speech at Fulton, Missouri, on March 5, 1946: "There never was a war in history easier to prevent by timely action than the one which has just desolated such great areas of the globe. It could have been prevented, in my belief, without the firing of a single shot, and Germany might be powerful, prosperous and honored today, but no one would listen and one by one we were all sucked into the awful whirlpool." In risking a world war over Poland, Hitler not only staked the existence of his own nation, but the preeminence of Europe in the world, a preeminence that Europeans had come to take for granted in the 20th century.

The idealism of Woodrow Wilson and the American Republic had offered alternative solutions in 1919 to the centuries-old tradition of European diplomacy and war. Far from becoming a beacon, it had remained but a brief flash, illuminating the battle-scarred face of Europe.

22 | The Second World War

The outbreak of the Second World War brought to a climax the deep political and moral crisis of 20th-century Europe, laid bare in the First World War and compounded by its aftermath. Initially, the Second World War seemed to be fought for the same reasons and with the same aims as the First World War: the failure of the European states to devise an effective concert for the preservation of peace, the German drive for hegemony over Europe, and the clash of Western democracy with German authoritarianism. Both the geographic and ideological scope of the Second World War became much wider and more complex, however. In Europe, the frontiers and the democratic ideals which the settlement of 1919 had tried to uphold came under attack not only from Germany and Italy, but also from Soviet Russia, which shared in Hitler's annexations of the early phase of World War II. In the Far East, Japan was not content with picking up a few islands or concessions vacated by one European power, but rather aimed at hegemony over all of Asia, from India to the Pacific.

The United States, a reluctant and belated member of the World War I alliance, was threatened in its own existence at an early stage of World War II and was forced to throw its resources and manpower into the balance in two widely separated theaters of the globe.

The European state system, which had emerged from World War I under the illusion of continuing world dominance because of the American withdrawal and the paralysis of Russia, would soon find itself utterly destroyed by Hitler and desperately dependent on the military power of the United States and Soviet Russia for its liberation and regeneration.

The moral limitations of total war, already shaken by the experience of the First World War, would suffer a complete breakdown in the Second World War, with the extermination of millions of civilians, the massive population transfers and expulsions, and the indiscriminate bombing of civilian targets.

The colonial peoples of the world, grown restless with the First World War, would soon demand complete emancipation from their weakened and impoverished European masters, and alter a world balance which in its general outlines had stood unchanged for centuries.

The scientific progress of the West, accelerated by the exigencies of World War I, would accomplish its most awesome breakthrough with the development of nuclear fission and rocket propulsion. Both would furnish mankind for the first time with a potential for undreamed-of destruction or improvement of his own world and the exploration of others.

THE BALANCE OF POWER

THE MILITARY BALANCE

Before the outbreak of the Second World War, Nazi propaganda had done its best to convince the Western democracies of Germany's crushing military superiority and hence of the futility of any Western opposition to Hitler's political plans on the continent of Europe. German propaganda had been effective largely because of the demonstration of German and Italian air power during the Spanish Civil War. The German bombing of Guernica and the Italian air raids against Barcelona had led the French and British governments to believe that Germany would open hostilities against them with "knock-out blows" against the Allied capitals from the air.

The German military potential had vastly grown between the Munich Conference and the German attack on Poland; but the military balance at the outset of the war was far more favorable to the British-French-Polish coalition than either Nazi propaganda or the outcome of the early campaigns seemed to suggest.

On land the combined forces of Poland, Britain, and France outnumbered Germany's fifty-two divisions. In naval power, the Western democracies enjoyed a crushing superiority, since the German navy, dwarfed by the Treaty of Versailles, had remained the stepchild of German rearmament under Hitler. The German pre-war naval program, called "Plan Z," had contemplated the construction of six super-battleships, two aircraft carriers, and numerous other craft. It had counted, however, on another decade of peace, and the German navy had a mere twenty-seven ocean-going submarines and two pocket battleships ready for action when the war began.

Germany's military advantage over the Allies was not one of numbers but consisted rather in the revolutionary adaptation of two new weapons born in the First World War, the tank and the aircraft. Ever since the carnage of the Somme and Verdun, military experts had attempted to restore mobility to the warfare which had bogged down in the trenches of France. Several Allied veterans of the First World War, J. F. C. Fuller and Lidell Hart in England and Charles De Gaulle in France, became the prophets of modern mechanized and armored warfare. They advocated the formation of armored divisions to break the enemy's linear defense, which no amount of massed artillery had ever really broken on the western front. Winston Churchill, as Minister of Ammunition, had urged the use of airborne troops, as early as 1917, to break the costly deadlock in France. These Allied advocates of mobile warfare, ignored in their own countries, greatly influenced the development of German military tactics before the outbreak of the Second World War. General Heinz Guderian created the German armored divisions which, supported by German air power and sometimes airborne troops, accounted largely for the speed of German victories during the early campaigns.

THE ECONOMIC BALANCE

In a war of attrition, the availability of raw materials was more significant than the mere balance of armaments, as the experience of World War I had clearly shown. The Allied victory of 1918 was achieved, in part, because of the strangulation of the German war economy by the British blockade. Although Nazi Germany had made strenuous efforts under its Four Year Plan to achieve economic self-sufficiency, the Germany of 1939 was even less prepared to wage a long war of attrition than the Germany of 1914 because of its inadequate stockpiles of strategic raw materials, especially oil. Because of the raw material sources lost to Germany under the Treaty of Versailles, the German war economy of 1939 depended heavily on imports, such as oil from Rumania and Russia, iron ore from the Swedish mines of Kiruna, and nickel from the Finnish mines at Petsamo. The effects of the British blockade, imposed in 1939, were mitigated, however, by German-Soviet economic collaboration under the trade agreement of August, 1939, as long as Stalin chose to supply Hitler with the economic needs of war.

Britain and France, on the other hand, controlling the oceans of the world by virtue of their sea power and possessing colonial empires of their own, could draw freely upon the resources of the world in their struggle against a continental power like Germany.

THE POLITICAL BALANCE

By obtaining the non-aggression pact with Russia on August 23, 1939, Hitler seemed to have tipped the political balance of Europe in his favor and created conditions favorable to his military aggression against Poland. The long-range effectiveness of the German-Soviet entente depended, however, on future military developments in Western Europe and the ability of the two dictators to agree on an ultimate demarcation of German and Russian power in Eastern Europe. Effusive public protestations of mutual trust and friendship notwithstanding, there lingered an element of suspicion in German-Russian relations from the start of World War II, both sides recognizing the pragmatic nature of the agreement of August, 1939, and the possibility of a subsequent change.

543

Fascist Italy, although a political as well as a military ally of Nazi Germany since the conclusion of the Pact of Steel of May, 1939, declined to enter the war on Hitler's side in September, in view of her military unpreparedness. In vain, Mussolini had attempted to avoid a general war over Poland by seeking to arrange a last-minute Great Power Conference for a peaceful solution of the Polish problem in the manner of the Munich Conference of September, 1938.

The United States still stood far apart from the events of Europe in 1939, largely because of the prevailing isolationist sentiment of the American public. President Roosevelt's statement that even a neutral could not be asked to "close his mind or his conscience" reflected a widespread American sympathy for the Allied cause in Europe, but the stringent provisions of the American neutrality legislation of 1939 prohibited even a limited intervention on behalf of Poland, France, or Britain. American diplomatic efforts to save European nations threatened by aggression, such as were made on behalf of Finland in November, 1939, thus remained as ineffectual as had been Roosevelt's appeal to Germany, Italy, and Poland in late August, 1939.

In 1939 the war was still fought within the narrow confines of the European world, with the two World Powers Russia and the United States interested spectators but not participants.

THE CAMPAIGN IN POLAND

Whether the Allied advantage of superior resources could be brought to bear against Germany depended on the Allied ability to contain German offensive power, as in 1914, or on their willingness to carry the war into Germany at an early stage. Both opportunities offered themselves to the Western democracies in September, 1939, but, for a variety of reasons, they failed to take advantage of either.

The Western declaration of war on September 3, 1939, forced Hitler, in effect, to wage a two-front war. Since German military power was inadequate for a simultaneous offensive against Poland and France, Hitler massed the bulk of his army — all of his armored divisions and most of his air force — against Poland, the weaker of his enemies. Germany's western border and, with it, the Ruhr, the heart of German armaments production, thus remained exposed to Allied attack for most of September. Germany's fortifications in the west, the so-called *Westwall,* were both incomplete and thinly manned. Begun only in 1936, the Westwall was inferior to the French Maginot line, whose fortifications, begun in 1929, were complete in 1939.

The French government had promised Poland, as early as the spring of 1939, to launch an air and land offensive against Germany from the west within sixteen days of Polish mobilization. The French army confined itself, however, to a few insignificant skirmishes against the Saar, which never assumed the character of an offensive and forced no German withdrawals from the Polish campaign.

The sluggishness of the Western military response to the German attack on Poland had its roots in a number of circumstances. To begin with, the Allies withheld their air power for fear of German retaliation. The British government of 1939 remembered the panic, which German Zeppelin and airplane raids had caused among the civilian population of London in 1916 and 1917. Both Britain and France began to evacuate their capitals in September, 1939, and British civil defense authorities held forty-four million gas masks in readiness in expectation of a German gas attack from the air.

The French army, for its part, had abandoned the offensive spirit of 1914 for a purely defensive posture. Remembering the First World War, especially Verdun, France looked for military survival and victory to the Maginot Line. The initiative of the attack was to be left to Germany. A German offensive against the Western Powers, it was hoped, would recoil before the French line of fortifications. Should Germany break through Belgium, as she had done in 1914, the mobile mass of French and British armies, stationed behind the Franco-Belgian frontier, would halt and destroy such an attack.

Poland thus stood alone between the German toops advancing from the west and a hostile Soviet Union in the east. Poland's chance of prolonged resistance was reduced further by the ambitious plans of the Polish army, which were out of all proportion to Poland's military capability. Rather than building strong defensive positions behind Poland's natural lines of defense, the San, Narev, and Vistula rivers, which straddled the line of the German advance, Marshal Ryz Smigly contemplated launching a Polish offensive into East Prussia. Lacking in modern armaments, especially in air power and tanks, Poland's thirty infantry divisions, together with their cavalry, soon lost the initiative to an enemy with superior armaments and a revolutionary doctrine of war. German armored and mechanized divisions, closely supported from the air, drove deep wedges into Poland from west, north, and south. By September 19, 1939, the mass of the Polish army was trapped and destroyed in a series of battles between the Vistula and the Bzura. The Polish government had departed for Rumania on September 16, 1939. Warsaw alone, under heavy German artillery and air bombardment, rejected all German calls for surrender until September 28, when a shortage of food and water ended the resistance of the Polish capital.

Hitler had given his first demonstration of lightning warfare, or *Blitzkrieg,* in a campaign that lasted twenty-eight days and destroyed a nation of thirty million people. Although the world was shocked by the speed of the German victory, the Western military leaders did not draw the

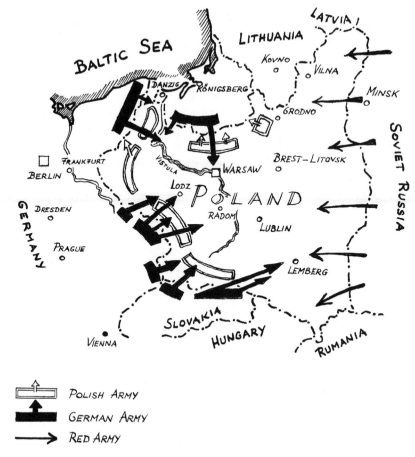

The German and Soviet attack on Poland. September 1939.

proper conclusions from it. The new German tactics of rapidly moving armored divisions, supported from the air, might have been feasible in the open plains of Poland, it was argued, but would they succeed equally well against an enemy firmly entrenched in modern fortifications?

THE FOURTH PARTITIONING OF POLAND

Russian troops had moved into eastern Poland on September 17, 1939, to occupy those parts promised to the Soviet Union under the Stalin-Hitler pact of August, 1939. The timing of the Soviet move was carefully chosen. Stalin had resisted German pressures for an earlier Russian intervention and moved his forces only after the Polish government had gone into exile. Also, in the new Soviet-German border and friendship agreement signed on September 28, 1939, Russia agreed to move the German-Russian demarcation line further east and closer to the Curzon Line of 1920. Stalin thus hoped to minimize the odium of aggression which the partitioning of Poland had attached to Russia. The Soviets pointed out that an effective Polish government had ceased to function and that the areas acquired were inhabited primarily by Ukrainians and White [Byelo] Russians.

The Western Powers, having gone to war to uphold Poland's independence, limited their reaction to the fourth partitioning of Poland to weak protests, for fear that a stronger stand would only cement the German-Soviet entente.

The people of Poland, having enjoyed independence but briefly after a century and a half of servitude, entered upon their darkest period of suffering. Germany annexed half of German-occupied Poland outright, turning the remainder into a German "Government General" under Nazi governor Hans Frank. Frank's first proclamation to the people of Poland, on October 26, 1939, gave a foretaste of German occupation measures to come. German troops, Frank's message stated, had restored order to Poland and had eliminated the threat to European peace; Poland had been a state built upon the dictated Peace of Versailles and it would never rise again.

By eliminating an independent Polish state, in September, 1939, Hitler had realized a German foreign policy aim that had been pursued in various guises as far back as the days of the Weimar Republic. The German victory had been achieved, however, at the price of a general European war which put Germany's own existence in question and which Hitler would soon find difficult to terminate by either military power or political persuasion.

As for the Poles now living under Russian rule, their sentiments may be surmised from underground leaflets soon to appear after the arrival of the Red Army. One such leaflet proclaimed that Russia had deprived the Poles of bread, sugar, and meat and bestowed on them prisons, concentration camps, and German friendship.

THE WESTERN STALEMATE

Western military inaction during the Polish campaign encouraged Hitler to believe that the governments of Britain and France might yet be persuaded to recognize the German gains in Poland, through a negotiated peace, once Western public opinion had been satisfied after the formal declarations of war. Hitler's peace offer to the Western Powers, made on October 6, 1939, on that basis was rejected. Prime Minister Neville Chamberlain's reply stated in essence that Britain did not wish to exclude Germany from her rightful place in Europe but refused to submit to an uneasy truce interrupted by further threats.

Unable to get peace in the west on his own terms and uneasy about Stalin's intentions in the east, Hitler now wished to launch a German offensive in the west as soon as his troops were transferred from Poland. The aim of Hitler's projected fall offensive, which was ordered repeatedly but never launched, was to have been the seizure of the Low Lands and the channel coast of France. From these areas, Hitler intended to strike at Britain's sea lanes with German air and naval power. Poor weather, and the reluctance of the German generals to commit their troops so soon after the Polish campaign, led to the postponement of the German attack.

The French High Command, on the other hand, also stuck to its defensive plans throughout the fall and winter of 1939-1940 and awaited the German onslaught behind its strong defenses. Thus a strange and quiet war descended on the western front such as the First World War had never seen. Both sides exchanged propaganda broadcasts across the trenches and sometimes even music, but rarely fire. The lull worked to Hitler's advantage. While Germany increased the size and improved the training of her armies, the Western powers failed to induce Holland and Belgium to coordinate their defenses with those of France and Britain. The two small neutrals, mindful of the fate of Poland, feared to provoke Germany by accepting the western invitation. Instead, Queen Wilhelmina of Holland and King Leopold of Belgium embarked on a futile mediation policy on November 7, 1939, in "the fateful hour before the war in Western Europe had begun its full course."

SOVIET EXPANSION IN THE BALTIC

As the war in western Europe entered its quiet autumn stalemate, another war erupted in the Baltic area in the wake of Soviet agression. The absence of Western political power in the Baltic, thanks to the Western preoccupation with the war against Germany and Hitler's own blank check to Stalin, enabled Russia to seek to regain her 1914 western frontiers in stages. Following the Russian occupation of eastern Poland, Stalin launched the military penetration of the three Baltic states, Latvia, Lithuania, and Estonia. Between September 29 and October 11, all three countries were forced to sign treaties of "mutual assistance" which granted naval and air bases to the USSR. Finland was next. Reviewing earlier demands for the lease of the Finnish islands of Suursaari and Koivisto, made as early as 1938, Stalin now added the demand for the port of Hanko on the Finnish mainland. In addition, the Russo-Finnish border near Leningrad was to be moved by some fifty miles to improve the defenses of Leningrad. As Stalin told the startled Finnish delegation which had arrived in Moscow, it was the border that had to be moved, not the city of Leningrad.

Finland refused to be intimidated, although she could count on little else besides the public sympathy of the Western democracies. Pres-

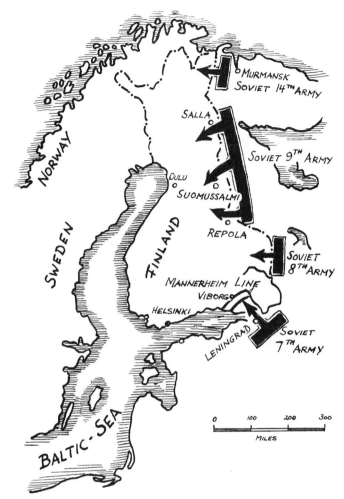

The Soviet attack on Finland, November 1939-February 1940.

ident Roosevelt's effort to intervene on Finland's behalf in Moscow was brushed aside cynically by Molotov. Whereas the Soviet Union had granted Finland liberty and independence after the First World War, Molotov stated, the United States had not acted in like manner with regard to the Philippines and Cuba.

On November 30, 1939, Russia opened hostilities against Finland and installed a Finnish Communist puppet government under Otto Kuusinen at Teriojoki on the Finnish-Russian border. With Kuusinen, Stalin signed an agreement on December 2, 1939, which granted Russia all that Helsinki had denied. The League of Nations branded Russia as an aggressor on December 14, 1939, but it was not moral censure by an organization grown feeble and ineffective that Stalin feared.

Rather, the Soviets were unpleasantly surprised by the brilliant performance of Finland's tough little army of 300,000 men, supported by an air force of 150 aging and obsolete aircraft. Not only did the Finns hold superior Russian forces at bay between November, 1939, and January, 1940, but they annihilated a number of Russian divisions in the winter battles of Suomossalmi in January, 1940. The longer Finnish resistance lasted, the greater Russian fears became that the Western powers might intervene and rob the Russo-Finnish war of its localized character.

THE SCANDINAVIAN INTERLUDE

The Russo-Finnish conflict very nearly merged with the western war against Germany at the beginning of 1940 because of strategic decisions reached by the Allied Supreme War Council on February 5, 1940. Ever since the speedy collapse of Poland in September, 1939, France had been seeking an opportunity to establish a "second front" in Germany's flank, in order to deflect German power from the French border. For this reason, France had sought unsuccessfully to enlarge the Franco-British-Turkish mutual assistance pact of September 28, 1939, into an alliance of Balkan nations against Germany. Finland's struggle against Soviet aggression had aroused the admiration of the people of France and Britain, who demanded action in support of Finland. The Allied Supreme War Council thus decided to combine a Western relief action for Finland with a military occupation of Norway and Sweden. The latter would deprive Germany of the much-needed Swedish iron ore.

In the end, it was Finland which declined the Western offer of military assistance for fear of becoming embroiled in the larger war in progress in Western Europe. Moscow shared this concern and, after wearing down Finnish resistance in February, 1940, made peace with Finland in the Treaty of Moscow on March 13, 1940. Finland lost South Karelia, together with the Karelian Isthmus and the city of Viborg, the Salla district in central-northern Finland, and a portion of the Fisher Peninsula in the far north. Hanko and a number of islands in the Gulf of Finland were leased to Russia but Petsamo, with its valuable nickel mines remained with Finland. All in all, the peace was costly for Finland, but it preserved Finland's sovereignty for the time being and spared her the horrors of becoming a battlefield of the Great Powers of Europe. Whether the Moscow treaty was a final settlement of Russian claims or merely a truce depended on the further course of the Second World War, as the Finnish government knew only too well.

THE INVASION OF NORWAY

Finland had made peace and the governments of Norway and Sweden protested vigorously against Allied plans regarding Scandinavia.

The Western Powers proceeded nevertheless with mining operations of Norwegian coastal waters, used by German ore-ships. They also held an invasion force in readiness should Germany retaliate with landings of her own in Norway.

A German decision to invade both Norway and Denmark had been reached in principle as early as December, 1939, after the German

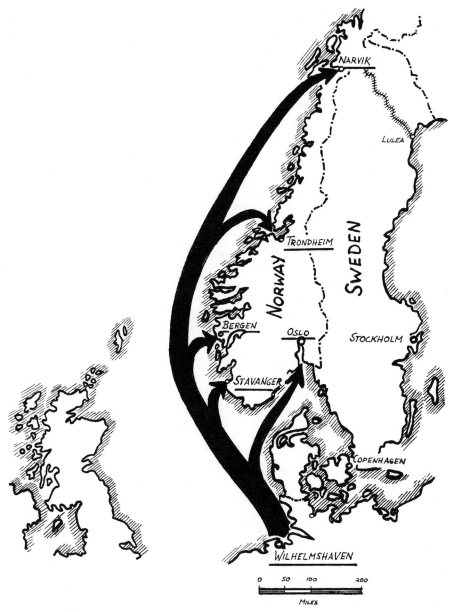

The German invasion of Norway and Denmark, April 1940.

Naval Chief, Grand Admiral Raeder, had pointed out the importance of Norway to Hitler. By sheer coincidence, the German and Allied plans concerning Scandinavia reached fruition at almost the same moment, the German invasion of Denmark and Norway proceeding on April 9, 1940.

The German occupation of Denmark was not resisted, but the German amphibious landings along the coast of Norway, from Narvik in the north to Oslo in the south, entailed serious risks for the invader, in view of Germany's naval weakness. A resolute and early intervention of the Royal Navy could have sunk the German troop convoys and turned the German gamble into a disaster. In fact, the German landings achieved surprise, and, once established on Norwegian soil, the German troops enjoyed the advantage of air superiority over the belated British intervention.

The Norwegians had defended their neutrality in a brave but futile struggle, although they inflicted painful casualties on the German fleet. Norwegian coastal batteries sank the German heavy cruiser *Blücher* as it tried to force its way into Oslo Fjord. Not until April 12 and April 13, however, did the British navy strike back with an attack on Narvik, which destroyed virtually the entire German destroyer force in Narvik Fjord. British landings in the vicity of Trondheim and Narvik achieved temporary success, the port of Narvik falling into British hands on May 28, 1940. The ominous turn of events in the Battle of France since May 10, 1940, forced the Allies, however, to retire from the Norwegian campaign, after evacuating the Norwegian government and king to Britain.

With the conquest of Norway, Germany had acquired important air and naval bases from which she could threaten the British sea lanes in the North Atlantic. The Norwegian campaign also yielded to the Germans the plant at Vemork, then the only European plant capable of producing heavy water, an item of importance in the manufacture of an atomic bomb. Fortunately for the Allies, it was soon destroyed by Norwegian resistance forces.

The Allied defeat in Norway, coming as it did so soon after the fall of Poland and the Western Powers' inability to sustain Finland, had a doubly disconcerting effect on the small neutrals of Europe. Thus, Belgium continued to reject all British efforts to integrate the Belgian army into the Western defense plans right up to the German invasion of the Lowlands in May, 1940.

In Britain Germany's open flaunting of British sea power during the Norwegian campaign brought to a climax the public's dissatisfaction with Neville Chamberlain's leadership. The prime minister was besieged to resign and came under heavy attack from members of his own Conservative Party, one of whom hurled at Chamberlain Cromwell's words:

"Depart, I say, and let us be done with you. In the name of God, go!" On May 10, 1940, the day which opened the Battle of France, Winston Churchill succeeded as prime minister.

THE BATTLE OF FRANCE

When the long awaited German spring offensive was launched into Holland, Belgium, and northern France on the tenth of May, 1940, the opposing armies were roughly balanced in manpower and armaments. The Germans had committed a total of 136 divisions in the west, including ten armored divisions. The Allies had 137 divisions in the line. The number of German tanks amounted to about 2,500, that of the Western Powers to 3,000. In artillery, France possessed a marked superiority, whereas the Germans had the advantage in the air, outnumbering the French bomber force by 1:8 and the French fighters by 1:4.

Yet several factors worked to the disadvantage of the Allies, and aided in their becoming unbalanced and being defeated before the end of June, 1940.

The aim of the German attack was no longer merely the conquest of Holland, Belgium, and the French channel coast, as Hitler had proposed in the fall of 1939. Rather, the Germans intended to drive France out of the war altogether and destroy the British Expeditionary Force (BEF) in the process. The German strategy that was to achieve this ambitious goal was based on deception. The Western Powers were to be led into believing that Holland and Belgium were indeed the principal object of the German attack, a ruse that would lure the powerful French First and Seventh Armies, as well as the BEF, into Belgium. A much stronger German assault with armored divisions was to be launched meanwhile through the Ardennes forest in southern Belgium towards Sedan and across the weakly guarded Meuse crossings. The ultimate objective of this attack, which the Germans called appropriately "operation scythe," was to reach the French channel coast and to cut off the main body of the French and British forces in Belgium. The German ruse worked almost to perfection.

While the Germans were bombing Holland into submission through a massive air raid on Rotterdam on May 14, 1940, and while they stormed the powerful Belgian fort of Eben Emael through the use of airborne troops, it took the Allies several days to recognize that the German breakout at Sedan was the principal point of the attack.

Once the Germans had broken through at Sedan, they were able to employ their proven tactics of the Polish campaign. Armored and mechanized divisions, closely supported by dive bombers and fighters, pushed their way to the channel coast within ten days after the beginning

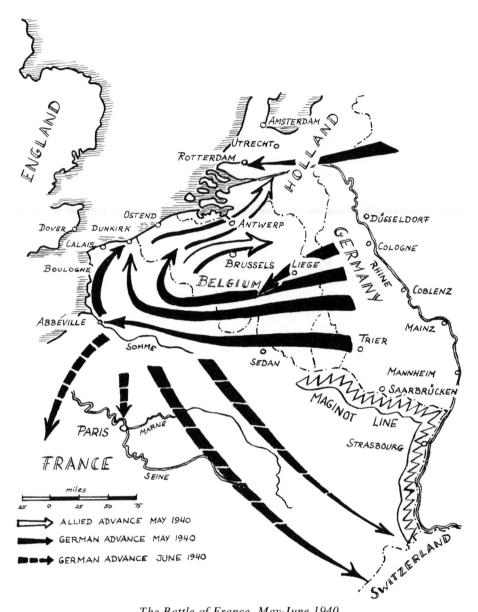

The Battle of France, May-June 1940.

of the offensive. By May 20, Abbéville was reached and the Allied front cut in half, with British, French, and Belgian forces trapped in an iron ring and the sea their only route of escape.

The German drive to the sea in a long and narrow corridor far behind enemy lines entailed great risks for the attacking forces as well, which an alert and determined opponent might well have turned to his advantage. The deployment of the French army in the spring of 1940 had left no strategic reserves, however, which might have crushed the extended German flank. The French mentality of linear defenses and continuing front lines failed to respond to the unforeseen emergency for which there seemed neither a precedent nor an answer under the rules of the last war. The few Allied counterattacks against the Germans' armored corridor either came too late or were undertaken with inadequate means. Soon the evacuation of the French and British armies, trapped in Belgium, became the foremost Allied task. Belgium's surrender on May 28, 1940, rendered the Allied situation even more critical, for it freed German forces for the pursuit towards Dunkirk, the last remaining port of embarkation.

By late May, 1940, the British government feared the worst and Winston Churchill was prepared to announce the greatest defeat in the history of the British army. Contrary to Churchill's fears and the pessimistic predictions of the British Admiralty, 340,000 Allied troops, the majority of them British, were carried to the safety of England's shores in an armada of pleasure boats and warships. The "miracle of Dunkirk" was due mainly to the sudden halt of the German troops advancing towards Dunkirk. Various explanations have been offered for it, among them Hitler's anxiety to save the German armored divisions for the second phase of the Battle of France and Göring's ambition to achieve the destruction of the entrapped forces with "his" air force. German air attacks on Dunkirk, although costly to the Allies, failed to halt the evacuation.

More important than the military significance of snatching the BEF from almost certain capture was the psychological impact on Britain in her darkest hour. The successful evacuation had revealed the limitations of German air and sea power after an unbroken series of German victories on land. The arms and vehicles of the BEF had remained on the dunes of Dunkirk, but its men were saved. However scarce their armaments in June, 1940, their very presence in England lent substance to Churchill's claim that any German attempt at invasion would meet with fierce resistance. The "miracle of Dunkirk" was overshadowed by the opening of the second phase in the Battle of France with the German attack on the Somme and Aisne lines on June 5, 1940. General Weygand, successor to General Gamelin after the Sedan debacle, pinned his hopes on the arrival of strong British air squadrons and upon the remote possibility of an American intervention in the European war. Until then, it was hoped, France could withstand the fury of the German attack alone, especially in view of the still unbroken defenses of the Maginot line.

To Britain, however, the Battle of France gave every sign of being already lost. After some very heated debates in London, Churchill withheld the fighter squadrons of the Royal Air Force (RAF) which

France so urgently requested. Their preservation was regarded as vital in Britain, since they, together with the Royal Navy, were the only defense left against an expected German invasion. The United States, although pledging material assistance to French premier Reynaud, could not meet his appeal for an American naval demonstration in the Mediterranean. France was alone. Her agony was increased when Mussolini declared war on France on June 10, 1940.

The United States, France, and Britain, foreseeing such a possibility, had tried in vain to keep the Duce satisfied by generous promises. If Italy retained her state of nonbelligerency now, she was offered the status of a belligerent power in any Allied postwar peace conference and due consideration of her "grievances." Mussolini, sensing larger gains at the expense of a mortally wounded France, cast his lot with Hitler. To make good his extravagant claims on Corsica and French North Africa, he needed, in his own words, "a few thousand dead."

From a military standpoint, the Italian intervention in the Battle of France was insignificant. The French army prevented any Italian breakthrough towards the Rhone Valley, and the French navy struck at Italian vessels vigorously from the first day. Meanwhile, however, the French lines on the Somme had broken. Paris fell on June 14, 1940, and even the Maginot line was pierced in several places in the final stage of battle.

With all hope of an organized resistance gone, the French army in retreat or in a state of shock, the government of France faced the agonizing choice between seeking an armistice and continuing the war from the colonies.

There was also the matter of the Franco-British agreement of March 28, 1940. Prime Minister Reynaud, who had succeeded Daladier on March 21, 1940, with the promise of a more vigorous prosecution of the war, had pledged in the agreement of March 28 not to enter into separate peace or armistice negotiations with the Germans except by mutual consent. Now confusion reigned in French government circles over how the pledge of March, 1940, could be reconciled with the French military situation of June, 1940. Former Prime Minister Herriot urged continuation of the struggle from North Africa. Marshal Pétain and General Weygand, on the other hand, advised an armistice, and Prime Minister Reynaud, under the strain of conflicting counsels, resigned on June 16, 1940, to be replaced by the 85-year-old Pétain. Winston Churchill had hoped to encourage the French government into prolonging the fight by offering a constitutional merger of the French and British empires. This startling project, which contemplated also a joint Anglo-French citizenship and fleet, came too late to influence the decision of the new French government.

Marshal Pétain, who had seen the French army of the First

World War suffer the agony of Verdun, concurred with the views of a large segment of the French army in 1940 that further resistance was useless and that an armistice must be sought forthwith. Pétain, like Weygand, took Britain's ultimate defeat for granted in June, 1940. No other course of events seemed probable to those who had regarded the French army as the finest in the world before the Battle of France and who had seen it defeated in a campaign of forty-three days.

The powerful French fleet was the greatest obstacle to winning Britain's consent to a separate Franco-German armistice. The British government took it for granted that the French fleet, if left in French bases, would fall into German hands sooner or later. Unlike Marshal Pétain and Admiral Darlan, the new French minister of marine, Winston Churchill did not trust Hitler's word that Germany would not touch the French navy.

ARMISTICE.

Without agreement on the future of the French fleet having been reached between France and Britain, Marshal Pétain signed the armistice with Germany on June 22, 1940. The Germans had arranged the ceremony in Marshal Foch's railroad car at Compiègne to erase their own memory of defeat at the hands of the Allies in November, 1918.

The Franco-German armistice stipulated the demobilization of the French fleet under German and Italian control. Germany promised not to use the French fleet for the duration of the war or to stake any claims on it in a future peace treaty with France.

German troops were to occupy three fifths of metropolitan France, including the entire French Atlantic coast as well as Paris. France was to bear the cost of occupation. France was permitted to retain an army of 100,000 men in unoccupied France—a figure which corresponded exactly to the size of the German army as fixed in the Treaty of Versailles. France was permitted, however, to maintain an army of roughly equal size in her North African territories. French prisoners of war were to stay in Germany until the signing of a final peace. German prisoners of war and political refugees, wanted by the Nazi government, had to be turned over to Germany.

Pétain's government considered the German terms harsh but not dishonorable. Above all, the French were surprised that the German demands did not include the surrender of French air and naval bases in North and West Africa. This omission reflected Germany's continental mentality, with its emphasis on Europe and neglect of areas beyond the European coasts. Significantly, it was from French North Africa that the Western Allies, Britain and the United States, were to launch their first invasion of German-dominated Europe at a later stage of the war.

SINKING OF FRENCH VESSELS

The British government put no trust in Hitler's "solemn assurances" not to seize the French fleet. The prospect of the French fleet in German hands, carrying German invasion troops across the channel to England, was so alarming that Churchill ordered the seizure or destruction of French naval vessels. All French ships in British ports were seized, and the French squadrons at Alexandria and Mers-el-Kebir were issued an ultimatum. They were given the choice between joining Britain and being disarmed in the French West Indies, far beyond the reach of Germany. A gentleman's agreement between the French Admiral Godefroy and Admiral Cunningham led to the internment of the French ships in Alexandria. At Mers-el-Kebir, the French naval base in Algeria, Admiral Marcel Gensoul rejected the British ultimatum on July 3, 1940. The British opened fire at point-blank range and sank three French battleships.

The incident at Mers-el-Kebir added fuel to the flames of French Anglophobia, nurtured by the feeling of having been deserted by Britain. Some of Pétain's cabinet members even demanded that France declare war on Britain. Marshal Pétain and General Weygand, however, merely severed official relations with Great Britain and ordered an ineffectual air strike against the British naval base at Gibraltar in retaliation.

THE POLITICAL DEATH OF THE THIRD REPUBLIC

The political end of the French Third Republic followed closely on the heels of its military collapse. Not since the great domestic political battles between the French Left and Right in the 1880's and 1890's had the prestige of French republicanism and democracy been so low as after the defeat of 1940. The full political spectrum of the French Right, ranging from Charles Maurras, who continued to publish his *"Action Française"* throughout the war in Lyons, to the monarchists, accused the Third Republic of having been responsible for the national humiliation of 1940. Military defeat was to be turned into political virtue and a new state was to be fashioned in the image of French conservatism. On July 10, 1940, Pétain prevailed upon the National Assembly to empower him with constitution-making authority. Through four constitutional laws, adopted on July 11 and July 12, the Third Republic was abolished and Vichy France emerged, referring to the French nation no longer as "Republic" but *"Etat Française."* Pétain became the chief of state, with legislative powers, and Pierre Laval his deputy and heir apparent. The new slogan of *"Dieu, Patrie, Famille, Travail"* replaced the more familiar *"Liberté, Egalité, Fraternité,"* and Vichy France strove towards a conservative reorganization of French society along corporate lines.

By creating an authoritarian state upon the ruins of the Third Republic, Pétain not only fulfilled the political yearnings of French Conservatism of more than fifty years but hoped to make France a more acceptable member of Hitler's projected New Order.

Not all French officers shared Pétain's defeatist attitude in the summer of 1940. Charles De Gaulle, who had led French armored forces with distinction during the 43-day Battle of France and who had subsequently served as undersecretary of state for war under Reynaud, did not give up the struggle against Hitler. When Pétain surrendered, he tried to form a French government in exile to carry on the struggle from London. "The war," De Gaulle broadcast from London, "has not been ended with the Battle of France. This is a world war." The response of the French colonies to De Gaulle's call was at first disappointing. Only in Chad, the Cameroon, and French Equatorial Africa did he gain a foothold in 1940. An attack by Gaullist forces on Dakar was repulsed by French troops loyal to Vichy on September 23, 1940, as were other Gaullist assaults on Syria and Lebanon. The great majority of French colonies remained loyal to Vichy and looked upon Pétain as their leader.

THE BATTLE OF BRITAIN

Hitler had won his victory over France with surprising speed and at relatively low cost. German casualties in the Battle of France of 1940 were fewer than those suffered by Germany in the single Battle of Verdun of 1916. Before going down in defeat, France had, however, inflicted severe casualties on the German air force, with over 900 German aircraft being put out of commission between May 10 and June 22, 1940, a loss that was to play its part in the coming air battle over Britain.

As late as July, 1940, Hitler entertained hopes of achieving a negotiated peace with Britain. On July 19, 1940, he addressed a "last appeal to the reason of Britain," promising to respect the British World Empire in return for British recognition of the changed balance of power in Europe. From the vantage point of a continental power, Britain's position seemed hopeless enough in the summer of 1940. With the fall of France, Britain was isolated politically and militarily. The United States, though sympathetic, was distant and as yet unprepared to intervene in the European war. The Soviet Union was hostile and itself bent on the destruction of the pre-war European state system in partnership with Hitler. German land, air, and naval forces were in control of the Atlantic coast of Europe from Norway to the Bay of Biscay.

Britain's air and sea power, however, were still unbroken, and in Winston Churchill England had found a war-time leader of rare courage, who refused to negotiate with Hitler on moral and political grounds. At a critical juncture in Europe's and England's destiny, Churchill staked the existence of the entire Empire on the struggle to restore the European balance and uproot the Fascist dictatorships.

Hitler, to his chagrin, was thus forced to seek a military solution to his unfinished quarrel with England. As in the days of Napoleon, a major continental power without a navy to match its huge army faced once again the perplexing task of invading the British Isles. The experience of Norway, however, had demonstrated the feasibility of landing troops against superior naval odds if they were protected by superior air power and launched as a surprise.

The element of surprise was lacking in the summer of 1940, and the success of the projected German invasion of Britain, code-named "Sea-Lion," thus depended on Germany's attainment of air superiority over Britain. The Battle of Britain led to the first major clash between opposing air forces. It also injected a new element of terror by introducing indiscriminate area bombing of cities by night, turning the conflict ever more into total war, which no longer distinguished between civilians and soldiers.

At the outset of the Battle of Britain, Air Marshal Hermann Göring, who directed the German attack, was confident that German air power alone could force Britain to her knees. An invasion, if necessary at all, would only be the final blow against an exhausted and demoralized Britain. The Germans were therefore the first to apply the theory of strategic air warfare, developed between the two world wars by such men as Air Marshall Sir Hugh Trenchard—the British Chief of Air Staff after

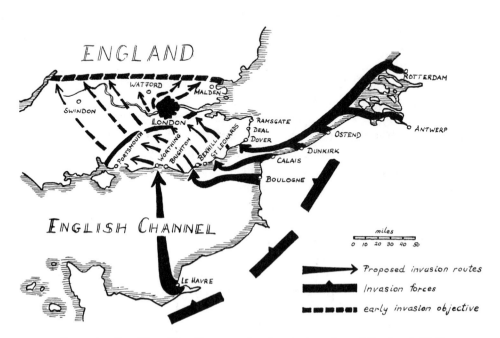

Operation Sea Lion: The German plan for the invasion of England, 1940.

World War I—J. F. C. Fuller and the Italian Giulio Douhet. These men had predicted in the 1920's that air power alone could decide the outcome of the next war if applied ruthlessly against the population centers of the enemy. "The direct attack against the moral and material resistance of the enemy," Douhet had predicted, "will hasten the end of the conflict and so will shorten the war. . . . Aerial warfare will be intensive and violent to a superlative degree, for each side will realize the necessity of inflicting upon the enemy the largest possible losses in the shortest possible time."

For the air assault against Britain, Germany had assembled three air fleets between Norway and Normandy, numbering some 1,000 fighter aircraft and 1,200 bombers. In keeping with its principal assignment, the destruction of the RAF fighter command, the German air force at first attacked British coastal shipping in an effort to draw out the RAF fighters. Not until August 13, 1940, which the Germans called "Eagle Day," was the German bomber offensive launched in earnest, however, because of the time required to replenish German aircraft losses of the Battle of France.

The RAF could muster only some 700 fighters, but it enjoyed other advantages, such as a radar warning system and efficient ground-to-air communications. The former enabled the British Fighter Command under Air Marshal Sir Hugh Dowding to detect German bombers during their approach or even at the time of their assembly over France. The latter permitted the maximum concentration of fighters at the focal point of battle. Finally, British pilots, when shot down, were often rescued in their own country, an advantage not shared by the attacking Germans.

The German bomber streams, attacking first at daytime and without adequate fighter cover, soon suffered such prohibitive losses from the eight-gun British Spitfire and Hurricane fighters that Göring was forced to switch to night attacks, beginning with August 24, 1940. By September 7, the German bombers had abandoned daylight raids on British fighter bases altogether, and concentrated on night raids on London. The German "Blitz" against London, though causing great damage to the people and city of London, was an admission of defeat. By the end of October, Britain had destroyed over 1,700 German aircraft. The German switch to night attacks had occurred just in time, however, because the British fighter bases and radar control (or Sector Stations), together with the RAF fighters, had taken a severe beating. Britain had lost nearly 700 fighters, but her aircraft production already surpassed that of Germany in the summer of 1940.

The great sacrifices of the RAF and its flying men were amply justified by the fact that Hitler had to abandon his invasion plans for September, 1940. Two German armies which had been earmarked for the invasion of Britain were soon absorbed in other theaters. The hundreds of ships and barges, assembled from as far away as the Baltic, were soon withdrawn, never to return for their intended mission.

Germany's failure to achieve air superiority over Britain or to bomb her into surrender had its principal cause in the disproportion between German aims and means. Göring proposed to achieve in seven weeks what took the combined air forces of Britain and the United States almost two years in the later stages of the Second World War: the destruction of the enemy's fighter defenses, the paralysis of his industry, and the domination of the air space over the invasion sites. The German air force, which tried to apply Douhet's doctrine of strategic air war, was not a strategic but a tactical air force. Although it had proven its worth in the support of German ground operations against Poland and France, it failed in its mission against the industries, air defenses, and supply centers of Britain. Its bombers were, by comparison with the RAF and U. S. bombers after 1943, too lightly armed, too small to carry large bomb loads, and too weakly escorted by German fighters. While Britain and, later, the United States applied the lessons of the Battle of Britain to their own bomber offensive against Germany, the German air force failed to develop a strategic bomber force for the remainder of the war.

German night attacks on London and other British cities continued throughout the winter of 1940/41 into May, 1941, when Hitler shifted 60 per cent of German air power to Eastern Europe in preparation for the assault on Russia. A German night raid on Coventry on November 14, 1940, cost the lives of 554 civilians. All in all, the Germans dropped some 67,000 tons of bombs on England during the "Blitz," killing an estimated 40,000 civilians.

Whereas the German Zeppelin raids on London in 1915 and 1916, which killed 500 civilians, had resulted in near panic, in 1940 the people of London endured the punishment from the air with grim determination. Churchill tried to retaliate during the Blitz with British night raids against German cities, including Berlin. The British Bomber Command was still too weak, however, to match the German effort, dropping only some 15,000 tons of bombs. Not for another year could Churchill make good his threat of 1941: "We shall mete out to the Germans the measure and more than the measure that they have meted out to us." By 1943 a single RAF area attack on Hamburg would claim more German civilian casualties than the entire Blitz had inflicted on the people of Britain between September, 1940, and May, 1941.

In Germany, the victory over France had been widely interpreted as the end of the war and scant attention was being paid to the bloody duel in England's skies. Now gloom followed the hasty overconfidence, as the war dragged on into the winter of 1940 and towards an uncertain future. Nor did the Nazi regime draw the proper economic conclusions from Hitler's inability to terminate the war in 1940. German armaments production continued at its leisurely pace, while Britain mobilized her war economy for an all-out effort and while Hitler contemplated extending the war to Russia.

THE AUTUMN STALEMATE OF 1940;
THE GERMAN-SOVIET CONFRONTATION
IN THE BALTIC AND THE BALKANS

Britain attempted to utilize the sudden pause which the Battle of Britain had imposed on Hitler's victories by arousing the two powerful neutrals, Russia and the United States, to the German danger. As early as June, 1940, Churchill had asked the United States to change its neutrality into a state of non-belligerency. Also, in anticipation of Italy's entry into the war, Britain had requested the use of fifty American destroyers.

The United States had ample cause to be concerned about Western hemispheric security. After the fall of France, the only European deterrent between the American Atlantic coast and the German-dominated Atlantic coast of Europe was Britain. Northwest Africa and Dakar, on the westernmost tip of Africa, were in the feeble hands of Vichy, and might soon fall under Axis domination as well.

President Roosevelt, on the occasion of his University of Virginia speech of June 10, 1940, had made the first public commitment to extend American material aid to the "opponents of force." During the Battle of Britain, the United States augmented Britain's own meagre stocks of arms and on September 3, 1940, gave Britain the requested fifty destroyers. In exchange, the United States leased British bases in the Western Hemisphere at Placentia Harbor in Newfoundland, on Bermuda, Antigua, St. Lucia, Trinidad, Georgetown, and Galleon Harbor. After the Battle of Britain, President Roosevelt was convinced of Britain's ability to hold out against the German threat if bolstered by American arms shipments. The Roosevelt administration thus persuaded Congress to adopt the Lend-Lease Act, signed into law on March 11, 1941. Lend-Lease tried, in Roosevelt's words, to "eliminate the dollar sign" from military aid. It empowered the President to 'sell, transfer title to, exchange, lease, lend or otherwise dispose of" American armaments. With an initial appropriation of $1.3 billion, the Lend-Lease Act was a powerful boost to Britain's defenses and lent substance to Roosevelt's pledge of making the United States the "arsenal of democracy."

The global repercussions of Hitler's victory over France were soon felt in Asia, adding new burdens to Britain and potential hazards to the United States. Japan, which had benefitted from the First World War by inheriting a portion of the German Pacific possessions, intended to reap even larger benefits from the paralysis of the Western democracies at the beginning of the Second World War. As Europe drifted towards war, Japan increased her pressures on Nationalist China, with whom she had been fighting intermittently since 1931. During the Munich crisis, Japan cut Hong-Kong off from China and shortly afterwards seized the island of Hainan in the Gulf of Tonkin. After the fall of Holland and France in May and June, 1940, Japan extended her sway into Southeast Asia by forcing Thailand into signing a treaty of "mutual assistance" and Vichy France into granting military bases to Japan in Indochina. The coming to power of Prince Konoye in July, 1940, bode ill for the cause of peace in Asia, Konoye being identified with the Japanese militarists.

Hitler intended to exploit the military pause following the Battle of Britain for the political consolidation of the German gains since 1939. While Britain was groping for ways to overcome her isolation, Hitler sought to increase it through the instrument of the Tripartite Pact, signed between Germany, Italy, and Japan on September 27, 1940. In its first part, the Tripartite Pact delineated the respective spheres of influence of the three signatory powers. Germany and Italy were to lead in the establishment of a New Order in Europe, Japan in the area of "Greater East Asia." In addition, all three powers pledged to assist one another with all political, economic, and military means if any one of them should be attacked by a power not presently involved in the European war or the Sino-Japanese conflict. As for Russia, the Pact stipulated that its provisions would in no way affect the relations of its members to the Soviet Union. The purpose of the Tripartite Pact was threefold: (1) to prevent a deeper American involvement in the European war, (2) to provide the framework for a European power bloc under German leadership, and (3) to open the path to stronger Nazi-Soviet collaboration.

As for the United States, Hitler feared that the Anglo-American destroyer-for-bases deal had secretly granted the United States bases in Europe, especially the Mediterranean. By including Japan in a formal alliance with Germany and Italy, the United States was to be threatened with the prospect of a Pacific war should it enter the one in Europe.

The project of a European power bloc required the consent not only of Italy, but Vichy France and Spain as well. It was towards this end that Hitler journeyed to France in October, 1940, to meet with Generalissimo Franco and Marshal Pétain. Hitler's meetings with Franco at Hendaye on October 23 and Pétain at Montoire on October 24, 1940, failed to persuade either Spain or Vichy France into joining the Tripartite Pact. The sympathies of Franco and of the Spanish foreign minister, Serrano Suñer, were decidedly on the Axis side, but Franco's political and military price went beyond Hitler's ability to pay. Spain desired French Morroco and demanded supplies of food, fuel, and armaments from Germany to offset the threatened American and British oil and grain embargo. Without German guarantees to this effect, Franco refused to authorize even a German attack on Gibraltar, for which Hitler had prepared forces for the spring of 1941.

Marshal Pétain, while still clinging to his conviction of a German victory, saw his main task in "contracting out" of the Second World War. He refused to join the Tripartite Pact, for fear that it might involve France in a war against Britain and turn France into a battlefield once more. Pierre Laval, Pétain's deputy, who was suspected by Pétain of maneuvering France into a position of war against Britain, was removed from his position on December 13, 1940, for this very reason. The most grievous blow to Hitler's political plans came from Mussolini, however, Hitler's closest European ally, as a result of Italy's independent action in the Balkans.

Mussolini had entered the Second World War in the expectation of waging a "parallel war" in the Mediterranean for Italian interests only. The absence of consultation on a military or political level between the Axis partners became a characteristic feature of the German-Italian alliance. Such "Summit meetings" between Hitler and Mussolini as took place from time to time on the Brenner pass or elsewhere, more often than not served the purpose of informing the other side of decisions already taken. Mussolini was also jealous and fearful of German power, especially when it began to encroach upon his own sphere of influence. By October, 1940, however, Germany had begun a troop build-up in the Balkans, for reasons to be presently discussed. It was partly to prevent the establishment of German power in the Balkans that Mussolini attacked Greece on October 28, 1940, from Albania without informing Hitler in advance. The Italian invasion of Greece, so lightly undertaken, threatened to become a source of great embarrassment to the Axis. Greece, although fighting unaided, not only repulsed the Italian invasion, but threatened to invade Albania as well. Mussolini was forced into a much larger military build-up than anticipated, for which the Albanian ports of Valona and Durazzo were ill-equipped.

The Italian-Greek war was harmful to the Axis cause for two reasons. First, it enabled Britain to secure a foothold on the European continent again, after Greece asked for British support. Churchill took immediate advantage of the Greek request for British aid and installed naval, ground, and air forces on the island of Crete, beginning on October 29, 1940. He wished to turn Crete into a "Scapa-Flow of the Mediterranean," from which British aircraft could strike against the Rumanian oil fields at Ploesti or the south of Italy. Second, it compelled Hitler to make preparations for a German military intervention in Greece as a result of the Italian debacle. Since the Italian defeat in Greece was soon followed by major Italian defeats in North Africa and in the Mediterranean at the hands of British ground and naval forces, Axis prestige suffered a serious blow towards the end of 1940. More important, the German political and military preparations in the Balkans for an attack on Greece aroused the suspicion and ill will of the Soviet Union, which Hitler also tried to include in the Tripartite Pact.

Before discussing the German-Soviet confrontation of December, 1940, it will be necessary to review the course of German-Soviet relations in the months before December, 1940.

Between the signing of the Stalin-Hitler Pact of August, 1939, and December, 1940, the climate of Soviet-German relations had taken a decided turn for the worse. Up to June, 1940, the terms of the Moscow pact had been mutually profitable. Russia had supplied Hitler with substantial shipments of grain, oil, phosphates, ore and numerous other strategic materials in exchange for German armaments and industrial equipment. Russia had rendered Nazi Germany political support by denouncing the British blockade, supporting Hitler's peace offer of October, 1939, and denouncing the Western Powers for waging an "imperialist" war. In September, 1939, Molotov had hailed the Stalin-Hitler Pact as the result of Stalin's "historic foresight."

Hitler had reciprocated by denying Finland any German diplomatic or military support during the Russo-Finnish war. The German invasion of Denmark and Norway also suited Stalin's aims, since it had minimized the danger of a Western intervention on behalf of Finland. The German-Soviet honeymoon cooled off perceptibly, however, with the German conquest of France.

Fearing both the sudden surge of German power and the possibility of a negotiated peace in the west, Stalin hastily collected the remaining prize from his 1939 agreement with Hitler. On the pretext that the Baltic states had secretly conspired against Russia, the Soviets occupied Latvia, Lithuania, and Estonia and incorporated them into the USSR by August 1, 1940. On June 23, 1940, the day after the signing of the German-French armistice at Compiègne, Russia demanded the surrender of Bessarabia from Rumania. Both in the Baltic and in Rumania, Stalin's annexations went beyond the Moscow pact of 1939. In Lithuania, the Suwalki district, an agreed German sphere of influence, was seized; in Rumania, the Northern Bukovina was annexed, in addition to Bessarabia.

Although Hitler had surrendered Finland and the Baltic states to the Russian sphere of influence and declared Germany's political disinterest in the Balkans in 1939, he had meanwhile acquired important stakes in both the Baltic and the Balkans. From Finland the German war economy received its nickel, and a troop transit agrement had been signed between Finland and Germany in September, 1940, to facilitate German troop transports to Norway. Rumania was Germany's principal supplier of oil next to the Soviet Union. Bulgaria had become vital to Hitler as a springboard for the invasion of Greece, projected for early 1941.

The Moscow pact of 1939 had also stipulated that Germany and Russia were to consult on matters of mutual concern. This pledge was ignored by both, however, in the course of the brief Balkan crisis from August to September, 1940, involving Rumania, Hungary, and Bulgaria, which nearly led to war between the three Balkan states. At issue were the revisionist demands of Hungary and Bulgaria, which pressured Rumania to return the territories acquired under the peace treaties of Trianon and Neuilly. Specifically, Hungary demanded the return of Transylvania, Bulgaria the restoration of the southern Dobruja. While Russia encouraged the Hungarian-Bulgarian demands, Germany and Italy settled the dispute through their diplomatic intervention. The Vienna Award of August 30, 1940, compelled Rumania to surrender northern Transylvania. The Treaty of Craiova of September 7, 1940, ceded the southern Dobruja to Bulgaria. The territory of rump Rumania, however, was guaranteed jointly by Germany and Italy, and Hitler sent German troops to protect the Rumanian oil fields at Ploesti in the guise of "military advisers." Stalin promptly ignored the German-Italian guarantee by occupying a number of Rumanian islands in the Black Sea delta of the Danube, in November, 1940. Furthermore, Bulgaria was urged to sign a treaty of mutual assistance with the Soviet Union.

In spite of these developments, Hitler had asked Soviet Foreign Minister Molotov to Berlin on November 12, 1940, to discuss the possibility of Russia's entry into the Tripartite Pact. The German hosts made a strong effort to convince Molotov that the war was as good as won by Germany, a contention belied by the fact that the RAF attacked Berlin during Molotov's stay. Hitler and Ribbentrop offered to Russia generous portions of the British Empire which they did not, in fact, control. Germany, Hitler said, was in the process of defeating the forty-five million people of Great Britain who had ruled an Empire of over six hundred million. Alluding to the U. S. lease of British bases, Hitler claimed that the United States had already begun to reserve for itself certain choice possessions of the British Empire in the Western Hemisphere. Russia's reward would lie in an expansion to the south, in the direction of the Persian Gulf. It was vital, Hitler told Molotov, that the Four Great Powers, Russia, Japan, Italy, and Germany, should set aside all their differences in order to exploit fully the opportunities offered by the dismemberment of the British Empire, a task which would keep them occupied for the coming fifty or one hundred years.

The Russians did not reject these vague promises, but they returned persistently to the concrete issues concerning Finland, the Balkans, and the Dardanelles. The Soviet reply of November 25, 1940, spelled out the Russian price for membership: German troops would be withdrawn forthwith from Finland; Russia and Bulgaria would sign a treaty of mutual assistance; Russia would obtain air and naval bases near the Dardanelles.

Russia's sphere of influence was to lie south of Baku and Batum in the general direction of the Persian Gulf, and Japan was to relinquish her coal and oil concessions in Northern Sakhalin. Turkey was to join the proposed Four Power Pact and be forced to do so by Russia, Germany, and Italy in the event of her refusal. Lastly, the Soviet government revealed its interest in the Jutland Straits, the Baltic exit into the North Sea, and proposed to discuss their future status.

The issue was joined. Hitler had wanted to buy off Russia with vague promises of future gains in Asia at the expense of a still undefeated Britain. Russia, by contrast, demanded greater power in European areas of long-standing Russian interest. Stalin's imperialism followed the tracks of Peter's and Catherine's, in order to bolster Russian defenses against the west—against Britain, for the moment, or Germany, should Hitler be tempted to move eastward in the future. In their confrontation over the Balkans, Stalin and Hitler found themselves the heirs of the bitter rivalries between three empires of days past: Austria-Hungary, Tsarist Russia, and Imperial Germany. Just as these rivalries had contributed to the coming of war in 1914, they played an important part in bringing about a rupture in German-Russian relations of 1941. Russia's insistence on concluding a pact of mutual assistance with Bulgaria, and Russia's repeated contention that Bulgaria was within her own "security zone" ran counter to Hitler's decision to use Bulgaria as the springboard for his attack on Greece.

In a larger sense, Stalin's sweeping demands and their fearless presentation by the pedantic Molotov confirmed Hitler's suspicion that Russia would not hesitate to make the most of German weakness in the east while the war against England was still undecided. The idea of destroying Soviet Russia by military force had occurred to Hitler as early as July, 1940, after Stalin's swift move into Latvia, Lithuania, and Estonia. Now it took concrete form when Hitler issued his directive of December 18, 1940, code-named "Barbarossa," for the invasion of the Soviet Union in the spring of 1941. Rather than seek a compromise through negotiations with Stalin, to escape the deadlock of December, 1940, emotion swayed the political decision of the Fuehrer. Resentment over Russia's imperialism now merged with Hitler's old enmity towards Russian Communism into a powerful stream of hate that no amount of warning could deflect from its fateful course.

The original purpose of Hitler's plan, as conceived in September, 1940, had been the isolation of Britain through a Europe united under German hegemony. The decision to attack Russia added a new foe of vast military potential before Britain was defeated in the west. Hitler had broken his own often-repeated maxim of not waging war on two fronts simultaneously. His own initiative now paved the way for the Grand Alliance and Nazi Germany's ultimate defeat.

Since Hitler had left his Japanese ally in the dark about the impending German invasion of Russia, Japan concluded a treaty of neutrality with the Soviet Union on April 13, 1941, without forewarning Hitler and in preparation of Japan's challenge to the United States in the Pacific. The Russo-Japanese agreement remained in effect throughout the war in Europe. Its existence was to have a significant effect on German military operations in Russia in 1941 and 1942.

THE STRUGGLE FOR THE MEDITERRANEAN: THE FIRST PHASE

While Hitler's project of a grand alliance was crumbling in the autumn months of 1940, the Mediterranean emerged as a major theater of war. After the Battle of France, Britain had been relieved of the necessity of maintaining large ground forces on the European continent and, having rescued her Expeditionary force at Dunkirk, did not view the fall of France as an unmitigated disaster for that reason. Britain was thus able to pay greater attention to the Mediterranean, where her stakes were high. In the Mediterranean, Britain could bring to bear her superior naval power against the Axis to maximum advantage. Since Churchill did not have to face the concentrated might of Hitler's armies in the Mediterranean, as in the brief and violent encounter of France, Britain could wage a peripheral campaign, for which she was best suited by national tradition and inclination.

The Mediterranean war is best remembered for its great armored battles in the deserts of Libya and western Egypt. Although these battles were to settle the issues in the last resort, the desert wastes of North Africa were not, in themselves, the major point at issue. Britain's interests rather ranged the whole length of the inland sea. Through the Mediterranean ran Britain's chief line of communication to India, Singapore, Malaya, and Australia. The oil fields and refineries of Iraq and Iran fuelled Britain's fleet. Egypt guarded the Mediterranean and Red Sea approaches to the Suez Canal.

At the outset, Britain's military and political hold on the theater was precarious enough. The withdrawal of France from the war forced Britain to patrol both ends of the Mediterranean with her navy. Algeria, Morocco, Tunisia in northwest Africa, and Syria at the eastern end of the Mediterranean had all remained loyal to Vichy, as had Dakar on the west coast of Africa and the island of Madagascar off southeast Africa. Gibraltar was safe from attack as long as Franco refused permission for the launching of a German invasion. Portugal, though neutral, had secretly coordinated her defenses with Britain since December, 1940, and agreed to joint action should Hitler invade the peninsula. Turkey's status as a non-belligerent, declared after the Italian entry into World War II, helped protect the British position in Iraq, as long as Hitler did not choose to march his armies directly over Turkish territory into the Middle East.

Britain's greatest assets were Italy's military unpreparedness and her confused strategy. The Italian naval command *(Supermarina)* possessed what appeared to be an imposing fleet, including six battleships and numerous cruisers. Italian naval effectiveness was seriously hampered, however, by the shortage of fuel, the lack of radar, and the absence of aircraft carriers. The Italian army in North Africa was lacking in motor transport and up-to-date tanks, a deficiency particularly serious in a theater where mobility and armor were of prime importance. Italian artillery pieces were often of World War I vintage, unable to harm British tanks.

Although inadequately armed, Mussolini pursued an ambitious strategy. Rather than seize the island of Malta and invade Egypt during the summer of 1940, when Britain was straining every effort against the German aerial assault, Mussolini dispatched Italian bombers to the Atlantic coast of France, where they participated in the German air offensive against London. Not until September, 1940, did Marshall Graziani invade Egypt from Libya with an army of over 300,000 men but few trucks to transport them. After the Italian capture of Sidi Barrani on September 18, 1940, Graziani halted to await the arrival of supplies. Although the Italian advance into Egypt had been inconclusive, Mussolini embarked on the invasion of Greece in October, 1940, and thereby scattered his forces still further. Of Mussolini, it was said that he would have dispatched Italian troops to the Pacific as well had the Japanese asked for them.

The British Commander-in-Chief Middle East, General Sir Archibald Wavell, had meanwhile assembled forces for a counterstroke. On December 9, 1940, the "lean, bronzed, desert-hardened and completely mechanized British force," as Churchill proudly called it, attacked and drove the Italians swiftly out of Egypt. Advancing into Libya, the British captured one Italian stronghold after another. Tobruk fell on January 22, 1941, Benghazi on February 7. By February 8, the British had reached the border of Tripolitania. At the end of its advance, the British desert army of about 25,000 men had captured 113,000 prisoners and 700 guns. In their spectacular victory in the desert, the British were materially aided by their mobility, naval support, and superior logistics, for British reinforcements and supplies could be carried by rail as far west as Mersa Matruh.

The desert victory was cheerful news to Britain at a time when German bombs were falling almost nightly on the British capital. "Our armies," thundered Churchill on December 23, 1940, "are tearing, and will tear the African army to shreds and tatters. . . ."

While Mussolini stood in danger of being expelled from North Africa altogether, his East African Empire was being overrun between

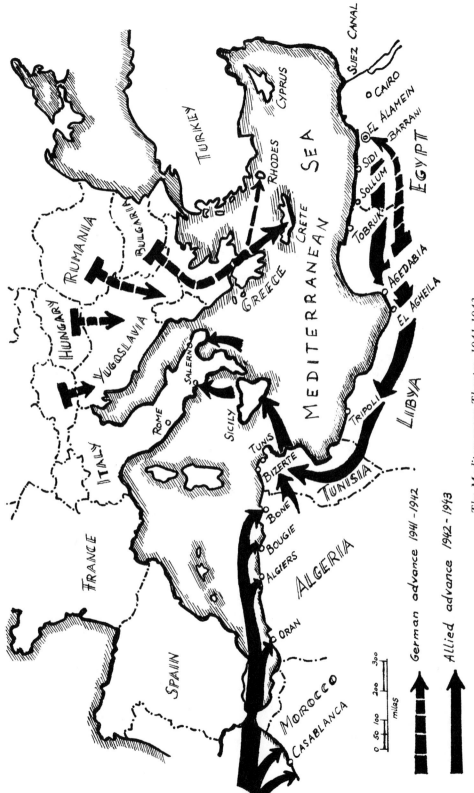

The Mediterranean Theater, 1941-1943.

SUEZ CANAL

CAIRO
EL ÁLAMEIN
BARRANI
SIDI
SOLLUM
TOBRUK
AGEDABIA
EL AGHEILA
TRIPOLI

EGYPT
LIBYA

MEDITERRANEAN SEA

CYPRUS
RHODES
CRETE
GREECE

TURKEY

BULGARIA
RUMANIA
HUNGARY
YUGOSLAVIA
ITALY
ROME
SALERNO
SICILY
TUNIS
BIZERTE
TUNISIA
BONE
BOUGIE
ALGIERS
ALGERIA
ORAN

FRANCE
SPAIN
MOROCCO
CASABLANCA

German advance 1941 - 1942

Allied advance 1942 - 1943

miles
0 50 100   200   300

January and May, 1941. In order to eliminate the Italian threat to the Gulf of Aden and the Red Sea, Britain occupied Eritrea and its principal sea port of Massawa in January, 1941. Ethiopia, attacked from British bases in Aden and Kenya, was under British control by May, 1941, following the surrender of the Duke of Aosta's forces.

The Italian defeats in Africa were accompanied by equally serious naval reverses in the Mediterranean. British torpedo aircraft, striking at the Italian naval base of Taranto on November 11, 1940, from the aircraft carrier *Illustrious* put half the Italian battle fleet out of commission. In the naval engagement at Cape Matapan, off the Greek coast, on March 29, 1941, Britain scored another naval victory, which increased the caution of the Italian fleet and facilitated the British landings in Greece.

THE BALKAN INTERLUDE

Within a short time after Britain's desert triumph of early 1941, several new developments altered the balance in the Mediterranean, so favorable to Great Britain up to that time. The principal factors responsible were, first, the German invasion of the Balkans and, with it, the appearance of superior German air power in the eastern Mediterranean in April and May, 1941. Secondly, the Germans sent an expeditionary force, the Afrika Korps, to Tripolitania in February, 1941, and, thirdly, British reverses in the Balkans produced a serious political crisis in the Middle East that threatened to evict Britain from Iraq.

In anticipation of the German attack on Greece in April, 1941, Great Britain had attempted to arraign as many Balkan states as possible against Germany. However, the mission of Foreign Secretary Anthony Eden and the Chief of the British Imperial General Staff, General Sir John G. Dill, undertaken for this purpose in early 1941, failed to win Turkey and Yugoslavia over to the side of Greece. In the diplomatic contest in the Balkans, Germany was the stronger by virtue of her proximity and her ability to exploit the rivalries of the Balkan nations. Germany used the Tripartite Pact to isolate Greece politically and militarily. Between November, 1940, and March, 1941, Hungary, Rumania, Slovakia, Bulgaria, and Yugoslovia had joined the Tripartite Pact. A coup d'état of March 27, 1941, by General Simovic ousted the Yugoslav government which had joined the Tripartite Pact, but it came too late to be of help to Greece. The new Yugoslav government of the 17-year-old Peter II, although not withdrawing from the Tripartite Pact, signed a treaty of friendship and non-aggression with Soviet Russia on April 5, 1941. Hitler responded by including Yugoslavia in his military attack on Greece, which was launched on April 6, 1941. By April 17, Yugoslav resistance had broken under the German attack launched from Austria, Hungary, and Bulgaria.

The collapse of Yugoslavia rendered the position of Greece hopeless also. General Papagos, the Greek chief of staff, had hoped to coordinate his forces with those of Yugoslavia to defeat the Italian army in Albania. The strongly fortified Metaxas Line, along the Greek-Bulgarian frontier, it was hoped, would check a German invasion from Bulgaria. Although Britain had committed some 57,000 troops to the defense of Greece, Greek resistance collapsed speedily. Within a few days after the opening of the German attack, the Metaxas Line was broken; Salonika was captured on April 9, and the East Macedonian army cut off. The second German blow of April 10, 1941, was aimed at the central Macedonian army and the British, and forced the Greeks to disengage from the Albanian front. Athens fell on April 27. Once more, as at Dunkirk in 1940, Britain had to evacuate an army from the European continent. This time the evacuation was rendered more difficult by the fact that the Germans controlled, not only all major Greek ports, but the air space over the open beaches as well. Still, the Royal Navy, supported loyally by Greek vessels, managed to rescue 47,000 troops, part of whom were used to bolster the defenses of Crete.

After their victory in Greece, the Germans quickly seized the strategic islands controlling the approaches to the Dardanelles and prepared for the assault of Crete.

BATTLE FOR CRETE

The Battle for Crete brought to a climax the Balkan campaign and caused a serious crisis for Britain, for it coincided with a number of other battles which taxed British forces to the limit. While Britain defended Crete in May, 1941, the Axis had launched a new thrust towards Egypt, a political revolt erupted in Syria, and British troops were needed in Ethiopia to overcome Italian resistance. British naval power, finally, was forced to muster all its strength in hunting down the German battleship *Bismarck* and her escort, the battle cruiser *Prinz Eugen,* which had broken out in the Atlantic in May, 1941, and posed a serious threat to British convoys.

Crete, the largest of the Aegean Islands and only 350 miles from Alexandria, was of prime importance to Great Britain as an air and naval base. Because of its strategic location, Britain had contemplated its occupation as early as May, 1940, a plan abandoned after the collapse of France. By May, 1941, the garrisons of Crete, under command of General Bernard Freyberg, had grown to 42,000. Freyberg knew that the German assault would come from the air since Germany had no naval forces of her own with which to protect a seaborne invasion and the Italian navy was reluctant to risk battle. In the Battle of Crete, Germany had command of the air, Britain of the sea. On May 20, 1941, 500 German transport aircraft set ashore thousands of airborne troops. In spite of their severe casualties, the German paratroops succeeded in capturing the air bases at Maleme,

Heraklion, and Retikon. Admiral Sir Andrew Cunningham's efforts to aid in the defense of Crete proved costly and, in the end, futile in the face of German air supremacy. The loss of six British destroyers and three cruisers during the Battle of Crete demonstrated the vulnerability of naval vessels to aerial attack, an experience to be confirmed seven months later by the sinking of the *Prince of Wales* and *Repulse* by Japanese aircraft. By the end of May, Britain could send neither naval nor air reinforcements to Crete, because of the demands which the breakout of the *Bismarck* and the Iraqi revolt made on British naval and air strength. By June 1, 1941, Britain had withdrawn from Crete, having rescued again some 17,000 troops. German casualties among paratroopers were so severe—some 6,500 out of a force of 22,000—that Hitler forbade further German airborne operations, including those planned against Malta.

IRAQI REVOLT

Shortly before the German invasion of Crete, Iraq's Prime Minister Rashid Ali el Gailani launched an anti-British revolt that threatened to deliver Iraq's oil and the strategic port of Basra on the Persian Gulf into Axis hands. Britain quelled the uprising, whose full significance Hitler apparently did not realize, by swift and improvised action. The stubborn British defense of the Iraqi airbase of Habbaniya and the rushing of troops from India to Basra led to the Arab defeat by the end of May, 1941. In response to Rashid Ali's appeal for German help, Hitler had dispatched a few airplanes which operated from Syria with the permission of the Pétain government. Beyond this, Hitler was not prepared to go, since he was anxious to concentrate all German forces for the impending attack on Russia, which opened on June 22, 1941.

Hitler's fixation with "Operation Barbarossa" blinded him to the opportunities which the German conquest of the Balkans and the island of Crete had opened up to him in the Middle East. In 1941 he might have seized the oil of Iraq at a price considerably smaller than his armies had to pay in their futile drive towards the Russian oil fields in the Caucasus in 1942. Thus, Hitler's decision to attack Russia not merely relieved Britain from the burden of the German air attack on London but enabled Britain to restore her shaky position in the Middle East and build her defenses in Egypt against the threat of an Axis invasion from Libya. Not only was Britain left free to deal with the pro-Nazi revolt of Rashid Ali, but she was able also to conquer Vichy-controlled Syria in a joint operation with Gaullist forces. By July 12, 1941, the Vichy forces under General Dentz capitulated to the Gaullist-British troops which had invaded Syria from Palestine.

The Axis threat to Egypt was not eliminated until November, 1941, however. In February, 1941, a small German expeditionary force under the command of General Erwin Rommel had landed in Tripolitania. In Rommel, the Italian High Command had acquired a resourceful general who combined the art of military bluff with a sound appreciation of the requirements of desert warfare. From the beginning of his African command, Rommel aimed not merely at the reconquest of Libya, which Wavell had overrun towards the end of 1940, but at the conquest of Egypt and a breakthrough into the Middle East. Rommel's boldness baffled his foes as much as it did his superiors. Having deceived Wavell about his real strength through the ample use of dummy tanks, mounted on *Volkswagen* chassis, he expanded a limited drive towards El Agheila at the end of March, 1941, into a full-scale offensive for the reconquest of Libya. After the capture of Benghazi on April 3, 1941, the Italian and German forces crossed into Egypt and took the strategic Sollum and Halfaya passes. The port of Tobruk, with its strong defenses and large supply stores, was by-passed after Rommel failed to take it by storm. Its successful defense by Britain throughout 1941 was a major cause of Rommel's eventual setback in November, 1941, for it denied the Axis a badly needed sea port and remained a thorn in its flank. Rommel's offensive had caught Wavell by surprise, and he was unable to dislodge the Axis from its newly gained stronghold in western Egypt. General J. C. Auchinleck, who had gained distinction by his swift move into Basra during the Iraqi revolt of April and May, 1941, succeeded Wavell as British Commander-in-Chief Middle East in the fall of 1941. Auchinleck counterattacked in November, 1941, with the aim of lifting the seige of Tobruk and expelling Rommel from Egypt. As during Wavell's offensive of December, 1940, Auchinleck enjoyed the advantage of superior logistics, his supplies arriving by rail, Rommel's over roads that stretched three hundred miles to Benghazi and over a thousand miles to Tripoli. The climax to Auchinleck's westward offensive came with the tank battle at Sidi Rezegh on November 23, 1941, which was turned into a British victory through Auchinleck's personal intervention. General Ritchie, having suffered heavy tank losses, wished to withdraw the British 8th Army back to Egypt and faced disaster when Rommel followed up his initial victory with a dash for the 8th Army's supply bases in the desert. The German search missed its mark, and the 8th Army rallied under Auchinleck's firm hand. After lifting the German siege of Tobruk, Auchinleck captured the Axis garrison at the Halfaya pass and forced Rommel to abandon Libya once more. Following his maxim that saving an army was more important than holding ground, Rommel retreated to Tripolitania. The campaign in Africa ended with a draw at the turn of 1941-42, neither side having accomplished its aim: the Axis had failed to conquer Egypt; the British had been unable to trap and destroy the Afrika-Korps. Rommel was granted another respite, during which he prepared the launching of another invasion of Egypt.

THE GERMAN ATTACK ON THE SOVIET UNION: THE BATTLE OF RUSSIA, JUNE TO DECEMBER, 1941

The conclusion of the Soviet-Yugoslav friendship treaty of April, 1941, and the subsequent overrunning of the Balkans by Germany had brought Soviet-German tensions to a new high point. Numerous warnings began to reach the Kremlin, both from well-meaning Western sources and Soviet intelligence, that Hitler was about to attack Russia. Stalin, it is true, had taken certain precautions against such an eventuality. His troops were massed from the Baltic to the Black Sea, and on May 6, 1941, he took the unprecedented step of combining his office of Secretary General of the Party with the post of Chairman of the Council of People's Commissars, previously held by Molotov.

Apparently Stalin paid no heed to warnings of a German invasion; rather, it seems that he expected Hitler to make new demands on the Soviet Union after the Balkans had passed under German control. No longer did Stalin persist in his own demands of November, 1940. Instead, he tried to break the ominous silence of Berlin through a policy of good will and even appeasement. Russian deliveries under current Soviet-German trade agreements were made promptly and an expansion of Soviet-German trade proposed. Russia expelled the diplomatic representatives of those countries which Hitler had overrun, and extended diplomatic recognition to the pro-Nazi government of Rashid Ali in Iraq. To break the persistent silence, the Soviet news agency Tass finally issued a communiqué which denounced all rumors concerning an imminent German-Russian conflict as "inventions" and "false and preposterous provocation" by the enemies of both countries. In Moscow, Molotov asked the German ambassador for the opportunity of another meeting with Hitler, to learn the causes of Germany's apparent "dissatisfaction." Russian consternation and disbelief following the German attack in the early morning hours of June 22, 1941, thus seems to have been genuine and helps explain the absence of firm direction of the Soviet defenses in the first days of the German-Soviet war.

German Aims; The Military Balance

At the beginning of the invasion of Russia, Hitler called his attack a "Crusade against Russian Communism," undertaken for the protection of European civilization. Nazi propaganda also alleged that the German invasion had come just in time to forestall a Russian attack on Central Europe.

Hitler's attack was neither an ordinary preventive war nor a crusade. Far from aiming at the liberation of the peoples of Russia from

Stalinist dictatorship, Hitler plotted their colonization by Germany. Russia, said Hitler, will be "Germany's India," and it was in Russia that the aims and practices of the Nazi regime were to reach their most bizarre and brutal expression. Hitler's own desire for the colonization of the Slavic East, as expressed in "Mein Kampf," now merged with earlier German colonizing schemes as practiced by Ludendorff after the Treaty of Brest-Litovsk. The German "Eastern Ministry" under Alfred Rosenberg, the leading Nazi ideologue, was to prepare the political dismemberment of Russia after her defeat, as well as the settlement of millions of German colonists. Hitler dreamed of a German Empire from the Volga to the Rhine which would eliminate the threat of Moscow once and for all. The face of Muscovy, in Rosenberg's words, was to be turned forever eastward, towards Asia.

The grandiose schemes of Nazi colonization were reflected also in Hitler's orders for the conduct of the war in Russia. Hitler made a conscious distinction between the war in the west, where rules of civilized warfare had been generally observed, and the east. On June 6, 1941, he issued his "Commissar Order," which denied captured political commissars of the Red Army the status of prisoners and ordered their execution by the German army. From the beginning, Hitler counted on a total and swift victory over the Soviet Union and hence made no effort to appeal to anti-Communist sentiment, latent especially among the Ukrainian people, nor did he take advantage of the friction between the Great Russians and the Non-Russian nationalities of the Soviet Empire.

Hitler's method of waging war greatly facilitated Stalin's endeavor to portray Soviet resistance as a patriotic effort against a brutal foreign invader, bent on the enslavement of all Russians. Stalin's successful appeal to patriotism contributed materially to Russia's survival when the outcome of the military campaigns hung in the balance.

GERMAN UNDERESTIMATION OF RUSSIAN STRENGTH

The military power of the Soviet Union was the great enigma of 1941, for Russia had shielded her military secrets from foreign scrutiny more than any other Great Power. Moreover, such evidence of Soviet military capabilities as was available was contradictory. Finland's brilliant defense during the Russo-Finnish war of 1939/40 had created the impression that the Red Army was a clumsy giant under timid leadership. In the undeclared war against Japan in Manchuria in 1938 and 1939, however, the Soviet Union had bested the Japanese army in many battles. Soviet military aid to the Republicans during the Spanish Civil War had revealed the high quality of Soviet tanks and military aircraft.

Hitler himself seems to have felt a certain uneasiness about his military venture against Russia, for he called it the "most difficult decision of his life." German army leaders, however, based their judgment on the

Russian performance in the Finnish war and hoped that Stalin's blood purge of 1938/39 had deprived the Soviet Union of the most capable military leaders, including the former Russian Chief of Staff, Tukhashevsky. Above all, the Great Purge seemed to indicate the general weakness of the Soviet system, and Hitler hoped that Stalin's empire would collapse like a house of cards, once "the door was forcefully kicked in."

THE GERMAN ADVANCE AND SOVIET RECOVERY

Hitler invaded Russia with an army not much larger than the one he had used against France in 1940, although German strength was

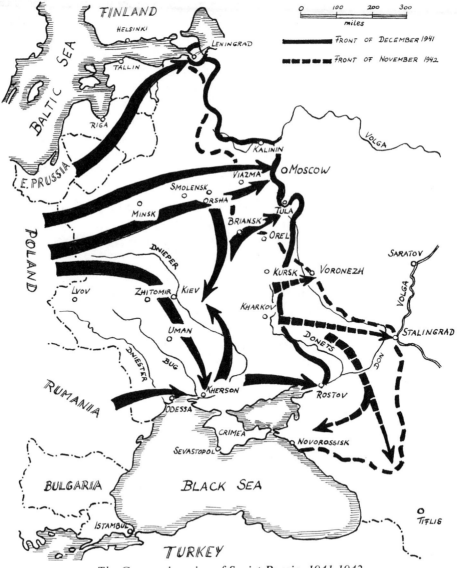

The German invasion of Soviet Russia, 1941-1942.

augmented by Finnish, Slovak, Hungarian, and Rumanian forces, whose governments joined in the attack. The military occupation of Western Europe and the demands of the North African campaign prohibited the formation of a major German strategic reserve to meet any unforeseen crisis in the Russian campaign. Nor did Hitler make provisions for a winter campaign, should Soviet resistance endure beyond the autumn months of 1941. On the German side, no margin was left for error, none for weather, or the exhaustion that might befall the invader.

According to Hitler's directive, the three German Army Groups, under the command of Leeb in the north, von Bock in the center, and Rundstedt in the south, were to annihilate the bulk of the Russian army in battles in western Russia before the start of winter and before it could retreat and make another stand in the vast spaces of the interior. The spearheads of the attack were to reach Kiev in the south and Smolensk in the center, and join with Finland's army in the north after the conquest of Leningrad. Following the expected defeat of the Red Army, a relatively small German force of sixty divisions was to occupy the line of the Urals and German air power would deal with remaining pockets of Soviet resistance in Asiatic Russia.

The clash between the three German Army Groups and the three Russian fronts opposing them, under Voroshilov, Timoshenko, and Budyenny, led to battles as varied as were the underlying causes of Russia's military strength and weakness. Soviet resistance alternated between determination such as Hitler's armies had encountered in no other theater of war and the surrender or desertion of whole units. Most important, however, the German strategy of encirclement by swiftly moving armored divisions, which had worked smoothly on the well paved roads of France, did not always succeed in Russia with its poor and muddy roads. Still, by August, 1941, the Germans had inflicted casualties on the Red Army that were more severe than any Western army could have withstood without a general collapse. Such battles of encirclement as the Germans were able to complete, at Byelostok, Minsk, Smolensk, and Uman, cost the Russians the staggering loss of some 700,000 prisoners and thousands of tanks. German successes had been greatest in the center, where the road to Moscow seemed open after the battle of Smolensk, but Leningrad and Kiev were still in Russian hands. Also, the German victories had been bought at a heavy price to the invaders. By August, 1941, the German sword had cut deeply into Russia but its point was blunted with the loss of a full third of German armored strength. No longer able to pour forth in all directions simultaneously, the Germans had to choose among objectives. The German army commanders favored Moscow, for both psychological and military reasons. The fall of Moscow would dim the fighting spirit of the remaining Soviet forces and deprive them of their chief communications and armaments center. On August 20, 1941, Hitler decreed otherwise. While holding back the German central front, where the Soviets had suffered their greatest defeats thus far, he ordered the capture of Leningrad in the north and of the Ukraine in the south. By seizing the Ukraine with its great mineral and agricultural riches, Hitler hoped to strangle the Soviet economy and thus hasten Russia's military collapse.

The Battle for the Ukraine resulted once more in great Russian losses and seemed to bear out Hitler's predictions of an early Russian collapse. In the battle of Kiev, the Ukrainian capital, over 600,000 Russian prisoners were taken in late September and Budyenny was forced into retreat. Rostov, the gate to the Caucasus, fell shortly thereafter. The magnitude of the Soviet defeat in the Ukraine prompted Hitler to change his strategy once more and order the attack on Moscow, which began on October 2, 1941.

The German drive on Moscow, code-named "Typhoon," shattered the better part of six Russian armies which became trapped in the battles of Vyazma and Bryansk during the early part of October. "I say this today," Hitler boasted on October 2, 1941, "because for the first time I am entitled to say it: the enemy is already broken and will never be in a position to rise again." On October 9 the chief of the German press office announced to the world that the war in Russia was over and that organized Soviet resistance had ceased.

Moscow's situation seemed hopeless enough, but the German victory celebration was premature. In mid-October Moscow gave many signs of panic. Most government agencies had departed for Kuibyshev in the Volga, and looting broke out among the civilian population. Members of the Communist Party were observed destroying their membership cards. Only Stalin seemed to keep his nerve, staying on in the Kremlin and awaiting his opponent's wrong move as the pincers of fifty German divisions were closing in on Moscow.

By October, 1941, the Soviet Union had lost more than half of its coal, steel, and iron industries, more than a third of its grain-producing areas, and nearly half of its railroads. Four million Russian officers and men had been captured since the beginning of the German invasion, and there was no immediate outside help in sight. Yet Russia survived and Moscow remained beyond Hitler's reach as a result of one of the most remarkable military recoveries in history.

The recovery was due, in part, to the exhausted state of the German army in Russia. By December, 1941, German casualties had risen to over 760,000 men, or 24 per cent of the German strength, and German armored divisions were down to one third of their initial complement. Nearly three thousand German aircraft were destroyed during the ten-month period after June 22, 1941. Hitler had no reserves left and the Quarter Master General of the German Army confessed by the end of November: "We have come to the end of our resources in men and material."

Stalin, on the other hand, was able to commit twenty-one fresh Siberian divisions to the Battle of Moscow, since the Soviet-Japanese neutrality agreement of April, 1941 freed him from the danger of a two-front war.

A further significant factor was the weather. The German operation "Typhoon" was first slowed down by the mud of October and November and then frozen into immobility by the sudden onset of winter, with temperatures falling to forty degrees below zero. The German mood of overconfidence changed as swiftly as the weather into one of despair and haunting visions of another Napoleonic rout or another Battle of the Marne. Lack of foresight and underestimation of the enemy had left the German army without protection against the rigors of the Russian winter. With disbelief, Soviet troops viewed the bodies of the German infantry, their feet frozen to tightly fitting boots. For all its mechanized equipment, the German army in Russia had remained ignorant of what every Russian child knew: the best and cheapest way of keeping one's feet from freezing was to wear loose boots, stuffed with newspaper.

Operation "Typhoon" had turned into a Russian blizzard. Russia's winter had come to her rescue, casting a chilling blanket over Hitler's proud divisions and scattering his armor over the frozen steppes like so many broken toys.

THE SOVIET COUNTERSTRIKE

The breakdown of the German attack on Moscow was the signal for a Soviet counterattack, launched on December 6, 1941. The Soviet winter offensive set out with the ambitious goal of shattering the German central and northern fronts, facing Moscow and Leningrad. In the south, a Russian counterattack had retaken Rostov as early as November. In the center, the Red Army came within the vicinity of Smolensk, whence the German drive on Moscow had begun. In the north, at Kholm and Demyansk, in a Russian battle of encirclement, over one-hundred thousand German troops were trapped. In a sense, Stalin repeated Hitler's mistake, however, of underestimating his opponent's remaining strength. The German forces trapped at Kholm and Demyansk, supplied from the air, held out until relieved in the spring of 1942. Hitler applied a strategy of no retreat, regardless of the consequences, for fear that a retreat would deliver the German army to the same fate that had befallen Napoleon's Grande Armeé in 1812. The Soviet winter offensive thus failed to annihilate the invaders, and its overall results merely confirmed the defensive victory of Moscow.

Hitler's prestige had suffered a severe blow, however, both among his own troops and in the world. As the Battle of Britain had revealed the limitations of German air power in 1940, the Battle of Moscow indicated the limits of German strength on land. Above all, it pointed out the inadequacies of German armaments production, which had failed to keep up with the vast losses incurred in Russia. Also the failure of "Barbarossa" created a crisis of confidence between Hitler and his generals. After dismissing the leaders of the German Army Groups in Russia and the commander-in-chief of the German army, Field Marshal Brauchitsch, Hitler assumed personal command of the German Army in December, 1941. Increasingly, the "iron will" of National Socialist ideology replaced the common sense of military strategy within the German army.

THE SOVIET UNION AND THE
WESTERN POWERS IN 1941

Although the Soviet government had watched Britain's struggle for survival in 1940 with indifference and even supplied Hitler's bombers with the fuel for their air attacks, Churchill promised all-out aid to Russia from the first day of the German attack. Old ideological differences were set aside, for Hitler was the common enemy. Britain could breathe freely for the first time within a year, for the Soviet armies engaged the mass of German troops which might otherwise have attempted an invasion in 1941. At the invitation of Russia, Britain concluded an agreement with the Soviet Union on July 12, 1941, pledging mutual support and excluding separate peace or armistice negotiations for the duration of the war. Almost from the start of the Anglo-Soviet alliance, Stalin demanded that a second front be established in the west. The Soviets suggested France or Norway as possible invasion sites and in addition asked for vast British military aid, especially tanks and aircraft. Persia, which had given evidence of pro-German leanings during the revolt of Rashid Ali in Iraq, was occupied jointly by Soviet and British forces, beginning on August 15, 1941. Persia was vital also as a supply route for Western military aid to Russia, since both the Baltic and the Black Sea were closed to Western convoys. Beyond the Persian operation, little military collaboration between Russia and Britain was achieved in 1941, however. Britain's own resources were inadequate for an invasion of Western Europe, at a time when British forces were engaged in North Africa and the ominous developments in the Pacific called for British reinforcements in Malaya. The "second front" in 1941 thus consisted of British air raids on Germany. On July 30, 1941, British carrier-borne aircraft attacked Petsamo in Finland, and the British bomber command stepped up its night raids against Germany.

Russia had also approached the United States for armed aid as early as July, 1941, with a request for industrial and military items valued at close to $2 billion. Reaction in the United States to Hitler's attack on Russia was not as clear-cut as it was in Britain, however, the United States not being at war with Germany and the memory of Stalin's attack on Finland still being very much alive. Some political quarters in the United

States even suggested that the German invasion of Russia had created the conditions for a negotiated peace between Germany and Britain. Others, including Harry Truman, voiced the opinion that the mutual destruction of Nazi Germany and Soviet Russia would be most advantageous to the United States. President Roosevelt, however, sent Harry Hopkins to Moscow in July, 1941, to ascertain Russia's needs. In August, during the Atlantic Conference with Churchill, the President made public his decision to aid Russia. In the Moscow Protocol of October, the United States pledged to deliver over $1 billion worth of matériel to Russia over a nine months' period. When Stalin observed that motorization would determine the outcome of the war, Roosevelt promised to send an additional 10,000 U. S. trucks per month. After the United States entered the war, Russia shared in the benefits of Lend-Lease, receiving a total of $11 billion worth of aid before the end of World War II. Apart from numerous other items, the United States gave Russia over 13,000 tanks and 400,000 trucks. Thanks to the American vehicles, Russian infantry divisions became more mobile than the German, a fact that soon became evident in the rapid westward surge of the Red Army after the Battle of Stalingrad.

COOLNESS OF ALLIANCE

In spite of the Anglo-Russian agreement of July, 1941, and the promise of military shipments by Britain and the United States, the political climate of the alliance remained cool. The coolness had its origin partly in the British failure to draw German strength away from Russia by establishing immediately a second front in Western Europe and partly in the nature of Soviet political demands, voiced cautiously as early as December, 1941. During the visit of British Foreign Secretary Anthony Eden to Moscow in December, 1941, Stalin gave a general idea of his views on the postwar order of Europe. Stalin proposed, in effect, to divide Europe after the war into new spheres of influence. Russia demanded the frontiers of 1940, including all the territories which she had annexed as a result of the Stalin-Hitler Pact of 1939. The Curzon line was to form the Soviet-Polish frontier. Britain, in Stalin's views, was to secure permanent military bases in France, Norway, and Sweden, if she desired. Germany was to be dismembered into several independent states. These views contained the seeds of future discord within the Grand Alliance after the United States had joined the war. Stalin's demands for the Curzon line and the frontiers of 1940 conflicted not only with the wishes of the Polish government in exile in London under General Sikorski but more generally with the principles of the Atlantic Charter, which Churchill had endorsed in August, 1941. In the Atlantic Charter, both Britain and the United States had rejected any territorial changes which did not accord with the freely expressed wishes of the people concerned.

THE JAPANESE ATTACK ON PEARL HARBOR; THE APPROACHING CRISIS IN THE ATLANTIC AND THE PACIFIC

Although not formally at war, the United States had been committed to a policy of containment of German power in Europe and Japanese power in Asia, since 1940. In the Atlantic, the growing American involvement was indicated by the acquisition of British bases from Newfoundland to the Bahamas, the establishment of U. S. strongholds on Iceland and Greenland, and the adoption of Lend-Lease. The Atlantic Charter of August, 1941, had announced the moral principles of the undeclared war which the United States was waging against the Axis. August, 1941, as noted earlier, also marked the beginning of American arms aid to Russia. Shortly after the Atlantic Conference between Roosevelt and Churchill, the United States assumed convoy duties in the North Atlantic, and on September 11, 1941, the President issued the "shoot first" order. The latter ordered American vessels to destroy German and Italian naval, land, and air forces "when encountered." Incidents in the Atlantic followed soon. At the end of October, 1941, a German submarine sank the American destroyer *Reuben James*. The United States had fully become part of the Battle of the Atlantic.

In the Pacific, the United States had responded to the Japanese penetration of Southeast Asia in the summer of 1940 with a policy of warning and subtle pressure. On July 25, 1940, President Roosevelt ordered the control of American oil and scrap iron exports, on which Japan heavily depended. In May, 1941, the President extended Lend-Lease to Nationalist China, and on July 26, 1941, all Japanese assets in the United States were frozen. The aim of American policy was to persuade Japan to retreat from the war with Nationalist China, which had been raging full-scale since 1937. Specific American conditions for peace in Asia were presented to Japan in a ten-point program on November 25, 1941. These included the demand for a complete Japanese military withdrawal from China and French Indochina and the call for Japanese support of Chiang Kai-shek. Furthermore, Japan was invited to join a proposed multipower non-aggression pact between the U. S., Great Britain, the Netherlands, Thailand, and the Soviet Union. Finally, Japan was asked to withdraw in effect from the Tripartite Pact with Italy and Germany. In return, the United States offered improved trade relations and future financial support of Japan.

The Japanese government, on the other hand, had reached a decision in principle, on July 2, 1941, to wage war against both Britain and the United States unless these powers acquiesced in Japan's defeat of China and the creation of a "Greater East Asian Co-Prosperity Sphere" under Japanese hegemony.

The conditions which General Hideki Tojo, the Japanese prime minister since mid-October, 1941, presented to the United States for a peaceful solution of the Japanese-American confrontation in Asia were thus completely incompatible with the American ten-point program. Tojo demanded an Anglo-American pledge of non-interference in the war in China and a promise not to establish bases in China, Thailand, or the Netherlands East Indies. The United States was even asked to lift the trade restrictions and thus, in effect, provide Japan with the means for further aggression. At the time when Tojo's special envoy to Washington, Saburo Kurusu, was ostensibly still engaged in negotiations with the United States, a Japanese fleet struck Pearl Harbor with a carrier attack in the early morning hours of December 7, 1941.

THE JAPANESE GAMBLE

In deciding on war, Tojo counted on a number of political and military advantages that seemed to minimize the risk of an open challenge to the United States in the Pacific. Manchuria was safe from Russian attack since the conclusion of the Soviet-Japanese neutrality pact of April, 1941, which Japan was careful not to break after Hitler's invasion of Russia. Neither Britain nor Holland could muster strong forces in defense of their rich Southeast Asian colonies. American naval forces, spread thin over two oceans since American involvement in the Battle of the Atlantic, were outnumbered in the Pacific by Japan. Even before the American naval disaster of Pearl Harbor, Japan enjoyed a naval superiority in every category, especially in aircraft carriers, with ten Japanese carriers facing three American in the Pacific. The Philippines, America's chief outpost in Asia, were surrounded on all sides by Japanese strongholds, from Formosa to the Carolines and the Marianas.

Japan expected the war to be short and, therefore, failed to develop a long-range strategy in conjunction with Germany for the defeat of the Allies. Germany declared war on the United States on December 11, 1941, following the Pearl Harbor attack, of which Japan had not informed Hitler in advance. Italy and most of the European Axis satellites followed suit. Japan, Germany, and Italy set up a joint Military Commission and signed a military agreement in January, 1942. The Military Commission was not, however, the Axis counterpart to the Combined Chiefs of Staff of Britain and the United States, for it did not discuss joint strategy. The terms of the military agreement, referring mainly to Axis naval coordination, were sufficiently vague as to be meaningless. The few German submarines which operated from Japanese bases in Malaya were soon withdrawn for want of cooperation.

The extent of mutual confidence between the Axis partners can best be gathered, perhaps, from Hitler's own description of his Japanese ally: "They lie to beat the band; everything they say has always got some background motive of deception. . . . If they've really got plans for something, we shall never hear about them. . . ."

THE MEANING OF THE
AMERICAN ENTRY INTO WORLD WAR II

With Pearl Harbor, the war which had begun in 1939 over the Polish corridor was turned into a global conflict with every ocean and continent of the world involved and every major power committed.

By attacking the United States, Japan had added the world's greatest industrial complex, largest skilled labor force, and most ample supply of strategic raw materials to the Allied cause, and had thereby dramatically altered the strategic balance of the war. The American economy, adapted for the needs of war by the War Production Board, the War Manpower Commission, the Office of Defense Transportation, and related agencies, soon produced nearly half of all the armaments manufactured by all belligerents of World War II. For example, in 1944, the United States turned out over 96,000 aircraft, as compared to 40,000 produced by Germany in the same year. Whereas German submarines were to sink a total of 14 million tons of Allied shipping, American shipyards produced 53 million tons of new shipping. American farming not only fed the armed forces of the United States, grown to over 12 million by the end of World War II, but helped to feed Soviet and British forces through Lend-Lease as well. The United States won the battle of production before Allied forces on land, sea, and in the air could turn the tide against the Axis in Europe and the Pacific.

Staggering as the American production feats were in themselves, the manner of their achievement was perhaps more impressive still. Of all the economies of the belligerent powers of World War II, that of the United States functioned with the least amount of government control and the least sacrifice to the civilian consumer.

Churchill, who, unlike the Japanese, fully appreciated the enormous productive power of the United States, happily recalled Sir Edward Grey's remark made before the First World War. The United States, the British Foreign Secretary had observed, was like "a gigantic boiler. Once the fire is lighted under it, there is no limit to the power it can generate."

Because of its larger resources, the United States alone among the belligerents of World War II could afford the mass production of conventional arms while launching the atomic bomb project at the same time. Germany's scientists had enjoyed a lead in atomic research before the outbreak of the war with the first splitting of the uranium atom by Otto Hahn in Berlin on December 17, 1938. During the war, Germany possessed neither the industrial capacity nor the organization for the successful conclusion of her atomic bomb project. Fortunately for the United States, the German and Italian dictatorships had driven some of the world's most renowned physicists to American shores, including Albert Einstein, Enrico Fermi, Leo Szilard, Eugene Wigner, and Edward Teller. They repaid American hospitality with outstanding contributions to the perfection of an American nuclear bomb in 1945.

THE POLITICAL MEANING OF THE AMERICAN ENTRY

During its early stage, the Second World War was waged between European powers which equated control over Europe with control over most of the world. With the formation of the Grand Alliance the political preponderance slipped from Britain to the United States — and Russia, with lasting consequences to the European world. The full significance of this development was not realized by all, including Winston Churchill, who continued to predict a thousand-year future for the British Empire in his speeches to Parliament and the nation of Britain.

No one could predict with certainty the length and breadth of American involvement in European affairs once Germany was beaten. As the war progressed, the United States gave growing evidence, however, that it would take a much stronger hand in shaping the postwar world, according to its own concepts and principles, which were not necessarily identical with those of Britain in every respect. The American resolve not to return to isolationism, as in 1920, was the direct result of Pearl Harbor, for the American participation in the Second World War was a matter of necessity, not choice, as the American entry into World War I had been. Both Houses of Congress reflected the American mood with the Connally and Fulbright Resolutions of November 5 and September 21, 1943, respectively, which endorsed the project of a new world organization and assured American participation in the future United Nations Organization. The ultimate meaning for Europe of America's abandonment of isolationism was, however, the prospect of a world transformed, in which the former colonial dependencies of Europe would graduate to political equality. Winston Churchill sensed the direction in which the wind was blowing when he opposed President Roosevelt's suggestion, made at the Quebec Conference of 1943, to issue a joint declaration on national independence for all colonies. Britain wished to limit the principles of the Atlantic Charter, notably the right of peoples to choose their own form of government, to Europe. The United States, mindful of its own revolutionary heritage and colonial emancipation from Great Britain, wished to extend them to the whole world. Significantly, the beginning of the European colonial retreat was to come in Asia, where Japan first unseated European colonial rule, only to be evicted in turn by the superior power of the United States.

THE FORGING OF THE GRAND ALLIANCE

"In the past we have had a light which flickered, in the present we have a light with flames, and in the future there will be a light which shines over all the land and sea." Thus Winston Churchill summed up the meaning of the United States entry into the Second World War for Britain. Following the British declaration of war on Japan on December 8, 1941, the United States and Great Britain established the most intimate alliance that any two Great Powers had ever managed to achieve in modern times. Its terms were largely unwritten, resting rather on a common language, outlook, and interest, and the personal esteem which the war-time leaders Roosevelt and Churchill felt for each other.

For purposes of military coordination and joint strategy, the two Powers formed the Combined Chiefs of Staff Committee, consisting of the respective heads of the three military services. For purposes of pooling ammunitions, a combined Munitions Assignment Board and Combined Raw Materials Board were set up in January, 1942. Top strategy decisions were usually worked out during the numerous personal meetings between the Prime Minister and the President. Not counting the Atlantic Conference of August, 1941, held before the U. S. entry into World War II, Roosevelt and Churchill met on seven separate occasions in places ranging from Washington, D. C., Hyde Park, Casablanca, Cairo, and Quebec, in addition to their meetings with Stalin at Teheran in November, 1943, and Yalta in February, 1945. During their first person-to-person meeting in Washington from December 22, 1941 to January 14, 1942 (Arcadia Conference), the President and Prime Minister agreed on the general guidelines of Allied military and political strategy. On the military side, the Arcadia Conference confirmed an earlier decision, reached during informal Anglo-American staff conferences in early 1941, that Germany was the more dangerous enemy and that her defeat should have priority over Japan's. Roosevelt and Churchill also agreed on the desirability of a joint American-British invasion of northwest Africa without fixing a specific date.

DECLARATION OF THE UNITED NATIONS

On the political side, the Arcadia Conference drafted the Declaration of the United Nations on January 2, 1942. Aside from reaffirming the principles of the Atlantic Charter, the Declaration of the United Nations pledged the support of its signatories to the common war effort and the refusal to make a separate peace with the Axis powers.

The coordination of military strategy between the Western Allies and the Soviet Union was less intimate than that achieved between the United States and Britain, since the Soviet Union was not included in the combined Chiefs of Staff Committee. Stalin was kept informed, however, of Western military plans, either through Churchill's personal visits to Moscow or at the summit meetings of the Big Three, especially at Teheran in November, 1943. Western-Soviet military coordination was to achieve its greatest effectiveness towards the end of the European war, in 1944, when the Russian summer offensive coincided with the Allied landings in Normandy, and in early 1945, when the Soviet winter offensive relieved German pressure in the west in the Battle of the Bulge. No effective scheme was ever worked out which would have permitted the "shuttle bombing" of Germany, by Allied aircraft starting in England and landing on fields behind the Russian lines.

The political cooperation of Russia within the Grand Alliance seemed assured when Stalin accepted the Declaration of the United Nations and signed a twenty-year alliance with Great Britain in May, 1942. Soviet-Western relations continued to be marred, however, by Russian suspicions that deepened as the date of an Allied invasion of France was postponed. The low point in Western-Soviet relations came in early 1943 when Stalin recalled his ambassadors from Washington and London. *Pravda,* the official Communist Party newspaper, even attributed the delay of the invasion of France to "small but influential groups in Britain and the United States, such as arms manufacturers and war suppliers, who place their private, selfish interests before those of the masses, to turn a bigger profit from the war."

Such charges and Japanese efforts to the contrary notwithstanding, Stalin did not consider a separate peace with Hitler. Nevertheless, the Soviet suspicions did not portend well for the continuance of the Grand Alliance after its military purpose had been achieved.

By the beginning of 1942, the United States, Britain, and Russia could look confidently to the ultimate defeat of Hitler, no matter how great their immediate reverses or how costly their future effort. The Grand Alliance of 1942, global in scope, embraced the majority of the world's population and resources. It was therefore on a very different level from the first anti-Hitler coalition of the Second World War, that of Britain, France, and Poland.

THE PACIFIC THEATER:
THE FIRST STAGE,
DECEMBER, 1941, TO JUNE, 1942

The Japanese surprise attack on Pearl Harbor was incidental to the main purpose of Japanese aggression in Asia. Its chief aim was the annihilation of the American Pacific Fleet in order to secure the eastern flank of the Japanese drive towards the East Indies, rich in rice and minerals. Even the first Japanese blow against the United States, although delivered as a complete surprise, was only a half victory. Japan had destroyed most of the American battleships anchored at Pearl Harbor, but she had failed to knock out the vast American fuel stores, nor had she damaged a single American aircraft carrier, the American carriers being out of port at the time of the attack. The great naval battles of the Pacific were to show, moreover, that the faster carriers and cruisers, not the battleships, were the decisive factor of naval power, battleships being used increasingly in support of landing operations. The United States was thus left with a fleet in being, which, though small, was to help contain Japanese expansion within a few months after the Pearl Harbor attack.

Nevertheless the Japanese possessed the initiative in the early months of the Pacific war, and their advance proceeded with the same precision and speed which had marked Hitler's Blitzkrieg in Europe. Within a few weeks after Pearl Harbor, Malaya, Hong-Kong, and Thailand were overrun. Singapore, with its British garrison of 60,000, was captured on February 15, 1942. Designed primarily as a naval fortress with defenses towards the sea, it fell an easy prey to Japanese air attack and the overland approach from Malaya. From Thailand, Japanese troops invaded Burma in January, 1942, and captured the capital, Rangoon, in March.

British naval disasters followed closely those on land. On December 10, 1941, the battleship *Prince of Wales,* veteran of the battle which had sunk the *Bismarck* in the Atlantic earlier in the year, was sunk by Japanese aircraft operating from Malayan bases, as was the battle cruiser *Repulse.* British sea power seemed to be swept from Asian waters, when a Japanese carrier force under Admiral Nagumo invaded and roamed the Indian Ocean at will and with impunity in early April, 1942. It sank two heavy British cruisers and the aircraft carrier *Hermes.* Another Japanese force destroyed over 130,000 tons of British merchant shipping in the Bay of Bengal at the same time. The British hastily withdrew their remaining capital ships to the safer shores of East Africa. By March, 1942, Borneo, Java, and Sumatra were in Japanese possession, following the defeat of a weak American, British, Dutch, and Australian force under the command of General Sir Archibald Warvell.

In the Philippines the Japanese had landed on Luzon on December 10, 1941, after destroying most of the American B-17 bombers on Clark Field in an air attack. After declaring Manila an open city, General Douglas MacArthur withdrew his forces gradually to the Bataan Peninsula and the island fortress of Corregidor. At Bataan and Corregidor, the Filipino and United States troops, outnumbered and short of supplies, made their last stand under General Jonathan Wainwright until forced to surrender on April 9 and May 6, 1942, respectively. General MacArthur, having pledged to return to the Philippines, was evacuated to Australia.

In the Central Pacific, Japan had seized the Caroline Islands from Britain, and Wake and Guam from the United States. In the Southwest Pacific, Japanese amphibious forces had landed on eastern New Guinea after wresting Rabaul in New Britain from its Australian defenders. Rabaul quickly became the principal Japanese naval and air base in the southwest Pacific.

By March, 1942, Japan had completed her program of conquest in less time and with fewer casualties than anyone, the Japanese included, had believed possible. The rich East Indies were the most valuable prize of the Japanese conquest, flanked by an extensive defense perimeter that extended from the Philippines to the central Pacific, New Guinea, New Britain, Malaya, and Burma. To protect its conquered island empire still further, Japan planned the isolation of Australia through the conquest of Port Moresby on New Guinea, which overlooked the Coral Sea. Also the Solomons, New Hebrides, New Caledonia, the Fijis, and Samoa were on the Japanese program of conquest. Finally, the American Pacific Fleet, especially the carriers which had survived the holocaust of Pearl Harbor, were to be challenged and destroyed in the course of a Japanese assault on the island of Midway and the Aleutians.

THE ALLIED RESPONSE, THE BATTLE OF MIDWAY

Because of the preponderance of American over British power in the Far East, the Pacific became mainly an American theater of operations. Burma and India were assigned to a British command, first under General Wavell, since 1943 under Lord Louis Mountbatten. The Southwest Pacific, including Australia and the Philippines, was assigned to the command of General MacArthur, the central Pacific to that of Admiral Chester W. Nimitz.

In spite of the "Germany first" strategy, adopted in the Arcadia Conference, the United States decided not to retire altogether from the war in the Far East. Admiral Nimitz and General MacArthur, on the contrary, waged an aggressive defense in early 1942 with what limited resources they possessed. American aircraft carriers raided Japanese bases in the Gilbert and Marshall islands in February, 1942, and on April 18, 1942, General Doolittle staged his famous air raid on Tokyo from the carrier *Hornet*. In the Battle of the Coral Sea of May 8, 1942, United States carriers fought their first battle with Japanese carriers. Although the United States lost the carrier *Lexington* in the engagement, the Battle of the Coral Sea saved Port Moresby from invasion and thus eliminated an immediate threat to Australia.

On June 4, 1942, a much larger Japanese fleet under Admiral Yamamoto clashed with an American carrier force under Rear Admiral

Spruance in the Battle of Midway. Admiral Yamamoto had cast away his advantage of superior numbers by splitting his attack force between two objectives, Midway and the Aleutians. While the Japanese seized the islands of Attu and Kiska in the Aleutians, they lost the Battle of Midway. At the cost of the American carrier *Yorktown* and one American cruiser, Rear Admiral Spruance sank four Japanese carriers, the *Hiryu, Soryu, Akagi,* and *Kaga,* the pride of the Japanese navy. More serious than the loss of carriers was that of experienced Japanese pilots, whose replacement proved difficult.

Attu and Kiska were retaken by the United States in 1943. But for the temporary occupation of American soil in the Aleutians, the Japanese navy might have won the great naval battle of June 4, 1942, for which it had prepared so eagerly in order to wrest naval control in the Central Pacific from the United States.

Midway signified the end of Japanese expansion in the Pacific, six months after the attack on Pearl Harbor. Instead of seeking further conquests, Japan was forced to concentrate on defending those islands already gained. The conditions for an American counteroffensive had been met. Slowly, the initiative would pass from Japanese to American hands.

THE GERMAN ATTACK ON RUSSIA, THE SECOND PHASE: JUNE TO NOVEMBER, 1942; THE BATTLE OF STALINGRAD

Unable to advance along the whole length of the 1700-mile Russian front after the bloodletting of 1941, Hitler nevertheless intended to regain the initiative which Stalin had wrested from him in the Battle of Moscow. Hitler's directive of April, 1942, thus called for a German offensive along the southern portion of the Russian front. It ordered the German armies to march towards Stalingrad on the Volga, the Caucasus, and the Caspian Sea. The German aim was the strangulation of Russian communications on the Volga and the capture of the Russian oil that Hitler regarded as essential to a German victory. Beyond that, Hitler's lively imagination envisaged a juncture of German forces from the Caucasus with those advancing over Egypt in the Middle East.

Implicit in the German eastern strategy of 1942 was the danger of overextension, for German means were disproportionate to their aims. By 1942 Hitler increasingly had to have recourse to Italian, Rumanian, and Hungarian divisions to fill the gaps torn into German manpower as a result of the winter losses of 1941. By contrast, the German drive towards the Caspian Sea, if it succeeded, would extend the German southern front from Voronezh to Baku, a line of over 2,000 miles. The German chief of staff, General Halder, expressed misgivings about the risks involved from the beginning, but he, like other generals before him, was soon dismissed by Hitler, when his predictions were confirmed by the course of battle in late 1942.

Stalin did not passively await the beginning of the German assault. In early May, 1942, Timoshenko invaded the Ukraine to retake Kiev and disrupt the German offensive preparations. The Soviet offensive failed, but it delayed the opening of the German assault by some four weeks. At the end of June, six German armies, supported by satellite divisions, marched eastward towards the Volga and the Caucasus. Sevastopol, the fortress on the Crimean Peninsula, under German siege since September, 1941, fell on July 4, 1942. The German attack at first rolled on swiftly from the Donets to the Don rivers, but it failed to trap major Soviet forces. The Russians fought more flexibly than they had in 1941 and rescued the bulk of their armies across the Don. Also, the number of Soviet desertions was much smaller, thanks to Stalin's patriotic appeals to the Red Army of July 1, 1942, and the Russian knowledge of German treatment of Soviet prisoners of war. By August, 1942, the German spearhead had split in two, one approaching Stalingrad, the other moving towards the oil fields of Maikop and along the Black Sea Coast. At Maikop the retreating Russians had so thoroughly wrecked the installations as to render them useless. Baku and Grozny, the other major Russian oil fields, remained beyond the reach of German armored divisions, which had run short of fuel.

By September, 1942, the German Sixth Army had entered Stalingrad, where the Soviet 62nd Army under General Chuikov contested every house and cellar. The 62nd Army was fighting with its back against the western Volga bank. The visitor to Stalingrad, now named Volgograd, can see the spot where Chuikov made his heroic stand, marked by a lone tank turret.

To both sides, Stalingrad held more than strategic significance. During the Russian Civil War, Stalin had successfully defended the city, then called Tsaritsyn, against the Don Cossacks under Krasnov. His victory in 1918 had helped launch Stalin's career. Hitler, on the other hand, had staked his own reputation on the outcome of the battle. In another premature victory statement, made on November 8, 1942, during the Nazi rally at Munich, he claimed that Stalingrad was already his. No more Russian ships, he said, could sail up the Volga. If the Russians wanted to counterattack, Hitler added, let them, for they will be bled to death.

Stalin had made fewer speeches but more thorough preparations for victory. While the German Sixth Army was absorbed in house-to-house fighting in the city of Stalingrad, Zhukov, the deputy leader of the Soviet General Staff (STAVKA), had massed five armies under generals Yeremenko and Rokossovsky against the Rumanian divisions which guarded the flanks of the 6th Army. On November 19, 1942, the Soviet armies overran the Rumanian positions; on November 22, they closed the

FIGURE 17   *The successful defenders: Red Army anti-aircraft gunners at Stalingrad.*

ring, trapping over 220,000 German troops with their commander, Field Marshal Friedrich Paulus and twenty-four German generals. Hitler ordered them to hold out and promised them supplies from the air. To survive, the German Sixth Army would have required a daily minimum supply of 700 tons. The German air force was incapable of assuring such supplies, however, since in November, 1942, it was also engaged in airlifting Axis troops to Tunisia, following the Allied landings in northwest Africa.

Not only did German relief attacks fail to break the Russian siege of Stalingrad, but the German front on the Don River also disintegrated with the collapse of the Italian 8th Army. An even greater Soviet victory seemed in sight when Russian forces, moving towards Rostov, threatened to cut off all German armies in the Caucasus. The German front in southern Russia gave every sign of total collapse by the end of 1942. On February 2, 1943, the remnants of the German Sixth Army under Paulus surrendered. Some 90,000 men and immense masses of war matériel fell into Russian hands. Paulus, ironically, had played a key role in drawing up the plans for "Barbarossa" in 1941. His disillusionment with

Hitler after the disaster of Stalingrad was indicated when he and other cap-tured German generals formed the so-called "National Committee of a Free Germany," which broadcast appeals from Russia for the end of Ger-man resistance.

The German armies of the Caucasus managed to escape en-circlement by a narrow margin. Field Marshal Manstein managed to improvise a new German front in the Ukraine and even throw the Rus-sians out of Charkov on March 12, 1943. By March, 1943, the front in Russia was back to the initial line of June, 1942. Hitler's excursion to Stalingrad and the Caucasus had cost him fifty German and satellite divisions with no gains whatever to show. Coming within a few days of the tenth anniversary of the Nazi seizure of power in Germany, the defeat at Stalingrad greatly impaired Hitler's prestige in Germany, and some Ger-man officers began to plot his removal. Coming within a few weeks of the Allied landings in northwest Africa and Montgomery's victory in Egypt, the Battle of Stalingrad signified the end of the defensive phase of the war in Europe, as the Battle of Midway had indicated the turning of the tide in the Pacific.

NORTH AFRICA, THE SECOND PHASE:
MAY, 1942, TO MAY, 1943

At the turn of 1941/1942, Great Britain had sustained serious naval losses due to Japanese action in the Far East and Axis naval attack in the Mediterranean. By the end of 1941 twenty-six German submarines were operating in the Mediterranean. Together with Italian "human tor-pedoes," they put out of action three British battleships, the *Barham*,

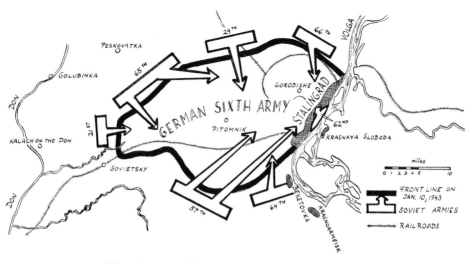

The German defeat at Stalingrad, January, 1943.

Queen Elizabeth, and *Valiant* as well as the British aircraft carrier *Ark Royal.* The *Prince of Wales* and *Repulse* were sunk by Japanese aircraft in December, 1941, as noted earlier. British naval losses had a direct impact on the course of the North African campaigns, for they enabled Italy to reinforce Rommel's Axis forces for another invasion of Egypt in the spring of 1942.

On May 26, 1942, Rommel launched his attack against the British position at Gazala on the Mediterranean and Bir Hakheim in the desert, which was strongly defended by the Free French Forces under General Koenig. French resistance delayed Rommel's offensive longer than anticipated, but by June, 1942, the Afrika Corps had reached Tobruk once again. This time Rommel's attack succeeded, and Tobruk was taken by Axis troops on June 21, 1942, with its vast stores of supplies and vehicles. The fall of Tobruk encouraged Rommel to seek a breakthrough towards Alexandria and the Suez Canal and beyond to the Persian Gulf. As Axis spirits soared at the prospect of victory, Winston Churchill came under attack in the House of Commons. Tobruk threatened to undo Churchill's career, as the fall of Norway had finished Neville Chamberlain's in May, 1940. Mussolini, not to be caught by surprise if Rommel captured Cairo, flew to Libya together with a white horse from which to view the Axis victory parade.

Rommel was anxious to keep the British 8th Army on the run, before it could be reinforced and make another stand in western Egypt. Thus the Axis offensive into Egypt began on June 22, 1942, the day after the surrender of Tobruk. It took Mersa Matruh in western Egypt on June 29, and reached El Alamein the following day. Only a short distance separated the Axis from the Suez Canal, but Rommel had to wait for reinforcements. He had started his offensive in May, 1942, with over 300 German tanks, of which 55 were left intact by the end of June. The German Afrika Corps presented a strange sight by the summer of 1942, most of its vehicles, including Rommel's command car, being captured British transport.

The outcome of the Battle of Egypt depended on supplies. By the summer of 1942, Britain had recovered sufficiently from the earlier naval losses to interdict Axis communications to North Africa. While Rommel's convoys suffered heavy losses, the British military build-up in Egypt proceeded smoothly. The successful defense of Malta and the British seizure of Madagascar in May, 1942, now paid full dividends. Britain had seized Madagascar from Vichy France for fear that either German or Japanese submarines might establish a base at Diego Suarez. With Madagascar in British hands, the long sea route around Africa was relatively safe. The British 8th Army under its new commander, General Bernard Montgomery, amassed considerable strength during August and September, 1942, with over 1,100 tanks and 150,000 men. Among the desert army's new tanks were hundreds of American Shermans, which Roosevelt had promised to a worried Churchill the day after the fall of Tobruk. Rommel, on his part, had few illusions about the meaning of such aid. During a visit to Hitler's headquarters in 1942, he had shown the Fuehrer an American armor-piercing shell, which Göring dismissed with the observation that the Americans knew only how to make razor blades. To this, Rommel replied that he would gladly have an American supply of "razor blades" for his own African forces.

Since the Quattara Depression, impassable to tanks and trucks, prohibited an outflanking of the El Alamein position from the South, Rommel had to attack it frontally. The two German assaults, made between July and late August, 1942, recoiled, the latter resulting in heavy German losses in the Battle of Alam Halfa. For an outflanking of El Alamein by sea, through amphibious landings in the British rear, the Germans lacked sea power.

On October 23, 1942, Montgomery struck back at El Alamein, having prepared his attack methodically and resisted pressures from London for an earlier assault. By November 1, the British 8th Army had broken through the vast German mine fields following the heaviest artillery bombardment of the whole African war. The British breakthrough had been achieved at the cost of five hundred British tanks, but Montgomery had another six hundred to spare with which to pursue the beaten Germans. Heavy rainfalls came to Rommel's rescue in early November, turning the desert into mud and slowing down the pursuing British armies. Although Rommel saved the bulk of his troops, he lost his equipment in Egypt. After the Battle of El Alamein and the successful Allied landings in northwest Africa on November 8, 1942, he regarded the war in North Africa as lost for the Axis and urged speedy evacuation of all troops to Italy. For reasons of political prestige and fears of an Italian defection, Hitler decreed otherwise and ordered a major German build-up in Tunisia.

THE ALLIED LANDINGS IN FRENCH NORTH AFRICA

The project of landing in French North Africa had been considered by Britain ever since the fall of France in 1940, because of the German failure to occupy the territories under the armistice with France. Roosevelt had evinced interest in the idea during the Atlantic Conference of August, 1941, and basic agreement was reached with Churchill at the Arcadia Conference at the turn of 1941/42. General George C. Marshall, U. S. Army Chief of Staff, believed, on the other hand, that an Allied landing in North Africa would squander resources and postpone an invasion of France, which he suggested for 1942. He even went so far as to threaten the shifting of American power to the Pacific unless Britain agreed to an early Allied invasion of France. Thus a basic disagreement on strategy developed between Britain and the United States, which was not fully resolved until 1944 and which had both military and political overtones. The British favored a Mediterranean strategy, first, because it would help them regain control over the inland sea, so vital to Great Britain; second, because Italy was the weakest link in the Axis chain and could be knocked out with less effort than Germany; and, third, because the Western Allies stood a better chance of keeping Soviet influence out of southeast Europe if they included the Balkans in their military operation. Finally, there was the remote prospect of breaking into Germany from the south, via Yugoslavia and Austria. The British approach was peripheral and partly politically motivated. The American was frontal and primarily military in conception.

These issues did not all come out at once but emerged rather gradually. They were resolved through compromise between Britain and the United States. In substance, the American view prevailed, since the main Allied attack against Hitler's Europe was to be delivered against France. For the moment, the British preference for Africa was adopted, however, with Allied landings in French North Africa proceeding on November 8, 1942. The chief risk of the Allied invasion lay in the question: What would Spain and Vichy France do? Thus far, Pétain had fought off every British attack on Vichy colonies to the best of his abilities, as shown in the British operations against Dakar in 1940, Syria and Lebanon in 1941, and Madagascar in 1942. Also, Pièrre Laval, fired in December, 1941, had returned to power in April, 1942. He and Admiral Darlan, commander-in-chief of all Vichy armed forces, were firm believers in an Axis victory. The United States, on the other hand, had maintained full diplomatic relations with Vichy and had established a vast network of agents in French North Africa with the aid of consul-general Robert D. Murphy. Through Murphy's influence and with the aid of General Henri Giraud, a veteran and hero of the Battle of France of 1940, it was hoped to secure a quick ceasefire should Vichy forces resist. Also, to minimize the effect of Vichy's Anglophobia, the overall command was entrusted to an American, General Dwight D. Eisenhower.

The three Allied task forces, carrying out operation "Torch," ran into stiff resistance nonetheless. Spain did not move, but Vichy naval forces at Casablanca, Oran, and Algiers fought back, and General Giraud turned out to be a disappointment. Few Vichy officers listened to him, the majority remaining loyal to Darlan, who happened to be in Algeria at the time of the invasion. When Darlan realized the scope of "Torch" — 35,000 U. S. troops were landed in Morocco, a further 39,000 at Oran, and a mixed U. S.-British force of 33,000 at Algiers — he readily switched sides. Eisenhower appointed Darlan French civilian chief in North Africa and made Giraud French military commander. Eisenhower's decision came under heavy attack in Britain and the United States, but it was justified on military grounds. The Allies were soon freed from their odious association with ex-collaborator Darlan when the Admiral was assassinated on December 24, 1942. De Gaulle's Free French forces were initially kept out of Allied politics in French North Africa, the situation being complex enough without their involvement. Pétain played a double game. While publicly condemning the landings and severing relations with the U. S., he secretly endorsed Darlan's move.

The Germans had observed the Allied naval concentrations at Gibraltar, but had mistaken them for preparations of another Allied convoy to the island of Malta. When surprised by the North African landings, they responded swiftly. On November 11, 1942, they moved into unoccupied France south of the Armistice Line, making Pétain their virtual prisoner and disarming the Vichy armistice army of 100,000 men. The French fleet at Toulon eluded them when it was scuttled before German eyes by orders of Admiral Delaborde on November 27, 1942. Sixty-two French war ships, including three battleships, sank to the bottom of the harbor.

On November 10, 1942, Hitler rushed Axis forces by air to Tunisia, in order to deny it to the Allies. The German airlift to Tunisia, as noted previously, coincided with the crisis of the German Sixth Army at Stalingrad, whose survival also depended on airborne supplies. In the end, Hitler was to lose both Stalingrad and Tunis, along with all the German troops committed to both battles.

THE BATTLE OF TUNISIA

As Eisenhower moved into Tunisia from the west, Montgomery's 8th Army had captured the port of Tripoli on January 23, 1943, exactly three months after the opening of the British attack at El Alamein. Mussolini, more dependent than ever on German support to keep a foothold in North Africa, implored Hitler to make a separate peace with Russia and throw his weight into the Mediterranean scales. Even if Hitler had wished to withdraw from his Russian campaign, he could hardly have done so after the Russian victory at Stalingrad. Still, Hitler heeded Mussolini's, not Rommel's advice, when he poured considerable German forces into the Tunisian bridgehead. The Axis position in Tunisia was hopeless from the start in view of the greatly augmented Allied air and sea power in the western Mediterranean. While trying to keep Axis troops in Tunisia supplied, Italy lost fourteen destroyers and 325,000 tons of merchant shipping to Allied air and naval action.

Rommel's efforts to keep the fronts, approaching from east and west, from closing in failed. A German attack against the American lines at the Kasserine Pass in late February broke down after initial successes. Rommel's effort to disrupt British offensive preparations east of the Mareth Line collapsed likewise in March, 1943. On March 27, 1943, Montgomery broke through the Mareth Line, and on May 7, American forces seized Bizerte. Tunis had been reached by the British two days earlier. The Battle of Tunisia yielded a bigger haul of Axis prisoners, nearly 250,000, than Stalingrad. Hitler was to miss the battle-hardened veterans of the Afrika Corps when he had to fend off Allied landings in Sicily and Italy.

The Tunisian theater had given American troops their first battle experience against German forces in World War II, although some officers knew their enemy from World War I. New names appeared that were to gain distinction soon in the battles of Italy and France: Omar N. Bradley, the strategist; George S. Patton, Jr., the controversial and hard-hitting tank commander; and Mark W. Clark, the diplomat and soldier. Tunisia was significant also in that it provided an opportunity for American and British officers and men to develop into a closely knit Allied team.

STRATEGIC AND POLITICAL DECISIONS AT CASABLANCA

The favorable turn of Allied military fortunes at Stalingrad, at El Alamein, and in Northwest Africa seemed to warrant further consultation on the highest level among Allied leaders. Roosevelt and Churchill thus invited Stalin to a summit conference. Since Stalin declined on the grounds of his involvement in the winter battles of 1942/43, the President and Prime Minister, together with their staffs, met at Casablanca from January 12 to 25, 1943.

In keeping with her "Mediterranean first" strategy, Britain wished to exploit the African victory by Allied landings in Sicily and Italy, with an eye on the possible entry of Turkey into the war on the Allied side. The United States, while agreeing to an invasion of Sicily, insisted on preparations for an invasion of France. In the Pacific, the United States was to maintain the initiative it had secured with the Battle of Midway. Among Allied military objectives, first priority was given, however, to the defeat of the German submarine menace, for, in January, 1943, the Battle of the Atlantic was far from won. Also, the Casablanca Conference laid the groundwork for the Allied strategic bomber offensive against Germany. Its objective, according to the directive for the Combined Chiefs of Staff, was "the destruction and dislocation of the German military, industrial, and economic system and the undermining of the morale of the German people to the point where their capacity for armed resistance was fatally weakened." Following the Casablanca Conference, President Roosevelt announced his "unconditional surrender" doctrine to an Allied press conference. This doctrine gave rise to controversy almost as soon as it was announced. The critics of the doctrine maintained that it prolonged the conflict in Europe unnecessarily by identifying the people of the Axis nations with their political and military dictators. The President himself interpreted the meaning of his doctrine, however, by emphasizing that "unconditional surrender" did not imply the destruction of the Axis populations, but merely of the "philosophies — based on conquest and the subjugation of other people." Roosevelt's motive appears to have been twofold. First, he wished to assure the Soviet Union that the Western Powers would not enter into separate discussions with the Fascist dictators. Soviet suspicions to that effect had been aroused by the Western dealings with Darlan, a Nazi collaborator. Second, Roosevelt wished to avoid any advance commitment to the enemy, such as had vexed President Wilson in his dealings with Imperial Germany.

EUROPE BETWEEN THE NEW ORDER AND ALLIED PLANNING

Before the outbreak of World War II, there were many, inside and outside Germany, who would have preferred to attribute Hitler's ideas, as expressed in *Mein Kampf,* to a youthful mind, unfettered by the experience of power or the burdens of political responsibility. Some twenty years after the publication of *Mein Kampf,* Nazi policy revealed a striking identity, however, with the geopolitical and racist themes of the Hitler of 1924.

Mein Kampf had interpreted the 20th century as a turning point which marked the decline of the older sea powers, grown wealthy through their colonies, and the beginning of a new era in which world power would rest on the domination of the Eurasian land mass by a single nation. Until the German reverses in the east towards the end of 1942, Hitler had every hope that Germany was on the threshold of world power through the domination of Russia. From its heart in Europe, Germany would rule over a vast and unassailable hinterland, covering European Russia and stretching to the Urals and beyond. The rest of Europe would be a mere appendix to the German-dominated Eurasian land mass. The older states of Europe would exist in varying degrees of dependency, determined by their loyalty to Hitler during the war or the ethnic make-up of their people.

Russia thus occupied the key position in Hitler's projected world empire, and in Russia German planning and policy assumed their most extreme form. "We National Socialists continue," Hitler had written in 1924, "where the development ended six hundred years ago. We end the eternal migration of Germans to the south and west of Europe and point to the territories of the east. We finish once and for all with the colonial and trading policy of the pre-war times and switch to the conquest of new soil. If we speak of new soil in Europe today, however, we are thinking primarily of Russia. . . . The gigantic empire of the east is ripe for collapse. We have been chosen by fate to witness a catastrophe, which will bring the most striking confirmation of the validity of race theory."

Nazi agencies, including Rosenberg's Eastern Ministry and the SS, planned in detail the settlement of millions of German colonists in Poland and Russia and the mass transfer or expulsion of the indigenous populations. A "General Plan East," prepared in 1941, contemplated moving some 80 per cent of all Poles out of Europe, possibly to Brazil. Sixty-five per cent of all Ukrainians and 75 per cent of all White (Byelo) Russians were to be transferred to western Siberia. The problem of the high birth rate of the Great Russians was to be solved by a "consciously negative population policy" through the denial of medical services and the promotion of high infant mortality.

The long-range goals of Nazi policy in Russia were fore-shadowed by the nature of the occupation methods. During the initial stages of the invasion, the German army was frequently greeted with good will and the expectation of deliverance from the Soviet system. Ukrainian nationalists in particular, such as Stephen Bandera, hoped for the establishment of an independent Ukraine with German help. Such hopes were soon dashed. The Ukrainian peasant, who expected the restoration of his land, soon discovered that the German conquerors merely took over the Soviet state and collective farms and operated them, if anything, more ruthlessly, for German ends. Of the four million Soviet prisoners captured by the end of 1941, one third died of starvation or disease during the first winter of the Russian war. Ruthless economic exploitation, deliberate cultural and educational impoverishment, the mass recruitment of slave labor, and mass reprisals against the resistance which these policies evoked, became the pattern of German rule in Russia.

Hitler's treatment of Russia also condemned to insignificance the so-called Vlasov movement. Andrey Vlasov, a captured Soviet general and former Russian adviser to Chiang Kai-shek, established a "Russian Liberation Committee" in German-occupied Smolensk on April 12, 1943. It appealed to Russians on both sides of the front to aid in the overthrow of the Stalinist dictatorship. Vlasov compared his movement for the liberation of Russia from Communism with Prussia's war of liberation against Napoleon in 1813. Germany, Vlasov said, could now repay the debt of Prussia and help create a "single and indivisible Russia." Vlasov's claim to equality with Germany condemned his movement to a mere propaganda role, tolerated by Hitler but never taken seriously.

Hitler's invasion of Russia set into motion another Nazi policy rooted in the ideas of *Mein Kampf:* the extermination of the European Jews. With the retreat of the Soviet armies in 1941, the Nazi regime at first killed thousands of eastern Jews in haphazard fashion through mass shootings. Beginning in December, 1941, a much more elaborate and systematic machinery was set rolling, which aimed at the destruction not only of Jews in Poland and conquered Russia, but of all Jews in every part of German-dominated Europe through poison gas. Heydrich and Eichmann were the names, Chelmno, Belzec, Sobibor, Treblinka, Maidanek, and Auschwitz were the places, that spelled the death of millions in the worst holocaust of racial persecution in the history of modern Europe.

Nazi rule in western Europe was less overt in its objectives than in the east, but in the case of Norway and Holland, at least, it aimed at an eventual "Anschluss." Because of the alleged ethnic affinity of Norwegians and Dutch with Germans, the Nazi regime was particularly anxious to incorporate both Norway and Holland into the German Reich. On April 9, 1940, the day of Germany's invasion of Denmark and Norway, Hitler exclaimed: "Just as Bismarck's Reich emerged from the year 1866, the Greater Germanic Reich shall rise from this day." Soon after the arrival of German troops, all political parties in Holland and Norway were dissolved, and the attempt of native Nazi revolutions made. In Holland, Hitler relied on the Dutch Nazi leader Anton A. Mussert and his *Nationaal-Socialistische Beweging der Nederlanden,* in Norway on Vidkun Quisling and his *Nasjonal Samling.* Mussert and Quisling, being little more than puppets of the Nazi governors Seyss-Inquart and Terboven, attracted no mass following among their countrymen. In the end, German rule in Norway and Holland depended as much on bayonets as it did in the less favored eastern territories.

The longest and most successful of resistance movements in Nazi-occupied Europe was that of Yugoslavia. Following the German Balkan campaign of 1941, Yugoslavia had been dismembered into an Italian-controlled Croatian satellite, an Italian protectorate over Montenegro, and a German-occupied Serbian rump state, roughly of the same size as the Serbia of 1914. Soon the occupying powers were faced with two resistance forces: the "Cetniks" of General Draza Mihailovic, and the Communists under Tito. Mihailovic, who represented the Yugoslav government in exile under King Peter, entered into an occasional alliance with the occupying powers to combat the Yugoslav Communists and assert Serbian supremacy over the Croats. Tito's resistance was unequivocal, however, and so successful that it earned the grudging admiration of Hitler and the full support of Churchill, who dropped the controversial Mihailovic. Tito, Hitler said, deserved the title of "Marshal" far more than some of his own generals, for Tito had survived all German attempts to capture or destroy his forces.

What stands out from Nazi plans for a New Order in Europe is the paucity of ideas and the total disregard for European history and values. The New Order threatened to efface not only past frontiers but some of the most cherished principles of European civilization — above all, the sanctity of the individual opposite the power of the state. Even Mussolini, Hitler's mentor and closest ally, felt uneasy at the prospect of a total German victory. "I wonder," he confided to Ciano, "if at this time we do not belong among the vassal nations. And even if this is not so today, it will be so on the day of total victory for Germany."

EUROPE IN ALLIED PLANNING OF 1943; THE MOSCOW FOREIGN MINISTERS' CONFERENCE; THE TEHERAN CONFERENCE

In 1943 the Grand Alliance was still more concerned with the military task of defeating Germany than with political plans for postwar Europe. However, the meeting of the three foreign ministers, Hull, Eden and Molotov, in Moscow in October, 1943, and of Roosevelt, Churchill, and Stalin at Teheran in November, 1943, led to an exchange of political views and to preparations for future political decisions. At Moscow, the foreign ministers reached general agreement on the establishment of a future international world organization, based on the sovereign equality of peace-loving states and designed to maintain international peace and security. U. S. Secretary of State Hull would have liked the conference to accept also the substitution of the trustee principle for colonialism, a move blocked by the British foreign secretary. Soviet objection scuttled a British project for an Austro-Hungarian-Bavarian federation, to be created after the war. Churchill hoped that such a "peaceful, cowlike federation" would add to the stability of central eastern Europe after the war. Russia suspected the project as a thinly disguised Western effort to restore the Habsburg Empire and secure Western influence in the Danube Basin. The three powers thus agreed merely to restore an independent Austria with the frontiers of 1938. The foreign ministers also agreed to try the Nazi leaders for war crimes and to install a European Advisory Commission for the study of Allied policy in postwar Germany.

The principal decision of the summit meeting at Teheran was military. Roosevelt and Stalin overruled Churchill's project of extending Western military operations in the Mediterranean from Italy to the Balkans. The main assault of the Western powers for 1944 was to be launched against France.

This military decision had obvious political implications, however, for it left the task of evicting Hitler from the Balkans to Russia with all the implied opportunity of future Soviet penetration. All three powers agreed on the desirability of dismembering Germany as the best safeguard for future peace in Europe. President Roosevelt submitted a detailed plan for the break-up of Germany into five parts and for United Nations control over the Kiel Canal, the city of Hamburg, and the industrial centers of the Ruhr and the Saar. Stalin seems to have attached less significance to political dismemberment than to drastic measures against the German

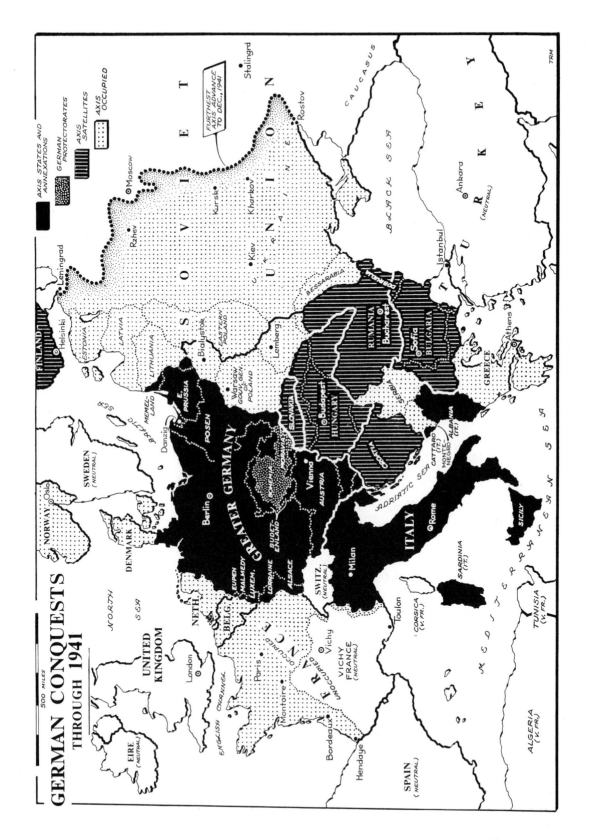

GERMAN CONQUESTS
THROUGH 1941

500 MILES

Legend:
- AXIS STATES AND ANNEXATIONS
- GERMAN PROTECTORATES
- AXIS SATELLITES
- AXIS OCCUPIED

FURTHEST AXIS ADVANCE TO DEC., 1941

EIRE (NEUTRAL)

UNITED KINGDOM

London

ENGLISH CHANNEL

NORTH SEA

NORWAY

Oslo

SWEDEN (NEUTRAL)

DENMARK

NETH.

BELG.

EUPEN
MALMEDY
LUXEM.
LORRAINE
ALSACE

FRANCE

OCCUPIED

UNOCCUPIED

Paris

Montoire

Bordeaux

Hendaye

Vichy

VICHY FRANCE (NEUTRAL)

SPAIN (NEUTRAL)

Toulon

CORSICA (V. FR.)

SARDINIA (IT.)

Rome

ITALY

Milan

SWITZ. (NEUTRAL)

GREATER GERMANY

Berlin

SUDET-ENLAND

BOHEMIA

Vienna

AUSTRIA

POSEN

E. PRUSSIA

Danzig

MEMEL-LAND

BALTIC SEA

FINLAND

Helsinki

Leningrad

ESTONIA

LATVIA

LITHUANIA

GOV. GEN. OF POLAND

Warsaw

Bialystok

EASTERN POLAND

Lemberg

SLOVAKIA

Budapest

HUNGARY

SERBIA

CROATIA

MONTE-NEGRO

ALBANIA (IT.)

CATTARO (IT.)

BESSARABIA

RUMANIA

Bucharest

BULGARIA

Sofia

GREECE

Athens

ADRIATIC SEA

MEDITERRANEAN SEA

ALGERIA (V. FR.)

TUNISIA (V. FR.)

SICILY

SOVIET UNION

Moscow

Rzhev

Kursk

Kharkov

Kiev

UKRAINE

Rostov

Stalingrad

CAUCASUS

BLACK SEA

Istanbul

TURKEY (NEUTRAL)

Ankara

TRM

army, for he suggested shooting 50,000 German officers as a preventive measure against future German militarism. Stalin demanded the port of Königsberg for the Soviet Union, to which the Western powers did not object. The remainder of East Prussia as well as Upper Silesia was to go to Poland. On Churchill's suggestion, the Curzon Line was accepted as the tentative eastern frontier of postwar Poland. The question of the Baltic states, which Russia had annexed in August, 1940, was not open to discussion as far as Stalin was concerned. Their peoples, in Stalin's words, had expressed "in plebiscites their desire to join the Soviet Union."

From the first exchange of views on the postwar order of Europe on the summit level, it was apparent that the Soviet Union did not intend to relinquish any of the gains made while the Stalin-Hitler pact was in effect. In some areas, notably the Balkans, Soviet influence might even go beyond that of 1941. Churchill, the only leader at Teheran rooted in pre-war concepts of European power balance, foresaw the trend of coming events more clearly than did Roosevelt. The defeat of Churchill's views at Teheran foreshadowed the future Soviet-American preponderance in European affairs. It also indicated that the European state system was not likely to emerge from an Allied victory over Hitler in the form of the pre-war status quo. Russian influence in eastern Europe would predominate, and European influence in the world at large was likely to diminish once the United Nations had become a functioning world organization.

THE FIRST BREACH IN THE AXIS WALL: THE ALLIED LANDINGS IN SICILY AND ITALY

A full two months passed between the end of the Tunisian campaign and the Allied invasion of Sicily on July 10, 1943. American veterans of the Pacific island war against the Japanese might well have anticipated fearful losses and a prolonged campaign, for Sicily, properly defended and fortified, could have been a formidable obstacle to an invasion. By July, 1943, Italy had lost the stomach for total war, however, once its colonial empire was gone and its unprotected cities exposed to Allied air attack. Moreover, Hitler had sacrificed an entire army in Tunisia, and the demands of the Russian front kept German strength in Sicily to a minimum.

The huge Allied invasion force, totalling 470,000 troops and exceeding that which would land in Normandy in 1944, thus went ashore with little difficulty. The Allied landings were undertaken along the south and east coasts, in the Gulf of Gela, and near Syracuse, rather than close to the Messina Strait where they might have prevented the evacuation of Axis troops to southern Italy. After capturing the principal ports of

Augusta, Palermo, and Syracuse, the U. S. 7th Army under Patton and the British 8th Army under Montgomery fanned out across the island in an effort to trap the Axis garrison before it could make good its escape across the Messina Strait. The Germans fought a skillful delaying action in Catania and around Mt. Aetna, however, and evacuated 45,000 of their own together with 60,000 Italian troops.

The 38-day campaign for the conquest of Sicily had demonstrated in the European theater what the United States already knew from the experience in the Pacific: No enemy coast could repulse an Allied invasion under the weight of naval gunfire and the umbrella of superior Allied air power. The Sicilian campaign had also given further proof of the success of Allied teamwork, first tried in Tunisia. Eisenhower had exercised supreme command, with British Field Marshal Sir Harold Alexander as his deputy. Admiral Cunningham and Air Marshal Tedder, both British, headed the combined naval and air forces.

The Allied conquest of Sicily soon yielded military and political benefits that ranged from the Mediterranean all the way to Russia. Hitler's nervousness about Italy's position in the war led him to withdraw forces from the Russian front when the largest tank battle of the east, at Kursk, was in full swing. In the Mediterranean, Allied shipping lanes were safe from Axis attack for the first time since 1940. Above all, the Allied landings on Sicily provided the final push which toppled the Italian dictator and opened the way for an Allied-Italian armistice.

Turkey, to Britain's disappointment, still resisted all pressures to enter the war on the Allied side. Churchill's journey to Turkey, undertaken soon after the Casablanca Conference, failed of its purpose. The Turks still feared the threat of German air power more than they trusted the Allied ability to defend Istanbul. The Dardanelles, gateway to Russian Black Sea ports, thus remained closed to Allied convoys, as they had after the abortive Gallipoli campaign of 1915.

THE FALL OF MUSSOLINI; THE ALLIED LANDINGS IN ITALY

Mussolini's strategy of fighting a "parallel war," apart from the World War proper, had collapsed once Italy was brought face to face with the superior might of Britain and the United States in the Mediterranean. By 1943, all that was left of Mussolini's dream of Roman Empire was a precarious Italian foothold in the Balkans, where Mussolini had set up a Fascist satellite in Croatia. On June 10, 1940, when Italy had cast her lot with Hitler, Mussolini had broadcast to his people: "It is the struggle of fertile and young people against people who have become sterile and are in process of decline." At last, the hollowness of Fascist rhetoric had been revealed. By July, 1943, Mussolini was, by his own admission, the "most hated man in Italy."

The Italian King, Victor Emmanuel III, never on cordial terms with the Duce, now tried, with the help of the army, to spare Italy the pain of unconditional surrender by toppling Mussolini. Even a majority of the Fascist Grand Council joined, when it stripped Mussolini of his supreme command in a dramatic session on July 24, 1943. Mussolini, tired and aged beyond his sixty years, accepted the coup d'état and his subsequent imprisonment without a fight. Shifted from place to place, he was finally sent to a mountain hotel on the Gran Sasso in the Abruzzi, whence a German commando freed him on September 12, 1943. While moving Mussolini to Germany, Hitler prepared "Case Axis," a surprise move to disarm all Italian divisions within German reach, from southern France to Greece.

Marshal Pietro Badoglio, the new Italian prime minister, professed publicly his loyalty to the Axis alliance but secretly approached the Allies with the offer of switching sides. The Allies refused to enter into any political bargaining, however, and insisted on unconditional surrender, which the Badoglio government accepted on September 3, 1943. According to the terms of the armistice, Italy had to hand over her fleet and air force and secure her ports and air bases until the arrival of the Allies. This was easier said than done, for by the time that the armistice was announced by Eisenhower on September 8, 1943, the Germans had put into effect "Case Axis" and gained military control of most of Italy, including Rome. When the Allies landed at Salerno on September 9, 1943, the Germans were waiting in strength. The Allies had failed to capitalize on the political collapse of Italy. Badoglio and the Italian king had failed to prevent Italy from being turned into a battleground, with painful consequences for her people and her ancient monuments.

For a variety of reasons the Italian campaign became a frustrating and disappointing experience for the Allies. President Roosevelt and a reluctant Winston Churchill had agreed at Washington in May and August, 1943, to give priority to the Allied invasion of Normandy, scheduled for May, 1944. Allied resources for the Italian campaign were thus limited from the beginning. The nature of the Italian terrain and weather added their burden, what with mountains, mud, and rivers swollen by autumn rains. Also, the German defense, directed by Field Marshal Albert Kesselring, was skillful and flexible, unlike the German strategy in Russia, which sacrificed whole armies for the sake of holding ground. The Germans had expected the Allies to follow up the political collapse of Italy with landings far in the north or even airborne seizures of the Alpine passes between Austria and Italy. When they realized the Allied intention of fighting up the boot of Italy, they built powerful defenses in the Apennines from the Ligurian to the Adriatic seas. Meanwhile, the German troops in southern Italy fought a delaying action, exacting a maximum of

Allied casualties as they retreated slowly north, from one prepared defensive line to the next.

The landings of the U. S. Fifth Army at Salerno on September 9, 1943, turned, in General Mark W. Clark's words, "into near disaster," for they were undertaken without the customary advance naval bombardment in order to achieve surprise. After dropping 3,000 tons of bombs on the German defenses, the Fifth Army overwhelmed the opposition, however, and reached Naples by October 1, 1943. The British 8th Army, which had encountered little opposition in its landings at Reppo and Taranto on September 3, 1943, had meanwhile captured the strategic air base at Foggia and linked up with Mark W. Clark. From Foggia, Allied bombers could strike conveniently against targets in Rumania and Austria.

After Naples, the Allies forced the German "Volturno Line" but came to a halt before the "Gustav Line," which rested in its western flank on Monte Cassino, the site of the ancient Benedictine monastery with a commanding view of the approaches from the south. Before Monte Cassino, all Allied attacks collapsed between November, 1943, and May, 1944. The Allies tried to unhinge the Gustav Line by landing two divisions behind the German front at Anzio in January, 1944. Anzio threatened to turn into another fruitless slugging match, for the Allies failed to exploit the initial surprise. Hitler, sensing the opportunity of a tactical victory, rushed 20,000 troops to Anzio to drive the Allies into the sea. An attack by Clark across the Rapido, to relieve German pressure at Anzio, broke down under heavy casualties. Between January and May, 1944, the Anzio Battle cost the Allies 59,000 casualties, but the capture of Monte Cassino finally forced the Germans into a general retreat.

Allied soldiers of many nationalities, ranging from Poles to New Zealanders, had taken part in the Battle of Monte Cassino and lost their lives in this, the most bitterly fought battle of the entire Italian campaign. The endless rows of Allied graves at Cassino bear witness to the fierceness of the struggle, which also claimed among its victims one of Europe's finest Christian monuments in the old Cassino abbey. The German retreat from the Gustav line did not halt until it reached the Apennines, 180 miles to the north of Rome. Rome, the first Axis capital to fall into Allied hands, had been declared an open city and abandoned by the Germans on June 4, 1944. General Sir Henry Maitland Wilson, who had replaced Eisenhower as Allied Supreme Commander in the Mediterranean, wished to exploit the victory for an immediate pursuit of the enemy, before he had found time to get entrenched in the "Gothic Line" in the Apennines. Wilson proposed to land at Trieste and carry an Allied offensive into Austria via the Ljubljana gap.

D-Day in Normandy came within two days after the fall of Rome, however, demanding all Allied landing craft. Additional troops and landing craft had to be withdrawn from Italy in preparation for the landings in southern France, scheduled for August, 1944. Although the "Gothic

Line" was pierced with the capture of the Giogo and Futa passes in September, 1944, the River Po was not reached until the spring of 1945.

Although high in cost and slow in gains, the Italian campaign had tied down between twenty and thirty German divisions at various stages, which Hitler might have used either in Russia or France. With the invasion of France, Germany was forced to fight on three European fronts.

THE TWO ITALYS AFTER 1943

The political division of Italy followed its military division into Allied- and German-held portions of the peninsula. Political life in Allied-occupied Italy was characterized by considerable bickering among Italian politicos, whom Churchill called a "cluster of aged and hungry politicians," and some disagreements among the Allies. On November 10, 1943, an Allied Control Commission was set up for occupied Italy, but the Badoglio government was permitted to stay in power. On October 13, 1943, the latter declared war on Germany, a move of no military consequence though it secured Italy the status of a co-belligerent on the Allied

The Allied advance in Italy, January, 1944-January, 1945.

side. More important than the military contribution of Badoglio was that of the Italian partisans in northern Italy, who formed the Committee of National Liberation of Upper Italy (CLNAI) and soon established contact with the Allies. The partisans blew up German communications and rescued downed Allied airmen.

Badoglio soon ran into difficulty with Italian émigré politicians, many of whom had returned from the United States. Count Sforza, Benedetto Croce, and the Communist Palmiro Togliatti refused to support Badoglio and the King, whom they regarded as compromised by his long association with Mussolini. Victor Emmanuel, popular with Winston Churchill for he had delivered the Italian fleet, was retained, however, until the occupation of Rome. After that, the King abdicated in favor of his son, and a new government was formed under Ivanoe Bonomi, a former Italian premier.

Hitler was severely shaken by Mussolini's overthrow. Less concerned with the collapse of Italian military power, he feared that the example of a successful palace revolution in Italy might stimulate a similar development among disaffected German generals or induce lesser Axis satellites to leave the sinking Nazi ship. Hitler was therefore anxious to maintain the illusion of a Fascist Italy, united in alliance with Germany, by setting up a puppet state in northern Italy under Mussolini. At Salo on Lake Garda, the capital of the "Italian Social Republic," Mussolini eked out a precarious political existence under the watchful eyes of his German guards. Embittered by the King's desertion, the Duce reverted to the social radicalism of his youth, while displaying an anti-semitism which had been largely absent from the Fascist regime of earlier years. Those members of the Fascist Grand Council who had voted for his overthrow on July 24, 1943, and who were in his hands, including his son-in-law, Count Galeazzo Ciano, were tried and executed by a special court in Verona. In the final stages of the Fascist Republic, Mussolini was not spared the humiliation of witnessing the German annexation of Trieste, Goricia, and the South Tyrol, Italy's gains of the First World War. As German resistance collapsed in northern Italy in April, 1945, Mussolini was captured and shot by Italian partisans on April 29, 1945. In Milan, where Fascism had had its beginnings, Mussolini's body was displayed in gruesome fashion after the execution.

THE LIBERATION OF RUSSIA: FROM KURSK TO MINSK, JULY, 1943, TO JULY, 1944

On July 5, 1943, five days before the Allied landings on Sicily, Hitler launched his last major offensive on the Russian front at Kursk and Orel. The attack was motivated largely by reasons of prestige, to erase the impression of Stalingrad and give proof of the unbroken offensive power of the German army. The battle, which led to the biggest clash of Russian and German armor thus far, ended in a German defeat. Not only were the Russians well prepared to meet the assault, of which they had fore-knowledge, but the Red Army of 1943 was better equipped, more self-confident, and more ably led than that of 1941 or 1942. A new generation of battle-hardened and experienced Russian generals had emerged from the earlier trials: Rokossovsky, Malinovsky, Konev, Vatutin, and Zhukov.

After the Battle of Kursk, the initiative passed permanently into Russian hands. Russian superiority in men and matériel was such that the Soviets were able to launch several offensives at widely separated points and from one season into another. Although the Germans continued to commit the bulk of their armies to the Russian front in 1943 and 1944, they were driven from one crisis to another, never gaining a breathing spell or regaining the initiative. The Soviet advance was also facilitated by Hitler's rigid strategy of no retreat, which was intended to retain the allegiance of the German satellites, Finland and Rumania, and to hold on to important economic resources, such as the ore and coal of the Donets Basin. Beginning with 1943, the Russians became the masters of mobile warfare and encirclement, while Hitler reverted to a strategy of linear defense.

The first Russian blow, delivered on July 12, 1943, forced the German central front to abandon Smolensk and withdraw towards the old Russo-Polish frontier. In October, 1943, three Soviet armies, under Vatutin, Rokossovsky, and Konev, forced the Dnieper on the southern front, and captured Kiev in November, 1943. By March, 1944, the Russians had entered Bessarabia and by May, 1944, had cleared the Crimea of German troops. In the north, a Soviet offensive had retaken Novgorod and lifted the German siege of Leningrad, by January, 1944. Between the beginning of the Russian summer offensive of 1943 and the opening of 1944, the Red Army had liberated three quarters of German-occupied Russia and inflicted such severe casualties on the retreating Germans that the outcome of the summer battles of 1944 could not remain in doubt.

The Soviet summer offensive of 1944 coincided with the Allied landings in Normandy and the Allied offensive in Italy. While the Allied forces captured Rome on June 4, 1944, and landed on the beaches of Normandy on June 6, Russia unleashed her attack in the east on June 10, 1944. The German fronts in Italy, France, and Russia were thus subjected to simultaneous attack, making the shifting of German reserves along interior lines impossible.

The first Russian attack was directed against the Finnish front, for Finland had shown signs of weakening after the siege of Leningrad was broken. After the Russian breakthrough on the Karelian Isthmus and the fall of Viborg, Marshal Mannerheim renewed earlier peacefeelers and asked for a separate armistice. Like Badoglio in Italy the year before,

Mannerheim hoped to save Finland from becoming a battlefield when the Axis cause was apparently lost. Unlike Italy, Finland had never signed an alliance with Hitler and had maintained its independence from Nazi politics, as shown by Finland's protection of its Jewish minority from Nazi arrest and persecution.

FINNISH ARMISTICE

The Russo-Finnish armistice of September 19, 1944, confirmed the Moscow Treaty of 1940. Beyond that, it required Finland to pay $300 million in reparations, surrender Petsamo, and intern German forces still on Finnish soil. German troops remained, however, in northern Finland until the war's end, causing more damage than Finland had suffered in all the years of war against Russia.

The main Soviet attack fell on the German central front in White Russia on June 22, 1944, the third anniversary of Hitler's invasion of the Soviet Union. By July 3, 1944, Minsk, the White Russian capital, was liberated. During the Battle of White Russia, Germany suffered her worst defeat in the east thus far, with twenty-eight German divisions destroyed and 350,000 men killed or captured. Of the German Central Army Group, only eight divisions survived, scattered over a front two-hundred miles long. Exploiting their immense victory, the Soviets broke through to the Baltic, and reached the vicinity of Riga by the beginning of August, 1944.

RUMANIAN ARMISTICE

Russian successes in the south were on an equally large scale. Following the invasion of Rumania by Malinovsky and Tolbuchin on August 20, 1944, the Rumanian government of Antonescu was overthrown and King Michael requested an armistice, which was granted on September 12, 1944. The position of Bulgaria was peculiar in that it had never declared war on Russia or participated in Hitler's invasion of 1941. As the Soviet armies approached, Bulgaria declared herself neutral on August 26, 1944, and asked the German troops to leave. Russia responded by declaring war on Bulgaria, ousting the Bulgarian government, and installing a Soviet puppet regime in Sofia. Malinovsky then broke into southern Hungary and Tolbuchin into Yugoslavia, capturing Belgrade on October 19, 1944.

Hungary might well have emulated the Rumanian and Finnish example, but for the German military occupation, which had ousted the Horthy regime when it tried to send peace feelers to London.

By the end of summer of 1944, the Russians stood once more at the Baltic and in the Balkans. In Poland their attack had come to a standstill at the gates of Warsaw. Anticipating a Soviet occupation of the Polish capital, the underground Home Army under General Bor-

Koromovski, which was loyal to the Polish government in exile in London, staged an uprising against the German garrison. The purpose of the uprising was to establish a functioning Polish administration, independent of the Soviet-sponsored "Polish Committee of Liberation" installed at Lublin.

The Polish uprising caught the Germans by surprise, but the Soviet armies did not make a move to come to its aid. Nor did Stalin grant landing permits to Allied aircraft which attempted to supply General Bor from the air. After a struggle which lasted sixty-three days, the Germans crushed the insurrection. Warsaw lay in ruins and Soviet-Western relations had suffered a serious crisis of confidence.

THE TURNING OF THE TIDE ON THE SEAS
AND IN THE AIR:
THE BATTLE OF THE ATLANTIC

While the Soviet armies decimated Hitler's strength on land, American and British air and sea power won control over the Atlantic and the air space over Europe. Prior to the engagement of major German ground forces by the Western Allies in Normandy in 1944, Soviet Russia tended to minimize the Western effort in the air and on the seas. Russia, primarily a land power, measured military gains in terms of enemy divisions destroyed on the ground.

The air and sea war was as vital to Allied victory, however, as were Russia's operations on the ground, for it assured the flow of arms to Britain and paralyzed the German war economy to the point of collapse by early 1945.

Although small in numbers, the German navy under the command of Admiral Raeder struck hard at Britain's sea lanes from the beginning of the war. German surface raiders, some in the disguise of neutral merchantmen, operated in the Atlantic, the Indian Ocean, and the Pacific, sinking a total of 235,000 tons of British shipping within the first year of the war. The pocket battleship *Graf Spee* destroyed a further 50,000 tons before her captain scuttled the ship when cornered by a superior British force off Montevideo on December 17, 1939. The *Scheer,* the *Spee's* sister ship, sank 100,000 tons before returning to Germany in late 1940.

With the establishment of German naval bases at Brest, Lorient, St. Nazaire, and Bordeaux, as well as on the coast of Norway, the German navy hoped to close the ring of the sea blockade around the British Isles. In May, 1941, a task force, consisting of the *Bismarck,* then believed to be the most powerful battleship afloat, and the cruiser *Prinz Eugen,* sailed into the Atlantic from Norwegian bases. The *Bismarck* raid coincided with the Battle of Crete in the eastern Mediterranean, which absorbed a large part of British Mediterranean sea power. Churchill would rather lose Crete than see his Atlantic convoys annihilated, and thus ordered the Gibraltar-based Force H to join in the hunt for the *Bismarck*. In its first clash with the Royal Navy on May 24, 1941, the *Bismarck* sank the *Hood,* Britain's largest and fastest capital ship. Three days later the Home Fleet and Force H caught up with the German intruder and sank the *Bismarck* before it could reach the safety of the German naval base of Brest.

The sinking of the *Bismarck* ended German efforts to attack the North Atlantic routes with heavy surface vessels, but soon Britain was gripped in a far more desperate struggle against the German submarines, or U-Boats. Although Britain had again adopted the convoy system in 1939, proven in the battle of 1917, it was of little value because of heavy losses in escort vessels during the British evacuations of 1940 and 1941, from Dunkirk, Greece, and Crete. Also, German submarines, unlike those of 1917, now operated in large groups, or "wolf-packs," whose tactics the German submarine commander Admiral Doenitz had devised before the outbreak of World War II.

During the first phase of the German submarine offensive against British shipping, from July, 1940, to March, 1941, Britain lost two million tons of merchant shipping. Italian submarines, operating also in the Atlantic, added another 130,000 tons for the same period. In 1942, Allied shipping losses exceeded for the first time the building capacity of Allied shipyards, with 7.7 million tons destroyed and only 7.1 million tons newly built. The sharp increase in Allied shipping losses was due, in part, to German submarine operations along the U. S. east coast and in the Gulf of Mexico after the U. S. entry into the war. German submarine attacks against convoys bound for Russia were so successful that such convoys were discontinued along the arctic route in late 1942. One Allied convoy, sailing from Iceland to Russia on July 4, 1942, lost twenty out of thirty-three vessels when attacked by German aircraft and submarines from Norwegian bases.

The high rate of Allied shipping losses continued into early 1943, when German submarine strength reached its peak. In May, 1943, Allied countermeasures began to take effect, however. By that date, one German submarine was being sunk for every 10,000 tons of Allied shipping lost. Previously, the rate had been one German submarine for every 100,000 tons. Altogether, the Germans lost 237 submarines in 1943. The German goal of sinking 900,000 tons per month in 1943 was not attained. Instead, Doenitz was forced to break off the Battle of the Atlantic.

The Allied victory was due to improved command, new tactics, and a scientific lead. The British Anti–U-Boat Warfare Committee, established and directed by Churchill since 1942, shifted its tactics from the passive escorting of convoys to search and destroy operations against submarines before they could approach a convoy. To this end, special task forces were created, called "support groups" in the Royal Navy and "hunter-killer groups" in the U. S. Navy, consisting of aircraft carriers and destroyers. Long-range aircraft, operating from Iceland, Greenland, and Northern Ireland were able to close the "Black Pit," an area of the North Atlantic where German submarines had been immune to air attack before. Increasingly, Allied aircraft were able to intercept German submarines in the Bay of Biscay before they could reach the open Atlantic. Allied radar, superior to German, helped locate surfaced German submarines at night or in fog and thus deprived them of their principal advantage, that of surprise.

German efforts to counter the Allied methods by the use of new weapons either failed or came too late. Neither torpedoes with acoustic homing devices nor the "snorkel," an airbreathing device which permitted submarines to stay submerged, altered the balance in the Atlantic after 1943.

As in other theaters and campaigns, the Axis had come dangerously close to victory in the Battle of the Atlantic; nearly fourteen million tons of Allied shipping had been sunk. But for the turning of the tide in 1943, Churchill might have seized southern Ireland by force of arms as a last desperate resort, to bolster the defense of Britain's vital sea lanes.

THE BOMBER OFFENSIVE AGAINST GERMANY

The strategic directive for the Allied bomber offensive against Germany had been laid down at the Casablanca Conference, as stated earlier. It called not only for the destruction of German industry from the air but also the demoralization of the German civilian population through area bombing. The Casablanca directive thus combined the American and British views on air strategy. Both hoped to inflict enough punishment on Germany from the air to render an actual invasion of Western Europe unnecessary and force Germany into surrender by air power alone. The two air forces differed in their approach to the common end, however: the United States Army Air Force hoped to cripple Germany by knocking out key industries, such as plants for the manufacture of ball-bearings, aircraft, synthetic oil and rubber, in precision daylight attacks. The RAF hoped to bring about the collapse of German civilian morale or even stimulate revolt against the Nazi regime through night attacks on German cities. The latter view was taken by Air Marshal Harris, chief of the RAF Bomber Command since February, 1942, and Professor F. A. Lindemann (Lord Cherwell), scientific adviser to the Prime Minister, as well as Churchill himself. The aim of the RAF Bomber Command, in Harris' words, was to bomb Germany "city by city and ever more terribly in order to make it impossible for her to go on with the war." Churchill added: "The severe, ruthless bombing of Germany on an ever increasing scale will not only cripple her war effort . . . but will create conditions intolerable to the mass of the German population."

By 1943 the Allies possessed both the aircraft and bases for a strategic air offensive against Germany. Compared to the German bombers of the "Blitz" of 1940, American and British bombers of 1943 were more advanced in armaments, range, and bomb load. The American "B-17" and "B-24" and the British "Lancaster" could carry bomb loads of up to 4,000 pounds over a range of nearly 3,000 miles. Southern England remained the principal launching point, but Libya and later Italy were also used for strikes against targets in Rumania and Austria.

After the adoption of a "Combined Bomber Plan" in June, 1943, the 8th U. S. Air Force under General Carl A. Spaatz and the 9th U. S. Air Force under General L. H. Brereton began regular daylight raids, while the RAF bomber command continued to strike at population centers at night. The American daylight raids of 1943 were undertaken without long-range fighter escorts, and losses were extremely heavy. A low-level attack against the Rumanian oil fields at Ploesti on August 1, 1943, resulted in the loss of fifty-four four-engined B-24's out of a force of 177. In an attack on the German naval base at Kiel on June 13, 1943, twenty-two out of sixty B-17's were shot down. A daylight raid on the ball-bearing plants of Schweinfurt on October 10, 1943, led to the loss of sixty B-17's and damage to another 138 out of a total force of 291 bombers.

The British had meanwhile carried out some of the heaviest night raids of the war. On July 24/25, 1943, over 3,000 RAF bombers dropped close to 9,000 tons of bombs and incendiaries on Hamburg, obliterating one third of the city and killing some 42,000 civilians.

At the beginning of 1944, the American daylight offensive came into its own when long-range fighters became available and German fighter opposition declined. Beginning with a 1,000-plane raid against German aircraft factories on February 20, 1944 — a date known as the opening of "Big Week" in the 8th Air Force annals — the German fighter industry became the principal target. After dropping nearly 10,000 tons of bombs within the "Big Week," the USAF had gained air supremacy over Germany by March, 1944. Germany had become, in the words of the German fighter chief Galland, "a house without a roof." Beginning with April, 1944, the daylight offensive concentrated on German oil plants with devastating results to the German air force and armored divisions. Oil, always a scarce commodity in the Germany of World War II, threatened to dry up completely in 1944. The German oil bottleneck nullified all the gains which the German armaments industry had made in 1944 in spite of the Allied bomber offensive. Under the leadership of Albert Speer, German armaments output reached its highest peak of the war in September, 1944. Although Germany produced 40,000 aircraft in

1944, there was not enough fuel either to train new pilots or to get the new fighters off the ground.

By early 1945 Germany had become a passive object of air attack, its communications wrecked, its cities destroyed, and its armies largely immobilized. The heaviest of all fire bomb raids fell on the city of Dresden in the final weeks of the war, which, although undertaken with conventional bombs, claimed more victims than the nuclear attacks on Nagasaki or Hiroshima. All in all, the USAF had dropped 600,000 tons of bombs on Germany, the RAF 900,000. Of the two approaches to strategic bombing, adopted in the Combined Bomber Plan of 1943, the American had proved the more successful from a military point of view. By 1945 the RAF had laid waste every major German city between Hamburg and Dresden, Cologne and Berlin, but the hoped-for collapse of civilian morale or revolution against the Nazi regime had not come. What paralyzed Germany in 1945 was not so much her lacking will to fight but rather her inability to fight because of American precision raids on oil and communications.

German attempts to retaliate against Britain between 1942 and 1945 through air raids of her own failed, mostly because of the limited number of German bombers. The so-called German "Baedecker raids" of 1942, while damaging cultural sites such as Canterbury, had no effect on Air Marshal Harris' resolve to continue with the policy of fire bombing. The German "Baby Blitz" of early 1944 against London likewise accomplished little more than feeding Goebbels' propaganda machine. More serious was the bombardment by German "V-1" and "V-2" rockets beginning on June 10 and September 8, 1944, respectively. General Eisenhower believed that these weapons, if employed in larger numbers and at an earlier date, might have prevented the Allied invasion of Normandy in June, 1944. Of the two new German weapons, the "V-2" was the more dangerous, for it was a ballistic missile with a one-ton warhead, flying at supersonic speeds and arriving without warning. Against "V-2" bombardment, London was defenseless. Altogether, the bombardment of London with German rockets claimed some 10,000 civilian lives, a fraction of the casualties that some German cities suffered within a single RAF night attack.

THE ALLIED INVASION OF FRANCE

The Teheran Conference had put to rest the Anglo-American debate over the preference of the Mediterranean or Normandy as the principal target of Allied attack in 1944. The Casablanca Conference had laid the groundwork for the pre-invasion planning through the establishment of COSSAC (Chief of Staff to the Supreme Allied Commander) under British Lieut. General Sir Frederick Morgan. With the appointment of General Dwight D. Eisenhower as Allied Supreme Commander in January, 1944, COSSAC gave way to SHAEF (Supreme Headquarters, Allied Expeditionary Force). SHAEF was an Allied team in every respect, with Air Marshal Sir William Tedder as deputy supreme commander, Admiral Sir Bertram Ramsay in charge of the Allied Naval Expeditionary Force, and Air Marshal Sir Trafford Leigh-Mallory in command of the combined air forces.

Prior to Eisenhower's appointment, others had been considered for the post of Supreme Commander, among them U. S. Army Chief of Staff General George C. Marshall and Sir Alan Brooke, Chief of the Imperial General Staff. More than any other high-ranking Allied commander, however, Eisenhower possessed the human qualities which alone could hold a team together in time of trial and crisis. Others might have encountered difficulties in reconciling such forceful personalities as Patton and Montgomery, or in establishing the close confidence that reigned between Eisenhower and the Prime Minister.

Normandy, rather than the Pas-de-Calais, had been chosen by Morgan as the invasion site, for its defenses were weaker and the element of surprise would be greater. Considerations of tide, moonlight, and sunrise had narrowed the choice of time to a few days in May or June, 1944. Elaborate logistical support of the invasion forces had been arranged through the construction of two artificial harbors in "Operation Mulberry," one each for the American and British beachheads. Allied control of the air was assured from the beginning with two U. S. air forces, the RAF bomber command, and the British Tactical Air Force.

German Preparations

In spite of the fronts in Italy and Russia, Hitler could still muster sixty divisions for the defense of France in June, 1944. Their combat value was not always equal to that of the invasion troops, however, for they were lacking in mobility, depending on bicycles or horse-drawn transport. Also, Germany had no air power worth mentioning left in France in 1944. The defenses of the German "Atlantic Wall" varied in strength, the most powerful being those of the Pas-de-Calais. Complex underwater obstacles, more formidable than any the United States had encountered in the Pacific, guarded vital stretches of the beaches.

As opposed to the unified command and purpose of the Allied invasion forces, disagreement reigned in the German command. Rundstedt, the German Commander-in-Chief West, wanted to destroy the invasion forces in a mobile war in the interior of France. Rommel, in charge of coastal defenses, and aware of Allied air supremacy from his African days, regarded the battle—and the war—as lost unless the Allies were pushed back into the sea on the first day of battle.

THE FIRST STAGE: THE BATTLE OF THE BEACHHEAD

In spite of adverse weather and heavy seas, Eisenhower ordered the invasion to proceed in the early morning hours of June 6, 1944. While airborne troops descended behind German lines, American troops went ashore on Omaha and Utah beaches, the British further to the north on beaches code-named Gold, Juno, and Sword. Allied air power and naval gunfire gave effective support and German reinforcements were slow in arriving since the bridges across the Seine and the Loire had been destroyed in the pre-invasion bombardment. Also, the Germans persisted in their error that the Normandy landings were a diversion only, to be followed by bigger landings in the Pas-de-Calais, which never came.

Still German resistance was stubborn and not until the end of June had Allied strength grown sufficiently for the first breakout from the beaches. On June 18, American forces sealed off the Cotentin Peninsula, and by June 30, Bradley had captured Cherbourg. Allied spirits, raised high by the successful landings, had given way to fears by the end of June that another stalemate was in the offing in Normandy such as had occurred in Italy the year before. The German ring of containment around the beaches was nearer the breaking point, however, than the Allies generally realized. On July 3, Hitler fired Rundstedt, and Rommel predicted the imminent collapse of the German front in Normandy in mid-July, 1944.

THE SECOND STAGE: THE BREAK-OUT INTO NORMANDY

Two weeks after Rommel's warning to Hitler, the U. S. First Army captured Avranches and thereby opened the gap through which the First and Third Armies poured into Normandy and Brittany. The forces of Field Marshal Guenther von Kluge, Rundstedt's successor, were now in danger of complete encirclement unless speedily withdrawn. After the German failure to cut off the American breakout in the Battle of Mortain, 90,000 German troops were trapped in a pocket between Mortain and Falaise. The Battle of Falaise marked the end of organized German resistance in Normandy. While the U. S. First Army completed the destruction of the encircled German forces, Patton's Third Army had raced towards the Seine and crossed it at several places by August 24, 1944. Paris was captured the following day, the honor of entering Paris first among Allied troops being given to the 2nd French Armored Division under Jacques LeClerc. Hitler had ordered the destruction of Paris before it fell into Allied hands. The German commander, General Dietrich von Choltitz, disobeyed his orders, and Paris did not burn.

In the south of France, American and French forces had meanwhile carried out operation "Anvil" (or "Dragoon") with landings on the Mediterranean coast on August 15, 1944. Although "Anvil" was launched at the expense of Allied strength in Italy, it secured Marseilles intact. The gaining of a major French sea port was especially important to the Allies

FIGURE 18   *D-Day 1944: U. S. troops during a lull in the battle on the Normandy beachhead.*

in view of the thorough destruction of Cherbourg, whose facilities did not become fully available until December, 1944. The Mulberry harbors, severely wrecked in the Atlantic gales of late June, 1944, had been rendered largely useless.

GERMAN OFFICERS' REVOLT

As military disaster fell upon the German armies in east and west in July, 1944, a conspiracy of German army officers tried to assassinate Hitler on July 20, 1944. The conspiracy included high-ranking officers, such as Rommel and Kluge, as well as officers who had fallen out of favor with Hitler before the war, such as former Army Chief-of-Staff Ludwig Beck. Some of the conspirators were men of high motives, who had come to regard Hitler's dictatorship as criminal. Among them may be

621

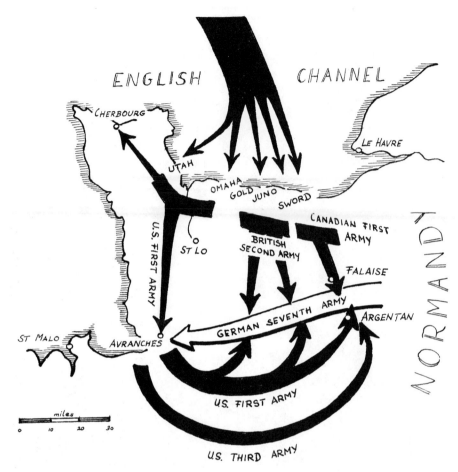

D-Day and the Battle of Normandy, 1944.

counted Colonel Claus Schenck von Stauffenberg, who placed the bomb at Hitler's feet. Hitler survived the blast, as if by miracle, a fact which confirmed his own conviction of Providential mission. Whether Hitler's death in 1944 would have altered the Allied policy of unconditional surrender must remain a point of speculation. That it would have ended the war in Europe sooner and thus have preserved countless lives and many cities may be assumed.

THE AUTUMN STALEMATE

By August, 1944, the military situation on all three fronts seemed to suggest the imminent collapse of Germany. In the east, the Russians had torn a gap two hundred miles wide in the German front and annihilated an entire German Army Group. In Italy the Gothic Line was pierced. In France the German retreat from Normandy had been turned into a rout. The chief difficulty of the Soviet and Western armies now was to bring up enough supplies for a sustained pursuit.and knock-out blow of the enemy before he had regained his balance.

On the western front Montgomery had liberated Brussels on September 3 and taken Antwerp on September 4, 1944, its port facilities largely intact. Further east, the U. S. First, Third, and Seventh Armies, as well as the French First Army, were rapidly approaching the German border. By September, 1944, the Allied armies lacked the supplies, however, to keep up the pursuit along the entire front, which now stretched from the North Sea to Switzerland. The Atlantic sea ports had either been thoroughly wrecked or were still defended by German garrisons which Hitler had left behind during the German retreat from Normandy. Antwerp, though in Allied hands, could not be used until November 28, 1944, owing to German control of the islands commanding its approaches to the North Sea. The French railroad network and rolling stock had been largely destroyed by Allied air power during the Normandy campaign.

THE ALLIED STRATEGIC DILEMMA

Since Allied supplies were inadequate for an invasion of Germany along the entire front, Montgomery proposed to limit the offensive to the Allied left wing. In a reverse application of the German Schlieffen Plan of 1914, he wished to hold the Allied right and, using Paris as the pivot of his movement, unleash the Allied left wing for an invasion of Holland, a drive to the Ruhr, and a thrust to Berlin. By a daring breakout into the heart of Germany along a narrow front, Montgomery hoped to end the war before the close of 1944 and free London from the ordeal of German rocket bombardment.

Eisenhower, an advocate of a "broad front" strategy against Germany, gave only limited approval to Montgomery's scheme. Two U. S. airborne divisions were assigned to Operation "Market Garden," which was to capture the bridges across the Dutch waterways, straddling Montgomery's advance into Holland. Operation "Market Garden," launched on September 17, 1944, failed in its objective. Although the Allies captured eight bridges, the ninth—and most important—across the Lower Rhine at Arnhem, eluded them. In an unexpectedly severe German response, the British Frist Airborne Division was badly mauled and had to be withdrawn.

Rundstedt, recalled by Hitler on September 5, 1944, skillfully conducted the German defense, which made extensive use of the old German fortifications of 1939, the "Westwall" or "Siegfried Line." The war of rapid movement gradually gave way to a battle of attrition before the German lines. The U. S. First Army captured Aachen on October 21, 1944, the U. S. Third Army took Metz on November 19, and the U. S. Seventh Army occupied Strasbourg on November 23. After that the Allies halted, awaiting reinforcements and supplies to prepare for the Rhine crossing in early 1945.

HITLER'S LAST HOPES; THE BATTLE OF THE BULGE

With Allied forces closing in and the specter of military defeat looming ever larger, Hitler turned to the memory of Prussia and the Seven Years' War for comfort and encouragement. Just as the Prussia of Frederick the Great had survived military defeat through the break-up of the Austro-French-Russian coalition in 1762, so Nazi Germany would in the end prevail because of the disintegration of the Grand Alliance of the Second World War. As the Western Powers and the Soviet Union fell to quarrelling, Germany, "like a spider in the web" would hold the balance in Europe once more. To hasten the collapse of the Soviet-Western alliance, Germany must deal only a few more forceful blows to demonstrate her unbroken will to resist. That will, Hitler hoped, had been strengthened by the doctrine of unconditional surrender and the publicity given to the "Morgenthau Plan," which had called for the pasturization of a defeated Germany.

The historical parallel which Hitler drew was tempting but, alas, misleading. Western-Soviet disagreements there were, and they had mounted since the summer of 1944. Stalin's refusal to aid the Warsaw uprising of the Polish Home Army appeared to the Western Powers as a cynical betrayal of Polish patriots for the benefit of Polish Communists. As Hitler's armies evacuated Greece in the fall of 1944, civil war between Greek Communists and non-Communists erupted, in which Britain intervened by force of arms on behalf of the non-Communists. Poland and the Balkans thus emerged as key areas of future Soviet-Western disagreements.

But there was still tremendous good will towards Russia in the Western democracies and faith in the alliance as a foundation for a better postwar world. Nazi policy had burned all bridges and neither Stalin nor the Western Powers felt the need of Hitler's aid when their armies stood at the threshold of total victory.

The political hopes which Hitler attached to his last military gamble, the Battle of the Bulge, were thus based on an illusion from the start. The military expectations, too, as events soon proved, were set too high.

While the Allied Armies were preparing for the assault on the Rhine, Hitler had assembled a reserve of some twenty-four divisions, including strong armored forces. On December 16, 1944, this force attacked the Allied front at its weakest point in the Ardennes forest, at the juncture of the U. S. First and Third Armies, where seventy-five miles of front line were guarded by four divisions. These were either battle-weary or new to combat in Europe. The aim of the German offensive in the Ardennes was no less ambitious than to inflict another Dunkirk on the Allies. The German armored divisions were to cross the Meuse, take Antwerp, and annihilate the Allied armies fighting in Belgium.

Initially, the German attack achieved complete surprise and caused considerable confusion, for few Allied leaders had thought the German army capable of a major offensive after the beating of Normandy. After its early gains, the German advance soon ran into difficulties, however. The German dash for the Meuse, the first principal aim of the offensive, was slowed down by the stubborn defense of the Ardennes road junctures, such as Saint-Vith and Bastogne. These road junctures were vital to the Germans for the unleashing of their full armored power in the thickly wooded terrain. American units, often improvised, isolated, or surrounded, snapped back with fierce opposition once the initial panic had worn off. The defense of isolated Bastogne by the 101st Airborne Division was the most successful of these actions. At Bastogne, General Anthony C. McAuliffe hurled his unorthodox "Nuts" to the Germans when they demanded his surrender. On December 26, 1944, Bastogne was relieved by the tanks of Patton's Third Army, which had wheeled north in record time over snowbound and icy roads.

Montgomery, in temporary command of all Allied forces north of the "bulge," had meanwhile rushed powerful forces to the Meuse, which threw back all German attempts to cross the river. What had begun as a dangerous German break-out on December 16, 1944, promised to turn into an Allied victory by early January, 1945. With their spearhead halted, the Germans found it increasingly difficult to hold their extended flanks. Rather than see his armies cut off once more, Hitler reluctantly withdrew in the course of January to his original position. Also, beginning on January 12, 1945, the German eastern front was set ablaze by the Soviet winter offensive, which forced the shifting of German troops to the east.

In December, 1944, Hitler had tried to repeat his spectacular success of 1940, which had been won over much the same ground; but his opponent of 1944 was not the same as that of 1940. Whereas the French army of 1940 never recovered from the shock of May 10, 1940, the Allies of 1944 regained their balance within days of the German attack. In 1940 Hitler had been able to commit his entire army in the west and had possessed the advantage of air superiority. In 1944 he fought on three fronts and exposed his columns to devastating air attack once the December mists had risen from the battlefield. Allied casualties during the Battle of the Bulge were high, especially American, with 76,000 killed,

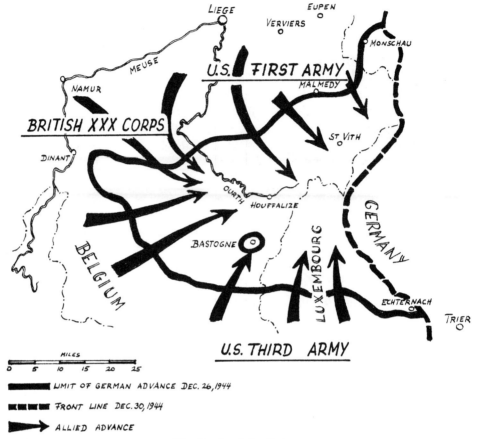

LIMIT OF GERMAN ADVANCE DEC. 26, 1944

FRONT LINE DEC. 30, 1944

ALLIED ADVANCE

The Battle of the Bulge.

captured, or wounded. The only military advantage gained by Germany was, however, the postponement of the Allied assault on the Rhine by a few weeks.

THE FINAL BATTLES IN EAST AND WEST

The Soviets crowned their long advance from the banks of the Volga to the Vistula with a crushing blow against the German central front in Poland in January, 1945. The Soviet offensive of January 12, 1945, undertaken with vastly superior tank and infantry forces, rang the death knell of the Third Reich. After the conquest of Warsaw on January 17, 1945, Zhukov and Konev drove in a broad sweep into the heart of Germany, capturing Upper Silesia in mid-February and reaching the Oder by early March, 1945. With the loss of Upper Silesia, Germany was deprived of her last great armaments center not yet completely gutted from the air. Having reached the Oder, Zhukov was only some sixty miles east of the German capital, from which Hitler directed his diminishing armies.

Russian advances on the flanks had closely followed those in the center. After the capture of Köenigsberg on April 9, 1945, German resistance in East Prussia collapsed. In the final holocaust of Hitler's Germany, there was no Battle of Tannenberg to prevent a Russian breakthrough to Berlin. Marshal Rokossovsky's forces broke through the Masurian Lakes and crossed the battlefields of World War I fame, where the tsarist armies had been stopped in August, 1914.

In the south the Soviets awaited the collapse of a local German offensive for the relief of Budapest, which the Russians had invested since December, 1944. By mid-February the Hungarian capital was in Russian hands and on February 20, 1945, Hungary signed an armistice with Russia. Hungary pledged to pay $300 million in reparations to the U. S. S. R., Yugoslavia, and Czechoslovakia, and declared war on Germany. After the conquest of Hungary, Malinovsky and Tolbuchin entered Austria and captured Vienna on April 13, 1945.

Along the Oder, the Soviet offensive had meanwhile come to a temporary halt in the face of stiffening German opposition. Except for a bridgehead at Kuestrin, the Soviets failed to force the Oder until mid-April, 1945. In Hitler's underground bunker, wild flights of fancy alternated with moods of deep depression and the awareness of a rapidly approaching end. Again the "Miracle of the House of Brandenburg" was invoked, which had saved Frederick the Great at the end of the Seven Years' War. Goebbels took refuge in astrology, predicting a turning of the tide after the middle of April and peace by August, 1945. When news of President Roosevelt's death reached the Bunker, it was acclaimed as the hoped-for miracle which would save the Nazi regime. Only after the collapse of the last German effort to halt the Russian encirclement of Berlin on April 21, 1945, did Hitler admit defeat and prepare his suicide. For Goebbels' propaganda, there remained the task of assuring the proper setting for the Fuehrer's death amidst the vast funeral pyre which Berlin had now become. After dictating his "political testament," which echoed his hatred for the Jews, and after appointing Doenitz as new Reichspresident, the Fuehrer shot himself on April 30, 1945. His bride of less than fourteen days, Eva Braun, joined him in death, as did Goebbels with his family.

The Western armies, held at bay until March, had meanwhile crossed the Rhine and shattered all coherent opposition to its east. Following the capture of Cologne by the U. S. First Army, the latter seized the Rhine bridge at Remagen intact on March 7, 1945. Before the battle-damaged bridge collapsed under German fire, four U. S. divisions had raced across and secured a foothold on the eastern bank. Other Rhine crossings followed rapidly by Patton's Third Army at Oppenheim and Montgomery at Wesel at the end of March. By April 1, 1945, the U. S. 9th Army and U. S. 1st Army had encircled the Ruhr, with three quarters of a million men entrapped in it. By April 18, the Battle of the Ruhr was over, and more than 300,000 German prisoners were taken. By April 25, 1945, Germany was cut in two when the U. S. First Army linked hands with the First Ukrainian Army at Torgau on the Elbe, deep in the heart of Germany. The imminent collapse of German resistance in Italy was indicated by the efforts of SS General Karl Wolff to arrange for a separate surrender of German troops in northern Italy.

As German resistance approached its end on all fronts, suspicions among the Allies began to cloud their victory. Beginning with January, 1945, several high placed Nazi officials had tried to persuade the Western Allies to allow the Germans to stop fighting in the west while continuing the war against Russia. Such proposals, made first by Nazi Foreign Minister Ribbentrop and later even by Heinrich Himmler, were turned down. The Western powers remained faithful to their pledge, under the United Nations Declaration of 1942, not to enter into separate armistice or peace negotiations with the enemy.

Stalin's suspicions were not put to rest, however, and he made bitter accusations against President Roosevelt before the latter's death on April 12, 1945. Soviet behavior in Poland and the Balkans since the Yalta Conference, of which more will be said presently, had, on the other hand, aroused Western suspicions. Winston Churchill, in particular, feared that Stalin would not keep the promises made at Yalta once Hitler was defeated. He therefore favored an Allied military thrust as far east into Germany as conditions would permit, including a Western capture of Berlin. The Western powers could thus improve their bargaining position with Stalin and force him to honor his pledges before their armies retreated into the pre-arranged occupation zones of Germany.

Churchill's urgings had little impact on the final battles. Montgomery succeeded in sealing off the Western Baltic by occupying Luebeck before the Russians reached it. Eisenhower was less motivated by postwar political considerations than by military needs. Anticipating grave Western casualties in an assult on Berlin and suspecting strong German forces in Bavaria and western Austria—the "Alpine Redoubt"— he directed his armies mainly towards the latter. Berlin was thus taken by Soviet forces alone on May 2, 1945. The "Alpine Redoubt" proved rather an illusion; but for a brief battle for Nuremberg, German resistance collapsed speedily all along the line.

German forces in Italy surrendered on May 2. At Rheims, the seat of SHAEF, General Jodl surrendered unconditionally on May 7, 1945. On May 8, 1945, the surrender ceremony was repeated in Berlin for the benefit of the Russians, with General Keitel affixing his signature to the surrender document. On May 21, 1945, the short-lived government of Admiral Doenitz was arrested at its seat in Flensburg on Eisenhower's order. The war in Europe had come to an end.

The collapse of Nazi Germany, April-May, 1945

THE YALTA CONFERENCE

Allied preparations for the political future of Europe had not kept pace with the advance of Allied armies into Germany. At a time when Soviet armies had overrun the Balkans and Poland and were driving into the heart of Germany, "the whole shape and structure of postwar Europe," in Churchill's words, "clamored for review." At the Dumbarton Oaks Con-

629

ference between August and October, 1944, the U. S., Great Britain, the U. S. S. R., and China had agreed on the basic structure of the proposed United Nations Organization, but they had failed to reach agreement on the question of the Great Power veto in the Security Council nor had they settled Russia's claim for sixteen seats in the General Assembly.

The basic question before the last summit conference between Roosevelt, Churchill, and Stalin, arranged at Yalta for early February, 1945, was whether the Grand Alliance, which had functioned so well as a military instrument, would also succeed in laying common ground for an enduring peace. Would Russia compromise on the UN? Would the Big Three be able to agree on common principles for the nations liberated from the Nazi yoke and those emerging from Nazi satellite status? What was Allied policy on postwar Germany to be, and would Russia join the war against Japan?

The chief difficulty of the Big Three at Yalta was how to reconcile the lofty principles of the Atlantic Charter with the territorial aspirations of Russia. Before going to Yalta, the United States had evinced high optimism in the United Nations as an instrument of peace and compromise. The United Nations, U. S. Secretary of State Cordell Hull said, would in itself eliminate "the need for spheres of influence, for alliances, for balance of power, or any other of the special arrangements through which, in the unhappy past, nations strove to safeguard their security or promote their interests."

Winston Churchill, though also a believer in the United Nations, was less sanguine about its peacemaking capacity, and would have preferred a concrete understanding on the demarcations of Great Power influence in postwar Europe. Thus, when German control over the Balkans passed to the Soviets in October, 1944, the Prime Minister and Foreign Secretary Anthony Eden had gone to Moscow to determine the extent of future Soviet influence in the Balkans. The agreement reached between Stalin and Churchill in Moscow used percentages as guidelines of the relative influence that Britain and the Soviet Union were to exercise. The precise meaning of influence thus defined was not spelled out, however. In Bulgaria, Rumania, and Hungary, Soviet influence was to predominate, with 75-80 per cent. In Yugoslavia the division was to follow an even 50-50 per cent. In Greece, where Britain had landed small forces, Stalin promised to stay out.

The Soviet Union, which had lost more men in the Second World War than the United States and Great Britain combined, was anxious to protect its security by extending its sway as far west as possible. The governments within the Soviet sphere of influence, to be considered "friendly" to Russia, would have to be predominantly Communist.

The agreements reached at Yalta obscured, rather than solved, the contradictions implicit in the Western and Soviet positions, for they gave the appearance of agreement in principle and compromise on details. Therein lay the source of future disappointment and controversy.

DECLARATION ON LIBERATED EUROPE

Western hopes for Soviet cooperation were high when Stalin subscribed to the "Declaration on Liberated Europe" at Yalta. The three powers agreed to assist "the peoples liberated from the domination of Nazi Germany and the peoples of the former Axis satellite states of Europe . . . to create democratic institutions of their own choice."

UN COMPROMISE

Soviet-Western differences over the UN, left unsettled at Dumbarton Oaks, were solved by compromise. Russia settled for three rather than sixteen seats in the General Assembly, while Britain secured individual representation for her dominions. The United States was content with one seat. The Soviet Union accepted the American compromise formula on the Great Power veto. Stalin agreed to the opening of the first UN meeting at San Francisco in April, 1945, and promised Soviet participation.

POLAND

In the Polish question, the Western powers agreed to draw the Soviet-Polish frontier roughly along the old Curzon Line, the city of Lvov and the oil rich parts of Galicia also going to Russia. At Yalta, Stalin thus secured essentially the same border with Poland that Hitler had agreed to in the Soviet-German border and friendship agreement of September, 1939. Poland's western borders were to be fixed in a final peace settlement, it being understood that Poland would be compensated at Germany's expense. Churchill opposed the extension of the Polish western frontier to the Oder and the western Neisse, however, on the grounds that "overindulgence with German food" might lead to the "death of the Polish goose."

The conflict between the Soviet-supported "Lublin Committee," recognized by Stalin as the lawful government of Poland, and the Polish government in exile in London was to be resolved by compromise. Stalin agreed to the formation of a "Provisional Government of National Unity" with the inclusion of London Poles. A Commission of Three, consisting of Molotov, the U. S., and British ambassadors in Moscow, was to aid in its establishment. Free elections were to be held in Poland as soon as practicable.

GERMANY

No specific plan for the dismemberment of Germany was adopted at Yalta, although the powers upheld the principle of Germany's political dismemberment. The question was referred to the three foreign ministers for further study. Agreement was reached on the postwar occupation zones, France being admitted as a fourth occupying power with a seat on the Allied Control Commission. Berlin, deeply inside the Soviet zone of occupation, was to be administered by all four powers and divided into occupation zones also. Agreement was further reached on German reparations in principle, though not on their extent. German reparations were to consist of capital equipment, current production, and German labor. The United States, against the opposition of Great Britain, accepted the sum of $20 billion, suggested by the Soviet Union as a basis for future reparations discussions.

Asia

Stalin pledged to join the Western powers in the war against Japan after the war in Europe had ended. Russia's price for entering the Pacific war was agreed upon mainly in personal negotiations between Stalin and Roosevelt, from which both Churchill and the American Secretary of State Edward R. Stettinius were largely absent. Russia was to regain the territories lost to Japan in the Treaty of Portsmouth of 1905. In addition, the Soviet Union was to receive the Kurile Islands, in Japanese possession since 1875, and Russia was to receive control over Port Arthur and the Manchurian railway. The autonomy of Outer Mongolia was to be guaranteed by international agreement. The latter concessions at the expense of China were made without advance agreement or consultation with the government of Nationalist China. No promise was extracted from Stalin to discontinue Soviet support to the Chinese Communists after the conclusion of the Pacific war.

Roosevelt's concessions to Stalin at Yalta were made, it should be noted, at a time when Soviet aid in the defeat of Japan was still regarded vital, since American strategy counted on an invasion of the Japanese homeland.

The overall Western impression gained at Yalta was optimistic. To some the conference appeared as "the dawn of a new day," and Roosevelt, upon returning home, summed up the Yalta meeting as "the end of the system of unilateral action, exclusive alliances and spheres of influence."

EARLY WESTERN DISAPPOINTMENTS

Soviet action in Poland and the Balkans shortly after Yalta soon deflated Western optimism. The Moscow Three Power Commission, which was to have assisted in the establishment of the Provisional Government of National Unity for Poland, broke down under Molotov's obstruction. With the Lublin Committee, now installed in Warsaw,

Stalin signed a treaty of assistance, as though it were the permanent government of Poland. On March 28, 1945, fifteen leaders of the Polish Home Army were arrested after being tricked into negotiations with the Soviet general Ivanov under false assurances of safe conduct.

In Rumania, Soviet deputy foreign minister Andrei Vishinsky had engineered a *coup d'état* on February 27, 1945, resulting in the ouster of General Radescu's government and the installment of a Communist puppet regime under Petra Groza.

As the war ended in Europe, Churchill expressed his misgivings about a new division of Europe so soon after the common triumph over Hitler had been achieved: "There is not much comfort in looking into a future," the Prime Minister wrote to Stalin, "where you and the countries you dominate plus the Communist Parties in many other states, are all drawn up on one side, and those who rally to the English speaking nations . . . are on the other. It is quite obvious that their quarrel would tear the world to pieces and that all of us leading men on either side who had anything to do with that would be shamed before history."

THE PACIFIC THEATER:
THE ALLIED ADVANCE, 1942 TO 1945

U.S. STRATEGY FOR THE DEFEAT OF JAPAN

Midway, as noted earlier, had marked the end of Japanese expansion in the Pacific and the beginning of the American counterattack. In planning the ultimate defeat of Japan, the American Joint Chiefs of Staff had to consider the vast distances of the Pacific theater, the nature of Japanese resistance, often stronger than any encountered in Europe, and the fact that the United States shouldered the burden of the Pacific war almost alone. The atomic bomb project was in its infancy in 1942, unknown to most and unsure of ultimate success. American strategy thus had to rely on the conventional means of war, and aim at the invasion of the Japanese homeland from the start.

Of the three possible routes of approach to the Japanese home islands, two were ruled out early in the war. (1) The United States could launch an invasion from the north, via the Aleutians. The Japanese feared such an attack and tied up strong forces in Hokkaido, the northernmost of the Japanese main islands, throughout the war. After considering such an approach briefly, U. S. planners dropped it. (2) Japan could be invaded from the Chinese mainland. This route was not considered for long in view of the poor caliber of the Chinese Nationalist Army and the difficulties of supply. (3) There remained the thrust from the southwest and central Pacific, which was ultimately chosen.

Australia and Hawaii became the starting points of a long dual advance across the southwest and central Pacific that leaped from one island group to another until it converged upon the Philippines and Okinawa in the Ryukyus. As American air and sea power grew in strength, Nimitz and MacArthur found it possible to by-pass Japanese strongholds and render them harmless through sea and air blockade without the cost of an invasion. The time- and life-saving technique of "island-skipping" was first successfully employed during the Solomons campaign against the strongly held island of Kolombangara. Later, it was used on a grander scale against Rabaul in New Britain, the Carolines, and Mindanao Island in the Philippines.

THE BATTLES OF THE SOUTHWEST AND CENTRAL PACIFIC

Most of New Guinea and the Solomons were cleared of Japanese forces between August, 1942, and the summer of 1944 in bitter and sometimes costly fighting. The center of Japanese resistance in the southwest Pacific was Rabaul, in New Britain, from which the Japanese dispatched powerful naval and air forces against the American operations in the Solomons and on New Guinea. In the Battle of Savo Island of August, 1942, fought in the course of the Solomons campaign, the United States suffered one of its worst naval defeats, with four cruisers sunk. Soon Rabaul was neutralized, however, under the attacks of Halsey's carrier-based planes. A Japanese convoy, sailing from Rabaul to New Guinea in February, 1943, was intercepted and destroyed in the Battle of the Bismarck Sea. Japanese efforts to prevent American landings on the Island of Bougainville in the Solomons with ships and planes launched from Rabaul, led to the Japanese defeat in the Battle of Empress Augusta Bay in November, 1943.

In the same month the American central Pacific offensive had evicted Japanese forces from Makin, Tarawa, and Apamama in the Gilberts. In February, 1944, Kwajalein and Eniwetock were seized in the Marshalls. The American central Pacific drive reached its climax with the invasion of the Marianas in June, 1944, when 120,000 U. S. troops, sailing from faraway Hawaii and the Solomons, attacked Saipan, Tinian, and Guam. The Japanese attempted desperately to fend off the invasion, for American possession of the Marianas would bring all of Japan within striking range of B-29 bombers. In the Battle of the Philippine Sea of June 19, 1944, Admiral Raymond A. Spruance fought off a Japanese fleet under Vice Admiral Ozawa, with the loss of three Japanese carriers. Coming within a short time after D-Day in Europe, the American landings in the Marianas and the Battle of the Philippine Sea gave powerful evidence of the American ability to wage war offensively in two widely separated theaters of the globe.

With the capture of the Marianas, the American air offensive against Japan began in earnest. Beginning with the B-29 raid of November

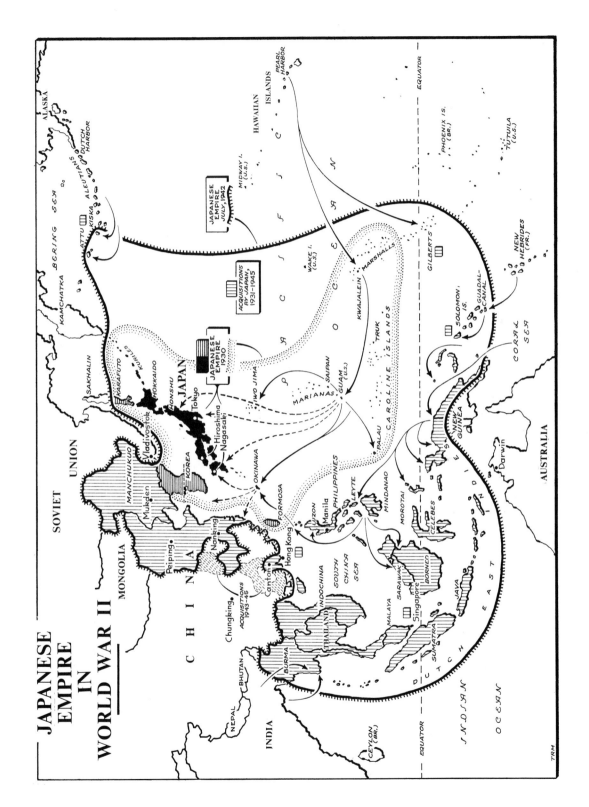

JAPANESE
EMPIRE
IN
WORLD WAR II

ALASKA

BERING SEA

KAMCHATKA

ALEUTIANS
DUTCH
HARBOR

KISKA

ATTU

JAPANESE
EMPIRE
JULY, 1942

MIDWAY I.
(U.S.)

HAWAIIAN

ISLANDS

PEARL
HARBOR

EQUATOR

PHOENIX IS.
(BR.)

TUTUILA
(U.S.)

SOVIET

UNION

MONGOLIA

SAKHALIN

KARAFUTO

KURILES

HOKKAIDO

HONSHU

JAPAN

Tokyo

Hiroshima
Nagasaki

ACQUISITIONS
BY JAPAN,
1931-1945

WAKE I.
(U.S.)

JAPANESE
EMPIRE
1930

IWO JIMA

SAIPAN

GUAM
(U.S.)

MARIANAS

KWAJALEIN

MARSHALLS

TRUK

CAROLINE ISLANDS

GILBERTS

SOLOMON
IS.

GUADAL-
CANAL

NEW
HEBRIDES
(FR.)

CORAL
SEA

MANCHUKUO

Mukden

Vladivostok

KOREA

OKINAWA

PALAU

NEW GUINEA

Peiping

CHINA

Nanking

FORMOSA

Hong Kong

Canton

LUZON

Manila

PHILIPPINES

LEYTE

MINDANAO

MOROTAI

CELEBES

Darwin

AUSTRALIA

Chungking

ACQUISITIONS
1943-45

THAILAND

INDOCHINA

SOUTH
CHINA
SEA

SARAWAK

BORNEO

NEPAL

BHUTAN

INDIA

BURMA

MALAYA

Singapore

SUMATRA

JAVA

DUTCH

EAST

INDIES

CEYLON
(BR.)

EQUATOR

INDIAN

OCEAN

PACIFIC

OCEAN

TRM

24, 1944, from Saipan, Tokyo came under steady air bombardment. An incendiary raid of March 9, 1945, destroyed much of residential Tokyo and killed 83,000 people. By early 1945 the Marianas-based fleet of B-29's had grown so powerful that it could carry out both day and night attacks on Japanese industries and cities. Before the nuclear attacks on Hiroshima and Nagasaki, over 160,000 tons of bombs were dropped on Japan and nearly a quarter of a million civilians killed.

In Japan the loss of the Marianas led to the fall of the Tojo government, which had plunged Japan into war in 1941. Thoughtful Japanese leaders regarded the war as lost, but the prevailing atmosphere of militarism prevented their speaking up or taking action to end a struggle that had become useless.

THE CAPTURE OF THE PHILIPPINES, IWO JIMA, AND OKINAWA

By-passing Mindanao Island, American troops landed on Leyte in the Philippines on October 20, 1944, and at Lingayen Gulf on Luzon on January 9, 1945. Once more, powerful Japanese naval forces tried to prevent the American landings and were driven off with heavy losses to themselves. In three separate naval engagements of late October, 1944, known collectively as the Battle for Leyte Gulf, the Japanese fleet lost four aircraft carriers and was turned back. Manila fell in early March, 1945, Corregidor shortly thereafter. For Douglas MacArthur the return to the Philippines had much the same emotional meaning as the British return to France had had for Churchill in June, 1944: both had suffered defeat at the outset and both had returned in victory to the scene of their earlier defeat.

The tiny island of Iwo Jima in the Bonin group became the site of one of the bloodiest battles of the Pacific war in February, 1945. Both Japan and the United States regarded the island as vital for reasons of air power. To the Japanese Iwo Jima was, in effect, an unsinkable aircraft carrier, from which they could intercept Japanese-bound B-29's. For the United States, possession of Iwo Jima was desirable as an emergency base for crippled, home-bound B-29's.

Within four days after their landings on Iwo Jima, on February 19, 1945, American Marines had taken Mount Suribachi, commanding the southern end of the island. Japanese resistance on the remainder of Iwo Jima was not broken until mid-March, 1945. The extraordinary ferocity of the battle was reflected in the casualties which both sides suffered. Of an estimated 20,000 Japanese defenders, only some one thousand survived. American casualties numbered seven thousand killed and wounded.

After the fall of Iwo Jima, the U. S. Tenth Army landed on Okinawa in the Ryukyus, only some three-hundred miles to the south of Kyushu, the southernmost of the Japanese home islands. Fighting at their doorstep, the Japanese put up a desperate resistance with a reckless expenditure of lives. American casualties under Kamikaze attacks gave a foretaste of the cost of an invasion of Japan. Japanese suicide planes sank thirty American vessels and damaged ten battleships and thirteen aircraft carriers. Both the American and Japanese army commanders on Okinawa died before the end of battle in June, 1945, General Buckner from a Japanese shell, General Ushijima by his own hand.

THE INDIA-BURMA-CHINA THEATER

While the United States was driving Japan from its island empire in the southwest and central Pacific in a long campaign, the Japanese conquests in Malaya, Burma, and on the Chinese mainland had remained relatively secure. After the loss of Singapore and with the growing demand which the North African theater made on British resources, the best that Britain could hope for in Southeast Asia was to hold the line. The isolation of Nationalist China and mutual suspicions between Chiang Kai-shek and the British rendered the British position in the Southeast Asian theater more difficult still. The American participation in the Southeast Asian theater, though smaller in scale than in the Pacific, was significant, mainly in providing air power and supplies and training Nationalist Chinese forces. Major General Joseph Stilwell became Chiang's chief of staff and, in addition, assumed numerous other duties in the China-India-Burma theater. Stilwell was commanding general of U. S. forces in Burma, China, and India, supervised Lend-Lease to China, and acted as liaison man between the British Southeast Asian command and Nationalist China. Furthermore, Stilwell organized the airlift across the Himalayas, the "Hump," and supervised the training of Nationalist Chinese forces, some of which had retreated to India during the Japanese invasion of Burma in 1942.

In vain Stilwell attempted to launch an offensive for the reconquest of Burma in 1943, largely because of his disagreement with Chiang, who preferred the use of American air power to the use of his own troops against the Japanese. An offensive by American-trained Nationalist Chinese forces from India into northern Burma in October, 1943, bogged down after the conquest of the Taro Plain. Stilwell's outspoken criticism of Chiang, which earned him the nickname of "Vinegar Joe," led to his replacement by Major General Wedemyer in October, 1944.

By 1944 the United States had abandoned plans for a major ground attack in the China-Burma theater, but China remained important for its strategic air bases until the conquest of the Marianas.

Major Allied ground operations in Burma did not start until the fall of 1944. British forces, attacking along the central-southern front reached the road juncture of Meiktila by March 28, 1945, and took Rangoon and Prome in early May, 1945. Meanwhile, American and Nationalist Chinese forces had reached the old China-Burma border and opened the Burma Road.

THE POTSDAM DECLARATION AND JAPAN'S SURRENDER

On July 26, 1945, ten days after the first American nuclear test bomb had been fired at Alamagordo, New Mexico, President Truman, Prime Minister Churchill, and Generalissimo Chiang Kai-shek called on Japan in the Potsdam Declaration to surrender unconditionally. On the same day, the American cruiser *Indianapolis* delivered the warhead for the first atomic bomb to the B-29 base at Tinian in the Marianas.

The Japanese government under premier Admiral Suzuki had been searching for a negotiated peace for some time prior to these events, hoping to enlist the good offices of the Soviet Union. Russia, however, had pledged to enter the war against Japan at Yalta and thus not only ignored the Japanese overtures, but refused to renew the Soviet-Japanese non-aggression pact of 1941 after its expiration in April, 1945. Japan's diplomatic isolation was complete, her military situation hopeless. American ground forces were at the doorstep of Japan in Okinawa, Japanese cities lay in ruins, and Japan's life lines to the East Indies and Manchuria were cut by American submarines, which had destroyed over five million tons of Japanese merchant shipping. Still, the Japanese government rejected the Potsdam Declaration for fear that its acceptance by Japan would destroy the monarchy. Only the dropping of the nuclear bombs on Hiroshima and Nagasaki on August 6 and 9 respectively convinced the Japanese Supreme Council for the Direction of the War of the futility of further resistance. Russia had entered the war against Japan on August 8, 1945. On September 2, 1945, Japan signed the document of unconditional surrender on the deck of the U. S. battleship *Missouri* in Tokyo Bay.

Bibliography

CHAPTER 1

Albertini, Luigi, *The Origins of the War of 1914*, 3 vols., (London, 1952/54)
Fay, Sidney B., *The Origins of the World War*, 2 vols. (1928–30)
Feis, Herbert, *Europe: The World's Banker, 1870–1914* (Clifton, N.J., 1930)
Feldman, Gerald D., ed., *German Imperialism, 1914–1918: The Development of a Historical Debate* (N.Y., 1972)
Fischer, Fritz, *Germany's Aims in the First World War* (N.Y., 1964)
Hantsch, Hugo, *Leopold Graf Berchtold, Grandseigneur und Staatsmann*, 2 vols. (Graz, 1963)
Hayes, Carlton I. H., *A Generation of Materialism 1871–1900*. (N.Y., 1963)
Langer, William L., *European Alliances and Alignments, 1871–1890* (N.Y., 1931)
———, *The Diplomacy of Imperialism*, 2 vols. (N.Y., 1935)
Lee, Dwight E., ed., *The Outbreak of the First World War*. (N.Y., 1970)
Remak, Joachim, *The Origins of World War I* (N.Y., 1967)
Ritter, Gerhard, *Staatskunst und Kriegshandwerk*, 3 vols. (Munich, 1959)
Schmitt, Bernadott E., *The Coming of the War 1914*, 2 vols. (N.Y., 1930)
Stavrianos, Ls., *The Balkans 1815–1914*. (N.Y., 1963)
Taylor, A. J. P., *The Struggle for Mastery in Europe, 1848–1918* (N.Y., 1954)
Tuchman, Barbara W., *The Proud Tower* (N.Y., 1966)

CHAPTER 2

Baldwin, Hanson W., *World War I* (N.Y., 1962)
Falls, Cyril, *The Great War* (N.Y., 1959)
Gatzke, Hans W., *Germany's Drive to the West* (Baltimore, 1950)
Grebler, Leo and Winkler, Wilhelm, *The Cost of the World War to Germany and to Austria—Hungary*. (Yale, 1940)
Lidell, Hart B. H., *The Real War 1914–1918* (Boston, 1930)
———, *Strategy* (N.Y., 1967)
Pitt, Barrie, *1918 The Last Act* (London, 1962)
Roth, Jack J., ed., *World War I: A Turning Point in Modern History* (N.Y., 1967)
Tuchman, Barbara W., *The Guns of August*. (N.Y., 1962)

CHAPTER 3

Adams, Arthur E., ed., *The Russian Revolution and Bolshevik Victory*, (Problems in European Civilization, Boston, 1960)
Balabanoff, Angelica, *Impressions of Lenin* (Ann Arbor, 1968)
Carr, Edward H., *Studies in Revolution* (N.Y., 1964)
———, *The Bolshevik Revolution*, 3 vols. (N.Y., 1950–53)
Charques, Richard, *The Twilight of Imperial Russia* (N.Y., Toronto, 1965)
Crossman, Richard, ed., *The God that Failed* (N.Y., 1963)
Deutscher, Isaac, *Stalin: A Political Biography* (N.Y., 1967)

————, *The Prophet Armed* (N.Y., 1954)
————, *The Prophet Unarmed* (N.Y., 1959)
————, *The Prophet Outcast* (N.Y., 1965)
Dmytryshyn, Basil, *USSR, A Concise History* (N.Y., 1965)
Drachkovitch, Milorad M., ed., *The Revolutionary Internationals 1864–1943* (Stanford, 1966)
Fischer, Louis, *Men and Politics* (N.Y., 1966)
Geiger, Kent H., *The Family in Soviet Russia* (Cambridge, 1968)
Hendel, Samuel and Braham, Randolph L., ed., *The USSR after 50 years* (N.Y., 1967)
Kennan, George F., *Russia Leaves the War*
————, *The Decision to Intervene* (N.Y., 1967)
McNeal, Robert, *The Bolshevik Tradition. Lenin, Stalin, Khrushchev* (Englewood Cliffs, 1963)
Moorehead, Alan. *The Russian Revolution* (N.Y., 1958)
Page, Stanley W., *Lenin and World Revolution* (N.Y., 1959)
Payne, Robert, *Stalin* (N.Y., 1965)
Pipes, Richard, *The Formation of the Soviet Union: Communism and Nationalism 1917–1923* (N.Y., 1964)
Plamenatz, John, *German Marxism and Russian Communism* (London, N.Y., Toronto, 1954)
Reshetar, John, *A Concise History of the Communist Party of the Soviet Union* (N.Y., 1964)
Rubinstein, Alvin Z., *The Foreign Policy of the Soviet Union* (N.Y., 1966)
Trotsky, Leon, *Literature and Revolution* (Ann Arbor, 1960)
Ulam, Adam B., *Expansion and Coexistence* (N.Y., 1968)
Von Laue, Theodore H., *Why Lenin? Why Stalin?* (Philadelphia, N.Y., Toronto, 1971)
von Rauch, George, *A History of Soviet Russia* (N.Y., 1957)
Wilson, Edmund, *To the Finland Station* (Garden City, N.Y., 1953)
Wolfe, Bertram D. *Three Who Made a Revolution* (Boston, 1955)
————, *Communist Totalitarianism* (Boston, 1956)

CHAPTER 4

Berlau, Joseph, *The German Social Democratic Party 1914–1921* (N.Y., 1949)
Bernstein, Eduard, *Die Deutsche Revolution* (Berlin, 1921)
Ebert, Friedrich, *Schriften, Aufzeichnungen Reden* (Dresden, 1962)
Gay, Peter, *The Dilemma of Democratic Socialism* (N.Y., 1952)
Groener, Wilhelm, *Lebenserinnerungen* (Goettingen, 1959)
Hanak, Harry, *Great Britain and Austria–Hungary During the First World War* (N.Y., 1962)
Hantsch, Hugo, *Die Geschichte Österreichs* (Graz, Vienna, 1962)
Horn, Daniel, *The German Naval Mutinies of WW I* (Rutgers, 1969)

CHAPTER 5

Albrecht-Carrié, René, *The Meaning of the First World War* (Englewood Cliffs, 1965)
Bailey, Thomas A., *Woodrow Wilson and the Lost Peace* (N.Y., 1944)
————, *Woodrow Wilson and the Great Betrayal* (N.Y., 1945)

Czernin, Ferdinand, *Versailles, 1919* (N.Y., 1965)

Holborn, Hajo, *The Political Collapse of Europe* (N.Y., 1951)

Lederer, Ivo Jr., ed., *The Versailles Settlement* (N.Y., 1960)

Mantoux, Etienne, *The Carthaginian Peace* (Pittsburgh, 1952)

Mayer, Arno J., *Politics and Diplomacy of Peacemaking. Containment and Counterrevolution at Versailles, 1918–1919* (1967)

Thompson, John M., *Russia, Bolshevism and the Versailles Peace* (Princeton, 1966)

CHAPTER 6

Aron, Raymond, *The Century of Total War* (N.Y., 1954)

Carr, Edward H., *German–Soviet Relations between the two World Wars 1919–1939* (1966)

———, *International Relations between the two World Wars* (1947)

Eden, Anthony, *Facing the Dictators 1923–1938* (Boston, 1962)

Eubank, Keith, *The Origins of World War II* (N.Y., 1969)

Feis, Herbert, *Three International Episodes* (N.Y., 1966)

Galbraith, J. K., *The Great Crash, 1929* (Boston, 1955)

Gilbert, Martin, *Britain and Germany Between the Wars* (N.Y., 1967)

Hilger, G. and Meyer, A. G., *The Incompatible Allies: A Memoir–History of German–Soviet Relations, 1918–1941* (1953)

Kleine Ahlbrandt, W. L., ed., *Appeasement of the Dictators* (1970)

Lafore, Laurence, *The End of Glory* (Philadelphia, 1970)

Lee, Dwight E., ed., *Munich* (Cambridge, 1970)

Loewenheim, Francis L., *Peace or Appeasement?* (1965)

Meyer, Henry C., *Mittleleuropa in German Thought and Action 1815–1945* (1955)

Nogueres, Henri, *Munich* (1965)

Schultze, Ernst, *Ruhrbesetzung und Weltwirtschaft* (1927)

Snell, John L., *The Outbreak of the Second World War* (Lexington, Mass., 1962)

Taylor, A. J. P., *The Origins of the Second World War* (N.Y., 1961)

Thorne, Christopher, *The Approach of War, 1938–1939* (N.Y., 1967)

Ulam, Adam B., *Expansion and Coexistence* (N.Y., 1968)

Wiskemann, Elizabeth, *The Rome–Berlin Axis* (1949)

Wolfers, Arnold, *Britain and France between two Wars* (N.Y., 1966)

Woolf, S. J., ed., *European Fascism* (N.Y., 1968)

CHAPTER 7

See bibliography for Chapter 6

CHAPTER 8

See bibliography for Chapter 6

CHAPTER 9

Gopal, Ram, *British Rule in India* (London, 1963)

Graves, Robert and Hodge, Alan, *The Long Week-End* (N.Y., 1963)

Bibliography

Griffiths, Percival, *The British Impact on India* (Hamden, Conn., 1965)
Harari, Maurice, *Government and Politics of the Middle East* (Englewood Cliffs, 1962)
Lewis, Martin, ed., *The British in India* (Boston, 1962)
Mowat, Charles L., *Britain between the Wars 1918–1940* (Chicago, 1955)
Raymond, John, ed., *The Baldwin Age* (1961)
Reynolds and Brasher, *Britain in the Twentieth Century 1900–1964* (Cambridge, 1966)
Rock, William R., *Neville Chamberlain* (N.Y., 1969)
Semmel, Bernard, *Imperialism and Social Reform* (N.Y., 1968)
Strachey, John, *The End of Empire* (N.Y., 1964)
Taylor, A. J. P., *English History, 1914–1945* (N.Y., and Oxford, 1965)

CHAPTER 10

Bain, Chester A., *Vietnam, the Roots of Conflict* (Englewood Cliffs, 1967)
Brogan, D. W., *France under the Republic* (1940)
Colton, Joel, *Léon Blum, Humanist in Politics* (N.Y., 1966)
Dalby, Louise Elliott, *Léon Blum, Evolution of a Socialist* (1963)
Derfler, Leslie, *The Third French Republic* (N.Y., 1966)
Greene, Nathanael, *From Versailles to Vichy* (N.Y., 1970)
Luethy, Herbert, *France Against Herself* (1957)
Pierce, Roy, *Contemporary French Political Thought* (N.Y., 1966)
Sedgwick, Alexander, *The Third French Republic, 1870–1914* (N.Y., 1969)
Shirer, William L., *The Collapse of the Third Republic* (N.Y., 1969)
Thomson, David, *Democracy in France since 1870* (N.Y., 1964)

CHAPTER 11

Deakin, F. W., *The Brutal Friendship* (N.Y., 1966)
Fermi, Laura, *Mussolini* (N.Y., 1966)
Halperin, S. William, *Mussolini and Italian Fascism* (N.Y., 1964)
Kirkpatrick, Ivone, *Mussolini: A Study in Power* (1964)
Nolte, Ernst, *Three Faces of Fascism* (N.Y., 1966)
Salvemini, Gaetano, *Under the Axe of Fascism* (1936)
——, *The Fascist Dictatorship in Italy* (N.Y., 1967)
Tasca, Angelo, *The Rise of Italian Fascism 1918–1922* (N.Y., 1966)
Weber, Eugen, *Varieties of Fascism* (N.Y., 1964)
Wiskemann, Elizabeth, *Fascism in Italy: its Development and Influence* (London, 1969)

CHAPTER 12

Bergsträsser, Ludwig, *Geschichte der Politischen Parteien in Deutschland* (Munich, 1955)
Bracher, Karl Dietrich, *Die Auflösung der Weimarer Republik* (Stuttgart, 1957)
Brook-Shepherd, Gordon, *Dollfuss* (London, 1961)
Craig, Gordon, *From Bismarck to Adenauer, Aspects of German Statecraft* (N.Y., 1965)
Dahrendorf, Ralf, *Society and Democracy in Germany* (N.Y., 1967)
Erich, Eyck, *A History of the Weimar Republik,* 2 vols. (N.Y., 1970)

Fischer, Ruth, *Stalin and German Communism* (Cambridge, 1948)
Gulick, Charles A., *Austria from Habsburg to Hitler,* 2 vols. (1948)
Halperin, S. William, *Germany Tried Democracy* (N.Y., 1946)
Holborn, Hajo, *A History of Modern Germany, 1840–1945* (N.Y., 1969)
Pinson, Koppel S., *Modern Germany* (N.Y., 1959)
Ringer, Fritz, K., ed., *The German Inflation of 1923* (Oxford, 1969)
Sering, Max, *Germany Under the Dawes Plan* (London, 1929)
Schacht, Hjalmar, *The Stabilization of the Mark* (N.Y., 1927)
Stampfer, Friedrich, *Die Ersten 14 Jahre der Deutschen Republik* (Offenbach,
    1947)
Stern, Fritz, *The Politics of Cultural Despair* (N.Y., 1965)
Tobias, Fritz, *The Reichstag Fire* (N.Y., 1964)
Von Schuschnigg, Kurt, *Austrian Requiem* (1947)
Zöllner, Erich, *Geschichte Österreichs* (Vienna, 1961)

CHAPTER 13

Jelavich, Charles and Barbara, *The Balkans* (Englewood Cliffs, 1965)
_____, *The Balkans in Transition* (Los Angeles, 1963)
Macartney, C. A. and Palmer, A. W., *Independent Eastern Europe* (St. Martin's,
    1966)
Pounds, N. J. G., *Eastern Europe* (Chicago, 1969)
Royal Institute of International Affairs, *The Balkan States* (1936)
_____, *The Baltic States* (1938)
Seton-Watson, Hugh, *Eastern Europe between the Wars 1918–1941* (N.Y.,
    1967)
Zischka, Anton, *The Other Europeans* (London, 1962)

CHAPTER 14

Bonjour E., et al., *A Short History of Switzerland* (Oxford, 1952)
Childs, Marquis, *Sweden: the Middle Way* (Yale, 1947)
Derry, T. K., *A Short History of Norway* (London, 1957)
Edestein, Harry, *Division and Cohesion in Democracy, A Study of Norway*
    (Princeton, 1966)
Kohn, Hans, *Nationalism and Liberty: The Swiss Example* (1956)
Mazour, Anatole G., *Finland between East and West* (N.Y., 1956)
Soloveytchik, G., *Switzerland in Perspective* (1954)
Thürer, Georg, *Free and Swiss* (Miami, 1970)
Tomasson, Richard F., *Sweden: Prototype of Modern Society* (N.Y., 1970)
Wvorinen, John H., *A History of Finland* (N.Y., 1965)

CHAPTER 15

See bibliography for Chapter 3

CHAPTER 16

Bullock, Alan, *Hitler, A Study in Tyranny* (N.Y., 1964)
Domarus, Max, ed., *Reden und Proklamationen 1932–1945. Adolf Hitler,* 4 vols.
    (Munich, 1965)
Ellis, Howard S., *Exchange Control in Central Europe* (Cambridge, 1941)

Goebbels, Joseph, *Der Angriff* (Munich, 1935)

Hitler, Adolf, *Mein Kampf.* Translated by Ralph Manheim, (1962, Boston)

Kogon, Eugen, *Der SS-Staat* (1947)

Leber, Annedore, *Für und wider, Entscheidungen in Deutschland 1918–1945,* (Annedore Leber-Mosaik-Verlag, 1962)

Mau, Hermann and Krausnick, Helmut, *Deutsche Geschichte der Jüngsten Vergangenheit 1933–1945* (1956)

Mosse, George L., *The Crisis of German Ideology.* (N.Y., 1964)

Schoenbaum, David, *Hitler's Social Revolution.* (N.Y., 1967)

Shirer, William L., *The Rise and Fall of the Third Reich.* (N.Y., 1960)

Snell, John L., ed., *The Nazi Revolution* (Problems in European Civilization, Boston, 1959)

Speer, Albert, *Inside the Third Reich* (N.Y., 1971)

Wheaton, Eliot B., *Prelude to Calamity* (N.Y., 1968)

CHAPTER 17

See bibliography for Chapter 11

CHAPTER 18

Payne, Stanley G., *The Spanish Revolution* (N.Y., 1970)

_____, *Franco's Spain* (N.Y., 1967)

Robinson, Richard A. H., *The Origins of Franco's Spain* (Pittsburgh, 1970)

Thomas, Hugh, *The Spanish Civil War* (N.Y., 1963)

CHAPTER 19

See bibliography for Chapter 10

CHAPTER 20

Barnouw, A. J., *The Dutch; a Portrait Study of the People of Holland* (1940)

Kalken, F. Van, *Histoire de la Belgique et de son Expansion Coloniale* (1954)

Petit, J., *Luxembourg Yesterday and Today* (1953)

Rousseau, A., *Belgium and Luxemburg* (1950)

CHAPTER 21

See bibliography for Chapter 6

CHAPTER 22

Baldwin, Hanson, *Battles Lost and Won* (N.Y., 1966)

Boelchke, Willi A., ed., *The Secret Conferences of Dr. Goebbels, The Nazi Propaganda War 1939–43* (N.Y., 1970)

Buchanan, Russel A., *The United States and World War II* 3 vols., (N.Y., 1964)

Churchill, Winston S., *The Second World War,* 6 vols. (Boston, 1948–53)

Dallin, Alexander, *German Rule in Russia 1941–1945* (1957)

de Gaulle, Charles, *The Complete War Memoirs of Charles de Gaulle,* 1940–46, 3 vols. (N.Y., 1968) de la Gorce, Paul-Marie, *The French Army* (N.Y., 1963)

Feis, Herbert, *Churchill, Roosevelt, Stalin. The War They Waged and the Peace They Sought* (Princeton, 1967)

Gibson, Hugh, ed., *The Ciano Diaries* (N.Y., 1945)

Jacobsen, H. A. and J. Rohwer, eds., *Decisive Battles of WW II* (N.Y., 1965)

Kriegstagebuch, des O.K.W., *1940–1945* 6 vols. (Frankfurt a. Main, 1965)

Langer, William and Gleason, S. Everett, *The Undeclared War* (1953)

Liddell, Hart and Basil, Henry, *History of the Second World War* (New York, 1971)

———, ed., *The Rommel Papers* (New York, 1953)

Lochner, Louis P., ed., *The Goebbels Diaries 1942–1943* (N.Y., 1948)

Manstein, Erich von, *Lost Victories* (Chicago, 1958)

Morison, Samuel Eliot, *The Two-Ocean War* (Boston, 1963)

Ritter, Gerhard, *The German Resistance* (N.Y., 1958)

Snyder, L. L., *The War: A Concise History, 1939–1945* (N.Y., 1962)

Thompson, Laurence, *1940* (N.Y., 1966)

Tompkins, Peter, *The Murder of Admiral Darlan* (N.Y., 1965)

Trevor-Roper, Hugh R., *Blitzkrieg to Defeat: Hitler's War Directives 1939–1945* (N.Y., 1965)

———, ed., *Hitler's War Directives* (London, 1964)

———, *The Last Days of Hitler* (N.Y., 1947)

Wilmot, Chester, *The Struggle for Europe* (Westport, Conn., 1972)

Woodward, Llewellyn, *British Foreign Policy in the Second World War* (London, 1962)

Wright, Gordon, *The Ordeal of Total War 1939–1945.* (N.Y., Evanston, Ill., London, 1968)

Index of Subjects

Index of Subjects

652

Index of Persons

Index of Persons